D. W. Davies E. Holler E. D. Jensen S. R. Kimbleton
B. W. Lampson G. LeLann K. J. Thurber R. W. Watson

Distributed Systems – Architecture and Implementation

An Advanced Course

Edited by B. W. Lampson, M. Paul, and H. J. Siegert

Springer-Verlag New York Berlin Heidelberg Tokyo

Editors

Dr. B. W. Lampson
Xerox Corporation, PARC
3333 Coyote Hill Road, Palo Alto, CA 94304 / USA

Prof. Dr. M. Paul
Prof. Dr. H. J. Siegert
Institut für Informatik, Technische Universität München
Arcisstraße 21, D-8000 München 2

Originally published as Vol. 105 in the series
Lecture Notes in Computer Science
First Edition 1981
ISBN 3-540-10571-9 Springer-Verlag Berlin Heidelberg New York
ISBN 0-387-10571-9 Springer-Verlag New York Heidelberg Berlin

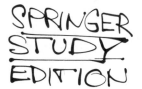
SPRINGER
STUDY
EDITION

ISBN 0-387-12116-1 Springer-Verlag New York Berlin Heidelberg Tokyo
ISBN 3-540-12116-1 Springer-Verlag Berlin Heidelberg New York Tokyo

9 8 7 6 5 4 3 (Third printing, 1985)

Printed and bound by R.R. Donnelley & Sons, Harrisonburg, Virginia.
Printed in the United States of America.

Preface

The papers comprising this volume were prepared for and presented at the Advanced Course on Distributed Systems—Architecture and Implementation, which was held from March 4 to March 13, 1980 at the Technische Universität München. It was organized by the Institut für Informatik, and jointly financed by the Ministry for Research and Technology of the Federal Republic of Germany, and the Commission of the European Communities.

Architecture and implementation of distributed systems have become more and more important and are receiving considerable attention. Several reasons for this observation can be identified:

1. The dramatic advance in microelectronic technology has made it possible to increase the number of components per chip by a factor of ten every two years. In the near future it will be feasible to implement on one chip a large CPU, such as an IBM 370/168, with about 130,000 logic gates. At the same time we have seen a significant cost reduction for CPU-processing, storage and transmission of data.

2. There is a growing need for increased availability and reliability of computer systems. Examples can be found in various application areas like computers in aircraft, medical applications, defense systems, production plant control and many others.

3. The price-performance characteristics of hardware and software components indicate that it might be more economical to achieve high performance not through the use of extremely complex high speed single components, but rather by utilizing dedicated computing units working independently in parallel.

Research on distributed systems is in progress within universities as well as in industry and in governmental organizations. Several experimental systems are in the design or implementation phase. There are some topics which are already quite well understood, e.g., hardware interconnection, interprocess communication, synchronization and atomic transactions. But there are other topics which are not well understood at all, e.g., the architecture of distributed systems, design choices, resource management, and verification and testing in a distributed environment. We can expect that many more questions and problems will arise in the future, since we do not yet have the necessary experience with distributed systems in operation.

Due to the fact that distributed systems are in an early research stage, the material presented during the course was concerned with established results as well as development trends, first ideas towards solutions for some unsolved problems, and important questions not yet investigated. It should be noticed that the contents of the lectures were selected according to the goal of the course, which was to concentrate on the total system view of a distributed system and not merely to present isolated single aspects.

With great pleasure we take this opportunity to express our gratitude and appreciation

> to the lecturers, who have spent considerable time not only discussing the course contents during the preparation period but also and foremost preparing excellent lecture notes,

> to Butler Lampson, who acted as editor of this book, and to Xerox Corporation for allowing him to use their facilities for producing the course notes and final book copy,

> to Sara Dake, Dr. Lampson's secretary, who did a large part of the work required to assemble this book, and

> to all members of our staff who have helped to organize this course.

We are confident that these lectures will prove rewarding for all computer scientists working in the area of distributed systems.

M. Paul
H. J. Siegert

Contents

Richard W. Watson, University of California Lawrence Livermore Laboratory [1]

Stephen R. Kimbleton and Pearl Wang, National Bureau of Standards [3] (14.1-14.6)
Butler W. Lampson, Xerox Palo Alto Research Center (14.7-14.9)

1. This work was performed under the auspices of the U.S. Department of Energy by the Lawrence Livermore Laboratory under contract No. W-7405-ENG-48.

2. This work was done jointly with Howard Sturgis.

3. This work is a contribution of the National Bureau of Standards and is not subject to copyright. Partial funding for the preparation of this paper was provided by the U.S. Air Force Rome Air Development Center (RADC) under Contract No. F 30602-77-0068. Certain commercial products are identified in this paper in order to adequately specify the procedures being described. In no case does such identification imply recommendation or endorsement by the National Bureau of Standards, nor does it imply that the material identified is necessarily the best for the purpose.

4. Much of the discussions and concepts contained in this section are based upon real systems and experiments conducted by associates of the author. Rather than rewrite these experiments, the authors of the papers describing the experiments allowed the author to excerpt material and descriptions. For this a very substantial debt of gratitude is owed to L. D. Anderson, T. O. Wolff, L. J. Schlecta, B. R. Manning, and R. C. DeWard for permission to use their works.

5. The NSW case study is based on information given in design specifications, overviews and tutorials listed in the references. The author is very much indebted to Robert Thomas of Bolt, Beranek and Newman and Dick Watson from Lawrence Livermore Laboratory for kindly providing most of the information material listed.

6. This section is excerpted from papers written by my colleagues David Boggs, Dave Gifford, Jay Israel, Robert Metcalfe, Jim Mitchell, John Shoch, Howard Sturgis, Ed Taft, and Chuck Thacker. I am especially indebted to Dave Gifford for the entire contents of 17.4.

Chapter 1. Motivations, objectives and characterization of distributed systems

1.1. Motivations

Specialists generally agree that distributed computing is made possible by the price-performance revolution in microelectronics on the one hand and the development of efficient and cost effective interconnection structures on the other hand. But changes in technology can be a driving force only because they make it possible to match user needs which tend to become more and more sophisticated. These are the two major motivations for distributed systems.

1.1.1. Technological changes

1.1.1.1. Microelectronics technology

Semiconductor technology has made dramatic advances over the last years (LSI and VLSI). The raw cost of fabricating a given logic element (processor, memory, peripheral controller) has been declining by a factor of 10 every three years over the last decade. Another way of looking at technological advances is to compare sizes of memory on one chip: from 4 Kbits in 1973, it has moved to 256Kbits in 1979. The present density of logic on a chip is such that any complex logic element can be built with a few chips at a cost lower than 1000 US$. Current prices may fall in the future because of even larger production volumes and because of the rapidly developing trend for standardizing chip interface logic. As the cost represented by the hardware in general has been a constantly decreasing factor, software development costs are now the prominent factor, which can be kept low enough only by taking advantage of cheap and sophisticated hardware as much as possible. It has become easier and cheaper nowadays to buy a multiple processor system than to invest in a large and complex multiprogrammed uniprocessor. Finally, because hardware has become less expensive and more flexible, individual processor efficiency can be de-emphasized with the result that operating systems should not include any more costly software implemented mechanisms aimed at "optimizing" hardware utilization.

1.1.1.2. Interconnection and communication technology

In conventional multiprocessor systems, processors communicate through shared memory. For many practical reasons, e.g. geographical dispersion, or operational objectives, e.g. modularity, it is now more common to provide each processor with some storage facility. Processor/memory elements can cooperate, exchange messages and behave as a single system only if they are interconnected through a convenient communication medium. We see this architectural trend in most recent multiple processor systems. Indeed, the concept of architectures centered around a shared communication medium, as illustrated by DEC's bus-based PDP-11 series, is in no way a new idea. What is new is the generalization of this approach as well as the physical sizes contemplated for current and future multiple processor computing systems.

In 1964, Rand Corporation published a series of reports which contained the description of a new concept: packet-switching. Since then, many experimental and public computer communication networks have been built, based on packet-switching subnets which carry traffic between computers and terminals across arbitrary large distances. Because of the growing importance of computer-communication networks, international organizations, like ISO and CCITT, are working at the definition of standards which would ease the problem of interconnecting heterogeneous processing elements. Future computer-communication networks may not all use packet-switching technology. However, the demonstration that such networks may be built and used at a cost which is highly competitive compared to conventional telecommunication networks costs has been a very strong incentive for users to consider the possibility of distributing processing elements across regions and countries and still having immediate access to any of these elements from anywhere.

More recently, so-called local area computer networks have developed extremely rapidly. Intended for computing systems limited in size, these networks make use of such simple and cheap technologies as twisted pairs, coaxial cables, radio transmission as well as of more sophisticated technologies like fiber optics. Local area interconnection media allow for the wiring of a campus, a building, a factory, etc. and they can handle a reasonably large number of processing elements. Several experimental local area computer networks have been in use for years. The feasibility as well as the cost-effectiveness of this approach have been widely demonstrated. Local area computer networks are now becoming commercialy available from some manufacturers. Users are led to decide whether they would keep on using a big mainframe installation or rather move to a local network of smaller processing elements. Clearly, as interconnection techniques tend to be more and more mastered, it is becoming more and more reasonable to envision the building of any large or small distributed computing system out of several processing elements. For the same reason, the interconnection of a number of distributed systems through a small or large network is also achievable with the current technology.

1.1.2. User needs

Parallel to the decline of hardware costs and the development of interconnection technologies, there is a general trend for introducing computing systems into almost every business-oriented or leisure-oriented activity, as well as improving computing system interfaces. Also, new system architectures are needed to meet economic or managerial user constraints.

Increased sophistication

New application areas for computing systems represent an extremely large market for the data processing industry. However, it is not a matter of producing and selling more existing computing systems. "New" users are not willing to buy systems having complex and "hostile" interfaces. They want a simple external access language for using services, not physical resources, which should be permanently available. Furthermore, the set of services offered should be expandable at will. These "new" users and "current" users as well assume that computing systems may now be tailored to their individual needs. User requirements can only be fulfilled by building systems which meet the objectives described under section 1.2. We will see in the following why such systems have to be distributed.

Managerial issues

Not all organizations exhibit a centralized functional structure. There is a growing reluctance from users to buy a conventional and centralized data processing system, which tends to impose a centralized style of management on an organization, when activities are by nature decentralized. Such an artificial distortion between the managerial/functional structure of an organization and the architecture of the computing system being used may result in large money losses. For example, it may turn out to be extremely profitable to provide each department, each line unit, with its own small computer. Local tasks are run and controlled by the people who understand them best; these people being fully responsible for results, it may be expected that the job will be done seriously enough.

Economical considerations

The possibility of installing processing elements at those locations where computing power is needed brings another advantage which is reduced communication costs. Probably, a lot of processing can be conducted on local processing elements, as opposed to all processing being handled by one central but remote big mainframe. In a federation of processing elements, communication requirements for accessing any processing element are much less demanding than those of a central processing element serving all processing elements. Another way of explaining this is to imgine a set of dispersed conventional terminals requiring access to a set of services. Most configurations are organized as stars, with all terminals linked individually to a common and unique mainframe. If we provide terminals with some local – and cheap – "intelligence", either by making terminals looking like processors or by "concentrating" them on a number of special-purpose processing elements, it is probable that most traffic will be kept local and that remote traffic will require less communication hardware, shared more efficiently, thus inducing lower communication costs.

Finally, for minis and micros, there is evidence that Grosch's law does not hold. This factor of dis-economy of scale may also be a good incentive for considering the choice of a distributed system. To summarize, technological advances in storage/processing logic and interconnection structures have made it possible to reduce hardware costs dramatically. This has attracted a large community of new users. Also, users of existing computing systems are not all pleased with the quality of services obtained from existing systems. There seems to be a convergence between what is desired and what may be achieved. We now analyze more carefully what is desired i.e. what the objectives of distributed systems are.

1.2. Objectives

As well as motivations, objectives may not be all meaningful to a particular system and probably not equally important. Objectives listed below constitute what is usually expected from distributed systems in general.

1.2.1. Increased performance

Whatever the progress in technology may be, the processing power obtained out of a single processing element will certainly be less than the processing power of a multiple processor system. This is not revolutionary. However, sources of contention and bottlenecks which are known to exist in conventional multiprocessors, e.g. shared memory based interprocessor communication, central process scheduler, should be removed. Interconnecting several processing elements which cooperate on a single activity via some decentralized technique to perform overall system control is probably the only way to enhance performance. Short response time and high throughput can be achieved through the partitioning of global system functions into tasks that each of several processing elements, specialized or not, can handle individually. This results in a parallel execution of simultaneous conflict-free requests without incurring the cost of context-switching. Overall system control is needed to detect and resolve possible conflicts without impairing parallelism and asynchrony in processing.

1.2.2. Extensibility

An extensible system is thought of as a system which can be easily adapted to a changing environment without disrupting its functioning. This implies that the design of the system should not be changed. We see two kinds of environmental changes:

Modification of performance requirements: what is usually necessary is either to replace some general-purpose processing elements with specialized ones, or to add more processing elements to the existing system, or to replace existing processing elements with functionally identical but better performing elements. One may also wish to reduce a system configuration because performance constraints have relaxed. It should be possible either to add or to plug out processing elements dynamically without disturbing the system.

Modification of functional requirements: one may wish to expand the set of services a computing system provides. This may prove to be practically impossible in numerous cases because of early design and implementation choices or because of the software development effort required. By designing from the begining a computing system as a set of a variable number of processing elements which provide for a variable number of functions, it should be possible to integrate new functions at low incremental costs. This objective of extensibility implies that it is easy to interconnect processing elements, which may be heterogeneous, which means also that the overall design is modular in essence.

A modular architecture which, as we shall see, is one of the characteristics of distributed computing systems, has the following advantages:

> *simpler system design*: instead of using a general purpose computing system for executing a variety of possibly independent tasks, the different elements of a distributed system can be each specialized to do a limited set of tasks. This simplifies the design of each element and reduces the complexity of the overall system design. Consequently, development and maintenance costs will be reduced.

> *ease of installation*: an extensible system may be installed incrementally, this leading to low-cost initial configurations and easing the problem of debugging a particular implementation.

ease of maintenance: as processing elements may be added to or withdrawn from the system at any time, it becomes possible to unplug any element in order to check its functioning as well as to replace it on the spot by another correct element. Furthermore, if the system includes several functionally identical elements, maintenance and utilization phases may overlap without disturbing user activities.

1.2.3. Increased availability

Technological advances and know-how help to build hardware which is more and more reliable. Identical progress is developing in the software area. However, the probability that a fault, an error or a failure occurs is non-zero for any physical system. Most reliability mechanisms developed for conventional systems rely on redundant hardware e.g. TMR, redundant software e.g. different versions of an algorithm run in parallel, redundant data e.g. checkpoints and journals. However, a single fault, error or failure can jeopardize the correct functioning of these mechanisms. Basically, the availability of a system including some single critical resource, e.g. a CPU, is very low as it depends directly on whether or not this single resource is operational. The existence of several processing elements in a system raises the opportunity for utilizing mutual inspection techniques which allow for automatic detection, diagnosis and recovery. If processors cooperate in a decentralized manner and if they check each other in adherence to some specific protocol without relying on a single "central" processing element, it becomes possible to take full advantage of redundancy in hardware, software and data so as to obtain fail-soft computing systems i.e. systems which keep on running in spite of faults, errors or failures. The availability of a distributed system is then closely related to the degree of redundancy embedded in the system. To which extent is a system able to survive failures is a notion akin to availability which has been referred to as resiliency. For a given function, a computing system is said to be n-resilient if the function is not disrupted as long as at most n failures are experienced by the system at the same time.

1.2.4. Resource sharing

The term "resource" should be taken in its widest sense. For example, a resource may be a physical device, external to the computing system, and which happens to be necessary for conducting activities within the system (e.g. sensors). Another example is a database which is maintained on some particular processing element and which contains data useful to a number of processes. A resource may also just be a processing element which can be assigned processes dynamically. Resource sharing involves load sharing and transparency to implemented architectures. Resource sharing should not be restricted to remote access to a variety of resources. What is required is some system-wide control of all activities for the purpose of achieving optimal and dynamic resource allocation and thus optimal resource sharing.

1.2.5. Comments

Going through the presentation of these ojectives, the reader may have noticed a few points. First, objectives are somehow inter-related. For instance, response time may be kept below a given value by adding more processing elements when the external load is expected to increase in the future (performance-extensibility relationship) or by absorbing temporary overflows through automatic load sharing (performance-resource sharing relationship). Similarly, extensibility is an objective akin to increased availability to some aspects because there may well be no difference at all, as regards executives, between a processing element which is plugged out for maintenance purposes and a processing element which has failed suddenly. Second, we have tried to avoid paraphrasing. Indeed, it is easy to expand the set of objectives by adding such items as "adaptability to geographical dispersion", "reduced communication costs", "high reliability", etc. We believe that such goals are included in the four objectives presented in the above. Describing them as separate objectives would only add confusion. Third, all objectives apply to distributed systems in general, i.e. to large computer networks, local area computer networks and multiple processor systems. Fourth, there is one remanent concept behind all of the objectives, that is the concept of system-wide control. It should be recognized from now on that none of these objectives can be met if executives do not embed some system-wide control technique.

1.3. Characterization

We will not try here to define what a distributed system is. The technical and commercial litterature is full of such definitions which contradict each other and which, in many cases, are so fuzzy that it does not mean anything to adopt or to reject them. Actually, a definition is useful if it helps one to infer principles and guidelines for the design of distributed systems. In the following, we will therefore attempt to identify what are believed to be the most interesting and important characteristics of distributed systems.

1.3.1. What is distributed?

Most computing systems include all of the following ingredients: hardware, system software, system data, user software and data. It may look attractive to label "distributed system" any system which has some of these ingredients distributed. Then, it remains to be explained what it means to speak of distributed hardware, distributed software and distributed data. To this end, it is possible to follow three different approaches which are:

- characterization of distribution solely in terms of physical features
- characterization of distribution solely in terms of logical features
- characterization of distribution in terms of both physical and logical features.

Physical characteristics

It may be somewhat difficult to distinguish distributed systems from centralized ones only from the observation of physical characteristics. For example, one may decide to say that within a processing unit, the logic of a register and the logic of the multiplier are distributed because they are not exactly residing at the same place. Similarly, two disk drives connected on the same I/O channel may be said distributed. However, one has the intuition that physical components should be more "distributed" because otherwise, all computing systems could be labeled "distributed". Then the question of how far apart should components be located so as to speak of a distributed system? In other words, if a 100 miles long leased telephone line is inserted between two processing elements which happened to be located in the same room and if this modification can be kept transparent to the operating system, have we moved from a centralized system to a distributed one? This is simply an example of the more general question: when using some metrics for physical distances, frequencies, bandwidth, etc., what are the correct thresholds which allow to differentiate between centralized and distributed systems? Will everybody agree on some given thresholds?

Defining distribution only in terms of logical characteristics is one way to alleviate the problem. However, if we want to meet some of the objectives assigned to distributed systems — increased availability for example — some modular and redundant hardware, data structures and software components are necessary. Should we consider that modularity and redundancy are characteristics equivalent to physical distribution? We need to express the fact that some objectives cannot be met by a computing system whose hardware would include only one processing element, as opposed to a multiplicity of processing elements. It seems that physical distribution is a pre-requisite. It seems also that this is not sufficient to characterize what is meant by distributed system. What are then the logical features behind the concept of distribution?

Logical characteristics

It is possible to build a list of logical criteria which can be found in the literature. A partial list could be:

- multiplicity of general-purpose resource components
- interconnected communicating processing elements having apparent or hidden levels of control
- system transparency
- system-wide executive control is performed by several processes without hierarchical relationship and which do not have a coherent view of the entire system state
- processes have disjoint address spaces and communicate via explicit message passing.

We have selected five criteria which seem to constitute most widely accepted characteristics.

Logical and physical characteristics

In this book, we will use the term "distributed system" to refer to a computing system which has the following characteristics:

(1) it includes an arbitrary number of system and user processes;

(2) the architecture is modular, consisting of a possibly varying number of processing elements;

(3) communication is achieved via message passing on a shared communication structure, (excluding shared memory);

(4) some system-wide control is performed, so as to provide for dynamic interprocess cooperation and runtime management;

(5) interprocess message transit delays are variable and some non-zero time always exists between the production of an event by a process and the materialization of this production at the destination process premise (different from the observation of the event by the destination process).

These characteristics may be interpreted as general rules to be observed for designing distributed systems which would meet the objectives presented in section 1.2. It is fair to say that specialists generally agree on these characteristics although the discussion is still open on the exclusion of memory from the set of possible communication media.

1.3.2. What is new ?

The relationships between objectives and characteristics (1), (2) and (3) are obvious. As explained in section 1.2.5, characteristic (4) is a vital one. But why characteristic (5)? Characteristic (5) expresses a very fundamental and important physical constraint which must be taken into account explicitly for the design of a control technique which would not be in contradiction with the objectives of distributed systems. Let us elaborate on this. Most existing systems utilize control techniques which are based on the premise that all processes constituting the executive share a complete and consistent view of the entire system state. This is achieved via the utilization of a particular – and unique – entity which regulates the activities of the executive processes. We will refer to these techniques as centralized ones. In distributed systems, the existence of such a unique entity is ruled out. Then, because of characteristic (5), it can be shown that it is impossible to build or to observe a complete and consistent view of the system state in those systems which also have characteristics (1), (2) and (3). Therefore, centralized control techniques are not suitable for these systems.

At this point, it is important to realize that system designers have the responsibility of deciding, for every system, which levels of abstraction should embed centralized or decentralized control techniques. There is probably no choice left as regards the lowest levels, e.g. communication. Conversely, options are left open for higher levels of abstraction. For example, one may decide that a distributed system is obtained by providing for an extra layer of software on top of existing operating systems implemented in each processing element. This result in the development of what is called a network operating system. Similarly, one may consider that every processing element in a distributed system should host one instantiation of a virtual and global operating system. Such a global operating system would include a global executive, also instantiated on each of the processing elements and which would achieve, in particular, some system-wide control of processing activities. Clearly, global executives can be centralized or distributed, depending on the way control is performed.

For example, a number of multiprocessors which exhibit characteristics (1), (2) and (3) and which use a centralized system-wide control technique have been built and are being used. They work correctly because:

(i) all processes constituting the executive rely on some unique entity for obtaining a view of the system state which is unique; consequently, these processes make consistent decisions

(ii) the relative shielding between what the instantaneous system state really is and its representation communicated to the executive processes is always kept small enough.

Such designs are perfectly acceptable. However, it should be recognized that corresponding systems do not meet the objectives of distributed systems. In physically distributed systems, the system state representation is partitioned and scattered all over the different processing elements. The control of all executive functions normally done within processing elements must be done among processing elements. Because of characteristic (5), executive processes in charge of performing system-wide control have to work under the following constraints:

(1) processes may each have a different view of the system state; consequently, these processes may make inconsistent decisions

(2) the shielding between what the instantaneous system state really is and its representation communicated to these processes may not be negligible.

Consequently, the new problem and the key issue are the design of control techniques which would meet the constraints of distributed systems. To our knowledge, there is currently no computing system embedding decentralized control techniques at all levels of abstraction. Rapid progress should be expected in the near future.

Chapter 2. Distributed system architecture model

2.1. Introduction

The area of distributed systems is new and not well defined. The purpose of this chapter is to provide an informal conceptual framework for organizing the discussion of distributed system design goals, issues, and interrelationships, provide some common terminology to be used in the following chapters, and provide an overview of some common design issues. We refer to this framework or *reference architecture* as the *Distributed Systems Architecture Model* or simply as the *Model*. The remainder of the book elaborates the Model and presents alternative approaches to its realization. Besides serving as an organizing framework for the material of this book, we believe, the Model is useful in the design, organization, and analysis of a distributed system. The Model is shown in figure 2-1.

The Model contains three dimensions. The vertical dimension represents a distributed system as consisting of a set of logical layers. This book is primarily organized according to this axis. Each layer and sublayer has design and implementation issues unique to itself as well as a range of issues common among all the layers. These common issues are shown as a second dimension on the horizontal axis. The problems presented by each common issue and the appropriate solutions to it may be the same or different in each layer. The third dimension, shown perpendicular to the page, concerns issues reflecting the global interaction of all parts of a distributed system on whole-system implementation and optimization. This dimension is poorly understood. It is shown here primarily as a reminder of its importance and the need for research to improve our understanding. Each of these dimensions is discussed in detail in the sections to follow.

There are many problems and solutions in common between distributed and nondistributed systems. However, distributed systems introduce new problems due to the physical separation and heterogeneity of their components and multiple controlling administrations:

- Naming (identification), protection, and sharing issues resulting from the heterogeneous systems.

- Translation issues resulting from heterogeneous control and data encodings and representations.

- The need for a message based interprocess communication (IPC) model because memory sharing is not practical between distributed components.

- Distributed service and resource structures.

- New sources of errors and potentially more complex error-recovery.

- Need to maintain consistency among multiple copies of information.

- Synchronization and other control problems resulting from distributed state information and arbitrary message delay.

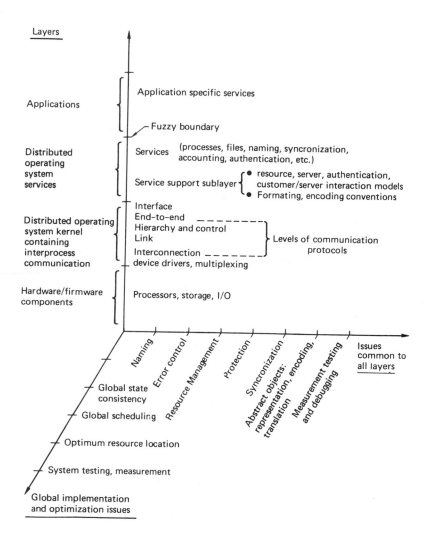

Figure 2-1: Distributed system architecture model

- Accounting and resource management issues resulting from multiple controlling administrations.

- Efficiency problems resulting from the variable communication delay and bandwidth of between components.

- More complex verification, debugging, measurement problems.

Many existing system models and mechanisms cannot be extended to deal with these problems. The Model does, we believe, provide a framework for solutions to them through the techniques of layering, the creation of abstract objects, and message passing.

2.2. Layers and interfaces

The concept of modular and layered design or levels of abstraction has been widely accepted as good software engineering practice and is shown in figure 2-2. Associated with a *layer N* are two *interfaces*. Each layer *N* provides at the interface to layers *N* + 1 and higher a well-defined set of services. Layer *N* is in turn implemented using the services provided through interfaces with layers *N* - 1 and lower. The layers may be partially ordered since many abstractions at higher levels may involve only some or none of the abstractions at some particular level below (see Chapter 11 for an example). The classification of levels can also vary depending on one's point of view. For example, in an internetwork environment, where two networks are each used as a logical link in the other, the end-to-end protocol of each would be positioned in a level hierarchy differently depending on whether one was viewing the structure from one or the other network [Section 6.8, Shoch 80b]. Another example is the need of apparently lower level device drivers to convert messages to I/O commands and interrupts to messages. A number of other situations of this kind are described in the ISO Reference Model documentation [ISO 79]. It seems to us that layering while a useful conceptual tool has a number of subtleties yet to be explicated before it can be applied formally in modeling all aspects of real systems [Parnas 72, 79]. Layers only interact through their interfaces. Layering is advantageous because:

- The internal structures, mechanisms, encodings, and algorithms used within a layer are not visible to other layers.

- Complex systems can be broken down into more easily understood pieces.

- The system can evolve more easily because the algorithms and mechanisms implementing a given layer can be changed without affecting the service offered, providing the service offered at the interface remains unchanged.

- Alternate services can be offered at layer *N* + 1, but share or multiplex the services of layer *N*.

- Alternate implementations for a layer can coexist.

- A layer or sublayer can be simplified or omitted when any or all of its services are not needed.

- The confidence in the correct operation of a layered system is more easily established by testing and analysis of each layer in turn.

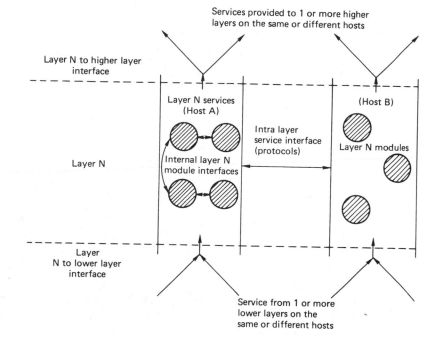

Figure 2-2: Layers, interfaces, and protocols

Creating a distributed system architecture requires

(1) decomposing the system into layers and sublayers according to some set of criteria;

(2) specifying the services to be offered by layer N to higher layers;

(3) specifying the services layer N requires of lower layers.

The services of layer N may be further decomposed into modules. The modules implementing a service of a given layer may in turn be distributed. Modules, like layers, provide at their interface a well-defined set of services and their internal implementation is not visible on the other side of this interface.

Decomposition of a system into layers and modules is an iterative and somewhat arbitrary process. The following guidelines for layer or module specifications are suggested in [ISO79].

- Use a reasonably small number of layers.
- Provide interface at points where the service description and number of interactions can be made small.
- Provide separation to handle functions that are clearly different in process or technology.
- Utilize past experience.
- Group related functions.
- Localize function.
- Provide boundaries where interfaces can be standardized.
- Provide appropriate levels of abstraction.
- Allow layers to be bypassed.

The above description identifies two interfaces, one between adjacent layers and one between cooperating modules within a given layer. An *interface* is defined as a set of conventions for the exchange of information between two entities. It consists of three components:

- A set of visible abstract objects (see the next section) and for each a set of allowed operations and associated parameters.
- A set of rules governing the legal sequences (sequences that will not result in an error indication) of these operations.
- The encoding and formatting conventions required for operations and parameters (data).

One of the problems in any new field, such as distributed computing, is lack of agreed terminology [Enslow 78]. Within the distributed computing literature we find the term *protocol* used where the term interface as defined above seems operationally equivalent. The term *protocol* is often, but not always, used to connote an interface between two distributed (remote from each other) cooperating modules of the same level; i.e. *peer modules*, located on heterogeneous systems. Whereas, attempts have been made to have the term *interface* connote the conventions for communication across adjacent layers or in some sense between dissimilar local entities [Pouzin 78].

Sometimes a distinction is made between the terms *service* or *function* and *interface*, where the terms service or function of a layer refer to an abstract specification of generic primitives, their results and their sequencing [Pearson 80], while the term interface is a detailed specification of how to obtain the service on a particular implementation [Sunshine 79]. There is the connotation in networking literature that services or protocols require universal agreement or standards, while the details of an interface are generally a local implementation option. If we want to be able to achieve program portability or relocatability within a distributed system in order to achieve reliability or other goals, then interfaces between adjacent layers will also require standardization. If all these terms are to have distinct meanings, then much sharper definitions are needed than we are prepared to give.

2.3. Abstract objects as a unifying concept

The Model is centered around the creation of a distributed or decentralized operating system (DOS), also often called a network operating system (NOS).

One of the major design goals of a DOS is to provide users access to real and abstract *objects* or *resources* [Jones 78b] in which the distributed nature of their implementation is hidden as far as practical, and in which all *objects* (system and user defined) are named, communicated with, shared, and protected uniformly. The system can be extended by creating new *resources*, using existing ones as components. Real objects are entities such as processors, secondary storage, I/O devices etc. DOS abstract objects or resources are entities such as processes, files, directories, virtual I/O devices, databases, clocks, and accounts, which computing experience has shown to be a useful set of basic building blocks for creating higher level objects. Objects at each level in turn interact through and are created out of lower level resources.

The generality is that each layer of the model and its internal modules provides its services by defining a set of objects which can only be accessed through well defined interfaces. Each *type* of resource is *specified* by:

- A set of data structures visible at the interface (its *representation*) and

- A set of *operations* or *functions* and associated *parameters* that can be performed on the representation.

Chapter 11 contains an excellent example of the use of layered abstraction.

Two resources are of the same type if and only if they have the same *specification*. The representation for a given object type and the operations on this *representation* are implemented by one or more modules called, object managers or resource servers, or simply *servers*. Servers can be implemented by hardware/firmware or a set of procedures, processes, etc.

The implementation details of a resource representation are of concern only to a particular *server*. Two different servers of a resource of type, say file, might internally structure the files they manage quite differently, while presenting externally at the interface, the same representation and operations. This characteristic is important in dealing with the heterogeneity that results when distributed systems are built on top of existing operating systems or implemented directly on the hardware/firmware components of many vendors.

One can recognize two kinds of objects, *active* and *passive*. Passive objects (I/O devices, messages, communication channels, files, directories, accounts, etc.) must be acted upon by active objects for the content of their representation to change. Active objects can change the content of their own representations as well as the content of the representations of other objects.

We call the primitive active DOS object of the model a *process*, where a process is informally understood to be a procedure (a set of commands) executing on a real or virtual processor (virtual processors may multiplex one or more real processors). Processes in turn are thought of as controlling, managing, or creating all types of DOS and application objects. Computers that only execute a single program are considered to consist of a single process. All communication is between processes, i.e. interprocess communication (IPC). Processes are implemented on *hosts*, data-terminal-equipment (DTE) in CCITT terminology. Hosts may have arbitrarily complex structures (many physical processors may be considered a single *host*, or a single physical processor may be considered many hosts), one or more network interfaces, and one or more network addresses. Host is a rather elusive concept. It generally has the connotation of a uniform local environment for processes (the names, structure, locality of processes on a given host have something in common).

Processes interact by sending each other objects called *messages*, usually in the form of *requests* and *replys*. (The view of interprocess communication (IPC) within the application layer may explicitly be that of sending messages or making procedure like calls [Lauer 79]. Remote procedure calls are discussed in Chapter 14. Even if the *procedure call interface* model is used in a distributed system, the reality is that messages are being exchanged. Therefore, we use the message view here.) A pair of processes carrying on a conversation we will call *correspondents*. A *message* is the smallest unit of data that must be sent and received between a pair of correspondents for a meaningful action to take place. The resulting primitive form of a message passing and process oriented model for a distributed system is shown in figure 2-3.

A given process can operate in either or both *server* and *customer* or *client* roles at different times. A customer process accesses a resource by sending *requests* containing operation specification and parameters to the appropriate server. The server may then satisfy the request by accessing data structures local to it or by sending additional requests to other servers to aid it in carrying out the original request. When a request is satisfied, the server sends replies containing an indication of success or failure and results (if any). Messages that contain directives or declarations that the receiver must interpret, *control messages*, are distinguished from messages that contain information simply to be stored, printed, displayed, or otherwise passed on without interpretation, *data messages*. The distinction between data and control appears in all layers of the Model. Data messages are logically just parameters of requests and replys, that because of their size, are sent separately.

Besides the customer and server processes being distinct, the handler of replies *may* be a different process from the requester, or a different address within the requester than that used to send the request. Further, the sources and sinks for data *may* be different processes than the original requester or server. In general a customer or server system may be built with multiple cooperating processes, each process handling one or more different roles. We elaborate this idea of roles in Section 2.4.4. The layers of the Model are now introduced.

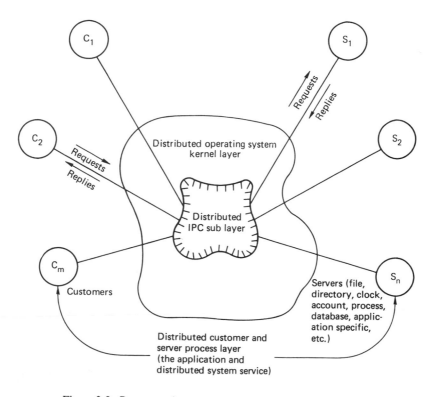

Figure 2-3: Process and message passing distributed system model

2.4. The model layers

2.4.1. Introduction

The Model consists of four basic layers, meeting the layering guidelines listed in Section 2.2, derived from the concept of objects and their interaction presented above:

1) A *hardware/firmware component* layer: processors, memories, I/O units, keyboard terminals, devices for data collection and physical process control, etc. All passive components are assumed to have an active element (host) either embedded within them or associated with them in some way that implements one or more controlling processes. All communication with and between passive components takes place through their associated processes.

2) A *distributed operating system kernel* layer that provides:

(a) component drivers for interfacing a component's I/O structure to the message passing model, such as converting interrupts into messages, and messages into I/O commands, and for providing the basis for creating abstract processes, files, devices or other most primitive objects;

(b) any foundation needed to support component multiplexing;

(c) basic mechanisms required for protection and security; and

(d) an interprocess communication service. The IPC service also provides the most primitive process synchronization mechanism. Because of the emphasis placed here on the IPC service, we often simply call this kernel layer the IPC or communication layer.

3) A *distributed operating system service* layer that provides services useful to a wide variety of applications, as well as implements basic resource allocation and multiplexing policies. This layer consists of sublayers of processes, providing services built on each other, starting with a basic process creation, management, and destruction service, the *process server*. Other primitive services allow access to storage outside a process's memory space and other hardware components.

4) An *application* layer that contains processes that provide application dependent services.

The dividing line between these last two layers is fuzzy because all processes are logically treated uniformly in the sense that they communicate and access each others services by message passing, although some may be permanently resident in the memory of a processor for efficiency, require special privileges to communicate with a kernel driver [Donnelley 79], be specially trusted as part of a distributed protection system, or implement their service in terms of that provided by others.

2.4.2. Need for a distributed operating system

An important characteristic of the Model, mentioned earlier, is that it explicitly recognizes the need to create a distributed operating system. Most of the existing literature on distributed systems or computer networking architecture has focused on interprocess communication. This is only natural as much of the work during the past decade has been concentrated on learning how to physically interconnect and achieve interprocess communication between heterogeneous systems. Developments to date have made possible valuable services such as, access to remote interactive programs from terminals on heterogeneous systems, simple file transfer (primarily text files), and electronic mail. However, there have been very few applications of resource sharing or distributed computing as defined in Chapter 1. Current network architectures consist of one or more function-oriented protocols, such as virtual terminal or file transfer protocols, built on top of an IPC protocol layer [Crocker 72, Pouzin 78]. The potential offered by computer networking to support resource sharing and distributed computing cannot be realized with such architectures because [Kimbleton 76, Thomas 78, Watson 80b, White 76]:

• No basis is provided for easily creating, in a modular fashion, new resources or services out of existing ones. For example, one cannot use existing file transport servers as foundations for a distributed data management system.

• Each programmer desiring to provide or use a new network sharable resource must face anew all the problems on the common issue axis of the model as well as interface to the protocols of the IPC layer. Every service uses different identifier, request/reply formatting, and other conventions, for example.

- The terminal user or programmer must know the different naming and other access mechanisms required by the network, each host, and each service. He must log in to his local host, use a network access program, and then log in to his target host(s), each possibly using different conventions.

- The setting up of accounts and other administrative procedures are awkward. The user must explicitly establish accounts and receive billing from each administration controlling a host with resources he wishes to use.

- They fail to adequately recognize that many distributed applications are more naturally transaction than stream oriented, that is, a request is sent and a reply is received, with no implication that further conversation need ever take place. The result is that extra delay and messages are required at each level of the architecture to open and close *connections* (initialize and destroy error control, resource management, protection, etc. state). Because a message at one level can generate several at the next level, this overhead can be high.

We believe these problems can be eliminated or minimized and a firm basis provided for distributed systems if a different point of view is taken, namely, that what is required is that a distributed operating system layer be explicitly created with a structure centered around a well designed distributed kernel/interprocess communication facility. These DOS and IPC layers must:

- Turn a collection of distributed hardware/software resources into a coherent set of real and abstract objects or resources. The IPC and DOS layers must support naming, sharing, protection, synchronization, intercommunication, and error recovery.

- Multiplex and allocate these resources among many distributed computations or processes.

They must provide this functionality in the face of the problems of heterogeneity and physical separation of components mentioned earlier. The ISO Open Systems Interconnection Reference Model is a start in the DOS direction, and it and the Model here have commonality with respect to the IPC layer and what we define in Section 2.4.4 as service support functions [desJardin 78, ISO 79, Zimmerman 80]. Let us now discuss each of the four layers briefly.

2.4.3. Application layer

The service provided by the Application Layer is clearly dependent on specific applications. The needs of an application or set of applications will define the services required of the DOS layer. Process management, communication, information management, virtual I/O, clocks, accounting, authentication are the usual services needed in various forms by all applications.

There are currently few distributed application systems in the sense of the definition of Chapter 1 and so this area is the least well understood, but the following design areas can be identified as important:

Application Structure—The issue here is how to organize and structure the processing, data and other application resources both physically and logically [Enslow 78]. The types of questions that need answering are:

- How should processing be distributed? Should it be distributed to achieve functional separation, closeness according to some measure, a given level of fault tolerance, or other goal? For example, on a functional basis, all activity supporting databases might be placed on one set of hosts, while heavy numeric computational activities would be placed on a different set of hosts. Measures of distance may be associated with improving responsiveness, throughput, or communication costs. Text editing and graphic I/O display processing, or command language interaction for an application may be moved close to human users, while computation associated with the application's mathematical models may be remote. To improve reliability or responsiveness, the same generic processing functions may be available at several locations [Chapter 18, Shapiro 77]. One of the important factors that will affect the freedom an application developer has to organize processing is how data type representation and translation are handled [Section 2.5.7, Chapter 14]. For example, there may be real economic motivation to distribute a large numeric application between low cost mass produced mini/midi computers and large scale systems, yet differences in word length and floating point number representations may prove difficult to overcome.

- How should application processes be organized for control and communication? Are the application processes organized in a linear chain, tree structure, or more general network? Is the control of the application distributed or centralized [Chapter 8]? How do the application processes maintain synchronization [Chapter 12]?

- How should data be distributed? Should files be replicated at each processing node, partitioned so that only some of the data exist at given nodes, or should some other organization be used? One can imagine distributed business applications where some of the data collected by each business organizational entity is only needed locally, some is frequently or occassionally used by other entities, while some is required for processing needed to operate the business as a whole. The decisions on how to organize the data will depend on costs (money, reliability, responsiveness, etc.) and on available mechanisms to support consistency of multiple copies, maintain synchronization of access and so forth [Chapter 13, Bernstein 79].

- What mechanisms are required to support different data and processing organizations [Saltzer 78b]? Mechanisms are required on at least two levels, those required within the distributed application itself such as those for maintaining synchronization or data consistency, and those required to support distributed application development, debugging, and maintenance [Section 14.7].

Language Issues—There are important common questions associated with programming, human terminal user, and distributed operating system interface languages for distributed systems. What features should be in these languages in addition to those desirable in a nondistributed system [Feldman 78, Lauer 79, Liskov 79]? One view of distributed system design is that it endeavors, using layers of abstraction, to create the illusion of a nondistributed system at some level. How pure should this illusion be; how many of the distributed system naming, error control, resource management, and other mechanisms should be visible and under user control in the various languages or be handled automatically (if possible) below these interfaces? For example, should users be able to specify at which physical locations processing is to be performed or data are to be stored? It may be important to provide such visibility and control to achieve performance goals. If a host system crashes, and direct network access exists to its secondary storage, should the system automatically attempt to move the representation of a process or data to another host and continue, or should the human user be explicitly required to perform such recovery operations? Knowing how error recovery is performed and being able to control it may be important for efficiency or security reasons.

The distributed system model should not prejudice the answers to the many questions asked above. Much research is needed to develop the mechanisms and criteria that will enable a methodology to be created to answer these questions. Much of the material in Part C is also applicable to applications.

2.4.4. Distributed operating system service layer

The services provided by the DOS layer are the conjunction of the services provided by its distributed servers, such as those mentioned above. The underlying services required by the DOS layer are access by its most primitive servers to the kernel component drivers (logically very restricted, privileged processes that communicate with the underlying physical objects by interrupts and priviledged commands, and communicate with higher level objects via the message based interprocess communication facility). The DOS area is somewhat better understood than that of applications. Some example prototype systems are under development and in the paper design stage [Clark 80; Donnelley 79; Farber 73; Fletcher 80; Forsdick 78; Jensen 78; Kimbleton 76,79; Lantz 79,80; Livesey 79; Millstein 77; Peebles 75,80; Thomas 73,78; Watson 80b,c; Wittie 79].

The user characteristics of needed DOS services have a great overlap with their counterparts for nondistributed systems. From the application point of view the interface language to the DOS layer is likely to look very similar in distributed and nondistributed systems because the basic types of objects required in each is the same. While, as mentioned in the previous section, there is a question about how much of the resource management, error control and other idiosyncrasies of a distributed system to make visible at the DOS interface, the same need exists to be able to create and destroy resources, interrogate their status, read and write their data structures, account for their usage, and start and stop them. The main new issues introduced with distributed operating system services are associated with their internal organization and implementation. These issues show up in meeting the three goals below and in the areas common across all layers, discussed in Section 2.5.

Chapters 8 discusses a spectrum of distributed operating systems. At one end of the spectrum are DOS's characterized by their having been built on top of existing operating systems, having resources allocated on a local basis, and having each host computer under local administrative control [Kimbleton 78]. Those at the other end of the spectrum are characterized by having been built as the native system on each host computer, and by having all resources managed, administered, and allocated globally [Jensen 78]. An important question is how can tools, such as editors, compilers, database management systems, that were implemented to run under an existing local OS be inserted, without a major rewrite, into a new DOS based system [Chapters 14, 18, Millstein 77]. Because of current vendor hardware constraints, the desire to use existing software, and their general expected utility, we believe systems at the NOS end of the spectrum to be common in the future.

Common NOS goals are the following.

The prime design goal is that a process (program), terminal user, or programmer have a uniform coherent view of distributed objects. Processes, programmers, and terminal users should not have to be explicitly aware of whether a needed resource is local, remote, or distributed. To the extent possible, host boundaries should not be visible. This does not mean that programs or users have no control over where a process is to be run or other resource is to be located or that they cannot learn the locations of resources. It means that a user need not (although he may) program differently or use different terminal procedures depending on resource location and that network operations and the idiosyncrasies of local hosts can be largely or completely hidden. Of course, performance may depend on the relative location of objects. One consequence of this goal is that if a resource or its controlling server is relocated for economic, performance, or other reasons to another system in the network, then at most a new identifier (address) is required, but no changes are required in the program logic or resource access mechanisms.

A second goal is that the structure be efficiently implementable and usable as the base *native* operating system on a single system of common current architecture [Donnelley 80], as well as be implementable as a *guest* layer [Peebles 80, Thomas 78] on existing operating systems that support appropriate interprocess communication [Haverty 78]. By the former condition we mean that, when implemented as the native operating system, access by local user processes to local services should be as efficient and no more involved in terms of the number and kind of messages or system calls exchanged than is common on existing nondistributed operating systems. [Donnelley 79] gives an example of the latter. We believe that a NOS architecture (assuming current vendor systems) can be made independent of the number and kind of underlying components, although different architectures, in detail, will exist depending on the assumptions made about the commonality that exists on the base systems.

Initially many DOS's will likely be implemented as guest systems, on top of existing OS's, but over time, as part of the evolution toward distributed computing, we expect that the structure of base OS design to evolve toward that required for a DOS. Layering a DOS on top of an existing OS implies creating a layer of servers that support the standard service interface and internally implement the service in part or in whole by calling on the corresponding existing OS services to accomplish their task.

A third important goal is extensibility, implying:

- That users can easily add new services built on existing services without requiring system programmers to add new resident or privileged code. (Some services may be made resident or privileged for performance enhancement, but that is a separate issue.)

- That the basic DOS structure not require the DOS to spring full blown into existence with all possible services to be useful; in other words that it can start with a few services as needed by initial applications and evolve.

- That systems desiring to participate in the DOS as users of or providers of a single service be able to do so with minimal implementation.

The abstract object model described in Section 2.2 forms a good base for meeting the above goals. While all objects within the DOS layer are provided by processes, these resources can be built up in sublayers starting with primitive resources built from the basic facilities of the underlying hardware/firmware components and increasing in abstraction and application orientation. For example [Chapter 19], on systems providing access to disk storage, there might be a primitive server providing primitive objects such as disk segments to be read and written.

At the next level a basic file server can be supplied organizing the disk storage into file objects considered as segments of elements, such as bits or bytes, which can be randomly read and written. No translation of data types would take place. At the next level might be a variety of servers offering more elaborately structured file objects, associated access methods, and automatic data translation. Additional levels might support further information object refinement such as provided by data management systems, etc. These servers for all these layers of abstract objects can all be distributed, including the disk segment object server connecting the disks directly to a network can provide performance and reliability advantages [Thornton 80; Watson 80c]. Similar hierarchies of service can be provided for other resources.

Within current network architectures, protocols are defined for services such as file transfer, remote job entry, and virtual terminals. These types of services would be provided within the Model somewhat differently. Instead of being separate, special, unique services, they would be provided by more general DOS servers such as those handling files or terminals. For example, whole file transfer would be just a special case of random copying of information from one file to another. The file server used would be at the appropriate level of abstraction to deal with the desired data types and their translation between heterogeneous systems. At the very least, if a specific server were useful for whole file transfer, it would be built on lower levels of DOS file servers and not itself be considered a primitive service. Similarly virtual terminal definitions [Davidson 77] would be built into the DOS terminal service just as they are on a nondistributed OS. In other words, the focus would be on the definition of general purpose abstract objects and operations that can be used as building blocks for objects of a higher levels of abstraction, rather than on elaborate definitions of restricted objects and operations focused on restricted modes of information transfer.

A Service Support Sublayer

One important layer or sublayer (shown in figure 2-1 as the Service Support sublayer) missing in most current distributed system or network architectures defines standards in areas such as logical server and resource structures; protection, error control, resource management models, request/reply syntax, control and data representations, and even many operations that can easily be made common across a wide range of DOS and application level services. Recognizing this commonality (the common issue axis of the model) and specifying conventions to support it in a well defined DOS sublayer of protocols is important for two main reasons:

- Each new standard or special service does not have to be designed from scratch to deal with these issues anew, thus facilitating the addition of new servers. A run-time environment can be created to support this commonality as special support processes, a set of library routines, or other building block mechanism.

- Recognizing the commonality across services facilitates creation of a uniform, coherent interface language for DOS services, easing learning and use.

The areas where conventions are usefully specified fall into roughly two groups: A sublayer concerned with standard format and encoding of messages, requests/replies, data and parameters and their automatic translation between forms on heterogeneous systems [Forsdick 79, White 76], and a sublayer concerned with models for the logical structure of applications, servers, resources, and their interaction, yielding standard semantics of request and replies for operations common across all or most services and standard mechanisms for dealing with the issues common to most services (the common issue axis of the Model). Development of such models, we believe to be a fruitful area for research. The creation of standard data and control formats is discussed further in Section 2.5.7. An example of the direction that one might go in creating a lowest DOS layer defining standard models for objects, servers, and customer/server interaction are now outlined [Fletcher 80, Watson 80b].

Uniform Object or Resource Model

A typical resource can be viewed as a data structure (possibly distributed) consisting of two major parts:

- *The heading or resource state record* contains named fixed fields of information of various lengths and types, such as creation time, last access time, account to be charged for the resource, security level, access rights, identity verification, mnemonics or other commentary, etc.

- The *body* is the resource proper. Its structure varies depending on the nature of the resource. For example, a basic file body could be an array of bits or records labeled by consecutive natural integers, while a directory body could be a list of lower level machine-oriented names labeled by higher level human oriented names in the form of character strings.

Only a few functions are required to cover the vast bulk of operations performed on basic DOS layer resources. Application layer objects such as text editers, compilers, modeling codes, etc., may have extensive special function sets. All operations involving querying or modifying resource headings, or reading or writing resource bodies are actually special cases of generic *copy* or *move* functions. Functions are needed to *create* and *destroy* entire resources. Another group of functions is needed for dealing with access control and passing of names. Some important functions apply only to certain kinds of resources; active resources, such as processes, must be *started* and *stopped.*

Uniform Server Model

Besides handling requests for operations on resources, servers need to maintain state information for varying periods of time, for a single request, or across multiple requests. Supporting the representation and customer process access of this state in a uniform manner across servers seems useful. Some characteristics desirable in such a model are:

- Allow servers to reliably maintain and if necessary recover state across multiple messages.

- Allow state information after one operation to be defaulted as input parameters for succeeding operations.

- Share state information across two or more *associations*, where an association is defined by a pair of unique origin, destination process addresses.

- Be able to operate on state information even when an association is blocked by lower-level flow control.

- Support parallel services on a single association.

- Allow interrogating the state of an operation while it is in progress from the same or a different association.

- Be able to distinguish and specify when and where replies for an operation are to be sent and from which parallel entity the reply is coming.

- Be able to abort, suspend, restart an operation.

- Provide for the above services in general, but require only a minimal implementation when a server only supports sequential operations and does not require state to be saved across operations.

[Fletcher 80] outlines a server model meeting many of the above needs.

Customer-Server Interaction Model

Customer (application) and server systems may be structured as multiple communicating and cooperating processes. A general model defining the main roles of each and their communication patterns can be specified, allowing conventions supporting this model to be developed. The goals of such a model and associated supporting conventions are:

- To specify the roles and associated addressing points visible at customer and server interfaces, thus providing for the distribution of roles.

- To specify how all communicating entities can know each others' interface addresses, and authenticate the right of another to send them a message or request a service.

- To specify which functions and which request/reply sequences can be directed to which interface addresses.

- To provide mechanisms for detecting a crash of a partner and handle higher level error control generally.

- To provide for a form of higher-level flow control or other resource management functions.

- To provide mechanisms to support error recovery.

Synchronization of cooperating processes is assumed to be handled with a higher-level DOS service built on a primitive *Wait* mechanism supplied by the IPC layer. Such a model should require minimal message or other overhead when roles are not distributed. An example where the distribution of roles might exist is the following, illustrated in the model of figure 2-4. An application system is structured as a master process controlling one or more subordinate processes. The subordinate processes act in the role of requesters. Each requester could control its own data source or sink process. Replies indicating the outcome of operations are to be sent directly to the master or replyee. Master and subordinates send, internal to the application system, request and reply control messages to each other to synchronize their activities. The server could be a file server consisting of the supervisory server that maintains master catalogs and implements policy controlling file migration, device controlling processes that manage particular devices such as disks or mass stores and actually control the data transfers. Devices could be directly attached via intelligent controllers (separate processes) to the network allowing direct transfer of data between source and sink [Thornton 80]. To support the distribution of these roles, the primitives for DOS services and their associated parameters must be appropriately designed to obey conventions enabling each party to obtain the address of the other parties with which it must communicate, be able to validate that processes sending it messages are authorized to do so, and meet other of the needs outlined above. Other aspects of the customer-server interaction would include error recovery [ISO 79, Chapters 11, 15] and protection [Donnelley 80, Nessett 80].

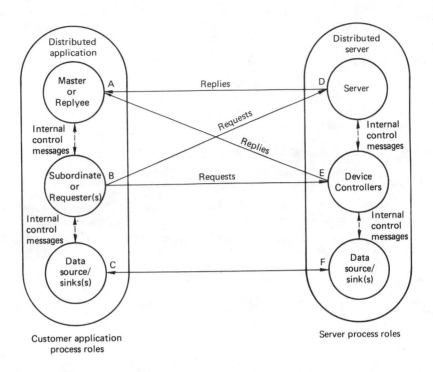

Figure 2-4: Customer/server interaction, data movement model

2.4.5. The distributed system kernel or interprocess communication layer

Earlier we mentioned that the distributed kernel layer consists of

(1) an interprocess communication service;

(2) the minimal software necessary to

    (a) create a message oriented interface to the input/output (I/O) structure of hardware/firmware components,

    (b) provide a basis for creating process, primitive memory, and I/O resources,

    (c) establish the basis for system protection,

    (d) provide the foundations needed to support component multiplexing.

The services to be provided in the kernel could vary depending on assumptions about the underlying hardware support, physical and personnel security, and applications to be supported. We believe the strategy most likely to be successful, particulary with current hardware and operating architectures and a heterogeneous component and administrative environment, is to place the minimum functionality possible in the kernel. For example, within a microcomputer supporting only a single process (program) that uses DOS services supplied elsewhere, the only part of the kernel required would be IPC and initialization support provided as a package of procedures; while within a large multiprogramming system supporting many processes and other resources such as disk files or clocks, the kernel would require modules to allow processes to be created and multiplexed, disks to be read and written, and the clock to be read. Responsibility for process, disk, and file management would still reside within server processes outside the kernel. Such processes might have special privileges and trust, although logically they would be at the same level as other processes [Donnelley 79]. With respect to protection, the kernel might only support address integrity at boundaries where there are trusted IPC routing nodes, leaving resource protection a server process responsibility outside the kernel. [Peebles 80] places additional functionality in the kernel as an example. Issues in kernel design relevant to distributed and nondistributed systems are discussed by [Popek 78b]. How the parts of the distributed kernel needed on each host are implemented will vary from system to system depending on the type of host and whether it is built from the hardware/firmware up or is built on an existing OS. Protection is discussed in Section 2.5.6 and Chapter 10. We will focus here on the IPC service. Of all the layers of the Model, the IPC layer is best understood because most of the work in networking over the last decade has been focused here [McQuillan 78a, Pouzin 78].

IPC Service

Design goals for the IPC service are that it:

- Allow each communicating entity complete autonomy and control over its own resources and state.

- Place no a priori restrictions on which processes can communicate with which others. Knowing a process's address should be sufficient to communicate, subject to possible access control restrictions.

- Assure the privacy and security of communication.

- Efficiently support transaction and stream oriented services and applications.

- Allow all components, customer/server roles, and abstract objects, including data sources and sinks, to be distributed.

- Provide for user extensibility, location independence, and a uniform user view, by allowing communication among all processes to use the same mechanism and form, whether local or remote, user or system provided.

- Allow a system to participate in the distributed system by just supporting the IPC service.

The IPC facility must provide the following five basic services at the IPC interface (discussed in more detail in Chapter 7), in order to meet the above goals:

- Identification—a unique systemwide *global* process identification or addressing scheme is required. These names may or may not be location independent (see Chapter 9). It should allow processes to have more than one address (ports). One of the objects provided by the IPC service is a logical communication channel called an *association*, defined by an (origin, destination) address pair.

- IPC data elements—the basic IPC level interface data object (bit, byte, etc.) must be chosen and provision made for their transmission.

- Data stream synchronization – there must be some way to mark elements or insert marks in the data stream at an origin process and pass these marks to a destination process to provide known points from which to create higher level data objects such as messages, and establish synchronization of control state. The supporting IPC transport mechanism may segment and package them into transport units such as packets for transmission.

- Status – it must be possible for origin and destination to determine the state of the current communication, to know what data were successfully sent, received or may be in trouble.

- Autonomy – either end of an association channel must have complete control over its own resources and activity. This implies the ability to Abort data queued for sending or buffers queued for receiving and to control their own Wait conditions. No inactivity or incorrect operation of the other end should be able to permanently block a process.

Ideally one would like to provide these services with no errors, with perfect flow control (senders send only at the rate receivers can receive) and complete privacy and security. This is not possible in a real distributed environment. There are costs and tradeoffs in achieving approximations to these desires. Therefore, additional information may be required to be passed across the IPC interface to help the IPC service choose its algorithms and allocate its resources appropriately. The goal is to provide the above services independent of the underlying communication mechanisms.

To support the IPC service in a distributed environment requires an IPC layer architecture consisting of sublayers illustrated in figure 2-5:

- IPC layer interface
- end-to-end protocols
- network hierarchy and control protocols
- link protocols
- hardware/firmware interconnection technologies.

Each of these sublayers supports as their main objects communication channels and provides for their naming, error control, protection, synchronization, allocation, and the representation of the information objects they carry. Let us consider these briefly from the bottom up.

Interconnection Technology

The hardware/firmware components are used as network *nodes*. There are a wide range of technologies for interconnecting these nodes with physical channels depending on their distance from each other, bandwidth, delay, and cost tradeoffs.

Interconnection mechanisms and their characteristics are discussed under the heading of *hardware/firmware interconnection technologies* in Chapter 4.

Links

A pair of nodes, independent of the technology used, are said to be joined by a *link*. Links generally have well specified properties, such as, that information passing across them cannot get out-of-sequence, they are full duplex (information can simultaneously be sent and received in both directions), and there is some procedure to know when all previously sent information has

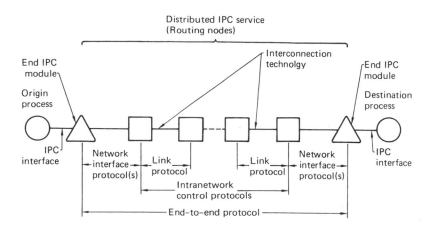

Figure 2-5: IPC layers in use

passed out of them [Fletcher 79, Sloan 79]. The job of controlling the transmission of information across links is performed by *link protocols*. Links transport units of information called *frames* usually structured as a header containing address and control information, a body containing data, and a trailer containing redundancy used for error checking. These protocols can be designed based on the link properties above. Design considerations for link protocols are discussed in Chapter 5.

Networks

Linked pairs of nodes can be combined in many topologies to create hierarchies of interconnected nodes called *networks*, where a given network may itself be composed of networks, an *internet*, shown in figure 2-6. A network is usually identified by the controlling administrative agency, interconnection technology, or protocols used. There are many design issues associated with network hierarchies, particularly when they are composed of multiple networks, examples are: interfacing to them, routing information through them, congestion control, optimum topology, and error control being examples. It is this area that is referred to as as *Hierarchy* and is discussed in Chapter 6. Networks transport objects called *packets*, usually structured as a header containing address and control information and a body containing data.

End-to-end Protocols

In order for processes to send messages to each other, a global distributed system addressing structure is needed. This addressing structure also allows the transmission mechanisms offered by lower level services to be multiplexed. Further, while lower sublayers of the IPC layer may provide error or flow control on a hop-by-hop (across a link or network) basis, it may still be useful to provide such services on a true end-to-end basis between the communicating processes. It is the function of an *end-to-end* or *transport* protocol to provide the above services. End-to-

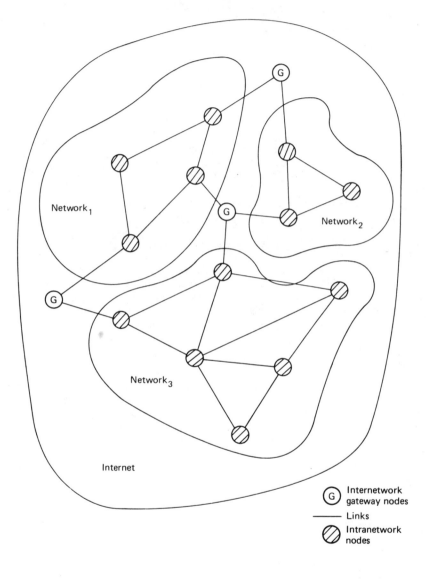

Figure 2-6: Nodes, links, networks

end protocols transport objects, called packets with the same structure as network packets. A given end-to-end packet, however, may be segmented and carried in several network packets. IPC interface objects such as messages may be segmented and be carried in several end-to-end packets. A range of end-to-end protocols is possible from the simplest that only provides an addressing structure useful to support routing, but that provides no guarantees on information delivery or flow control — to the more complex that offers guarantees about correct delivery, flow control and possibly other services. There are intermediate points in the design spectrum as well. Information on *type-of-service* passed across the IPC interface can allow the appropriate protocol to be selected. End-to-end protocol design issues are discussed in Chapter 7.

IPC Interface

The *IPC layer interface* must support the handling of sending, receiving, status, abort, block/wakeup primitives, including details of how addresses, data and other IPC information are passed as parameters. The IPC interface is discussed in Chapter 7.

The way the Model's IPC service would work is the following. Destination identifier information passed across the IPC interface is examined by a routing module to see if the destination is local or remote. If the destination is local, then local delivery mechanisms are invoked. If the destination is remote, then an end-to-end protocol module is invoked which in turn invokes network interface or link protocols. The information, *message* (logical object passed across the IPC interface), to be delivered is segmented into objects used for transmission called *packets, frames, blocks* (shown in figure 2-8) depending on the level of protocol. These are then transmitted.

2.4.6. Hardware/Firmware Components

Most existing hardware/firmware components were designed to be used in standalone or closely-coupled (shared memory) nondistributed system configurations. While most of these components can be used in a distributed system environment, it is important to raise the question of whether or not their design is most appropriate for a message oriented, heterogeneous, communication environment. This is an area that has not received sufficient attention.

The design areas where useful research and development are needed include considering:

- Changes to component I/O structures to provide for more efficient IPC. With current architectures there is considerable processing overhead associated with forming, receiving, and handling packets and frames of information and placing them on or taking them from transmission media. Converting interrupts into messages and messages into channel and device commands is another source of inefficiency that might be eliminated.

- Support for dealing with the heterogeneity problems of data representation and encoding. There is a need in this area for standards and for hardware/ firmware translation assistance.

- Changes to support system state information: its distribution, synchronization, interrogation, and modification.

- Mechanisms to aid efficient implementation of privacy, access control, protection, and security.

- Placing more intelligence in the components so that they can be directly connected to networks and participate in the entire architecture.
- Features to support remote measurement and diagnosis.
- Support enabling much of the architecture to be placed in firmware or special frontend systems.

Some of the current work in component design for explicit use in distributed systems is discussed in Chapters 16 and 17.

2.5. Issues common to all layers

2.5.1. Introduction

Several important design issues reappear at each layer and sublayer of the architecture. The nature of the problems associated with a particular area can be different at each layer, requiring different mechanisms for their solution, or the problems can be very similar, even the same, and identical mechanisms may be appropriate. The mechanisms used in dealing with a particular issue at each layer interact. Models for the basic resources supported within a layer and their interaction are required before mechanisms can be developed. Two of the questions asked as part of overall global system optimization are:

- Do these issues need to be dealt with in every layer?
- If not, within which layer(s) or sublayer(s) should each of these common issue areas be best handled?

A discussion of these common areas brings out many of the characteristics of distributed systems not found in nondistributed systems. We now introduce each issue so that the reader is made aware of them and can read each of the following chapters to see in detail how they can be handled within each layer of the Model.

2.5.2. Identifiers (Naming)

Identification is an area at the heart of all computer system design. An identifier is a symbol string designating or referencing an object. It is useful to review some of the understanding about from experience with nondistributed systems directly applicable to distributed systems as well.

- Identifiers are used for a wide variety of purposes, such as protection, error control, resource management, locating, and sharing resources and as a means to build more complex objects out of simpler atomic ones by including the names of the latter in the former.
- Identifiers exist in different forms at all levels of a system architecture. To access, locate, reach a specific object requires mapping of higher level identifiers using appropriate context, possibly through several intermediate levels, to identifiers of specific locations. The latter identifiers are often called *addresses*.
- Identification, protection, error control, synchronization, and resource management mechanisms often interact. One has to be careful in understanding how design choices in one affect goals and choices in the other.

- Identifiers appear in different forms, some convenient for people, others convenient for machine processing; some are unique within a global context for the whole system, others are unique only within a local context.

- Choice of an identification scheme and supporting mechanism can affect the ease or possiblity of achieving goals such as to allow:

    - Efficient transaction oriented as well as stream applications.

    - Sharing of objects (multiplexing of resources such as communication channels at one level by those at another is a special case).

    - Relocation of objects without changing references.

    - Inclusion of objects within others without identifier conflicts.

    - Multiple copies of logically identical objects.

    - An application and DOS level view of a uniform identifier structure applicable to all types of resources.

    - A system seen as a space of identified objects rather than as a space of host computers containing objects.

Related to the mapping of identifiers (addresses) at one level into those used at another is the process of *routing* information from one object to another. Routing can be considered the level of identifier mapping that results not in another identifier, but in actually reaching the referenced object over a sequence of communication channels. Routing can occur at any level of the architecture and is invisible to the levels below. In routing, the identifier of the destination object for a unit of information at one level is mapped

(1) into the name of the next module that is to handle that unit, and

(2) the name of communication channel over which the unit and its destination identifier are to be forwarded.

Routing is an important technique used to interconnect distributed heterogeneous systems.

Important issues associated with identification are:

(1) achieving uniqueness at some level,

(2) deciding on the number of levels of identifiers and interlevel mapping mechanisms, and

(3) determining size and structure of identifiers at each level.

Identification is an area where much is yet to be done to create a unified understanding of how the above goals can be achieved. Developments in this area to date have been largely ad hoc and the interactions of identification at all levels of an architecture are not well understood. Identification is discussed in many of the chapters, particularly Chapter 9.

2.5.3. Error control

Error control is concerned with detecting and trying to recover from errors and failures of different types. Error control mechanisms can be very simple, such as designing the form of state information or request/reply exchange so that duplication will not cause harm or omissions will be filled by information in later messages; or more elaborate such as those used to assure consistency of update of multiple information copies [Chapter 14], or that used with *atomic transactions* of Chapter 11. It seems clear that no single error control mechanism meets all needs or is appropriate at all layers and for all services in a layer. Developing error control mechanisms at any layer of a distributed system is complicated by three problems:

- Identifiers used for the objects being error controlled generally occupy finite length fields and thus must be reused when the field cycles. If it cannot be guaranteed that old information with a given identifier no longer exists in the system when the given identifier is reused, a hazard in the error control mechanism will exist.

- The distributed state or redundant information needed for error control must be correctly initialized or maintained in the face of arbitrary message delays, message errors, possible old identifiers, and system crashes.

- Information needed for error control itself must be transmitted across a hazardous environment, where it can be misaddressed, lost, damaged, duplicated, or missequenced.

In general, perfect error control (detection and correction of all errors) cannot be achieved at any given layer of the Model because all three of the above problems cannot be completely solved simultaneously within a given layer. All that is possible is to decrease unrecoverable error frequency (disasters) by increasing the probability of error detection and recovery. Error control mechanisms at a given layer must be developed around a knowledge of the types of errors that can occur, their frequency, the structure of the service being protected, and assumptions about the handling of the above three problems.

Determining whether or not to apply error control and choice of an error control mechanism at a given layer will depend on trading off costs involved in the mechanism and the costs of undetected or unrecovered errors. If error control is applied at lower levels, then the probability of undetected or uncorrected errors may be low enough that higher levels may choose not to provide additional error control. Alternatively, if higher levels are known to provide error control, then lower levels may not need to provide error control. Or for efficiency error control may be required at several levels. This whole area of global optimization by appropriate placement of error control in an architecture is not well understood.

As an illustration of the difficulties in designing error control for a distributed system let us assume we are creating a service and see what problems we encounter in trying to achieve perfect error control. The service and its error control are built on and supplied through the IPC layer. What can be assumed about the error control supplied by the IPC layer? The IPC can at best

(1) guarantee an arbitrarily low probability of misaddressed, damaged, missequenced information, and

(2) either guarantee information is not lost or that it is not duplicated, but not both [Belsnes 76].

This situation results because end-to-end protocols supporting the IPC service require a positive acknowledgement to guard against lost information. This acknowledgement can fail to be returned. The failure to receive an acknowledgement can result because the original information got lost and no acknowledgement was generated, or the information arrived safely and the acknowledgement got lost. These possibilities can occur due to transmission errors or destination failure. (We assume that the acknowledgement is not generated until the information is safely stored or acted on, not usually always practical.)

If the origin retransmits the original information, the possibility of duplication is introduced. A well designed end-to-end protocol can detect such duplication. But suppose after some number of retransmissions and waiting for an acknowledgement, none arrives. The end-to-end protocol generally will give up and report a problem to the next level service. What should the next level service do? If it blindly waits and then tries again, duplication can occur. If it does not retransmit, information could be lost.

The service has two choices. If the semantics of its requests were such that repetition would not cause a problem (overwriting a state variable rather than incrementing it is an example), then it could simply be repeated. If its requests were not of this nature, then it needs to interrogate the destination's state before deciding what to do. This implies that the destination was maintaining state information about the identity of requests received or that the origin was maintaining state enabling it to determine from the state of the destination whether or not the request in question was acted on, and that this origin or destination state could not have gotten lost or damaged in a failure that caused the original acknowledgement to get lost. Guaranteeing that the state information needed for error control by a customer or service is not lost is either an act of faith in local hardware, such as disks to survive a crash without loss of information, or requires storing redundant state locally or remotely, which can bring us recursively back through the same problems. In summary, we can decrease the probability of undetected and unrecoverable errors, but we cannot make them impossible. These issues are discussed further in Chapters 7, 11 and 15. An excellent introduction to error control is contained in [Randell 78].

2.5.4. Resource management

There are a wide range of resources being locally managed within each service and layer of the Model, memory for object representations, buffer space, access to communication channels, communication bandwidth, CPU cycles, address space, access to hardware/firmware components, etc. Allocating and scheduling resources at the various distributed system nodes is usually based on local decisions because of needs for local autonomy (administrative and technical) and because knowing how to allocate and schedule on a global basis is not well understood [Chapter 8]. Resource management and state information management for all the common issues are intimately related.

In many distributed systems, one would like to use resource and state management philosophies at all levels that could achieve both low *delay* and high *throughput*. Delay is defined as the time interval between when a process is ready to send a message until the first useful bit of the message reaches the destination. Delay is affected not only by the transmission and queuing properties of the IPC transport mechanisms, but also by the number of overhead set up messages at one or more layers that may have to first be exchanged to reserve resources, map identifiers, authenticate the sender, initialize state variables, etc., before the desired request or data can be sent.

Throughput is defined as the number of useful data bits per second that reach the receiver in some interval. Throughput is affected not only by transmission and queuing characteristics of the IPC transport mechanisms, but also by the amount of identification, control, protection and other overhead information that must encode or accompany the meaningful user data object bits.

Developing mechanisms that can achieve both low delay (desired in transaction oriented applications) and high throughput (desired in stream oriented applications) is a difficult task.

Tradeoffs exist between quantity and duration of retention of state information, amount of overhead information carried with messages, and the number of messages needed to initialize state information. The state and message overhead information required is a function of the resource management, naming, error control, protection and other services being supported. It can therefore be stated that levels of these services can also be traded off against delay and throughput. For example, if one wants high throughput but only wants to retain state information and allocate resources during a conversation, one can use initial exchanges of messages to set up the state and resources required during the conversation. The result may be high delay caused by these setup messages. One can reduce the number of setup messages by

(1) increasing the overhead information in a message to make it more self contained,

(2) retaining state information and resource allocation over longer periods of time,

(3) just sending the desired message on the assumption that the receiver will usually have adequate resources to handle it, or

(4) some combination.

If the receiver has inadequate resources it can treat the message as a reservation request and either queue or reject it, requiring retransmission. Techniques (1) and (3) can reduce throughput.

The important conclusion from the above is that mechanisms to achieve both low delay and high throughput will require relatively long term retention of some state information and some preallocation of resources and appropriate placement of functionality in various layers [Watson 80d]. The goal is to find techniques that minimize the state and preallocated resources required for naming, error control, protection, buffering etc. while yet keeping enough, possibly with some tradeoff with overhead information carried in messages, to achieve the desired delay-throughput balance. Often one is satisfied if the user does not have to explicitly deal with setup messages, but can operate in a transaction oriented mode with the system automatically supporting high throughput if many messages are sent close together in time. There may be a delay penalty for the initial message to setup state and allocate needed resources. Caching and demand allocation strategies are example approaches.

One of the questions for distributed system design is how many of the above strategies and algorithms should be visible and user controllable? This question and the tradeoffs above exist at all levels of the model. They are often the subject of vigorous debate such as that between advocates of datagrams and fixed route virtual circuits as the basic IPC transport mechanisms [Section 6.6]. It is our experience that careful choice of models and mechanisms, and willingness to retain some state and utilize some extra bandwidth can yield resource and state management approaches providing good delay-throughput balance. With user visible controls this balance can be shifted to improve either goal. An example is a timer based error control mechanism useful in an end-to-end protocol that achieves the desirable error control characteristics of virtual circuits and the delay characteristics of datagrams [Fletcher 78]. Similar desirable properties for naming, synchronization prototection, and other issues can, we believe, be developed.

Two terms associated with resource management are frequently used in distributed and nondistributed systems *flow control* and *congestion control*. Flow control generally refers to mechanisms at any layer of the Model for regulating the flow of information between a specific pair of correspondents, nodes on each end of a link, customer and server processes etc. A flow control mechanism tries to regulate the rate at which senders send to the rate at which receivers have resources to receive. Congestion control refers to system wide mechanisms to prevent global or partial system overload, for example, with network resources used to store and forward packets of information between all pairs of correspondents. The two mechanisms clearly interact. Improperly designed flow and congestion control mechanisms can lead to deadlocks or deadlock like situations [Donnelley 78, McQuillan 77]. The interaction between flow and congestion control are not well understood [Grange 79, Nessett 79b]. These mechanisms also interact with resource allocation implementation decisions within each node or server to affect pairwise and overall system performance [Sunshine 76]. Resource management is briefly discussed again in Section 2.6.

2.5.5. Synchronization

The term *synchronization* refers to mechanisms used by cooperating entities to coordinate access to shared resources or order events. Example forms of synchronization are delimiting data units; coordinating the initialization, maintenance, evolution, and termination of distributed shared state information used for protection, resource management, data translation, and error control; and ordering access by processes to shared information [Chapter 12]. General issues associated with synchronization can be highlighted by considering synchronization of distributed state. The distribution and coordination of state information is one of the main sources of problems in a distributed system. In a nondistributed system, using shared memory, all cooperating entities "see" the same state. This is not the case in a distributed system.

Even without errors or node failures, it will be impossible for each entity in a cooperating set to maintain the same view of their total state as the others, due to the arbitrary delays for messages updating or reporting state. When one then introduces the possibility that reports of or requests for state change can be damaged, duplicated, missequenced or lost, or that entities can fail in modes forgetting all or parts of their own and others state, the new problem is introduced of creating system organizations and mechanisms that allow stable and correct operation to be maintained in the face of these possibilities [Chapter 11]. Error control and synchronization interact strongly. The problem of initializing a set of distributed cooperating entities to a point where each has the necessary state and knowledge, or some level of confidence, that the others have the necessary state to proceed is a new problem. Examples of reliable state synchronization difficulties between two entities are given in [Section 7.9, Pouzin 78]. The problem is significantly increased in difficulty as the number of parties is increased beyond two [Chapters 12, 13].

2.5.6. Protection

The protection needs are the same in distributed and nondistributed systems; namely to ensure that:

- Only authorized entities can read, modify, or manipulate resources.
- Unauthorized entities cannot prevent authorized entities from sending, modifying, or manipulating resources.
- Only authorized entities can communicate.

The problems that must be overcome in a distributed system to meet these needs are significantly complicated by the reoccurring themes of heterogeneity, physical distribution, and multiple controlling authorities. Protection mechanisms must be built on a determination of the threats to be protected against and a set of assumptions about what can be ultimately trusted as safe or secure. There are three basic questions:

- To what extent can the communication system be trusted?

- To what extent can each hardware/firmware component and its local distributed operating system kernel be trusted?

- To what extent can the physical and personnel security at a host, node, or site be trusted?

All security systems are built on some level of trust within a single host. Within a single host either all processes trust one another, constitute a single protection domain, or all processes can only access each other and each others resources through a well defined and defensible interface, such as the IPC mechanism. In other words, they cannot directly access each other's memory or state except through establishing their right to do so through a trusted process server [Popek 78b]. All processes outside the component must also be guaranteed to follow the same access rules.

If one trusts the local DOS kernels or special servers, such as verified and tamper proof special devices, then encryption techniques can be used to:

(1) protect the information in transit against errors,

(2) to protect the communication system against threats such as passive "wiretapping,"

(3) establish safe authentication protocols (identifying each communicating party to the others), and

(4) detect deliberate message modification or playback

(5) allow secure passing of access control between processes. [Chapter 10, Donnelley 80, Kent 77, Needham 78, Nessett 80, Popek 78a-79, Simmons 79, Smid 79].

Encryption can be used in mechanisms at all levels of the model.

Encryption requires each party to have a matching encryption key or a pair of keys. These keys must be distributed by a safe, trusted mechanism and be securely stored. If a large number of dynamically established encryption channels are to be used, then a small number of secure semipermanent channels (keys or key pairs) must exist, along with a trusted key distribution center (possibly distributed), to be used to safely create the dynamic channels. This situation implies that

(1) special devices and each local kernel or a process must be able to protect keys against theft or forgery, and

(2) if dynamic establishment of encrypted channels is to be used to reduce the risks inherent in safely keeping large numbers of keys on a long term basis, a transaction oriented system may be difficult to create.

The latter problem may not exist if an encrypted channel does not have to be set up for each transaction, for example by use of public key encryption techniques [Section 10.4].

If processes can only access each other through a defensible interface, then each server can be made responsible for the protection of its resources by requiring processes accessing resources to prove their right to do so, in the desired mode. On nondistributed systems variants of *capability* or *access list* techniques are used [Section 10.5, Jones 78a]. In the capability technique the accessing process presents a token or capability (a protected identifier) whose possession constitutes proof of right of access [Denning 76, Dennis 66, Fabry 74]. This implies that it should be impossible to use forged, copied, or stolen capabilities. On a nondistributed system, these guarantees are made by keeping them in a trusted place, usually the operating system kernel. Because of the possibilities of system heterogeneity, multiple controlling administrations, and different levels of physical and personnel security, it may not be possible to provide such guarantees in a distributed system. Therefore, it may be just as well to allow capabilities to be stored, read, and written in user process memory. Servers can then encrypt capabilities or embed passwords within them to protect them against forgery [Needham 79b], but if they can be seen in memory dumps or within the communication media and be reentered then they can be compromised [Watson 80b]. Encryption based mechanisms offer a solution to this problem [Donnelley 80, Nessett 80].

One can also use access list based mechanisms to protect against capabilities being seen and then reentered, but these must be based either on use of addresses that the IPC layer guarantees cannot be forged or on the use of some other token that cannot be forged or stolen. These latter tokens usually are derived from some more fundamental guarantees such as unforgeable addresses, secure kernels, or key encryption and trusted key distribution.

In summary, interconnecting many different protection domains that are mutually suspicious is an area needing much work. This is particularly the case if each domain implements different protection policies. Protection is discussed further in Chapter 10.

2.5.7. Object representation, encoding, translation

Within each layer and across each interface of the architecture, meaningful objects must be defined. Objects may be those at the application or DOS levels such as files, processes, directories, sequences of requests or replies that must be treated as atomic, single requests, or data parameters; or be at the IPC level such as packets, frames, etc. The representation and encoding of these objects must be specified. Objects used for data transmission must be reliably delimited. When objects move from one host to another, translation between different representations of corresponding object representations and encodings must take place to deal with heterogeneity between interconnection technologies, networks, host computers, and operating systems. The common strategy is to translate from a local representation at the origin into the standard abstract representation visible at the object interface and then back into the local representation at the destination. Therefore each system does not need to translate its local representation to all possible other local representations. One of the important characteristics of languages and runtime environments for use in distributed systems is that explicit *type* information must be passed with all names or units through all layers where automatic translation may be required. Objects at each layer are usually of the form *header, body*, where the header contains type information needed for translation, length and other control information; and the body contains a data structure of typed data elements.

Objects used for communication may be considered as *data* or *control* information. What is control at layer n is treated as data at layer n-1. Both data and control information may require error or flow control. It is usually useful at each layer to be able to maintain separation of data and control, so that they can exist unambiguously on the same association between sender, receiver addresses, to simplify data and control translation, allow independent error flow control between them.

As an example of how control and data might be represented to support separation and translation, figure 2-7 shows how a DOS or Application layer request, reply, data message might be packaged into a message to be handled by the IPC layer according to conventions established within the DOS layer.

The IPC layer is assumed to support a data unit called a message containing uninterpreted octets delimited by beginning-of-message (BOM) and end-of-message (EOM) marked octets, shown in (a). The Service Support sublayer could then define additional structure for messages as now described. It is useful to provide separation of data and control messages to aid translation, transmission efficiency, and their transparent intermixing on a single association. This is accomplished with the Mode Octet in (b). Providing for 256 control and data modes is useful to support translation: Different data modes could encode data messages as various forms of strings, bits, characters, integer records, etc. Different control modes could indicate the form of token encoding being used, network standard, or for efficiency form X for host type X, thus not requiring translation when processes on two hosts of the same type X are correspondents.

Control mode messages contain requests and replies encoded as a series of statements. Each statement contains a function code and parameters and is delimited by the next function code or EOM. Function codes and parameters are encoded into tokens. A control message containing one or more statements is shown in (d). A control mode message containing a single statement is shown in (e). Each token is shown encoded as per (f) and (g). Each token is explicitly typed to provide for translation and is delimited by a length in octets. "Usage" indicates the purpose of the token such as function, account identifier, first a bit address, resource identifier, etc. Separating usage and type simplifies translation as only a few basic types are required such as bit string, character string, integer, and floating point number. Explicit designation of usage supports error checking, parameter default, position independence, and easy addition of new services through addition of new parameter usages. Other message and token encodings are suggested by [Forsdick 79, Postel 79, Rashid 80, White 76]. It would be inefficient for each data item in a data message to be individually typed. For data messages, the data-type information can be known in three ways: implicitly by the nature of the service or address, conveyed in control messages, or explicitly encoded in the message data-mode code as mentioned.

Figure 2-8 shows how the IPC layers of protocol would package a message assuming the message can fit in a packet. Within the IPC layer there may also be typed control packets or frames not shown here. When different networks are interconnected packet as well as higher level formats may have to be translated [Section 6.8].

In summary, providing explicit object type information and translation of object representations and encodings is one of the important mechanisms for dealing with heterogeneity. Developing conventions for request/reply formatting as in figure 2-7 and supporting message translation for each environment with a service, package of library routines process, or other way should facilitate use and creation of new resource types and services. Translation is discussed extensively from several points of view in Chapter 14, and again in Chapter 18.

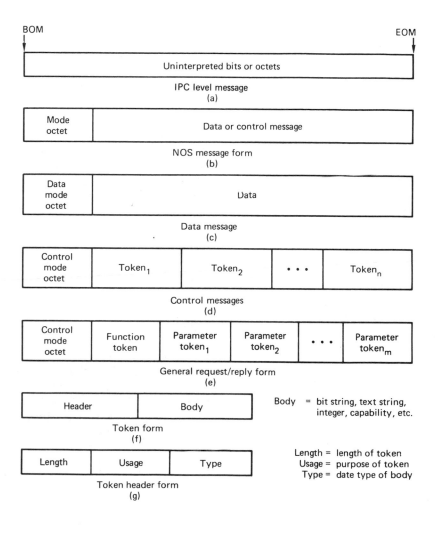

Figure 2-7: Message structure

2.5.8. Testing, debugging, and measurement

We have lumped these three together because systems suffer from logical bugs, performance bugs, and hardware/firmware malfunctions in which measurement is an important diagnostic tool, as well as being important in its own right for studying the effect on performance of various mechanisms and policies. It is also useful in achieving a better understanding of how the system works. These issues are involved enough in nondistributed systems, but become even more complex in a distributed system with its heterogeneous components, multiple controlling administration, and distributed state. For example, it may be impossible to stop the system or a particular component, gain sole access to the system or a component, achieve repeatability, place breakpoints, or single step the system. With automatic error control, failures and bugs may go undetected unless error control events are monitored. There is much research and development needed to create adequate tools and mechanisms in this area. While it is a motherhood statement to say measurement and diagnostic aids need to be built in at all levels of the Model from earliest design, a goal rarely followed in nondistributed systems, we see little hope of distributed system success if it is not followed. Mechanisms known to be useful at all levels of the architecture are error logging or counts, the ability to loop communication back from varying points in the layers, tracing paths traveled by units of information, obtaining relative timestamps at each node on a path, and counting and logging other events. Section 14.7 discusses these issues further.

2.6. Global implementation and optimization issues

There are reasons to believe that better performance or lower cost could result if local decisionsResource scheduling, allocation, and control in most existing distributed systems have been handled primarily on a local per node basis. The adaptive routing system used within the Arpanet communication subnet is an interesting exception [McQuillan 78a].

There are reasons to believe that better performance or lower cost could result if local decisions could be influenced by the global system state. Knowing what this global state is at any time is very difficult or may be impossible.

Global optimization issues revolve around the following type of questions:

- how can the scheduling and allocation of the resources on each component, such as processes on a processor be affected to achieve global performance or other goals;
- assuming relocatable objects, how, when, and which objects should be moved to be relocated with which others, for example, should processes move to be located near their associated data objects or vice versa;
- how is global consistency maintained if multiple copies exist, for example, through use of caching techniques;
- what special name mapping or other hardware may be required to support global optimization?
- how do mechanisms and services at one layer interact with those at another.

Other areas where global optimization of distributed control might be useful have been touched on in previous sections. This is one of the least well understood areas of distributed systems. Some of what is known is discussed in Chapter 8.

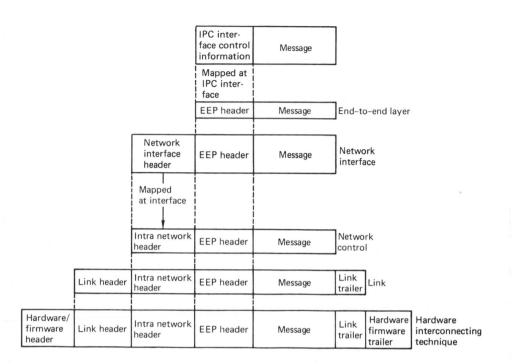

Figure 2-8: Message wrapped in possible set of IPC layer protocol units

2.7. Conclusions

We have presented a general multidimensional model for a distributed system architecture that, we believe, usefully serves to unify design issues, analysis, system organization, and should be useful in establishing standards for required interfaces. We have also introduced design goals and issues that will be discussed, along with details of useful mechanisms, further in later chapters. The central features of the model are that it emphasizes

- layering and modularity,
- the need to explicitly create a distributed operating system built around a unified view of objects or resources and their servers,
- the need to abstract and understand the common issues at all levels,
- a message based IPC, and
- the need to support both transaction and stream oriented services and applications.

Chapter 3. Interprocess communication layer: Introduction

3.1. Introduction

This section of the book discusses design issues, strategies and concepts associated with the interprocess communication layer of the model. The discussion will consider the following main issues: hardware interconnection technology, link level protocols, network hierarchies, and end-to-end protocols. At the lowest levels of this layer are many electrical design issues, such as driver/receiver design, which are not addressed here. Because of implementation dependencies, some terms may be difficult to define precisely. In these cases, we will provide what we feel is a reasonable definition and assume that like the definition of a set, although we can not precisely define the concept, we can recognize such entities and intuitively feel that we have a reasonable (number of reasonable) definition(s).

3.2. Transmission medium

Generally, the lowest level consideration in the design of a communication system is the transmission medium selection. Typical media include: common carrier circuits (lines), twisted pair (and variants), stripline, coaxial cable (and variants), waveguides, optical fibers, satellites, radio, cable TV systems, and value added networks. The medium provides the physical connections between the fundamental points or nodes in the distributed system. It is upon the physical medium that the remainder of the system is designed and built. Figure 3-1 summarizes the most important characteristics of the previously mentioned media.

Some of the entries in this list most designers would consider a physical medium: e.g., twisted pair. However, the list also contains medium which may be considered "logical" rather than physical, in the following sense: they are medium in place and can be purchased (rented or leased), but substantial detailed design of the medium itself is not required: e.g., common carrier lines, cable TV systems, and value added network communication subsystems (backbone networks).

Further, there are a number of trade-offs concerning transmission medium selection. The listed media contains concepts suitable for analog (common carrier lines) as well as digital data (twisted pair). Many lines may be utilized in a dedicated, shared, or combination of dedicated and shared mode of operation. Some designs may find that development of a private facility is more satisfactory than use of a public one. Some systems may use more than a single medium. The system design could require multi-point capability rather than point-to-point designs. Lastly, supplier choice is a difficult question. Figure 3-2 summarizes the major concerns in each of the above areas.

PHYSICAL MEDIA

OPTICAL FIBERS
— HIGH BANDWIDTH
— LIGHTWEIGHT
— SMALL
— NO INDUCED NOISE
— SECURITY
— LOW ERROR RATES
— POTENTIAL LOW COST
— NO RADIATION
— ELECTRIC ISOLATION
— REQUIRES SPECIAL OPTICAL
   INTERFACES AND CONNECTORS

SATELLITE
— HIGH BANDWIDTH
— LONG DELAYS
— LONG DISTANCE
— BROADCAST
— EAVESDROPPING

RADIO
— BROADCAST
-- MOBILE
— LONG DISTANCE
— LOW COST
-- EAVESDROPPING

TWISTED PAIR
— CHEAP
— LOW SPEED
— SHORT DISTANCE
— LONG DISTANCE USE MODEM
— LIGHTWEIGHT
— EASY TO SPLICE

STRIPLINE
— CHEAP
— LOW SPEED
— SHORT DISTANCE

PHYSICAL MEDIA (CONT.)

COAX
— CHEAP
— HIGH SPEED
— BROADCAST OR POINT-TO-POINT
— NOISE IMMUNITY
— LIGHTWEIGHT
— MEDIUM DISTANCE
— MEDIUM SPEED

WAVE GUIDES
— HIGH BANDWIDTH
— BULKY
— DELICATE
— MECHANICALLY INFLEXIBLE

LOGICAL MEDIA

COMMON CARRIER CIRCUITS
— LOGICAL MEDIA
— AVAILABLE
— LEASE
— CARRIER MAINTAINS
— CONFIGURATION FLEXIBILITY
— LONG DISTANCE
— SPEED VARIANTS

CABLE TV
— LOGICAL MEDIA
— MIGHT BE IN PLACE COAX
— AUDIO OR VIDEO

VALUE ADDED NETWORKS
— LOGICAL MEDIA
— MAINTAINED BY CARRIER
— WIDE AVAILABILITY
— LEASED
— CHARGED FOR USAGE
-- LONG DISTANCE

Figure 3-1: Media characteristics

3.3. Hardware paths

Using the transmission medium, we can establish a hardware path between two computers that wish to communicate. This path can be simply viewed as making a connection. The connection may be multiplexed, it may be point-to-point, etc. Further, between the actual computers, there may be an intervenor. Thus, the hardware path may connect two intervenors rather than the computers associated with the intervenors. A hardware path may also be used to interconnect the computer with the intervenor.

ANALOG
 — MODEMS
 — WIDE AVAILABILITY
 — WIDE CHOICES
 — MANY SPEEDS
 — TELEPHONE
 — WELL-DEFINED ERROR CHARACTERISTICS

DIGITAL
 — CHEAP
 — LOW NOISE SUSCEPTIBILITY
 — FUTURE

DEDICATED
 — HIGH COST PER USES
 — NO CONTENTION OR SHARING
 — LOW DELAY
 — NOT SUITED FOR BURST TRAFFIC
 — SIMPLE

SHARED
 — LOW COST
 — BANDWIDTH LOAD DEPENDENT
 — QUEUEING DELAYS
 — ADDED HARDWARE

PRIVATE
 — SHORT DISTANCE
 — USE INEXPENSIVE MEDIA
 — USER INSTALLS
 — USER MAINTAINS
 — VARIETY OF CHOICES

PUBLIC
 — LONG DISTANCE
 — LOW INSTALLATION EXPENSE
 — LEASE OR RENT
 — CARRIER MAINTENANCE
 — SPECIFIC CHOICES
 — FLEXIBLE CONFIGURATION

SINGLE
 — SIMPLE
 — LACK OF FLEXIBILITY

MIXED
 — COMPLEX
 — TRAFFIC MATCHING

POINT-TO-POINT
 — COMPLEXITY OF GROWTH RATE
 — SIMPLE TO CONTROL
 — BUFFERED I/O

MULTI-POINT
 — LOW COST
 — COMPLEX CONTROL
 — QUEUEING DELAYS

COMMON CARRIER
 — EXPENSIVE
 — LOW SPEED (300 BPS)
 — VOICE (1200 BPS TO 9600 BPS)
 — WIDEBAND
 — CAN CHOOSE ANALOG OR DIGITAL
 — CAN CHOOSE DEDICATED OR SHARED

SPECIALIZED CARRIER
 — MCI : MICROWAVE
 — WU : MAILGRAM

Figure 3-2: Media tradeoffs

3.4. Links

We define a link as the communication path between two computers. The link may be composed of several hardware paths which may include intervenors. This link may be viewed at a functional level; i.e., there is a link level protocol which specifies the format and functions allowed to occur. It is from this link level protocol that we will hierarchially build a system design.

3.5. Intervenors

The typical intervenor is a switch. The switch is generally thought of as a store-and-forward computer; i.e., the switch is a message or packet switch. For the sake of simplicity at this point, we will simply define a message to be a bit string which has a format consisting of a header, information, and trailer fields. A packet is an ordered, fixed length subpart of a message. A switch then is a device which receives messages or packets and performs some operation on the received entity. A typical operation may be to determine the "optimal" route from the current switch to the desired destination of the message. In this case, the switch must determine a route and transmit the message. The destination (or source) of the message may be another switch or a computer.

The intervenor provides a service; i.e., the intervenor implements or helps to implement the communication function. There are two major types of intrevenors. We must warn the reader here that it may be impractical to determine which type of intervenor is used, because the intervenor may be implemented as a set of functional levels. At the level which the user can access, see, test, etc., the user may not be able to devise experiments which allow him to determine the structure of lower levels. The two primary types of intervenors are: circuit/virtual circuit switches and message/packet/datagram switches. The major characteristics of these concepts are summarized in figure 3-3. The choice of a medium may dictate a switching concept; i.e., system design requirements which demand medium and topologies, along with system concepts which tend to keep bits ordered, will find circuit switch (virtual circuit) concepts to be advantageous. At some level of abstraction, a virtual circuit may be constructed on top of a datagram service.

```
         VIRTUAL CIRCUIT
           -- COULD BE PERMANENT
           -- LEASED LINES
           -- ASSIGNED TIME SLOTS (FDM OR TDM)
           -- DIAL UP ACCESS
           -- COULD BE IMPLEMENTED USING PACKET SWITCH
              OR BROADCAST CHANNEL CONCEPTS
           -- VOICE SUITABILITY

         DATAGRAM
           -- INDEPENDENT DATA ROUTING
           -- SIMPLE CONCEPT TO IMPLEMENT
           -- TRANSACTION ORIENTATION
```

Figure 3-3: Switch concepts

3.6. Protocols

Protocols are agreements or conventions. These agreements generally specify the allowable messages and operations, the sequence of information and the encoding rules. Protocols describe the basic data elements allowed. They establish the agreements via which the data elements are transmitted. Finally, the protocol definition constructs a standard communication channel (virtual path) between communicating devices. Typical considerations include data elements (bits, characters, packets, messages, files and jobs), agreements (code conventions, formats, path speeds, control sequences), and virtual path (addressing structures, priorities, sequencing, error control, flow control, bootstrapping, etc.).

The link level protocol is the lowest functional level protocol. Below the link level is the physical/electrical interface level. It is from this base that we will build a hierarchy of levels (possibly one level) which will allow for end to end communication between the initial source and final destination packet switch. Figure 3-4 shows a simplified protocol hierarchy adopted from [McQuillian 78].

Figures 3-5, 3-6, 3-7, and 3-8 illustrate another view of a set of generic protocol levels and some mappings of common systems onto this structure, taken from [Cerf 78]. Difficulties associated with defining a link and link level protocol will be discussed in the next section.

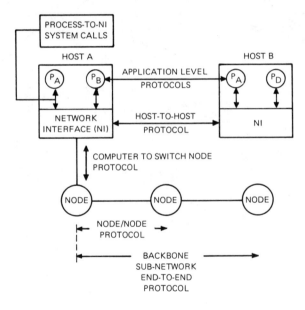

Figure 3-4: Typical hierarchy of protocols

PROTOCOL LAYER	FUNCTIONS
APPLICATION	FUNDS TRANSFER, INFORMATION RETRIEVAL, ELECTRONIC MAIL, TEXT EDITING, ETC.
UTILITY	FILE TRANSFER, VIRTUAL TERMINAL SUPPORT
SUBSCRIBER END-TO-END	INTERPROCESS COMMUNICATION (E.G., VIRTUAL CIRCUIT, DATAGRAM, REAL TIME, BROADCAST)
NETWORK ACCESS	NETWORK ACCESS SERVICES (E.G., VIRTUAL CIRCUIT, DATAGRAM, ETC.)
INTRANET, END-TO-END	FLOW CONTROL, SEQUENCING
INTRANENT, NODE-TO-NODE	CONGESTION CONTROL, ROUTING
LINK CONTROL	ERROR HANDLING, LINK FLOW CONTROL

Figure 3-5: Generic protocol structure

APPLICATION			
UTILITY	FILE TRANSFER	VIRTUAL TERMINAL	DIRECTORY LOOK-UP, FILE ACCESS
END-TO-END SUBSCRIBER	STREAM PROTOCOL		
	RELIABLE PACKET PROTOCOL		
NETWORK ACCESS	BROADCAST DATAGRAM		

LINK CONTROL			

Figure 3-6: Ethernet structure

APPLICATION	RJE	ELECTRONIC MAIL	
UTILITY	TELNET	FTP	
END-TO-END SUBSCRIBER	NCP	TCP	NVP/NVCP
NETWORK ACCESS	PERMANENT VIRTUAL CIRCUIT		DATAGRAM
INTRANET, END-TO-END	FLOW CONTROL, SEQUENCING, MESSAGE REASSEMBLY		
INTRANET, NODE-TO-NODE	ADAPTIVE ROUTING, STORE AND FORWARD, CONGESTION CONTROL		
LINK CONTROL	NON-SEQUENCED, MULTI-CHANNEL ERROR CONTROL		

Figure 3-7: Arpanet structure

UTILITY	TERMINAL HANDLING X.28, X.29
END-TO-END SUBSCRIBER	
NETWORK ACCESS	X.25, PERMANENT OR TEMPO-RARY VIRTUAL CIRCUITS
INTRANET, END-TO-END	MULTIPLE VIRTUAL CIRCUITS, FLOW CONTROL
INTRANET, NODE-TO-NODE.	ROUTING, STORE/FORWARD, CONGESTION CONTROL
LINK CONTROL	HDLC

Figure 3-8: PTT structure

3.7. Protocol properties

Protocols will be viewed as agreements.

There are several important properties of protocols that we will discuss: interlocking, hierarchial nature, protocols vs. interfaces, standards, internetting, and multiplexing.

Many common protocols utilize a concept called request/acknowledge interlocking. Sometimes this concept is known as handshaking. Interlocking provides for a controlled transfer of data over a transmission media. It specifies the sequence of operations necessary to send one unit of information.

Protocols are hierarchial in nature. They can be viewed as a layered structure on which higher levels of protocols are built. This course will discuss the link level and end-to-end level protocols necessary for interprocess communication as well as the hierarchial nature of protocols in more detail later.

Between layers there are agreements usually called interfaces. However, since interfaces have many of the same properties of protocols we tend to use the terms interface and protocol interchangeably in this book. The usual distinction made between protocol and interface is as follows: protocols provide rules for communication between similar processes, whereas interfaces provide rules for communication between dissimilar processes. For the remainder of this book we will make no sharp distinction between intra and inter layer agreements .

Because of the existence of distributed systems, there exist today many "standard protocols." These standards specify the most important features of the protocol. Each device in a distributed system then provides an implementation of the standard protocol. It is possible that we may wish to interconnect two distributed systems. Unless, these systems use the same protocol structure, we will have to provide a device called a gateway. The gateway provides protocols for internetworking.

There are a number of design issues involving protocols, such as error control, naming, routing, and flow control. These issues are hierarchial in nature, and the designer can expect to encounter them at each level in the protocol structure. For example, consider naming: not only is naming a consideration at all levels of a layered structure, but the choice of a naming scheme impacts internetworking designs. [Shoch 78] clearly points out the hierarchial nature of names. The hierarchial nature of other issues such as routing, flow control, etc., are not as obvious and/or "easy" to articulate as is the case for naming.

Because protocols exist as a layered structure, it is possible that a protocol may be able to simultaneously support several instances of higher level protocols. This concept is known as protocol multiplexing [Cohen 79].

Link level protocols are discussed in detail in Chapter 5; end-to-end or transport protocols are treated in Chapter 7. The hierarchial nature of protocols will be investigated in further detail.

3.8. Interconnection structure

A distributed processor is physically implemented by connecting the host processing nodes with some form of an interconection structure. This structure provides a hardware base upon which protocols are layered to provide a match between the hardware structure and the designed software structure. Physical connections and lower level protocols generally connect nodes in a point-to-point fashion, although some systems use broadcast or multi-point connections. The primary decisions concerning the interconnection structure are to select the node locations at which hosts connect into the communication structure, to determine a system topology which allows delay goals and anticipated traffic loads to be met, and to determine appropriate policies to implement the decisions.

To determine which of many structures is most appropriate, tradeoffs must be made between performance and service goals. Typical performance goals include delay, throughput, and efficiency. Typical service goals include availability, security, data integrity, and message integrity.

Many attempts have been made to classify topologies. Most schemes identify two strategies: point-to-point and multi-point. The most discussed structures are stars, rings/loops, irregular networks, fully interconnected networks, and broadcast systems. Figure 3-9 illustrates the important differences between point-to-point and multi-point schemes, and figure 3-10 illustrates the most widely discussed structures. The primary performance goals can be measured as indicated in figure 3-11. Service goal measurement is indicated in figure 3-12.

```
POINT-TO-POINT
   – PATH IS SETUP
   – CIRCUIT SWITCH
   – MESSAGE/PACKET SWITCH

MULTI-POINT
   – SOURCE TRANSMITS TO MORE THAN
     ONE RECEIVER
   – NUMBER OF SOURCES TRANSMIT TO A
     CENTRAL RECEIVER
   – BROADCAST
   – POLLING
```

Figure 3-9: Strategies

```
DELAY
   – TIME FOR A SINGLE BIT TRANSIT
   – MEASURE: AVERAGE RESPONSE TIME
   – DISTANCE DELAY
   – TRANSMISSION DELAY
   – PROCESSING DELAY
   – QUEUE DELAY
   – RTT (REAL TIME TRAFFIC) GBT (GUARANTEED BANDWIDTH
     TRAFFIC) AND LDT (LOR DELAY TRAFFIC) NEED LOW DELAY
   – LDT – INTERACTIVE COMPUTING
   – RTT – REMOTE TELEMETRY
   – GBT – DIGITAL SPEECH

THROUGHPUT
   – BITS IN MESSAGE DIVIDED BY TIME TO DELIVER MESSAGE
   – MEASURE – PEAK TRAFFIC LEVEL
   – MEDIA BANDWIDTH
   – PROCESSING BANDWIDTH
   – HTT (HIGH THROUGHPUT TRAFFIC) NEEDS HIGH THROUGHPUT
   – HTT – FILE TRANSFER
```

Figure 3-11: Performance goal measures

RING/LOOP

STAR

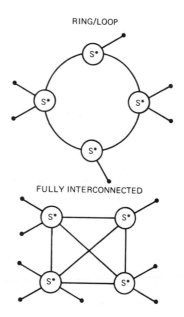

IRREGULAR

FULLY INTERCONNECTED

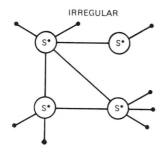

BROADCAST

S* — SWITCH

TOPOLOGY DESIGN ISSUES

PERFORMANCE
  — DELAY
  — THROUGHPUT
  — RELIABILITY
  — ROBUSTNESS

CONSTRAINTS
  — CIRCUIT SPEEDS
  — DISTANCE
  — ERROR RATES
  — SUBSCRIBER LOCATIONS
  — COSTS

PROBLEM
  — DON'T VIOLATE CONSTRAINTS
  — MINIMIZE COST
  — MAXIMIZE PERFORMANCE

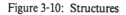

Figure 3-10: Structures

AVAILABILITY
  – DOWN TIME
  – MTBF
  – MTTR

DATA INTEGRITY
  – BIT ERRORS
  – ERROR RATE

MESSAGE INTEGRITY
  – MESSAGE LOSS
  – RATE OF MESSAGE LOSS

SECURITY
  – MESSAGE MISDELIVERY
  – RATE OF MESSAGE MISDELIVERY

Figure 3-12: Service goal measures

3.9. Multiplexing

When transmitting a signal on a hardware path, the path may have to be shared for efficiency reasons. This "shared path" is usually implemented using multiplexing. There are four main forms of multiplexing, illustrated in figure 3-13:

1) TDM – time division multiplexing.

2) STDM – statistical time division multiplexing.

3) FDM – frequency division multiplexing.

4) SDM – space division multiplexing.

3.10. Arbitration

It there is to be a shared path, there must be a way of controlling the path. This concept is called arbitration; that is, there exists with a shared path some way of determining what device is transmitting. In some systems this is done with the reception of correct data by a device (broadcast or contention channels). In other systems, the devices compete for allocation of the path before they transmit. The choice of arbitration method will have a substantial impact on the amount of device buffering, system throughput, etc. obtained from a particular topology.

3.11. Computer networks versus distributed computers

So far in this book, most of the discussion has been based on the concept of computer networks. Networks are one form of a distributed system. However, there are interconnected sets of processor-memory pairs which satisfy the definition of a distributed system which are not networks; rather, they are attempts to utilize processor-memory pairs to build a computer; e.g., HXDP, the Honeywell Experimental Distributed Processor [Jensen 78]. The functional design considerations at the interprocessor communication level apply equally well to both networks and distributed computers. Importantly, the user may not care that a system is distributed. In fact,

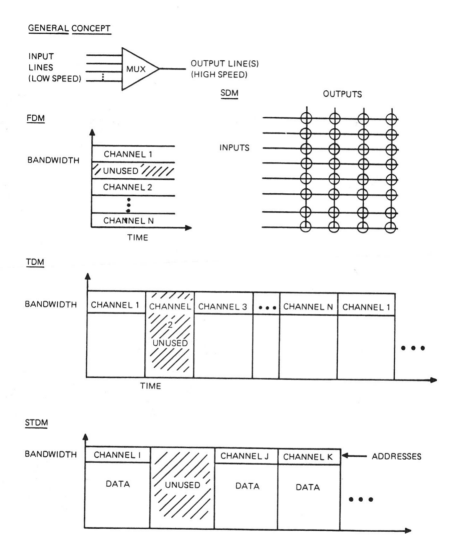

Figure 3-13: Multiplexing concepts

the effect of protocol levels may be to centralize the user's view at some level. Thus, even though networks and distributed computers may look quite similar from the hardware perspective, they differ in the user view, degree of centralization of user view, and level of abstraction at which the user view becomes centralized. The degree of centralization is primarily due, in the case of HXDP, to the desire to build a computer based upon use of processor-memory pairs.

3.12. Summary

A number of important concepts were introduced in this section. First is the idea of a layered structure of protocols which are used to match the hardware and software characteristics. Second is that a distributed processor is not necessarily a network, it could also be a distributed computer; however, the same design regime applies to both concepts. Lastly, is a definition and overview of a number of concepts which will be more fully developed later in this book.

Chapter 4. Hardware interconnection technology

4.1. Introduction

Distributed systems must be based on a hardware structure. The reference model described earlier noted the various levels on which the system can be developed. This chapter provides a set of concepts which define the lowest level of structure and the transmission technology upon which all other layers will be built.

4.2. Topologies

There are many classification schemes which attempt to illustrate the types of configurations of networks or distributed systems that are available. Some of these illustrate only the topological structure. Others include additional features which claim to illuminate the "important" topological features of distributed systems.

We will begin with a simple idea, point-to-point connection versus multi-point connection, and then build up to a hardware structure concept which illustrates features of topological taxonomies and how topology impacts path allocation. We will conclude with some example system concepts.

4.3. Point-to-point

Consider the case in figure 4-1. This figure illustrates the most basic concept of point-to-point connection; i.e., there exists a unique connection between individual pairs of nodes within our overall system. Clearly, by careful incorporation of these connecting paths, we can construct an arbitrarily complex system. However, to move information between two points which are not directly connected, a link must be established. This link may contain several connecting point-to-point paths, and possibly an intervening device. It is not required that transmission of data be performed in a store and forward manner; rather, a circuit between two nodes could be established through several intermediate nodes without store and forward techniques.

4.4. Multi-point

Figure 4-2 illustrates the concept of a multi-point system. In this system, a node may simultaneously connect to a number (N>1) of nodes. In such a system it is possible to "broadcast" information to a number of nodes simultaneously. It is possible to do a similar logical function of broadcasting in a point-to-point system, but the simultaneity is lost. In a point-to-point system, the "broadcast" must occur sequentially. We can build an arbitrarily complex system using multi-point connections also. Further, the mechanism of connection may be a simple multidrop coax, so the multi-point connection scheme is not very complex.

CONCEPT

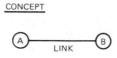

EXAMPLE SYSTEM

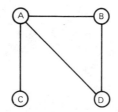

Figure 4-1: Point-to-point interconnection concept

CONCEPT

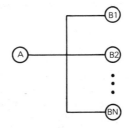

EXAMPLE SYSTEM (BUS STRUCTURE)

Figure 4-2: Multi-point interconnection concept

4.5. Taxonomies

Many researchers have attempted to utilize the concept of point-to-point and multi-point systems to describe the spectrum of distributed systems. Figure 4-3 illustrates the topological taxonomy of [Chen 74]. This taxonomy assumes that a set of PMS-level elements form the basic nodes; it was probably the first attempt to describe such systems.

```
BASIC
    SERIAL
        STAR, GENERALIZED STAR
        LOOP, GENERALIZED LOOP
    PARALLEL
        TRUNK
        CROSSPOINT
COMPLEX
    HIERARCHICAL
        TREE, GENERALIZED TREE
        OTHER
    OTHER
```

Figure 4-3: Chen topology taxonomy

The [Sieworek 74] Taxonomy (figure 4-4) attempted to illustrate the overall properties of distributed processors. The dimensions of the taxonomy allow for more than PMS-level elements, and include such issues as circuit versus message switching and deadlock handling. The topological decriptors however, are only a small portion of the taxonomy.

Anderson and Jensen [Anderson 75] described a systematic approach to the interconnection structure. This concept allows such processors as shared memory multi-processors to be included; in this course we have defined such systems to be not-distributed. However, if the shared memory is used solely for message communication, it then can be viewed as a form of a path. The resulting taxonomy is shown in figure 4-5.

Boorstyn, and Frank [Boorstyn 77] describe a simple formulation of the topology design problem as a set of constraints and cost measures. The performance of the network is to be maximized consistent with the constraints, while minimizing the cost measures. This formulation is summarized in figure 4-6.

Although many topologies are possible, there are primary topologies. In order of interconnection complexity these are:

1) irregular

2) broadcast

3) ring/loop

4) star

5) fully connected.

Figure 4-7 gives examples of these common topologies.

```
TOPOLOGY
    PHYSICAL SIZE
        LOCAL
        GEOGRAPHICALLY DISTRIBUTED
    PHYSICAL INTERCONNECTION PATTERN
    NONHOMOGENEOUS NODES
        BIPART GRAPH
    HOMOGENEOUS NODES
        SPANNING TREE
        FULLY CONNECTED GRAPH
SWITCH
    CENTRALIZED
    DISTRIBUTED
MEMORY
    DISTRIBUTION
        LOCAL
        SHARED
        HIERARCHY
    ADDRESSIBILITY
DATA PATHS
    CONCURRENCY
    WIDTH
        SERIAL
        PARALLEL
        SERIAL   PARALLEL
DATA DISCIPLINE
    CIRCUIT SWITCHED
    MESSAGE SWITCHED
ARBITRATION ALGORITHM
DEADLOCK
    PREVENTION
    AVOIDANCE
    DETECTION AND RECOVERY
```

Figure 4-4: Siework topology taxonomy

```
TRANSFER STRATEGY: DIRECT
    PATH: DEDICATED
        TOPOLOGY: DISTRIBUTED CONTROL LOOP
        TOPOLOGY: COMPLETE INTERCONNECTION
    PATH: SHARED
        TOPOLOGY: COMMON MEMORY
        TOPOLOGY: COMMON DISTRIBUTED CONTROL BUS
TRANSFER STRATEGY: INDIRECT
    ROUTING: CENTRALIZED
        PATH: DEDICATED
            TOPOLOGY: STAR
            TOPOLOGY: CENTRALLY CONTROLLED LOOP
        PATH: SHARED
            TOPOLOGY: COMMON CENTRALLY CONTROLLED BUS
    ROUTING: DECENTRALIZED
        PATH: DEDICATED
            TOPOLOGY: REGULAR NETWORK
            TOPOLOGY: IRREGULAR NETWORK
        PATH: SHARED
            TOPOLOGY: BUS WINDOW
```

Figure 4-5: Anderson/Jensen taxonomy

GIVEN: MINIMIZE:

TERMINAL AND HOST LOCATIONS   COST = (SUBNET LINE COST)
TRAFFIC REQUIREMENTS   + (SUBNET NODE COST)
    TERMINAL TO HOST   + (LOCAL ACCESS LINE COST)
    HOST TO HOST   + (LOCAL ACCESS HARDWARE COST)
DELAY REQUIREMENTS
RELIABILITY REQUIREMENTS
CANDIDATE SITES FOR COMMUNICATION
  SUBNETWORK NODES
COST INFORMATION

SUBPROBLEMS:

DESIGN SUBNET
DESIGN OF LOCAL DISTRIBUTION NETS

SUBPROBLEM PARAMETERS WHICH INTERACT:

SUBNET NODE NUMBER AND LOCATIONS
TERMINAL/HOST ASSOCIATION TO NODES
DELAY REQUIREMENTS — SUBNET AND LOCAL
RELIABILITY REQUIREMENTS — SUBNET AND LOCAL

Figure 4-6: Abstraction of [Boorstyn 77], topology design problem formulation

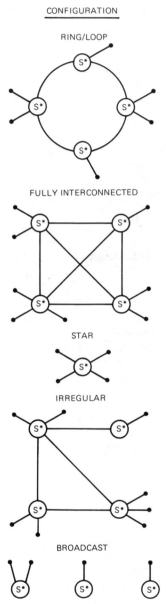

CONFIGURATION   EXAMPLES

RING/LOOP

NEWHALL LOOP
DCS
RINGNET
PIERCE LOOP
ISU NET
DLCN
SPIDER

FULLY INTERCONNECTED

IBM ATTACHED SUPPORT
PROCESSOR SYSTEM
MERIT

STAR

NPL
OCTOPUS
KUIPNET
LABOLINK
SNA
DATAKIT
AN/USQ-67

IRREGULAR

ARPANET

BROADCAST

ALOHANET
ETHERNET

S* — SWITCH

Figure 4-7: Examples of important topologies

There is a large amount of interaction between the connection structure and the higher level system design issues. Topology design is a difficult problem. Many topologies have simply evolved. Figure 4-8 shows the results of a study to illustrate the response routing impacts of a set of particular topologies [Sahin 78] on a set of particularly defined cost measures. Such highly theoretical investigations are interesting, but are difficult to generalize, interpret and use in any practical way.

4.6. Distributed system interfaces

At the higher levels in the model, a distributed system does not directly see the system topology. Further, the system does not know whether the topology is implemented using point-to-point or multi-point technology. What the system does see is two primary design decisions defining its interfaces to the communication structure: datagram interface, virtual circuit interface, and a logical extension of a virtual circuit interface, the terminal emulation interface. The datagram concept is distinguished by the characteristic that each datagram transmitted is completely self-contained; i.e., it includes within its structure all necessary control and address information. The virtual circuit, on the other hand, appears to the host to provide a dedicated point-to-point link between the source host node and the destination host node. Thus, the system operates as if a series of transmissions occurs between the hosts, rather than viewing each datagram individually. The terminal emulation concept uses a view of the system in which each unit appears to the network and the network appears to the host as a terminal. The properties of these interface concepts are summarized in figure 4-9.

Figure 4-10 illustrates the interface of several well known distributed systems in terms of interface and operation properties. Clearly, from the interconnection level, we see the similarity between what computer architects usually view as distributed systems, and what network designers view as geographically distributed networks. Since both system concepts use similar interconnection techniques, we must conclude that the point at which they become conceptually different (if they do) is somewhere higher in the model.

NETWORK	INTERFACE	OPERATION
ARPANET	DATAGRAM	STORE AND FORWARD PACKET SWITCH
AUTODIN II	DATAGRAM	STORE AND FORWARD PACKET SWITCH
DCS	DATAGRAM	BROADCAST PACKET SWITCH
ETHERNET	DATAGRAM	BROADCAST PACKET SWITCH
TELENET	VIRTUAL CIRCUIT	STORE AND FORWARD PACKET SWITCH
TYMNET	VIRTUAL CIRCUIT	STORE AND FORWARD "FRAMES" OVER POINT TO POINT CIRCUITS

Figure 4-10: Summary of major system properties

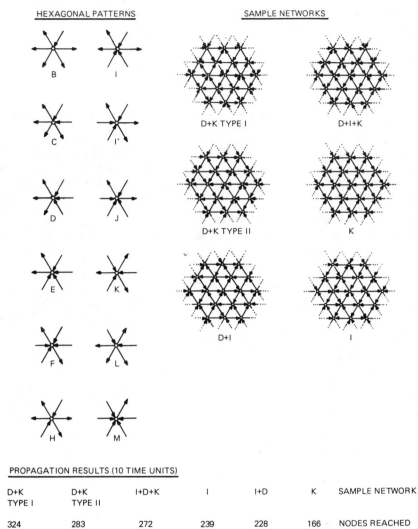

Figure 4-8: Hexogonal topology impacts on routing

EFFICIENCY RESULTS

SAMPLE NETWORK	EFFICIENCY ORDER	ADJACENCE INDEX	PATH INDEX
D+K TYPE I	1	4.5	6
D+K TYPE II	2	4.5	4.5
I + D+K	3	4.12	1.5
I	4	4	0
I+D	5	3	1.5
K	6	0	3

DEFINITIONS

ADJACENCE INDEX — A POINT IS ASSIGNED FOR EACH CHANNEL THAT IS ADJACENT TO A CHANNEL OF LIKE ORIENTATION.

PATH INDEX — A POINT IS ASSIGNED FOR EACH DIRECTION FOR WHICH THERE IS A STRAIGHT PATH. DIVIDE THIS SCORE BY THE NUMBER OF ADJACENT PARALLEL PATHS POINTED IN THE SAME DIRECTION.

Figure 4-8(cont): Hexogonal topology impacts on routing

DATAGRAM
    EACH DATAGRAM HANDLED SEPARATELY
    NO GUARANTEES AS TO LOSE, DUPLICATION, ETC.
    REASSEMBLIED INTO PROPER ORDER
    PROTOCOL FLEXIBILITY

VIRTUAL CIRCUIT
    APPEARS TO PROVIDE A CIRCUIT AND A SUSTAINED
      SEQUENCE OF TRANSMISSIONS
    RECOVERS LOST DATA, ELIMINATES DUPLICATION, ETC.
    ORDER IS MAINTAINED ON A LOGICAL CHANNEL
    DESIRE COMPATIBILITY TO CIRCUIT CONCEPTS

TERMINAL EMULATION
    EXTENSION OF VIRTUAL CIRCUIT
    HOST SENDS BIT STREAMS
    HOST APPEARS AS A SIMPLE TERMINAL

Figure 4-9: Datagram, virtual circuit, and terminal emulation interface concepts

4.7. Path allocation

In developing a path structure there is the issue of path allocation.   In point-to-point interconnections, the path is dedicated and therefore allocation is not an issue.   If the path is multi-point then a determination must be made as to which device is "allowed" to transmit. Some media such as multidrop coax bus structures may be utilized to construct a bus. In some modes of operation a device may broadcast information to many devices.   In other modes, a device may transmit to a single receiving device.   It is the path allocation scheme which determines how the path is actually used, regardless of its capabilities.   In a sense, all communication over a path could be regarded as point-to-point. The transmission of information at some level of the system is from a process to another process, and thus from some processor to some other processor (point A to point B).

Even broadcast transmission of a message from process A to processes B_1, B_2, B_3, ..., B_N may be viewed as point-to-point if the message receipt must be acknowledged separately by each receiver. Clearly, there are many ways that a particular path medium may be utilized. The path allocation scheme selected determines how the path is used. Not all of the schemes described below are suitable for all media. The primary strategies involve either controlled or uncontrolled transmission by the source device.   In controlled techniques, the path allocation determines which device can transmit before transmission occurs. In uncontrolled transmission schemes, the source transmits, and if an acknowledgement of message receipt is correctly received by the source within a certain amount of time then the transmission has occurred correctly. Otherwise, the source must retransmit the message.   If the source retransmits, some algorithm must be employed to select the appropriate retransmission instant.

Controlled transmission schemes are of two primary types: implicit (also known as reservation) and explicit (also known as selection).   Some researchers call these algorithms arbitration algorithms.   Uncontrolled techniques are usually known as random access or contention techniques. Figure 4-11 illustrates a number of path allocation taxonomies [Levy 78], [Luczak 78], [Thurber 72], [Thurber 78], and [Chen 74]. The remaining discussion is based upon the taxonomy of Luczak, and discusses in order reservation, selection, and random access.

Reservation techniques operate by establishing "time slots" for transmission.   Once this reservation is made, the transmitting device has to adhere to the assigned schedule until the reservation is changed.   Clearly, the node knows when to transmit and needs no external stimulus. Information being transmitted cannot collide unless there is a fault in the system, since each node knows when to transmit. In some systems, slots are grouped into frames, and frames may be reserved as well as individual slots.   This type of technique will require close synchronization of devices to ensure that the node knows exactly when its time slot is scheduled. There are two primary subcases: static and dynamic reservations. Static approaches fix the time slot allocations; e.g., TDM. Dynamic techniques allow the time slots allocation to be changed; e.g., STDM. In static techniques, if a device does not use its slot, that slot is unused. Thurber et.al. [Thurber 72] view reservation techniques as a special case of selection techniques. The reason for this is as follows: in any type of selection technique, arbitration must be performed before the device is connected to the path. This time difference can be arbitrarily large, and can be made a fixed value. Thus, most reservation concepts could be viewed as a subcase of selection techniques. Lastly, reservation techniques using centralized and/or decentralized reservations are possible.

THURBER, ET AL
CENTRALIZED
        DAISY CHAIN
        POLLING (2 CASES)
        INDEPENDENT REQUESTS
DECENTRALIZED
        DAISY CHAIN (2 CASES)
        POLLING
        INDEPENDENT REQUESTS

THURBER/MASSON
CENTRALIZED
        DAISY CHAIN
        POLLING
        INDEPENDENT REQUESTS
        IMPLICIT
DECENTRALIZED
        DAISY CHAIN
        POLLING
        INDEPENDENT REQUESTS
        IMPLICIT

CHEN
ARBITER LOCATION
        DISTRIBUTED
        CENTRALIZED
                STATIC
                DYNAMIC
PRIORITY SORTING
        COMPARISON
        COUNTING
ADDRESSING
        PRIORITY
        UNIT
INFORMATION PASSING
        ENCODED
        DECODED

LUCZAK
CONFIGURATION
        BIDIRECTIONAL SHARED CHANNEL
        DUAL UNIDIRECTIONAL SHARED CHANNEL
CHANNEL ACCESS (ARBITRATION)
        SELECTION
        RANDOM ACCESS CONTENTION
                ACCESS CONTROL
                COLLISION RESOLUTION
                MESSAGE PROTOCOL
        RESERVATION

Figure 4-11: Path allocation taxonomies

LEVY

ARBITRATION CATEGORY	A) FIXED WITH RESPECT TO DATA TRANSFER	B) VARIABLE WITH RESPECT TO DATA TRANSFER
1) CENTRALIZED, PRIORITY	CENTRALIZED, PRIORITY, FIXED	CENTRALIZED, VARIABLE PRIORITY
2) CENTRALIZED, DEMOCRATIC	CENTRALIZED, DEMO-CRATIC, FIXED	CENTRALIZED, DEMO-CRATIC, VARIABLE
3) CENTRALIZED, SEQUENTIAL	CENTRALIZED, SEQUENTIAL, FIXED	CENTRALIZED, SEQUEN-TIAL, VARIABLE
4) DISTRIBUTED, PRIORITY	DISTRIBUTED, PRIORITY, FIXED	DISTRIBUTED, PRIORITY, VARIABLE
5) DISTRIBUTED, DEMOCRATIC	DISTRIBUTED, DEMO-CRATIC, FIXED	DISTRIBUTED, DEMO-CRATIC, VARIABLE
6) DISTRIBUTED, SEQUENTIAL	DISTRIBUTED, SEQUENTIAL, FIXED	DISTRIBUTED, SEQUEN-TIAL, VARIABLE

Figure 4-11(cont): Path allocation taxonomies

Selection techniques can be described in terms of a transaction between the source device and an "arbitrator" which determines when a device may connect to the path. Because of the arbitrator, it is possible to design the system without slots; i.e., how long a device is connected to the path and how many transactions occur is up to the arbitration algorithm, and may differ substantially between devices. The major selection techniques are discussed below; figure 4-12 indicates the most important features.

The different selection schemes can be roughly classifed as being either centralized or decentralized. If the hardware used for passing bus control from one device to another is largely concentrated in one location, we have centralized control. The location of the hardware could be within one of the devices which is connected to the bus, or it could be a separate hardware unit. On the other hand, if the bus control logic is largely distributed throughout the different devices connected to the bus, we have decentralized control. The various bus control techniques are described here terms of distinct control lines, but in most cases the equivalent functions can be performed with coded transfers on the bus data lines. The basic tradeoff is allocation speed versus total number of bus lines. The major control techniques are shown in figure 4-12.

With centralized control, a single hardware unit is used to recognize and grant requests for the use of the bus. At least four different schemes can be used, plus various modifications or combinations of these:

1) Daisy chaining
2) Polling
3) Independent requests

4) Implicit.

The implicit techniques are extensions of the independent request techniques described in Thurber and Masson [Thurber 78]. These techniques encompass the techniques usually associated with the concept of random access or contention techniques. Since we are using a parallel to Luczak's [Luczak 78] development in this book, the implicit techniques will not be discussed further.

Each device can generate a request via the common Bus Request line. Whenever the Bus Controller receives a request on the Bus Request line, it returns a signal on the Bus Available line, which is daisy chained through each device. If a device receives the Bus Available signal and does not want control of the bus, it passes the Bus Available signal on to the next device. If a device receives the Bus Available signal and is requesting control of the bus, then it does not pass the Bus Available signal on to the next device. The requesting device places a signal on the Bus Busy line, drops its bus request, and begins its data transmission. The Bus Busy line keeps the Bus Available line up while the transmission takes place. When the device drops the Bus Busy signal, the Bus Available line is lowered. If the Bus Request line is again up, the allocation procedure repeats. The Bus Busy line can be eliminated, but this essentially converts the bus control to a decentralized Daisy Chain (as described later).

The obvious advantage of such a scheme is its simplicity: very few control lines are required, and the number of them is independent of the number of devices; hence, additional devices can be added by simply connecting them to the bus.

A disadvantage of the Daisy Chaining scheme is its susceptibility to failure. If a failure occurs in the Bus Available circuitry of a device, it could prevent succeeding devices from ever getting control of the bus, or it could allow more than one device to transmit over the bus at the same time. However, the logic involved is quite simple, and can easily be made redundant to increase its reliability. A power failure in a single device or the necessity to take a device off-line can also be problems with the Daisy Chain method of control.

Another disadvantage is the fixed priority structure which results. The devices which are "closer" to the Bus Controller always receive control of the bus in preference to those which are "further away". If the closer devices had a high demand for the bus, the farther devices could be locked out. Since the Bus Available signal must sequentially ripple through the devices, this bus assignment mechanism can also be quite slow. Finally, it should be noted that with Daisy Chaining, cable lengths are a function of system layout, so adding, deleting, or moving devices is physically awkward.

Figure 4-12 illustrates a centralized Polling system. As in the centralized Daisy Chaining method, each device on the bus can place a signal on the Bus Request line. When the Bus Controller receives a request, it begins polling the devices to determine who is making the request. The polling is done by counting on the polling lines. When the count corresponds to a requesting device, that device raises the Bus Busy line. The controller then stops the polling until the device has completed its transmission and removed the busy signal. If there is another bus request, the count may restart from zero or may be continued from where it stopped. Restarting from zero each time establishes the same sort of device priority as proximity does in Daisy Chaining, while continuing from the stopping point is a round-robin approach which gives equal opportunity to all devices. The priorities need not be fixed, because the polling sequence is easily altered.

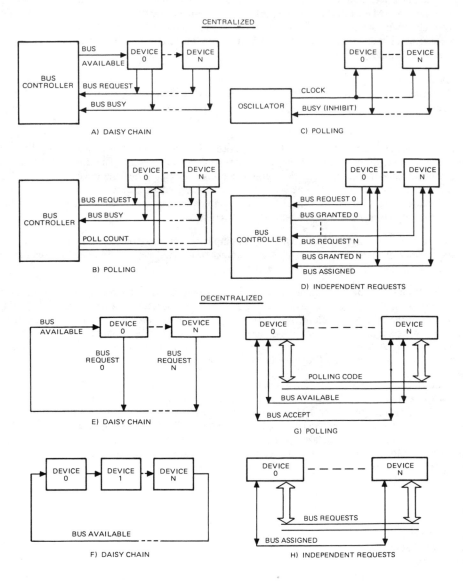

Figure 4-12: Bus arbitration techniques

The Bus Requests line can be eliminated by allowing the polling counter to continuously cycle except while it is stopped by a device using the bus. This alternative impacts the restart (i.e., priority) philosophy, and the average bus assignment time.

Polling does not suffer from the reliability of physical placement problems of Daisy Chaining, but the number of devices in figure 4-12 is limited by the number of polling lines. Attempting to poll bit-serially involves synchronous communication techniques and the attendant complications.

Figure 4-12 shows that centralized Polling may be made independent of the number of devices by placing a counter in each device. The Bus Controller then is reduced to distributing clock pulses which are counted by all devices. When the count reaches the value of the code of a device wanting the bus, the device raises the Busy line, which inhibits the clock. When the device completes its transmission, it removes the Busy signal and the counting continues. The devices can be serviced either in a round-robin manner or on a priority basis. If the counting always continues cyclically when the Busy signal is removed, the allocation is round-robin, and if the counters are all reset when the Busy signal is removed, the devices are prioritized by their codes. It is also possible to make the priorities adaptive by altering the codes assigned to the devices. Clock skew problems tend to limit this technique to small slow systems; it is also exceptionally susceptible to noise and clock failure.

Polling and Daisy Chaining can be combined into schemes where addresses or priorities are propagated between devices instead of a Bus Available signal. This adds some priority flexibility to Daisy Chaining at the expense of more lines and logic.

The third method of centralized bus control, Independent Requests, is shown in figure 4-12. In this case each device has a separate pair of Bus Request and Bus Granted lines, which it uses for communicating with the Bus Controller. When a device requires use of the bus, it sends its Bus Request to the controller. The controller selects the next device to receive service and sends a Bus Granted to it. The selected device lowers its request and raises Bus Assigned, indicating to all other devices that the bus is busy. After the transmission is complete the device lowers the Bus Assigned line, and the Bus Controller removes Bus Granted and selects the next requesting device.

The overhead time required for allocating the bus can be shorter than for Daisy Chaining or Polling, since all Bus Requests are presented simultaneously to the Bus Controlller. In addition, there is complete flexibility available for selecting the next device for service. The controller can use prespecified or adaptive priorities, a round-robin scheme, or both. It is also possible to disable requests from a particular device which, for instance, is known or suspected to have failed. The major disadvantage of Independent Requests is the number of lines and connectors required for control. Of course, the complexity of the allocation algorithm will be reflected in the amount of Bus Controller hardware.

In a decentrally controlled system, the control logic is (primarily) distributed throughout the devices on the bus. As in the centralized case, there are at least four distinct schemes, plus combinations and modifications of these [Thurber 78]:

1) Daisy Chaining
2) Polling

3) Independent Requests

4) Implicit.

The implicit techniques are extensions of the independent request techniques described in Thurber and Masson [Thurber 78]. These techniques encompass the techniques usually associated with the concepts of reservations and random access techniques. Since we are using a parallel to Luczak's [Luczak 78] development in this book, the implicit techniques will not be discussed further.

A decentralized Daisy Chain can be constructed from a centralized one by omitting the Bus Busy line and connecting the common Bus Request to the "first" Bus Available, as shown in figure 4-12. A device requests service by raising its Bus Request line if the incoming Bus Available line is low. When a Bus Available signal is received, a device which is not requesting the bus passes the signal on. The first device which is requesting service does not propagate the Bus Available, and keeps its Bus Request up until finished with the bus. Lowering the Bus Request lowers Bus Available if no successive devices also have Bus Request signals up, in which case the "first" device wanting the bus gets it. On the other hand, if some device "beyond" this one has a Bus Request, control propagates down to it. Thus, allocation is always on a round-robin basis.

A potential problem exists in that if a device in the interior of the chain releases the bus and no other device is requesting it, the fall of Bus Request is propagating back toward the "first" device while the Bus Available signal propagates "forward". If devices on both sides of the last user now raise Bus Request, the one to the "right" will obtain the bus momentarily until its Bus Available drops when the "left" device gets control. This dilemma can be avoided by postponing the bus assignment until such races have settled out, either asynchronously with one-shots in each device, or with a synchronizing signal from elsewhere in the system. A topologically simpler decentralized Daisy Chain is illustrated in Figure 4-12. Here, it is not possible to unambiguously specify the status of the bus by using a static level on the Bus Available line. However, it is possible to determine the bus status from transition on the Bus Available line. Whenever the Bus Available coming into a device changes state and that device needs to use the bus, it does not pass a signal transition onto the next device; if the device does not need the bus, it changes the Bus Available signal to the next device. When the bus is idle, the Bus Available signal oscillates around the Daisy Chain. The first device change terminates the oscillation and takes control of the bus. When the device is finished with the bus, it causes a transition in Bus Available to the next device.

Dependence on signal edges rather than levels renders this approach somewhat more susceptible to noise than the previous one. This problem can be minimized by passing control with a request/acknowledge type of mechanism such as used later for data communication, although this slows down bus allocation. Both of these decentralized Daisy Chains have the same single-point failure mode and physical layout liabilities as the centralized version. Specific systems may prefer either the (centralized) priority or the (decentralized) round-robin algorithm, but they are equally inflexible (albeit simple).

Decentralized Polling can be performed as shown in figure 4-12. When a device is willing to relinquish control of the bus, it puts a code (address or priority) on the polling lines and raises Bus Available. If the code matches that of another device which desires the bus, that device responds with Bus Accept. The former device drops the polling and Bus Available lines, and the latter device lowers Bus Accept and begins using the bus. If the polling device does not receive a Bus Accept (a Bus Refused line could be added to distinguish between devices which do not desire the bus and those which are failed), it changes the code according to some allocation algorithm (round-robin or priority) and tries again. This approach requires that exactly one device be granted bus control when the system is initialized. Since every device must have the same allocation hardware as a centralized polling Bus Controller, the decentralized version utilizes substantially more hardware. This buys enhanced reliability in that failure of a single device does not necessarily affect operation of the bus.

Figure 4-12 illustrates the decentralized version of Independent Requests. Any device desiring the bus raises its Bus Request line, which corresponds to its priority. When the current user releases the bus by dropping Bus Assigned, all requesting devices examine all active Bus Requests. The device which recognizes itself as the highest priority requestor obtains control of the bus by raising Bus Assigned. This causes all other requesting devices to lower their Bus Requests (and to store the priority of the successful device if a round-robin algorithm is to be accommodated).

The priority logic in each device is simpler than that in the centralized counterpart, but the number of lines and connectors is higher. If the priorities are fixed rather than dynamic, not all request lines go to all devices, so the decentralized case uses fewer lines in systems with up to about 10 devices. Again, the decentralized method offers some reliability advantages over the centralized one. Clock skew problems limit this process to small dense systems, and it is exceptionally susceptible to noise and clock failure.

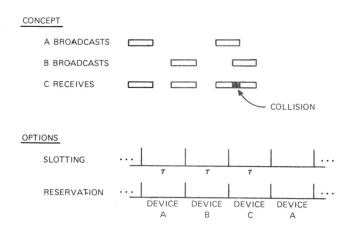

Figure 4-13: Random access/contention techniques

TECHNIQUE	CAPACITY UTILIZATION
PURE ALOHA	.18
SLOTTED ALOHA	.368
CARRIER SENSE ALOHA	.8 (OR ABOVE) ASSUMING USER STATIONS ARE CLOSE SO THAT DELAY IN LISTENING IS A SMALL FRACTION OF A SLOT INTERVAL.

Figure 4-13(cont): Random access/contention techniques

The basic concept of random access control is shown in figure 4-13. The idea is that devices desiring to transmit information transmit whenever they want. If no other device is transmitting and if no errors occur, the transmission completes satisfactorily. Otherwise, there is either a collision of information, i.e., information coming from two devices interferes with each other, or there is some other form of transmission error. Transmission errors are handled according to established system conventions as in any other technique. Collisions, like errors, require information to be retransmitted. However, something must now cause the devices which sent the colliding information to appropriately space their retranmissions so that further collisions are minimized. A simple technique would be to let the devices retransmit randomly. The main design issues involve access, collision detection and retry strategy. These are summarized in figure 4-14 and discussed below.

Transmission access to the path may be either slotted or unslotted. Slotted techniques allow devices to begin transmissions at specific times. Unslotted systems allow arbitrary transmission. Slotted techniques support a packet switching descipline if the time slots are of large enough duration to allow for transmission of a packet.

There are three primary strategies for collision detection: deaf, transmit and listen, and busy inhibit. The deaf strategy is also known as pure Aloha. In this case the transmitter waits for an acknowledgement of packet receipt. If such an acknowledgement does not arrive before a specified time period, then the transmission is repeated. The transmit and listen strategy works as follows: the source transmits and waits for a period of time (based upon propagation and system delays) and then listens. If the source when it is acting as a receiver detects a garbled message, it knows there was a collision. Lastly, a transmitter may monitor the path and transmit only if it hears no other device on the channel. In such cases it is possible (because of delays) that two devices may attempt to transmit at the same time and be unaware of each other until the transmissions have begun. Thus, if a device is tranmitting and it detects the presence of another transmitter, the device stops its transmission.

There exists numerous retry strategies which are useful once a collision is detected. Some of the most common are: random, adaptive, node delay, and reservation. The random delay strategy is non-adaptive. It operates on the concept that after a collision, the device retransmits at a time not related to or influenced by the number or frequency of collisions.   An implementation is to simply have all devices whose data collided randomly retransmit. Adaptive techniques attempt to be sensitive to the current usage level on the channel.   These procedures can be implemented

```
RANDOM ACCESS
ACCESS CONTROL
    SLOTTED
    UNSLOTTED
        DEAF (ALOHA)
        CARRIER SENSE MULTIPLE ACCESS (CSMA)
            COLLISION DETECTION
                RECEIVER ACKNOWLEDGMENT
                INTERFERENCE DETECTION
            DEFERENCE/ACQUISITION
                PERSISTENT CSMA
                    1 — PERSISTENT
                        UNSLOTTED (ETHERNET)
                        T — SLOTTED
                    P — PERSISTENT
                    NODE PRIORITY DELAY
                        FIXED
                        ROUND ROBIN
                NON-PERSISTENT CSMA
                    UNSLOTTED
                    T — SLOTTED


RANDOM ACCESS
    MESSAGE PROTOCOL
        MESSAGE ESTABLISHMENT
            SEPARATE PHASE
            INTEGRAL WITH MESSAGE TRANSMISSION PHASE
                NO RESPONSE ON FULL BUFFER (ETHERNET)
                NACK ON FULL BUFFER
                "IN-BUFFER" COLLISION MECHANISM
        ACKNOWLEDGEMENT
            MESSAGE-LEVEL ACK (ETHERNET)
            DEDICATED ACK INTERNAL




RANDOM ACCESS
    COLLISION RESOLUTION
        NON-ADAPTIVE RETRANSMISSION DELAYS (ALOHA)
        ADAPTIVE RETRANSMISSION DELAYS
            LOCAL
                BINARY EXPONENTIAL BACKOFF (ETHERNET)
                GEOMETRIC BACKOFF
            GLOBAL
        NODE PRIORITY DELAYS
        RESERVATION AFTER COLLISION
```

Figure 4-14: Random access design issues

globally or locally. Global techniques generally employ a network controller which periodically establishes the retransmission probabilities used by all devices. This can be done by a control message which is broadcast to all devices. Local techniques are generally driven by local observations of channel usage made while trying to transmit certain packets. Two important retransmission algorithms are: binary exponential backoff and geometric backoff. The node delay technique provides each node with a fixed unique delay time. If a collision occurs, then each node delays the appropriate time before transmitting. Lastly, the reservation technique reserves time slots for retransmission. To do this, the system must be able to ascertain the source(s) of a collision so that the reservations can be made.

Figure 4-15 illustrates some important throughput versus bandwidth characteristcs: pure Aloha, slotted Aloha, Ethernet measurements [Shoch 80] and delay curves derived by Franta [Franta 80].

BANDWIDTH VERSUS THROUGHPUT/DELAY

  — SIMULATION AND MODELLING CAN BE USED TO DERIVE THESE RESULTS
  — LIMITED NUMBER OF MEASUREMENTS
  — MEASUREMENTS SUPPORT VALIDITY OF RESULTS
  — LARGE NUMBER OF SYSTEM CONCEPTS

EXAMPLE

  — PURE ALOHA (.18 PEAK THROUGHPUT, 1/2e)
  — SLOTTED ALOHA (.36 PEAK THROUGHPUT, 1/e)

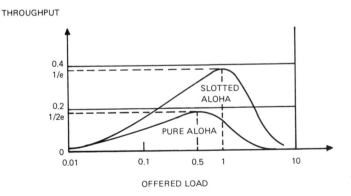

Figure 4-15: Throughput/bandwidth tradeoffs

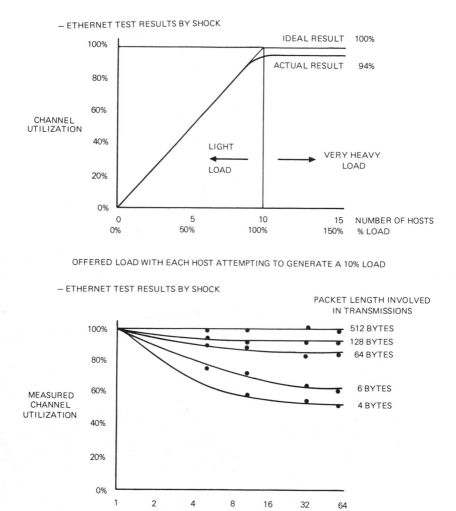

— ETHERNET TEST RESULTS BY SHOCK

OFFERED LOAD WITH EACH HOST ATTEMPTING TO GENERATE A 10% LOAD

— ETHERNET TEST RESULTS BY SHOCK

NUMBER OF HOSTS TRYING TO GENERATE A 100% CHANNEL UTILIZATION LOAD

Figure 4-15(cont): Throughput/bandwidth tradeoffs

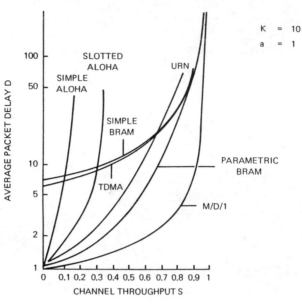

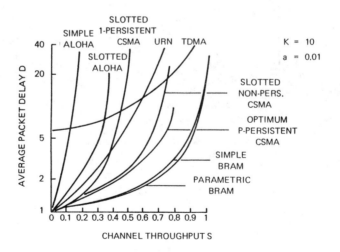

Figure 4-15(cont): Throughput/bandwidth tradeoffs

4.8. Bandwidth/throughput tradeoffs

Concerning a path there are a number of interesting tradeoffs that can be made. One of the most important of these is the difference between the theoretical channel capacity (bandwidth), and the actual maximum channel utilization possible (throughput); i.e., assuming that a channel has so many devices connected to it that it always has devices waiting to transmit, what is the throughput and further how do the throughput and bandwidth interrelate. For some common algorithms, figure 4-15 illustrates this important relationship [Schwartz 77], [Shoch 80] and [Franta 80]. One way to achieve high channel bandwidth usage is to increase the delay (queueing time) required to gain access to the system. The curves by Franta illustrate this relationship for some important system cases.

4.9. More on protocols

Protocols are defined as the basic agreements with which we define a system structure. Figure 4-16 illustrates the link X.25 protocols for use with some common systems. One problem is to determine just what a link protocol is. In figure 4-17, does a link protocol operate between Points A-A, Points B-B, or Points C-C. Clearly, the answer is dependent on the system. Since we are unable to define a link, we assume that the link protocol is the lowest functional level protocol, and that then all other protocols are made up based on that protocol. Further, note that maybe protocols are incorrectly viewed; i.e., there are really two levels which may contain sublevels: the operating system level and the communication subnetwork level. Then the link protocol is the lowest defined sublevel of the communication subnetwork level. Some common general purpose "standard" link protocols are illustrated in figure 4-18.

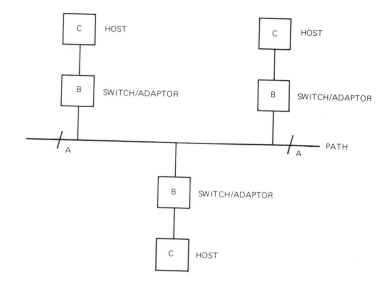

Figure 4-17: Link protocol ambiguity

SYSTEM

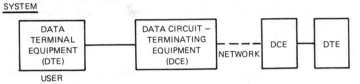

PROTOCOL HIERARCHY (SIMPLIFIED)

X.25 "LEVELS"

ELECTRICAL LEVEL — X.21, RS232, RS422
LINK LEVEL — ISO SUBSET OF HDLC
PACKET LEVEL — VIRTUAL CALLS
VIRTUAL TERMINAL

HDLC

01111110	ADDRESS	CONTROL	DATA	FRAME CHECK SEQUENCE
FLAG	ADR	CTL	DATA	FCS

MODES OF OPERATION

NRM — NORMAL RESPONSE MODE
PRIMARY STATION POLLS SECONDARY
STATION

ARM — ASYNCHRONOUS RESPONSE MODE
SECONDARY WAY TRANSMIT ANYTIME

Figure 4-16: Link protocols

SUMMARY

	DDCMP	BISYNC	SDLC
ERROR CONTROL			
RETRANSMIT	YES	YES	YES
ERROR RECOVERY	CYCLIC	CYCLIC (EBCDIC)	CYCLIC
ERROR DETECTION		VERTICAL 6-BIT	
		TRANSCODE &	
		LONGITUDINAL	
		(ASCII)	
INFORMATION ENCODING	NONE	ASCII OR EBCDIC	BIT ORIENTED
		6-BIT TRANSCODE	
LINE UTILIZATION			
FULL DUPLEX	YES	NO	YES
HALF DUPLEX	YES	YES	YES
SERIAL	YES	YES	YES
PARALLEL	YES	NO	NO
POINT-TO-POINT	YES	YES	YES
MULTIPOINT	YES	YES	YES
SYNCHRONIZATION			
SYNCHRONOUS	YES	YES	YES
ASYNCHRONOUS	YES	NO	NO
DATA TRANSPARENCY			
COUNT	YES	–	–
CHARACTER STUFFING	–	YES	–
BIT STUFFING	–	–	YES
BOOTSTRAPPING	YES	NO	NO

Figure 4-18: Common "standard" link protocols

FORMATS

DDCMP

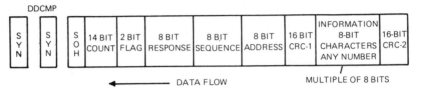

BISYNC

SDLC

SDLC CONTROL FIELD
FORMATS

FORMAT BIT	7	6	5	4	3	2	1	0
INFORMATION TRANSFER	0		← N_S →		P/F		← N_R →	
SUPERVISOR	1	0	← C_1 →		P/F		← N_R →	
NON-SEQUENCED	1	1	← C_2 →		P/F		← C_2 →	

$C_1 = 00$ READY TO RECEIVE – RR

10   NOT READY TO RECEIVE – RNR

01   RETRANSMIT STARTING WITH FRAME N_R – REJ

C_2 SPECIFIES A NUMBER OF COMMAND/RESPONSE FUNCTIONS

Figure 4-18(cont): Common "standard" link protocols

4.10. Buffers

From the perspective of the link and interconnection structure, there must be an interface to a node; most probably this interface is a buffer. There are two reasons for this. First, generally the node does not wish to be involved in all instances of transmission, e.g., every bit. Second, buffering capability allows the use of variable speed devices in a system. In some systems, the buffer is associated with the processors; in others, with a node, and hence possibly with many processors. Lastly, the buffer can be associated with the link rather than a specific processor; e.g., Network Systems HYPERcache^{TM}.

4.11. Case studies

Figure 4-19 illustrates three important distributed system concepts: broadcast (Ethernet), loop (DLCN), and bus (HXDP).

4.12. More on networks versus distributed computers

In the introduction, we discussed the difference between networks and distributed computers. This section will elaborate. There are two primary concepts of distributed systems because distributed systems evolved from two major perspectives: networks and distributed computers. Networks evolved from the perspective of data communications. Distributed computers evolved from the perspective of computer architecture. From the hardware level, however, the design issues are more a difference in kind rather than fact; i.e., both perspectives describe protocols, structured layers, etc. However, the tradeoffs to implement a system may differ substantially. Networks, for example, may have a substantially different structure due to the fact that nodes may be separated by very large distances. Several systems and their properties are illustrated in figure 4-20. One example system of particular note is the Sperry Univac DPS. As configured it is not, according to our definition, a distributed system. However, if the VATS were removed it would satisfy the definition. Further, DPS, like HXDP, was designed as a distributed computer. Arpanet illustrates a network.

Part of the difficulty in distributed processing is that in all three example systems of figure 4-20, the user interfaces to the system as if it were a uniprocessor. Thus, the user may not be aware of what type of system his job is executing on, unless the user desires certain features (special hardware, availability, electronic mail, etc.) which would normally not be available on a centralized system. It is important to understand that many system concepts provide a centralized user interface. The level at which this occurs is important. We must ask ourselves whether the user should see any impact of hardware distribution above the interconnection level.

4.13. Summary

A number of important ideas were discussed in this chapter: the concepts of point-to-point versus multi-point communication, topology, and path allocation. Important properties of specific systems were presented for comparison to each other.

SUMMARY

	ETHERNET	DLCN	HXDP
INTERFACE TO COMMUNICATION SUBNET	DATAGRAM BROADCAST MODE	DATAGRAM SHIFT – REGISTER INSERTION	MESSAGE (DATAGRAM) SYNCHRONOUS TIME SLOT ALLOCATION
OPERATION	PACKET SWITCH ARBITRARY LENGTH PACKET CO-AXIAL CABLE	PACKET SWITCH MULTIPLE VARIABLE LENGTH MESSAGES SHIFT REGISTERS/ LINES	SHARED BUS MESSAGE LENGTH 256 WORDS DOUBLE SHIELDED TWISTED PAIR

BLOCK DIAGRAMS

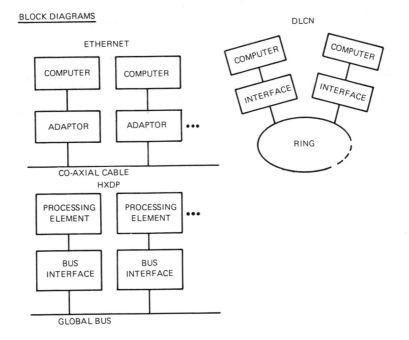

Figure 4-19: Important system concepts

SUMMARY

	DPS	HXDP	ARPANET.
MEMORY	SYSTEM WIDE SHARED WITH VAT IN SYSTEM EVEN THOUGH PHYS-ICALLY DEDICATED TO A COMPUTER	DEDICATED TO COMPUT-ERS	DEDICATED TO HOST COMPUTERS
TOPOLOGY	RING	GLOBAL BUS	IRREGULAR NET
DISTRIBUTED	NO	YES	NO
NOTES	VAT ALLOWS VIRTUAL SYSTEM TO APPEAR AS A MULTIPROCESSOR BUT WITHOUT VAT SYSTEM IS A LOOP/ RING TYPE DISTRIB-UTED SYSTEM	DISTRIBUTED COMPUTER	NETWORK WHOSE COM-MUNICATION SUBNET-WORK FORMS A DISTRIB-UTED SYSTEM

BLOCK DIAGRAMS

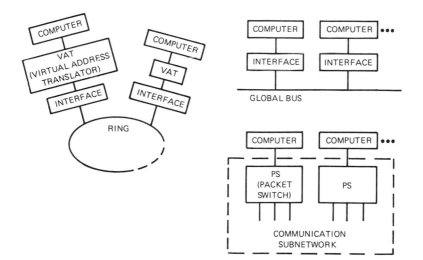

Figure 4-20: Networks versus distributed computers

Chapter 5. Link level

5.1. Introduction

A link is viewed as an abstraction of any physical route linking two separate entities. More precisely, a link is a passive communication path used to move frames among two entities. We say that communication is point-to-point. A communication path may include either one or several hardware paths. A frame is an abstraction of a block; it has a header, a body and a trailer. Only the header and the trailer are utilized by a link protocol.

A link protocol serves the purpose of performing and monitoring the exchange of frames between two communicating entities. It is probably easy to get convinced that such a characterization of a link protocol is acceptable for any level of abstraction in a communication system. What we would like to do is to identify unambiguously what is usually referred to as a link protocol in some intuitive manner. Such protocols have been designed:

- by manufacturers: e.g., DEC's DDCMP, IBM's SDLC;
- within the framework of computer network projects: e.g., LLL's Scull, Arpanet IMP-IMP protocol, Cyclades' MV8 protocol;
- by standardization bodies: e.g., ISO and ECMA's HDLC.

Recognizing the fact that processes utilize a hierarchy of point-to-point protocols to achieve point-to-point communication, we will therefore isolate that level of point-to-point protocols which do not use other point-to-point protocols (other than electrical protocols, possibly). These protocols will be referred to as "link protocols". Like any other point-to-point protocols, link protocols must embed mechanisms which cope with noise, failures and speed differences [Sunshine 75].

While being transmitted, frame content may be corrupted or frames may be lost. An error control mechanism is needed to guarantee that all frames to be transmitted are eventually received by the receiving entity and that the undetected error rate (undetected changes) is smaller than a predefined value.

The sending entity and the receiving entity may not process frames at compatible rates. Therefore, a flow control mechanism is needed to guarantee that a receiving entity does not get flooded with frames being sent too rapidly by a sending entity.

Some extra control information is used for error and flow control purposes. This control information, which constitutes "synchronization data" and which circulates over the link, must remain unambiguous in the face of damage, losses, duplicates and desequencing. Most popular error control mechanisms work as follows. For every frame being transmitted, the sender keeps a copy and sets up a timer. When time is up and no acknowledgment has been received from the receiver, or if a negative acknowledgment is received, a copy of the frame is transmitted again. This process is repeated until either an acknowledgment is received or until a maximum number of attempts is reached. Every frame is accompanied by a checksum (redundant data). Checksuming every received frame allows a receiver to decide whether an incoming frame is correct or not. In case no error is detected, a positive acknowledgment is returned. In case an error is detected, either no positive acknowledgment is returned or a negative acknowledgment is sent to the sender. Frames are also sequentially numbered in order to cope with desequencing, duplicates and losses.

Different flow control mechanisms have been suggested. They all are aimed at solving a fundamental problem in distributed systems, that is the absence of uniqueness in space and time. Pseudo-time, state information, etc. is used by flow control mechanisms to "synchronize" the communicating entities. Among most popular flow control mechanisms, one may find:

- pure alternate schemes (only one in-transit frame at a time)
- window-based schemes (several in-transit frames at a time, incremental allocation information)
- state-exchange schemes (several in-transit frames at a time, premises upon which the decision of sending a frame has been taken).

In order to illustrate these concepts, we have selected three different link protocols.

5.2. HDLC

HDLC is a bit-oriented link protocol intended to cover one way, two way alternate or two way simultaneous frame transfers between stations which are usually buffered. This protocol has been designed as a standard intended for the interconnection of heterogeneous equipments. It is an NPAR-like protocol (Negative/Positive Acknowledgment and Retransmission) based on the "window" concept.

5.2.1. Frame structure

The HDLC frame structure is described in figure 5-1. A flag is a delimiting bit sequence which is looked for by a receiving station. The address field contains the address of the destination station. The control field serves different purposes depending on the kind of frame it belongs to. This is described in figure 5-2.

Flag	Address	Control	Information	FCS	Flag
01111110	8 bits	8 bits	∷	16 bits	01111110

Figure 5-1: HDLC frame structure

The information field is any sequence of bits. The Frame Check Sequence is a 16 bit long cyclic redundancy checksum. In order to provide for a "transparent" transmission of bit sequences, no flag configuration should appear in the information field. To this end, the transmitting station will insert a 0-bit after every sequence of five consecutive 1-bits. This 0-bit will be removed from the body of the frame by the receiving station. Adjacent frames are separated either by flags, or by a sequence of 1-bits including at least seven bits.

	CONTROL FIELD BITS						
BIT ORDER	1	2	3	4	5	6	7	8
I frame format	0	N(S)			P/F	N(R)		
S frame format	1	0	S	S	P/F	N(R)		
U frame format	1	1	M	M	P/F	M	M	M

N(S) = Send Sequence Number   N(R) = Receive Sequence Number

P/F = Poll/Final Bit   S = Supervisory Bits   M = Modifier Bits

Figure 5-2: Control field

5.2.2. HDLC elements of procedure

The HDLC protocol is based on the notion of primary and secondary stations. A primary is permanently responsible for the control of the link. It generates commands and interprets responses. A secondary interprets received commands and generates responses. A combined station includes the functions of both a primary and a secondary. HDLC elements of procedure apply to two basic configurations:

- unbalanced configuration, with one primary and one or more secondaries;
- balanced configuration, with two combined.

We present below the essential characteristics of the elements of procedure. For more details, we refer the reader to [ECMA 79], [ISO 76] and [ISO 77].

5.2.2.1. Commands and responses

Information frames

The function of the I frames is to transfer across a link sequentially numbered frames containing an information field. The numbering is modulo 8 (128 for extended control field formats). Each I frame has an N_S and an N_R sequence number. N_S is the sequence number of the frame being transmitted. N_R indicates that the station transmitting the N_R has correctly received all I frames numbered up to N_R-1.

Supervisory frames

S frames are used to perform basic supervisory functions such as acknowledgment, polling, flow control and error recovery. Each S frame contains one sequence number N_R, which is used to acknowledge all I frames numbered up to N_R-1. The meaning of the Supervisory bits is given in figure 5-3. RR is used to indicate that the originating station is ready to receive an I frame. REJ is used to request retransmission of I frames starting with the frame numbered N_R. RNR is used to indicate a temporary inability to accept additional I frames. SREJ is used to request retransmission of the single I frame numbered $N_S = N_R$.

S FRAMES	BITS	
COMMANDS / RESPONSES	3	4
RR – Receive Ready	0	0
REJ – Reject	0	1
RNR – Receive Non Ready	1	0
SREJ – Selective Reject	1	1

Figure 5-3: Supervisory bits

Unnumbered frames

U frames are used to extend the number of control functions. Instead of listing the commands and responses which are currently defined, we felt it more useful to give an example of how to utilize a specific HDLC option (see 5.2.2.3).

5.2.2.2. Use of poll/final bit

The Poll bit (P) is used in a command to solicit a response or sequence of responses. The Final bit (F) is used in responses. For example, in Normal Response Mode (unbalanced configuration), the primary can solicit I frames by either sending an I frame with the P bit set to 1 or by sending certain S frames (RR, REJ, SREJ) with the P bit set to 1. In NRM, the secondary sets the F bit to 1 in the last frame of its response. Following transmission of such a frame, the secondary cannot transmit until a command with the P bit set to 1 is received.

5.2.2.3. An example

We propose to describe the Unbalanced Configuration, NRM, Extended Sequence Numbering HDLC option. Basic commands and responses are:

- I, RR, RNR, SNRME, DISC as Commands
- I, RR, RNR, UA, DM, FRMR as Responses.

Link setting: the primary transmits SNRME command (Set Normal Response Mode Extended) to initiate a link with one secondary station. The addressed station, upon receiving SNRME correctly, sends back a UA response (Unnumbered Acknowledgement). DM is used to report a status where the secondary is logically disconnected from the link.

Link disconnection: the primary sends DISC command to the addressed station. The secondary should return a UA response.

Exchange of information: primary to secondary: the primary station should send the I frames with the control field format shown figure 5-4.

BIT ORDER	1	2	------	8	9	10	------	16
I frame	0		N(S)		P/F		N(R)	

Figure 5-4: Extended control field

Secondary to primary: after the secondary has received an I frame correctly, it will take one of the following actions:

- if it has a message to send, it will acknowledge by setting N_R to one higher than the received N_S, and sending an I response with its own address in the address field
- if it has no message to send, but it is ready to receive I frames, the secondary will send back a RR response after setting N_R to one higher than N_S.
- if it is not ready to receive I frames any more, it sends back a RNR response after setting N_R.
- if it is unable to receive the current frame, it sends back a RNR response without incrementing N_R.

Recovery: frames with an incorrect FC are discarded. Frames with an incorrect sequence number are discarded. The secondary transmits FRMR at the first opportunity. An information field is used with FRMR which provides the reasons for the rejection.

5.3. The Arpanet IMP-IMP protocol

5.3.1. The protocol

The purpose of the Arpanet IMP-IMP protocol [McQuillan 77] is to move frames (which are called packets) between adjacent switching nodes (IMPs) in full duplex mode. It is an ASCII oriented PAR-like protocol (Positive Acknowledgment and Retransmission) based on the concept of parallel logical channels. A link is a collection of logical channels. Eight logical channels are maintained between each pair of IMPs (32 between Satellite IMPs). On each channel, the flow control window is set to 1.

The way the IMP-IMP protocol works is as follows. At both the sender and receiver end of a logical channel a one bit sequence number and a used/unused bit are kept. These bits are initialized to zero. When a frame must be transmitted, the sending IMP looks for an unused channel. If all channels are marked used, the frame is kept waiting. If some channel is unused, it is marked used and the frame is sent. The state of the sender sequence number is included with the frame. Upon receipt of a frame with no transmission error, an IMP checks the frame's sequence number against the receiver sequence number for that channel. If they match, the frame is accepted and the receiver sequence number is complemented.

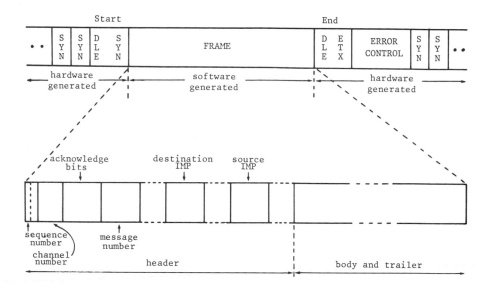

Figure 5-5: Inter-IMP frame format

The receiver returns an acknowledgment at the first opportunity (piggy-backed in frames going the other way, or in "empty" frames generated by the receiver). The receiver sequence number is returned with the acknowledgment. Upon receiving an acknowledgment, a sending IMP checks the acknowledgment sequence number against the sender sequence number for that channel. If they do not match, this means that the frame has been received correctly. The copy of the frame is discarded by the sender, the channel marked unused and the sender sequence number complemented.

Clearly, other cases indicate the occurence of duplicates (frames, acknowledgments). Duplicate frames are discarded but acknowledged. Duplicate acknowledgments are ignored. Actually, all eight (or thirty-two) receiver sequence numbers are transmitted with every acknowledgment. This is to inform a sender as soon as possible whether a frame must be retransmitted or not. The utilization of odd/even bits to detect lost and duplicate frames was first suggested in [Bartlett 69]. Because of possibly large differences in frame sizes (from a few bits up to 1008 bits), short frames (interactive traffic) may experience large waiting times for transmission in case channels are kept busy by large frames (bulk trafic). In order to keep service time reasonable for short frames, the IMPs maintain two queues for each link. Short frames are serviced before any regular frame.

Frame format

The format of IMP-IMP frames is shown figure 5-5. Arbitrary sequences of bits may be transmitted in the body of a frame. DLE-doubling is used for providing transparency, as follows. If the data in the body contains a DLE character, this character is doubled by the sending IMP hardware. When a receiving IMP detects a double DLE, it removes one DLE character from the data stream.

5.4. The Cyclades MV8 protocol

5.4.1. Introduction

The Arpanet IMP-IMP protocol does not embed any particular strategy for selecting one logical channel from all unused channels. Furthermore, frames are viewed as being either short or regular. The purpose of the MV8 protocol is to differentiate among short frames (0-15 octets), medium frames (16-127 octets), and long frames (128-255 octets), in the hope that a convenient servicing strategy will provide a sufficiently short transmission delay for short frames and a sufficiently large bandwidth for long frames.

5.4.2. The protocol

The basic MV8 protocol is similar to the Arpanet IMP-IMP protocol. A link between adjacent switching nodes is viewed as comprising eight "virtual" channels. The operation of a MV8 virtual channel is identical to the operation of an   IMP-IMP logical channel i.e., it is either used or unused, and both ends of a virtual channel keep a one bit sequence number. However, the channel allocation scheme is different. Channel 0 is reserved for short frames, which may also be sent prior to any other waiting frames on channels 1 through 7. Medium frames can only be sent on channels 1, 3, 5 and 7. Long frames can only be sent on channels 2, 4 and 6. This static allocation scheme is intended to achieve a fair sharing of the available bandwidth between medium and long frames.

A variation of this scheme allows for adaptation to traffic changes. The MV8 Channel Stealing protocol uses the MV8 preallocation scheme, except that free channels can be stolen from one category for another one if that latter category is predominant. Stolen channels are returned to their "owners" when a matching frame has to be transmitted (preemption is not employed). The behaviour of MV8, MV8/CS and the IMP-IMP protocol which would process frames on a FIFO basis (only one queue per link is maintained) have been simulated and compared. Results are reported in [Le Lann 78]. Significant differences in terms of waiting times for short frames and buffer occupancy delays for both medium and long frames are evidenced only for a link utilization ratio greater than 50%. For any ratio above that value, whatever the traffic pattern, only MV8 and MV8/CS provide for a constant transmission delay for short frames. However, important savings on buffer occupancy delays are possible with MV8/CS as compared to MV8. In some cases (ratios of short, medium, long frames = 1:1:1 and link utilization ratio = 0.7, or ratios = 1:8:1 and link utilization ratio = 0.6), such savings may be as high as 50%.

5.4.3. Frame format

Figure 5-6 shows the MV8 frame format. The text is a variable length field ($<$ 255 octets). The header length is 96 bits. This facilitates formatting on most types of computers. The identification field is left for the user to identify his frames.

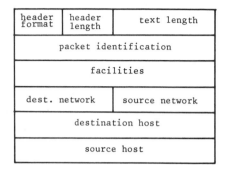

Figure 5-6: MV8 frame format

5.5. Conclusion

Link protocols are designed so as to move frames between communicating entities in a reliable fashion. Clearly, absolute reliability is not achievable. Consequently, processes which belong to higher levels of abstraction and which require better reliability must be provided with some additional mechanisms. This is the purpose of other communication protocols built on top of link protocols (see Chapters 6 and 7).

Chapter 6. Hierarchy

6.1. Introduction

A communication sub-network can be built according to a single, uniform principle. One such example is the ring network, in which all the stations are connected in a loop with unidirectional communication and employ a protocol allowing the stations to share their communication resources. For such a system there is often a straightforward design procedure which handles all its aspects. For example, in the many analyses of loop systems that have been published, delay has beem plotted against throughput for a given number of stations, with a certain, defined protocol. Problems such as lock-up or starvation can, by ingenuity, be solved entirely for these simple systems. Other examples of these sub-networks based on a single uniform principle are the star network, with all switching carried out by a central computer. Some kinds of Aloha network are of this type.

On the other hand, practical networks are usually more complex and incorporate a variety of principles in one combined system. For example, they could have a central switching computer and a number of satellite multiplexers. To analyse these is more difficult and in many cases there is no set of complete design rules so that arguments about the best routing method or how to reduce congestion could go on indefinitely. Mostly, these complex systems are built on a hierarchical principle in which one type of network operates within a certain region and these regions are connected together by a "super network" employing the same or a different principle. One result of this complexity is to introduce a whole new class of problems which will be discussed in these lectures.

In the study of distributed computing, there are other hierarchies which must not be confused with this one. We are speaking here of a hierarchy of connection and of control in the sub-network. There are also hierarchies or layered structures for protocols, which are quite different.

There are several reasons why a hierarchical structure is used.

- The first of these is the distribution of the network's terminals or nodes in a clustered formation. This might be the geographical layout of villages and towns (which shapes the telephone network) or might be the individual buildings in a large campus.

- The second reason is that different principles are needed at different levels of the hierarchy because different economic rules apply. A long- distance network is usually over-connected for reliability and at the top level of a telephone hierarchy is even fully connected. At the lowest level, the lines out to individual terminals are an expensive part of the whole system and cannot be duplicated. Furthermore, the need to duplicate them is doubtful, since the loss of single terminals counts less than the major disconnection of a large network.

- A third reason for hierarchies is organisational. A company may have its own switching centre which feeds into a national network. This in turn joins in an international network. The jurisdiction of the company, national PTT and collection of PTTs is different.

- A fourth reason for hierarchical construction is the sheer problem of size. Above a certain size, for example, a mesh network of roughly uniform structure uses excessive amounts of switching. Therefore a hierarchy is used incorporating, for example, local, regional and national meshes.

Examples

Figure 6-1 shows a ring network which connects together a number of star systems. A ring is often a good local network, but perhaps each room has its own ring station, and several terminals or computers in each room need individual ports, so some kind of local switching is employed.

Figure 6-2 shows a converse form of the same structural elements, a star network in which the branches are rings. This is precisely the form of the Spider network built at Bell Laboratories. Perhaps there is a limit to the length of a single ring and a convenient way to join together a number of rings is by bringing them to a central point. There have also been theoretical studies in which a number of rings are connected together by 'super ring'.

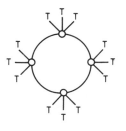

Figure 6-1: A ring network connecting stars

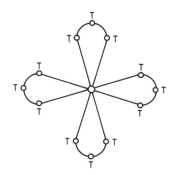

Figure 6-2: A star network connecting rings

Figure 6-3 shows a very common case, an overall mesh network in which local distribution is handled by star networks. This is the form of the telephone system.

Figure 6-4 shows a single principle, the multi-drop line, being used at two levels. Bank terminal networks have been constructed in this manner.

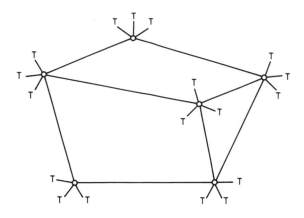

Figure 6-3: A mesh network connecting stars

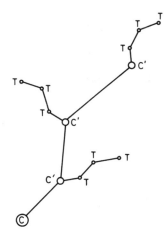

Figure 6-4: A multi-drop network of multi-drop lines

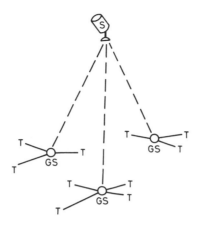

Figure 6-5: A satellite star connecting surface stars

Figure 6-5 shows a satellite system, perhaps of the Aloha type with local distribution by stars networks of surface cables.   Both levels of the hierarchy are stars but the design and the operational characteristics are quite different.

Figure 6-6 shows a system which is not hierarchical in form.   In this case a satellite network connects a new centres and the network is completed by means of a mesh.   Neither of the subsystems is clearly at the centre or on the periphery of this network.   Therefore it can be operated in a number of different ways.   For example, the surface mesh could carry traffic wherever possible, diverting it to the satellite system only when its capacity was exceeded.   This would be the method adopted if satellite delay makes this mode of transmission less desirable. Alternatively, the satellite system might have such low cost that traffic would move to the nearest satellite node in order to employ satellite transmission even if the number of hops was thereby increased.   This would be desirable if further extensions to the surface network were known to be costly.   The analysis of complex networks should extend to such systems, even though the word 'hierarchy' is not appropriate.

We choose to regard a simple mesh network also as a hierarchy in which the links between nodes form one level and these are connected into a mesh making a higher level of the hierarchy. The notion is apt because both link and mesh need attention to flow control, error control etc.

6.1.1. The problems of a hierarchy

The problems can be summarised as addressing, routing, flow control and congestion avoidance.

A distinction is usually made between the *name* of a terminal and its *address*.   This allows the name to be chosen conveniently for human use, while the address may be determined by the structure of the network.   For example, each local network might have its own prefix as in the telephone system with completely local control of the addressing within each local network.

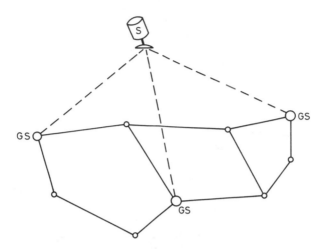

Figure 6-6: Satellites augmenting a mesh

Routing is trivial in unidirectional rings, stars or satellite systems, but meshes offer alternative routes and give rise to a routing problem. This takes its most interesting form for mesh networks generally. Even the taxonomy of routing methods in mesh networks is now a complex question. Fortunately, most of the methods studied have proved to have some merit, and the design of a routing philosophy is never a critical factor. Routing interacts with flow control and congestion avoidance.

The joint problems of flow control and congestion avoidance can both be seen as an aspect of buffer management [Kahn 72]. If there were adequate capacity for all the traffic aimed at a network these problems would not arise. They come from the various performance limitations in the network components. One of the limitations is line capacity. Nevertheless, lines cannot go into congestion by themselves. They will continue to carry their maximum traffic. Similarly, any well-designed switching node has a traffic limit, but it does not slow down or stop as this limit is approached.

On the other hand, a complete mesh network can certainly grind to a halt, much in the same way that a road system ceases to carry even the traffic of which it is basically capable when too much is thrown at it. The limitation which causes this behaviour in networks is primarily that of the buffers used to store the traffic waiting for onward transmission. It might be though that the solution was to increase the amount of storage available. Unfortunately, the only effect of this with overlead conditions is to make the network store more traffic and hence increase the delay. Rather it is necessary to find efficient ways to employ the buffers and use as little storage as possible.

We must distinguish between flow control and congestion avoidance. The aim of flow control is to hold back traffic from entering the network when the network is under stress. The meaning of this varies according to the network. For example, in the telephone network the origination of new calls is inhibited. In a packet network, new virtual calls could be inhibited but, since existing calls can increase their rate of traffic flow, there must ultimately be a limitation to accepting new packets. Thus flow control keeps open the internal economy of a network at the expense of admittance delay. This does not result in long queues of traffic waiting to enter the network, since most terminals or applications pace themselves according to the traffic they can send or receive. But all operations must slow down if the network is under pressure.

Flow control can be exerted by the network nodes, using their knowledge of the traffic state (which is usually rather local), or it may be imposed on virtual connections or actual circuits set up through the network, so that they cannot admit data until the earlier data has been acknowledged. Another form of flow control is applied to the network as a whole by restricting the total number of packets it is allowed to hold [Davies 72].

Congestion avoidance usually concerns the network as a whole. For example, the simple Aloha system has a strict limit on total traffic and, as this is approached, it goes into a congested state in which no messages are delivered and all incoming messages are endlessly repeated. Such a congested state is good for no one. It would be better to partition the available capacity in small amounts to each active subscriber. This is an extreme case.

Mesh networks also show something of this property if their design is faulty. The general characteristic of congestion is shown in figure 6-7. It can be found in systems as widely different as computer networks, road transport and river flows.

This congestion must be distinguished from overload. The well-designed network, under overload, organises itself to carry traffic at its maximum capacity and, when the load is reduced it recovers almost at once to its former state. Congested systems, like the simple Aloha network, when overloaded do not recover or recover very slowly.

This behaviour is rather similar to 'lock-up'. Lock-up is often regarded as simply a logical error which can be removed by better protocols. A simple example is the lock-up caused in the Arpa network when all the buffers in a node could be reserved by outbound packets, so that two full nodes could stare at each other [Kahn 72]. Such a simple error can be avoided merely by reserving one buffer for receiving. The theoretical design of deadlock-free store and forward systems is now understood, though the general solutions are not practical ones.

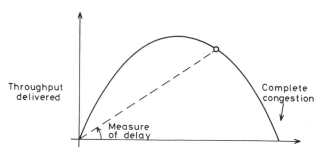

Figure 6-7: Congestion

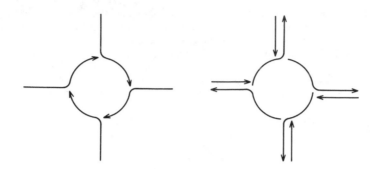

Figure 6-8: Lockup in a single traffic circle

In our experiments, when we examined congestion in a badly-designed mesh network (by stopping the simulation and making a post-mortem) we found 'near lock-up' conditions. These are not lock-ups in the strict sense, and they would disperse if the traffic were removed, but they were sufficiently close to make most of the packets involved to wait for others to move. An example would be a traffic circle filled with traffic in which only one exit was open.

The two possible priority rules in the traffic circles shown in figure 6-8 illustrate the possibilities for complete lock-up. With priority to incoming traffic it will happen whenever sufficient traffic is offered. With priorities to circulating traffic there cannot be a lock-up by this mechanism alone. Yet as figure 6-9 shows, a set of traffic circles can still produce a complete lock-up.

A solution is known, in principle, by means of buffer management. We arrange that each time a packet is handled by a node it increases in priority level. Then each node has buffers of different priority classes, with at least one buffer available in each class (one is sufficient). The packet may enter a buffer of lower class but not one of higher class than its own grade of priority. An alternative rule, which works as well, is to increase the packet priority level only when it finds its own priority level occupied at a node and has to move for a buffer of one level higher.

The result of this scheme is to provide, in effect, a network of many different levels, like a complex system of overpasses. The higher level buffer allows a method of escape from each level. The snag is that packets may visit a large number of nodes and hence a large number of buffer classes is required.

Figure 6-10 illustrates a scheme using similar principles, but with only three priority classes. This distinguishes three classes of traffic at a node; packets entering the system at that point, packets leaving it and packets passing through. All three can make demands on the buffers available. On the principle that a packet that has been handled many times is therefore more valuable the first priority is given to packets leaving the network. Since they are leaving, their occupation of the buffer is, in any case, temporary. The second priority is given to packets in transit and the third priority to packets entering.

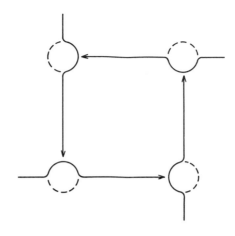

Figure 6-9: Lockup in a set of traffic circles

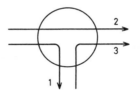

Figure 6-10: A three-priority scheme

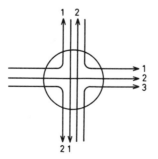

Figure 6-11: Typical priority rules for a hierarchical network

In a hierarchical network there may be a fourth and fifth class of packet namely those moving up to and coming down from higher levels. In the telephone network it has been a principle that traffic coming down from the higher level has the highest priority, though in this case the rule is applied to priority in the use of trunks that can be seized from either direction. Figure 6-11 shows a typical set of priority rules for a node in a hierarchical network, but it must be said that, when tried experimentally, this did not prove to be a solution to congestion avoidance.

6.2. Arpanet as an example

Routing

The basic data carrier in Arpanet is the packet, which finds its own route to the destination given in its header. An adaptive routing algorithm is used [McQuillan 77]. Each node forms a table giving the expected times of travel to each destination for each of the routing decisions, i.e., each line out from the node. A packet takes the path of smallest delay. The position at each node can be summarised by a table giving, for each destination, the best routing choice and the corresponding delay. This table is the one used for routing. We can call it the abbreviated table.

To update the tables, each node sends a copy of its abbreviated table to all it neighbours. From the table received on link x, a node can construct the expected delays for packets sent to any destination over this link. To do this it takes the received table and adds a constant time representing the delay in reaching the next node through link x. Now the node has formed a new table showing the expected delays for each destination in each direction. From this it forms the abbreviated table as before. This process can be shown to converge to a good solution if conditions are almost steady. It represents the algorithm by which the best route to each destination could be calculated iteratively. Under changing conditions the result is not so clearly optimal.

In the steady state it can easily be seen that packets will move steadily towards their destination, not ping-ponging between nodes or circulating around any loops. But if there is a sudden change in network conditions, for example the loss of a node, the intermediate states reached during adaption can very well have ping-ponging or other looping behaviour. Experimentally it was shown in the Arpanet that, on occasions, a few packets would take an extraordinarily long time to reach their destination because they had been trapped in a loop while the routing tables settled down ot a new state. Methods of preventing this have been devised but, as an additional precaution, protocols for packet networks are designed so that heavily delayed packets will not cause bad errors.

Another phenomenon found in the Arpa network was that good news travels fast and bad news slowly [McQuillan 74]. Suppose that a line, previously broken, opens up. Immediately, a certain node may greatly reduce its estimated delay to a certain destination. At each update, this good news will be passed on to the next surrounding ring of nodes and it will steam through the network at the rate of one hop per update.

In the contrary case, assuming that a line breaks down there will than be some larger delay estimates at a neighbouring node N. At the next update, the surrounding nodes will not react correctly to this change because they each still believe that their neighbours have a fast route via N. Some packets during this time will circulate round N, acting on the false information that fast routes via N exist. To make bad news travel faster, it was merely necessary to hold down the routing decision even when the evidence pointed to changing it. Thus if packets were directed towards N, when this had its delay estimate increased, the routing decision in the neighbouring nodes would not be changed and so their delay estimate would have to recognise N's problem and increase at the next update.

The Arpanet routing method has recently been changed. In the older version, each node made a routing table from local knowledge. These tables could be inconsistent while delay patterns were changing, and thus packets could be trapped for a while in loops. In the new method, a node estimates the delay to its neighbours, and when these change significantly it broadcasts an update to all the other nodes. Then all nodes calculate the best routes, using the same data and getting the same results. At most the routing tables at different nodes could differ during the broadcasting process, for a very brief interval.

Though the broadcast and the complete routing calculation are bigger tasks than those they replace, efficient methods were discovered and the updates are now done much less frequently than before, since the rapid adaption was found to be illusory.

Flow Control

When the Arpa network was first designed, flow control was little understood and congestion behaviour had not been simulated. It was seen that to allow packets to enter without restraint would be dangerous and therefore that, in some way, their exit from the network must be echoed back to the source to let more packets in. It was also obvious that if this was done on a single packet basis the throughput would be very limited. The decision made was to handle acknowlegement not for one at a time for as many as eight. These eight formed the message, a kind of 'super packet' which the Arpa network offered to deliver as a whole, with the packets in the correct order. This was done by reassembling the message at the destination. The first packet of a message to arrive would have to reserve a buffer space at the destination node sufficient for reassembling a full eight-packet message, since the depth was unknown.

The end-to-end message protocol did the acknowlegement with a RFNM or 'request for next message' which returned from the destination when the message had been delivered. This allowed the source to begin sending another message. This was designed to produce good through-put as well as fast handling of single packet messages. But it also produced reassembly lock-up.

Messages could arrive at a destination from many places and the first packet, in each case, would reserve the reassembly buffer. When all the available space was reserved it was still possible for the initial packets of new messages to arrive, looking for space. Under heavy traffic it could happen that all the packets waiting to enter the destination belonged to new messages while the re-assembly buffers were left waiting for packets that were stacked further back in the queues. It might seem that this could be overcome by destroying the unlucky packets and relying on the end-to-end protocol to re-send them. But this only postpones the problem to a higher level of traffic.

What had to be done to avoid reassembly lock-up was to make a change in the end-to-end protocol. Any message of more than one packet was required to reserve its buffer space in advance and, if there was no space, to wait for it at the sending end. When a buffer had been reserved for a message, there was a good chance that this message was part of a data stream that had further messages to follow. Thus the rule was introduced that after a message had been delivered, being a buffer, the returning RFNM would invite new messages straightway. Only if they did not come in time would the reserved buffer at the destination be relinquished. Thus the connection had two states. In one of these states it could handle single packet messages without formality but multi-packet messages needed a reservation first. In the other state, the reservation existed and would be maintained so long as the flow continued. These two states are established, not between hosts, but between a source and a destination node.

This was one of three lock-ups discovered early in the Arpanet history [Kahn 72], the others being the staredown mentioned earlier and an indirect store and forward lock-up analogous to the interaction between the four traffic circles shown in figure 6-9.

Other routing methods

The need for adaptive routing has often been argued [McQuillan 77]. The value of adaptive routing in shifting traffic away from congested areas only applies during the approach to overload. Simulation studies show that it is only effective over a small range of traffic flows and has little value in this role. It is, of course, most important for the diverting of flows after a line breakdown or a node failure. But this does not require automatic adaption on the Arpa model. For example, the SITA network for airline reservations [Brandt 72] recovers from node or line failure by changing to new routing tables retrieved from a store of many such tables.

Fixed routing, in which the destination rigidly determines the route at each node, tends to concentrate traffic on certain routes. There is a form of alternate, non-adaptive routing where traffic is split by the nodes over several different routes by either random or regular time division. Simulation studies have shown that flows in a network can be well balanced with only two alternative routes in use between any node pair. After a failure, new routes may have to be found. Thus there are many routing strategies as effective as the Arpanet scheme.

The routing mechanism must be seen as a single distributed system covering the whole network. Therefore a failure at any part can be very damaging. For example, on one occasion some digits in a store failed and caused the routing table to indicate a zero delay to a certain destination. The good news travelled fast until all traffic fof that destination was routed to the faulty node, which collapsed. After such events, extreme precautions were introduced into the routing algorithm, which tests storage and software frequently.

6.3. Addressing, routing and congestion in large mesh networks

Figure 6-12 shows three local meshes connected by a small number of 'trunk lines' to form a larger network. This could represent the way in which national networks of neighbouring countries are joined up. There is no single point of entry for transit packets passing on to other networks. In this respect, the airline routes with their major transit centres like London or Frankfurt are better designed. Almost the only feature that such a mesh offers is the possibility of area addressing.

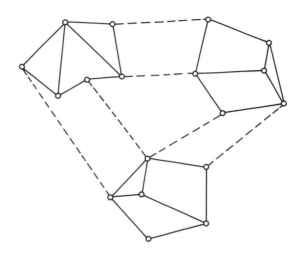

Figure 6-12: Local meshes connected by trunks

The telephone network shows a much stricter hierarchy of connection [Gimpelson 74]. This is only possible in very large networks.   Each telephone has its own local exchange. Exchanges with a community of interest may be directly connected (broken line) and calls are also allowed between two exchanges via one intermediate or *tandem* exchange, as shown in figure 6-13. But none of these direct lines will exist when the local exchanges are far apart. There is always a connection from a local exchange to an exchange on a higher level, the secondary level. Many local exchanges, of course, will connect each secondary level exchange. Again, at this level there may be direct connections and each secondary exchange connects to a tertiary level. In our diagram, all tertiary exchanges have direct connections, that is they form a fully connected network.

The bold lines in the figure represent connections which are always present. A number of different broken lines exist such as, in some networks, the direct line from primary to tertiary. The bold lines in our network represent tree structures coming down from each tertiary node. This is the meaning of the 'strict hierarchy of connection' but many direct routes also exist, for connections where is a high usage.

The routing rule in telephone systems is to use the direct routes or 'high usage routes' if they exist. The hierarchy routes (which always exist) are then used as overflows. A call from A will look for direct routes to F, E, D or C in that order, falling back on B if all else fails. Each node uses a similar procedure. For example, if a call from A has reached C this will test for direct routes to F, E, D in that order and, in the case shown in the figure, it will find a route (if all lines are not engaged) via E which will have no alternative to the direct route to F. This routing rule has the immense advantage that it can never produce loops. A loop condition is serious in a telephone network, because it produces an inefficiently routed circuit which is occupied for the whole of a call.

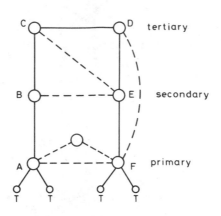

Figure 6-13: The strict hierarchy of the telephone network

A strict hierarchy of connection is not found in present-day packet switched networks simply because they are not yet big enough to justify the number of connections involved. Thus routing in hierarchical packet meshes cannot follow the simple rules used in the telephone network. Figure 6-14 shows what can be expected. Here there are four local networks each having a 'super node' so that long distance traffic can sensibly use these as transit centres. There is not a direct route from every switching centre to the secondary centres as in the telephone network. But like the telephone network, where two switches have sufficient traffic, there may be direct connections like those shown in the figure.

If the telephone routing philosophy is employed, preference is given to direct routes before the hierarchical routes are tried. It might be sufficient to use the number of hops as the measure for optimum routing. In simulation studies of a two-level network it was found desirable to balance the amount of traffic travelling at the two levels in order to increase the total carrying capacity. In the simulation this was done by adjusting the routing tables but in practise something more automatic would be needed.

Some routes never use the high level network (for example between stations in the same area) some always use the high level, and only a small proportion of source-destination pairs really need to make a choice. For these we could provide a pair of alternative routes, one of which uses the high level, the choice between them depending on an overall, network-wide measure of the pressure on the two parts of the network.

Something like this global control has been found necessary in the telephone network [Gimpelson 74]. In normal operation, alternate routing can be quite helpful, even when calls within the Eastern USA travel via California. The time zones can make this profitable. When the network is under stress after a major disaster (as happened with the Alaskan earthquake) alternate routing makes matters much worse by occupying lines and switches unnecessarily. Then a general decision is made to switch off the alternate routing options.

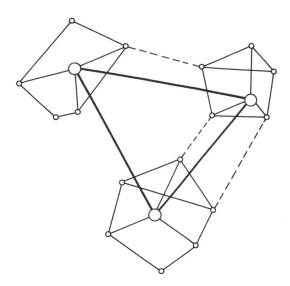

Figure 6-14: A looser hierarchy of packet-switched networks

Congestion avoidance in multi-level networks is a very difficult problem [Kerr 76], though we have empirical rules which seem to work well in single level networks. For example, the buffer priorities mentioned earlier and a refusal to use an alternate route when one hop from the destination were found completely effective in a single level network. But simulation studies of two level networks have failed to produce a complete answer. For example, isarithmic control (the control of the total number of packets in transit) at the upper level with the usual priority rules in the lower level gave good performance in one model we tried. But isarithmic control is not safe. Like counting the number of cars entering and leaving a carpark to determine whether it is full, the estimate should be updated by direct counting from time to time. But a fault in an isarithmic network can deprive it of carrying capacity very quickly. Therefore, the theoretical studies have shown no satisfactory solution to congestion control in a two level network. These studies were made with datagram networks having no end-to-end control. Either the use of virtual circuits (of which more later) or the use of flow control mechanisms between datagram ports might have simplified the problem.

6.4. Topology optimization

Topology optimization is a favourite subject for theses and theoretical papers [Gerla 77, Fratta 73, Frank 70, Boorstyn 77, Maruyama 78]. But the layout of most networks is determined from inadequate traffic figures, and with no certainty about the likely growth or the geographical changes that will occur later. Therefore optimum solutions may not last long, and the network will never be fully optimized again because all the connections cannot be uprooted. So there may be a gap between the theory and the practice.

Topology is only one aspect of the optimization problem and interacts with all the others. Thus we have to assume a routing and flow control method in order to calculate the delays which enter the optimization problem. Usually this is done by greatly simplified rules to speed up the optimization process.

A very few topology problems have exact solutions, such as the minimum spanning tree shown in figure 6-15, for which there are several effective algorithms. Most topology problems must be solved by heuristic methods, usually the choice of a likely topology and then gradual change to it, adopting any change which improves the optimizing parameter. The problem can be formulated in a large number of ways, for example to minimise average delay at a given traffic level, to maximise traffic level at a given delay, in each case using certain connectivity constraints. The heuristic methods may take an indefinite amount of time and are never certain to produce a true optimum. In practise, very good results can be obtained with a rather small number of iterations.

Probabilistic methods of calculation, such as these, should not be looked down upon. There are many computing problems for which exact algorithms exist which have hopelessly long running times while probabilistic algorithms will obtain the same result more quickly with high probability. For example, the best method for factorising very large numbers is of this kind. In all difficult problems, such as NP-complete problems, probabilistic methods seem to be winning.

6.5. Packet versus circuit switching

The choice between packet and circuit switching is often argued by committed people as a matter of religion. Both switching methods have a place [DaviesDW 79].

A simple rule for the best use of these methods is that packet switching suits short messages at irregular rates whereas circuit switching suits long messages passing at a steady rate. On this basis, circuit switching would be the choice for voice and packet switching for terminal traffic.

The treatment of signals before transmission can make a difference. Traditional facsimile transmission of unprocessed bit streams would be suited to circuit switching, but redundancy can be removed from this signal and this results in an irregular data rate. So the more efficient facsimile transmission methods are better suited to packet switching than circuit switching. There

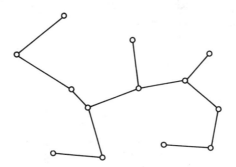

Figure 6-15: A minimum spanning tree

have been arguments in a number of papers recently that packet voice is economic, but these refer to private networks using leased lines and to the sharing of the network by voice and data. It is very unlikely that packet voice be adopted in public networks.

Interfacing equipment and its software has a significant cost. In spite of its complexity, the X.25 interface is ideally suited to a multiplexed port for computer operation. The alternative of a time-division multiplexed stream of bits is less convenient and requires complex hardware to put it into a form suitable for computer processing. In practice, it will be such considerations as interfaces, available software and hardware and habits built up by the use of existing systems which determine the switching method used.

Extreme views has been expressed. One of these says that, whatever advantages packet switching may have, the need for a fully integrated network will mean that all data is carried in 64Kbit/s channels or multiples thereof. But there has been no pressure to fully integrate the telex and telephone networks. The true situation is that networks are integrated at many levels, in their common use of carrier facilities, buildings and local networks but that the services required are different and in some cases the switches will be different, too.

At the other extreme there are enthusiasts who believe that packet switching can take over all of telecommunications and this is unlikely.

The state of development of the two switching arts is very different. Circuit switching has received an enormous investment resulting in the specialised hardware of switching matrices. Packet switching has been based on simple adaption of standard computers. It is not surprising that today's packet switches are limited in their handling capacity. As the traffic requirement for packets increases, assuming that enough revenue is being generated development effort will be employed and the cost per packet switched can decrease by an order of magnitude in a very short time. Therefore a study of present-day economics, which tends to include writing-off of the development of each new design of switch, is misleading.

There is a theory that the two switching methods are really equivalent and that very fast circuit switching will be developed and can provide the same functions as packet switching. In principle, this is possible but the development in circuit switching takes place for the requirements of telephony and nothing expensive is introduced unless it has some value for this primary purpose. Therefore the speed of switching in an integrated network will remain that suitable for telephone systems and be measured in seconds rather than milliseconds. Since digital telephone switching methods are suitable for bulk high-speed transmission it will be far better to employ any extra development money for the improvement of packet switching technology.

6.6. Datagrams and virtual circuits

The terms *datagram* and *virtual circuit* occur frequently in the computer networking literature associated with network interfaces, services, implementation, protocol design, and standards activities. The terms represent both mechanisms and philosophies. There is an ongoing debate about whether both approaches should be available at network interfaces, whether low level network design should provide virtual circuits on a datagram base in a layered fashion or directly implement fixed route virtual circuits in an unlayered fashion, and whether network architectures at all levels should use datagram (transaction-low delay, minimum message) or virtual circuit (preallocation, prenegotiation of resources) style philosophies [Section 2.5.4, Akkoyunlu 74,

DiCiccio 79, IFIP 79, Manning 78, Rinde 76, Roberts 78, Walden 72, Watson 80b,c,d]. This debate extends beyond technical to political, legal, and market strategy issues [Pouzin 76a]. Below we outline the datagram and virtual circuit concepts, their implementation, and the main points of the argument.

6.6.1. Datagrams

A *datagram* is a finite length packet of information, consisting of *header* and *data*, that can be sent from an origin address to a destination address independently of all other datagrams sent. The header of the datagram generally contains origin and destination addresses, datagram identifier, and possibly other control information dependent on the network environment and type of datagram service offered as shown in figure 6-16 [ANSI 79, Boggs 80, CCITT 79, Postel 79a, McQuillan 77]. For example, most networks using datagrams offer no guarantees that datagrams will be delivered, be undamaged, be unduplicated, or arrive in the order in which they were sent. Nor is end-to-end flow control provided. In other words, datagram delivery is on a best effort basis. If further service guarantees are desired, additional levels of protocols can be provided or optional services can be added to the datagram facility.

For example, it might be useful to know if a datagram could not be delivered. This information, a negative acknowledgement (NAK), might be valuable for diagnostic purposes or to increase the efficiency of highter level services. An option could be provided allowing the user to request such a service. NAK service requires each datagram to be uniquely identified. Similarly it might be useful to have a positive acknowledgement that the datagram was delivered, also requiring a datagram identifier. Such services require cooperation from the nodes that interpret the datagram header.

Another issue associated with datagram service design is the maximum size allowed for datagrams. A given network or internetwork environment may consist of various interconnection technologies and channel bandwidths that require constraints on the maximum size of the datagrams they can handle in order to fairly multiplex their communication channels. This implies either that there be an agreement that no datagram will be larger than a certain size on all links or networks, or that datagrams may have to be segmented and later reassembled. To allow for this possibility requires additional control information in the datagram header [Cerf 78, Postel 79a].

A datagram implementation is conceptually quite simple. When a datagram arrives at a node that performs routing, the destination address is examined to determine whether it designates an address within the node or one outside the node. If the address is one outside the node, the routing tables specify which link leaving the node should be used to route the datagram. As discussed in [Sections 6.2, 6.3, DaviesDW 79, McQuillan 78a], many static, dynamic, and alternate routing strategies are possible. Once a datagram has been sent from the origin, routed by an intermediate node, or passed to the destination process, no state information about it need be retained. It is important as discussed in Chapter 7 and [Watson 80d] to be able to bound the lifetime of datagrams in order to support reliable higher level protocols. A basic datagram service is the simplest packet switched transport service that a network can offer. Its appeal is that it is:

(1) the natural base transport mechanism for use with several hardware interconnection technologies, such as broadcast networks,

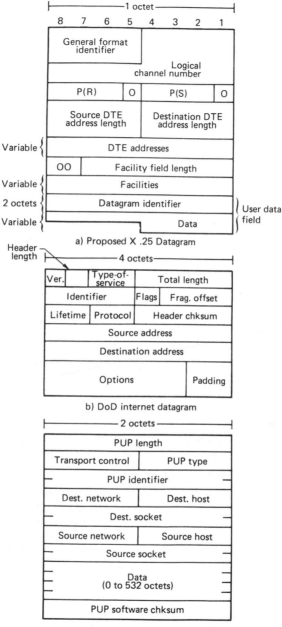

Figure 6-16: Example datagram formats

(2) is directly usable for certain classes of applications without additional layers of protocols,

(3) provides for a small, simple software interface,

(4) is a flexible easily extensible foundation to support

   (a) a variety of addressing modes and

   (b) a range of layered higher level protocols providing additional service [Boggs 80], including virtual circuits, and

(5) easily supports robust automatic recovery from link and node failures through alternate routing.

6.6.2. Virtual circuits

A *virtual circuit* (VC) is a logical channel between an origin and destination address pair, an *association*, in a packet switched network through which all packets sent are guaranteed to arrive in-sequence. Virtual circuits differ from physical circuits in that there is variable delay between packet arrival, and the error control used in VC implementations make VCs more reliable. Like physical circuits, virtual circuits can be permanently established for a particular association (*permanent* VCs) or be established dynamically (*switched* VCs). Besides the in-sequence packet delivery guarantee, virtual circuit service may also provide guarantees against duplicate, damaged, and lost packets, and other services such as flow control.

Any protocol that provides services for associations requiring state information of any kind to be established, maintained, and destroyed defines *connections*. For example, if one wanted to provide encrypted protection of the data sent in datagrams on an association, each end would require a key to be stored for use in encryption and decryption; thus defining a connection. If the service offered on a connection includes a guarantee maintaining data sequence, then the connection becomes a virtual circuit. Virtual circuits can be implemented (Figure 6-17):

(1) on top of a datagram service (a *layered* VC)

   (a) with the sequencing provided by an end-to-end protocol for process-to-process communication [Pouzin 76a,78],

   (b) or with the sequencing provided between origin and destination packet switches within a communication subnet [McQuillan 77], or

(2) by preestablishing fixed routes between the origin and the destination (an *unlayered* VC) [Rinde 76,77].

In the layered VC case (a), the interface to the network is a datagram interface while the service seen by a process is a VC; all information necessary to connect, maintain, and disconnect the VC is invisible to the network and is carried within the data of datagram packets. The intermediate nodes maintain no state after handling each datagram. In the layered VC case (b), origin and destination packet switches maintain state. All packets on a VC must go through these two nodes, intermediate nodes do not, however, have to maintain state information after handling a datagram. The network interface might support a datagram as well as VC interface to allow users direct access to the network's underlying datagram facility. In the unlayered VC case, state information on a per VC basis must be maintained at all nodes along the route of the VC and the network interface would be a VC interface. It might be difficult or expensive to also support a datagram interface and service for such a network because either a parallel datagram

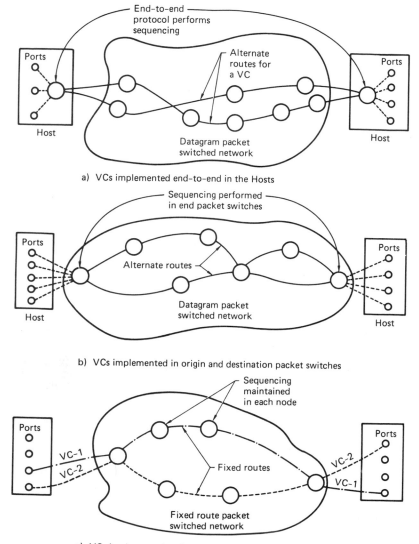

a) VCs implemented end-to-end in the Hosts

b) VCs implemented in origin and destination packet switches

c) VCs implemented as fixed routes

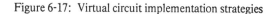

Figure 6-17: Virtual circuit implementation strategies

implementation would be required or, internal to the network, each datagram would in effect set up and tear down a VC as it passed through the net. From the above discussion it should be clear that there is a distinction between datagram or virtual circuit interfaces and services.

It is proposed that the X.25 protocol interface offer a *fast select* optional service [CCITT 79]. When the user specifies the fast select facility in the Call Establishment packet (see Section 6.7, Figure 6.7-3) it can include up to 128 octets of data in this packet. The state information for the Call is established normally. The destination of the fast select packet can then include up to 128 octets of data in the Call Accept packet or can include up to 128 octets of data in a Clear Indication packet disconnecting the VC. Fast select, while not reducing the network overhead required to set up the VC state, could reduce the number of packets involved, possibly useful in a transaction oriented environment.

There are two basic approaches to setting up an unlayered VC: centralized and distributed. In the centralized approach, packets requesting the establishment of a VC are directed to a central, possibly replicated, VC supervisor that maintains information on network topology, resources, and resource utilization [Rinde 76, 77]. This supervisor determines the best route according to network resource balancing criteria and sends messages to a selected sequence of nodes initializing state information for a fixed VC route. This state includes specification of the neighbor node to use for the VC and a short name for the VC. Similarly, packets requesting VC disconnection are sent to the central point so that it can update its tables and send messages to the nodes forming the VC, requesting them to destroy the state information associated with that VC.

In the distributed approach, the destination address in the VC establishment packet, along with other network state information, is used by routing algorithms at each node traversed by the packet to decide where to route it next, in effect an internal to the network datagramlike service. Each node traversed either establishes VC state or because of load rejects the packet. As part of the VC state, the node associates with the VC name the name of the next link it is to use for routing the packets for that VC.

A design issue associated with the unlayered approach concerns, what node and link resources to preallocate along the VC route besides state record space at each node; for example, link bandwidth and packet buffer space in the nodes can also be preallocated.

It is common in VC or connection oriented protocol designs and implementations to separate connection or VC establishment and disestablishment from the data transfer phase in order to provide rendezvous [Section 7.2.2] and reliable connection opening and closing [Section 7.9.5]. This phase separation is not required if it is assumed that no old packets from previous connections exist in the network when a connection or VC are closed, or if a timer based protocol is used [Fletcher 78, Watson 80a]. The establishment packet requires full origin and destination identifiers for the association to be connected, but a shorthand, temporary VC identifier for the association can be created and used during data transfer both at the interface in a layered VC and within the network with an unlayered VC. This means interface or internal network packet headers for VC data packets can be quite small, as they only require the temporary shorthand VC identifier; one of the arguments for this approach. Other appealing aspects of VCs are that existing applications designed around use of physical circuits may map more easily to a VC service, and that congestion control during data transfer is more easily handled. The main pro and con arguments for datagrams and VCs are now discussed.

6.6.3. Datagrams vs virtual circuits

The argument is not primarily one of datagrams vs VCs because connection or VC protocols are necessary in order to provide many useful services. The debate is about where the responsibilty should lie for definition of connections and VCs and what services to provide, if any. The datagram vs VC controversy revolves around flexibility, extent of network control, current vs future applications and markets, and economic tradeoffs between communications and processing and memory. There are many subtleties. We can only touch on the main issues and cannot explore all the levels of rebuttals.

The proponents of a datagram interface supported by an underlying datagram service (independent of whether or not there is also a VC interface) make several points:

1. Flexibility—If the underlying network implementation supports a datagram interface and service, then VCs can be implemented in the hosts or in the end packet switches as shown in figure 6-17. If services are implemented in the hosts, a wide variety of connection or VC protocols can be used, as most appropriate for an application. If the underlying implementation is datagram and VCs are implemented at the end packet switches, then the question exists: should a datagram interface and service also be available? If a datagram interface and service is not supported, then there is less flexibility to design appropriate higher level protocols. If an unlayered VC implementation is chosen, even less flexibility exists. A particular VC network interface or unlayered implementation may not provide the most appropriate services for all applications; therefore it is better to allow flexibility so that the required services can be provided by an appropriate end-to-end protocol. For example, we and others believe that, the form of interprocess communication most suitable for use in distributed operating systems (DOS) should be message or transaction oriented [Akkoyunlu 74, Lantz 80, Liskov 79, Livesey 79, Manning 78, NSW 76, Rashid 80, Watson 80a]. Much of the communication in a DOS will consist of short control messages between parties that will send a message, receive a reply and may not converse again [Section 6.7.10]. In other words, the communication patterns will be of a very bursty nature, exactly what packet switched datagram based networks were designed to deal with.

Similarly, applications such as credit checking, point of sale, many aspects of office automation, and certain of those for database querying and updating are likely to have these same characteristics. Transaction oriented VC protocols that provide full error control also exist to support these applications [Fletcher 78, Watson 80a]. Other examples where conventional VC protocols may be inappropriate involve realtime applications such as packetized speech and data collection, where achieving a low and uniform delay or maximum throughput may be more important than an occasional erroneous or omitted packet [Sproull 78, Swinehart 79]. These applications are not well suited to conventional positive acknowledgement/retransmission VC protocols. Still other applications, such as teleconferencing and electronic mail or applications involving the synchronization of multiple associations, may be best supported by broadcast, logical, or group addressing protocols which may be difficult or uneconomic in a VC environment [McQuillan 78b].

The supporters of a datagram interface and service are concerned that if only a VC interface is provided and supported by an unlayered VC implementation, the above lines of development may be precluded or be made impractically expensive. For example, a particular VC implementation could lead to tariff structures that would force VC networks to be used at higher levels much as physical circuit networks are now used by implementers of packet networks.

Namely, nodes will be connected with permanent or switched VCs which will then be multiplexed with higher level datagram or transacaction oriented connection protocols. Managing underlying multiplexed, switched VCs could become a complicated resource management task, unnecessary if direct access to a datagram service were available.

Unlayered VC advocates argue that for the user a fast select facility may be just as convenient for many of these needs as a datagram service.

2. Use of alternate routes—To achieve increases in throughput, parallel routes and pipelining are useful [McQuillan 78a]. These are easily supported with a datagram implementation with resequencing being handled at or near the ends. System robustness is also achieved by use of alternate routes when links or nodes fail. The end users do not have to be aware a problem occurred or be subjected to the delays involved in recreating a new route. Even if VCs are implemented on a datagram base in a particular network, public data networks are planning to use the X.75 VC protocol for network interconnection. This will rule out alternate routes between networks [Cerf 78, DiCiccio 79, Grossman 79]. VC advocates, on the other hand, argue that VC reconnection procedures, without data loss, are possible; that the lack of support for these in X.25 is an oversight that can be corrected [Rinde 77, Roberts 78].

3. End-to-end protocols are required within the host in any case—End-to-end protocols (EEP), datagram or VC, are required to provide the unique address space needed for distributed system support, to create a viable internetwork environment, to provide end-to-end error or flow control, and possibly end-to-end encryption or other services. Given the need for an EEP, the argument is made that a lower level VC mechanism introduces unnecessary redundancy [McQuillan 78a]. The counter argument is that the network may need internal VCs to best manage or protect its own resources and that clients who trust the network's claims of assurance will not have to implement their own end-to-end protocol or that simpler EEPs can be used.

4. Simpler interface—The datagram proponents argue that the amount of code required for a datagram interface is much smaller than that for a VC interface. This factor could be an important economic consideration in supporting microprocessor based terminals and special services or applications. VC advocates counter that for standard VC protocols such as X.25 most of the code can be moved to a low cost LSI chip.

5. Natural for some technologies—Datagram interface and service are most natural for use with network interconnection techniques such as those using broadcast technology (buses, rings, packet radio and satellite). Currently geographical networks public and private are dominant in terms of focus of attention and experience. However, we believe a good case can be made that within a decade high performance local networks using broadcast technology will be dominant.

6. Internetworking—Internetworking seems simpler and most robust if networks are interconnected at the datagram level as shown by experience within Xerox [Boggs 80] and the ARPA community [Cerf 78b]. Datagram advocates are also concerned that the different internal network VC implementations and resulting VC service and tariff differences will make it difficult to extend applications developed on one VC network across others.

The proponents of an unlayered VC implementation make the following points:

1. Communication cost—The cost of communication circuits needed for geographically distributed and public networks is decreasing much more slowly than that of processors and memory. Therefore, it is more economical to trade off the memory used for preallocation of VC state and packet buffers for smaller packet headers; thus, requiring less per packet communication bandwidth overhead. For value-added-networks, that must explicitly lease lines from a common carrier, this argument can be quite strong. Within a PTT, the argument is weaker as they can install high bandwidth lines at much lower true cost; internal accounting practices may distort the true economics. Use of small headers also makes more practical combining packets from several VCs going out on the same link into a single link frame, further reducing overhead of frame headers.

The above argument does not hold when the link bandwidth rises upwards of 100's kilobits/sec or higher, typically the case in local networks. In these regions, the main limitation on link utilization results from the number of frames that can be placed on or be taken from the link, or be processed by network nodes. These limitations result from operating system and I/O structures of existing systems. Within a decade or so new communications technology, broadcast satellite, packet radio, light pipes applicable to geographically distributed networks should allow much more economical high bandwidth lines [Jacobs 78, Kahn 78].

Datagram advocates question whether a significant savings truly exists when the entire VC economic picture is examined, either from the user's or from the public network administration's total system point of view. For the user, total costs include local access lines to the public network and required VC interface resources. Local access lines are often not highly utilized and therefore larger packet headers may not be significant. More complex interfaces, on the other hand, may be costly. With respect to the public network administration, it may have considerable investment in existing switching equipment at the nodes. Can this equipment be easily expanded to take advantage of newer low cost processing and memory capacity? The increasing importance of local networks raises even more questions about total system economics. A question the advocates of each approach ask the other is do network management costs increase faster in one or the other (VC management in VC networks, and routing and congestion management in datagram networks).

2. *Existing applications*—VC advocates point out that most current operating system structures and network applications (timesharing terminal interface and bulk data transfer) are naturally suited to VC interfaces and unlayered implementations. [Lavia 79] has argued that some VC services are also most appropriate for classes of transaction oriented services. In other words, they argue that there is not adequate market demand for a datagram service. Datagram advocates counter with the flexibility argument given earlier.

3. *Congestion and Flow Control*—The argument is made that because

(a) there is state information being kept on a per VC basis in each network node and at the network interface, and

(b) that initial VC routes can be carefully chosen,

that VC interfaces and unlayered implementations offer better congestion and flow control than datagram implementations; that there are no possibilities for store and forward lockup and congestion oscillations as in datagram networks [Rinde 76a,77].

However, datagram advocates argue that as understanding of routing and congestion control increase; this argument will grow weaker [Manning 78]. The datagram advocates go on to point out that while VCs might simplify congestion control during the data transfer phase, they just move congestion problems to the VC establishment phase or require under utilizing some resources [DaviesDW 79, Nessett 79].

4. Security — VC advocates also point out that many of the transaction oriented applications will require authentication and data transfer protection that may require message exchange overhead to validate digital signatures and distribute encryption keys. They claim security is naturally associated with VCs and that these operations are naturally handled at VC set up time.

Datagram advocates counter that these issues are best considered at other levels of an architecture; that they can be handled with a simpler mechanism that does not require the overhead of authentication or key distribution messages for each request/reply exchange; that authentication and key distribution message exchanges, if needed, may themselves be transaction oriented with third parties.

The above pro and con arguments have a strong flavor of longer term network application potential and economics versus present application and economic realities. Neither side's arguments are conclusive. In the longer term, both datagram and virtual circuit networks will exist and techniques for their effective utilization and interconnection will develop.

6.7. Network interfaces

6.7.1. Introduction

For the purposes of this discussion we will assume that the networks to which an interface is desired are packet switched networks. The point at which networks begin and end, and thus the point of interface to them, varies with different network environments. We will distinguish between two classes of network terminals:

(1) those capable of forming, and processing packets: *hosts*;

(2) those only capable of sending or receiving streams of bits or bytes: *devices*.

Examples of the former are all general purpose host computers and other devices with embedded micro/minicomputers. Examples of the latter are interactive keyboard and hard-copy or glass terminals interfacing with people, printers, and other peripherals. In order for the latter to be interfaced to a packet network, they must first be interfaced to a processor capable of packet handling. These systems can be special purpose dedicated device controllers or general purpose host computers. The systems for interfacing keyboard terminals are called terminal concentrations (TC), terminal interface processors (TIPs), packet-assembler-disassemblers (PAD's), and related names. These systems may be provided by the user or a network administration [CCITT 77b, Opderbeck 78]. They effectively convert terminals into logical hosts. In the remainder we concern ourselves with hosts.

There are two basic strategies for interfacing hosts to each other or with networks,

(1) interface them as pseudo devices (tape or disk drives, keyboard, or RJE terminals, for example), or

(2) interface them using a protocol family explicitly designed for computer-computer communication.

These protocols have properties such as symmetry (neither end is viewed as master or slave and the protocol implemented at each end is identical), error control (the link is protected against: lost, damaged, duplicate, out-of-sequence data), flow control (information flows across the channel at a rate or in quantities that the receiver can accept), and the ability to support multiplexing (a single channel can be used to support multiple conversations). In the sections below we examine each of these alternatives.

6.7.2. The pseudo device interface strategy

One common strategy for interfacing a host to a network or another host is to make the network or other host appear as a peripheral device that the host already has software to handle, or vice versa to make the host look like a keyboard terminal or other device for which the network already supports an interface, such as to a PAD.

If the network is viewed as a keyboard terminal, then several problems arise. First, how can the host computer initiate conversations with more then one destination? Further, because there is no addressing mechanism, the link to the network cannot be multiplexed. These problems are usually dealt with by using many physical links in the interface and treating the entities interconnected in this way as so many keyboard terminals. Second, the link from a computer to a keyboard terminal has inadequate automatic error control. This is not a serious problem if a person is sitting at the end of the link because he can handle error recovery. Third, most computer operating systems occasionally broadcast messages to all attached keyboard terminals, and interactive applications use many special characters as part of their user interface. An attached computer posing as a keyboard terminal must contain fairly elaborate programming to recognize and deal with these generally unwanted streams of characters. Fourth, flow control is strictly by rate rather than quantity, possibly with start (XON) or stop (XOFF) signals which create problems if they can get lost or if information must be discarded. They can also limit the potential throughput possible. Fifth, transparency issues arise when certain characters have predefined meaning and it is not possible to transmit arbitrary bit streams, or if it is possible to switch to a mode allowing an arbitrary bit stream, it may not be possible to switch back.

Using a peripheral interface such as that of a disk or tape drive also creates difficulties, as the following experience taken from [Watson 78] illustrates. When it was decided to interconnect high-speed, 18K-line/minute printers and COM units into the Lawrence Livermore National Laboratory Octopus network, a supposed short cut was taken by designing the interface to simulate a tape drive. The rationale for this action was to eliminate software modification in the host computers. The result was the creation of an asymmetrical, noncommunication type interface.

The printer/COM subnetwork required the ability to communicate status information back to the hosts. Rather than sending messages, the available tape drive signaling mechanisms were used, such as "parity error," "at load point," etc. with new meanings. As a result the output software on the host side had to be rewritten anyway. Using the simulated tape drive approach is causing interfacing and other problems for new types of host computers. Also, due to the lack of symmetry of the hardware, reinforced by a unidirectional data flow protocol, restrictions are placed on possible future directions for the evolution of this service.

The conclusion from the above discussion is that network interfaces should be communication oriented rather than device oriented; that is, symmetrical rather than assymmetrical, master/master rather than master/slave, and general data and control transfer should take place via error and flow controlled messages rather than by device-specific signals.

6.7.3. Importance of symmetry

It is very important that interfaces and protocols be symmetrical and support master-master rather than master-slave communication. The reasons for this are that

(1) each end needs to be autonomous (to be able to initiate conversations, rather than requiring polling, and to be able to control its own resources and Wait conditions [Haverty 78]) and

(2) one cannot predict ahead of time in what patterns one may desire to interconnect systems.

Lack of symmetry in hardware or software interfaces either restrict network evolution or require special intermediate modules to convert one interface sex into another. For example, lack of symmetry in the Arpanet high level protocols has restricted evolution or caused other problems [Davidson 77, White 76]. Early versions of the international standard HDLC protocol were also lacking in symmetry, which have since been largely corrected, although X.25 LAPB still uses the address field in an assymetrical way [Fletcher 79b]. Assymmetry in the X.25 packet level protocol required modification for use in the X.75 internetwork interface [CCITT 78a]. Insisting on symmetry, except where it can be clearly shown that it cannot or should not be achieved, has proved to be an important design discipline.

6.7.4. Need for error checking at all levels

It has been a fairly common practice to assume hardware interfaces will function without errors. This assumption was made in the Arpanet Host-Imp interface, and the errors that have resulted, while infrequent, have caused problems which were one motivation for the development of the Transmission Control Protocol [Cerf 74, Postel 79b]. This assumption has also been made by vendors in the design of channel and other interfaces, causing lost or damaged packet problems [Watson 78]. The Arpanet Imp-Imp link interface uses a cyclic redundancy check, but no check between the link interface and Imp memory. This resulted in problems which were solved by placing an additional software generated and checked checksum on link frames [Crowther 73]. The X.25 packet level was designed assuming that the link level provided an error free service. In fact this is impossible and analysis of the packet level shows that hazards exist as a result [CCITT 80]. These types of experiences, and the general lack of ability to predict future topology, expected problems, applications, and forms of interconnection technology, require that hardware/software network interfaces at all levels of a network architecture have the ability to detect and recover from errors.

6.7.5. Flow and congestion control

Without a reliable flow control mechanism across an interface, information can be lost, flow may be erratic or stopped altogether, or serious inefficiencies may result if flow or congestion control are handled by simply discarding information, counting on error control mechanisms for recovery. Flow control mechanisms are discussed in Chapters 5 and 7.

6.7.6. Full duplex interface

Nodes are generally both senders and receivers of information. If a half duplex network interface is used, then problems of flow and congestion control are increased. In networks where the sender does not reserve the receiver's interface before sending, packets may have to be stored within the network or be discarded, creating unnecessary retransmissions if the interface is sending (or receiving). If the interface must be reserved, then forms of lockup can exist causing performance problems [Donnelley 78]. These problems can be severe when a single service node is heavily used by many others [WatsonW 79, 80]. These resource contention problems are considerably reduced if full duplex network interfaces are used.

6.7.7. Datagram versus virtual circuit interfaces

The main issues in datagram versus virtual circuit interfaces were discussed in Section 6.6.4.

6.7.8. Xerox PUP as an example datagram interface and service

The Xerox PARC Universal Packet (PUP) system uses an internetwork datagram interface. The datagram format was shown in figure 6-16. The goal is for any two hosts in the internetwork environment to be able to communicate as long as the networks on which the hosts are connected are interconnected [Boggs 80]. The switching nodes in the PUP internet are host computers. The PUP datagram is routed from PUP node to PUP node until it arrives at its destination. Within the PUP internet whole networks as well as physical communication channels are treated as single logical links. A network or link driver in each PUP node, including origin, embeds the PUP datagram within whatever protocol(s) are required to move the PUP across the next physical and/or logical link. All networks are assumed to support a minimum/ maximum packet size and that if segmentation is required it is done on an intralink (logical or physical) basis. That is, reassembly takes place at the other end of the link before further routing of the PUP datagram takes place. The datagram level implements the global process-to-process address space. Routing and congestion control can be as simple or complex as desired.

6.7.9. X.25 as an example VC interface

This section briefly reviews the X.25 interface [CCITT 77a]. Because X.25 is a widely accepted international standard, it is important that those considering the design of distributed systems understand fully both its strengths and limitations. X.25 is designed to specify the interface between entities called Data Terminal Equipment (DTE) and Data Circuit-termination Equipment (DCEs). The former are any devices capable of operating as hosts (operate in packet mode). DCEs are viewed as packet switches supplied by a vendor, usually a Public Data Network, although any two computers could be interfaced with X.25, where each logically is both a DTE or DCE as seen by the other (lack of symmetry in the X.25 design introduces extra complexity in this application). The X.25 interface is defined by a hierarchical protocol family consisting of three levels:

1) A physical level (level-1) defining the mechanical and electrical connection between DTE and DCE. It uses the standard X.21 protocol at this level for defining a full duplex synchronous channel. We discuss this level no further.

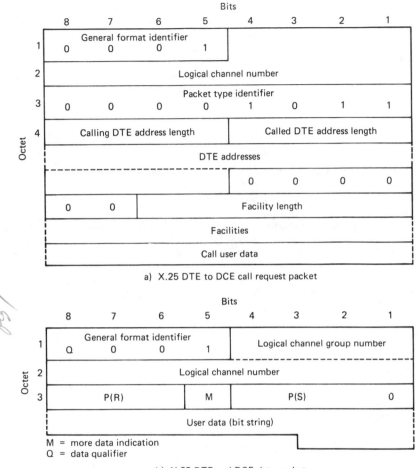

a) X.25 DTE to DCE call request packet

b) X.25 DTE and DCE data packet

Figure 6-18: X.25 Call request and data packet formats

2) A link level (level-2) management of the physical link is defined by a level-2 protocol based on a subset of the international standard HDLC for achieving link initialization, framing, transparency, and error and flow control.

3) A packet level (level-3) that defines virtual circuits or *logical channels* between DTE and DCE. It is an internal network implementation issue how to bind the two logical channels at origin and destination into a full duplex VC between origin and destination network addresses.

The packet level is defined as a local DTE/DCE protocol, although some services may optionally be given end-to-end significance. The packet level does not support error recovery. It depends on the level-2 protocol to to provide an error free link. Level-3 provides DTE/DCE flow control on a per logical channel basis, defines an out-of-data-band channel for one byte messages, called an *interrupt* service, allows units of information larger in size than a packet to be delimited, allows for flagging packets as next level data or control, and provides for resynchronizing the data stream in case of network problems. It has been proposed that networks, at their option, also support a datagram interface and service [CCITT 79]. We now briefly review how levels 2 and 3 of X.25 function and then discuss some of the implications in using X.25 in the design of distributed systems. For presentations in greater depth on the operation of X.25 see [DaviesDW 79, Fletcher 79b, McQuillan 78a, Opderbeck 78, Rybczynski 76]. Some X.25 packet formats are shown in figure 6-18.

X.25 level-2 transmits information across a link as objects called *frames* having the structure of figure 6-19a. Level-2 consists of two sublevels, a bit protocol that requires each bit in the link to be examined, and a frame level that utilizes frame header information. The bit protocol specifies how frames are delimited, data transparency is achieved, and redundant information is used to detect damaged frames. The frame level is used for link initialization, assurance, and flow control. It is beyond the scope of this section to discuss the operation of level-2. However, we need to point out two facts, it is impossible for a protocol at any level to provide perfect error control unless:

(1) all control as well as data messages are error controlled and

(2) the state information needed at each end to achieve error control can not be damaged or lost.

(3) identifiers used for error control are not reused while previously sent units or their acknowledgements with a given identifier exist or can be resent.

No protocol can meet these conditions perfectly. The result is that X.25 level-2 frames can be lost or duplicated as a result of link reset and node failure recovery procedures. This situation has implications for level-3.

Briefly X.25 level-3 works as follows. When a DTE wants to establish a virtual circuit, it chooses a logical channel number and sends a CALL REQUEST packet (figure 6-18a) to its DCE containing origin and destination addresses. This packet has room for specifying optional special facilities such as meaning of an acknowledgement (local or end-to-end significance), reverse charging, fast select, or to change default packet or flow control window sizes, and some limited user data, useful in identifying or validating the origin to the destination. The CALL REQUEST packet is transmitted through the network until it reaches the DCE associated with the destination DTE. This DCE selects a local logical channel number and forwards the packet as an INCOMING CALL packet (same basic format as a CALL REQUEST packet) to the addressed DTE. The called DTE can accept or reject the call. In the former case, a CALL ACCEPT packet is returned. In the latter case, a CLEAR packet is returned to the calling DTE containing the reason. X.25 phases are shown in figure 6-20, and the wrapping of level-3 packets in level-2 frames is illustrated in Figure 6-19b.

Once the call has been accepted a full duplex VC has been created and the two DTEs enter a data transfer phase. In this phase it is assumed that no error control of packets is required because level-2 provides an error free link. Sequence numbers are used at level-3 for acknowledgement and flow control on each DTE/DCE logical channel. Depending on prior agreement, a DTE can

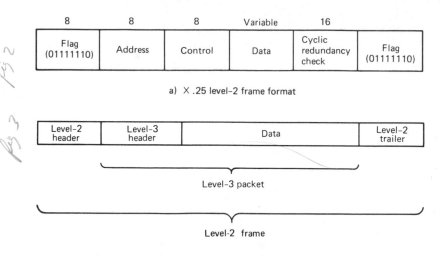

a) X .25 level–2 frame format

b) X .25 Level-3 Packet Wrapped in a Level-2 Frame

Figure 6-19: X.25 Frame and packet within frame formats

have a given number of packets outstanding with sequence numbers relative to the highest sequence number so far acknowledged by the DCE. Flow control can also be affected by special RECEIVE-NOT-READY and RECEIVE-READY packets. We have mentioned earlier that level-2 cannot provide perfect error control. During the data transfer phase, level-3 relies on knowing when level-2 must reset in order to reset each logical channel at its level. RESETS or RESTART may also be generated if a level-3 packet must be discarded for network congestion control or other reason. When a DTE receives a RESET or RESTART packet it can not know the state of some packets previously sent because acknowledgment does not necessarily have end-to-end significance. A description of several other hazards in X.25 that can lead to lost, duplicated, or missequenced packets is contained in [CCITT 80]. This can lead to duplicate or lost packets.

6.7.10. Implications of X.25 for distributed system design and implementation

The implications for distributed system design of X.25 derive from the following:

(1) although a datagram interface and service have been proposed, many networks may only support the VC interface and service,

(2) the X.121 international addressing standard used with X.25 does not adequately support a large enough locally assignable address space for use with private networks and distributed systems generally [CCITT 78b],

(3) there are a number of assurance hazards, and

(4) possible tariff policies associated with its use.

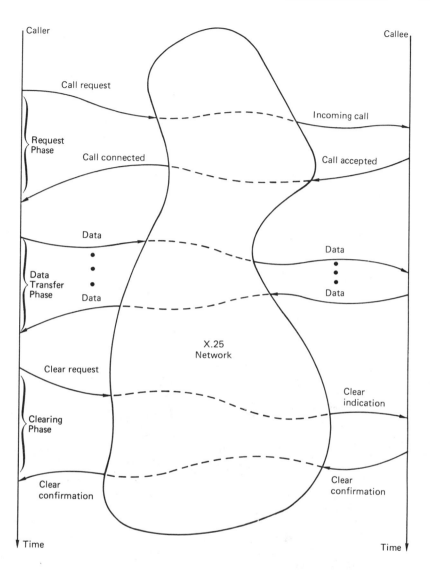

Figure 6-20: X.25 Call establishment, data transfer, and clearing phases

Items 2 and 3 imply the need for an end-to-end protocol [Chapter 7]. Let us briefly consider the implications of items (1) and (4) using an example distributed application. We assume all communication is over VCs.

A natural way to implement a distributed system might be to organize it into distributed cooperating application processes accessing services from distributed cooperating server

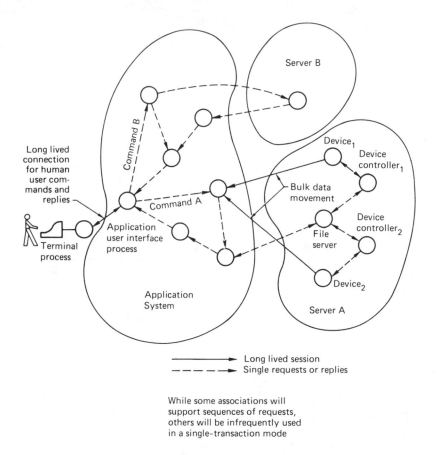

Figure 6-21: Example distributed system organization

processes. A human user controlling such an application will in general be connected to one of the application processes. As that application process executes the user's commands, it may send further commands to various servers or other cooperating application processes. These in turn may generate coordination and other requests to additional processes as shown in figure 6-21 [Livesey 79]. Most, if not all, of these secondary, tertiary etc. requests and associated replys will be single messages while some may involve the transfer of large amounts of data in several messages. Virtual circuits may be appropriate for the terminal connection and the bulk data transfers, but the communication pattern between particular pairs of processes involved in the exchange of the secondary and tertiary control commands may change depending on the nature of the terminal users original request. These interactions are more appropriately handled by a transaction oriented mechanism. An application designed for an X.25 network with a datagram service might not interface to one with only a VC service.

The application system designer must decide how to manage needed VCs. Should VCs be opened permanently between all possible pairs of correspondents, opened and closed for each request/reply pair, or should some other VC management scheme be used. The answer will depend heavily on the expected usage patterns and given tariff structures. The tariff structures in Public Data Networks are dependent on how they implement VCs. They can include costs for opening and closing VCs and the time the the VC is open, as well as for the number of packets or amount of data transferred. Alternatively the designer may choose a more constrained system organization to minimize the number of possible pairs of correspondents.

6.7.11. Network frontends

One goal that some workers have felt desirable is to develop an approach to network interfacing that would require:

(1) minimal changes to the host operating system and

(2) minimal network related processing within the host.

They want to achieve this goal without the disadvantages of the peripheral or keyboard terminal interface approach discussed in Section 6.7.2. Their proposed approach is to provide a separate network frontend (NFE) computer to handle end-to-end network protocols [Day 79b]. The network frontend idea is illustrated in figure 6-22. As a minimum, the end-to-end transport protocol would be moved into the NFE, although other possibilities include moving higher level protocol functions to the NFE as well.

The host-to-NFE protocols would be a family of layered interfaces as with X.25. At the lowest layer would be one or more levels of interface to achieve the reliable transfer of uninterpreted bits between the host and the NFE. This could be shared memory, or a parallel or serial hardware channel interface and link control protocol supported by the local host hardware and operating system. At the next layer there would be a packet protocol for multiplexing the link and for providing packet error and flow control across the interface. (Up to this point X.25 or just the packet level of X.25 built on some other lower level interface appropriate to the host could be used.) At the next level there would be a protocol for control of:

(1) the end-to-end transport protocol,

(2) possible internetwork protocol functions required in the NFE not directly mappable from the packet level of the host-to-NFE interface, and

(3) higher level end-to-end protocols.

One view of a NFE is that it is a protocol translation gateway (discussed in Section 6.8.2) with a one host network on one side. This approach is predicated on the assumption that the close host-to-NFE linkage and compatibility will allow the associated host-to-NFE interface protocols to be simpler and more easily inserted or grafted on the host operating system than if the end-to-end and other protocols required for a heterogeneous network were implemented in the host. One expected result is that, except for a small host specific layer, most of the implementation in the NFE can be host independent and thus usable with many vendors equipment. Another expected result is that there will be less network code required in the host, and fewer other host resources required.

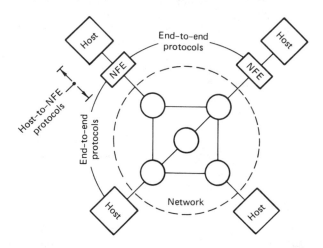

a) Network view

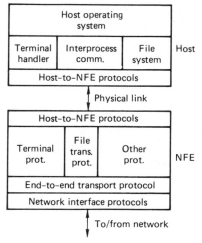

b) Host to NFE view

Figure 6-22: Network front end concept

The host, for example, would not need to perform data and control unit translation, word boundary alignment, message reassembly, and possibly more complex error control and other functions needed on an end-to-end basis. Also gains in increased network throughput and lower delay may be achieved for certain types of hosts [Poh 79]. The disadvantages of this approach are the loss of true end-to-end error control and other services, potential lack of flexibility to add new network services, and the possibility that it might not fit into a distributed operating system architecture.   One can view, we believe, the XNOS work described in Chapter 14 as a very sophisticated NFE.   Because experience with this approach is still in early experimental stages it is too early to fully evaluate its potential and limitations.

6.8. Distributed systems and internetwork design issues

6.8.1. Introduction

Many distributed systems will be implemented in an *internetwork* environment.   All the server and customer processes are not going to be available on host computers attached to a single network.   Different networks can be identified by differences in interconnection technology, protocol architecture, or controlling administration.   A likely type of environment is that of figure 6-23:

- One or more high performance private local networks providing access to centrally administered high performance, capital intensive resources (processors, mass storage, I/O).

- One or more private local networks providing connection of intelligent terminals and I/O devices, and micro/mini/midi distributed processors.

- One or more public data networks providing access to service bureaus offering special database and processing services, and interconnecting private hosts and geographically distributed private local networks.

Each of the above networks is going to use a different interconnection technology to most cost/effectively provide its services.   One network may, for example, use a 10's - 100's megabit/sec broadcast bus or ring with quite sophisticated interface (including buffering for network to host speed matching) [Hohn 80, Thornton 79, 80]; another may use packet radio or broadcast satellite technology [Kahn 78], or a simpler 1 - 5 megabit/sec broadcast bus such as Ethernet [Metcalfe 76, Clark 78], or on a national or international scale, irregular mesh store and forward packet switch technology [McQuillan 78a].   The number of packet switching interconnection technologies available is growing rapidly [Chapter 4].   Given this environment, a distributed system architecture must deal with network interconnection issues.   During the past decade attention has focused on rather slow geographically distributed networks and their interconnection.   However, with the trend to place increasing computing resources local to users in their offices and terminals, high performance local network design and interconnection issues will become, we believe, dominant during the coming decade.   Below we discuss some of the central problems in network interconnection.   Excellent discussions of internetwork design issues are contained in [Cerf 78, DiCiccio 79, Gien 79, Grossman 79, McQuillan 78a, Sunshine 77].   A number of internetwork issues are also discussed in Section 7.11.

6.8.2. Levels of network interconnection

The goal is simply stated.   Processes needing to communicate should be able to do so whether they are on the same host computer, on different hosts on the same network, or are on different hosts on different interconnected networks.   There may be delay or throughput performance differences, however, depending on their relative locations.   The question is, how can this goal be achieved, and what design issues are raised in achieving it?   We ignore the legal and political

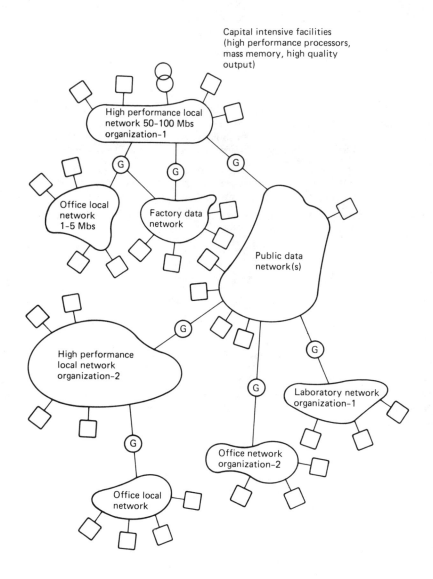

Figure 6-23: Example internetwork environment

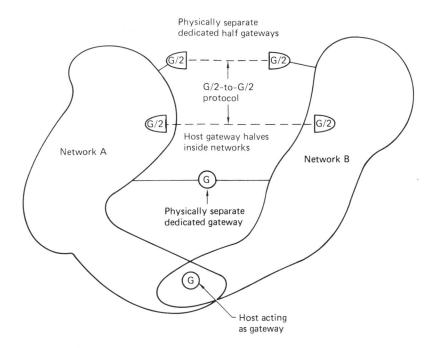

Figure 6-24: Gateway configurations

issues as a simplification here [Cerf 78, Mathison 78]. We are also primarily concerned with interconnection of packet networks, although some of what is said applies to interconnection of any form of network. Different networks are going to have different packet, addressing, interface, protocol, error control, protection, resource management, accounting, and other structures and algorithms. If they did not, then there would be little reason to consider them different networks. Therefore, translation at one or more levels is required to effect interconnection. The collection of hardware and software interface and translation services necessary to effect network interconnection has come to be called a *gateway*. A gateway may exist as a separate well defined hardware/software node, exist in host computers, or be split between two gateway halves with an intragateway protocol between each half as shown in figure 6-24. The function of a gateway is to provide a termination point for some of the intranetwork protocol services, translate other services, and be transparent to still yet other services used within each of the networks to which it is connected. The functions to be performed within a gateway depend on the interconnection strategy. Networks can be interconnected at any level where equivalent services exist within each network. To achieve equivalent services at the gateway interface, the services of one or both networks to be interconnected may be augmented by a layer of functions within the gateway or within gateways and hosts as shown in figure 6-25. How policy, as opposed to service, differences in networks to be interconnected should or could be overcome by use of gateways is not understood. For example, two different networks could support different security policies. One allowing read-up but not write-down, the other

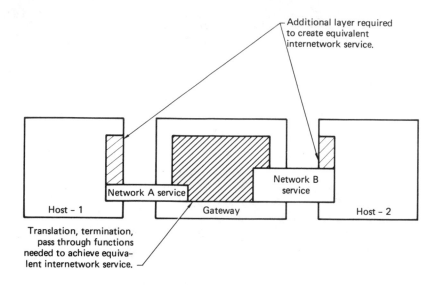

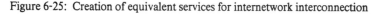

Figure 6-25: Creation of equivalent services for internetwork interconnection

vice versa. Each would be secure by itself, but interconnecting them would support both read-up and write-down, violating security in both. Ignoring this area of needed research, let us consider possible points of interconnection.

Packet Switch Interconnection

A packet switch may be an independent hardware/software node or be a logical entity within a general or special purpose host. At this level within a given network here is:

(1) a standard packet format defining a network address space and maximum packet size, and

(2) higher level conventions for routing, error, flow, and congestion control, accounting, and other services.

For interconnection to take place at this level, there has to be some internetwork homogeneity. Each network would have to be based on datagrams or virtual circuits, use the same internetwork address structure, and have routing and other mechanisms that are identical or reasonably map between each other. Given the assumed environment of figure 6-23, this assumption seems unrealistic, particularly in a rapidly changing networking technology environment. Certainly local and geographically distributed networks are going to use very different technology and internal policies.   This, however, is the approach being taken for interconnection of Public Data Networks. They are going to use a variant of X.25 called X.75 to affect interconnection as shown in figure 6-26 [CCITT 78a, Cerf 78, Roberts 76]. X.75 will not be offered as a means to interconnect private and public networks. The gateway half in each network will terminate X.25 services not supported by X.75 and pass certain X.25 services such as Call Establishment through transparently end-to-end. Other services such as error and flow control will be handled stepwise across each network and between gateway halves. The use of a VC internetwork interface has the problems for use within a distributed system discussed in Section 6.7 [DiCiccio79, Grossman 79, IFIP 79]. Networks that are interconnected in this way can be considered a new larger network as far as the distributed system designer is concerned and be dealt with as a single entity.

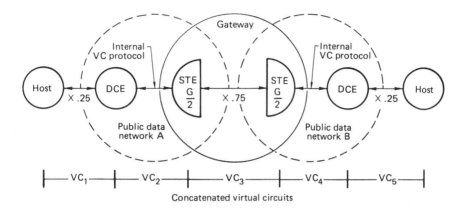

Figure 6-26: Interconnection of public data networks using X.75 virtual circuits

Protocol Translation Gateway Interconnection

A protocol translation gateway may be a dedicated hardware/software node or be special software implemented within a general purpose host. It is assumed that there are equivalent protocol services in each of the networks to be interconnected.

Protocol translation gateways are attached to each network as hosts. In its pure form all protocols at all levels are translated stepwise at each gateway from those used in one network into those used in the next. No common end-to-end protocols are assumed as shown in figure 6-27. There are serious problems with this approach which restrict its applicability to special situations, generally those limited to only requiring a single gateway to be traversed. These problems stem from the possible lack of internetwork address support within the layers of each network's intranetwork protocols, and difficulties of finding matching equivalent sets of services at all levels. Protocol translaton gateways can also be difficult to build and use. With this approach users may have to explicitly contact the gateways to establish routes and define appropriate service connections. For example, to move a file, the user may

(1) have to explicitly move the file from the origin host into a gateway using the file transfer protocol of the first network,

(2) log into the gateway and move the file to the next gateway or destination using a second file transfer protocol and so forth.

One could imagine creating higher level services to perform this staging on behalf of the user, but intervention at the gateways to deal with routing is still required. One could also imagine

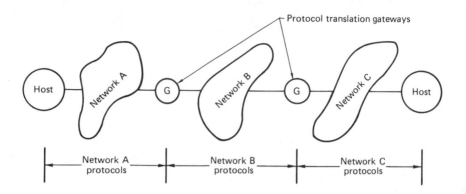

Figure 6-27: Protocol translation gateway interconnection

additions being made to each intranetwork protocol to support internetwork addressing or other services as shown in figure 6-25, but then local network autonomy may be compromised. Some of the techniques described by Kimbleton in Chapter 14 may also be applicable to protocol translation gateway design.

The protocol translation approach seems to us a stopgap technique until the field can develop further standards, except possibly if it is restricted to the case where network interface or transport protocols are augmented with internetwork addressing and are stepwise translated from those of one network to those of another, while higher level services are provided on an end-to-end internetwork basis. Even here one has the restriction on higher level services that they can only use those transport services available on all networks.

Internet Gateway Interconnection

The internet gateway may be a dedicated hardware/software node or be special software implemented within general purpose hosts. With this approach it is possible for any organization to set up its own internetwork environment without requiring agreement between different network administrations or vendors on a common network interface, or internal network structure and implementation. It provides for

(1) interconnection with either a basic datagram or virtual circuit service and

(2) full network autonomy.

All communicating systems use a common set of end-to-end protocols. For these reasons we believe that the internet gateway approach is practical and likely to be a common mechanism used to create an internetwork environment.

The model is quite simple. One creates a new network that has as nodes, *internet nodes*, all host computers containing customer or server processes, and gateways (processes within general purpose hosts or special dedicated systems). Existing networks become logical links within the new internet network. The system is shown in figure 6-28. One then specifies an end-to-end

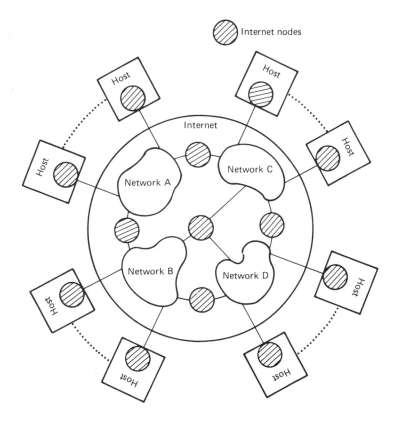

Figure 6-28: Internet gateway interconnection

internetwork protocol family.   Existing examples have been based on an internet datagram interface and service [Cerf 74, Boggs 80, Clark 78, Cerf 78a, Postel 79a, Watson 80a]. We believe a datagram service is more appropriate to use in local networks where broadcast, multidestination, and transaction oriented applications will be very important. We assume an internet datagram service in the following discussion, although an internet VC service could also be imagined [Gien 79, Grossman 79]. The only requirement on the interconnected networks is that they carry packets, the size of which can vary from network to network. A standard internet packet format is defined containing an internetwork address that can be used for routing purposes at each internet node.   At each internet node the internet packets are wrapped in whatever host-to-network, intranetwork, or other protocols are necessary to transport them to the next internet node.   At the next internet node the internet packets are unwrapped and the process is repeated if necessary.   In other words networks are treated as logical links. Summarizing, the services required of an internet node, illustrated in figure 6-29, are:

- Interprete internet addresses and map them to an intranet address for the next internet node along the route. (Problems of access control to different networks is part of the routing problem.)

- Wrap internet packets in intranet protocol headers and trailers.

- Deal with the problem of different packet size constraints on each logical or physical link of the internet (some component networks may directly support the internet datagram interface and service). Internet packets may have to be segmented (*fragmented*) into smaller packets, and then be reassembled at an appropriate point [Section 7.11.3].

- Handle flow and congestion control.

- Handle accounting and billing.

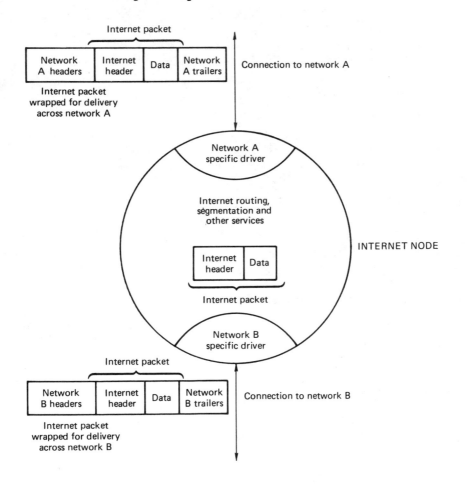

Figure 6-29: Internet node showing packet wrapping function

On top of a internet datagram service one can then build whatever additional end-to-end transport and other services are required to support the Model of Chapter 2. In effect, the internet design problems are the same as for any single datagram network, where different link bandwidths may impose variable maximum packet sizes, where different link technologies may require use of different lower level protocols, and where different links may have security level, access, or other constraints. The only really new factor that has been introduced is the possible need to deal with different accounting and billing systems, although there are likely to be more complicated routing issues due to different network tariffs, access controls, and service structures. Let us consider each of the above areas briefly.

Addressing and Routing

The general issues are discussed in Chapter 9. Currently the proposed standard international addressing structure (X.121) does not support a large enough address space for general distributed system use [CCITT 78b]. Proposals exist for extensions, but at this time one has to assume that a separate internet address structure would have to be created. These addresses would have to be mapped to an X.121 address when an X.25 network must be used. If logical processes or services can migrate from network to network, then a flat internet address structure is required. If processes do not migrate or only migrate within a network, then a hierarchical address structure of the form **network, within-network** can be used. Gateways would route internet packets on the basis of the **network** field until a gateway on the final network was reached; that gateway would then utilize the **within-network** portion to route it to the final destination.

Some networks may not allow through traffic, or have other restrictions related to access. These are factors that must be involved in routing decisions along with tariff structures and available services. Routing is likely to be more complex in many internet environments than in single networks because of these complicating factors. For example, an internet datagram may contain information about the type-of-service desired (throughput, delay, whether this packet is part of a stream, a transaction etc.). This type-of-service information could affect the routing decision. One route from a given gateway to the destination may require setting up a virtual circuit, while another may go through two datagram networks to reach the destination; the former might provide better throughput, while the latter might provide better delay characteristics. The appropriate routing choice would then depend on the desired service.

The routing algorithms and supporting mechanism can be fixed or adaptive as with a single network. We assume that it is desirable to have more than one gateway between networks to support alternate routing.

Wrapping

After the routing decision is made as to which network the internet packet is to be sent through next, the internet packet can be passed to a module (network or link driver) to be wrapped in appropriate interface, or other intranetwork protocols needed for its transport (figure 6-29) [Shoch 80b]. The type-of-service or other control information in the internet packet can be used to establish appropriate services for the next stage. At the other end of the logical link the internet packet is unwrapped by the link driver and is passed to the internet module for the next routing decision.

We now consider handling of virtual circuit networks as components in a datagram internet. One strategy is to use a single permanent VC between each internet node and multiplex internet datagrams on that VC. This is justifiable in the case where there is adequate traffic or the need for low delay (no VC establishment requirement) is great; the former may be the case between gateways. The other strategy is to use switched VC's in a multiplexed node. In this way, a VC is set up between internet nodes when needed. Depending on tariff and other resource management considerations, the VC can be left intact for some period, with other datagrams being multiplexed on it. Management of VC resources becomes a problem like managing any other resource in an nondistributed system.

Segmentation

Different networks or links of different bandwidths are likely to support different maximum packet sizes, particularly high performance local networks and public data networks. Different strategies for internet packet segmentation and reassembly are discussed in Section 7.11 and by [Shoch 79].

Flow and Congestion Control

The areas of flow and congestion control are not well understood for single networks [DaviesDW 79, Grange 79, McQuillan 78a, Nessett 79a], and the problems are compounded when networks with very different throughput rates, such as high performance local networks and public data networks, interconnect. Techniques that work with a mixed datagram and VC network environment and an environment with possible variable routing constraints are needed. Until more understanding is gained, use of simple packet discard to resolve congestion is probably a reasonable strategy.

Accounting and Billing

On the assumption that the internet is under the control of a single administration, this administration can subscribe to each network and receive a bill from that network. The bill from each network is likely to be based on different tariff structures; datagram networks will charge on a per packet related basis; VC networks on some combination of VC setup, VC connect time, and per packet basis. Both types of networks may also include other charges related to type-of-service parameters. Just receiving a bill is not all that is required. Routing strategies and their evaluation are going to interact strongly with tariff structures. There probably is going to be a need to keep a finer grain of traffic statistics at gateways so that the billing information can be suballocated. This need interacts with the need for statistics for diagnostic and other purposes.

6.8.3. Conclusions

We have examined a number of different strategies for network interconnection and concluded that the internet gateway strategy with a common end-to-end network protocol architecture is what is required for use with a distributed system. Successful internets have been built around a datagram interface and service using this approach. An internet must deal with the same issues that a single network must handle, addressing, routing, segmentation, error control, flow and congestion control, as well as accounting and billing. There is not yet much experience with internetworking, and so how best to deal with these issues is not well understood. It appears that routing may be more complicated because of the interactions among networks with different performance, interfaces and services (datagram or VC), tariff structures, and access controls. A useful list of research questions associated with internetworking is contained in [Cerf 78b]. In addition to the problems described there, one should add the problem of handling multiple levels of security control and protection when networks with different security policies are interconnected.

Chapter 7. IPC interface and end-to-end (transport) protocol design issues

7.1. Introduction

At the heart of a distributed system is the Interprocess Communication (IPC) service. An end-to-end (process-to-process) protocol (EEP) is required to support the IPC service in a distributed environment characterized by: heterogeneous process identification schemes, fluctuating bandwidth, arbitrary delays, communication errors, and multiple networks and interconnection technologies. EEPs have also been called *transport* or *host-host* protocols, transport because their function is to transport uninterpreted units of information, bits, bytes, messages etc. between an *origin* process and a *destination* process; host-host because they allow processes on one host to communicate with processes on another.

The design details of an EEP are critically dependent on the IPC service to be provided (pairwise, multidestination, or broadcast communication; transaction or virtual circuit; etc.) and on the assumptions made about the services offered by underlying protocols and technology (error control, protection, resource management, datagram, virtual circuit, etc.). For example, some claim that EEPs designed to be used strictly in an X.25 virtual circuit environment can be somewhat simpler than those required in a datagram environment because they can (1) utilize the X.25 guarantees that information will arrive at the destination insequence and unduplicated, (2) that after a virtual circuit close all information for that virtual circuit will have been purged from the network, and (3) utilize X.25 backpressure flow control instead of end-to-end flow control [DaviesDP 79, DaviesDW 79, ECMA 80]. As discussed in Section 7.4 and 7.9 we believe there are serious dangers in making such simplifying assumptions with respect to future evolution and the known hazards in X.25 [CCIT 80, Watson 80d,e].

While there is a growing concensus on the main EEP design problems, there is by no means agreement or complete understanding as to the best techniques to use to solve all of them nor consensus on the exact nature of the IPC service that should be supported. It is beyond the scope of this chapter to discuss all the design alternatives and their advantages and disadvantages. Therefore, we content ourselves with presenting major issues, one or two design approaches for dealing with each, and discuss our current preferences. We give pointers to the literature for more detail or alternate points of view. This chapter is organized as follows: First, we define a desired IPC service and an environment in which it must operate; then we outline the EEP design problems and mechanisms for their solution required to support the defined service in the specified environment.

7.2. IPC service

7.2.1. Desired IPC characteristics

Before an EEP can be specified, we need to define the IPC service to be supported. An IPC must be based on a model of process interaction structure and the types of data that processes will exchange. The following IPC characteristics are compatible with the Model of Chapter 2:

- No apriori restrictions should be placed on which processes can communicate with which others. Processes should see the same IPC interface (service) independent of whether they are communicating with local or remote processes. Local host or network idiosyncrasies should be largely or completely hidden. Just knowing another process's identifier or name should be sufficient to enable communication to take place, assuming the right to communicate exists. In other words, we do not want to limit IPC structures to trees of processes, although it should be possible to build such structures on the basic IPC service for use by specific applications.

- Symmetric communication should be supported between equal and autonomous partners. Each partner must have full control over its interaction with the other, deciding when it is willing to communicate, how much of its resources it is willing to allocate to a given conversation, and what events it is willing to be blocked on until they occur.

- Efficient transaction (low delay, minimum message) and stream oriented (high throughput) styles of communication should be supported. Most distributed operating system services are transaction oriented: a customer process issues a request for service, and a server process replies and no additional conversation need ever take place; underlying protocols supporting the service should not require the delay and communication overhead of additional messages if possible. Achieving efficient transaction support requires minimizing the number of overhead messages that must be exchanged before and after the data message to map and bind identifiers, and set up and release state information required for the type of service desired. In this way, delay, network traffic, and host overhead are kept to a minimum. Achieving efficient stream support requires maximizing bulk data transfer throughput. This requires minimizing communication and packet handling overhead.

- No restrictions should be placed on the length or content of the basic meaningful application data units.

- The basic IPC service should not limit or bias the direction that higher level programming language or application IPC may take.

7.2.2. The IPC interface

An IPC service is defined by the abstract objects and operations on these objects visible at the *IPC interface*. Below we define a simple basic IPC service. There are two main types of objects visible at the interface, communication channels and the data objects transmitted over these channels.

Communication channels

In order for processes in a distributed system to be able to communicate without a priori restrictions or identifier mapping and binding overhead, there needs to be a system wide *global* identifier space. A pair of (origin, destination) identifiers, called an *association*, define the IPC communication channel object. (The type of IPC service being discussed in this chapter is that for an association. Providing a reliable multidestination or broadcast IPC service is not currently a well understood problem.) Logically there is an association in existence at all times between all possible origin, destination address pairs, each represented by a state record. Data flows on an association insequence and unduplicated. In practice, most associations are inactive and their state records contain default values and do not need to occupy real resources. The state record for an association contains pointers to information to be sent or empty buffers to receive information, pointers to information successfully sent or received, pointers to information in doubt or trouble and indications of the cause of the trouble, specifications of block and wakeup conditions, and other information. Pointers will also exist to other implementation state information such as EEP state records for this association if origin and destination are not in the same machine.

An alternate point of view is that processes communicate not over channels but with ports (destination identifier), the origin identifier is not delivered or knowable [Rashid 80]. The association view seems to us more general because using the Receive From Any mechanism, discussed below, it supports the port view as a special case. The association view also does not preclude support for origin identifier based access list protection and allows independently flow controlled streams to the same destination identifier.

Some IPC services define two channels per association, one for normal data transfer, and one often referred to as an *interrupt*, or *expedited data unit* channel providing for the rapid transmission of a small amount of data, not blockable by the flow control on the normal data stream [Cerf 78a, Clark 78, ISO 79, Opderbeck 78, Postel 80b, Pouzin 78]. Logically, interrupt channels are usually attached to a different destination address than that for the normal data channel, namely that of a process or module controlling the one receiving the normal data flow. Therefore we see no reason why a separate association should not be used when an application needs a second channel [DaviesDP 79, Watson 80d]. This has the further advantage that the destination for the "interrupt" can be logically and/or physically fully separated from the process it is controlling. We expect such separation to be common in distributed systems. Higher level conventions for how such interrupt server addresses can be known are easily established.

The argument for defining both a normal and expedited channel for each association is that for many EEPs opening and closing connections (see Section 7.9) is expensive relative to the cost of supporting two channels [Clark 78]. If the "interrupt" server does exist on a different host a separate association will still be required, however.

In a perfect IPC service the underlying delivery mechanism would support a channel that

(1) was completely reliable, no duplicated, lost, damaged, or missequenced information,

(2) had uniform and acceptable delay and throughput performance,

(3) safeguarded the privacy and security of all communication,

(4) delivered information optimally at the maximum rate at which the destination can receive it, and

(5) achieved these services at an acceptable cost with no required tradeoffs.

In fact, there are tradeoffs among the above factors. Therefore, a practical IPC interface may support the passing of control information to assist the IPC layer in making appropriate tradeoff and internal resource allocation decisions. In many IPC and protocol specifications this class of help from the user is often referred to as *type-of-service, option*, or *facilities*.

Data objects

Lowest level data object: Some agreement must be reached on the size and encoding of the lowest level data object to be communicated between processes. The bit or 8-bit byte (octet) are commonly used.

Higher level data objects: There must be some way to mark the above basic data elements or insert marks in the data stream at the origin and have these marks passed to the destination. The set of contiguous elements between marks form higher-level data objects, the *IPC service units*. There may be one or more IPC service units, depending on the nature of services specified. Our current preference is to keep the IPC service as simple as possible and specify additional services, such as typed data units and checkpoint restart units, at the DOS and Service Support levels [Chapter 2]. Therefore, a single IPC service unit seems sufficient; higher-level conventions can use this IPC service unit to construct further data objects and structures. The boundaries of IPC service units can also be used by the end processes to establish known points for the synchronization of their control state, and as aids in detecting anomalous conditions. The IPC interface must support the transparent passing of IPC service units (any bit pattern can be transmitted).

The details of how the data is passed across the IPC interface, whether in objects structured as queues, circular or block buffers, is a local implementation issue and does not affect the basic nature of the IPC service, although choices made here have some performance interactions with EEP design decisions [McQuillan 78a, Sunshine 76].

IPC operations

We describe the needed functionality at the IPC interface as a set of primitives. Clearly it could be provided with other primitives or mechanism.

Sending and Receiving: Associations can be viewed as always logically existing, therefore no special operations are required to open or close them. Operations are required to *Send* and *Receive* information on a specified association. It is useful to support chaining of data or empty buffers in the *Send* or *Receive* mechanism. State records for an association only need to be allocated when the association is in a non default state. The IPC interface state record for the association is not in its default condition when

(1) there is data to be sent or buffers available to receive,

(2) the user has not read the latest status change, and

(3) an EEP module is maintaining state information for an association.

The above interface description is in contrast to one requiring an explicit association or connection opening primitive before a data transfer phase can be entered. The data transfer phase is then followed by an explicit connection close primitive. Such an interface style requires parallel sets of primitives to support both transaction and stream applications [Burruss 80,

Pearson 80], may limit experimentation at higher levels with other styles, and does not offer, that we can see, any additional user services.

In order for data to be exchanged on an association there must be both *Send* and *Receive* operations outstanding. Determining that matching *Sends* and *Receives* exist for the same association requires a *Send* and *Receive rendezvous*. When both ends of an association are on the same host it is relatively easy to determine if this condition exists. When the two ends are remote from each other, one or more messages must be sent. Normally receivers, such as a server, issue a *Receive* indicating they are willing to receive a request from *any* process or a group of processes. Generally this is accomplished with some shorthand notation and representation in the interface without an exhaustive list being maintained of acceptable correspondents. Sometimes special passive *Listen* primitives are used as the notation for this condition. A specific association is defined when a message from one of the acceptable origin addresses arrives. The rendezvous location could be at the origin, destination, or at an intermediate point [Walden 72]. Rendezvous at the sender or even intermediate points is not generally used because of the extra message traffic and state that would be generated and the problems of rendezvous in the Receive Any situation, including protection. Instead rendezvous is usually handled at the receiver.

The question is immediately raised how much information should be sent from sender to receiver to determine if a rendezvous exists. If a complete message is simply sent on the assumption (for control messages) that the receiver is normally ready, the case for most well designed servers, then low average delay results. For larger data message transfers, data transfer would usually begin after receiving a higher level confirming message. If the receiver was, in fact, not ready and the request was not queued, then later retransmission would be required, thus utilizing some unnecessary bandwidth. We believe appropriate conventions can be established at all levels of the Model to achieve good delay and throughput balance [Section 2.5.4, Fletcher 80].

Status: It must be possible for each end of an association to determine the state of its current communication:

(1)   to know what data has been successfully sent,

(2)   know when data can be sent,

(3)   know what data has been correctly received, and which Sends or Receives may be in trouble and the nature of the problem.

This information is maintained in the state record for an association. A *Status* primitive to interrogate this information must be provided.

Autonomy : It is very important that communicating processes be in a master-master rather than master-slave relationship to each other. This implies that processes be able to *Abort* data queued for sending or buffer elements queued for receiving based on timeout or other criteria, and that they be able to control or specify their blocking and wakeup conditions using a *Wait* primitive. Therefore, inactivity or incorrect operation of the other end or of the communication mechanism cannot permanently block a process unless it so chooses [Haverty 78]. Customer and server processes may utilize quite different styles. Customer processes will often send a request and wait until a reply is received ("remote procedure call"). Servers should not be blocked based on any particular customer's behavior. Some reliable timeout mechanism associated with wait events must be provided also.

Some EEPs reflect the IPC interface *Abort* operation through to the other end as a *Reset* command or require a *Purge* operation to remove any data in transit from the network. It is possible to design EEPs that do not require either [Watson 80a].

Other. Additional services not logically essential, but practically useful, are optional **Send** parameters to turn on diagnostic and measurement facilities; the ability to echo, trace, and timestamp data being examples. Other needs are met by supplying at the interface whatever information is needed to support authenticating the right to use the IPC service and provide the ability to account for IPC usage.

7.3. Example IPC service model

An example summarizing the discussion of the previous section based on the model of figure 2.3 is now presented. Figure 2-3 is repeated here as figure 7-1.

The structure shown in figure 7-1 supports an IPC service where a message is the IPC service unit. We assume messages use octets as the basic element. Messages are of arbitrary length and are

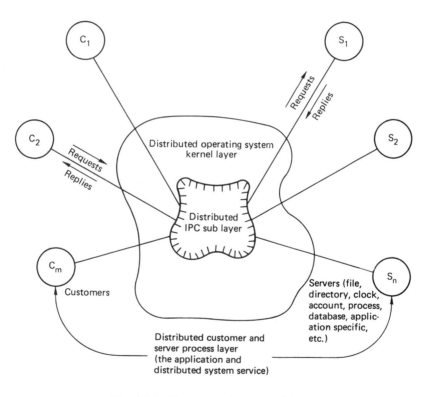

Figure 7-1: Message passing IPC model

delimited by bits marked with beginning-of-message (BOM) and end-of-message (EOM) marks. These marks are assumed transmitted as part of IPC service "headers" between origin and destination identifiers. These marks:

- Allow the origin and destination processes to use different buffer sizes and management strategies,

- Allow messages to be segmented in transmission and properly reassembled,

- Provide points for data resynchronization after a failure,

- Provide well defined points in the data stream for starting a parse or other operation,

- Provide wakeup indicators.

Messages are assumed reliably delivered (not lost, missequenced, damaged or duplicated) or an error notification is presented at the interface. Recovery from such an error is considered a higher level issue handled by conventions within the DOS service support layer [Chapter 2], or by application or DOS service specific conventions. Messages are exchanged between identifiers. A given process can have several identifiers. At the interface to the IPC layer there is no concept of establishing connections or virtual circuits, only that of sending and receiving messages, possibly in pieces, bounded by BOM and EOM marked bits where appropriate. Any state records required to support the service are assumed to be managed automatically below the interface.

The information at source and destination transmitted across the interface to and from the IPC layer is shown in figure 7-2. It could be handled in 1-5 primitives.

Send and *Receive* primitives include:

- Destination and origin identifiers.

- BOM, EOM marks.

- Uninterpreted message content.

- Privacy/Security level.

- Type-of-service and other information as appropriate.

- Possible timeout limits.

Rendezvous is assumed to take place at the receiver.

Wait, Abort, and *Status* are also required interface primitives. *Wait* is the basic process synchronization mechanism. A process can *Wait* or not, at its option, for any of its pending *Sends* or *Receives* to complete. Centralized or distributed servers to support semaphores or other higher-level synchronization mechanisms can be constructed on top of this primitive service [Chapter 12]. *Abort* allows any pending or active *Sends* or *Receives* to be cancelled or stopped. The *Status* operation returns appropriate status information on any pending sends or receives. A particular implementation using a single primitive is described by [Donnelley 79].

IPC interface models based on explicitly opening and closing connections and virtual circuits are described by [Bochmann 79, Burruss 80, DaviesDP 79, DaviesDW 79, ECMA 80, Hertweck 78, Pearson 80]. Related and alternate example IPC models are discussed in [Akkoyunlu 74, Baskett 77, Cheriton 79, Farber 73, Feldman 78, Lantz 80, Liskov 79, NSW 76, Peebles 80, Rashid 80, Ward 80].

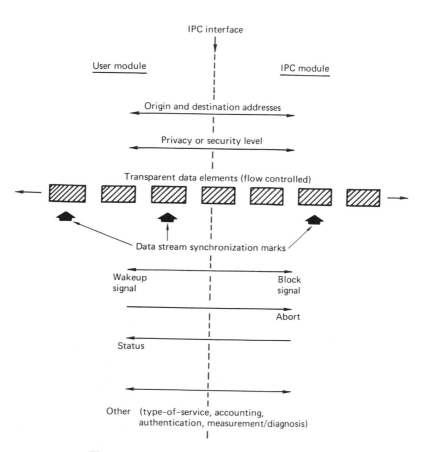

Figure 7-2: Information passed across the IPC interface

7.4. Underlying IPC environment

Before we can discuss the design issues of an EEP to support the IPC services above we need to say a few words about the underlying environment in which it is expected to operate. The fundamental assumption based on the network experience of ourselves and others [Boggs 80, Cerf 78b, Watson 78] is: *The network environment is in a constant state of evolution.* This changing environment results from the interplay of three factors:

- The constant growth in a network's user community and their creative ability to think of new applications and ways to use a distributed environment.

- Rapid changes in computer and peripheral technology and economics.

- New opportunities offered by improving hardware/firmware interconnection technology and economics.

The implications of the above factors are:

- It is potentially a dead end to make simplifying assumptions for EEP design based on the services provided by an existing lower level interconnection technology, topology, or protocol, because in all likelihood all of these will be changing over time.

- The environment will contain multiple local, geographically distributed, private, and public networks and interconnection technologies. In particular, we believe high performance local networks will come to be dominant in the years ahead.

- Bandwidths on various links and networks are likely to vary widely from a few kilobits/second (kbs) to tens of megabits/second (Mbs).

- Delays may also vary widely from milliseconds on local networks to seconds on satellite based networks or in congested networks.

- The IPC architecture must be layered and modular to simplify the introduction of new and the evolution of old technology.

- All forms of errors are possible in such a heterogeneous environment, including: lost, damaged, misaddressed, duplicated, and missequenced information.

- No guarantees on privacy or security can be assumed on all links or networks.

- There will be both stream and transaction oriented applications.

The last implication is particularly important in choosing a network architecture and EEP design philosophy. The basic philosophy can be stream oriented (preallocation of resources, preinitialization of state information) or transaction oriented (datagram, selfcontained messages). We believe that the inherent transaction orientation of the DOS services underlying a distributed system and the greater application flexibility possible with a transaction oriented base should lead one to choose a transaction orientation as the foundation of an architecture. We believe increasing use of local networks will foster transaction oriented applications. We believe stream oriented services can be easily and economically built on a transaction oriented base, but the converse is not true. For example, consider the difficulty of adding a datagram service to an unlayered virtual circuit implementation or the extra messages and delay in using certain protocols for transactions [Watson 80d]. This is an area of considerable technical, economic, and political controversy, however, as discussed in Section 6.6.

Based on the above assumptions, the EEP must be an internetwork protocol [Cerf 74]. This means as a minimum that it must support a unique address space across multiple networks, and deal with possible segmentation (fragmentation) and reassembly of EEP packets resulting from different lower level network or link packet size constraints [Shoch 79]. It also implies that there is an *internet* constructed of end nodes and gateways between networks. The internet nodes must be able to interpret at least part of the EEP headers and perform segmentation and reassembly as well as internet routing. Some networks may also directly use address and control information in EEP headers in their intranet routing and network control level protocols. Internetwork issues are discussed further in Section 6.8.

7.5. Services required by an EEP of the next lower level

Another aspect of an EEP's environment is the set of services provided by lower level protocols. The minimum services an EEP requires from link or next lower level protocols are:

1) EEP packets (header and data) can be treated by the lower level as uninterpreted data and be passed transparently in both directions across the interface.

2) The next lower level will inform the EEP module of failure in transmitting an EEP packet, if known.

3) The EEP level can know, a priori or otherwise, what minimum and maximum packet sizes, if any, are supported.

4) There is implicit or explicit flow control across the EEP to next lower level interface.

5) The EEP level needs to be able to know relevant lower level status (link up/down for example).

Another requirement useful for assurance is:

6) The EEP level can know, a priori or otherwise, how much time a packet spent on each logical or physical link, including time within software modules [Sloan 79, Watson 80b].

7.6. Levels of end-to-end services

The explicit and implied IPC services of Section 7.2.2 provide the following:

1) A global process identification or address space.

2) An IPC data element, data transparency and the grouping of these elements into larger units.

3) Protection (security, privacy).

4) Delivery assurance (error control): no misaddressed, lost, damaged, duplicated, or missequenced elements.

5) Flow control.

6) Diagnostics; measurement.

7) Other (priority, etc.)

If an EEP is designed to support all of these services, we will call it a *full-service* EEP. The necessary support mechanisms, however, are likely to have some service impact in terms of reduced throughput or increased delay, as well as in terms of required processing and buffer resources. A *minimum-service* EEP on the other hand needs to only support services (1) and (2) above and only as much of the others as may affect routing. Such a service is likely to have greater throughput and less delay, with the obvious tradeoffs of no guarantees on delivery, no flow control, etc. It provides a minimum transaction oriented service if the address space is large enough or can be managed so that addresses can be permanently assigned. The full and minimum-service EEPs represent the poles on a spectrum of EEP designs illustrated in figure 7-3. Internetwork gateways [Section 6.8] or other routing nodes may be involved in EEP services such as 3, 4, 6, 7.

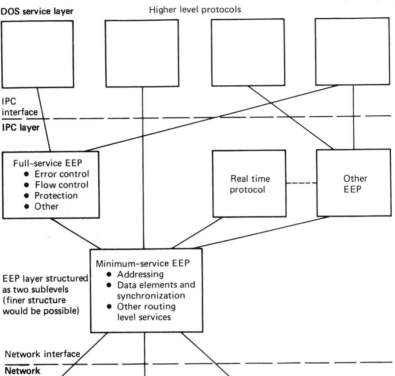

Figure 7-3: Two level structure for EEP service

There exist applications that require the full-service EEP (i.e. file or bulk data transfer), while others require maximum throughput or minimum delay, can tolerate errors, or do not require flow control (i.e. realtime data collection, packet voice) [McQuillan 78a, Sproull 78].

To accomodate this range, EEP's or EEP families have been designed either explicitly layered [Boggs 80, Postel 80a,b] or internally layered with the ability to specify the level of service desired [Cerf 78a, ECMA 80, Watson 80a]. With the explicitly layered approach one designs a base EEP to supply services (1) and (2) above. On top of this protocol other EEP's can be built to supply additional services. With an internally layered EEP, the users specify the level of service required at the interface, and different levels of implementation are possible depending on the user needs. We now move on to discuss issues and mechanisms associated with supporting each of the services above in the type of environment assumed earlier. These EEP design issues are summarized in figure 7-4. Much of the discussion applies to communication protocol design at all levels.

7.7. Origin, destination identifiers

One of the functions of an EEP is to support the global IPC identifier space. Host computers use a variety of process identification schemes. This heterogeneity is made invisible by mapping local process identifiers to global identifiers and vice versa. A given process can have several identifiers. There are two main design issues, the size of the identifier space and the structure of the address. The choice of an identifier structure has a significant impact on how identifiers can be mapped into routes, the size of the maps required at a particular node, whether the mapping can be distributed, whether identifiers can be dynamically bound, and ease of network extension or reconfiguration. It is important that the identifier space allow for internetwork process

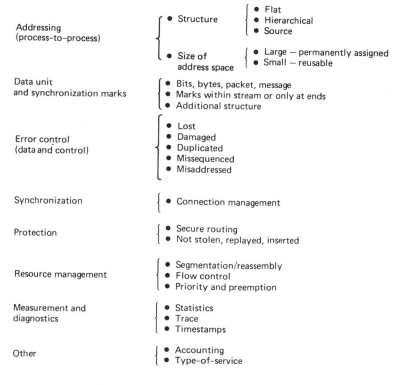

Figure 7-4: End-to-end protocol design issues

communication [Section 6.8]. Having a large enough identifier space is important in achieving a transaction oriented design. We assume that the same origin or destination identifier can be used in multiple associations. Identification is discussed in greater detail in Chapter 9 and in [Abraham 80, Cohen 79; McQuillan 78a,b; Pouzin 78; Shoch 78] as well as the papers cited at the end of Section 7.3.

7.8. EEP data objects and data stream synchronization marks

The main requirement in the choice of a basic EEP data object is that it be a unit common among the intercommunicating heterogeneous systems. The bit is clearly the universal common denominator. Many new computer systems have word sizes that are multiples of 8 bit bytes or octets or have byte manipulation instructions. Therefore, the octet has been commonly chosen as the basic EEP element because it is more efficiently handled than the bit on many current machines.

Communication between machines where one or more uses a word size that is not a multiple of an octet requires higher level conventions to designate the last meaningful bit in the last octet, when the octet is the basic unit. An EEP may support one or more higher level data units for error or flow control, or to provide delimiters in the data stream for use by higher level conventions (the BOM/EOM marks discussed earlier).

Protocols have been designed [DaviesDP 79] in which the only points in the data stream that are logically marked (as seen at the interface) are the beginning and end of a stream. This results in having to introduce primitives into the interface such as *connect, disconnect, connection reset, explicit forcing of data delivery* whose primary purpose is to impose synchronization marks on the stream. We believe, as stated above, that they unnecessarily complicate the interface and underlying EEP and obscure the basic IPC needs.

We believe a more appropriate approach is based on recognizing that the communicating end processes communicate in terms of integral units meaningful to their applications. We will call these units *messages*. A message may be a request for service consisting of op-code and request parameters, a reply containing a resultcode and result parameters, or meaningful units of data such as a disk sector, record, byte, or other application dependent data structure. The key characteristic of a message, whatever its internal structure, is that it is the smallest unit of data (an atomic unit) that must be completely received before a meaningful next level action can be initiated. Messages can be passed across the interface as whole units or in pieces depending on local implementation design decisions (we prefer the latter). The important requirement is that points in the data stream be marked as Beginning-of-Message (BOM) and End-of-Message (EOM) and that these marks or marked data elements be passed from the origin process to the destination process. The EOM has the semantics that it is also a wakeup signal and forces delivery of message data. A BOM arriving with no intervening EOM also is a wakeup and data delivery signal for data associated with the previous message. We believe that it is important that messages can be of arbitrary length so that the end processes can fit their natural atomic data units within them. Using the message approach, the special calls listed earlier do not have to appear in the IPC interface or be supported by the underlying EEP.

EEPs transport data in objects called *packets*. A packet consists of *header* and *data* parts. The header contains origin and destination addresses and control information needed to support the

EEP's services. The data part contains data objects. There are two general approaches to conveying BOM/EOM marks: insert them in the data stream or note their presence by use of control flags in EEP packet headers. The former requires that the EEP service scan all data, hence, is inefficient. Therefore, we prefer BOM/EOM marks to be carried in the headers, even though this means that at most one message can be in an EEP packet.

7.9. Error control and EEP state synchronization

7.9.1. Introduction

At every level of protocol there are two types of information, control and data. A protocol provides some service with respect to the data. Control information is sent between and interpreted by the cooperating protocol modules to provide the protocol's service. Error control deals with achieving both reliable data and control transmission, although the latter is often overlooked in EEP design.

Providing error control at the EEP level requires information to be carried in EEP packet headers and possibly control packets and to be maintained at each end in state records on a per association basis. Perfect error control is only possible if the following three conditions are met:

1) The identifiers of EEP units used for error control are not reused while previously sent units or their acknowledgements with the same identifier are still in the network (requiring either a guarantee on maximum-packet-lifetime, a method of flushing the network(s), or unique for-all-time identifiers).

2) The error control state information maintained at each end is never lost or damaged.

3) The error control information transmitted between each end is itself error controlled.

These three conditions cannot always be perfectly achieved and many of the design issues associated with error control center around doing as well as possible in the face of this reality.

While EEP state information is being maintained a *connection* is said to exist. The state records are called *connection records*. State information is also required associated with resource allocation and other aspects of the service provided by the EEP. An important part of error control is proper synchronization of state information at each end in the face of arbitrary transmission delays, transmission errors, and crashes and deadstarts at the ends.

The error control mechanisms required at any level of protocol depend on what assumptions can be made about the service provided by lower level protocols, both in terms of error rates and expected types of errors. For example, if the probability is high that information can be damaged or very large packet delays exist, then use of error correcting codes may be required, whereas if the probability of information being damaged is low and delays are small, then use of simpler error detecting codes and positive acknowledgment/retransmission procedures are more efficient. Similarly assumptions about whether packets of information (data and control) can be missequenced, duplicated or omitted affect the design of the protocol. With most current network interconnection technologies and lower level protocols, we believe the following two assumptions provide a reasonable basis for EEP error control design:

- Information can be damaged, lost, duplicated and missequenced.

- Errors of the above type will happen infrequently.

In the sections to follow we examine error types and appropriate end-to-end error control mechanisms.

7.9.2. Error types and implications

Before discussing error control mechanisms, it is useful to review the types of errors that must be defended against and some of their implications. Error types and control mechanisms are summarized in figure 7-5.

Damaged Packets:

Packets can be damaged when bits in the header or data part are changed while they are:

- On the communication media.
- Transported across interfaces.
- Stored in the memory of origin, destination, or intermediate nodes.

Damaged
    Cause: Bits changed on communication media, at interfaces, or in node memory.
    Detection: Checksum or other error detection code, or encryption/decryption
    Recovery: Discard, Nak or timeout and retransmission, error correcting code

Lost
    Cause: Damage to header, discarded by routing node (congestion, deadstart, exceeded lifetime)
    Detection: Failure of origin to receive a Ack or Nak in timeout period.
    Recovery: Retransmission

Duplicate
    Cause: Origin EEP or lower level protocol retransmission.
    Detection: Sequence numbers
    Recovery: Discard

Missequenced
    Cause: Retransmission, alternate routes.
    Detection: Sequence numbers
    Recovery: Hold until preceding data arrives, discard and retransmission

Misaddressed
    Cause: Address damage
    Detection: Checksum
    Recovery: Discard and retransmission

Figure 7-5: Error types, causes, detection/recovery mechanisms

In the entire technology chain from origin to destination, if there was overlapped, lower level checking for damage on all steps or links in the chain, then end-to-end checking would probably be unnecessary, but experience with existing systems shows that this overlap does not usually exist. For example, there is usually a cyclic redundancy check coupled with positive acknowledgment/retransmission in link level protocols used to improve the reliability of physical transmission channels. This checking is often performed in special hardware as the bits enter or exit the channel. Between the time the information is moved from memory to the hardware creating the check and after leaving the checking hardware, gaps in protection exist. Experience with the Arpanet IMP to channel interfaces showed that simple software checksums set in one IMP's main memory and checked in the next were required [Crowther 73]. Given the evolving multitechnology nature of the environment, likely to be common to the distributed systems under consideration here, it seems prudent to assume that such gaps will exist and that both header and data should be protected. Headers need to be protected between those nodes using or modifying them and data should be protected end-to-end or step-by-step with no gaps between origin and destination. The header information may be modified in route due to packet segmentation (fragmentation) or updating required at routing nodes, thus requiring checksum recomputation. For privacy/security and efficiency purposes, it is important to recognize that damaged headers could lead to packets being misaddressed or having incorrect security information and thus such packets should be destroyed as early as possible.

Lost packets:

Packets can be lost (omitted) due to four main causes:

- Damage to header or data is detected by a routing node or the destination EEP module requiring it to be destroyed or not accepted.
- Routing nodes or EEP modules may destroy packets as part of crash recovery procedures, congestion control, or limiting packet lifetime.
- End node crash with loss of state information.
- Protocol specific procedures [CCITT 80].

Lower level protocols can reduce the probability of the first cause (by retransmitting), but there is no way they can protect against the others. Higher level mechanism must be provided on an end-to-end basis to detect and recover from these situations.

Duplicate packets:

Duplicate packets can be created from three sources:

- The positive acknowledgment/retransmission mechanism used at the EEP level to recover from lost or damaged packets. This mechanism retransmits the packet when an acknowledgement is not received within a reasonable expected time. This event can occur if the acknowledgment gets lost or the data gets lost. The former would cause duplication.
- If a node at the link level fails to get an acknowledgment on one link after a reasonable number of retrys, it may try an alternate link. If the first link or the first node had a problem after the packet had been forwarded and only the acknowledgment was lost, then a duplicate could be created.

- An examination of the procedures used by many existing protocols and routing nodes in restarting or reconnecting after failure show that duplicates can get created due to loss of state information [CCITT 80].

Only end-to-end protection can protect against the above.

Missequenced packets:

Packets can get missequenced from two main causes:

- If there are alternate paths between origin and destination (on datagram networks for example) and packets traveling different routes have different transmission delays, then packets sent at a later time can arrive before ones sent earlier.
- If a packet must be retransmitted on a link, then it will be out-of-order. This is the most likely cause of missequencing.

Protocol specific procedures may also cause missequencing [CCITT 80].

End-to-end resequencing is required if these conditions apply.

As an example of the end-to-end confusion that can be introduced by the specific procedures of lower level protocols consider X.25. In a network supporting X.25, a packet or series of packets may be acknowledged at the interface and then later a *Reset, Restart* or *Clear* command can be received indicating network trouble. This can happen if the network gets congested and discards packets or the lower level link protocol Resets, for example. The origin is left in a confused state not knowing which outstanding packets made it to the end destination. This results because X.25 control information may not have end-to-end significance. If the application blindly retransmits, duplicates may be introduced. If it blindly does not retransmit, packets may lost. [CCITT 80] describes several other possible hazards introduced by X.25 procedures.

7.9.3. Need for end-to-end error assurance

Given that we believe it difficult to predict future network topology, interconnection hardware and interfaces, and the lower level protocols to be used, we feel it best to assume all the above types of errors can occur. Step-by-step error control mechanisms cannot protect against all the above errors, and in fact may introduce several of them. Further, if circuit switching technology is used to interconnect some of the nodes, there is an increased probability of packet damage. Therefore, we conclude that end-to-end error control must be provided.

7.9.4. Error control mechanisms used while a connection exists

We now examine the common mechanisms used to protect against the above error types. These mechanisms can be used with transaction or stream oriented protocols.

Damaged packets:

We have already mentioned checksums as the most common mechanism used to detect damaged packet headers or data. The main question here is the choice of an algorithm and size of the checksum. Since these checksums may be implemented in software, one criteria is ease of computation. Experience with the software checksum used in the IMP-IMP communication on the Arpanet, mentioned earlier, showed that a very simple checksum was effective [Crowther 73]. The Transmission Control Protocol (TCP) is currently using, for example, the 16-bit one's complement of the one's complement sum of all 16-bit units [Postel 80b]. [Fletcher 79b] gives another easy to compute and effective checksum. If an end-to-end checksum is employed on some size unit of data (segment), then that unit must be delimited and reassembled at the destination and the checksum checked before it can be passed onto the next level and acknowledged End to end encryption can also be used for error detection if some redundant information is provided [Kent 77].

In an internetwork environment, use of end to end checksums or encryption can introduce some subtle problems. For example, consider an environment where both high and low performance networks are interconnected. The maximum packet and checksum or encryption segment sizes appropriate for use in a high performance network could cause long, variable acknowledgment delays, depending on whether the destination was reached by high or low performance networks. To get around this problem could require the origin to have knowledge of network topology and routing strategies in order to properly adjust retransmission timers (see below). An alternate checksum strategy is to use an overlapping stepwise checking procedure. A possibility is to place separate checksums on both packet headers and data. When packets are fragmented [Section 7.13], the checksums of the new data fragments are compared with the checksum of the original packet data before transmission in order to provide protection across the period that the packet is in the routing node. This procedure provides end-to-end safety if packets do not require fragmentation and less, but we believe adequate, safety if fragmentation is required in exchange for considerable implementation simplification. If a damaged packet is simply discarded when it is detected as erroneous, a lost packet is created and the mechanism below is used for recovery.

Lost packets:

The mechanism in widespread use to protect against lost packets is *positive acknowledgment/retransmission*. The sender transmits a packet and then waits an interval for a positive acknowledgement (ACK). This interval is usually slightly larger than the average round trip time for a packet and its ACK to be generated and traverse the network. If an ACK is not forthcoming in that interval, the unacknowledged packet is retransmitted. This procedure is repeated some number of times until the origin EEP module gives up and reports a problem to its user process.

The choice of a retransmission interval is an important factor affecting average packet delay and network efficiency [Sunshine 76]. If the interval is too long, large average delays can result. If the interval is too short, average delay may be less, but network efficiency is decreased due to the possibility that packets may be retransmitted unnecessarily. This choice is further complicated in an internetwork environment average delay is quite route dependant.

When a packet is detected as damaged within the routing network or at the destination, retransmission may be speeded up by sending a negative acknowledgment (NAK) to the origin.

The NAK may arrive before the retransmission timeout occurs and thus reduce average packet delay by triggering earlier retransmission. If packets are lost primarily due to destruction of damaged or timed out packets, then use of a NAK can permit large retransmission intervals, easing the problems mentioned above. NAKs can also be useful in providing diagnostic information. If packets are damaged more frequently than packets are lost, so that NAK's usually effect recovery, the retransmission interval can be set longer thus increasing network efficiency. A NAK based mechanism is not sufficient by itself for error control because data packets can be lost from causes that would not allow NAKs to be generated; furthermore, the packets containing NAKs can get lost. Therefore, a NAK mechanism can at best increase efficiency or reduce average delay. For this reason some EEPs do not use a NAK, although we favor its use, in addition to positive acknowledgment, for its efficiency and diagnostic benefits.

An acknowledgment mechanism is based on being able to identify the units acknowledged. Therefore, some unit must be chosen for identification, such as: bits, octets, messages, segments, or packets. The size of the unit chosen for error control should be relatively small. For example, if units such as messages are numbered and they are larger than a packet size, failure of a piece of the message to arrive at the destination may require the entire message to be retransmitted. Larger units, as mentioned above, can also cause large variable acknowledgment delays. If packets can be segmented into smaller packets during routing, as discussed later, packets are not an appropriate unit. Therefore, units such as bits, octets, or a few octets seem the most appropriate error control units. We discuss the choice of a unit again later as other mechanisms require an identifiable unit; the EEP can be simplified if the same unit can be used for more than one need.

Units are numbered sequentially. The identifier is called a *sequence number (SN)*. An acknowledgment usually indicates the SN of the next unit the receiver expects to receive. The SN acknowledged also usually implies acknowledgement of all previous numbers. Therefore, if an ACK is lost, ACKs of succeeding units will acknowledge previous units. Similarly, duplication of ACKS will cause no difficulty because they just confirm what is already known.

The size of the field chosen to represent SNs is finite and therefore SN arithmetic is performed modulo 2^n, where n is the number of bits in the SN field. SNs will wrap around which means care must be taken to avoid having two different units or their ACKs or NAKs with the same SN number in the network at once. If we define the term *maximum-packet-lifetime (MPL)* to be the longest time a packet can exist in the network, R as the maximum time a sender will keep retransmitting a packet, and T as the maximum new SN generation rate (often maximum transmission rate), then, assuming new units are transmitted at the maximum rate even while retransmission takes place, one requirement on the length of the SN field n is,

$$2^n > (\text{MPL} + R) * T.$$

This inequality assures that a sender generating SNs at the maximum rate will not reuse a SN until the receiver is guaranteed to have received all previous instances. This is illustrated in figure 7-6. At point (1) the sender transmits a packet P_i Assume this packet and all retransmissions, (during retransmission interval R), except the last are lost and that the last retransmission takes time MPL to cross the network. At point (2) all instances of packet P_i with SN i have been removed from the network. A more stringent condition is actually required because there must also be no ambiguity in the meaning of ACKs. A receiver may wait a time A before generating an ACK, shown as point (3) in figure 7-6, and ACKs may live an MPL, shown as point (4) in figure

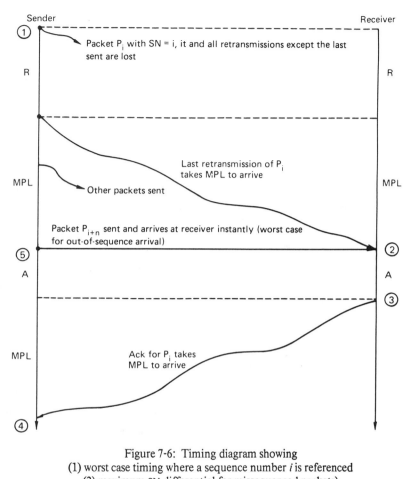

Figure 7-6: Timing diagram showing
(1) worst case timing where a sequence number i is referenced
(2) maximum SN differential for missequenced packets)

7-6. Therefore to assure that an old ACK of a given SN is not confused as acknowledging a more recently sent unit with that SN, the condition required is,

$$2^n > (2*\text{MPL} + R + A)\,T.$$

This condition assures that a sender generating SNs at the maximum rate will not reuse a SN until it is guaranteed that any ACKs of that SN have arrived or no longer exist in the network. We also note the obvious that for fixed values of n, MPL, R and A, an upperbound on the value of T is determined. With different transmission and retransmission strategies other inequalities would result.

Duplicates:

SNs are also used for duplicate detection. At any point in time the receiver knows what SN it is expecting next. We will call this SN the *left-window-edge (LWE)*, because at any point in time for assurance and flow control reasons, the receiver is only willing to accept units with SNs within a particular range called the *acceptance window*. Assuming we have chosen our SN field size according to the condition above, this implies that all SN's outside the range

$$\text{LWE} < \text{SN} < \text{LWE} + 2^{n-1}$$

should be rejected as duplicates, where the arithmetic is modulo 2^n. This acceptance window condition results because the maximum difference in SNs for two out of sequence unduplicated packets results if

(a) all transmissions and retransmissions of a packet P_i are lost except the last,

(b) the last retransmission of P_i takes MPL to reach the receiver, and

(c) while slightly before it arrives, point (5) on figure 7-6, a packet P_{i+n} is transmitted and instantly arrives at the receiver, point (2) figure 7-6.

If the sender was transmitting SNs at its maximum rate, then

$$\text{SN}_{i+n}\text{-SN}_i = T(\text{MPL} + \text{R}) < 2^{n-1}.$$

Any SNs outside the range above must be those of duplicates. The inequality above defines the maximum size acceptance window under the stated assumptions. Normally the acceptance window is much smaller than $\text{LWE} + 2^{n-1}$ because buffer space for receiving is the critical factor limiting the range of acceptable SNs. Duplicate detection is discussed further below.

Missequenced (out-of-order) packets:

A missequenced element is one with an SN not equal to the LWE but within the acceptance window. The inequality above defined the boundary in the circular SN space between duplicate and missequenced SNs. Two choices exist for handling a missequenced element:

(1) it can be held until its predecessors arrive, on the assumption they will follow shortly and all can be acknowledged before the senders retransmission interval elapses, thus increasing efficiency; or

(2) it can be discarded, with retransmissions providing correct ordering thus simplifying implementation.

If the average round trip time is quite large, for example on satellite links, such that several elements are likely to be in the network, then selectively being able to indicate which elements are missing can increase efficiency. For example if the sender has sent elements 2, 3, 4, 5, 6 and element 3 gets lost, the receiver can only ACK 2. The sender will time out and retransmit 3, 4, 5, 6 even though the receiver already may have 4, 5, 6. If the receiver could indicate it had up to 6 but was missing 3 some increase in efficiency might result. The extra complexity of such mechanism and savings must be traded off against the expected frequency of such events. We know of no EEP with such a selective NAK mechanism.

7.9.5. Connection management

Knowing when and how to reliably initialize (open) and reset or discard (close) EEP state information is called *connection management*. Connection management occurs at all protocol levels. Because of the possibility of duplicates and missequenced packets and end node crash with loss of state there are many subtleties in this area and we can only sketch the main issues. For more detail see [Fletcher 78, Garlick 77, McQuillan 78a, Sunshine 78, Watson 80d]. We believe that design choices made in the connection management and address areas have the greatest impact on whether or not efficient transaction support can be provided.

Reliable connection opening

Duplicate packets can create problems in reliably opening and initializing a connection. We desire to satisfy the following conditions relative to duplicates:

1) If no connection exists and the receiver is willing to receive, then no duplicate packets from a previously closed connection should cause a connection to be opened and duplicate data accepted by the next level (user) program. This is the "replay" problem, where a series of old duplicates could cause a connection to be opened and the data replayed to the receiver from one or more packets.

2) If a connection exists, then no duplicate packets from a previously closed connection should be acceptable within the current connection.

Let us consider these problems in order. Problem (1) results because there has to be some way to indicate that a new connection is being established and what the initial sequence numbers (ISNs) at each end are to be. This "opening" indication can be signaled by the use of a control flag in the packet header. A packet with such a flag "ON" is a dangerous packet, particularly if it should contain data. In the three-way-handshake mechanisms, discussed below, we call this flag the "OPEN flag". The OPEN flag only appears ON in the first packet sent over a connection. In the particular timer-based mechanism discussed below there is no OPEN flag, instead a packet starting a "run" of contiguous SNs has a data-run-flag (DRF) ON. More than one packet in a connection may have the DRF flag on, as described in [Fletcher 78]. Problem (1) results, for example, if a previous connection had just closed, the receiver was in a state ready for a new connection, and the EEP had the rule that when data arrived, either in a packet with the OPEN flag ON, or with acceptable SNs following a packet with the OPEN flag ON, it was passed to the next-level program. Then the arrival of an old duplicate OPEN packet with data from a previous connection would be accepted and the data passed to the next level. Further, even if the old OPEN packet did not contain data, but was followed by old duplicate data packets with acceptable contiguous SNs to that contained in the old OPEN packet, then they would be accepted and passed to the next level program as an undetected replay. These conditions result because the receiver has discarded all state information about a connection once it has closed the connection and thus has no way to recognize an incoming packet with the OPEN flag ON as an old duplicate. When such a packet arrives, the receiver proceeds to open a connection.

To guard against this problem three mechanisms have been proposed, the three-way handshake [Sunshine 78], the unique socket address [Clark 78], and use of timers [Fletcher 78]. A fourth mechanism is also possible, namely at the point where a connection is closed all packets associated with the connection are flushed from the network. Achieving this latter condition in a large store and forward packet switched (datagram) network is not really practical. It is our view

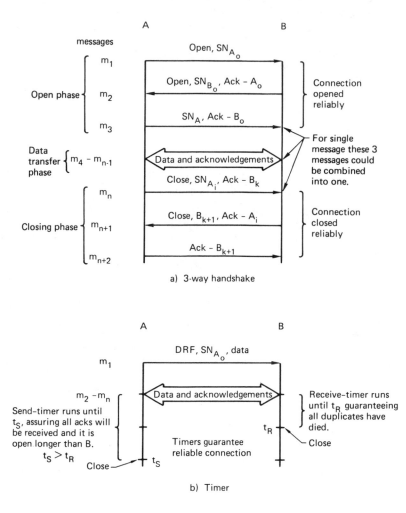

Figure 7-7: Three-way handshake and timer connection management

that the unique socket address approach is just a modified version of the three-way handshake as it effectively relies on an exchange of confirmation messages to detect the duplication. Therefore, we will limit our discussion to the explicit three-way handshake and timer-based mechanisms illustrated in figure 7-7 which for simplicity assumes only A sends data to B. We first discuss the three-way handshake mechanism and then the timer mechanism.

The three-way handshake protects against replay by not allowing data to be passed to the next level program until the successful exchange of three messages. It works as follows, shown in figure 7-7a:

Assume that node A wishes to communicate with node B in a full-duplex conversation.

1) A sends B a packet with the OPEN flag ON and an ISN, A_0.

2) B acknowledges the receipt of A_0 in a packet with the OPEN flag on and containing its own ISN, B_0.

3) A in a third message acknowledges receipt of B's ISN, B_0. A could include data with the first or third messages, but it is only on arrival of the successful acknowledgment by A of B's ISN, B_0, that B would pass data to the next (user) level. It is also important for B not to acknowledge data until it receives the third message and has safely delivered the data. The reasons for these restrictions are the following: Assume that the initial message from A was an old duplicate. B has no way of knowing this, so it responds as above. However, when A gets B's acknowledgment of this old duplicate opening packet, it can recognize that it does not acknowledge any SN that it has sent and send a reset. Further, B could crash with loss of memory after acknowledging the data and before safely delivering it. Therefore, causing an undetected data loss.

A can perform the former recognition because either it is closed with respect to B or, if it is opening a new connection to B, it picks a new ISN larger modulo 2^n than any used on "recent" connections with B. (This ISN can be chosen in a variety of ways; for example, by mapping the value of a monotonically increasing timer into the SN field [Garlick 77]. The length of the SN and clock fields, as discussed above, must be chosen large enough such that the mapping will not wrap around within a maximum-packet-lifetime.) It is thus important to note that the three-way handshake approach does make an implicit assumption about a bound on maximum-packet-lifetime in its choice of SN and clock field lengths.

Given that A can recognize that B is not acknowledging a valid SN, it can reply with an error or reset signal rather than an acknowledgment of B's ISN. In effect, in the absence of any state information from past connections, B checks whether or not the OPEN packet is a duplicate by asking A to confirm it.

If a connection is not yet established and an old duplicate from a previous connection arrives without the OPEN flag ON, then the old duplicate will be rejected.

There are a number of subtleties with the opening procedure above, such as what happens if any of the three messages get lost, or if both A and B try to open simultaneously. These are discussed in some detail in [Garlick 77, McQuillan 78a, Postel 80b, Sunshine 78].

Problem (2) exists when there is an open connection and a packet from a previous connection arrives. For the three-way handshake there are two cases: either the OPEN flag is ON or it is OFF. If the OPEN flag is ON, it is rejected immediately as it is recognized as being an old duplicate for this reason. If the OPEN flag is OFF, there is no way to distinguish this packet from a valid one for this connection if its SN is within the receiver's window of acceptable SN values.

The three-way handshake based approach solves this problem by trying to choose an ISN for a connection that makes this case acceptably improbable as discussed above.

The timer-based approach solves the above problems simply by having both sender and receiver maintain connection records long enough to guarantee that all duplicates have died out, information flow is smooth, and all transmissions, retransmissions, and acknowledgements have arrived at their destination, if they are ever going to arrive. The receiver maintains its connection record long enough to detect all duplicates. While the receiver maintains its connection record it will only accept units with sequence numbers in its acceptance window. In order for the sender to be sure to generate acceptable SNs, it must maintain its connection record as long or longer than the receiver, as well as long enough to recognize all acknowledgments that it may receive. These two connection records are under control of a Send-Timer and Receive-Timer respectively. These timers do not have to be synchronized, but are expected to run at the same rate. The mechanism requires bounding the sender's retransmission interval (R), maximum-packet-lifetime (MPL), and the time the receiver will hold a unit before acknowledging it (A).

The rules for timer intervals, control of the timers, setting of header control flags, SN selection, and packet acceptance for a particular timer protocol are developed in [Fletcher 78] . They are quite simple. If one defines a quantity,

$$Dt = MPL + R + A,$$

then safe values for use in initalizing the timers are:

$$\text{Receive-Time} = 2*Dt$$

$$\text{Send-Time} = 3*Dt.$$

The Send-Timer is reinitialized whenever a packet containing a new SN is transmitted. The Receive-Timer is reinitialized whenever a new SN is acknowledged. The Data Run Flag (DRF), mentioned above, is set ON in packets sent when all previously sent SNs have been acknowledged, allowing receivers to detect missequenced packets before it has initialized its state. When the Receive-Timer is non-zero only packets with SNs in the acceptance window can be accepted. When the Receive-Timer is zero only a packet with its DRF ON is acceptable. If the Send-Timer is non-zero, then the next contiguous SN to that contained in the connection record must be used when a new element is to be sent. If the Send-Timer is zero, then any ISN can be used because no old duplicates exist in the network. With this mechanism no exchanges of messages are required to reliably open or close connections. Therefore it provides both a reliable transaction and stream oriented service. Connection records are automatically maintained only when needed. Also no problems exist when both ends of an association simultaniously begin sending. Protocols using explicit connection opening and closing packets, but not a three-way handshake could also be augmented with a timer mechanism to provide reliable connection management [Watson 80e]. Different timer intervals would result.

The closing problem

A connection has been closed if the connection record either no longer exists or could be discarded (contains default values).

Assume that a full-duplex connection has been established, that an exchange of data has been taking place, and that one side A has no more data to send and wishes to close the connection. The main problem is to achieve a graceful close; namely A should stay open until all its sent data have been Acked or allowed time for an Ack to arrive until it has received all information B wishes to send, and until it has received all B's retransmissions, and vice versa. Other forms of closing are possible where one side unilaterally ends the conversation or will no longer receive. We are not concerned with these here. The following exchange will accomplish the graceful close using the three-way-handshake approach (shown in figure 7-7a):

1. A sends an indication to B that it is ready to close, i.e., has no more data to send.

2. B acknowledges receipt of this signal in some reliable way and continues sending its data.

3. B eventually indicates with a final data packet that it has no more to send.

4. A acknowledges the last data element sent by B and acknowledges B's desire to close.

5. B, on receipt of this acknowledgment, tells A to actually complete the close.

B can destroy its record at this point.

Even though A knew earlier, after step 3, that both it and B had no more data to send, it cannot close, since its acknowledgment of B's final data might have gotten lost, causing B to retransmit. On receipt of this retransmission, had A closed, A would have either ignored the retransmission or returned an error indication of some kind. The net result in either case would have been to leave B in a state of confusion where it does not know whether its last data had actually been received by A. The result of this possible confusion is that B might assume A had crashed before receipt of its last data and therefore open a new connection to resend the last data, thus causing duplication. With the above algorithm, if B's final "close it" message gets lost, the worst that can happen is that A is left with an inactive connection record. If B does not receive an acknowledgement of its last close it retransmission within a period 24 MPL + A, then it can report an error to its user program. Thus a timer is required.

Since connection record space may be an important resource to A, it can protect itself with an appropriate time-out after step 4. The length of such a time-out contains another form of implicit assumption about maximum-packet-lifetime and the length of time B will continue to try and retransmit if the acknowledgment(s) from A is (are) not getting through; a subtle point, but one dealt with explicitly with the a timer-based assurance mechanism. We have included it in the interest of describing the safest algorithm. Thus, in the absence of retaining special state information, another three-way handshake is required for a graceful close from the point where the last data is sent and final closing can be performed.

A graceful close can be achieved without a three-way closing handshake using the timer-based approach, outlined above, which guarantees state information is kept long enough for the desired closing conditions to be satisfied [Fletcher 78].

Crash detection and recovery:

When one side of a conversation crashes with loss of memory, it must recover with all connections closed and operate so as to require new connections to be reliably opened. This is called the half open connection problem [Sunshine 78]. For three-way handshake protocols there are some subtle issues associated with this problem in the interaction of the choice of an ISN and rate of SN generation that can lead to the need to resynchronize SNs in the middle of a conversation unless one assumes that all packets sent before the crash had died before restarting [Garlick 77, McQuillan 78a, Sunshine 78]. Simplifications can be achieved by waiting an interval 2MPL + A before reinitializing connections [Watson 80d], but there is then some hazard because explicit bounds on MPL are not guaranteed. Timer-based protocols must also wait a time based on MPL, R, and A before resuming so that all packets sent before the crash by either end have died. Because explicit bounds on MPL, R, and A would normally be guaranteed with a timer-based approach there is no hazard on restart.

In summary, considerable care must be exercised in connection management if a reliable protocol is to be developed.

7.9.6. Comparison of three-way-handshake and timer approaches

The difference between three-way-handshake and timer-based approaches are that one uses extra messages, while the other uses timed retention of state information to achieve reliable connection management. In a distributed operating system containing transaction oriented services and supporting transaction oriented applications we feel a timer-based approach is more desirable as it does not require special opening and closing packets and the required delay to reliably send a single message. As few as two messages are needed, one containing data, the second containing the acknowledgment. Using the 3-way handshake approach a minimum of five messages are required to send one data message as reliably as an EEP can [Belsnes 76]. There is also additional delay because data cannot be delivered until 3 messages have been exchanged. In some network architectures connection opening and closing type overhead has to be borne at each of several levels. This overhead, we believe, is unacceptable, not primarily because of the raw bandwidth consumed, but because of the cost and delay involved in generating messages, forming them into packets, placing them onto the transmission media, and buffering and handling them along the way (packet handling). Our experience and that of others show that general operating system overhead for packet handling may require several times the time required for actual protocol processing.

The timer approach is based on the fact that the total time of existence of a packet, including the interval between its first and last transmission, its maximum lifetime within the routing network, and the delay before it is acknowledged by the destination, can and should be explicitly bounded. The three-way-handshake protocols are also implicitly based on bounding the above factors in choice of SN field size, waiting time after a crash, requirements on ISN selection, and the interval chosen for reliably timing out connection records at the closing. Therefore, we believe that in order to support reliable protocols all networks and protocols should explicitly have mechanisms to explicitly bound the above factors.

Because overhead messages are not required to open and close connections with the timer mechanism and connection records can automatically be removed when timed out, connections are quite inexpensive. A criticism of the timer based approach is that inactive connection records must be kept until their associated timers time out. In order to archieve a reliable close this is in fact also true of the 3-way handshake protocols [Postel 80b] and the timeouts are comparable because they must consider the same MPL, R, and A factors discussed earlier. In practice the above factors can be bounded such that only a small number of inactive connection records will exist at any time. Further timer based protocols do not have the increased complexity of careful ISN selection and the handling of extra state transitions introduced by the OPEN and CLOSE flags. A detailed comparison between these approaches is contained in [Watson 80d].

In summary all EEPs designed to provide assurance are timer based, implicitly or explicitly, and a simpler protocol results if this fact is explicitly recognized in the system design.

7.9.7. Bounding maximum-packet-lifetime

Simplified, the lifetime of a packet can be strictly controlled by including a field in the packet header that is initialized by the origin and counted down by intermediate nodes. Each node, including the destination EEP module, must count at least once, more if it holds the packet longer than one time unit (tick). The packet is discarded if the count reaches zero before the packet is delivered. This mechanism requires nodes to know how long they hold a packet and how long a packet is on the previous link. If the link is a physical link, the latter is easily calculated. If the link is a logical link that has internal buffering and can hold a packet for an indefinite time period, such as a whole network between end nodes or gateways, without an MPL bound, then the protocols used on that logical link can be layered with a simple protocol that guarantees a conservative estimate of the transit time. This mechanism can also be used if the link level protocol does not report the time the packet is held by the link protocol module.

The idea is that each link frame is time-stamped by the sender so that the transit time can be computed by the receiver. Conceptually each end of a full duplex link has a send and a receive timer. On link (not EEP connection) initialization each receiving half sends its timer value to the

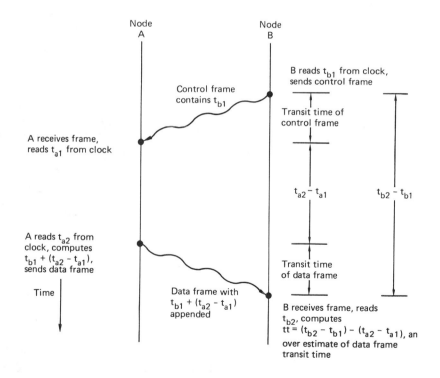

Figure 7-8: The transit time of a data frame is overestimated to be $tt = (t_{b2}\ t_{b1})\ (t_{a2}\ t_{a1})$

other end's sender half, which uses this value to initialize its link sender timer. (No other synchronization is required.) The sender places its link send timer value in each logical link frame. The receiver subtracts this value from its link receive timer value to estimate time on the link. This mechanism assures that the transit times are always overestimated, never underestimated, because of the delay in the original initialization exchange. The basic idea is shown in figure 7-8 taken from [Sloan 79], where Node B initializes Node A's link send timer. The details of protocols taking into account clock drift and link errors are presented in [Sloan 79, Watson 80d]. Routing nodes are also assumed to destroy all packets on recovery from a crash as part of the MPL bounding process.

7.9.8. Reliable control information

The final error control issue we will discuss is the protection of control information. Control information is transmitted between protocol modules at each end and not between the actual end-user processes. (The protocol modules may, however, be considered part of the user's code.) One can protect the control information by including it within a SN space, and thus the same mechanisms used for protecting data can protect control information from being lost, damaged, duplicated, and missequenced. It is important that data flow-control mechanisms of the protocol not block control information flow. This can happen when control information is transmitted within the same SN space as the data.

One solution is to provide a separate logical channel for the control information. One can accomplish this by assigning the protocol modules different addresses from those used for the end-user processes (a separate association) or by creating a control sub-channel [Garlick 77].

Instead we prefer the following mechanism. We feel the approach to be described will be simpler to implement and is more in keeping with the servo-mechanism nature of the communication process. The mechanism is based on formulating the meaning of control information so that its loss or duplication does not matter. This is accomplished by requiring it to fit one of three conditions: (1) report state about the sender, (2) report the sender's current view of its correspondent's state, or (3) describe the data in the packet in some way. The state reporting format gives the current known value of state variables rather than stating an increment to a variable. We call this model for dealing with control information the state exchange model, each end is participating in a feedback servo loop reporting its current view of their combined state [Fletcher 79b]. An end reports its view of the combined origin, destination state when its state changes (which occurs whenever data is sent, buffer availability changes, etc.) or its view of the combined state does not agree with that reported by the other end. Then if a packet is lost under condition (1) above, state information, possibly more up-to-date, will appear in later packets and if duplicated it will just cause the overwriting with an identical value of some state register content. In condition (2) above, loss or duplication will be detected at the receiver and the appropriate control information regenerated and sent as appropriate. In case (3) above, state is associated with the data, and the mechanisms for dealing with data loss or duplication will be invoked and lead to appropriate recovery. If packets are missequenced incorrect state may be set but generally it can be expressed so that this causes no problem and is self correcting by the above mechanism, although an exception is described later in Section 7.11.4. We saw the state exchange model in use earlier with the sequence number ACK/retransmission mechanism. In general, formulating requests and state reports so that they are idempotent (capable of repeated delivery without harm) is useful at all architecture levels if it can be done [Chapter 11, Liskov 79].

Control information requiring frequent communication is generally placed in packet header fields piggybacked with data. Infrequently appearing control information can be included, when needed, in optional header fields or separate control packets.

7.10. Protection

There are several issues here: Information must be protected from (1) being sent to the wrong destination, (2) being stolen, (3) being replayed, (4) claiming to come from another origin, (5) being surreptitiously inserted, and (6) appearing on a link or network of the wrong security or privacy level. Some of the mechanisms available at the EEP level are the following: To protect against delivery to an incorrect destination, header checksums can be used to protect address, security level and other sensitive header information, and routing algorithms can ensure that the security levels of links and packets are appropriately matched. To protect against data being stolen, end-to-end encryption can be used [Section 10.3, Kent 77, Needham 78, Popek 79]. Replays and insertions can be detected with encryption mechanisms and sequence numbers [Kent 77]. Protection from packets being sent by one origin claiming to be another origin and assuring packets have the appropriate privacy or security level for each link or network requires use of trusted gateways or routing nodes between domains of trust. The former can also be achieved with encryption based mechanisms.

7.11. Resource management

7.11.1. Introduction

The main resources that must be managed within the IPC layer are address space, buffers, and bandwidth. Within the routing network fair allocation of bandwidth and buffers may dictate different size packets for different networks or links. There may also be a need for priority mechanisms.

7.11.2. Identifier space

Management of identifier space allocation simply means knowing what identifiers are available to be allocated to processes. That is, knowing which are in use, or have been used if the space is large enough not to require their reuse. The main problem is maintaining this information safely across crashes. If identifiers are reused, then provision must be made to assure packets from previous associations using a given identifier are unacceptable (connection management discussed earlier). Mechanisms for maintaining identifier usage information are outside the EEP and are not discussed here.

7.11.3. Segmentation and reassembly

The EEP is assumed to operate in an environment with multiple networks, and multiple link technologies and bandwidths. This internet environment may place maximum or desired minimum packet size constraints on different physical or logical links between internet nodes in order to fairly allocate bandwidth or buffers. This environment may require packet segmentation and reassembly. There are two approaches to packet segmentation or fragmentation as summarized by [Shoch 79] and shown in figure 7-9.

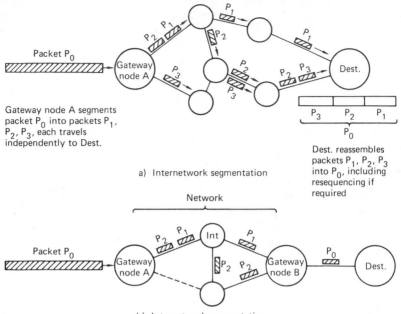

Packet P_0

Gateway node A segments packet P_0 into packets P_1, P_2, P_3, each travels independently to Dest.

Dest. reassembles packets P_1, P_2, P_3 into P_0, including resequencing if required

a) Internetwork segmentation

b) Intranetwork segmentation

Figure 7-9: Inter and intranetwork segmentation and reassembly

With *internetwork segmentation* an EEP packet can be segmented into several smaller packets, if it is too large for a link or network it is about to enter. Each of these smaller packets travels independently to the destination where reassembly takes place. This is the approach used in the Internet Protocol design [Postel 80a]. Rules need to be established for how to form the headers of the new packets from the information in the original. A unit must be chosen for identification purposes so that the original packet can be correctly reassembled at the destination. Simplification results if this unit is the same one used for error control; efficiency results if the unit is small [Cerf 74].

With *intranetwork segmentation* a link or network specific driver segments the original packet into smaller packets for transport to the next internet node, wraps each in the necessary lower level protocol(s), and ships them to the next internet node, where the original is reassembled appropriately sequenced by the lower level protocol for transport across the next internet link. The Xerox PUP system uses this approach [Boggs 80].

If internet links have specified desired minimum frame or packet sizes, there are two approaches to reassembly during routing. One requires state information to be maintained on a per association basis at routing nodes, assumes relatively stable routing, and the ability to recognize higher level data units such as messages. This approach trys to assemble either a minimum size packet or whole message for an association before forwarding it. The second approach combines several EEP packets destined for the same next internet node into a single lower level protocol frame or packet. The next node then makes its routing decisions on the EEP packets and makes up new frames as appropriate for its outgoing links. The second approach seems considerably simpler and more flexible.

There is currently not much practical experience with segmentation/reassembly. The problem could be avoided if all networks would support an agreed minimum packet size and all packets never exceed this size. Given the wide range of interconnection technologies and bandwidths, and rapidly changing communication technology, the appropriate maximum packet sizes for different networks are likely to vary widely and restricting packet sizes may lead to serious inefficiencies. Therefore, we believe a general segmentation mechanism should be supported.

7.11.4. Flow control

Resources are required at the receiver to process and store received packets. *Flow control* is the mechanism used to regulate the flow of information from the sender to the receiver at a rate or in a quantity that the receiver can handle. The main receiver resource is buffer memory, although access to the network interface and CPU cycles may also be important. There are a wide range of buffer management strategies possible. One goal of a well designed flow control mechanism is that the origin not send information faster than the receiver can absorb it, independent of the particular buffer management strategy chosen.

There are a variety of possible flow control mechanisms possible [Cornafion 79, Grange 79, Pouzin 76b]. Maximum or average rate based mechanisms, while useful for some applications, are not easy to use in an environment with variable delays and bandwidths. Instead most EEP flow control mechanisms are built around limits on the quantity of information sent. Mechanisms that allow an end to simply specify it is willing to receive N more units without sequence number information, such as used in the Arpanet host-host protocol, run into difficulties because loss or duplication of such messages can create uncertainty. Therefore, designers have gone to mechanisms that not only specify how many units a receiver is willing to receive, but in effect the sequence numbers of the units it is willing to receive. These mechanisms are robust in the face of lost or duplicated flow control information, i.e. they use the state exchange model mentioned in [Section 7.9.8]. The most common flow control mechanisms are built around the *window* or *credit* concept. The basic idea works as follows. (Assume for now that the unit used for flow control is the same as that used for error control.)

ACK packets contain the SN of the next expected unit, LWE. To support flow control a number relative to the LWE called the *window* is also included. The window, when added to the LWE, specifies the highest sequence numbered unit the receiver is willing to receive.

If protocols require that the origin never have more elements outstanding than indicated by the latest window received, the protocol is said to enforce a conservative sender strategy. If the window is only considered advisory and senders can choose to send more on the assumption that due to network delays its information is always slightly out of date and that by the time its elements arrive at the receiver they can be accommodated, an optimistic sender strategy is supported [Garlick 77, Cornafion 79]. There is the possibility, of course, that no buffer space will be available and therefore information will have to be discarded and then be retransmitted. Similarly, receivers in choosing values for the window can operate on conservative or optimistic strategies by allocating windows based on actual buffer space available, (conservative strategy), or based on average receiver or network bandwidth (optimistic strategy). The interaction of the buffer allocation and flow control mechanisms can affect the efficiency and potential bandwidth possible [Sunshine 76].

Having outlined the window flow control concept, two questions need answering, on what size unit or units should flow control be performed, and how is it determined how many of these units to advertise. In trying to answer these questions, one quickly recognizes that flow control is not fully understood nor is there much real experience with alternate proposals. The problem arises from the desire for a mechanism and choice of a flow control unit(s) that:

- Reflects the nature of the resources being protected and

- Allows efficient transmission on an association independent of the widely varying implementation choices possible.

For example, consider a possible interaction between one possible choice for flow control unit and buffer strategy [Garlick 77, McQuillan 78a].

There are two basic buffering strategies, circular or infinite queue, and block buffers. Assume flow control units are bits rather than messages. With the circular buffer, the last bit of a message is followed in the buffer by the first bit of the next message with some appropriate mark. There is thus a one to one correspondence between bits advertised in windows and buffer bits available, independent of the number of messages sent. With the square buffer strategy, when a bit marked as an end-of-message arrives, the entire buffer is usually returned to the user program even if it contains unused space. Each new message starts a new buffer. Therefore, with a block buffer mechanism, if 1000 bits are available in a buffer block and are advertised as the window and a one bit message arrives, the entire 1000 bit buffer is returned and the window immediately goes to zero. If the sender had sent several messages into the network whose total data count was less than 1000 bits, as a result of receiving the advertised window, all but the first would be rejected as a result of window overflow. Thus, there would have been unnecessary network traffic that could be compounded due to retransmissions. Had the sender known that only one message up to 1000 bits was acceptable, it could have adjusted its sending strategy appropriately.

One possible solution would be to choose the message as the flow control unit. Then the questions arise how does each EEP know how large messages can be; how does an EEP interface know how many messages to associate with the user's buffers; what if independent of the buffers supplied by the next level user, the EEP module is itself supplying buffers for out-of-sequence reassembly or other purposes; what if the user's buffers are swapped or paged to disk? On the assumption we want to support a transaction oriented service, requiring prenegotiation of message or buffer sizes should not be required. Nor do we believe the protocol should have built in assumptions about one or a few specific resource allocation strategies. One might consider allowing the window to reflect two units, such as messages and bits, and then depend on information being passed across the user interface from the next level to aid the EEP modules in setting parameters in their flow control and sending strategy algorithms. Another view would be that the buffer strategy offered by the operating system should be compatible with the nature of the applications and EEP being supported. Information from NAKs might also be used to aid adaptive flow control algorithms. If a receiving system is managing a buffer pool, [Nessett 79a] has suggested it might be useful for the sender to send information with each packet (advisory only) indicating the remaining amount of information to be sent. In summary there are still many questions needing answers in the flow control area.

When the sender's combined state indicates that the receiver has no receive space, a zero length window exists. There is a problem associated with reliably opening zero length windows resulting from the possibility of lost or missequenced packets [Garlick 77]. For example, if a receiver sends a packet advertising a zero window, then sends a packet advertising a positive window, and the latter arrives first; the sender will "think" that a window renege has taken place and thus may not send while it awaits a new positive window indication. Here is an example where missequenced control information can cause a problem. This problem can be solved if the out-of-sequence arrival can be detected or senders periodically send (generally header-only packets) into zero windows forcing the receiver to reply with its current state.

7.11.5. Priority

Priority is a resource management issue associated with both intermediate nodes and end modules. Priority information can be used to aid the scheduling of access to network interfaces, links, and buffers. Two priority scheduling strategies are possible, preemptive and nonpreemptive. In the former, if a lower priority operation is being performed when a higher priority one arrives, then the lower priority one is immediately terminated. With respect to packet handling this may imply overwriting a buffer or stopping a transmission. Preemptive strategies may be implemented either allowing the preempted operation to be continued, restarted, the preempted resource to be regained if backup or other storage exists, or not. With a nonpreemptive strategy existing operations are completed or resources freed before scheduling is undertaken. Priority information in packet headers is required. Such mechanisms can interact strongly with error and congestion control, thus increasing delay variability and throughput. Arguments have been made that in a properly designed packet network average delay should be low enough that priority and preemption do not need to be explicitly dealt with [McQuillan 78a]. Within military networks used for command and control as well as normal administrative and other tasks, these concepts may, however, require explicit attention. There is little experience with these concepts in existing packet switched networks.

7.12. Measurement and diagnostics

When error control exists in a system, then the system can operate correctly in spite of failures, yet it is important to know that failures have occurred. Therefore, statistics are needed on events such as checksum failures, number and type of NAKs, number of retransmissions, and number of missequenced packets. Timestamps and traces of routes traversed are also useful. This information is needed to detect and fix problems. Performance problems as well as errors are common in systems as complex as the ones we are describing. Performance problems result from incorrect setting of timers, inappropriate algorithms or parameters for determining flow control windows, poor buffer management strategies, and so forth. To effectively deal with the above, EEPs need to support measurement and diagnostic aids. Control fields or packets can be used to specify the above services.

7.13. Conclusions

The previous sections have outlined major IPC and EEP design issues. We emphasized the need to clearly understand the IPC service desired. An interface that supports the sending and receiving of arbitrary length messages provides for both transaction and stream oriented applications. We believe that connection management (opening and closing state information) need not and should not be made visible at the IPC interface because it biases the design away from support for transaction applications and provides no additional, in our understanding, user service. The choice of EEP mechanisms is not only dependent on the services to be offered, but also on assumptions about the services provided by the next lower level. We indicated that design decisions based on simplifying assumptions such as that the underlying environment will be X.25 or other particular protocol may limit future evolution toward a more general internetwork (local and public) environment or deeper analysis may show that the assumptions cannot be fully guaranteed.

Designing an EEP is not a simple task. There are many subtlte interactions between EEP mechanisms and implementation decisions. Some areas such as error control are quite well understood, while other areas such as addressing, protection, and resource management require more research and experience. We have emphasized that to achieve a transaction orientation, attention to decisions made in all areas of EEP design is required. Areas critically impacting a transaction orientation are identification, connection management, and flow control. It is desirable in these areas to find mechanisms that do not require opening or closing message exchanges to reliably send a single data message. Achieving a stream orientation (high throughput) requires minimizing packet acceptance and processing overhead [Bunch 80], using as large a packet as possible, and using a large data to header space ratio. Designing a full service EEP and its implementations to support high performance is not well understood, particularly the interaction of resource management features of the protocol and mechanisms used in the implementation or between communicating implementations and other protocol levels. Other areas needing research are EEP specification, verification, and validation [BBN 80, Sunshine 79].

Chapter 8. Distributed control

8.1. Abstract

Executive control concepts and mechanisms have evolved primarily in a highly centralized uniprocessor context, surrounded by the rather centralized (e.g., hierarchical) structures of nature and human society. At least partially as a consequence of this, there is currently some difficulty envisioning more "decentralized" control concepts and designing corresponding mechanisms. To help stimulate thought in this area, we present a conceptual model of the spectrum of control alternatives from maximally centralized to maximally decentralized. The model is not intended either to provide a quantitative measure of decentralization, or to ascribe attributes (e.g., "better") to points in the spectrum – instead, its illumination should greatly facilitate the subsequent performance of these endeavors.

While decentralization of control is a logical matter, our centralized legacy includes important assumptions about communication characteristics which underly most control mechanisms if not also the concepts. These assumptions are frequently either not explicitly recognized, or ignored as being conceptually insignificant. This has resulted in control mechanisms originally intended for one communication environment (e.g., shared primary memory) being naively reimplemented in another (e.g., disjoint primary memories) with adverse consequences for their performance and even correctness. Thus, the search for new decentralized control concepts and mechanisms should carefully consider that the environment will often impose communication attributes which are unconventional in the executive control context.

8.2. Introduction

Computer systems are usually considered to be "distributed" on the basis of such aspects as user access, system geography, processing, or data being decentralized. The aspect which is least frequently decentralized is *control* (i.e., resource management). There are rational arguments (outside the scope of this paper), and even some evidence, for the hypothesis that various types of decentralized control offer significant potential benefits (e.g., improved modularity and robustness) under certain conditions. Unfortunately, there is little commonality of view on what "decentralized" (or even "centralized") control means. This seems to be a consequence of intellectual inertia imparted by the rather centralized (e.g., hierarchical) organizations which predominate in nature and human society – the more decentralized alternatives are only recently beginning to be perceived in any sort of conceptual fashion. In addition, the initial scarcity of processor resources focused the attention of system software designers on uniprocessors, where they developed the current foundations of traditional operating systems. As processor hardware became less costly, multiple processors were connected to shared primary memory (forming "multiprocessors"), because most of the uniprocessor software concepts and structures could be successfully retained with minimal modification and augmentation. One consequence of this historical milieu and evolution was that many of the premises on which these traditional operating system concepts were strongly based are now very often so taken for granted that they have become transparent–they are either not recognized explicitly, or believed to be universally valid. This makes it difficult to see where they may be inherently centralized and how more decentralized alternatives might replace them. Instances of more or less decentralized control have arisen in various aspects of computer system design, but almost inevitably in an ad hoc fashion–particular approaches are used accidentally or out of convenience or necessity, rather than through consideration of fundamental principles. A systematic method of selecting among control alternatives, based on a more complete perspective of the decentralization issues, will be necessary to meet some of the challenges posed by contemporary application and architectural trends.

To help stimulate thought in this area, we present a conceptual model to illuminate the spectrum of control decentralization alternatives from minimal (centralized) to maximal. We have four objectives for this model:

- contribute to an improved understanding of the fundamental nature of "decentralization," particularly with respect to control;

- assist in the formulation of a common frame of reference and terminology for discussing control decentralization;

- clarify the perception of relative differences and similarities among specific instances of control;

- facilitate the synthesis of control policies and mechanisms which are as decentralized as desired.

The model is not intended to provide predictions or quantitative evaluations, nor does it ascribe attributes (e.g., "better," "more robust") to different points in the control spectrum. These endeavors are important but difficult to accomplish without the results sought from our model.

The primitive object in this model is a *resource*, which is an abstract data type (i.e., set of operations which collectively define its behavior). Resources exist at different levels of abstraction–in computer systems these tend to range from the user interface at the top, to the bottom hardware. (A type is implementation-independent, so hardware may appear at any level and is not per se a level of abstraction [Jensen 1980].) A resource is encapsulated by one or more *controllers* (also data types) which abstract it and thus themselves become resources at higher levels. This abstraction, called *control*, consists of effecting the decisions and actions involved in regulating access to (e.g., sharing) the resource, as well as implementing the resource data structures and operations visible to its users.

This model considers control in terms of *activities* at specific levels of abstraction. It is founded on the principle that an activity is "decentralized" if there is no unique, special lower level entity (e.g., a monitor, a bus arbiter) which can enforce a consistent view of the activity state on the entities participating in that activity. ("Consistency" is the invariance of predicates defined on the state [Eswaran 1976].) Instead, either there is no such enforcement, or there are multiple such special entities (a similar view is expressed in [Le Lann 1979]). The absence of enforcement generally implies that it is not possible to prove activity consistency, although the system or application may allow it to be achieved with some (perhaps very high) probability.

Figure 8-1 illustrates this in the context of a store and forward network (such as Arpanet). At level *l* there is an activity of sending a message from one host to another- the source host message output buffer must be made consistent with the destination host message input buffer. That activity is decentralized because its consistency is achieved by the three IMP's below at level *k*. The IMP's engage in activities requiring consistency which depends on pairs of modems communicating bits with each other at level *j*– thus, those activities at level *k* are decentralized. For the modems to attain consistency of transmitted and received bits, the transmitting modem's clock at level *i* provides timing signals which are embedded in the data stream – therefore, a pair of modems communicating at level *j* is a centralized activity.

When there are multiple special lower level entities which enforce consistency of an activity, their number and relationships determine the *degree* to which that higher level activity is decentralized. This model proposes that the important aspects of those relationships are based

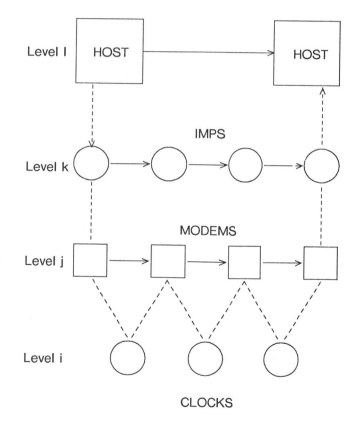

Figure 8-1: Activity decentralization at levels of abstraction

on the notion of *multilateral* control--the nature of multiple controller participation in the management of resources, both individually and collectively.

It is sometimes helpful to think of the model in geometric terms--the factors which determine the degree of control decentralization can be considered the edges of a multi-dimensional construction which bounds a "control space." This formulation suggests characterizing the construction according to such properties as vertex identification (the extreme cases of each factor), edge (factor) metric, and edge orthogonality (independence of factors).

8.3. The control space

In this model, there are five major factors which determine the degree of control decentralization. The first three deal with control of individual resources, and the last two with control of the resources collectively.

8.3.1. Individual Resource Control

Individual resource control is fundamental, because every resource is controlled but some only individually and not collectively. The degree to which the control of a single resource is decentralized is a function of the number of controllers it has, and of the relationships among them.

There are many different ways in which multiple controllers may all participate in the management of the same resource--for example:

- successive, where all management activities are performed for a period of time by one controller, and then by another, in some serial sequence;

- partitioned, where each controller performs a different management activity (e.g., function), whether consecutively or concurrently;

- democratic, where all controllers perform each management activity by negotiation and consensus among equals.

Many of the various multilateral management forms exhibit different degrees of decentralization. This model distinguishes them on that basis according to two factors: *consentience* and *equipollence*.

In the sense intended here, "consentience" is the extent to which a particular management activity for a resource is carried out by all its controllers together. Consentaneity may take place with or without any real concurrency. Activities each may have different degrees of consentience. The most centralized case is where only one controller performs a particular instance of the activity on the resource, as exemplified by autocracy and partitioning--figure 8-2 illustrates this for all the activities. The most decentralized case is where every controller for the activity is involved in every instance of it (see figure 8-3), as with successive and democratic control.

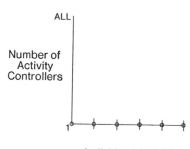

Figure 8-2: The maximally centralized case of consentience

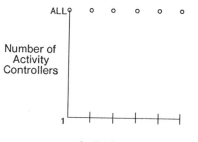

Figure 8-3: The maximally decentralized case of consentience

"Equipollence" is the degree of equality with which management authority and responsibility are distributed across the multiple controllers for a particular activity. It may be different for each of the various management activities. Equipollence can be visualized by plotting the responsibility and authority for each controller participating in the activity, as shown in figure 8-4 – a scalar metric for equipollence is then the inverse of relative dispersion. The maximally centralized case, typified by autocracy and partitioning, is where one controller has all responsibility and authority for the activity and no other controller has any (figure 8-5). Succesive and democratic control are instances of the maximally decentralized case of equipollence, where every controller is equally capable of participating in the activity (as seen in figure 8-6).

The per-activity measures for consentience and equipollence can be viewed as a 2-dimensional construction enclosing the control decentralization space for any given activity (shown in figure 8-7). Similarly, the scalar measures for all the activities corresponding to a particular resource can be combined to represent the control decentralization space for that resource. This combination could be (for example) the average of the per-activity measures, weighted by some system- or application-dependent coefficients such as "importance" or frequency of execution. (However, one must resist any temptation to quantify the model beyond its intent and

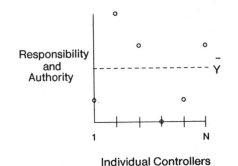

Individual Controllers

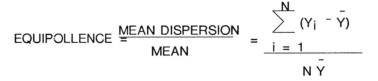

Figure 8-4: Equipollence

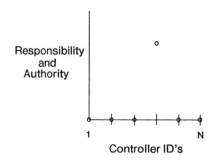

Controller ID's

Figure 8-5: The maximally centralized case of equipollence

suitability.) In both the activity and resource cases, one corner of the space (minimum consentience and minimum equipollence) is the maximally centralized point–autocracy. Diagonally opposed to that corner is the maximally decentralized point (maximum consentience and maximum equipollence), exemplified by democracy. Successive is an intermediate case where equipollence is high but consentience is low. The maximum consentience/minimum

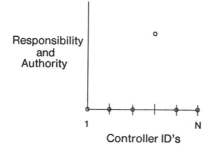

Figure 8-6: The maximally decentralized case of equipollence

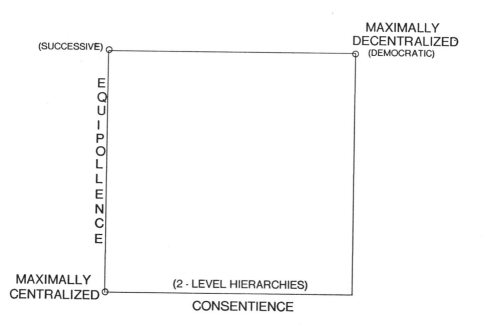

Figure 8-7: A graphical representation of the first two decentralization factors

equipollence corner is more difficult than the others to associate with an obvious resource management technique. While the minimally and maximally decentralized cases of control can readily be identified, most points within the construction are more difficult to order solely on the basis of their consentience and equipollence coordinates. This is because (at least at the present time) there appears to be nothing intrinsically more decentralized about greater consentience than about greater equipollence--a function of the two must be selected which determines decentralization ordering. That function takes into account the relative significance of each factor, depending perhaps on the motivations and requirements of a particular system analysis or synthesis effort. It currently appears sufficient to use a linear weighting, but additional experience with decentralization of control will probably further illuminate this issue.

The third factor which contributes to the degree of control decentralization is the number of controllers an activity has. The most centralized case is where only one controller is involved in the activity, such as when control is autocratic or partitioned (illustrated for all activities in figure 8-8). The most decentralized case is where all controllers of the resource participate in the activity (figure 8-9)–in principle, control can be decentralized in this respect without limit by adding controllers, so there is no unique endpoint.

Either the per-activity or the per-resource 2-dimensional construction can be viewed with the corresponding number of controllers as a 3-dimensional spectrum of control decentralization, as seen in figure 8-10. Neither consentience nor equipollence are affected by the number of participants–for example, the democratic and successive vertices of figure 8-7 become edges in

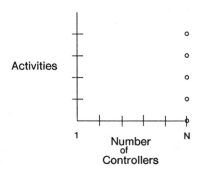

Figure 8-8: Number of controllers: maximally centralized case

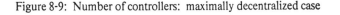

Figure 8-9: Number of controllers: maximally decentralized case

figure 8-10. However, the most centralized endpoint of the third factor is an exception because when there is only one controller, consentience and equipollence are both necessarily zero. This is reflected in the geometric representation by the $X = Y = Z = 0$ corner being the only one which exists on the XZ plane. The same issue regarding ordering of points in the space which arose when the first two factors were considered jointly is germane here – control decentralization is some function of all three factors, the first two being (in our current view) more significant.

8.3.2. Collective Resource Control

Very often resources are controlled not just as separate entities but also collectively in accordance with more global objectives and constraints (i.e., as a system). The three factors above do not account for the extent to which this latter aspect of control is decentralized, even by combining the per-resource results. The precept of multilateral resource management can be applied here as well to derive two factors that determine the degree to which *system-wide* control is decentralized.

The first of these factors (the fourth in our model) is the percentage of of all other controllers in the system with which each controller performs multilateral management. An aggregate (e.g., the mean) of the percentages in this vector is a suitable scalar metric. Combining the per-controller percentages with unity weighting seems reasonable because controllers (unlike resources) generally appear to have uniform importance with respect to the degree of decentralization. The maximally centralized case is where no controller participates in the multilateral management of

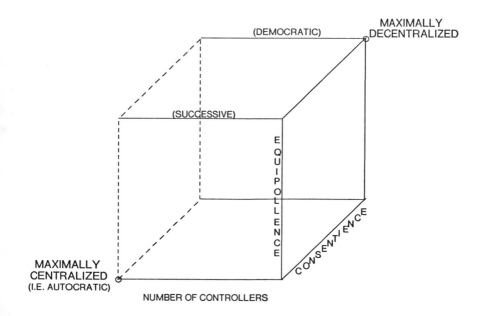

Figure 8-10: A graphical representation of the first three decentralization factors

any resource--the resources are partitioned into disjoint subsets, each of which is managed independently of the others by one controller. The maximally decentralized case is where every controller participates with every other in the multilateral management of at least one resource. Figure 8-11 illustrates five cases ordered in increasing degree of control decentralization according to this factor.

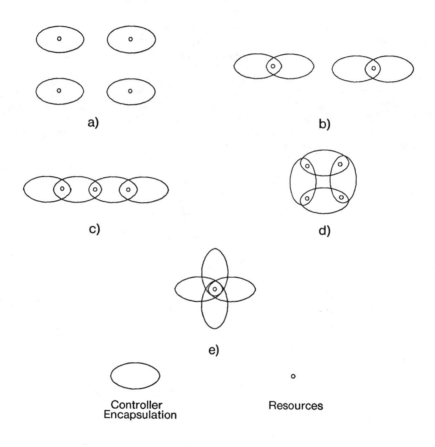

Figure 8-11: Ordering by number of controllers which participate in each instance
of multilateral resource management

The second system-wide factor (number five in the model) is the number of resources involved in each instance of multilateral management. The scalar metric which suggests itself is derived from the vector by summing the number of resources in the system which are managed by at least two controllers. The maximally centralized case is where no resources are multilaterally managed, and the maximally decentralized case is where all resources are multilaterally managed. In figure 8-12, five cases are shown ordered in increasing degree of control decentralization on this basis.

Together, the fourth and fifth factors provide a measure of system-wide control decentralization, as illustrated in the construction of figure 8-13. If no controllers multilaterally manage, then obviously no resources are multilaterally managed, and vice versa. Thus, $X = Y = 0$ is the only point which exists on the lines $X = 0$ and $Y = 0$. The maximally centralized point in the construction is that no controllers multilaterally manage any resources; diagonally opposed is the maximally decentralized point where every controller participates in the management of every

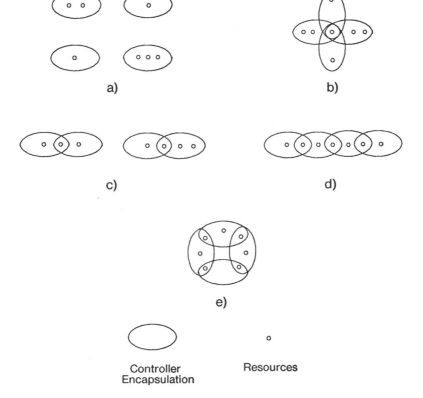

Figure 8-12: Ordering by number of multilaterally managed resources

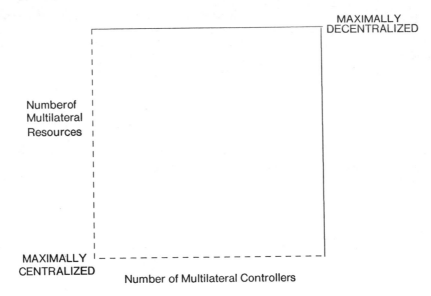

Figure 8-13: System-wide control decentralization

resource. Beyond that, ordering of cases in the space depends on the relative importance ascribed to each of the two factors by the particular function (as with the first three factors). A useful method for doing this is to perform a sum of products using the vector forms of the metrics. The cases in figure 8-14 are in ascending order of system-wide control decentralization according to this measure.

The two global factors can be viewed in conjunction with the 3-dimensional per-resource construction as a 5-dimensional representation of the control spectrum. The edges corresponding to the fourth and fifth factors are orthogonal to the others, but obvious boundary conditions do not exist--the maximally centralized collective case implies the maximally centralized individual case.

There is a five-dimensional control decentralization construction corresponding to any particular level of abstraction, and in general a computer system will be represented at a different point in each. For example, a computer network could have:

- rather decentralized control at the user interface level, provided by a so-called "network operating system";

- rather centralized control at the executive level, because the host operating systems are autonomous;

- rather decentralized control at the communication subnet level, as a consequence of both the hardware and the routing algorithm designs.

The implications of a system's representative point position at one level of abstraction on those at any other level are largely unknown at this time, especially for the more decentralized cases.

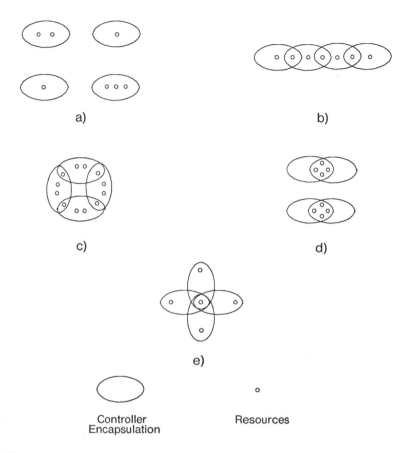

Figure 8-14: Ordering by number of resources multilaterally managed by number of controllers

While decentralization of control is a logical matter, physical communication issues are often an important factor-- this is discussed next.

8.4. Communication and the decentralization of control

Multilateral resource management clearly necessitates that the participating controllers share some information. Some of this information may be static- e.g., an a' priori model of other controllers' known or expected strategies, tactics, and even algorithms. Other information may be dynamic, including models of observed behavior and estimates of current state of the other controllers. Static information can be easily shared through seperate copies, but dynamic information sharing requires communication among the controllers. Our centralized executive control legacy includes important assumptions about communication characteristics which underly most control mechanisms if not also the concepts.

Communication involves two conceptually distinct aspects: the production, and the manifestation, of signals--the relationship between these two we term signal *observability*. Examples of poor observability include signals which: are erroneous, lost, duplicated, spurious, or received out of transmitted order; have variable, unknown delay (see [Le Lann 1977]), or long delay with respect to the rate at which the system state changes. Signal observability has three important factors: completeness, latency, and synchronization.

Completeness of signal observability is the extent to which a controller can see any signal it wants to–more specifically, it is the set of probabilities for each controller that it can observe each signal in any particular set of signals. Some of these probabilities may be conditional on certain aspects of the system state. The best (i.e., least constraining) case is that every controller can always observe every signal; the worst (i.e., most constraining) case is that no controller can ever observe any signal.

Latency of signal observability is the extent to which a controller can see a signal in time for it to be useful. To be more precise, it is the set of probabilities for each controller that it can observe each signal in any particular set of signals any necessary amount of time before the next signal is sent (e.g., in time to respond, or to affect which signal is sent next). As with completeness, some of the probabilities may be conditional. The best case is that every controller can observe every signal within any arbitrarily small amount of time after it is sent; the worst case is that no controller can observe any signal until after all signals in the set have been sent.

Synchronization of signal observability is the extent to which all controllers can see signals in the same sequence–more exactly, the probability for each controller in any particular set of controllers that it can induce any particular ordering (according to time, priorities, atomicity of operations, etc.) on any particular set of signals. As before, some of the probabilities may be conditional. Depending on the circumstances, synchronization of signals may be either weak or strong: the former means that the controllers are all able to agree on a common ordering, but it may not be the one desired–e.g., that in which the signals were sent with respect to a hypothetical global time reference; the latter means that the controllers are all able to establish the desired sequence–e.g., the actual sending order with respect to their own (asynchronous) time references. The best case is that every controller can determine whatever ordering is desired on all signals; the worst case is that no controllers can determine any common ordering of any signals. Between these lie cases where only partial or probabilistic signal synchronization can be achieved.

Typically, each level of abstraction has different signals, and communication at one level is carried out by the next level down. Signal observability at the lowest system-wide level, interprocessor communication, is particularly important because it can impact the behavior of higher level communication and control.

When the interprocessor communication mechanism is shared primary memory (as in uniprocessors and multiprocessors), signal observability is normally very good. The performance, and even correctness, of nearly all conventional centralized executive control techniques assume and depend on that. For example, figure 8-15 shows a standard producer/consumer situation–consistency of the activity is enforced by a single synchronizing entity, based on the premise that there is a high degree of signal observability (e.g., synchronism) between the producer in the critical section and the synchronizer. But when the interprocessor communication mechanism is explicit I/O (e.g., buses) rather than shared primary memory, signal

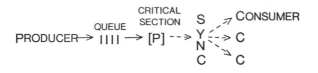

Figure 8-15: Centralized synchronization

observability is normally much worse–communication protocols may help alleviate part of the problem (the usual packet switching errors such as duplications), but cannot help and even exacerbate other parts (e.g., delays). The difference between the memory and I/O interprocessor communication cases is essentially one of observability error probabilities, but this conceptually insignificant *quantitative* difference may necessitate a conceptually significant *qualitative* difference in control (just as different memory technology speeds lead to different management approaches for primary and secondary memories). Thus, conventional centralized software mechanisms originally intended for one communication environment (e.g., shared primary memory) may be inappropriate and even counterproductive if naively re-implemented in systems with reduced signal observability (e.g., disjoint primary memories).

An important consequence of this is that it is not now generally feasible for most multiple-processor machines without shared main memory to have a conceptually singular operating system in the same sense as a uniprocessor or multiprocessor–that is, one which integrates the processors into a *computer* by attempting to manage all the executive level resources in the best interests of the whole system. Instead, most such machines are constrained by the current state of the operating system art to being a *network*–there is a seperate operating system for each processor, the executive level resources are partitioned, and each partition is managed locally for the good of just that small piece of the system. In many applications (e.g., resource-sharing networks), such an arrangement may be adequate or even necessary (for technical or nontechnical reasons). But in many others (e.g., real-time control), having only local and no global executive control appears to greatly reduce the potential extent to which certain important attributes, such as robustness and modularity, can be provided on a system-wide basis.

Depending on the individual system and application, it may be possible to extend certain centralized control schemes to less favorable signal observability conditions. However, the general solution to the problem of achieving a high degree of decentralized system-wide executive control requires creation of new concepts and techniques which are designed explicitly to function correctly and efficiently despite poor signal observability. In particular, this implies algorithms which make "best effort" resource management decisions based on information which may be inaccurate and incomplete. Such generalization of signal observability premises may prove to be beneficial in centralized control environments as well.

To the best of our knowledge, only one computer system has been designed and implemented for the express purpose of studying decentralized control [Jensen 1977, Boebert 1980]–a new such system is now being developed at Carnegie-Mellon University. Some steps in the direction of decentralized control have been taken at levels above (e.g., concurrency control in multiple-copy data bases [Thomas 1978]) and below (e.g., routing in packet-switching communication networks [Schwartz 1980]) the executive level, where the control functions are simpler and less general, and the resources usually somewhat less abstract and less dynamic. Related efforts include decentralized problem solving in artificial intelligence [Lesser 1979]), and perhaps relevant ideas might be gained from such fields as stochastic decision making, fuzzy and probabilistic logics, etc. [Gupta 1977].

8.5. Acknowledgement

I am grateful for the helpful comments from my associates at C.M.U., Honeywell's Systems and Research Center, and elsewhere.

Chapter 9. Identifiers (naming) in distributed systems

9.1. Introduction

Identification systems (often called naming systems) are at the heart of all computer system design. We have chosen to use the neutral term identifier rather than name because we want to be able to distinguish between various kinds of entities used to designate or refer to objects at all levels of the architecture and normal usage of the word name gives it a more specific connotation (see below). In spite of the importance of identifiers, no general unified treatment of them exists, either across computer science or within subareas such as programming, operating, or database management systems. These two statements are particularly true of distributed computing. A useful introduction to identification issues associated with operating systems, with applicability to distributed systems, is given by [Saltzer 78a]. Other introductions to the subject specifically aimed at distributed systems are contained in [Abraham 80, ISO 79, Livesey 79, McQuillan 78a-b, Pouzin 78, Shoch 78, Zimmerman 80]. It is premature (at least for ourselves) to attempt a definitive discussion of identification. Instead, we briefly review some general properties, design goals and issues associated with the topic, and then present some concrete examples in distributed systems. The central point we wish to make is that identification is not a topic to be treated lightly, in an ad hoc manner, or in isolation from other distributed system needs such as protection, error control, and resource management, although this often has been the case.

An *identifier* is a string of symbols, usually bits or characters, used to designate or refer to an object. These objects and their identifiers may be visible at the interfaces between layers of the Model, between modules of the same layer, or may be embedded and used strictly within a module. We are primarily concerned in this chapter with identifiers used at interfaces between layers. In particular, we focus on identifiers used with the objects defined by the DOS layer and their relationship with and use of lower level identifiers. The important use of identifiers, such as sequence numbers, between modules of the same layer for error control, synchronization, and resource management is discussed in many of the other chapters. The use of identifiers for protection is discussed in Chapter 10 and briefly later in this chapter. Some general characteristics of identification systems are:

- Identifiers are used for a wide variety of purposes, referencing, locating, scheduling, allocating, error controlling, synchronizing, and sharing of objects or resources (information units, communication channels, transactions, processes, files, etc.). One can use an identifier to refer to an object's value(s) or to refer to the object itself. Identifiers are used in either sense when constructing more complex objects out of simpler component objects. Associated with an identifier, implicitly or explicitly, is the *type* of the designated object [Chapter 2].

- Identifiers exist in different forms at all levels of a system architecture. [Shoch 78] has made a useful informal distinction between three important classes of identifiers widely used in distributed systems, *names, addresses, and routes*:

"The *name* of a resource indicates **what** we seek,

an *address* indicates **where** it is, and

a *route* tells us **how to get there.**"

Names, addresses, and routes can occur at all levels of the architecture. Names used within the interprocess communication layer have often been called terms such as *ports, or logical or generic addresses* as distinct from *physical or specific addresses*. Where useful, we also follow this convention. If an identified object is to be manipulated or accessed, the identifier must be *mapped* using an appropriate *mapping function* and *context* into another identifier and ultimately the object as shown in figure 9-1. In general, an identifier is mapped in one *context* into another identifier that is subsequently evaluated in yet another context. Identifiers used at different levels referring to the same object must be *bound* together, statically or dynamically. Commonly one maps names into addresses and addresses into routes, although one could also map a name to a route and a route to an address, etc.

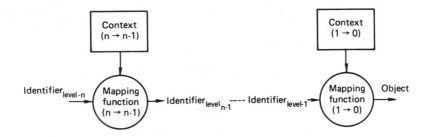

Figure 9-1: Mapping of identifiers through *n* levels to the represented object

- An identification system consists of the symbol alphabet(s) out of which one or more levels of identifiers can be formed, the structure or rules for forming identifiers, and the mapping/context mechanisms used to bind and *resolve* identifiers at one level into identifiers at lower levels. If objects can be relocated, shared, created, or destroyed, then mechanisms are needed for updating the appropriate contexts.

- Identification, protection, error control, diagnostic, and resource management mechanisms often interact. One has to be aware of how design goals or choices in one of these areas affect those in the others. The introduction of ideas such as data types associated with identifiers allow error control and user convenience also to be tied to the identification scheme.

- Choice of an identification scheme can affect whether or not it is possible, easy, or efficient to achieve the goals listed in the next section.

- There are many possible ways to designate the object(s) desired: by an explicit name or address (object x or object at x), by content (object(s) with value(s) y or values $>$ expression), by source (all "my" files), broadcast identifier (all objects of a class), group identifier (all participants in subject V), by route (the object found by following path Z), by relationship to a given identifier (all previous sequence numbers), etc.

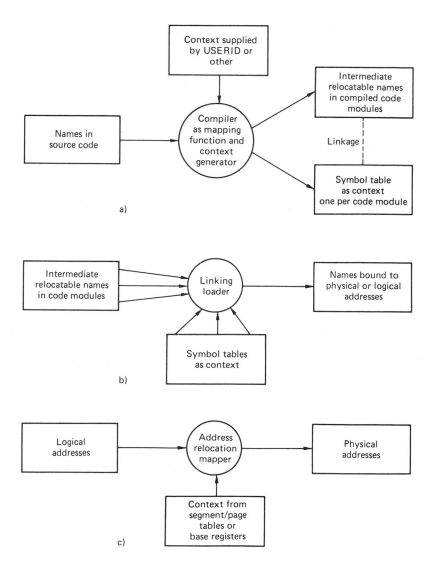

Figure 9-2: Example of levels of identifier mapping in a programming/ operating system

As an illustration of the above points consider the familiar programming/operating system environment shown in figure 9-2. The programming language allows programmers to choose names from a very large symbolic name space for objects such as other programs or data structures in a form convenient for people. These names are translated into intermediate machine-oriented name forms that at load time are mapped with the aid of context (symbol tables) to locations in an address space. If static relocation is used, the intermediate names are bound to addresses in the processor's physical main memory and relocation at runtime is not possible. Runtime relocation is desirable to improve system utilization and to provide for virtual memory in a multiprogramming system. To meet these needs, another level of naming, mapping, binding can be introduced by having the loader bind the intermediate names to identifiers in a one dimensional logical-address space. These logical-addresses are then *dynamically bound* at runtime to physical-addresses with the mapping and context supplied by base registers or page tables. Even with this additional level of naming, problems still exist with respect to ease of sharing of program and data objects, and allowing them to grow dynamically without address conflicts. These problems can be resolved by adding yet another level of identification and context as in the Multics segmentation mechanism [Watson 70].

Below the level that a main memory address is produced, additional information, routing, address mapping, and control mechanisms may be involved to improve performance through use of one or more levels of memory caching. At higher levels of naming, the naming mechanisms of programming, file or information management systems, and those of address systems may be kept separate or be unified with significant usage and implementation implications [Saltzer 78a]. Protection and resource allocation mechanisms are usually tied to these mechanisms.

The important point of the above example is that by adding additional levels of identifiers and associated mapping and context, we are able to improve our ability to relocate, extend, or share objects. Or stated another way, gains are achieved if names do not have to be bound to addresses or routes until they are used, i.e. *dynamic binding*. Only recently have the needs for dynamic name binding and supporting mechanisms begun to be explored for use in distributed systems [McQuillan 78b].

The problems introduced to the design of identification systems by distribution result from the heterogeneous nature of component systems, each with its own possible local identification system for memory addressing, files, processes, and other objects; and problems introduced in maintaining distributed context and mapping information, compounded by delays and errors in message transmission and local system or network crashes. The questions that we want to address are:

- What type of identifiers are required at each of the levels of the distributed system architecture model to meet the goals below,

- Where should context be maintained and mapping performed between different levels of identifiers, and

- How should we deal with heterogeneity.

One set of answers to these questions is given in following sections.

9.2. Identifier goals and implications

There are many possible identification system goals for a distributed system, several being identical to those for nondistributed systems. Some of the more important ones and their implementation implications are:

- Efficient support of transaction as well as session oriented services and applications. In a *transaction* oriented system, the application has the identifiers of one or more resources on which it desires to perform a given operation and receive a reply, with no implication that these resources or the operation may ever be used again. In a *session* oriented system, on the other hand, it is assumed at the start that a stream of operations may be requested over time against an identified set of resources. Efficient support of transaction oriented applications and services implies that we want to minimize, at all levels of the Model, the delay and number of messages that must be exchanged before and after the actual message is sent to perform the desired function. With respect to an identification system, this means that we want to minimize the number of messages that must first be exchanged to initialize or map identifiers held at one level into identifiers directly usable by another level.

  This identifier mapping usually involves message exchanges and allocation and deallocation of identifier space and context. Minimizing this overhead requires large enough unique identifier spaces such that directly usable identifiers can be permanently allocated and permanent context can exist either self-contained within the identifier or elsewhere. Supporting efficient stream applications implies that we want to perform identifier mapping at most once before or during the first access.

- Support at least two levels of identifiers, one convenient for people and one convenient for machines. There should be a clean separation of mechanism for these two levels of identifiers. For each form of DOS identifier a related goal is that it have the same general structure for all types of resources. Other properties desired in these two forms of identifiers are somewhat different. A machine-oriented identifier should be a bit pattern easily manipulated and stored by machines and be directly useful with protection, resource management, and other mechanisms. A human-oriented identifier, on the other hand, is generally a human readable character string with mnemonic value. At some point in time and layer of the Model, human-oriented identifiers must be mapped into machine-oriented ones.

- Allow unique identifiers to be generated in a distributed manner. If a central unique identifier generator is required, complicating efficiency and reliability issues are introduced that do not occur if identifiers can be generated in a distributed manner. Structured identifiers are required to support this goal, although the structure does not have to be visible.

- Provide a system viewed as a global space of identified objects rather than one viewed as a space of identified host computers containing locally identified objects. Similarly, the identification mechanism should be independent of the physical connectivity or topology of the system. That is, the boundaries between physical components and their connection as a network, while technologically and administratively real, should be invisible, to the extent possible, and be recognized as logically artificial. If these boundaries are represented in identifiers, it should be within a unified identifier structure, such as a hierarchical form. (We do not intend that users cannot discover or influence an object's location.)

- Support relocation of objects. The implication here is that there be at least two levels of identifiers, a name and an address, and that the binding between them be dynamic. Also implied are mechanisms for updating the appropriate context for the required mapping when an object is moved.

- Allow multiple logically equivalent *generic* servers for particular resource types. The implication here is that a single identifier at one level can be dynamically bound to more than one address at a lower level. When mapping takes place one object is chosen according to some set of criteria associated with resource management, error control, or other constraints.

- Support use of multiple copies of the same object. If the value(s) of the object is only going to be read or interrogated, one set of constraints are imposed. If the value(s) can be written or modified, tougher constraints are imposed to achieve consistency between the contents of the distributed multiple copies and an ordering of reads and writes applied against the objects [Chapter 13]. Multiple copies are expected to be required frequently in distributed systems to achieve performance, reliability or robustness goals. More than one level of identifier and dynamic binding is implied.

- Allow multiple local user defined identifiers for the same object. What is implied here is that there be unique global identifiers for objects and at least one level of local identifier. Mechanism to bind local and global identifiers is required. The needed local context must be bound in turn to an object or human user, for example. An identification system must be able to switch context as appropriate.

- Support two or more resources sharing or including as components single instances of other objects, without identifier conflicts. This desire implies the need for local identification domains for each object and context switching mechanisms as above. For efficiency, the appropriate level of object granularity must be chosen. Granularity at the level of processes or servers, as in the Model, seems an appropriate level given current hardware architecture. Implicit in the last two goals is the need for a two dimensional identifier space consisting of a pair of identifiers *identifier-of-context, identifier-of-object*.

- Allow many different objects to share the same identifier. Such a need is useful to support broadcast, or group identifiers for conferencing or other applications. At least two levels of identifiers and one-to-many mapping are required.

- Minimize the number of independent identification systems needed across and within architecture levels. This requires recognition of commonality of need.

- All of the above goals may be desirable or be supported by different mechanisms at each layer of the Model, or be supported by mechanisms spanning layers as described later.

The sections below outline issues and mechanisms that can be used to create identification systems that meet one or more of the above goals. Whether an efficient identification system(s) can meet all the above goals for a distributed system with existing hardware/firmware components is an open question. Some of the goals are potentially contradictory such as the goal to achieve a transaction orientation and goals requiring multiple-levels of mapping.

9.3. Unique machine-oriented identifiers

It must be possible at some level of the Model to uniquely identify every object in the global system. On this foundation one can build higher level identification constructs to support the goals above. The question is how to create a *global* unique identifier space in a heterogeneous environment, where each *local* identification domain may use one or more different schemes to create identifiers unique within itself. Global identifiers are resolved within a global, possibly distributed, context; local identifiers are resolved within local contexts. One strategy for creating a global identifier space, called hierarchical concatenation in [Pouzin 78], is to create a unique identifier for each identification domain, usually a host computer, then to concatenate to the unique identifier for the domain the identifiers used within that domain. The RSEXEC system used this approach [Thomas 73]. This is one form of the pair (identifier-of-context, identifier-of-object-within-context). This particular scheme has the disadvantage that the form and length of identifiers used within heterogeneous domains may vary so widely that it may be awkward or inefficient for applications to be prepared to deal with them. It can also have the disadvantage that host computer boundaries are explicitly visible.

The alternative is to develop a standard, uniform global identifier form and space for all resources and some way to partition this global space among the local domains, which then map their local identifiers to these global identifiers. Binding of local identifiers to global identifiers can be permanent or temporary. This mechanism immediately introduces a level of indirection with some of the advantages desired: local identifiers can be chosen as most appropriate for their local language or operating system environment, several local identifiers can be mapped to the same global identifier or vice versa, and the global identifier can be reassigned if objects are relocated.

In order to outline the issues associated with creation of a uniform, unique, machine-oriented, global, identifier space, we now describe a scheme usable with the Model of Chapter 2. We call these entities *object-identifiers*. In review, the Model has the following properties:

- Processes are the fundamental communicating objects.
- All objects or resources are managed by server processes.
- Resources are created, manipulated, and destroyed by customer processes sending request messages to server processes and in turn receiving replies.

These properties are reflected in the identification scheme.

We envision the standard form for DOS object-identifiers as being defined by the Service-Support sublayer of the DOS [Section 2.4.4, Watson 80b, Fletcher 80] as a special data type. Object-identifiers can be unstructured or structured. In order to allow distributed generation, requires structured object-identifiers. It seems natural to allow each (possibly generic) server to generate object-identifiers for the objects it serves. This is allowed if object-identifiers have a structure with two components *server-identifier, unique-local-identifier*. To provide uniform identifiers, each of these components has a standard structure, which could be as simple as specifying a maximum variable length. We now discuss how each of these identifier components can be obtained, first the unique-local-identifier.

Each object type is represented at the interface by a data structure (usually abstract). A given server implements this structure as some real structure. A particular object exists as an instance of one of these real structures located at a particular place. This object, in the general heterogeneous case, will have a *local-implementation-identifier* unique within the local domain of the server. It is the responsibility of the server to create unique-local-identifiers according to the standard form, and to bind them to its local-implementation-identifiers: The idea is shown in figure 9-3. The server generates unique-local-identifiers in any convenient way, subject only to the constraints of the standard, such as a maximum length. Because different implementations of servers for the same type of object may desire to use different unique-local-identifier forms, it is best if holders of a global identifier do not attach meaning to them.

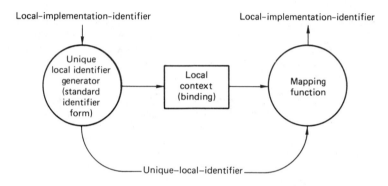

Figure 9-3: Generating and mapping unique-local-identifiers from/to
local-implementation-identifiers

If there are several copies of an object, each instance has a unique local-implementation-identifier within the context of its server and location. When an object is relocated it gets a new local-implementation-identifier, and its implementation representation may change. However, in either of the two cases above, the multiple copies of an object or the relocated object, the object can still have the same object-identifier if the same server is involved. If the object can be relocated across servers, then additional constraints are imposed on identifier form and binding. Now we discuss how the server-identifier is obtained.

The IPC layer has to have identifiers for all processes in order to perform its message delivery service. We will call this IPC name an *address*. An address is bound to an object by routing context. Other terms have been used for this level of name such as *port*, *socket*, and *mail box*. Addresses are discussed further later. It is useful for processes to have more than one address, enabling parallel error and flow controlled conversations between two processes, partitioning of services, or other purposes (figure 9-4). It is also useful to associate one identifier (logical-address) with several physical processes (process local-implementation-identifiers) so that services can be relocated, or forms of generic services can be created where any of several processes can provide the same logically equivalent service. Figure 9-5 illustrates the above. The IPC or higher levels must map this name to a specific server's. This mapping can take place at the origin to a specific hierarchical address or be distributed [McQuillan 78b].

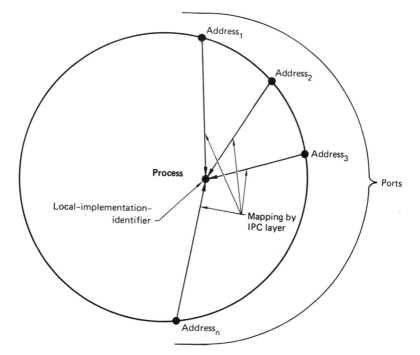

Figure 9-4: A process with multiple addresses or ports

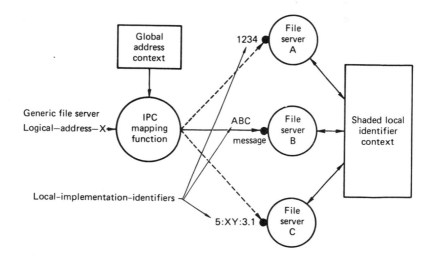

Figure 9-5: Generic file servers, IPC mapping routes address X to one instance (ABC)

Given origin and destination addresses and a message, one of the IPC layer services is to find a path or *route* from origin address to destination address along which to move the message as shown in figure 9-6. One or more routes (for robustness preferably the latter) may exist. The IPC layer maps addresses to routes. The last step in the routing maps an address to a process's local-implementation-identifier. Processes obtain their addresses from a process server. A process server either obtains addresses from the IPC service, if they are unstructured, or it may be able to construct them, if they are structured according to known rules. All process servers must form addresses according to global system rules. A process server binds addresses to process local-implementation-identifiers by setting routing tables as appropriate. If a service is relocated, the process server can rebind the address to a new process local-implementation-identifier and make appropriate changes to other routing tables. The mechanism to set routing tables would involve a routing table server, and is intimately tied to strategies for routing [Chapter 6, McQuillan 77,78a], and is a topic outside this section.

If an address is bound to many generic server processes simultaneously, the IPC routing algorithm will deliver messages to one, based on appropriate internal criteria, such as the "closest." If the generic server supports sessions, then future messages of the session must be directed to the instance first reached. Such servers would return a specific address as part of their request/reply protocol.

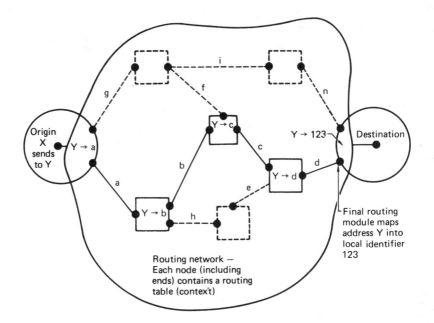

Figure 9-6: Router maps address *Y* to route *abcd* to local-implementation-identifier for object

It seems reasonable to use an address of a server as the server-identifier in the object-identifiers needed for its objects. Complete object-identifier mapping is shown in figure 9-7. The identifier form that results *address, unique-local-identifier* either provides or supports many of the identification goals listed earlier:

- For transaction oriented applications, the address needed to send a request can be directly obtained from the object-identifier or can be known in some a priori way. Dynamic binding supported by caching mechanisms may be required also.

- It is machine-oriented and can be used easily to create human-oriented identification mechanisms at higher levels.

- Identifiers can be generated in a distributed way.

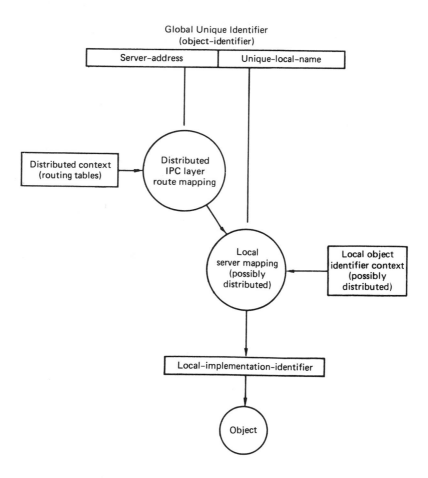

Figure 9-7: Mapping of unique global name (object identifier)

- A global space of uniquely named objects is created.

- With appropriate constraints on unique-local-identifiers and use of server logical-address, it directly supports object relocation and provides for generic servers and multiple copies. (Context in the IPC layer and in the servers may have to be changed.)

- If a new type of resource is constructed using existing ones as components, there is no identifier conflict and the inclusion of server addresses in the component identifiers can be directly useful to the new server.

The remaining goals can be achieved with a higher level identification mechanism such as that described below. It should be pointed out that processes have in effect two forms of identifiers associated with them, object-identifiers used as parameters in requests for services applied to them (the address part being the address of a process server) and addresses used to send them messages in regard to services performed by them. Let us now see how this identifier form can be used with protection mechanisms.

Two basic access control mechanisms are capability and access list control [Jones 78a, Chapter 10]. A *capability*, in the most general sense, is just a trusted identifier (object-identifier) with additional redundancy for protection. Possession of a capability is sole proof of right of access, with the modes of access associated with that capability [Dennis 66, Denning 76, Fabry 74]. An *access list* control mechanism requires, in addition to the object identifier, another trusted identifier representing the accessing *principal*, the entity with which access rights are associated. This trusted identifier might be a password, address, or other identifier form. Both mechanisms share in common the need to trust that an identifier, the capability in the former, and the trusted identifier in the latter, cannot be forged or stolen and then be used. Encryption or other use of redundancy and assumptions about what components (i.e. local operating systems, physical security and communications) can be trusted form the basis for deciding which approach to use and how to create a workable system [Watson 78]. Secure passing of capabilities in a DOS is discussed in [Donnelley 80, Nessett 80]. Authenticating that humans or processes are who they claim to be or are acting on behalf of whom they claim are topics not fully understood in distributed systems. Some of the issues are covered in [Section 9.3, Kent 77, Needham 78, Popek 78] and the last references above. The object-identifier in a system being designed at the Lawrence Livermore National Laboratory (LLNL) is a capability and has the form shown in figure 9-8. It consists of the following fields:

- The *address* is the address of the server that manages the resource. Often a process uses the address in one of the capabilities in a request message to determine where to send the request.

- The *properties* are a set of standard bits and fields that indicate to a customer process the resource type, access mode, resource lifetime, security level, etc. It is state information included in the capability to reduce messages to the server.

- The unique-local-identifier is used by the server to identify and locate the specific resource designated, and possibly for other server-dependent purposes.

- The redundancy, if present, guards the unique-local-identifier part of the capability against forgery. Encryption can also be used for this purpose [Chaum 78, Needham 79a,b].

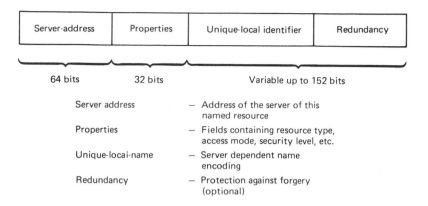

Server-address	Properties	Unique-local identifier	Redundancy

64 bits	32 bits	Variable up to 152 bits

Server address	— Address of the server of this named resource
Properties	— Fields containing resource type, access mode, security level, etc.
Unique-local-name	— Server dependent name encoding
Redundancy	— Protection against forgery (optional)

Figure 9-8: LLL standard capability form as example machine oriented identifier

An important need in all identification systems, whether global or local, is to be able to create unique identifiers in the face of crashes that can cause loss of identifier generator state information. One common mechanism is to use a clock guaranteed to continue operating across failures and that will not recycle during the period within which the needed identifiers must be unique [Garlick 77]. In exchange for the simplicity of this mechanism one may require rather long identifiers, depending on the granularity of clock interval needed. An alternative mechanism that can yield shorter identifiers, but increased complexity, can be built using two or more levels of storage or more than one storage device. One approach is to structure the identifier in a hierarchical fashion with one field for each level. One field normally is associated with main memory. A counter is kept on each level containing the highest value of the associated field assigned. The current values of these fields are cached in main memory. When a lower level field is about to cycle or the associated device crashes, the next higher level counter is incremented and lower levels are reset. Using the stable storage concept of Chapter 11, two levels of storage are sufficient for a safe efficient generator mechanism.

9.4. Human-oriented names

Higher-level naming contexts are required to meet the needs of human users for their own local mnemonic names, and to assist them in organizing, relating, and sharing objects. Higher-level names also can be used to provide for multiple copies and to support object relocation [Livesey 79]. Higher-level naming conventions and context can be embedded explicitly within particular applications or be supported by special name servers. Mapping from a high-level name to a machine-oriented identifier can be through explicit context of (high-level, machine-oriented) identifier pairs or implicitly by having some algorithmic or other relationship between the structures of the identifiers. An example of a higher level naming mechanism embedded in a distributed application is the mechanism used in the ARPANET mail service, where the name mapping takes place in several steps. For example, when a mail item is sent to the name DWATSON@BBN, the address of a mail server on a BBN computer is obtained from a table. The structured mail message is sent to this address. This service in turn will forward the message to an equivalent service on the specific BBN machine identified BBNB where the name DWATSON is mapped to the standard name of the file where my mail is stored.

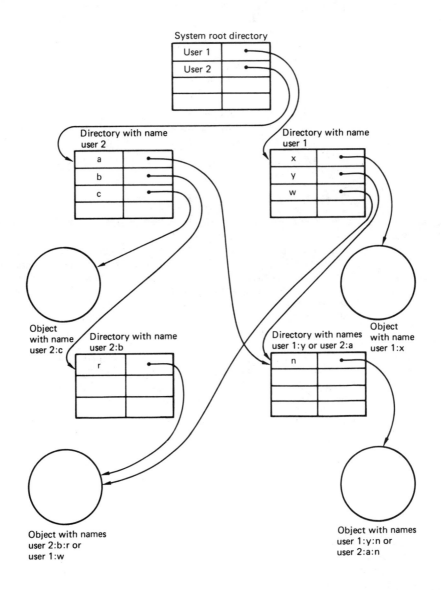

Figure 9-9: Naming graph with shared multiply named objects

One view of database management systems is that their main function is to provide a general purpose higher-level naming mechanism. Although they usually store object representations and values, the items stored could just be the object-identifiers described above. The NSW uses database management techniques to provide human-oriented names [Millstein 77]. The design of database management systems allowing servers and databases to be distributed is a special domain in its own right beyond the scope of this section [Chapter 13, Bernstein 79].

Another mechanism used to create higher-level names is a *naming graph* implemented with *directories or catalogs.* These latter, in current operating systems, generally only contain names for files, but they can just as well be generalized to contain names for any resource. Capabilities, object-identifiers, or other form of identifier for any type of resource can be placed in a directory and given a mnemonic name. Since capabilities to directories can themselves be placed in directories, the directories constitute a naming graph as shown in figure 9-9.

The leaves of the naming graph are names of resources other than directories; the non-leaf nodes are directories. The *path-name* of a resource is the sequence of branches (directory entries) traversed from the root to a node. A given resource may be reachable by several paths thus allowing users to share resources, each being able to specify his own path name. Directories could be extended to maintain machine-oriented names for multiple copies of a resource [Reed 77]. Directories are managed by directory servers. Directory servers can be simple or complex. For example, in its simplest form, a directory server would have primitives for storing pairs (mnemonic name, machine-oriented-name) and retrieving machine-oriented names given a mnemonic name from named directories. Utility or other applications programs would be responsible for tracing down a naming graph according to a pathname to obtain the machine-oriented names at the leaves. It would also be possible to provide this latter service in a directory server.

One could also envision extending the directory service to provide message forwarding to processes identified by path-names. [Livesey 79, Reed 77] have proposed incorporating this service within the IPC layer. Saltzer gives a detailed discussion of the design issues associated with naming graph mechanisms [Saltzer 78a]. [Donnelley 80] discusses the relationship of directory and protection mechanisms.

Additional implementation and efficiency issues are introduced when there are multiple directory servers and the individual directories and other resources in a particular naming graph can be distributed [Thomas 78]. Tracing a path-name through a distributed naming graph may require exchanges of many messages. [Thomas 78] proposes mechanisms that attempt to create optimum location for directories, files and processes. This is just one example of the general issue of optimal, global location of resources when a particular object contains many other objects as components [Saltzer 78b]. The solution is likely to involve caching strategies, either explicitly under user control or automatically handled by servers or the IPC service. Until this problem area is better understood, at least in the case of directories, we believe that one should proceed slowly by only providing a simple directory server and leaving object and directory location and object-identifier caching as a user visible task.

Mapping of human-oriented names to object-identifiers is shown in figure 9-10. Separating machine-oriented identification (the object-identifier) and human-oriented naming allows:

- Servers, other than human-oriented name servers, to only have to deal with object-identifiers, and

- Several forms of application dependent and general purpose higher-level name services to be provided.

Ease of use or efficiency might be achieved for some applications and services if some servers other than name servers also implemented higher-level naming context, although this is not logically required [Fletcher 80].

9.5. Addresses and routing

The concepts of addressing and routing are introduced here in the context of the IPC layer, but they can exist at higher levels as well, using related mechanisms. Two of the services offered by the IPC layer are to provide a global identifier space of unique process addresses and to provide whatever mechanism is required to route information from one address to another. Addressing and routing are intimately related because routing is the level of identifier mapping that allows actual access to processes. There are two main design issues, the size of the address space and the structure of an address. The choice of an address structure has a significant impact on how addresses are mapped into routes, the size of the maps required at a particular node, whether the mapping can be distributed, and ease of network extension or reconfiguration [Shoch 78a, McQuillan 78a, Sunshine 77a,b]. Having a large enough address space is important in achieving a transaction oriented design as discussed later.

There are two forms of addresses in common use, single level or *flat*, and *hierarchical*. (Another form of address which explicitly specifies the route, a *source* address, has also been proposed as

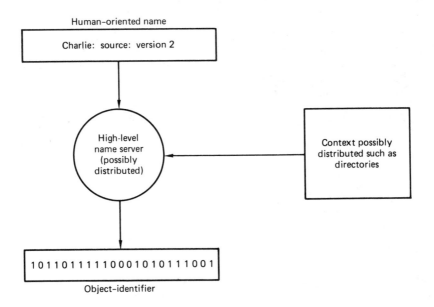

Figure 9-10: A high-level name server maps human-oriented names into a machine-oriented name

being useful in internetworking and in network extensibility [Cerf 78b, Sunshine 77a,b].) With flat addresses, every routing node must maintain context to map all possible addresses. Therefore, potentially large routing tables or contexts must be provided at every routing node. If processes can be relocated without restriction or generic servers are constructed of component processes that can be located anywhere in the network environment, then flat addressing is required. Flat addresses may also be mapped into hierarchical addresses at the origin. The amount of context required at the origin can be reduced by a variety of techniques such as caching and broadcast searching when the cache fails [McQuillan 78b]. Higher level system design is often simplified if the ease of relocation offered by flat addresses is provided. Flat addresses are particularly attractive in environments supporting an efficient broadcast service. Flat addresses can be generated in a distributed manner by partitioning the address space.

Hierarchical addresses, because of information prebound in their structure, require less address-to-route context to be stored at each routing node. For this reason hierarchical addresses are normally used in mesh network environments. A hierarchical address consists of concantenated fields defining subtrees (i.e. network, cluster, host, process). That is, the address of a process reflects the hierarchical logical geometry of the network. Hierarchical addressing is illustrated in figure 9-11 and works as follows. The further away the destination is, in terms of the chosen hierarchy, the sooner the left-to-right parse is stopped. A node's routing algorithm maps an address field's value into the name of one of the node's outbound links or indicates that the next field should be treated with a further map. The decision process is repeated until successful or unsuccessful completion is indicated. This means that every routing node need not store information about every potential individual destination. Every branch down the hierarchical address tree could contain a different number of levels and a different fan-out at each level, i.e., fields within the address are not necessarily uniform in number or size in different subtrees. Hierarchical addressing can cause routing inefficiencies if a partition of the logical tree is geographically dispersed, because routing decisions may route all traffic for that partition to the same place even though the next decision may route packets within the partition to widely separated points [Shoch 78]. Within the hierarchical framework, one can provide for generic services and process relocation. A portion of the address space, characterized by a standard value for the leftmost bits, is set aside for this purpose. The routing tables in each node of the network then point to the nearest "representative" of a generic service or must be updated when an address is rebound to another process. Other IPC implementation choices can provide for logical addresses by using two levels of global addresses within the IPC level, flat and hierarchical, and map from flat addresses to hierarchical addresses at the origin. Various hybrid combinations are possible as discussed in [McQuillan 78b]. Routing is of course simplified with interconnection technologies such as broadcast bus, ring, etc. Routing is a special topic in its own right and is discussed further in [Section 6.3].

The above discussion introduced addressing and routing in the context of the IPC layer of the Model. In general it is important to restate that these functions can exist at any architecture level. An excellent example is reported by [Postel 79] where routing takes place at the application level for an internetwork electronic mail service. Postel discusses the identifier interactions and mapping between architecture levels. Routing can take place within the DOS layer, for example, when multiple processes are cooperating to provide a single service and the service has one logical-address. Name mapping in Naming Graphs (previous section) is another example.

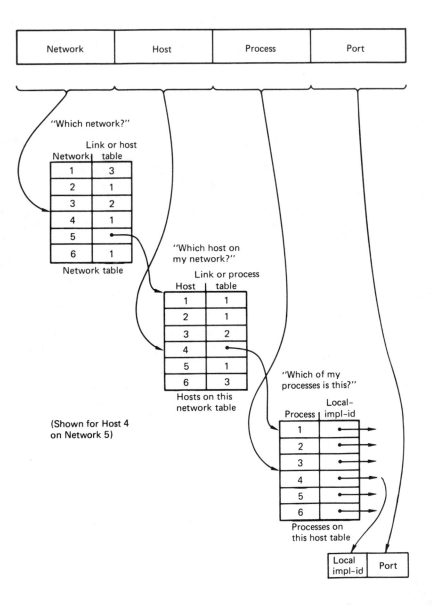

Figure 9-11: Relationship of hierarchical address and routing table structure

Another topic needing attention is the size of the address space. The network address space should be large enough that every process can have several addresses and none of the addresses has to be reused, even after the process is destroyed (assuming reasonable lifetime for the system). This feature is important as one element in achieving a transaction oriented system, because a process does not first have to send a message to a well known logger or connection establishment address, present a higher level name, and then be allocated a logical channel, socket, or other reusable address before entering a data transfer phase. There are also error control and security problems associated with using small reassignable addresses, in that old packets from a previous use of a given address may be in existence, or on recovery from a crash an address may be reassigned while one end of a previous association using that address still is sending to it.

The argument against large addresses, on the order of 64 bits, is that they increase the size of packet headers and thus may increase memory resources at intermediate and end nodes for packet and association state storage and increase the overhead on transmission bandwidth. With the rapid decrease in memory cost we believe that the first point is insignificant. The second point appears more serious, but a closer look at networking experience shows that there are two critical resources, the overall communication bandwidth available, and the time and resources required to create or process a packet and place it on or take it off the communication media. The latter often is the main limitation on throughput. Charging algorithms of public networks clearly recognize this situation by charging on a per packet basis. There is a relatively small overall incremental cost to sending additional bits, header or data, in a packet.

We believe the gain in flexibility for the system architecture, through use of larger address fields, are worth the incremental cost of increasing header size. This argument is particularly true for networks using high bandwidth links and is weaker when low speed links are used [Section 6.6]. In general, we agree with [Clark 78] that tradeoffs between increasing header size and complicating an application or protocol design or implementation favor using increased header information.

The pros and cons of fixed versus variable length addresses and headers revolve around tradeoffs between ease of extensibility and ease of implementation and packet processing. There is considerable controversy in this area. We believe that eventually variable length addressing will probably prevail, but as this is written the supporters of fixed length addresses tend to prevail.

One final topic needs discussion, the use of different address spaces at each level of IPC protocol. Each layer of IPC protocol defines a space of unique addresses for the entities that it connects with its abstract channels. Each pair of addresses (source, sink) at every level define a logical information channel (such channels could support a range of services depending on the protocol (i.e. datagram, virtual circuits, etc.). Providing for addressing, and thus channels, at each level of protocol is important because it allows:

- Channels at higher levels to be multiplexed on a single channel at a lower level for efficiency or other reasons; each higher level channel must have its own name,

- A single channel at a higher level to be multiplexed across many lower level channels for increased reliability or performance; the date elements for each higher level channel must be named because such splitting can cause out-of-sequence delivery, and

- Different protocols at a given level to use the same lower level protocol and be multiplexed on the same lower level channels.

For example, as mentioned in Section 9.7, a carriers X.25 virtual circuit (VC) tariff structure might make it more economical to set up a VC between a pair of hosts and then multiplex many end-to-end associations (simultaneously or sequentially) on that VC, than to use a separate VC for each association [Hertwick 78]. Many VC's in turn are multiplexed on a single link as shown in figure 9-12. Identifier multiplexing can also be generalized across the architecture at the DOS and Application levels as well.

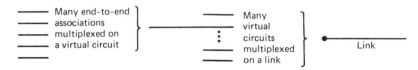

Figure 9-12: Example showing levels of protocol addressing
multiplexed on next lower level channel

It is also possible to multiplex protocols at one level on those at another without providing a separate address space in each [Cohen 79, Boggs 80]. [Cohen 79] points out that, while it is possible to merge layers in an implementation, the protocol and channel multiplexing flexibility inherent in a layered architecture is lost.

9.6. Conclusion

We have outlined characteristics and design goals for identification in a distributed operating system. We then presented an example identification system that met many of these goals, elaborating design issues as we proceeded. This identification scheme consisted of:

- Human-oriented name servers that provided for mnemonic names, sharing and organization of objects, and

- Unique, global machine-oriented identifiers structured as unique server addresses (supplied by the IPC service) and unique identifiers local to servers.

The human-oriented name service could be embedded in application processes or be provided by general purpose name servers using database management or directory techniques. The objects stored by these servers are the unique, global, machine-oriented identifiers (object-identifiers), for any type of resource. Other servers need only concern themselves with object-identifiers. We showed how binding would be handled between identifiers from heterogeneous identification domains and how naming at the Application, DOS Kernel/IPC layers interact.

We also discussed how an identifier generator could create unique identifiers in the face of system crashes and interactions between addressing and routing. It was pointed out that addressing and routing can occur at any level of the architecture.

We believe that the area of identification system design is an area with many open questions. One important need is to unify the many existing concepts and mechanisms. Another is to develop appropriate lower level hardware/firmware to support the desirable dynamic binding in an efficient manner.

Chapter 10. Protection

If a number of users employ the same computer system, they may need protection against one another. They could need protection against malicious attempts of one user to use objects or parts of the system which belong to another or against accidents which result in one user's program interfering with parts of the system belonging to another.

Protection can be applied to data, program, the use of computer power, the use of storage space, storage media or peripherals. Protection can therefore be described as control of *access* to all these things.

The techniques used to protect one user against another's malicious attempts must also be able to protect a user against hardware and software faults, which could have similar effects. Accidental software errors could equally well have been the results of malicious attempts; protection again malicious actions, since they are designed to cause trouble, is more difficult than protection against bugs. So, even if we chose to assume that all our users are blameless, have the same interests at heart and will never interfere with one another, the protection methods to be described would still have some useful function.

10.1. Basic protection needs

Some part of the system, which is concerned with access control, must be able to identify the users and the processes which are working on their behalf. Users can identify themselves, so the system just has to verify their identity. Identity verification by password, by physical keys such as a magnetic striped card or by personal characteristics such as a dynamic signature is a broad subject that will not be treated here. We shall be concerned, however, with methods by which one part of the system transfers its knowledge of the identity of the user to another. This is part of the process of *authentication* of messages.

We spoke already about parts of the system which *belong* to one user. In writing this, we were beginning to assume a protection model. Access control must follow rigid rules and these use such concepts as *ownership* or *classification of level of security of data* or *protection domains*. To describe a protection system we must describe in detail the model which it is using.

In one of the simplest models, each program or piece of data has an owner--a single user in a special relationship to this object which allows him to change other's rights of access to it. In yet another commonly used model, each piece of data or program is classified at a certain level of secrecy and each user has clearance to access from a certain level of secrecy downwards.

The first of these models, often called *discretionary access*, allows enormous freedom in the patterns of access which can be set up. The effect of this is to make it almost impossible to determine the pattern of access which is reached after many changes have been made.

The second of these models follows the military classification concept, and raises the problem of how to classify any newly-created objects. The only safe rule is to give it the highest classification of any of the material used in its production. This results in a gradual upward migration of security level so there have to be methods of reducing the classification of material by human decision.

The basic needs of a protection system are:

(a)   to define the model in such a way that the users can understand it and its implications for their particular protection requirements.

(b)   to implement the model.

(c)   to prove that the model implemented coincides with the model defined.

Such is the difficulty of the subject that probably none of these steps has yet been carried out in a satisfactory manner. The only hope of doing so is to use a very simple model indeed. For example, if the users are isolated from each other and cannot use the system to interact with one another, the definition of access control is easy and it may then be possible to achieve and prove a correct implementation.

The protection model has two aspects, static and dynamic. The static model describes the rights of access of users to objects in the system. The dynamic model shows how these rights of access can be changed by the users. This gives rise to further needs in the protection systems, the need to review the access rights which exist and the need to withdraw or revoke access rights. The latter may or may not be possible.

10.1.1. Protection in distributed systems

If we have a good protection model and the method of implementing it for a non-distributed system, we might try to apply this to a distributed system by setting up a distributed access control mechanism. There are probably better ways to design distributed systems. For example, a user may have an intelligent terminal to which only he has access. His sharing with other users might be confined to the storage and retrieval of data and programs as files. In this kind of distributed system, the *file servers* implement the access control. Later we shall describe authentication servers and servers which *certify* digital signatures. By keeping the functions of these servers relatively simple, we have some chance of understanding the protection model and being sure that it has been implemented correctly.

We shall find that this method of design removes some of the possibilities for clever protection features which have been provided in monolithic systems. It is a worthwhile sacrifice if it provides better protection.

The distributed system which is made of parts separated by some distance – a geographically distributed system – gives rise to the additional need to protect the communication sub-system. For practical purposes, any communication system that is not in a single, physically isolated enclave, can be regarded as open to *line tapping*, the reading of data.

A threat which is less easy to evaluate is *active line tapping* which means the changing of data on the line. Some scenarios for attack on communication systems require, as figure 10-1 shows, a processor to read signals coming in on the line and, from them, construct new signals which go onwards to the destination. This is extremely difficult to do, without being detected. Nevertheless, the possibility of an active line tap must be considered in analyzing the security of a communication system.

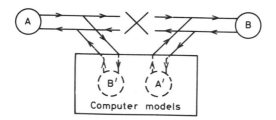

Figure 10-1: Active line tap

The technique for protecting the communication system against such malicious attempts is cryptography. Cryptographic techniques are used not only for protecting the secrecy of communications (which also prevents active line taps) but also for *authenticating* messages. Authentication means assuring the receiver that the message came from the reputed source and that it travelled to him without being modified. Privacy and authentication are complementary functions. We shall find that authentication has unexpected shades of meaning and that new technology is needed to achieve all that may be required.

For geographically distributed networks, in which the communication system is not fundamentally secure, cryptography can be considered as a piece of basic technology out of which the total protection system is built. Since cryptography is relatively unfamiliar and has been the subject of some basic new developments in the last few years, a large part of these lectures will be concerned with the application of cryptography to privacy and authentication. In the final part of these lectures we shall return again to the wider subject of protection and access control and see how cryptographic techniques can be used to develop control methods when we move from monolithic to distributed systems.

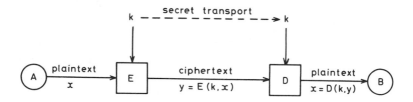

Figure 10-2: A single-key cipher system

10.2. Single key cryptography and the data encryption standard

Figure 10-2 shows the traditional view of a cryptographic system and introduces the notation which we shall use.

The encipherment function E must be matched to an inverse decipherment function D to restore the plaintext. The secrecy of the system cannot lie in these functions alone, because if they became known, any secrecy would be lost and could only be restored by finding new pairs of functions. For this reason, each function has an additional variable k which is known as the *key*. An important principle is that the nature of the functions E and D may be known to the enemy but this must not enable him to circumvent the secrecy unless he also knows the value of k.

For definiteness let us think of the cipher system as the Data Encryption Standard. This was developed by IBM and adopted for US non-classified Government use and has now taken on the function of a de-facto standard. For this cipher system, the plaintext x is a sixty-four digit binary number and so is the ciphertext. Encipherment associates each of the 2^{64} possible values of x with a different one of the 2^{64} possible values of y. It follows that D and E are mutually inverse functions in whichever order they are applied. Our figure implies that $D(k,E(k,x)) = x$ and it is also true that $E(k,D(k,x)) = x$ for all values of x in the 64 bit domain. This commutative property would not have been true if the ciphertext had contained more than 64 bits. Expansion of the message in the ciphertext is not usual in ciphers and is inconvenient, but there will be some examples of expansion among public key cipher systems.

Knowledge of y alone cannot give any information about x or k unless something is known about the plaintext x. This follows because each value of y can be produced by some value of x. If there is a stream of blocks forming the plaintext x which have some known statistical property then, given sufficient values of the corresponding stream y, it is possible, in principle, to discover the value of k. The amount of text needed was calculated by C. Shannon [Shannon 49] and is known as the *unicity distance*. The theory which gives this value does not correspond to practical crypto-analysis because it assumes unlimited computing power.

For example, suppose the plaintext is known to consist of English text in an 8 bit character code. If the redundancy of English text is such that each 8 character block carries 12 bits of information (for example) then there are only 4,096 different valid forms of the plaintext block x. Suppose, for the present, that the key k has 128 bits. If a single block of 8 characters of ciphertext is known, and we ran through all values of the key trying to see whether the corresponding plaintext produced by the function D was valid, the probability of success for each value k would be 4096 divided by 2^{64} that is 2^{-52}. Consequently, of the 2^{128} values of k, 2^{76} would give valid plaintext values.

If we had two consecutive blocks of ciphertext to work on, the single value of k would produce a pair of successive plaintext blocks which were valid with probability 2^{-104} and a number of keys which passed the test would be 2^{24}. Each time a block is added, the number of remaining keys is reduced by the factor 2^{52}. Consequently, after the third block has been used, a unique key will have been found. Figure 10-3 shows this process. We can see that the unicity distance depends on the size of key and the amount of redundancy in the plaintext. We can also see that in this case the method of calculation which reveals the correct value of key by *key exhaustion* is beyond the capability of present day computing power.

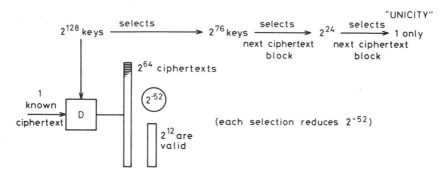

Figure 10-3: Testing and selection of keys – unicity

Unicity distance is a measure of the unconditional strength of cipher algorithm, the strength it would have if the enemy had unlimited computing power. In almost all practical cases the unicity distance is so short that this is not a practical way to judge the strength of the cipher algorithm. We have to consider methods by which ciphers could be broken with a practical amount of computing power.

For this purpose there are no certain guides. We have to try every kind of trick and every form of analysis we can devise and see whether the cipher system resists it.

10.2.1. Measuring the strength of a cipher system

One crude measure of the strength of a cipher system is the size of its key. If the key is small enough, then the criterion of unconditional security can be applied. For example, with a 10 bit key, the key can be found in only 1024 trials if the cipher text exceeds the unicity distance. Most commercially available cipher systems employ very long keys to avoid this.

If the key is long enough to resist this attack, we are involved with crypto-analysis in its more usual form, a collection of tricks and devices which is typically successful in breaking all but the most carefully devised cipher systems. Given that we have a full armory of cryptanalytic techniques, we can define the strength of a cipher system in terms of the kinds of data that a cryptanalyst needs to work successfully. The limit known as the unicity distance is far too stringent for this purpose except for the simplest of ciphers. For example, with monoalphabetic substitution of English text, the unicity distance has been estimated as about 30 characters and the more skillful amateur cryptanalysts who habitually solve these problems can work almost down to this limit. For the complex ciphers we shall be dealing with there is no possibility of achieving such a remarkable degree of success.

The least that a cryptanalyst can work with is a reasonable quantity of ciphertext and some accurate statistics of the plaintext. For practical cipher systems, the quantity of ciphertext needed is quite large.

When testing a cipher system to validate its strength we need to apply a stronger attack than the enemy can use and therefore we assume a greater degree of knowledge. The usual assumption is that corresponding sequences of plaintext and ciphertext are available. This *known plain text* criterion is realistic for a widely used cipher.

It is normally accepted that a cipher system is satisfactory if it can resist a cryptanalytic attack under the following conditions:

(a) the encipherment and decipherment functions are known.

(b) a substantial quantity of corresponding plaintext and ciphertext is given.

There is a further, even more stringent, criterion that is sometimes applied, called *chosen plaintext*. According to this criterion, the cipher should remain secure when, in addition to the above, the ciphertext is given to the cryptanalyst for a stream of plaintext which he chooses. This situation could arise if the enemy had captured an encipherment machine with the key installed in it, was unable to read the key from the machine, but could run the machine to encipher any stream of plaintext he desired. (There is a corresponding criterion which could be called *chosen cipher text*, which in some cases would be a different criterion for the strength of the cipher.)

All worthwhile ciphers are now expected to meet the known plaintext criterion. A cipher system proposed for very wide use such as the data encryption standard would be expected to resist also the chosen plaintext and chosen ciphertext attacks.

10.2.2. The data encryption standard

The data encryption standard algorithm is fully described in the Federal Information Processing Standards Publication No. 46. It is a block cipher, operating on 64 bits to produce a 64 bit cipher text and employing a 56 bit key. It is designed for implementation by LSI logic, and is rather inconvenient to carry out by a program in a general purpose computer. We propose neither to describe the cipher in detail nor to examine it from a cryptanalytic viewpoint. Within a space of several lectures it would only be possible to treat elementary methods of cryptanalysis as applied to relatively simple ciphers. It is perhaps sufficient to know that the DES has been validated by experts, but unfortunate that the experts are unable to describe their methods for reasons of national security.

The lack of public knowledge of the criteria employed by the specialists has come under criticism but seems to be unavoidable. The chief remaining criticism is the size of the DES key [Diffie 77]. By building fast LSI chips for testing keys under the known plaintext criterion, it would be feasible to find a key in one day using a machine operated in parallel with one million chips. See figure 10-4. The cost of the machine has been variously estimated at figures between 20 million dollars and 200 million dollars. There is no doubt that it is within the capacity of the governments of advanced nations to build such a machine. Nevertheless, it leaves the cipher sufficiently secure for all but the most extremely sensitive commercial applications.

Greater strength can be obtained by enciphering twice with two different keys. This is not as strong as a key of 112 bits would be with known plaintext because, if 2^{57} blocks of data could be stored and sorted into sequence, it could be broken. The plaintext is enciphered with all 2^{56} keys and the ciphertext is deciphered with all the keys, then the resultant values, still linked with their key numbers, are sorted into sequence. If two equal values are found, the pair of keys they are linked to will take the plaintext into the ciphertext and are a possible solution of the cryptanalysis problem. There will be about 2^{48} such matches. For each of these a second plain/cipher pair is

2^{56} different keys = 7.10^{16} approximately

one DAY = 8.10^4 seconds, approximately

Hence : to find a key in less than one day requires 10^{12} tests per second

The proposal :
$\begin{cases} \text{A chip is made which tests a key in 1 microsecond} \\ \\ \text{One million such chips are set to work in parallel} \end{cases}$

Estimated cost :   \$ 20,000,000   to   \$ 200,000,000

Figure 10-4: The DES-breaking machine

used to find the correct key-pair. The cost of doing this with present day technology is enormously greater than the key exhaustion machine and therefore double encipherment probably meets all conceivable requirements. However, double encipherment as an additional strength has not been publicly validated by the experts.

There has been some expert discussion of triple keying and triple encipherment with two keys and the weaknesses of the latter. Although these are good intellectual exercises, they have moved far beyond the grounds of feasible computation. They only become valid considerations when large advances in computing and storage technology are assumed.

It may be necessary to introduce an improved data encryption standard in ten or twenty years to allow for improved technology. This could use a 64 bit block and a 112 or 128 bit key. Long-term standardisation work for encipherment should take account of the future need for a longer key.

Figures 10-5 and 10-6 show how the data encryption algorithm builds up its strength by multiple operations using a highly non-linear function which depends on the key. It would be easy to devise a new version of the algorithm with a longer key.

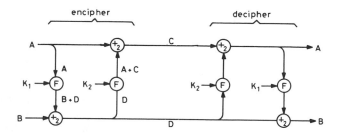

Figure 10-5: A very weak cipher with two rounds of the DES type

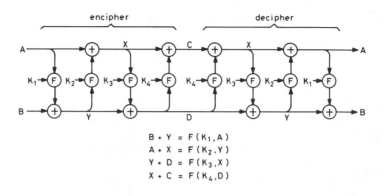

$$B + Y = F(K_1, A)$$
$$A + X = F(K_2, Y)$$
$$Y + D = F(K_3, X)$$
$$X + C = F(K_4, D)$$

Figure 10-6: A weak cipher with four rounds of the DES type

10.2.3. Block and stream ciphers

Block ciphers like the DES are convenient for mathematical analysis and are proving to be highly adaptable for practical use. In the history of the development of ciphers, they are a little unusual. In order to be secure, block ciphers must operate on sufficiently large blocks. In the secure form they were not possible until the heavy computation involved in securely enciphering a block of this size became feasible. Most ciphers, particularly in recent years, have been stream ciphers designed to operate on a continuous stream of characters and to deliver each character without having to wait for other characters to make up a block. Figure 10-7 shows the basic form of a typical stream system. The special problem it has is the initial setting of the key stream generator and the transmission of that setting to the other end.

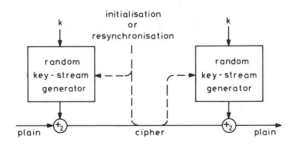

Figure 10-7: A typical stream cipher system

The data encryption standard algorithm can be used as a stream cipher by the feedback arrangement shown in figure 10-8. The two shift registers are both loaded with the cipher text stream while it is being transmitted and therefore should contain the same data. Hence the DES devices, which are both in encryption mode, produce the same output. The key stream which is added to the text is identical at each end.

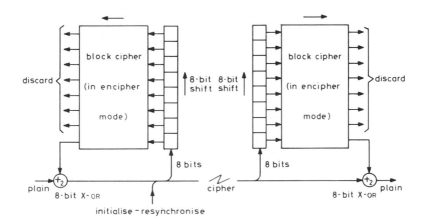

Figure 10-8: Cipher feedback (CFB) to produce a stream cipher system

The effect of the cipher feedback at the sender is that the transmitted text depends on both the initial setting used and also all the text transmitted to date. Nevertheless, an error on the line has only a temporary effect at the receiver, and in the case shown it alters nine octets. The system could be regarded as *self-synchronizing*. Any starting values could be used, and after eight octets have been transmitted the following octets would be correctly deciphered. It is desirable that the initial setting of the shift register at the sending end should be sufficiently random and not repeat itself in a predictable fashion.

Cipher feedback is particularly useful when the DES cipher is fitted into an existing system. Because each character is passed on by the encipherment unit as soon as it is received, this stream method of using the DES can often be regarded as *transparent* to the data it enciphers and deciphers. It has a speed disadvantage because it delivers only one octet for each operation of the DES algorithm.

10.2.4. Block chaining

If the individual blocks of a message are enciphered independently there are two dangers to security. The kind of redundancy which applies in computer-generated messages causes sections of messages to be relatively unchanged in form. For example, the headers of messages can be predicted with high probability. This means that certain blocks of a message may only carry effectively one or two bits of information. For these blocks, an analysis of the cipher text will soon solve what is effectively a simple substitution cipher.

If the format of the message is known to the enemy he may be able, without knowing the content of the message, nevertheless to change it in a useful way. For example, in a complex message which carries out a money transfer, only one or two blocks may be involved in specifying the amount of money involved. The enemy could be able, by substituting different values of these blocks, consistently to increase or decrease the money value without actually knowing what it is.

These tricks depend on the fact that blocks have been enciphered independently. By adopting a scheme which connects the blocks together during encipherment the tricks will be frustrated. This is known as block chaining. Figure 10-9 illustrates the recommended form of cipher block chaining. It employs feedback, but unlike the cipher feedback scheme described before, the data encryption algorithm is in the main path, not the feedback path. Encipherment at the sender is followed by decipherment at the receiver. Errors on the line, in this case, can affect two successive blocks.

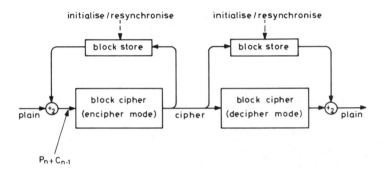

Figure 10-9: A recommended method for chaining blocks

The block chaining mechanism must be initialized by setting the value of the feedback/feed-forward registers. In the proposed standard, when a key is distributed to the communicating parties, an initializing variable (IV) associated with that key is also distributed. This same IV is used to load the registers at the beginning of every chain of blocks during the life of the associated key.

The scheme described thus far leaves one vulnerable feature. There is a tendency for messages to have beginnings which vary little. Until the variable part of the message is reached, the problem of block analysis which we described earlier remains. To overcome this, at the beginning of each chain, a serial number is transmitted and this *chain identifier* is incremented and not repeated throughout the life of the key and the corresponding IV. Although the chain identifier may be known to the enemy, since he does not know the IV, the value of stereotyped message beginnings is lost.

10.3. Application of a cipher system at different levels in the hierarchy

A communication subsystem is often hierarchical in structure. Distributed systems are built with the communication subsystem as a component. The structure of protocols which is formed above the communication system is also hierarchical in structure. Encipherment can be applied at any level. The different levels give it properties of convenience and security. We shall describe some of the effects of using encipherment at different levels in the hierarchy starting from the lowest level (the communication lines themselves) and working upwards.

(1) Line level. The communication lines are components of the communication subsystem and can be regarded, from the simplest viewpoint, as carriers of binary digits.

Encipherment can be applied to this binary stream. This is encipherment at the *line level*. A key is associated with each line, and there are as many keys as there are communication lines; not a difficult key distribution problem. Encipherment conceals everything that passes on the line and hence conceals the nature and amount of the traffic passing.

The main disadvantage of line level encipherment is that all information is handled in clear form while it is not on the lines. In some private systems this would be acceptable, but not in a public network where the employees of the telecommunication organization would have too easy an access to sensitive material.

(2) Link level. The link protocol operated on the communication lines handles information in a succession of frames. The contents of each frame can be enciphered, leaving the starting flag in the clear so that the frame structure is visible on the line. This is encipherment at the *link level*. It shares with the line level the property that key distribution is easy but that all the information is visible at any switching or multiplexing centre. The difference between these two otherwise similar applications of ciphers is that, using the frame structure, there is less obvious structure in the data being enciphered. For example, at the line level the cipher system might be occupied with enciphering zeros for much of its time. On the negative side, link-level encipherment reveals to a line-tapper the numbers and lengths of the frames being transferred.

(3) Communication sub-network end-to-end encipherment. Two users who establish a call or virtual call through the communication subsystem can employ encipherment to conceal all the data which they send through the network. The information carried by the subsystem then has its routing information (such as the headers of packets) in clear while the data carried on behalf of the users (such as the data field of packets) is enciphered.

Each two parties in communication must have a common key. Potentially, in a heavily used network this could result in a number of keys proportional to the square of the number of subscribers. Key distribution is a more difficult problem than it is at the line or link level. This application of a cipher system could be called the *packet level* or *circuit level* according to the type of subnet in use. The comparison between link level and packet level encipherment is shown in figures 10-10 and 10-11. Typically, in a packet system, encipherment would be applied immediately beyond the X.25 interface into the network. The users are then secure against both line-tappers and those who can tap the switching or multiplexing centres. For this increased security something must be paid.

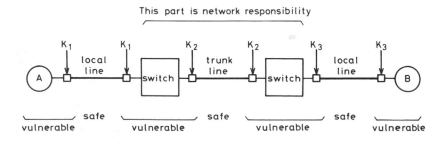

Figure 10-10: Link level encryption

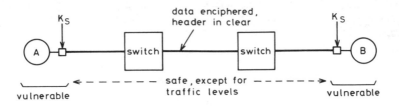

Figure 10-11: End-to-end encryption

The line tapper can now read the headers of packets or the routing information of circuits and discover the quantity and sources and destinations of messages. Thus traffic flow information is not longer concealed.

(4) Encipherment at the transport service. A transport protocol is designed to conceal the details of the communication subnet by giving them a uniform appearance to the user of the subnet. It will often be convenient to apply encipherment at this level. This gives a further degree of separation between users. A transport service may operate on behalf of many users through a single network port, such as an X.25 interface. Encipherment at the X.25 interface implies a protocol mechanism shared by these users and is a potential source of weakness unless its software is both faultness and protected from intrusion. Applying encipherment at the transport level means that individual users are responsible for their own encipherment. In most other respects it is similar to end-to-end encipherment over the communication subsystem.

(5) Encipherment at higher levels. Consider a higher level protocol such as a file transfer service. This could offer to provide the users with two different qualities of service, normal or enciphered. Alternatively, a program which employs the file transfer protocol could encipher its own files, having made an agreement with the receiver concerning the keys to be used and other aspects of the cipher system.

The higher the level at which encipherment is applied, the more information is given to the line-tapper by the *red tape* messages passed between the various protocols in use. On the other hand, there is more detailed protection between different users as the level of encipherment is pushed higher.

10.3.1. Key distribution

The exchange of keys for line or link level encipherment is a relatively straightforward, local affair. End-to-end, transport level or higher level encipherment requires keys to be established for each pair of users of the communication system. We can illustrate the principles by reference to a virtual call made through a packet network.

The duration of the virtual call can be called a *session*. The best security is obtained by establishing a new key for each session. A single mechanism must provide for establishing a session key whenever a call is made. In particular, if a call is broken any re-establishment will use a new session key. One convenient way to establish a session key is by means of a public key crypto-system, to be described below. But for the present, let us assume that we have available only the data encryption standard algorithm. In the case where the two subscribers A and B may not trust each other completely, they must have in common a trusted organisation which can help them with key distribution. Let us call this a *network security centre* or NSC.

Suppose that both A and B have already set up a secure communication path with the NSC. The keys employed will be called kA and kB. Each user must establish one such key to the security centre, which will give him a means for establishing session keys with any other user subscribing to the same security centre.

To distribute a session key the NSC generates the key ks and transmits it to each of the parties A and B. See figure 10-12. The keys as sent will be $E(kA, ks)$ and $E(kB, ks)$. In practice, the messages may contain other data, for example a serial number or time of day to ensure that live messages, not recordings of older ones, are being transmitted. Each of the communicating parties A and B is now able to decipher the message and retrieve the session key ks. At the end of the session, the session key is destroyed. No copy is kept by the NSC after it has distributed the key, because recovery from a failure would use a new session key.

There is a problem with this method as we have described it. Suppose that A initiates the call and requests a session key from the centre. If the message is passed as shown in figure 10-12 (a), the receiver of the call, B, must link up the message it receives from the centre with one it receives from A. This can be done by means of an identifier field, but it involves a procedure to cover the possibility of the messages arriving at B in two different sequences. It would generally be more convenient to carry the messages as shown in figure 10-12 (b), in which the NSC returns to the calling subscriber A both his own session key and the one destined for subscriber B. The cipher must resist known plaintext attack, for it gives A plaintext material in the form of ks with which to attack kB. In any case, subscriber A could have obtained such material by line-tap between the NSC and subscriber B. With this modified procedure, no *rendezvous* of messages is needed.

The scheme for session key distribution becomes slightly more complicated when there is a regional organization of Network Security Centres and the two communicating subscribers do

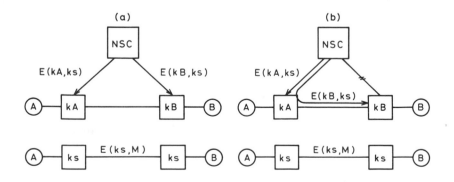

Figure 10-12: Distribution of a session key

not belong to the same centre. The choice between the two schemes shown in figure 10-12 is unclear. The scheme (b) which avoids a message rendezvous now requires a considerably longer communication path. International work on standards for encryption protocols has not yet approached this problem.

Work is proceeding to define standard protocols for setting up and operating secure links. The work has made most progress for the use of the Data Encryption Standard but it will also be applied to public key ciphers and to hybrid systems in which a public key cipher is used to establish a session key for the DES algorithm.

The protocols suitable for applying cryptography at one level of the network should be applicable, with only minor changes, to higher levels. The definition of standard protocols for secure communication must be adaptable in this way, so that encipherment is not limited to one level.

10.4. Public key cipher systems

The idea of encipherment with a public key was first described by Diffie and Hellman in 1976 [Diffie 76]. The first motivation for such a system was to simplify key distribution. A key that is public knowledge does not need the secret key distribution channel required by conventional cipher systems.

Figure 10-13 shows the principle of a public key cipher. Encipherment E and Decipherment D are functions defined by means of algorithms which are public. The essential difference from the conventional cipher is that the key used for encipherment, ke, is different from the key used for decipherment, kd. It is therefore at least possible that the encipherment key can be made public while the decipherment key is secret. This is strictly a one-way encipherment scheme. The receiver of information generates both keys, making only the encipherment key public.

If the system is to work, the encipherment and decipherment keys must be related. In the figure they are shown as being calculated by means of functions F and G from a starting key ks. In practice, these keys may each comprise more than one number. If the system is to have any chance of working securely, the function F must be a *one-way function*. This means that ke can

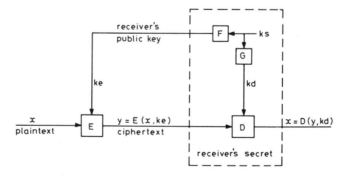

Cryptography using a public key

Figure 10-13: Cryptography using a public key

be calculated relatively easily from a knowledge of ks, but the inverse calculation, to find ks given ke is computationally infeasible. One-way functions are well known as a method for preserving the secrecy of passwords. Since a one-way function can be tabulated, in principle, and the inverse can be read from the inverted table, the function can be one-way only if its domain is large enough to preclude this as a feasible method of computing the inverse. It follows that ks and ke contain large numbers.

There is a condition that the functions D and E must satisfy. Since ke is public knowledge, for each value of this key the ciphertext y must be a one-way function of the plaintext. The function D must protect its key. Any one can generate ciphertext from chosen plaintext and these values can be applied to the function D. Regarded as though it were a conventional decipherment algorithm, it must resist a chosen plaintext attack.

These are necessary conditions for a satisfactory public key cryptosystem but they are not sufficient because the cipher system must resist a large variety of different forms of attack, some of them based on a knowledge of the special mathematical properties of the functions D and E. Because the two keys are different, it is feasible for the functions D and E to be the same and this is indeed true of the most famous of the public key ciphers, that due to Rivest, Shamir and Adleman [Rivest 78]. We shall refer to this cipher as the *RSA public key cipher*.

A public key cipher is especially fortunate if the range of values from which the cipher text y is chosen has the same size as the domain of x. Then the function E is a bijection and it follows that the transformation of a given value of y by the decipherment function D can be inverted by a subsequent operation of the function E. That is: $y = E(D(y))$ as well as $x = D(E(x))$. The significance of this will appear later.

In spite of the large domain of x, it might be possible to guess probable plaintext blocks, particularly if some part of the message format is fixed. The enemy could try large numbers of variants of *probable messages* to see which one generates the cipher text he has read from the line. For this reason, every plaintext block x should contain a random field of sufficient size to inhibit the guessing game. For example, 50 bits of random data would make the guessing

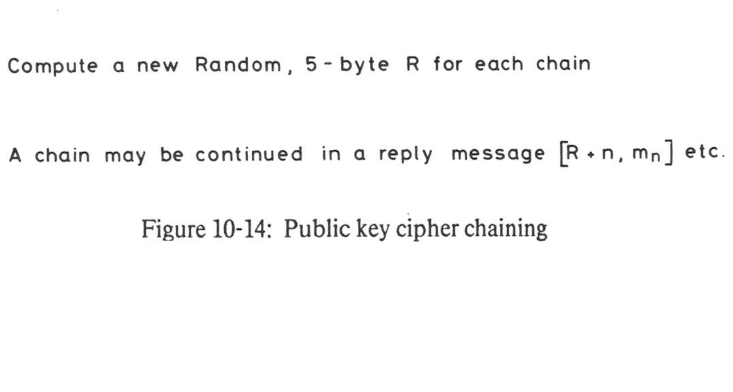

Divide message into 45 byte blocks $m_0 \; m_1 \; m_2 \; ----$

Concatenate Random number R with m_0 | R | m_0 |
$\xleftarrow{\hspace{2cm}}$
50 bytes

Send, enciphered, $[R, m_0]$, $[R+1, m_1]$, $[R+2, m_2] \; ----$

Compute a new Random, 5-byte R for each chain

A chain may be continued in a reply message $[R+n, m_n]$ etc.

Figure 10-14: Public key cipher chaining

method impracticable. Like any block cipher, a public key cipher should have its blocks chained together to prevent the construction of new messages by shuffling blocks of old ones. Cipher block chaining in the form used for the data encryption standard is not suitable because the message could still be interrupted and a different continuation added by the enemy without breaking the chaining rules. A satisfactory chaining method would be to use the random number field mentioned earlier, incrementing the value in this field by unity for each successive block in the chain. The same chaining number can be used in the return path to complete the authentication of the two correspondents. See figure 10-14.

10.4.1. The discrete exponential function

As a preparation for the description of the RSA cipher we shall give some information about the discrete exponential function and its one-way properties, and show how this can be used to exchange a secret key by means of public messages.

The arithmetic of integers can be made into a finite arithmetic if the result of an arithmetic operation is reduced to a residue, modulo p where p is a prime. For example, if $p = 17$ is the modulus, the result of $7 \cdot 5 = 35$ is reduced by subtracting multiples of 17 to give the value 1. The residue is a number lying in the range 0, 1, ... $p-1$. (It is the remainder left after division by the modulus p.) This *modulo p arithmetic* has a number of very convenient properties. It requires no negative numbers because $p-x$ will serve as the negative of x. Each number x other than 0 has a unique multiplicative inverse in this arithmetic system.

Given a number x in this arithmetic the result of multiplying n values of x together is the nth power of x, x^n, modulo p. It can also be regarded as the discrete exponential of n with base x. Thus if $y = x^n$ we can express the inverse as $n = \log y$ to base x. A useful property of this function, when p is large (for most values of p), is that y is a one-way function of n. The exponential is relatively easy to calculate but the logarithm, for large enough and suitable values of p, is infeasible to calculate. To calculate the exponential does not require n multiplications.

```
To  calculate   a 22          22 =   1 0 1 1 0    binary


Binary  exponent :                     1


    1        squared , x  a         1   a


    0        squared                a 2


    1        squared , x  a         a 4, a 5


    1        squared , x  a         a 10, a 11


    0        squared                a 22
```

Figure 10-15: Exponential calculation

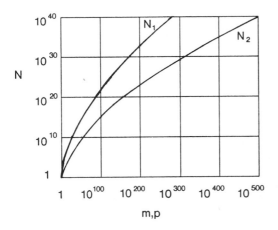

$N_1 = \exp\sqrt{2\ln(p)\cdot\ln[\ln(p)]}$ is the complexity of the discrete logarithm, modulo p.

$N_2 = \exp\sqrt{\ln(m)\cdot\ln[\ln(m)]}$ is the complexity of the factorisation of m.

Figure 10-16: The complexity of factorization and the discrete logarithm

By repeated squaring and multiplying, the number of multiplications needed to form the exponential is less than twice the number of bits in the binary representation of n. See figure 10-15. With large values of p, the computation is not easy, but the inverse, or logarithmic function is much harder to compute.

There is an easy method due to Pohlig and Hellman [Pohlig 78] for computing the logarithm if $p-1$ has only small factors. If we have a free choice, we should choose $p-1$ to be twice a prime number so that this alternative method of computation gives no advantage. Under these conditions the best method of calculating a logarithm requires a number of operations of the order

$$\exp\left([2\ln(p)\cdot\ln\ln(p)]^{\frac{1}{2}}\right)$$

The form of this function is shown in figure 10-16. If we are to have a complexity similar to that of the data encryption standard algorithm, which is 10^{17} operations, then p should be approximately a 220 bit number.

Given that the exponential is a one-way function, it can easily be used by two communicating parties X and Y to generate a secret key by means of public messages. The principle of this method is shown in figure 10-17. The two parties choose secret numbers x and y having already agreed on the modulus p and a base a.

The first step is for the parties to generate a^x and a^y respectively and exchange these values. Then X can form the expression $(a^y)^x$ and Y can form the expression $(a^x)^y$. Both these quantities are equal to a^{xy}, so they have a common secret key. The enemy who knows the values of p, a, a^x and a^y cannot form this quantity unless he is able to calculate finite logarithms.

Thus the one-way function and the commutative property of the exponential enable it to be used for "key distribution" by means of public messages. Note that the two participants, X and Y, must have a method for verifying each others identities.

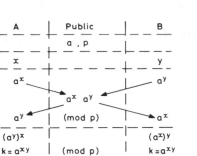

Figure 10-17: Exchange of a key by use of double exponentiation

10.4.2. The power function and its use in cryptography

A function we have been discussing, in the form $y = x^n$, can be regarded as a power function of x with constant n. It is a one-to-one mapping between the set of values $0, 1 \ldots p-1$, provided that n has no factors in common with $p-1$. For example, a prime value of n is always suitable.

The inverse of this function is easily calculated; it takes the form $x = y^m$ where m is to be derived from n and p. It is easy to show that m is a solution of the congruence $mn = 1$ (modulo $p-1$).

This can form the basis of a scheme of cryptography in which p is made public and the values of m, n are both secret keys. Like a public key system it has different keys for encipherment and decipherment, but it is not a public key system because knowing the value of the encipherment key n immediately gives access to the decipherment key m. Nevertheless it is a satisfactory cipher of the traditional kind with both keys secret.

It can be applied to secret communication without key distribution. Let M be sending a message to U by means of numbers in arithmetic modulo p. Figure 10-18 shows the principle. Both M and U devise cipher systems of the kind we have described, with secret keys which they keep to themselves. M enciphers and passes the message to U who enciphers with his key and returns it to M. M then deciphers using the decipherment key n, and passes the message back again to U who deciphers with his decipherment key v. Thus (at the cost of three transmissions instead of one) the message x has passed from one end to other. It is a curious cipher system because no keys have been transported. It is not a public key system but it has the same effect as distributing a key by the exponential method and then using it for transport.

10.4.3. The public key cipher of Rivest, Shamir and Adleman [Rivest 78]

The RSA cipher uses the same principle as the power function described above but "decouples" the encipherment and decipherment key by using, instead of the prime modulus p, a composite modulus $m = p \cdot q$ for which the factorization into p and q is kept secret.

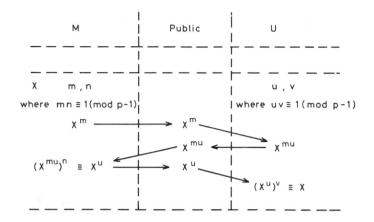

Figure 10-18: No key transport!

Encipherment of plaintext x to produce ciphertext y is

$$y = x^e \,(\text{modulo } m)$$

Decipherment of ciphertext y to produce plaintext x requires a decipherment key d chosen so that—

$$x = y^d \,(\text{modulo } m)$$

In a public key system the receiver of data has to generate both e and d so that he can make e public and keep d secret. To do this he uses his secret knowledge of the factorization of m. The relationship required is—

$$de = 1 \,(\text{modulo } \lambda) \text{ where } \lambda = \text{lcm}(p-1, q-1)$$

This λ is the least common multiple, the smallest number divisible by both $p-1$ and $q-1$, and can easily be calculated if p and q are known.

The principle of the Rivest cipher is summarized in figure 10-19. The public information is the modulus m and encipherment key e. The secret information is the factorization $p.q$, the consequent value of λ and the value of d derived from the congruence modulo λ. Then the receiver can carry out the decipherment function but no one else can.

One of the limits to the strength of the RSA system is the complexity of the factorization problem. The best known method of factorization has an expression for complexity—

$$\exp \{[\ln(m) \cdot \ln \ln(m)]^{1/2}\}$$

which is similar to the complexity of the discrete logarithm function. This was plotted in figure 10-16. The modulus (in this case a composite modulus) must be a number of 395 bits or more in size if the strength of the cipher is to be comparable with that of the data encryption standard.

A consideration of some proposed methods of breaking the RSA cipher without factorisation [Simmons 77] showed that both p and q should satisfy further conditions, rather like those for the prime p of the exponential method, in fact

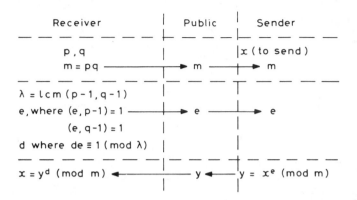

Figure 10-19: Summary of the RSA cipher system

- $p-1$ must have a large factor $p\,'$
- $p\,'-1$ must have a large prime factor $p\,''$
- The other prime q must satisfy similar conditions.

It is not difficult to find such primes, though the amount of computation is large. It can be estimated as around 1,000 times the encipherment time for the RSA algorithm.

A practical problem with the RSA algorithm is the relative difficulty of the encipherment and decipherment calculations. With small processors such as one would like to use, computation times for one block are measured in seconds or minutes. To achieve wide use it would be necessary to have special LSI hardware, perhaps a little more complex than the DES hardware, to speed up these operations.

10.4.4. The need for a digital signature

The traditional cipher system provides authentication. Assuming that the key has not been compromised, if a message is transmitted and deciphered satisfactorily it can be assumed to have come from the sender who shares the secret key. In this way, a sender and receiver are insulated, by their knowledge of the secret key, from all attacks by outsiders who do not know the key. They cannot read the text or substitute different texts.

There is one aspect in which the authentication provided by traditional cipher systems is incomplete. If the sender A and the receiver B do not entirely trust each other, it provides no way of resolving disputes between them. If A were to sign a document and B could not forge his signature the signed document would have legal strength. This means that A cannot claim not to have send the document since B can produce it in court and prove that it is A's signature. Furthermore B cannot generate documents of this kind and attach A's signature. We would like to have these properties in a digital system.

Clearly the signature must be a function of the whole message in such a way that no part of the message can be changed without invalidating the signature. Furthermore the signature must depend on secret information which only A knows, otherwise B could forge it. Yet there must also be public information which B can use to validate the signature. These seemingly difficult conditions can be met by the use of a public key cryptosystem like the RSA cipher.

Attempts have been made [Rabin 78] to generate signatures of this kind using a traditional cryptosystem such as the DES. These schemes have the great snag that the public information needed to validate the signature can only be used for one signature. A must go on generating large quantities of public information to provide for all the signatures he is going to make. In the public key system, the public keys remain useful for an indefinite number of signatures.

To illustrate the rather impractical methods needed without a public key system consider the signature for a single bit message—a message that can take either of the values 0 or 1. A can choose two values a and b which he associates with 0 and 1, and publish a one-way function of these values $F(a)$ and $F(b)$. His signature for the message value 0 would be the quantity a, which any receiver can check against the stated value of $F(a)$. The preparation consists of publishing the two values of the one-way function but this serves only for a single bit message and cannot be used again.

Figure 10-20 shows how a public key cryptosystem can be used to generate a signature. The public key cipher must be one in which the range of cipher text messages equals in size the domain of plaintext. Therefore the decipherment and encipherment functions can be operated in reverse order, as the figure shows. Now it is the turn of the sender to use his secret key to transform the message y. Anyone can take the sender's public key ke and use it to transform this message back into its plain form. Therefore the message is not secret but it can easily be shown to have been "signed". This is because only the possessor of the secret key kd could have transformed the message in such a way that, using the public key ke, it could be transformed back to plaintext. If there is any doubt as to what constitutes valid plaintext, some redundancy should be built into the message so that this can be used to check for a valid value of y.

This transformation need not be applied to the whole of the message; any one-way hash function of the message, of suitable length, can be used as the message y. In this way, the message can be enciphered for sending by the RSA system and the hash function of the message can be signed, also using the RSA system. Encipherment of the message uses the receiver's public key whereas

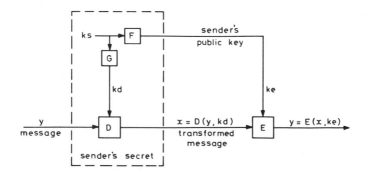

Figure 10-20: Signatures using a public key cryptosystem

signature uses the sender's private key. This is shown in figure 10-21. A suggested form for the hash function is shown in figure 10-22.

At the receiving end, the message can be deciphered and the hash function recalculated. The received signature can be transformed (by the encipherment function) and compared with the hashed message. If they are equal, the signature is valid. Any interference with the signature or the enciphered message will prevent agreement. When encipherment and signatures are combined in this way, since they employ the public keys of the sender and the receiver both the origin and destination of the message are authenticated to the other party.

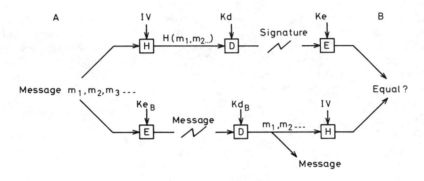

Figure 10-21: A separate signature

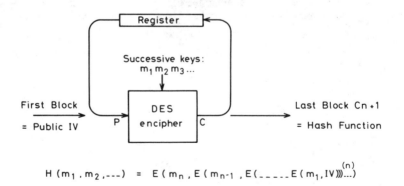

$$H(m_1, m_2, ---) = E(m_n, E(m_{n-1}, E(\_\_\_\_\_E(m_1, IV)))\overset{(n)}{...})$$

Figure 10-22: A hash function using the DES

10.4.5. The registry of public keys

Public key systems for encipherment and signature would be compromised if it were possible to substitute false values for the public keys. Users will need to change their keys, for security reasons. An enquiry to find the latest value of public key for some recognized participant in the scheme should therefore be handled by a *public key server*. The authentication of these keys is vital to the success of the scheme. This can be provided by having a signature for all the messages conveying public keys to the users. The public key of the key registry can be widely published so that falsifying it would be inconceivable.

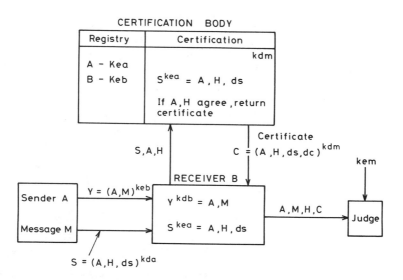

Figure 10-23: Certification

The following explains the notation:

Y -- ciphertext
S -- signature
H -- hash function of message M
ds -- date of signature
dc -- date of certificate
kea -- public encipherment key of A
keb -- public encipherment key of B
kda -- decipherment key of A
kdb -- decipherment key of B
kem -- public key of certification body
kdm -- decipherment key of certification body

A trusted authority must provide this service. Its software must be audited to ensure that it gives consistent answers to all enquirers. Then each owner of a public key can check as often as he likes that the value provided by the key registry is correct. It is very difficult to devise a more convenient scheme.

It has been objected [Popek 79] that users of this system can annnounce that their secret key has been compromised (having engineered the compromise themselves) and then claim that a number of the documents reputedly signed by them are forgeries. This is true, and it would be a criticism of any conceivable signature method. Fortunately, such behaviour would be very suspicious and could not be repeated. Like bankruptcy, it would not be a crime, but a warning to be cautious in business with the party concerned.

To guard against the revoking of very important signatures, they can easily be certified. To do this, the document and its signature are sent to the certification body, which examines and verifies the signature according to its records, then dates a certificate which it adds to the message and signature, signing the whole thing with its own key. It would be difficult for the signer to claim afterwards that his signature was a forgery. Certification is illustrated in figure 10-23.

Thus, in practice, the scheme of digital signatures by means of public key systems can be made as workable as any other similar institution. Ultimately it depends on a degree of trust, in this case trust of a single authority whose activities can be monitored by its users.

10.4.6. Other public key ciphers and signatures

Historically, the first public key systems to be described were methods of key distribution by which two correspondents could arrive at a common, secret key. With the exception of the exponential method described earlier, these are now of academic interest only.

The most interesting of the alternative public key cipher systems is the one based on the knapsack problem [Merkle 78]. This produces a cipher text which is expanded from the plaintext and hence it does not easily provide for digital signatures. There are methods for minimising the degrees of expansion, but it seems likely that the security of the method is reduced if the degree of expansion is made small. A number of variations of the knapsack system have been published.

A different application of the knapsack principle has been suggested for the purpose of digital signatures [Shamir 78]. All the knapsack schemes have a large size of key. For the original cipher scheme 100 numbers of 100 bits each are believed to be needed. Because there is no satisfactory analysis of the system's strength, the need for keys of this size is conjectural. A recent analysis suggests that order 150 knapsacks are necessary. For the signature scheme, the public key is double this size, that is 20,000 bits. The computational load of the knapsack methods is very small.

A cipher based on the use of the Chinese remainder theorem to solve simple equations, modulo a composite number, was suggested by Lu and Lee [Lu 79]. This system combined a compact key with the low computational requirements of the knapsack systems. Unfortunately, there seem to be a number of approaches to the breaking of this system and it cannot be considered secure.

For general utility, as soon as the special hardware is available, the RSA system is recommended for both cryptography and digital signatures. If a programmed method of cryptography, not requiring special hardware, is desired and the large key is acceptable, the knapsack encipherment method is available.

10.5. Access control

We return now to the wider subject of protection in computer systems and in particular to the control of access to objects such as files of data and programs.

10.5.1. The access matrix

Figure 10-24 shows schematically the way in which a matrix can be defined which expresses the access rights of the users of the system. The objects which may be accessed are represented by the index i and those things which access the objects are represented by the index j. The entry A_{ij} of the matrix contains the access rights of the user j to the object i.

When a user enters the system he is identified (by a password or whatever) and various processes are established to work on his behalf. The user passes on his access rights to these processes and may wish to limit their individual rights, perhaps in order to limit the extent of the damage caused by bugs. Thus the things represented by the index j, the actors in this drama, may be the users themselves or processes acting on their behalf. A group of these may share identical access rights and it is convenient to group these together and give them a single value of j. This can be done in different ways. A group of users, for example, can be considered jointly as a "principal"

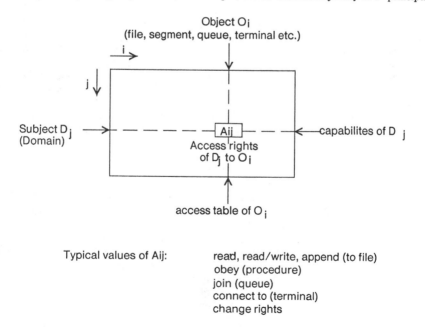

Typical values of Aij: read, read/write, append (to file)
                                obey (procedure)
                                join (queue)
                                connect to (terminal)
                                change rights

Figure 10-24: The access matrix

so that the rights defined for this principal are enjoyed by all the users which comprise it. Alternatively, a group of the actors which have the same access rights can be regarded, in the abstract, as comprising a protection "domain". This neutral word will be adopted here so the vertical axis of the matrix is labelled by the domains D_j.

The objects to which access are controlled vary according to the context, the commonest examples are data and programs but it is also possible for constructs such as queues to have access rights attached to their various functions, such as storing on a queue or taking from a queue. Peripherals and communication lines may also appear among the objects O_i.

The entry $A_{i,j}$ will define a form of access such as the right to read data, to write data, to obey programs, to append data to a file, to load a queue, to send data out on a particular communication line etc.

It must be emphasized that the access matrix we are describing is a concept, not something which is actually stored in a practical protection system. The difficulty in so doing would be its sparseness. Many files and programs are accessible only to their "owners" so there would be columns of the table containing only one entry. A practical system must devise ways of storing the information contained in the access matrix more compactly, and in such a way that it can be retrieved easily when needed.

10.5.2. The access control list

The column of the access matrix under O_i describes all those domains having access to that object. It is the access control list for O_i and since it can be stored without the empty elements of the matrix, it forms a compact description of access rights to to the object. It can be held in association with the object and checked when access is requested. This requires that there is a unique identifier for each of the domains D_j which is difficult to achieve in a distributed system.

We could, for example, give each separate system the right to control a subset of the domains. Users wishing to establish their membership of a domain would first access their 'home' system. The domain identifier used globally would be the concatenation of the local name and the name of the system which administers it. This name could be used, in enciphered form, as a capability to establish membership. For additional security it could be datestamped and have a limited life.

If the control of access is enforced at the obeying of every instruction, this must be done by special hardware. It becomes difficult if there are too many objects in play at one time. Consequently, access control of this kind is usually applied at relatively coarse levels such as to the whole of a file, considered as a single object. The implementation is further complicated by the indirectness of addressing in most large systems. Thus when an item in a file is first requested, the segment mapping onto the store is consulted and, if necessary, the file is retrieved from another level of the store hierarchy. Having established the access right to this file, or this segment, there is no need to repeat the procedure when subsequent instructions access this file, provided some risks are taken with the revocation of access. There is a danger, whenever access has been revoked, that this does not remove a user's right until he needs to retrieve his file again. The extent of the risk can be limited by a time limit on the use of a file without rechecking access rights.

10.5.3. Capabilities

An alternative way to store the access matrix is to take a row corresponding to one domain D_j and store these data with the domain, rather than the objects being accessed. Each element of the matrix is then called a *capability*. When an access is requested by a domain, the capability is presented, like a ticket, to verify that the access right does exist. The checking mechanism is then very simple, like a ticket inspector. It can act on the information presented and needs no other stored data.

When a new user is identified, very few capabilities are needed to establish all his access rights. It would be sufficient to identify one program to begin his work, and a catalogue containing the basic set of capabilities he needs. When he uses system programs, for example, they will have their own capabilities which they employ, but will not copy to him.

The convenience of capabilities allows them to operate at a detailed level, defining small areas of store, for example. Capabilities can be copied and passed on to other users or processes and they can be restricted before passing on. For example, a user's program may offer a small part of its working space to a subroutine which it invokes.

Capabilities must be unforgeable. Within a single system this is achieved by flagging all the words in a store with a single bit indicating whether or not they are capabilities. Processes working for users cannot create capabilities and can only modify them by restriction.

If the copying of capabilities is unrestricted, it soon becomes impossible to discover all the domains which have access to a particular object. Some systems have attempted to control this propagation of access by limiting the numbers of times a capability can be copied. For example, the copies of the original capability might themselves be made uncopyable. In other systems, capabilities may only be stored in "capability segments" so the system is able to review access with relative ease.

10.5.4. Access control lists combined with capabilities

Access control lists give a more rigid form of control, in which propagation can be limited and the extent of access reviewed. Capabilities give a simpler mechanism for checking. The two features can be combined by making the first access to a new object subject to the access control list and then generating a temporary capability so that further accesses are simplified. The validity of the capability could, for example, be one user session.

10.5.5. A simplified model for changing access rights

An access control system contains not only a matrix showing which subjects can access which objects and by what access methods, it must also contain rules for determining how these access rights can be changed. In a "discretionary system" the changes are made by ordinary users and the rights to change access rights are handled by the same system.

Access to an object can be made directly, using an existing access right or indirectly by changing access rights until the object becomes accessible. A long sequence of changes may be needed to reach a given object. Finding this sequence is a difficult puzzle. The difficulty can be expressed by considering this problem: Given a set of subjects and objects with their access rights (including rights to change access rights), can subject x achieve access of type y to object z? It can in general be shown that a complete (algorithmic) solution to this problem requires a number of operations which increases exponentially with the size of the problem. The size might be measured, for example, by the number of subjects added to the number of objects. So, for practical purposes, it is not feasible to discover the access possibilities latent in a given access matrix.

This 'complexity' result seems to be true for all discretionary access schemes which are reasonably flexible. It is not always true, and we shall now describe a simple protection scheme that was devised [Jones 78] in order to have an easy method of answering the question above. For this scheme there is a systematic way of discovering if x can achieve access of type y to object z in a number of operations proportional to the size of the problem. But even a small change to this *take-grant* system, to make it more flexible, seems to result in exponential complexity.

The take-grant system is described by means of a *protection graph*, in which the nodes of the graph are either the subjects, which can take action on behalf of users and are shown by filled circles, or the passive objects shown by unfilled circles, or objects not known to be either subjects or passive objects shown by circles with a slash. In the graph, a directed edge from one node to another is labelled by a set of symbols which can be called access privileges. Some of these will use letters such as a, b and others will be the specific rights t meaning *take* and g meaning *grant*. The *take* and *grant* rights are those by which the access rules in the graph are changed.

The rules for changing access rights take the form of four re-write rules, each having an obvious interpretation. The take and grant rules are shown in the two parts of figure 10-25. In the first of these, A exercises his *take* right to take from X the right a which X possesses towards node Y. The result of the re-write is that A now has access right a towards Y. In the second of these figures, A exercises his *grant* right by granting to X the access right a which he possesses towards Y. The result is to create a new access right from X to Y.

The other two re-write rules create and remove access rights which the node itself possesses. For example, as shown in figure 10-26, A can create a new node N and label the edge from A to N

excercising the 'take' right of A

excercising the 'grant' right of A

Figure 10-25: Exercising *take* and *grant* rights

excercising the 'create' right of A

excercising the 'remove' right of A

Figure 10-26: Exercising *create* and *remove* rights

with the access right *a*. Alternatively, if *A* has a number of access rights towards *X*, as shown in the second part of the figure 10-26, it may remove a subset of these. If it removes all access rights to *X* then the edge itself is deleted.

Given this basic set of re-writing rules, any given situation of access rights modelled in a graph can be modified sequentially using any of the re-write rules and exercising any of the take or grant rights which appear on the graph. Figure 10-27 shows an example in which the state of the system at the top of the figure is progressively modified by exercising take and grant rights. The right being exercised in each of the stages is shown by encircling the appropriate symbol and the new access right which this gives rise to is shown by the broken edge. The question that might be asked about the initial graph is "does this state of affairs give *A* the possibility of exercising the right *a* towards *B*?". The operation of the re-write rules which are shown in the figure shows that this can indeed be achieved. Note that only subjects (filled circles) exercise the rights to *take* and *grant*.

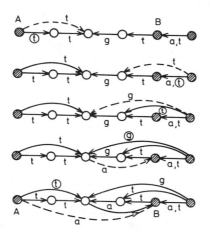

Figure 10-27: Can *A* acquire the right *a* towards *B*?

The value of this model is that it shows, at least in one simple case, that the potential accesses which may be achieved by the subjects exercising their various rights can be explored in a reasonable time. Unfortunately, this is not true for the more complex models which represent access control mechanisms at present in use. This fundamental difficulty in exploring all the implications of a discretionary access control system is, no doubt, one reason why non-discretionary systems based on the military model of classified information are often used.

10.5.6. Capabilities in a distributed system

Inside a single processor, capabilities are protected against forgery by a tag provided by the hardware. Only the operating system can create capabilities. Users may copy them to other users. Sometimes they can restrict them before copying to others. For example, a small piece of working space can be handed over, to receive the result of a procedure. We would like to extend these possibilities to a distributed system.

Figure 10-28 shows how capabilities can be protected by encipherment with a single-key cipher, like the DES. The server creates the capability C. Outside the server, only the enciphered form $E(s,C)$ is allowed to exist, where s is a key held secret by the server. Therefore, even though the coding of C is known, others than S cannot make them. There is no reason why the plaintext version of C should not go along with the enciphered form, if this is needed for housekeeping.

Anyone can copy $E(s,C)$, so in communication and in store it should be further protected. It is shown on the line between S and A as $E(sa,E(s,C))$, protected by the key sa held in common by S and A. For storage in user A's files it could be held in the same form. The figure shows it communicated under key ab to B then used by B to obtain access rights at S, which will recognise $E(s,C)$ as the capability no matter whence it receives it.

Figure 10-29 shows how a public key system can be used for the same purpose, obviating the need for the many secret keys to be communicated between the servers and users. The scheme is due to J. Fletcher and J. Donelley of Lawrence Livermore Laboratory. Server S has a secret key $\underline{S}$ and a public key S which is known to all the users. The notation for the keys of A and B is similar. The operations performed on messages are shown in reverse order of performance, as in an algebraic notation. Thus $\underline{S}C$ is the result of operating on the capability C using the server's secret key $\underline{S}$. Therefore it is the 'signed' form of C. If this is subsequently signed again with $\underline{S}$, then enciphered with A's public key A, the result is $A\underline{S}.\underline{S}C$, where the dot merely separates the signed capability, which propagates through the system, from the other signatures and ciphers which protect it on its journey.

The operations on the messages are shown in the smaller boxes. The stored values are shown in the larger boxes. For example, $A\underline{S}.\underline{S}C$ passes from S to A. This is operated upon by $\underline{A}$ then S then A, shown as $AS\underline{A}$ giving the result —

$$AS\underline{A}.A\underline{S}.\underline{S}C = A\underline{S}C$$

since $\underline{A}A = 1$ and $S\underline{S} = 1$, in effect. The first operation, A, removes the encipherment. The second, S, checks the signature. The third, A, re-enciphers for safe storage. In order to check the signature, $\underline{S}C$ should have added to it some recognizable redundancy. In fact, C probably has a recognizable form and can be read by means of another S operation. Provided that $\underline{S}C$ is propagated (since the server will recognize nothing else) the second signature by the server hardly seems necessary, though it gives the scheme a nice symmetry.

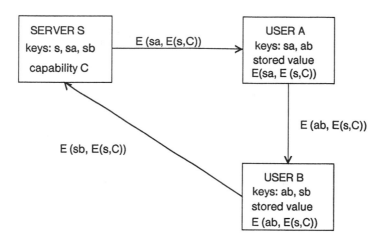

Figure 10-28: Encipherment of capabilities (DES)

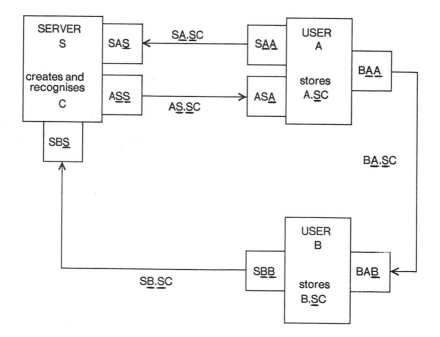

Figure 10-29: Public-key handling of capabilities

Each user handling the signed capability, $\underline{SC}$, treats it in the same way, deciphering it, checking the sender's signature, re-enciphering for storage the deciphering, signing and enciphering for transmission. The figure also shows how A would handle the capability when returning it to S for use.

The two schemes of figures 10-28 and 10-29 allow capabilities to be copied and propagated but not restricted. If A wishes to apply a restriction R to the capability before sending it on to B, this could be done by concatenating A's own message, addressed to S, with the capability, enciphered so that they cannot be separated. In the single key scheme: —

$$E(sa, E(s,C):R)$$

takes the place of $E(s,C)$. There must also be a plaintext format to indicate how such a composite capability should be interpreted by S. The notation : is used for concatenation. In the public key scheme,

$$S\underline{A}(\underline{SC}:R)$$

is used to replace SC. It is signed by A and enciphered for S. The server could replace these by a new signed capability incorporating the restriction after the first occasion that B presented them for use.

These capabilities $E(s,C)$ and SC are capable of propagation without limit. It would be possible for A to limit their validity to B, using B's identity b, in the forms: —

$$E(sa, E(s,C):b) \text{ or } S\underline{A}(\underline{SC}:b)$$

which the server would recognize only if they appeared enciphered under ab or signed with B, respectively.

10.5.7. The location of access control in a distributed system

In our early discussion we considered the network security centre as a method for distributing session keys for point-to-point communication. Any two parts of the system requiring communication could request a key and the NSC would provide it without imposing any access restrictions. To achieve this, each communicating party should have a terminal master key kt which is also held at the centre and used for the secure communication of session keys.

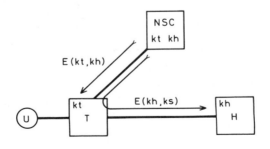

Figure 10-30: Key distribution $T-H$

Let us consider communication between the user U at the terminal T with the host H illustrated in figure 10-30. A convenient notation is that kt is the terminal key and kh is the host key, both of these being held also at the NSC. To communicate the session key ks when the terminal T calls the host H, this session key is sent to the terminal in two forms, $E(kt, ks)$ for use at the terminal itself and $E(kh, ks)$ for use at the host, travelling to the host via the terminal.

Suppose now that the user U also possesses a key ku stored on a magnetic striped card which verifies his presence at the terminal. The NSC is now asked to establish communication for the user U rather that the terminal T. At the other end, the communication is not to be with the host H in general but with a particular process P within the host. Let us assume that this process possesses the key kp which helps to identify it. The scheme shown in figure 10-31 has been proposed, originally by Branstad, to transmit a key for this user and this process.

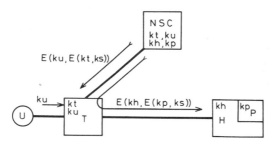

Figure 10-31: Key distribution $U-P$

The form of the key transmitted to the terminal is $E(ku, E(kt, ks))$. When the user has provided his key ku, and if the terminal contains the key kt, the terminal can carry out the double decipherment necessary to obtain the value of the session key ks. The message sent to the host via the terminal contains ciphered form of the session key ($E(kh, E(kp, ks))$). The cryptographic device at the host, having received kp from the process, can carry out the double decipherment necessary to produce the session key which will match the session key at the other end. Then an exchange of test messages in each direction will verify that the link has been established between U and P.

The additional security which this scheme offers will only be realized if both the user and the process are provided with positive identifications of the other party. We assume that the user has specified process P when making his call, and the message to the terminal carried along with the session key identifies that P is the other party in the conversation. Similarly, the message sent to the host should specify that the other party is U. The messages could be written as $E(ku, E(kt, ks, P))$ and $E(kp, E(kh, ks, U))$. This will verify to the host that the calling party is U and knows the key ku and, with sufficient internal security in the handling of the keys by the host, it will prevent "spoofing" by other processes in the host. Put another way, someone with access to the terminal key will not be able to masquerade as U and some process at the host site knowing the host key kh will not be able to masquerade as the destination process P.

The degree of control exercised by the NSC can be increased by including in it a form of access control. This requires a matrix showing which users are authorized to access which processes.

With this information, the NSC can prevent unauthorized connections and arrange that processes such as P receive only calls from users U already authorized to call them. But it is a moot point how far a host should delegate such access control to an NSC. It is probable that a host would maintain its own table to make an independent check, relying on the NSC to keep away undesirable callers but not trusting the NSC entirely.

The same kind of mechanism will serve equally well for inter-host communications, calls from host process to user or, in principle, from user to user. The example of U calling P probably represents the most common case.

The fineness of access control obtained in this way is very limited. If we are concerned with access to individual files, with different forms of access such as read, write etc., and even with control of access to particular data items, it seems very clumsy to allow an NSC to control this by having a great number of individual keys prepared in advance for this purpose. But there is a possibility for distinguishing between different modes of access to different computer services. For example, a data base may be maintained by one group of people and used by a much wider range of people who, by subscription, are allowed to access it by reading the data only. Both the "update" and the "read only" forms of access will probably be effected by a hierarchy of processes, but they can be initiated by two starting processes with keys in the manner shown in figure 10-31. Then again, a commercial data base may want to provide a "shop window" for any one to call for information about the system, and perhaps for some trial accesses to learn how good it is. This could be provided by a starting process which is open to all callers, whereas only subscribers would be allowed to call the starting process which exercises the whole data base. In this way, a relatively coarse form of access control could be applied to typical server hosts.

More detailed access control by a network security centre is indeed possible. The separation of users into broad classes would be retained but within each class there might be finer distinctions according to the details of the transaction requested. A need for a large number of different keys could be avoided if the NSC consults its access matrix and passes on to the destination host, along with the session key, a note of the kind of access required. It would block those forms of access which were not allowed in its matrix, and pass only the valid access requests on to the host. It is clear that, if pushed too far, this would result in duplicating access controls at the NSC and the host itself. It therefore seems unlikely that such a mechanism will be widely used.

Considered as an organizational problem, the NSC which functions only for key distribution is relatively simple. NSCs could be organized for one company, for a group of organizations, for a geographical region or nationally. By connecting national NSCs, in some way yet to be specified, the mechanism of key distribution could operate internationally. The main security consideration is a limitation of the number of places in which a particular terminal's or host's key is stored. A terminal that is used both on a company network and a national or international network will probably use a different terminal key for these different purposes. Therefore different kinds of NSC will not share keys and accesses which are external to the organization will easily been distinguished.

Session keys which are used with the data encryption standard can very well be distributed by means of a public key system. It is not difficult to see how terminal or user and host can exchange session keys without the need for a network security centre. Access control must then be provided at the host receiving the call, since the NSC no longer exists.

In the DES based system shown in figure 10-31, propagation of the authentication of user U to another host is difficult. For example, suppose that the host H shown must now make a call to another host on behalf of U and verify, in this second call, that the transaction is indeed on behalf of U. There is no obvious way to carry this information to a second host. Using a public key system, a signed message from U would be sufficient. An alternative possibility is that the second host has given its approval to this kind of access by providing U, or the terminal working on this user's behalf, with a capability. This capability can be passed on from host H to the second host, but it will require another session key known only to U and the second host if this capability is not to be "leaked" to the host H. This method will only provide for the propagation of user identity if the chain of hosts is known in advance. Without experience it is difficult to know if this is a realistic assumption. Certainly, the public key system promises to be much more convenient.

Chapter 11. Atomic transactions

11.1. Introduction

This chapter deals with methods for performing atomic actions on a collection of computers, even in the face of such adverse circumstances as concurrent access to the data involved in the actions, and crashes of some of the computers involved. For the sake of definiteness, and because it captures the essence of the more general problem, we consider the problem of crash recovery in a data storage system which is constructed from a number of independent computers. The portion of the system which is running on some individual computer may crash, and then be restarted by some crash recovery procedure. This may result in the loss of some information which was present just before the crash. The loss of this information may, in turn, lead to an inconsistent state for the information permanently stored in the system.

For example, a client program may use this data storage system to store balances in an accounting system. Suppose that there are two accounts, called A and B, which contain $10 and $15 respectively. Further, suppose the client wishes to move $5 from A to B. The client might proceed as follows:

> **read** account A (obtaining $10)
>
> **read** account B (obtaining $15)
>
> **write** $5 to account A
>
> **write** $20 to account B

Now consider a possible effect of a crash of the system program running on the machine to which these commands are addressed. The crash could occur after one of the write commands has been carried out, but before the other has been initiated. Moreover, recovery from the crash could result in never executing the other write command. In this case, account A is left containing $5 and account B with $15, an unintended result. The contents of the two accounts are inconsistent.

There are other ways in which this problem can arise: accounts A and B are stored on two different machines and one of these machines crashes; or, the client itself crashes after issuing one write command and before issuing the other.

In this chapter we present an algorithm for maintaining the consistency of a file system in the presence of these possible errors. We begin, in section 11.2, by describing the kind of system to which the algorithm is intended to apply. In section 11.3 we introduce the concept of an *atomic transaction*. We argue that if a system provides atomic transactions, and the client program uses them correctly, then the stored data will remain consistent.

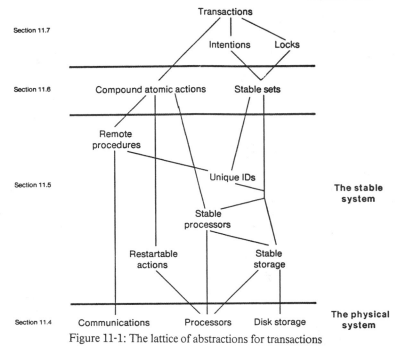

Figure 11-1: The lattice of abstractions for transactions

The remainder of the chapter is devoted to describing an algorithm for obtaining atomic transactions. Any correctness argument for this (or any other) algorithm necessarily depends on a formal model of the physical components of the system. Such models are quite simple for correctly functioning devices. Since we are interested in recovering from malfunctions, however, our models must be more complex. Section 11.4 gives models for storage, processors and communication, and discusses the meaning of a formal model for a physical device.

Starting from this base, we build up the lattice of abstractions shown in figure 11-1. The second level of this lattice constructs better behaved devices from the physical ones, by eliminating storage failures and eliminating communication entirely (section 11.5). The third level consists of a more powerful primitive which works properly in spite of crashes (section 11.6). Finally, the highest level constructs atomic transactions (section 11.7). Throughout we give informal arguments for the correctness of the various algorithms.

11.2. System overview

Our data storage system is constructed from a number of computers; the basic service provided by such a system is reading and writing of data bytes stored in the system and identified by integer addresses. There are a number of computers which contain client programs (*clients*), and a number of computers which contain the system (*servers*); for simplicity we assume that client and server machines are disjoint. Each server has one or more attached storage devices, such as magnetic disks. Some facility is provided for transmitting messages from one machine to another. A client will issue each read or write command as a message sent directly to the server storing the addressed data, so that transfers can proceed with as much concurrency as possible.

We follow tradition in using a pair of integers $\langle f, b \rangle$ to address a byte, where f identifies the *file* containing the byte, and b identifies the byte within the file. A file is thus a sequence of bytes addressed by integers in the range $1..n$, where n is the *length* of the file. There are two *commands* available for accessing files: a generalized *Read* command, and a generalized *Write* command. The generality allows information associated with a file other than its data bytes to be read and written, for example its length, or protection information associated with the file; these complications are irrelevant to our subject and will not be mentioned again. A client requests the execution of a command by sending a message containing the command to the appropriate server. When the command has been completed, the server sends a message to the client containing a *response*. In the case of a read command, this response will contain the requested data. For a write command, the response is simply an acknowledgement. It is necessary to provide interlocks between the concurrent accesses of different clients.

It should now be clear that our distributed *data storage* system is not a distributed *data base* system. Instead, we have isolated the fundamental facilities required by a data base system, or any other system requiring long-term storage of information: randomly addressable storage of bits, and arbitrarily large updates which are atomic in spite of crashes and concurrent accesses. We claim that this is a logically sound foundation for a data base system; if it proves to be unsatisfactory, the problem will be inadequate performance.

11.3. Consistency and transactions

For any system, we say that a given state is *consistent* if it satisfies some predicate called the *invariant* of the system. For example, an invariant for an accounting system might be that assets and liabilities sum to zero. The choice of invariant obviously depends on the application, and is beyond the scope of a data storage system. The task of the storage system is to provide facilities which, when properly used, make it possible for a client application program to maintain its invariant in spite of crashes and concurrent accesses.

A suitable form for such facilities is suggested by the following observation. Any computation which takes a system from one state to another can be put into the form

$$state := F(state)$$

where F is a function without side effects. A state is a function which assigns a value to each element (called an address) in some set (called an address space). In general F will change only the values at some subset of the addresses, called the *output set* of F; these new values will depend only on the values at some other subset of the addresses, called the *input set*.

That is, the function needs to read only those addresses whose values are actually referenced by the computation, and the assignment needs to write only those addresses whose values are actually changed by the computation. Such a computation will clearly be atomic in the presence of crashes if the assignment is atomic in the presence of crashes, i.e., if either all the writes are done, or none of them are. Two such computations F and G may run concurrently and still be atomic (i.e., serializable) if the input set of F is disjoint from the output set of G, and vice versa.

In pursuit of this idea, we introduce the notion of a *transaction* (the same concept is used in [Eswaren 76], and elsewhere in the data base literature, to define consistency among multiple users of a common data base). A transaction is a sequence of read and write commands sent by a client to the file system. The write commands may depend on the results of previous read commands in the same transaction. The system guarantees that after recovery from a system crash, for each transaction, either all of the write commands will have been executed, or none will have been. In addition, transactions appear indivisible with respect to other transactions which may be executing concurrently; that is, there exists some serial order of execution which would give the same results. We call this the *atomic* property for transactions. The client will indicate the commands of a transaction by surrounding them with *Begin* and *End* commands. If the client fails to issue the end transaction command (perhaps because he crashes), then a time out mechanism will eventually abort the transaction without executing any of the write commands.

Assuming this atomic property for transactions, consider how the previous example might be implemented by a client. The client first issues a *Begin* command, and then continues just as in the example in section 1. After sending the two write commands, he sends *End*. This transaction moves $5 from *A* to *B*. Notice that the client waits for the responses to the read commands, then computes the new balances, and finally issues write commands containing the new balances.

A client may decide to terminate a transaction before it is completed. For this purpose we have an additional command, *Abort*. This terminates the transaction, and no write commands issued in the transaction will take effect. Because the system also times out transactions, the *Abort* command is logically unnecessary, but the action it causes also occurs on a timeout and hence must be implemented in the system.

Thus, we have two groups of commands, which constitute the entire interface between the data storage system and its clients:

- Data commands: *Read, Write*
- Control commands: *Begin, End, Abort*

We shall return to transactions in section 11.7 after laying some necessary groundwork.

11.4. The physical system

To show the correctness of our algorithms in spite of imperfect disk storage, processor failures (crashes) and unreliable communication, we must have a formal model of these devices. Given this model, a proof can be carried out with any desired degree of formality (quite low here). The validity of the model itself, however, cannot be established by proof, since a physical system does not have formal properties, and hence its relation to a formal system cannot be formally shown. The best we can do is to claim that the model represents all the events which can occur in the physical system. The correctness of this claim can only be established by experience.

In order to make our assumptions about possible failures more explicit, and we hope more convincing, we divide the events which occur in the model into two categories: *desired* and *undesired*; in an fault-free system only desired events will occur. Undesired events are subdivided into expected ones, called *errors*, and unexpected ones, called *disasters*. Our algorithms are designed to work in the presence of any number of errors, and no disasters; we make no claims about their behavior if a disaster occurs.

In fact, of course, disasters are included in the model precisely because we can envision the possibility of their occurring. Since our system may fail if a disaster does occur, we need to estimate the probability p that a disaster will occur during an interval of operation T_O; p is then an upper bound on the probability that the system will fail during T_O. The value of p can only be estimated by an exhaustive enumeration of possible failure mechanisms. Whether a given p is small enough depends on the needs of the application.

In constructing our model, we have tried to represent as an error, rather than a disaster, any event with a significant probability of occurring in a system properly constructed from current hardware. We believe that such a system will have very small p for intervals T_O of years or decades. The reader must make his own judgment about the truth of this claim.

Our general theme is that, while an error may occur, it will be detected and dealt with before it causes incorrect behavior. In the remainder of this section, we present our model for the three main physical components on which the system depends: disk storage, processors and communication. In the next section, we describe how errors are handled; in general this is done by constructing higher-level abstractions for which desired events are the only expected ones.

11.4.1. Disk storage

Our model for disk storage is a set of addressable pages, where each page contains a status (*good, bad*) and a block of data. There are two actions by which a processor can communicate with the disk:

> **procedure** *Put*(*at*: *Address, data*: *Dblock*)
>
> **procedure** *Get*(*at*: *Address*) **returns** (*status*: (*good, looksBad*), *data*: *Dblock*)

Put does not return status, because things which go wrong when writing on the disk are usually not detected by current hardware, which lacks read-after-write capability. The extension to a model in which a *Put* can return bad status is trivial.

We consider two kinds of events: those which are the result of the processor actions *Get* and *Put*, and those which are spontaneous.

The results of a *Get*(*at*: *a*) are:

- (desired) Page a is (*good, d*), and *Get* returns (*good, d*).
- (desired) Page a is *bad*, and *Get* returns *looksBad*.
- (error) *Soft read error*. Page a is *good*, and *Get* returns *looksBad*, provided this has not happened too often in the recent past; this is made precise in the next event.
- (disaster) *Persistent read error*. Page a is *good*, and *Get* returns *looksBad*, and n_R successive *Get*s within a time T_R have all returned *looksBad*.
- (disaster) *Undetected error*. Page a is *bad*, and *Get* returns *good*, or if page a is (*good, d*), then returns (*good, d'*) with $d' \neq d$.

The definition of a persistent read error implies that if n_R successive *Get*s of a *good* page have all returned *looksBad*, the page must actually be *bad* (i.e., has decayed or been badly written; see below), or else a disaster has happened, namely the persistent error. This somewhat curious definition reflects the fact that the system must treat the page as *bad* if it cannot be read after repeated attempts, even though its actual status is not observable.

The effects of a *Put*(*at*: *a*, *data*: *d*) are:

- (desired) Page *a* becomes (*good*, *d*).

- (error) *Null write*: Page *a* is unchanged.

- (error) *Bad write*: Page *a* becomes (*bad, d*).

The remaining undesired events, called *decays*, model various kinds of accidents. To describe them we need some preliminaries. Each decay event will damage some set of pages, which are contained in some larger set of pages which is characteristic of the decay. For example, a decay may damage many pages on one cylinder, but no pages on other cylinders; or many pages on one surface, but no pages on other surfaces. We call these characteristic sets *decay sets*; they are not necessarily disjoint, as the example illustrates. Two pages are *decay related* if there is some decay set which contains both. We also assume a partitioning of the disk pages into *units* (such as disk drives), and a time interval T_D called the *unit decay time*. We assume that any decay set is wholly contained in one unit, and that it is possible to partition each unit into pairs of pages which are not decay-related (in order to construct stable storage; see 11.5.1). T_D must be very long compared to the time required to read all the disk pages.

A *decay* is a spontaneous event in which some set of pages, all within some one characteristic decay set, changes from *good* to *bad*. We now consider the following spontaneous events:

- (error) *Infrequent decay*: a decay preceded and followed by an interval T_D during which there is no other decay in the same unit, and the only bad writes on that unit are to pages in the characteristic set of the decay. Because units can be bounded in size, the stringency of the infrequency assumption does not depend on the total size of the system.

- (error) *Revival*: a page goes from (*bad,d*) to (*good, d*).

- (disaster) *Frequent decay*: two decays in the same unit within an interval T_D.

- (disaster) *Undetected error*: some page changes from (*s, d*) to (*s, d'*) with $d' \neq d$.

Other events may be obtained as combinations of these events. For example, a *Put* changing the wrong page can be modeled as a *Put* in which the addressed page is unchanged (error), and an undetected error in which some other page spontaneously changes to a new *good* value (disaster). Similarly, a *Put* writing the wrong data can be modeled in the same way, except that the written page is the one which suffers the undetected error. One consequence of this model is that writing correct data at the wrong address is a disaster and hence cannot be tolerated.

11.4.2. Processors and crashes

Our model for a processor is conventional except for the treatment of crashes. A processor consists of a collection of processes and some shared state. Each process is an automaton with some local state, and makes state transitions (executes instructions) at some finite non-zero rate. Instructions can read and write the shared state as well as the local state of the process; some standard kind of synchronization primitive, such as monitors, allows this to be done in an orderly way. For simplicity we consider the number of processes to be fixed, but since a process may enter an idle state in which it is simply waiting to be reinitialized, our model is equivalent to one with a varying but bounded number of processes. One of the processes provides an interval timer suitable for measuring decay times (see 11.4.1 and 11.5.1). The union of the shared state and the process states is the state of the processor. A processor can also interact with the disk storage and the communication system as described in sections 11.4.1 and 11.4.3.

A crash is an error which causes the state of the processor to be reset to some standard value; because of this effect, the processor state is called *volatile* state. This implies that the processor retains no memory of what was happening at the time of the crash. Of course the disk storage, or other processors which do not crash, may retain such memory. In a system with interesting long-term behavior, such as ours, a processor recovering from a crash will examine its disk storage and communicate with other processors in order to reach a state which is an acceptable approximation to its state before the crash. Since a crash is expected, it may occur at any time; hence a crash may occur during crash recovery, another crash may occur during recovery from that crash, and so forth.

Our model includes no errors in the processor other than crashes. The assumption is that any malfunction will be detected (by some kind of consistency checking) and converted into a crash before it affects the disk storage or communication system. It may well be questioned whether this assumption is realistic.

11.4.3. Communication

Our model for communication is a set of messages, where each message contains a status (*good*, *bad*), a block of data, and a destination which is a processor. Since we are not concerned with authentication in this paper, we assume that the source of a message, if it is needed, will be encoded in the data. There are two actions by which a processor can communicate with another one:

> **procedure** *Send*(*to*: *Processor*, *data*: *Mblock*)
>
> **procedure** *Receive* **returns** (*status*: (*good*, *bad*), *data*: *Mblock*)

The similarity to the actions for disk storage is not accidental. Because messages are not permanent objects, however, the undesired events are somewhat simpler to describe. The possible events are as follows:

The possible results of a *Receive* executed by processor *p* are:

- (desired) If a message (*good*, *d*, *p*) exists, returns (*good*, *d*) and destroys the message.
- (desired) If a *bad* message exists, returns *bad* and destroys the message.

There may be an arbitrary delay before a *Receive* returns.

The effects of a *Send*(*to*: *q*, *data*: *d*) are:

- (desired) Creates a message (*good*, *d*, *q*).

Finally, we consider the following spontaneous events:

- (error) *Loss*: some message is destroyed.
- (error) *Duplication*: some new message identical to an existing message is created.

- (error) *Decay*: some message changes from *good* to *bad*.

- (disaster) *Undetected error*: some message changes from *bad* to *good*, or from (*good, d, q*) to (*good, d ', q '*) with *d '≠d* or *q '≠q*.

As with disk storage, other undesired events can be obtained as combinations including these spontaneous events.

11.4.4. Simple, compound and restartable actions

Throughout this paper we shall be discussing program fragments which are designed to implement the actions (also called operations or procedures) of various abstractions. These actions will usually be compound, i.e. composed from several simpler actions, and it is our task to show that the compound action can be treated at the next higher level of abstraction as though it were simple. We would like a simple action to be *atomic*. An atomic action has both of the following properties:

- *Unitary*: If the action returns (i. e., the next action in the program starts to execute), then the action was carried out completely; and if the system crashes before the action returns, then after the crash the action has either been carried out completely, or (apparently) not started.

- *Serializable*: When a collection of several actions is carried out by concurrent processes, the result is always as if the individual actions were carried out one at a time in some order. Moreover, if some process invokes two actions in turn, the first completing before the second is started, then the effect of those actions must be as if they were carried out in that order.

Unfortunately, we are unable to make all the actions in our various abstractions atomic. Instead, we are forced to state more complicated *weak* properties for some of our compound actions.

Consider the effect of crashes on a compound action S. The unitary property can be restated more formally as follows: associated with S is a precondition P and a postcondition Q. If P holds before S, and if S returns, then Q will hold; if a crash intervenes, then $(P \vee Q)$ will hold. P and Q completely characterize the behavior of S.

The behavior of *any* action S in the presence of crashes can be characterized by a precondition P and two postconditions Q_{ok} and Q_{crash}. If P holds before S and S returns, then Q_{ok} holds. On the other hand, if there is a crash before S returns, then Q_{crash} holds. Sometimes we mean that Q_{crash} holds at the moment of the crash, and sometimes that it holds after the lower levels of abstraction have done their crash recovery. Notice that since a crash can occur at any moment, and in particular just before S returns, Q_{ok} must imply Q_{crash}. Notice also that the unitary property is equivalent to asserting that $Q_{crash} = (P \vee Q_{ok})$.

During crash recovery it is usually impossible to discover whether a particular action has completed or not. Thus, we will frequently require that S be *restartable*, by which we mean that Q_{crash} implies P (hence Q_{ok} implies P). If S is restartable and S was in progress at the moment of the crash, then S can be repeated during crash recovery with no ill effects. Notice that atomic does not imply restartable.

11.5. The stable system

The physical devices described in the previous section are an unsatisfactory basis for the direct construction of systems. Their behavior is uncomfortably complex; hence there are too many cases to be considered whenever an action is invoked. In this section we describe how to construct on top of these devices a more satisfactory set of virtual devices, with fewer undesired properties and more convenient interfaces. By eliminating all the errors, we are able to convert disk storage into an ideal device for recording state, called *stable storage*. Likewise, we are able to convert communications into an ideal device for invoking procedures on a remote processor. By "ideal" in both cases we mean that with these devices our system behaves just like a conventional error-free single-processor system, except for the complications introduced by crashes.

We have not been so successful in concealing the undesired behavior of processors. In fact, the remaining sections of the paper are devoted to an explanation of how to deal with crashes. The methods for doing this rely on some idealizations of the physical processor, described in section 11.5.2.

11.5.1. Stable storage

The disk storage not used as volatile storage for processor state (see 11.5.2) is converted into *stable* storage with the same actions as disk storage, but with the property that no errors can occur. Since the only desired events are ideal reads and writes, stable storage is an ideal storage medium, with no failure modes which must be dealt with by its clients.

To construct stable storage, we introduce two successive abstractions, each of which eliminates two of the errors associated with disk storage. The first is called *careful disk storage*; its state and actions are specified exactly like those of disk storage, except that the only errors are a bad write immediately followed by a crash, and infrequent decay. A careful page is represented by a disk page. *CarefulGet* repeatedly does *Get* until it gets a *good* status, or until it has tried *n* times, where *n* is the bound on the number of soft read errors. This eliminates soft read errors. *CarefulPut* repeatedly does *Put* followed by *Get* until the *Get* returns *good* with the data being written. This eliminates null writes; it also eliminates bad writes, provided there is no crash during the *CarefulPut*. More precisely, Q_{ok} for *CarefulPut* is the desired result, but Q_{crash} is not. Since crashes are expected, this isn't much use by itself.

A more complicated construction is needed for stable storage. A stable page consists simply of a block of data, without any status (because the status is always *good*). In addition to *Get* and *Put*, it has a third action called *Cleanup*. It is represented by an ordered pair of careful disk pages, chosen from the same unit but not decay-related. The definition of units ensures that this is possible, and that we can use all the pages of a unit for stable pages. The value of the data is the data of the first representing page if that page is *good*, otherwise the data of the second page. The representing pages are protected by a monitor which ensures that only one action can be in progress at a time. Since the monitor lock is held in volatile storage and hence is released by a crash, some care must be taken in analyzing what happens when there is a crash during an update operation.

We maintain the following invariant on the representing pages: not more than one of them is *bad*, and if both are *good* they both have the data written by the most recent *StablePut*, except during a *StablePut* action. The second clause must be qualified a little: if a crash occurs during a *StablePut*, the data may remain different until the end of the subsequent crash recovery, but thereafter both pages' data will be either the data from that *StablePut* or from the previous one. Given this invariant, it is clear that *only the desired events and the unexpected disasters for disk pages are possible for stable pages*. Another way of saying this is that *StablePut* is an *atomic* operation: it either changes the page to the desired new value, or it does nothing and a crash occurs. Furthermore, decay is unexpected.

The actions are implemented as follows. A *StableGet* does a *CarefulGet* from one of the representing pages, and if the result is bad does a *CarefulGet* from the other one. A *StablePut* does a *CarefulPut* to each of the representing pages in turn; the second *CarefulPut* must not be started until the first is complete. Since a crash during the first *CarefulPut* will prevent the second one from being started, we can be sure that if the second *CarefulPut* is started, there was no write error in the first one.

The third action, called *Cleanup*, works like this:

Do a *CarefulGet* from each of the two representing pages;
if both return *good* and the same data **then**
Do nothing
else if one returns *bad* **then**
{ One of the two pages has decayed, or has suffered a bad write in a *CarefulPut* which was interrupted by a crash. }
Do a *CarefulPut* of the data block obtained from the *good* address to the *bad* address.
else if both return *good*, but different data **then**
{ A crash occurred between the two *CarefulPuts* of a *StablePut* }
Choose either one of the pages, and do a *CarefulPut* of its data to the other page.

This action is applied to every stable page before normal operation of the system begins (at initialization, and after each crash), and at least every unit decay time T_D thereafter. Because the timing of T_D is restarted after a crash, it can be done in volatile storage. Instead of cleaning up all the pages after every crash, we could call *Cleanup* before the first *Get* or *Put* to each page, thus reducing the one-time cost of crash recovery; with this scheme the T_D interval must be kept in stable storage, however.

For the stable storage actions to work, there must be *mapping* functions which enumerate the stable pages, and give the representing pages for each stable page. The simplest way to provide these functions is to permanently assign a region of the disk to stable pages, take the address of one representing page as the address of the stable page, and use a simple function on the address of one representing page to obtain the address of the other. For example, if a unit consists of two physical drives, we might pair corresponding pages on the two drives. A more elaborate scheme is to treat a small part of the disk in this way, and use the stable storage thus obtained to record the mapping functions for the rest of stable storage.

To show that the invariant holds, we assume that it holds when stable storage is initialized, and consider all possible combinations of events. The detailed argument is a tedious case analysis, but its essence is simple. Both pages cannot be bad for the following reason. Consider the first page to become bad; it either decayed, or it suffered a bad write during a *StablePut*. In the former case, the other page cannot decay or suffer a bad write during an interval T_D, and during this interval a *Cleanup* will fix the bad page. In the latter case, the bad write is corrected by the *CarefulPut* it is part of, unless there is a crash, in which case the *Cleanup* done during the ensuing crash recovery will fix the bad page before another *Put* can be done. If both pages are good but different, there must have been a crash between the *CarefulPuts* of a *StablePut*, and the ensuing *Cleanup* will force either the old or the new data into both pages.

To simplify the exposition in the next three sections, we assume that all non-volatile data is held in stable storage.

11.5.2. Stable processors

A stable processor differs from a physical one in three ways. First, it can make use of a portion of the disk storage to store its volatile state; as with other aspects of a processor, long-term reliability of this disk storage is not important, since any failure is converted into a crash of the processor. Thus the disk storage used in this way becomes part of the volatile state.

Second, it makes use of stable storage to obtain more useful behavior after a crash, as follows. A process can *save* its state; after a crash each process is restored to its most recently saved state. *Save* is an atomic operation. The state is saved in stable storage, using the simple one-page atomic *StablePut* action. As a consequence, the size of the state for a process is limited to a few hundred bytes. This restriction can easily be removed by techniques discussed elsewhere in the paper, but in fact our algorithms do not require large process states. There is also a *Reset* operation which resets the saved state, so that the process will return to its idle state after a crash.

Third, it makes use of stable storage to construct *stable monitors*. Recall that a monitor is a collection of data, together with a set of procedures for examining and updating the data, with the property that only one process at a time can be executing one of these procedures. This mutual exclusion is provided by a monitor lock which is part of the data. A stable monitor is a monitor whose data, except for the lock, is in stable storage. It has an *image* in global volatile storage which contains the monitor lock and perhaps copies of some of the monitor data. The monitor's procedures acquire this lock, read any data they need from stable storage, and return the proper results to the caller. A procedure which updates the data must do so with exactly one *StablePut*. Saving the process state is not permitted within the monitor; if it were, a process could find itself running in the monitor after a crash with the lock not set.

Since the lock is not represented in stable storage, it is automatically released whenever there is a crash. This is harmless because a process cannot resume execution within the monitor after a crash (since no saves are permitted there), and the single *Put* in an update procedure has either happened (in which case the situation is identical to a crash just after leaving the monitor) or has not happened (in which case it is identical to a crash just before entering the monitor). As a corollary, we note that the procedures of a stable monitor are atomic.

A monitor which keeps the lock in stable storage is possible, but requires that a *Save* of the process state be done simultaneously with setting the lock, and an *Erase* or another *Save* simultaneously with releasing it. Otherwise a crash will leave the lock set with no process in the monitor, or vice versa. Such monitors are expensive (because of the two *StablePuts*) and complex to understand (because of the two *Saves*), and therefore to be avoided if possible. We have found it possible to do without them.

The state of a stable processor, unlike that of a physical processor, is not entirely volatile, that is, it does not all disappear after a crash. In fact, we go further and adopt a programming style which allows us to claim that *none* of its shared state is volatile. More precisely, any shared datum must be protected by some monitor. To any code outside the monitor, the possible changes in state of the datum are simply those which can result from invoking an update action of the monitor (which might, of course, crash). We insist that all the visible states must be stable; i.e., the monitor actions map one stable state into another. Inside the monitor anything goes, and in particular volatile storage may be used to cache the datum. Whenever the monitor lock is released, however, the current state of the datum must be represented in stable storage. As a consequence, the only effect of a crash is to return all the processes to their most recently saved states; any state shared between processes is not affected by a crash. This fact greatly simplifies reasoning about crashes. Note that the remote call mechanism of section 14.9 does not run on a stable processor, and hence does not have this property, even though all the procedures of later sections which are called remotely do have it

11.5.3. Remote procedures

In order to simplify the algorithm and our reasoning about it, we use the remote procedure calls of section 14.9 for all the communication among machines. These calls have the same semantics as ordinary procedure calls, except that the procedure may be executed more than once.

11.6. Stable sets and compound actions

Based on stable storage, stable processors, and remote procedures, we can build a more powerful object (stable sets) and a more powerful method for constructing compound actions, from which it is then straightforward to build atomic transactions. The base established in the previous section has the following elements:

- stable storage, with an ideal atomic write operation (*StablePut*) for data blocks of a few hundred bytes;

- stable processes which can save their local state, which revert to that state after a crash, and which can execute procedures on more than one processor, provided the procedures are restartable actions;

- stable monitors protecting data in stable storage, provided all the data is on a single processor, and each update operation involves only a single *Put*;

- no volatile data.

In this system the existence of separate processors is logically invisible. However, we want our algorithms to have costs which depend only on the amount and distribution of the data being accessed, and not on the total size of the system. This means that interrogating every processor in the system must be ruled out, for example. Also, the cost of recovering from a crash of one processor must not depend on the number of processors in the system. Rather, it should be fixed, or at most be proportional to the number of processes affected, i.e., the processes running on the processor which crashes. Finally, it should be possible to distribute the work of processing a number of transactions evenly over all the processors, without requiring any single processor to be involved in all transactions.

In order to handle arbitrarily large transactions, we need arbitrarily large stable storage objects, instead of the fixed size pages provided by stable storage, and we need arbitrarily large atomic actions instead of the fixed size ones provided by stable monitors. The purpose of this section is to construct these things.

11.6.1. Stable sets

A stable set is a set of records, each one somewhat smaller than a stable page. The stable set itself is named by a unique identifier, and may contain any number of records. All the operations on stable sets are restartable, and all except *Create* and *Erase* return an error indication unless executed between a *Create* and the next *Erase*. Stable sets have the following atomic operations:

Create(*i*: *ID*) creates a stable set named by *i*. If such a set already exists, it does nothing.

Insert(*s*, *t*: *StableSet*, *new*: *Record*) requires that *new* is not in *s* or *t*, and inserts *new* into both sets; one might be **nil**. *Insert* into *n* sets for any fixed *n* would also be possible, but is not needed for our application.

Replace(*s*, *t*: *StableSet*, *old*, *new*: *Record*) requires that *old* was inserted into *s* and *t* by a single *Insert* or a previous *Replace*. It removes *old* from *s* and *t* and inserts *new* into *s* and *t*.

IsEmpty(*s*: *StableSet*) returns true if *s* is empty, false otherwise.

IsMember(*s*: *StableSet*, *r*: *Record*) returns true if *r* is in *s*, false otherwise.

There are also two non-atomic operations:

Enumerate(*s*: *StableSet*, *p*: **procedure**) calls *p* with each element of *s* in turn. We will write such operations in the form **for** *r* **in** *s* **do** . . . for readability.

Erase(*s*: *StableSet*) which enumerates the elements of *s* and removes each one from *s*. If the element was inserted into another set *t* by the *Insert* which put it into *s*, it is removed from *t* also. If *s* does not exist, *Erase* does nothing.

We have no need for an operation which removes a single element from a set, and its absence simplifies some of our reasoning.

These operations have all the obvious properties of set operations. Since *Enumerate* and *Erase* are not atomic, we specify them more carefully: *Enumerate* will produce at least all the items *Insert*ed before the enumeration starts, if no *Erase* has been done; it will not produce any items which have not been *Insert*ed after it is over.

We have two implementations for stable sets. The first is designed to work efficiently on a single processor, and is extremely simple. We permanently allocate a set of pages in stable storage, with known addresses, to represent stable sets; these pages are called the *pool*. On each page we store an item of the following type:

```
type Item = record case tag: (empty, element) of
    empty: ();
    element: (s, t: ID, r: Record) end
```

The pages of the pool are initialized to *empty*. The elements of a set *ss* are those values *rr* for which there exists a representing page in the pool, i.e., one containing an *element* item *i* with $i.r = rr$ and ($i.s = ss$ or $i.t = ss$). To do *Insert*(*ss, tt, rr*) we find an *empty* page and write into it the item (*tag = element, s = ss, t = tt, r = rr*). To do *IsEmpty, IsMember* and *Enumerate* we search for all the relevant representing pages. To do *Replace*(*ss, tt, oo, nn*) we find the page representing (*ss, tt, oo*) and overwrite it with (*ss, tt, nn*). Note that *Insert* and *Replace* are atomic, as claimed above, since each involves just one *Put*.

A practical implementation using pools maintains a more efficient representation of the sets in volatile storage, and reconstructs this representation after a crash by reading all the pages in the pool. To make better use of stable storage, it also orders the pages of the pool in a ring, stores several items in each page, implements the *Erase* operation by writing an *erased* item rather than removing each item of the set, and recovers the space for the elements of erased sets as it cycles around the ring. The details of all this do not require any new ideas.

The utility of the pool implementation is limited by the need to read all the pages in the pool after a crash. We do not want to read all the pages of all the pools in the system when one processor crashes. Therefore a *wide* stable set, which spans more than one processor, requires a different approach. We assume that the value of a record determines the processor on which it should be stored (for both sets into which it is inserted), and that the unique identifier of the set determines a processor called the *root processor* of the set. The idea is to have a stable set called a *leaf* on each processor, and to use another stable set, called the *root* and stored on the root processor, to keep track of all the processors involved. All these sets can be implemented in pools. Each record stored in the root contains only a processor name; the records in the leaves contain the elements of the wide set. Operations involving a single record are directed to its processor, and are implemented in the obvious way. *IsEmpty, Erase* and *Enumerate* are directed to the root, which uses the corresponding operation of each leaf set in turn. *Enumerate* calls its procedure argument locally on each leaf machine.

The only tricky point is to ensure that elements are not added to a leaf until its processor is registered in the root set. To accomplish this, the *Insert* operations check whether the leaf set is empty, and if so they first call the root set's *Insert* to add the leaf processor. As a consequence, *Insert* is no longer an atomic operation within the implementation, but since extra entries in the root set are not visible to the user of the wide set, it is still atomic at that level.

11.6.2. Compound atomic actions

We need to be able to take a complex action, requiring many atomic steps, and make the entire action atomic, i.e., ensure that it will be carried out completely once it has been started. If the action *R* is invoked from a processor which never crashes, and all the actions which can be invoked concurrently with *R* are compatible, then this goal will be met, because the invoking processor will keep timing out and restarting *R* until it is finally completed. Thus, for example, if we assume that the client of our data storage system never crashes, then restartable actions are sufficient to provide atomic transactions. Since we do not want to assume that any processor never crashes, least of all the client's, someting more is needed.

In fact, what is needed is simply a simulation of a processor with a single process which never crashes, and our stable processors already provide such a thing. Consider the following procedure, to be executed by a stable processor:

procedure A = **begin** *Save*; R; *Reset* **end**

If R is a restartable action, then A is an atomic action. This is clear from a case analysis. If A crashes before the *Save*, nothing has been done. If A crashes after the *Reset*, R has been done completely and will not be done again because the saved state has been erased. If A crashes between the *Save* and the *Reset*, A will resume after the *Save* and restart R. The resulting execution sequence is equivalent to a single execution of R, by the definition of a restartable action.

11.7. Transactions

In this section we present algorithms for the atomic transactions discussed in section 11.3. The central idea behind them is that a transaction is made atomic by performing it in two *phases*:

- First, record the information necessary to do the writes in a set of *intentions*, without changing the data stored by the system. The last action taken in this phase is said to *commit* the transaction.

- Second, do the writes, actually changing the stored data.

If a crash occurs after the transaction commits, but before all the changes to stored data are done, the second phase is restarted. This restart happens as often as necessary to make get all the changes made. Any algorithm which works like this is called a *two-phase commit* [Gray 78].

To preserve the atomic property, the writing of the intentions set must itself be atomic. More precisely, consider the change from a state in which it is still possible to abort the transaction (i.e. none of the changes have been recorded in the files in such a way that they can be seen by any other transaction), to one in which aborting is no longer possible, and hence crash recovery must complete the transaction. This change is the point at which the transaction is committed. It must be atomic, and hence must be the result of a single *Put* action. The intentions set may be of arbitrary size, but it must be represented in such a way that its existence has no effect on the file data until this final *Put* has been done. In addition, care must be taken that the intentions are properly cleaned up after the transaction has been committed or aborted.

This idea is implemented using stable sets and compound atomic actions. The intentions are recorded in a stable set, and the locks needed to make concurrent transactions atomic are recorded in another stable set. The complex operation of committing the transaction (including carrying out the writes) is made into a compound atomic action.

We present algorithms for the following procedures to be called by clients: *Begin, Read, Write, End,* and *Abort.* The client is expected to call *Begin* on one of the servers, which we call the *coordinator* for the transaction. *Begin* returns a transaction identifier. The client then calls *Read* and *Write* any number of times on various servers, directing each call to the server holding the file pages addressed by the call. These calls may be done from separate processes within the client. When all the client's *Write* calls have returned, he calls either *End* or *Abort* on the coordinator.

If the client fails to wait for all his *Write*s to return, no harm will be done to the file servers, but their resulting behavior may not be that intended by the client. Each of the actions is designed to be atomic and restartable; thus even in the presence of server crashes, lost messages and crashed clients they are either fully performed or not performed at all. However, if the client does not repeat each *Write* call until it returns, he will be unable to determine which *Writes* actually occurred. Similarly, if he calls *End* before all *Writes* have returned, he can not be sure which of the outstanding ones will be included in the transaction.

We use the following data structures:

A *transaction identifier* (*TI*) is simply a unique identifier.

An *Intention* is a record containing

> t: a *TI*;
> p: a page address *PA* = **record** file identifier, page number in file **end**;
> a: an action *RW* = (*read, write*);
> d: data to be written.

Actually t and p are identifiers for the stable sets in which an *Intention* is recorded; we shall ignore this distinction to keep the programs shorter.

A *transaction flag* (*TF*) is a record containing

> t: a *TI*;
> ph: the phase of the transaction, *Phase* = (*nonexistent, running, committed, aborted*).

On each of the server machines we maintain sets containing these objects, and stable monitors protecting these sets, as follows:

- For each file page p, at the server holding the file page,
  a stable set *p.locks* (whose elements are *Intentions* which are interpreted as *locks*), a stable monitor protecting this set, and a condition *p.lockFreed* on which to wait for locks.

- For each transaction t, at the coordinator for the transaction,
  a root for a wide stable set *t.intentions* (containing *Intentions* which are interpreted as data which will be written when the transaction ends). A leaf of this set will exist on each server on which a file page is written or read under this transaction.

- At each server s,
  a stable set *s.flags* (containing transaction flags), a stable monitor protecting this set.

We first introduce two entry procedures on the set of transaction flags; these are not accessible to the client:

```
entry procedure SetPhase(t: TI, desiredPhase: Phase {not nonexistent}) = begin
    case GetPhase(t) of
        committed, aborted: {do nothing};
        running: overwrite with ⟨t, desiredPhase⟩;
        nonexistent: if desiredPhase = running then insert ⟨t, running⟩ in flags {else nothing}
    endcase;
entry function GetPhase(t: TI): phase = begin
    if ⟨t, phase⟩ B flags then return phase else return nonexistent end.
```

The *SetPhase* procedure is an atomic restartable action. It is designed so that the phase of a transaction will go through three steps: *nonexistent, running,* and then either *committed* or *aborted*. Moreover, only setting it to *running* can remove it from the *nonexistent* phase, and it will change from *running* to either *aborted* or *committed* exactly once.

Now we introduce the five client callable procedures. Two are entry procedures of the stable monitor for a page. Each should return an error if the page is not stored on this server, but this detail is suppressed in the code.

```
entry function Read(t: TI, p: PA): Data =
        var noConflict: Boolean; begin
        repeat noConflict := true;
                for i in p.locks do if i.t≠t and i.a= write then begin Wait (p.lockFreed); noConflict := false end
        until noConflict;
        Insert(p.locks, t.intentions, <read, nil>); return StableGet(p) end;

entry procedure Write(t: TI, p: PA, d: Data) =
        var noConflict: Boolean; var d'; begin
        repeat noConflict := true; d' := d;
                for i in p.locks do
                        if i.t≠t then begin Wait (p.lockFreed); noConflict := false end
                        else if i.a = write then d' := i.d;
        until noConflict;
        if d'=d then Overwrite(p.locks, t.intentions, <write, d'>, <write, d>)
        else Insert(p.locks, t.intentions, <write, d>) end;
```

The other three, which control the start and end of the transaction, are not monitor entry procedures. The *End* and *Abort* procedures which complete a transaction do so by calling an internal procedure *Complete*.

```
procedure Begin(): TI =
        const t = UniqueID(); begin SetPhase(t, running); CreateWideStableSet(t); return t end;

function End(t: TI): Phase = return Complete(t, committed)

function Abort(t: TI): Phase = return Complete(t, aborted)

function Complete(t: TI, desiredResult: Phase {committed or aborted only}): Phase = begin
        if GetPhase(t) = nonexistent then return nonexistent;
        Save {process state}; SetPhase(t, desiredResult);
        {now the transaction is committed or aborted}
        if GetPhase(t) = committed then
                for i in t.intentions do if i.a= write then StablePut(i.p, i.d);
        Erase(t.intentions) {also erases all corresponding entries in all p.locks
                                and signals all p.lockFreed conditions};
        Reset {process state}; return GetPhase(t) end;
```

A transaction will terminate either through an *End* or an *Abort*. Both of these commands may be running simultaneously, either because of a confused client, or because *Abort* is being locally generated by a server at the same time as a client calls *End*. Moreover, the remote procedure call mechanism can result in several instances of either *End* or *Abort* in simultaneous execution. In any case, the *phase* will change to either *aborted* or *committed* and remain with that value; which of these occurs determines the outcome of the transaction. Thus it is *phase* which makes *Abort* and *End* compatible.

We make four claims:

(1) If *phase* changes from *running* to *committed*, then all *Write* commands completed before *End* was first entered will be reflected in the file data.

(2) The only changes to file data will be as a result of *Write* commands directed to this transaction.

(3) If *phase* changes from *running* to *aborted*, then no *Write* commands will be reflected.

(4) After the first *End* or *Abort* completes, the wide stable set for *t* will have been erased and will remain erased and empty.

Claim 4 follows from the fact that both *End* and *Abort* eventually call *Erase*(*t*). Thus the set will have been erased. The set can not be recreated because the only call on set creation is in the *Begin* action, and each time *Begin* is called it will use a new unique id. Claim 3 follows from the fact that the only writes to file data pages occur in the *End* procedure; these writes will not occur if the *End* procedure discovers that *phase* has been set to *aborted*; finally, once *phase* has been set to *aborted*, it will remain set to *aborted*. Claim 2 follows from the fact that only *Write* can add intentions with $a = write$ to *t*.

Claim 1 follows from several facts. The fundamental one is that the body of *End* (following the *Save* and up to the *Reset*) is a restartable action. This action has two possible outcomes, depending on the value of *phase* after the *SetPhase*. If $phase = committed$, then the restartable action does nothing. If $phase = committed$, then it remains so forever, and *End* will embark on some useful work. This work will include *StablePut*(*i.p*, *i.d*) for any *write* intention *i* enumerated from set *t*. Any *Write*(*t*, *p*, *d*) command completed before *End* was called will have made such an entry in *t*, and the enumeration will produce it. All such entries will be produced because there will be no call on *Erase*(*t*) until at least one enumeration has completed without interruption from crashes.

11.8. Refinements

Many refinements to the algorithms of the last three sections can be made. A few have been pointed out already, and a number of others are collected in this section. Most of them are incorporated in a running system which embodies the ideas of this paper [Israel 78].

11.8.1. File representation

A file can conveniently be represented by a page containing an *index* array of pointers to data pages, which in turn contain the bytes (or the obvious tree which generalizes this structure). With this representation, we can record and carry out intentions without having to write all the data into the intentions set, read it out, and finally write it into the file. Instead, when doing a *Write*(*p*, *d*) we allocate a new stable page, write *d* into it, and record the address of the new page in the intention. Then only these addresses need to be copied into the index when carrying out the intentions. This scheme allows us to handle the data only once, just as in a system without atomic transactions. It does have one drawback: if pages are updated randomly in a large file, any physical contiguity of the file pages will soon be lost. As a result, sequential access will be slower, and the space required to store the index will increase, since it will not be possible to compress its contents.

11.8.2. Ordering of actions

It is easy to see that the sequential **for** loop in *End* can be done in parallel, since all the data on which it operates is disjoint.

A more interesting observation is that the writing of intentions into the *t* and *p* sets can be postponed until just before *End* is called. In this way it is likely that all the intentions can be written in a single *StablePut*, even for a fairly large transaction. The effect of this optimization is that the client's *Write* calls will not return until just before the *End*; a new procedure, say *GetReady*, would have to be added so that the client can inform the servers that he wants responses to his *Writes*. We can carry this idea one step further, and move the *GetReady* call from the client to the coordinator, which does it as part of *End* before committing the transaction. For this to work, the client must tell the coordinator what responses to *Writes* he is expecting (e.g., by giving the unique identifiers of the calls) so that the coordinator can check that the responses are in fact received. In addition, the other servers must return their *Write* responses to the coordinator in response to his *GetReady*, rather than to the client.

A consequence of this scheme is that a crash of any server *s* is likely to force transactions in progress involving *s* to be aborted, since the intentions held in volatile storage at *s* will be lost, and the client is no longer repeating his *Write* calls until he gets the return which indicates that the intentions have been recorded in stable storage. If crashes are not too frequent this is not objectionable, since deadlocks will cause occasional transaction aborts in any case.

A more attractive consequence is that write locks will not be set until just before the *End*, thus reducing the interval during which data cannot be read by other transactions [Gifford 79]. In order to avoid undue increases in the number of transactions aborted for deadlock, it may be necessary to resort to an "intending to write" lock which delays other transactions also intending to write, without affecting readers. These intricacies are beyond the scope of this paper.

11.8.3. Aborts

In a practical system it is necessary to time out and automatically abort transactions which run too long (usually because the client has crashed) or which deadlock. The latter case can be detected by some explicit mechanism which examines the locks, or it can be inferred from a timeout. In any case, these automatic aborts add no logical complexity to the scheme described in section 11.7, which is already prepared to receive an *Abort* from the client at any time.

When a deadlock occurs because of a conflict between read and write locks, a less drastic action than aborting the transaction holding the read lock is possible, namely to simply notify the client that it was necessary to break his read locks. He then can choose to abort the transaction, reread the data, or decide that he doesn't really care. It is necessary to require that the client explicitly approve each broken read lock before committing the transaction. The implications of this scheme are discussed in more detail elsewhere.

Conclusions

We have defined a facility (transactions) which clients can use to perform complex updates to distributed data in a manner which maintains consistency in the presence of system crashes and concurrency. We have seen that transactions can be implemented with only a small amount of communication among servers. This communication is proportional to the number of servers involved in a transaction, rather than the size of the update. We have described the algorithm through a series of abstractions, together with informal correctness arguments.

Chapter 12. Synchronization

12.1. Introduction

At every level of abstraction, processes which execute on processing elements (P.E.'s) can initiate operations. An operation at level j is implemented as a set of actions which are defined at some level i, with $i < j$. Again, what is viewed as an action from level j is in fact defined as an operation at level i. This model applies recursively at all levels. Operations, and therefore actions, manipulate resources. Resources will be abstracted as data objects. For example, a peripheral may be abstracted by its current state as defined by some finite state automaton. A file record will be abstracted by its content. Examples of actions which manipulate data objects are Read, Write, Create, Delete. A computing system is expected to meet some external specification at all times, in which case the system state will be said to be consistent. The purpose of synchronization mechanisms is to provide processes with some means whereby the system may be kept in a consistent state. The type of synchronization considered in this chapter is synchronization as achieved by executives. We will not discuss the synchronization features embedded in languages [Hoare 74, Brinch Hansen 78, Hoare 78, Ichbiah 79, Mao 80].

12.2. Consistency and atomicity

Data objects have semantic links with each other, that is to say their values must satisfy some constraints known as consistency constraints [Eswaran 76]. When an object is created, deleted, written, it may be necessary to create, delete, write some other data objects for consistency constraints to be satisfied. For every level of abstraction, a set of operations is defined. Each operation is defined in such a way that, assuming its input is a set of objects whose values are consistent, it will produce a set of new values which are also consistent. Therefore, states which need to be communicated or remembered among processes being consistent, processing is also consistent. In the absence of any particular assumption, the only way to preserve consistency is to guarantee that operations remain atomic. For example, operations are executed one after the other in a strictly sequential fashion. Enforcing atomicity for operations is a sufficient condition for satisfying consistency constraints. If specific assumptions may be expressed, then it is possible to relax the constraint of atomicity for operations and still preserve consistency. Such restrictive assumptions will not be made here.

Starting the execution of an operation only after the completion of the previous one leads to a particular kind of schedule called a serial schedule. In distributed systems, implementing only serial schedules could be very inefficient. Indeed, if actions activated by a given set of operations manipulate different objects, parallel execution of actions is not only possible but recommended. Furthermore, if actions which manipulate a given object and which belong to different operations can be issued "concurrently" and queued by the processing element hosting that object, the idle time separating the execution of two successive actions is smaller than when only one action at a time is being issued and processed. Consequently, what seems desirable is to allow for the interleaving of actions as much as possible so as to optimize performances. Corresponding schedules will be called interleaved schedules. Some interleaved schedules may be equivalent to a serial schedule. Therefore, they are consistent. But this is not always the case.

For example, let us consider a set of objects $X = [x_1, x_2, ..., x_n]$ being manipulated by two operations $A = [a_1, a_2, ..., a_n]$ and $B = [b_1, b_2, ..., b_n]$ where a_i (resp. b_i) stands for the action belonging to A (resp. B) which manipulates object x_i. Different interleaved schedules may take place, producing different final states for X. For every object x_i, one may have either $x_i(A,B) = b_i(a_i(x_i(0)))$ or $x_i(B,A) = a_i(b_i(x_i(0)))$, where $x_i(0)$ stands for the initial state of x_i. Let us assume that the consistency constraints indicate that only two final states are consistent which are either $X(A,B) : [x_i(A,B)$ for every $i]$ or $X(B,A) : [x_i(B,A)$ for every $i]$. These two final states are the only ones which would result from a serial schedule. In order to preclude other interleaved schedules taking place, one must guarantee that either $a_i \rightarrow b_i$ for every i or $b_i \rightarrow a_i$ for every i, where $\rightarrow$ stands for some arbitrary ordering relationship. Ordering actions serves the purpose of implementing atomic operations so as to preserve system state consistency. The notion of relative ordering of actions, of events, is very fundamental for establishing system specification and correctness proofs.

12.3. Event ordering and atomicity

The notion of which event "happened before" another one is usually intuitively based on physical timing considerations. Actually, this amounts to assuming implicitly that some universal time can be defined and observed identically from various locations. We know this to be meaningless. Practically, one may approximate some "universal time" with a given accuracy. However, it may well be unnecessary or impossible to express some system specification in terms of physical timing. Particular chronological orderings of events take place in computing systems because processes which produce these events obey specific rules (algorithms, protocols, etc.) which express relative orderings on sets of events as inferred from the system specification. These orderings allow processes which observe events to correctly implement system activities. Depending on the nature of these activities, either partial or total orderings of events are needed.

12.3.1. Partial and total orderings

A partial ordering , denoted by "$\rightarrow$" (read "happened before"), may be defined on any set of events produced by processes which exchange messages [Lamport 78].

(1) if a and b are actions in the same process and a comes before b, then $a \rightarrow b$

(2) if a is the sending of a message by one process and b is the receipt of the same message by another process, then $a \rightarrow b$

(3) if $a \rightarrow b$ and $b \rightarrow c$ then $a \rightarrow c$

The ordering is irreflexive if we have also:

(4) $a \sim\rightarrow a$ for any event a. ($\sim\rightarrow$ stands for "did not happen before").

As long as processes interact with each other by exchanging messages, it is possible to order some of the events which occur in different processes. The ordering $\rightarrow$ is only partial. For example, if for two events a and b we have $a \rightsquigarrow\rightarrow b$ and $b \rightsquigarrow\rightarrow a$ then it is impossible to tell which event happened before the other. These events are said to be concurrent. In particular, events occuring in processes which do not communicate with each other cannot be ordered. Depending on the constraints to be satisfied, this may or may not be acceptable. In some cases, as illustrated by the example given in section 12.2, it is necessary to order all events, even those produced by processes which do not interact with each other. One way to obtain a total ordering from the partial one defined above consists in defining a total ordering on the set of processes.

12.3.2. Atomic operations

Let us now use some given ordering $\rightarrow$ so as to define more precisely the notion of atomic operation. Consider a set of operations and let A and B be any two operations in this set. Let A^* and B^* be the sets of all actions a^* and b^* which access common resources. We will say that A is atomic for B (or the reverse) if either $a^* \rightarrow b^*$ or $b^* \rightarrow a^*$. Note that for any given common resource, one may have several actions a^* and several actions b^*. In other words, an operation is atomic if the following conditions are satisfied:

(1)   either all actions are completed or no action is completed

(2)   intermediate states are not visible to any other operation.

Atomicity is a well known concept. For example, conventional computer instructions (operations) are atomic due to the fact that such instructions are processed one after the other by a single P.E.. In distributed systems, actions belonging to a given operation may be processed by several P.E.'s, with no predictable timing relationship. Therefore, in distributed systems, the implementation of atomic operations probably requires some specific mechanism not needed in centralized systems.

12.4. Synchronization

It should be clear now that atomicity implies that it is possible to express / induce / enforce a particular ordering on any given set of events. This is the purpose of synchronization mechanisms. More precisely, we will say that synchronization is a way of expressing / inducing / enforcing either a partial or a total ordering on any set of events. At this point, we would like to draw the attention of the reader on a very fundamental issue in computing systems, which is the issue of computing delays. In conventional systems operated by a single P.E., it is usually possible to predict very accurately how long it takes for the P.E. to execute any given instruction (an operation). However, in general, the design of the executive is not based on knowledge of these figures. Therefore, it would probably be unreasonable to base the design of an executive for a distributed system on assumptions concerning computing delays. In distributed systems, computing delays include propagation delays (among the various processing elements), which makes it even more difficult to predict computing delays accurately enough. Let us illustrate these notions as follows. Consider a conventional system including a shared memory (figure 12-1). Process P produces an event E while processing some operation. In order to be observable , the production of E must be materialized, e.g. by updating a memory cell M. In conventional systems, the production and the materialization of E are not distinguishable by those processes (Q for example) which should observe the occurrence of E.

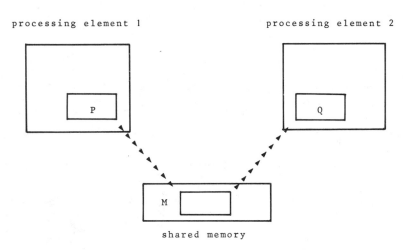

Figure 12-1: Production/materialization versus observation of an event in shared-memory systems

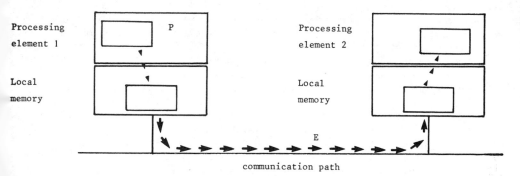

Figure 12-2: Production/materialization/observation of an event in a distributed system

Let us assume for a while that in distributed systems, processing elements do not share a common memory (this is not necessarily true for all distributed systems but the explanation applies in any case). For such systems, one may decide to materialize the occurence of an event either at the producer premises or at the consumer premises. In the first case, again, production and materialization are not distinguishable but observation is a two-step operation. In the second case, production and materialization are distinct (see figure 12-2).

Whatever the implementation, between production and observation, we have now introduced a new parameter which is the propagation delay between production and observation. For distributed systems where operation executions involve a number of processing elements, it is easy to see that variability in propagation delays may disturb any particular event ordering which was supposed to occur. Even worse, when propagation delays are supposed to be fixed, specific event orderings (e.g. consistent ones) cannot be predicted. Therefore the need for a particular synchronization mechanism to be used by producers and observers of events.

12.5. Synchronization and types of computing systems

Depending on how activities are conducted at a given level of abstraction in a computing system, it is possible to describe more precisely what is a consistent schedule in each case. We distinguish between producers of events/actions and consumers of events/actions. Producers and consumers are equivalent to customers and servers as introduced in chapter 2. Upon request, a producer initializes an operation. This may result in the firing of several actions. Actions are processed by consumers. In the general case, at any time before completion, an operation may require the firing of a new action. A representation of a multiproducer/multiconsumer system is given figure 12-3.

12.5.1. Fully replicated computing

Fully replicated computing refers to a situation where every action fired by any operation must be processed by all consumers. What is required is that all actions should be completed. If, for any reason, e.g., temporary overflow of one consumer, one action cannot be performed, then some particular decision must be made. It is important to realize that it is not simply a matter of achieving physical broadcasting of actions. Although physical broadcasting may help to implement efficiently the necessary synchronization mechanism, it is not a solution to our problem. In this context, the purpose of a synchronization mechanism is to guarantee that the ordering of actions processed by consumers is identical for all consumers.

12.5.2. Strictly partitioned computing

Strictly partitioned computing refers to a situation where one operation fires different actions at some consumers. For two different operations, the two corresponding sets of consumers may or may not overlap. For a given operation initiated at different times, the corresponding sets of consumers may be different. For this kind of system, the purpose of a synchronization mechanism is to guarantee that all interfering actions get ordered so that operations are kept atomic.

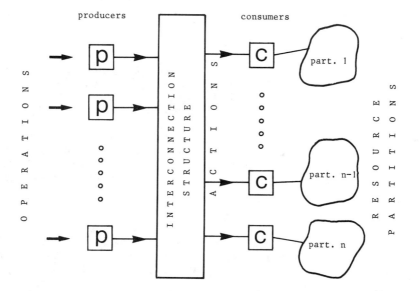

Figure 12-3: A multiproducer/multiconsumer model

12.5.3. Partitioned and partially replicated computing

This kind of computing refers to a situation where one operation fires either different or identical actions at some of the consumers. All comments made for both fully replicated and strictly partitioned computing apply to this kind of computing.

12.6. Event ordering — examples

We will examine examples of synchronization problems as they may arise at three different levels of abstraction.

12.6.1. Link protocols

The Arpanet IMP-IMP protocol has been described in chapter 5. As regards frame transmission on an IMP-IMP link, any ordering of frames is convenient. However, a specific ordering (strict sequencing) is enforced on the set of frames which circulate on a given logical channel. This is needed for error and flow control purposes. Identically, if a specific ordering of frames is required at a higher level of abstraction (e.g., sequencing of messages should be maintained between a sender and a receiver), such an ordering must be built a posteriori at this higher level.

12.6.2. Executives

One way of building a consistent schedule of operations at the level of executives consists in controlling all operations from a single locus of control, i.e., by enforcing mutual exclusion between competing operations. In centralized systems, Test-and-Set instructions, Semaphores, Monitors are synchronization tools which serve this purpose. These tools are well known and will not be described in further detail. When executives provide producers of actions with several synchronization tools, operations may have to be synchronized with each other by using more than one such tool. This is a common situation in distributed systems. What is then required is a synchronization mechanism which would allow for the building of a number of consistent schedules, one per producer of actions, such that the global schedule resulting from the interleaving of all individual schedules would also be a consistent one.

It is worth mentioning that in most computing systems, either centralized or distributed, and as far as executives are concerned, the effect of an action materializes as the modification of some process state. For example, a data item is updated, indicating that a resource has been either allocated to or released by some process(es). For a correct functioning of the system, it is mandatory for executives to be given a consistent view of those data structures which reflect the state of all processes they manage. Consequently, the problem of synchronizing operations at the executive level is in essence akin to the problem of synchronizing transactions at the level of abstraction corresponding to file or database management. Keeping a given data structure consistent is the objective. Differences between these two levels are differences in operation sizes and complexity, in data structure sizes, in frequency of operations, etc.

12.6.3. Database system nucleus

A database system nucleus is aimed at managing data objects on behalf of system users. A database contains a (usually large) number of objects. As explained in section 12.2, there are specific constraints to be satisfied to keep the database state consistent. Locks are tools which allow for the building of atomic operations. At the level of abstraction of database nucleus, an operation is usually called a transaction. Two kinds of locks may be used which are share-lock and exclusive-lock. Setting of a lock, releasing of a lock are examples of actions initiated by transactions. Simultaneous share-lock actions on one given object are compatible. Either simultaneous exclusive-lock actions or simultaneous exclusive-lock and share-lock actions are incompatible. For a given set of transactions T, it is possible to define different schedules [Eswaran 76].

Every schedule equivalent to a serial schedule is consistent. However, non serial schedules may also be consistent under specific conditions. A legal schedule is a schedule in which conflicting lock actions are not granted simultaneously. But legal schedules are not necessarily consistent. A well-formed transaction is defined as a transaction where each read action is preceded by a share-lock action and each write action is preceded by an exclusive-lock action. Furthermore, we may constrain transactions to initiate lock actions during a phase which should not contain any unlock action. Once an entity has been unlocked, lock actions are prohibited. This is the notion of two-phase locking. If each transaction in set T is well-formed and if locking is two-phase, then any legal schedule for T is consistent. This condition is a sufficient one. In order to express necessary conditions for a legal schedule to be consistent, it is required to make additional assumptions.

If consistency constraints are always satisfied, any transaction running at any time will be given a consistent view of the database state. We will say that (internal) consistency is achieved. In (fully or partially) replicated database systems, a particular kind of consistency constraints must be satisfied which state that all copies of an entity must be identical. In other words, a read action "broadcast" to all consumers retaining one such copy should not return two or more different values. This type of consistency is referred to as mutual consistency. For more detailed information on the problem of concurrency control in distributed file/database systems, we refer the reader to chapters 11 and 13. Let us now turn our attention to synchronization mechanisms intended for distributed systems in general.

12.7. Synchronization mechanisms for distributed systems

12.7.1. Centralized versus decentralized synchronization

For the purpose of implementing atomic operations, possibly at all levels of abstraction, it is possible to rely on a particular entity, to be referred to as a central synchronizing entity, which would be accessed by every producer each time an operation must be initiated. The term *synchronizing entity* is used to refer to such objects as hardware interlocks, semaphores, processes, etc. A synchronizing entity is said to be central if:

- it possesses a unique name, known by all processes which must synchronize with each other;
- at any time, any of these processes may access the synchronizing entity.

Some systems are designed so as to tolerate failures, in particular failure of the central synchronizing entity. Some recovery technique is provided to elect / choose / designate a new synchronizing entity when such a failure occurs. Between two consecutive failures, the definition given above applies. Whether recovery is conducted in a decentralized or centralized manner is a separate issue. Every synchronization mechanism which is based on the existence of a central synchronizing entity will be said centralized. Other mechanisms will be said decentralized. Clearly, the performing of a function (e.g., process scheduling, data access control) may or may not be controlled via a central synchronizing entity. In the first case, we will say that control of the function is centralized and that it is decentralized in the second case. From this analysis, it is possible to characterize some synchronization mechanisms.

Centralized mechanisms

- unique physical clock
- eventcount; although an eventcount may be implemented on several physical components (physically distributed), it still constitutes a unique entity to be used as such, e.g. by observers which read the eventcount
- static sequencer.

Decentralized mechanisms

- multiple physical clocks
- multiple logical clocks
- pair-wise shared variables
- circulating token
- circulating sequencer.

Let us now describe the essential aspects of some synchronization mechanisms. The presentation will be structured after a general classification. Only the basic features of the mechanisms will be presented. The interested reader is referred to the literature referenced throughout this section.

12.7.2. Centralized mechanisms

12.7.2.1. Utilization of a physical clock

The idea is to build a unique physical time frame within the system by providing for a single clock, as it is the case in centralized systems. Producers may use the physical timestamps either delivered by or read from the central clock to express some ordering on the set of actions they initialize. Although simple, this approach suffers many drawbacks. For instance, correct timestamping relies entirely on the possibility to receive correctly at all times the current value displayed by the clock. There is the danger that bad transmission may become an impediment for a desired ordering to take place. Also, an accurate a priori knowledge or a posteriori estimation of interprocess message transit delays is required. The degree of accuracy depends on the constraints put on the system. For example, it may be necessary for some systems using a satellite clock to take into account relativistic phenomena within the synchronization mechanism [Cohen 77], [Holt 78].

12.7.2.2. Utilization of a central process

Many examples may be given. For example, in distributed databases, concurrency control may rely on the existence of a unique process which receives all requests issued by producers which initiate actions. Synchronization is in fact achieved via the mutual exclusion performed by this central process. Solutions described in [Gray 78], [Menasce 77] and [Stonebraker 78] utilize conflict graphs, a technique designed initially for centralized systems for the purpose of avoiding or detecting deadlocks. Basically, each time a producer wishes to lock an entity, it sends a request to the central process. If the requested locks lead to a deadlock situation (e.g. by detecting a cycle in the graph), the decision to roll-back a transaction or to make the requestor wait is taken by the central process.

The issue of resiliency is addressed in [Menasce 77] and [Stonebraker 78]. In [Menasce 77], it is suggested to maintain several copies of the global conflict graph (lock table). When the central process fails, a new one is nominated. It is assumed that producers are arranged in a linear order. The nominee is the next process being alive in the chain. In [Stonebraker 78], the claim is made that several copies of the global conflict graph could become inconsistent. The solution suggested consists in designating a new central process when the previous one has failed (a predefined ordering of producers is supposed to be known) and to have producers sending lock requests again to this new central process so that the conflict graph may be reconstructed. As regards the database itself, these two solutions are based on the concept of primary/secondary copies. At any time, for every entity there exists a primary copy of this entity. A number of copies are maintained in order to survive failures. A centralized and resilient solution to the problem of maitaining mutual consistency of copies in fully replicated database systems has been described in [Alsberg 76]. This solution is also based on the existence of a primary copy (the central process) and several secondary copies. However, the problem of detecting and solving conflicts arising between concurrent transactions, i.e., how to implement atomic transactions, is not addressed in this paper.

12.7.2.3. Eventcounts

An eventcount as described in [Reed 77] is an object which keeps a count of the number of events in a particular class (e.g., actions) that have occurred so far. Three primitives are defined:

Advance (E) : increases the integer value of E by 1.

Read (E) : returns the "current" value of E. The value returned is a lower bound on the current value of E after the *Read*, and an upper bound on the value of E before the *Read*.

Await (E,v) : suspends the calling process until the value of E is at least v.

One important objective is to allow for concurrent execution of these primitives on the same eventcount, without using mutual exclusion as an underlying mechanism (e.g., hardware interlock). The notion of single manipulator eventcount is defined as an eventcount that works correctly as long as concurrent execution of *Advance* operations is avoided. For example, in a distributed system, an evencount can be built out of several single eventcounts (e.g., one per producer). Only the corresponding local producer can manipulate a given single eventcount. Under these conditions, an *Advance* operation on the global eventcount will advance the appropriate single manipulator eventcount. A *Read* operation on the global eventcount is done by reading the component single manipulator eventcounts, in any order, and summing the resulting values.

An implementation is described which guarantees that an *Advance* operation is atomic by representing the eventcount in Gray code in case only single-bit actions are available. It is shown also how a *Read* operation is performed, by fetching each single eventcount (or each bit) twice. Eventcounts are synchronization tools which can be used to design any synchronization mechanism for consumers and producers which can observe and signal the occurence of actions. The claim is made that the flow of information in eventcounts make the eventcount primitives attractive for secure systems that attempt to solve the confinement problem [Lampson 73]. It is not clear whether eventcounts adapt well to distributed systems which should survive element failures.

12.7.2.4. Static sequencer

Unlike eventcounts, sequencers can be used to totally order events in a given class (e.g., actions). Like an eventcount, a sequencer is a non-decreasing integer variable [Reed 77]. Only one primitive is defined:

Ticket(S) : returns the current value of sequencer S and increments S.

Unlike eventcounts, sequencers require a separate mutual exclusion mechanism for insuring that the Ticket primitive is atomic. The activation of two Ticket primitives by any two producers cannot be concurrent. There are two problems with static sequencers to be looked at carefully which are:

- how do corresponding synchronization mechanisms survive the failure of the sequencer?
- how is mutual exclusion achieved?

12.7.2.5. General comments

Clearly, as centralized approaches "adapted" to distributed systems do not meet the requirements of distributed systems, they miss some of the objectives of these systems. In particular, computing systems built under such approaches may not be highly available (e.g., crash of the unique clock, of the central entity) and they may exhibit poor performances (e.g., because of the bottleneck created by the central entity).

12.7.3. Decentralized mechanisms

12.7.3.1. Multiple physical clocks

The objective is also to obtain a unique physical time frame within the system so that consistent schedules may be derived from a total chronological ordering of actions occuring in the system. When several clocks are used it is not enough for the clocks individually to run at approximatively the same rate. They must be kept synchronized so that the relative drifting of any two clocks is kept smaller than a predictable constant. In [Lamport 78] a solution to accomplish this is given. The system under consideration is modelled after a strongly connected graph of processes with diameter d. Every process is provided with a clock and every t, a synchronization (sync) message is sent over every arc. A sync message contains a physical timestamp T. Upon receiving a sync message, if needed, a process should set forward its local clock to be later than the timestamp value contained in the incoming message. It is assumed that both a lower bound u and an upper bound $u + z$ are known for interprocess message transit delays. Let k be the intrinsic accuracy of each clock (e.g. $k < 10^{-6}$) and e the allowed drifting of any two clocks. If $e/(1-k) \leq u$ and $e \ll t$ then it is possible to compute the approximate value of e which is $e \simeq d(2kt + z)$.

Depending on the requirements as regards clocks relative drifting and the validity of the assumptions as regards transit delay boundaries, one may decide:

- either to take the risk of missing some sync messages from time to time, because of some excessively large message transit delays, thus achieving what could be called probabilistic synchronization,

- or not to take this risk. Then, if the upper bound chosen for message transit delays has to be rather large, one should evaluate the consequences as regards performances. The key parameter here is the ratio z/u. For example in Arpanet, z and u are in the order of several hundreds of milliseconds.

The use of timestamps to obtain orderings of actions in a distributed system was suggested first in [Thomas 76].

12.7.3.2. Multiple logical clocks

A logical clock as described in [Lamport 78] should be viewed as a function C which assigns a number to any action initiated locally. Such logical clocks may be implemented by counters. In a system where each producer owns a logical clock, the problem is to guarantee that the system of clocks satisfies some condition F so that a particular ordering may be built on the set of actions initiated by producers. For example, using the irreflexive partial ordering introduced in section 12.3, condition F would be as follows: for any actions a (in i) and b (in j), if $a \rightarrow b$ then $C(i,a) < C(j,b)$. In order to meet condition F, the following rules must be obeyed by producers.

Rule 1: each producer i increments $C(i)$ between any two successive actions.

Rule 2: if action a is the sending of a message m by producer i, then the message m contains a timestamp $T(m) = C(i,a)$. Upon receiving a message m, producer j sets $C(j)$ greater than or equal to its present value and greater than $T(m)$.

Any system of logical clocks satisfying condition F can be used to place a total ordering, denoted by $\ll$, on any set of actions. It is only necessary to use any arbitrary total ordering $<$ of the producers (e.g., by using their names). The ordering $\ll$ is defined as follows : $a \ll b$ if and only if either $C(i,a) < C(j,b)$ or $C(i,a) = C(j,b)$ and $i < j$. The synchronization mechanism defined by rules 1 and 2 and the total ordering $\ll$ allow for the building of consistent schedules of actions. The ordering $\ll$ is not unique and it may not be equivalent to a chronological ordering. This is why it may be necessary to implement a system of logical clocks on a system of several physical clocks (see previous section).

General comments

Synchronization mechanisms built out of several physical or logical clocks have the common characteristic that they are not based on mutual exclusion. This may be particularly advantageous in distributed systems.

12.7.3.3. Utilization of a circulating privilege

Synchronization mechanisms may take advantage of the fact that producers are given unique and permanent names. This defines a total ordering on the set of producers. Such an ordering may be used to view producers as being organized as on a chain or as on a loop. Each producer has a unique predecessor and a unique successor. Such a logical structuring does not imply any particular physical topology.

Pair-wise shared variables: A synchronization mechanism based on the concept of a logical ring has been presented in [Dijkstra 74]. Possession of a control privilege may be inferred by every producer from the observation of a variable shared with one of its two neighbours. Algorithms are given whereby a system being provided with any number of control privileges at initialization time reaches a *stabilized* state where there is only one such privilege in existence. The type of synchronization achieved by this mechanism is mutual exclusion. Failure detection, recovery and dynamic extension are possible with another mechanism based on a similar idea, which is described below.

Circulating token: The idea is to provide for a unique message having a specific format, called the *control token*. This token circulates permanently on a virtual ring of producers. At any time, only the producer which possesses the unique control token is entitled to initiate an operation (mutual exclusion). The token is then sent to the successor. Two requirements must be met; first, the virtual ring should be able to reconfigure itself whenever a producer or a portion of the communication subnetwork either fails or comes up; second, it is necessary to guarantee that at any time, there is one and only one token on the virtual ring. Protocols providing for failure detection and recovery have been presented in [Le Lann 77] and [Le Lann 78]. A protocol aimed at performing lost token detection and token regeneration is described below.

We assume that each producer owns a timer. A timer is reset upon reception of the control token (CT) or any other token (see further). Tokens on the ring circulate FIFO. This may be guaranteed by the use of an end-to-end protocol.

The protocol

- whenever a timer awakes, the corresponding producer generates an election token (ET) which contains the producer name. The timer is set again. We say that the producer has entered an election phase;
- whenever a candidate receives the CT before its own ET is back, it should cancel the election phase (and removes its ET when back);
- whenever a candidate receives an ET, it should record the name of the originating producer.

Let $S(i)$ be the list of candidate names known by candidate i (i stands for any producer name).

- whenever a candidate receives its own ET, it removes it from the ring, resets its timer and runs algorithm A.

A: if $i = \min S(i)$ then generate a new CT; set timer.

Let us demonstrate that with algorithm A no new CT is generated in case the CT is not lost and only one new CT is generated in case the CT is lost. Let us describe first the state-transition table of a producer (i) on the ring (see table 12-1).

Events

- 0: awaking of the timer
- 1: reception of the control token
- 2: reception of an election token, the identity of which is smaller than i
- 3: reception of an election token, the identity of which is larger than i

4: reception of election token i (after a complete revolution on the ring)

States

    a: idle, token timer is set

    b: election token timer is set and $i = \min S(i)$

    a^*: generation of the new CT and immediate switching to state a

Let us introduce the following notation:

$I(CT,x)$	$=$	instant of CT reception by producer x
$I(t(x),y)$	$=$	instant of reception of election token x by producer y
$I(x,0)$	$=$	instant of generation of an election token by producer x
$I(x,x)$	$=$	instant of occurrence of event 4
$\sim k$	$=$	non occurrence of event k

Let us imagine that two producers x and y generate "simultaneously" a new CT and let us show that this situation is impossible. Assume for example that identity $(x) < $ identity (y). Producer y will generate a new CT if and only if state(y) at $I(y,y)$ is b; this implies ~ 1 and ~ 2 between $I(y,0)$ and $I(y,y)$. Identically, assuming that x will generate a new CT implies ~ 1 between $I(x,0)$ and $I(x,x)$ as $x < y$. It is easy to show that a subset of these conditions leads to a contradiction. ~ 2 between $I(y,0)$ and $I(y,y) \rightleftarrows I(t(x),y) > I(y,y)$ for producer y. ~ 1 between $I(x,0)$ and $I(x,x) \rightleftarrows$ I(CT,x) $> I(x,x)$ with the CT received by x being generated by y. This constraint and the FIFO hypothesis imply that, for producer y, we have $I(t(x),y) < I(y,y)$.

This demonstrates that a new CT cannot be generated by two different producers during one token revolution on the ring. The new CT is generated in a finite time delay for which it is possible to compute an upper bound if maximum values are known for transit and processing delays. Any failure occurring during an election phase will only make the duration of this phase longer. This protocol is an example of a distributed mechanism which survives failures.

external events state (i)	0	1	2	3	4
α	β	α	α	α	α
β	β	α	α	β	α^{**}

Table 12-1: Producer state-transition table

1 : the action holds the
    smallest ticket

2,4 : reception of an action
      carrying a smaller ticket

3,4,6 : upon request of the
        operation producer

5 : the "prepare-to-commit"
    message has been acknowledged

7 : reception of the "commit"
    message from the commit
    coordinator

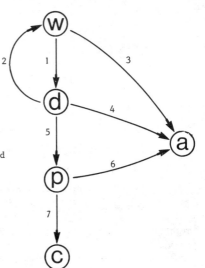

Figure 12-4: Circulating control token and sequencer

General comments

The efficiency of synchronization mechanisms which achieve mutual exclusion between producers depends greatly on the size (in time) of the critical sections. It is likely that when critical sections include exchange of messages between producers and consumers, such synchronization mechanisms would lead to poor performances.

12.7.3.4. Circulating sequencer

A circulating sequencer is a sequencer which circulates permanently on a virtual ring, via the control token mechanism (see figure 12-4).

Upon receiving the control token, a producer may activate a number of *Ticket* primitives and then send the control token to its successor on the ring. This is one way to achieve distributed mutual exclusion among processes which share a sequencer. In [Le Lann 78], a description is given of a protocol which makes the circulating sequencer mechanism resilient. This protocol makes use of a cycle number carried by the control token and incremented by that producer x for which the property $x >$ successor(x) holds. An algorithm is run by one of the two producers involved in a virtual ring reconfiguration in order to decide whether it is necessary to regenerate a new control token. This algorithm provides also for the regeneration of the cycle number as well as the sequencer value.

An example of utilization

Let p be a producer and n be the number of actions which are pending when p receives the token. A strategy may be to allow p to acquire exactly n consecutive tickets. In some cases, the necessity for an action to wait until the token is back before being ticketed may be judged unacceptable. Different algorithms which allow for anticipated selection of tickets are given in [Le Lann 78]. Depending on the strategy adopted for selecting tickets, consumers may use the total ordering inferred from ticket numbers either for avoiding inconsistent schedules (e.g., incoming actions are processed according to a strictly sequential ordering of tickets) or for detecting the occurrence of possibly inconsistent schedules and taking the appropriate decision. For example, conflicts between actions belonging to two (or more) operations are handled by giving priority to the action which carries the smallest ticket. Such a synchronization mechanism allows for the processing of operations which activate actions at any time before completion. This synchronization mechanism is used in conjunction with locking/unlocking protocols in Delta, an experimental distributed transactional system built within the framework of project SIRIUS (INRIA). Transactions manipulate files which are partitioned and partially replicated. Any transaction must be implemented as an atomic operation. All actions invoked for a given operation carry the value of the ticket allocated to this operation. Every action received by a consumer is acknowledged. A producer is notified any modification of the state of an action it has requested. Five states are defined:

waiting, W

done, D

prepared to be comitted, P

committed, C

aborted, A

The state transition graph of an action is given on figure 12-5.

For such actions as write, create, delete, no modification actually takes place in the system files. Such actions are processed within the execution context private to the originating transaction; they alter a copy of the objects requested. It is only when the *End* command is decoded by a

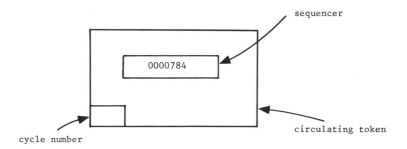

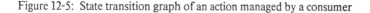

Figure 12-5: State transition graph of an action managed by a consumer

producer (*End* may be either *Commit* or *Abort*) that the modifications are executed and made visible to other transactions (in case of a *Commit*).   In case two operations have conflicts at different consumers, the conflict will be resolved identically by every consumer, and the decision will be immediate (move from state D to state A or to state W).   When an "older" action is received, i.e. which carries a smaller ticket, a consumer may decide either to roll-back (move to W) or to abort (move to A) the "younger" action.   When an action is made to wait, other actions fired by the corresponding operation are not altered.   When an action is aborted, the corresponding initiator will abort all other related actions.   Roll backs and aborts are kept transparent to external users.   In particular, in case of an abort, the corresponding transaction will be automatically re-submitted by the original producer.

It is easy to see that tickets define a total ordering on the set of actions initiated by producers. This is a sufficient condition to guarantee consistent schedules.   There is a large spectrum of decentralized mechanisms aimed at solving the consistency problem.   The mechanism briefly presented above represents one end of the spectrum in the sense that no information at all (except ticket values) is necessary for a consumer to correctly schedule competing actions.   At the other end of the spectrum, one finds mechanisms based on an actual representation of the system state, e.g. wait-for-graphs, conflict graphs [Gray 78, Menasce 77].   In between, one finds mechanisms based on partial knowledge of the system state [Rosenkrantz 78].   All these mechanisms are based on the assumption that roll backs and aborts are acceptable. The trade-off is between the overhead incurred for collecting state information and savings on unnecessary roll backs and aborts.   Depending on the type of transactions to be processed, one has the possibility to choose which mechanism seems more appropriate.

12.8. Evaluation criteria

Synchronization mechanisms do not have identical properties.   A number of criteria, useful for evaluation, are given below.   Their respective importance depends on the constraints put on the system.

Response time and throughput: any mechanism should take full advantage of the parallel nature of the system; parallelism and anticipation in synchronization as well as in communication may result in high throughput and short response times.

Resiliency: any synchronization mechanism should survive failures.   Actually, we need a more precise measurement of such a property which would express the number of simultaneous failures (of producers, of consumers) a mechanism may survive.   This is the notion of resiliency.

Overhead: costs of a given mechanism must be carefully evaluated, in particular the overhead as regards traffic (number and size of additional messages), processing (handling of additional messages) and storage (for synchronization information).

Convergence and fairness: when conflicts occur between operations, it may be necessary for a synchronization mechanism to avoid starvation of producers.   Furthermore, it may also be required that a given mechanism provides producers with equal rights.

Extensibility: if a mechanism allows for dynamic system reduction (it is resilient), then it is necessary to show how this mechanism matches the requirement of dynamic system extension. What this means is that the design of a synchronization mechanism should not be in contradiction with the objective of being able to reinsert or to add new processing elements into the system without disrupting its functioning.

Determinacy: a mechanism may be designed so that it always achieves some necessary synchronization. Such a mechanism may be characterized as being deterministic. Oppositely, a mechanism will be said probabilistic if it achieves some necessary synchronization only most of the time.

Recovery: how much help may be provided by a synchronization mechanism as regards error recovery? In particular, how easy is it for non failed elements to be kept in a consistent state when a failure or a succession of failures occur? How easy and how fast is it for repaired elements to reach a state known to be consistent with the global system state?

Connectivity: with some mechanisms, it is required for producers to be logically fully connected i.e., each producer must operate permanent connections with every other producer. Such a constraint may result in costs which can be high as compared with the costs incurred by mechanisms where producers know only about some neighbours.

Initialization: with a given mechanism, how easy is it to initialize the system and to let know to any process when it is allowed to produce or to consume actions ?

Expression of ordering relationship: when producers wish to enforce some particular ordering on a given set of operations, they may have to exchange messages so as to implement the desired ordering. However, depending on the synchronization mechanism used, the implementation will be more or less efficient. For example, it may be necessary for each producer to wait until its operation has been completed before it is allowed to fire the next producer. With some mechanisms, it is possible for each producer to fire the next one as soon as its operation has been initialized. Response time and throughput may be very different in both cases.

Constraints as regards utilization: is there any constraint brought by a given mechanism as regards utilization? For instance, is it possible to achieve any desired synchronization when operations do not pre-declare all actions to be initialized?

Understandability/simplicity: it is intuitively understood that formal correctness proofs will be easier to give if a mechanism is simple. This is important when observing that the number of situations which may arise from failures may become very large. Also, when time has come to implement a given mechanism, problems such as specifying, debugging, maintaining and modifying the corresponding software become preponderant. In this area like in many others, simplicity is welcome.

Chapter 13. Multiple copy update

13.1. Introduction

A computing system is said to be distributed if and only if its operation is based on *distributed control* at all levels of abstraction [Le Lann 79], apart from its physical characteristics. Distributed control, however, implies that a means be provided to all processes participating in a certain function at a given level of abstraction, which enables these processes to obtain a *consistent and identical view* of the function related global state of the system without the need to refer to a unique centralized data structure called system data base which in turn is controlled by a unique process. Thus all information describing the *global system state* has to be maintained in a decentralized database by means of intercommunication between all participating processes such, that a consistent and identical view of the global state is granted.

A look at the case studies given in Chapters 18 and 19 shows, that the concepts of existing network operating systems like the Works Manager of NSW follow these guidelines by providing *distributed system data bases* for maintaining global state information such as directories of process names, global file catalogues, user authorization and accounting information, tool descriptors, resource status etc.

The amount of information stored in a system data base is usually small as compared to the amount of information maintained by an application data base. System data bases are kept in main storage if frequent and fast access is necessary (e.g. resource allocation tables), but may as well be on secondary storage, if survival during system crashes is a requirement or if a larger amount of information has to be maintained as e.g. in the case of a global file catalogue.

As in the case of an application data base three types of distribution are possible, depending on the characteristics and frequency of requests for access and on the response time and reliability/availability requirements to be met:

A system data base may be

- *strictly partitioned*, in which case no duplicates of data base components (i.e. partitions) are provided
- *fully redundant*, i.e. only copies of the complete data base are distributed
- *partially redundant*, i.e. the data base is partitioned with certain partitions being stored as distributed copies

Multiple *distributed copies* of complete system data bases or of certain partitions of these data bases provide for reduced response time in the case of read only access requests, because data may be stored near to where they are used most frequently, and for higher availability/reliability in the presence of host computer crashes. Finally, distribution of partitioned data in general allows for incremental upwards scaling without major service disruption if additional information has to be accomodated by the data base.

Maintaining a distributed system data base to support distributed control requires that the distributed components of the data base, i.e., partitions and copies of partitions or multiple copies of the complete data base itself be kept consistent, such that the distributed processes exercising distributed conrol by means of accessing state information in the data base are able to deduce from this information a consistent and identical view of the global system state. This notion of data base consistency incorporates two aspects [Rosenkrantz 77]:

- *mutual consistency* of redundant copies
- *internal consistency* of each copy

Copies of a data base or of a partition of a data base are said to be mutually consistent if they are identical; since this is hard to achieve for every instant of time, where the data base is accessed, this constraint is usually relaxed to that it is only required, that multiple copies must converge to the same final state once all access activities cease. Whether this interpretation of mutual consistency is tolerable in a particular case or not depends on the application envisaged. *Strong mutual consistency* in the sense, that an access to a data base at a given point in time sees the same information, regardless of which copy is used, requires more complex and thus more costly coordination mechanisms than mutual consistency as defined above.

Internal consistency of a distributed data base refers, as in the case of a conventional data base, to the information content of the data base and involves two concepts:

- The concept of *semantic integrity*, demanding, that the stored data reflect accurately the real world modeled by the data base. This requires, that each transaction changing data base contents be verified not to violate semantic integrity constraints prior to committing any changes, a task which is no more difficult to achieve in a distributed environment than it is in a centralized one. Semantic integrity will thus be not considered further.

- The concept of *atomic transactions* [Chapter 11], requiring that either none or all of the actions caused by a transaction are reflected in the data base and in the information presented to the outside world as the transaction result. Since the transaction is only committed if it does not violate semantic integrity, atomic transactions guarantee data base internal consistency, and so does any *serial schedule* of atomic transactions. Thus for a distributed data base with its possibilities of concurrent transaction processing, mechanisms must be provided, which generate socalled serializable transaction schedules supporting the atomic appearance of transactions, i.e. schedules which are equivalent to serial schedules [Eswaran 76, Gray 75].

To summarize: distributed data bases with partial or full redundancy, i.e., data bases comprising multiple copies of data, require mechanisms which guarantee mutual consistency and atomic transaction processing and thereby keep their copies identical (as far as required by a given application) *and* internally consistent with respect to the total data base contents in the presence of concurrent updates.

In recent years quite a number of solutions to the problem of how to keep multiple copy data bases consistent in the above sense have been proposed, varying in quality of mutual consistency achieved, in performance, overhead, robustness with respect to failures, and assumptions made concerning the environment in which these mechanisms are to operate. Most of these proposals have yet to be implemented.

The proposals may be classified in various ways, e.g., according to the *basic synchronization techniques* used [Le Lann79] or whether *voting* is applied to come to an agreement on the global sequence of transaction processing to be observed by all host computers or not [Bremer 79].

In the following we give an outline of the general architecture on which the majority of the proposed solutions is based, then present some solutions using the classification proposed in [Bremer 79] and discuss available verification techniques, and finally evaluate the solutions described with respect to their applicability for maintaining multiple copy system data bases.

13.2. Basic architecture of multiple copy update mechanisms

The problem of maintaining the consistency of a distributed data base including multiple copies of data can be stripped down to the problem of coordinating the action of a set of distributed processes for the purpose of providing some service on behalf of a request from outside the system.

A model for an interprocess synchronization architecture as proposed in [Le Lann 79] seems to provide a useful basis for solutions to the more general of the above problems: A set of distributed processes, called *producers*, is responsible for accepting requests for internal activities (e.g. transaction processing) from outside; the corresponding actions are performed by sets of processes called *consumers*. Consumer actions are initiated by the producers by means of messages, which carry *action descriptors*. Since activities initiated by different producers may interfere with each other and thus lead to incorrect results (e.g. in the case of a distributed data base to mutual and internal inconsistencies), the *atomic property of requests* must be enforced by the producers, either directly by means of inter producer communication to reach a global agreement on the consumer actions to be initialized (voting) or by establishing an ordering of requests from which the consumers deduct the sequence of actions to be performed.

Figure 13-1 shows the producer/consumer interaction model. An *intercommunication medium* has to be provided, which allows for inter process communication between and within the sets of producers and consumers via logical channels (connection based intercommunication).

The use of *connection based intercommunication* results in several advantages:

- Messages are received in the same order as they are sent (with respect to a single source)
- Duplicate messages will be automatically discarded
- Permanent errors result in automatically closing the respective connection

Voting and ordering mechanisms may rely on the above basic communication system properties, but on the other hand will have to cope with the following deficiencies:

- Message delays are variable
- In the case of a missing response a communicating process is unable to decide, whether its correspondent has failed or no connection can be established because of a communication subsystem failure

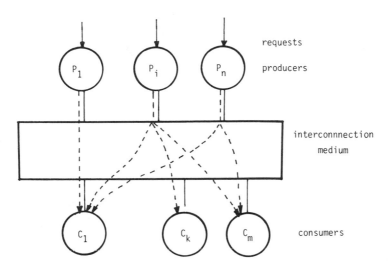

Figure 13-1: Producer-consumer model

On top of the above, two additional features are considered to be a must for any mechanism designed to coordinate consumer actions (producer activities):

- Crashes or removal of host computers resulting in the disappearance of producers and consumers must be allowed at any time.

- Integration or reintegration of host computers must be possible at any time.

The above interprocess synchronization architecture may be interpreted with respect to a distributed multiple copy data base environment as follows:

- The set of producers corresponds to a set of data base *access controllers*. Each transaction to be processed is submitted to exactly one of these controllers (e.g. the one being "closest" to where the transaction was generated). It is the task of this controller to obtain the permit to schedule this transaction for being processed. It is mainly by the kind of solution applied to obtain this permit that the various proposals for multiple copy update mechanisms can be classified.

- The set of consumers corresponds to a set of *storage processors*, the individual actions of which consist in the read and write operations forming the steps of the execution phase of a transaction. Storage processors are responsible for manipulating shared data.

In the case of a fully redundant data base a storage processor is associated with each data base copy. Update operations require, that a controller initiates identical actions at all storage processors and that either all or none of these actions are performed. In the case of a strictly partitioned distributed data base transaction processing results in *different actions* being initiated by a controller at some of the storage processors. Partial replication of partitions requires *identical actions* of corresponding storage processors.

In general, if operations of two or more controllers interfere with each other

- a correct *serialization* of storage processor actions has to be achieved (serializability of transaction schedules) to guarantee internal consistency, and

- if interference is with more than one storage processor, *compatible serializations* have to be achieved with respect to the storage processors involved to guarantee internal consistency, for strictly partitioned data bases and additionally mutual consistency in the presence of multiple copies of data.

The notion of a compatible serialization is illustrated best by an example. Suppose the concurrent transactions t_1 and t_2 result in actions $A_1(P)$, $A_1(Q)$ and $A_2(P)$, $A_2(Q)$ at storage processors P and Q, respectively. If $A_1(P){\rightarrow}A_2(P)$ is a correct serialization at P, then the compatible serialization at Q is $A_1(Q){\rightarrow}A_2(Q)$ ($\rightarrow$ denotes an ordering relationship).

To achieve serialization and compatibility of serializations may become a difficult task when not all storage processor actions are known in advance (which can be interpreted as a case of *dynamic resource allocation*). However, transactions in system data bases, in contrast to transactions in application data base systems, result in static controller operations where all data objects to be accessed are known in advance (*pre-claiming* of resources).

The process synchronization architecture described above is only to serve as a model which can be used to ease the understanding of the problems involved in maintaining distributed multiple copy data bases and to sketch the objectives which should be considered by any solution proposed. In particular, it does not plot the exact way of how to achieve compatible serialization; this may be achieved under the complete responsibility of the access controllers (e.g., by means of enforcing the atomic nature of transactions) or under the complete responsibility of the storage processors or under the responsibility of both sets of processes. Finally, producer and consumer functions may well be integrated into the same process.

It might be argued, that maintaining a distributed multiple copy data base for the purpose of supporting distributed control represents a distributed control problem by itself. This in fact is true, if regarded from a macroscopic point of view. In order not to end up with recursive solutions which are based on the availability of a solution to the problem they are supposed to solve, consistency control of distributed data must be based on mechanisms which establish temporarily centralized control at a microscopic level, in the sense that the actions being performed on the data base on behalf of a transaction are controlled by some *ordering relationship* imposed on the transactions competing for data base access. If such an ordering is *total*, it can be used to solve any contention among conflicting transactions.

Various proposals have been made of how to achieve a *total ordering of events* (a transaction being introduced into a system represents an event) in a distributed system [Chapter 12]:

- distributed physical clocks with synchronization by means of message exchange [Lamport 78]

- synchronized logical clocks [Lamport 78]

- eventcounts [Reed 77]

- sequencers [Reed 77, Le Lann 78]

These techniques, often referred to as basic synchronization techniques, are described in Chapter 12 and will not be further discussed here.

13.3. Solutions to the multiple copy update problem

The following model (c.f. [Bernstein 78]) seems to be adequate to describe a distributed system data base and the transactions that are run against it:

A data base D is defined as a set of data items,

$$D=\{x_1,...,x_m\},$$

with the granularity of data items being of no concern. Data items x_i may take values from $dom(x_i)$, $i=1,...,m$. Thus the state of the data base is an element of

$$dom(D)=dom(x_1)\times ... \times dom(x_m)$$

A transaction t_i, $i=1,2....$ is defined as a read operation R_i, during which the values of all variables constituting the so-called *readset* (or base variables [Thomas 78a]) of t_i are obtained from D, followed by a computation f_i, followed by a write operation W_i, which assigns values to the *writeset* (update variables) of t_i; readset$_i$ and writeset$_i$ specify the portion of D being read and written respectively by a transaction t_i; the computation f_i corresponds to the mapping

$$f_i: dom(readset_i) ---> dom(writeset_i)$$

For a set of transactions $t=\{t_i \mid i=1,2...\}$ being defined on a single centralized data base, the interleaved execution of transactions is modeled by a log L, defined as a string of symbols from the alphabet $S = \{R_i, W_i \mid t_i \in t\}$ such that

- every symbol from S appears in L exactly once
- for each i, R_i precedes W_i in L

Thus a log corresponds to a schedule [Eswaran 76]; a serial log is of the form

$$L = R_{i1} W_{i1} R_{i2} W_{i2}... R_{in} W_{in}$$

and represents the non interleaved execution of transactions (c.f. 13.1). If a log is equivalent to a serial log, i.e., if the execution of the transactions according to the log produces the same effect as a serial execution of the same transactions, then the log is called serializable.

An example for a log describing the interleaved execution of transactions is

$$R_1 R_2 W_1 R_3 W_3 W_2$$

In order for this log to be serializable the conditions

$$R_2 \cap W_1 = \emptyset \text{ and } R_2 \cap W_3 = \emptyset$$

must be met. The equivalent serial log would then be

$$R_1 W_1 R_3 W_3 R_2 W_2$$

A log as defined above refers to a single centralized data base. In such an environment enforcement of serializability may be achieved by locking the data items a transaction is to read or write:

- locking of all data items belonging to the readset and writeset of a transaction prior to execution, known as preclaiming, assures a serializable schedule if transactions are processed concurrently [Eswaran 76]; permanent blocking (deadlock) is prevented, if locking is always performed successively in the same order (w.r.t. the data items to be locked) [Havender68].

- If the data items accessed during transaction execution are not preclaimed (i.e. not locked in advance), serializability can only be achieved, as shown in [Eswaran 76, Bernstein 78], by means of a *two phase lock protocol* , which assures, that by the time a transaction releases its read-locks, it must have obtained all its write-locks. Since a two phase lock protocol does not avoid deadlocks, it must be combined with mechanisms for deadlock detection and resolution (including transaction back-up).

With both methods, concurrency is increased, if different *locking modes* are provided, depending on whether w.r.t. a given data item "dirty" reads concurrently to updates (no lock), concurrent reads only (read-lock), or no concurrent use at all (write-lock) are allowed [Gray 75].

In the case of a distributed data base a schedule described by a log as defined above, consisting of consecutive transaction steps, is not desirable, since it does not represent an efficient use of the parallel processing capability of a distributed system. What should be accomplished is a transaction schedule allowing for a maximum parallelism of transaction step executions. Again, if such a schedule is to guarantee consistency of a distributed multiple copy data base, it must be serializable, i.e., equivalent to a serial schedule, modeled by a log in which the write operation W_i of a transaction t_i has to be interpreted as simultaneous updates of redundant data items, if such· data items belong to the writeset of t_r.

As shown in [Schlageter 78], a "distributed" transaction schedule is serializable, if the distributed processing of each transaction belonging to such a schedule follows a *global two phase lock protocol*. However, a prerequisite for implementing global two phase protocols in a distributed system is the availability of *global locking mechanisms* to lock data items constituting readsets and writesets, regardless of the distribution and the number of copies of these data items.

To establish a global locking scheme, combined with some mechanisms, which allow to process transactions according to some given ordering relation, is the key of all distributed multiple copy data base update mechanisms.

If locks are always claimed at once by each transaction (preclaiming) and if all write-locks are released at once, we can think of each transaction as consisting of the steps

- request permission for execution
- execution step
  - read
  - write
- release permission for execution

Depending on whether permission for execution is achieved by voting among controllers/storage processors or by means of the use of control privileges, we can differentiate between solutions based on voting and non voting solutions.

To describe different proposals, a scenario with 3 distributed controllers A, B and C and two simultaneously arriving conflicting transactions, t_A and t_C is used, c.f. figure 13-2. Furthermore, it is assumed, that a copy of the data base is associated with each controller, and thus the controller performs all actions of the local storage processor.

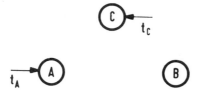

Figure 13-2: Scenario with 3 controllers and 2 simultaneously arriving transactions

13.3.1. Voting solutions

Voting solutions are based on the exchange of messages between controllers to come to an agreement on the global sequence of transactions to be performed on the distributed data base.

If controllers perform voting on a given transaction simultaneously and then proceed in common to the execution step as soon as agreement is reached, the voting procedure is called synchronous [Ellis 77, Holler 74, Mullery 75]. If voting on permission requests and execution for different transactions are allowed to be performed concurrently by controllers and storage processors, the voting procedure is called asynchronous [Bernstein 78, Thomas 78a].

In both cases, the sequencing decision is based on a total transaction ordering scheme (c.f. 13.2); it is assumed that for a given set of transactions the ordering can be deducted from a tag attached to each transaction.

Synchronous voting [Holler 74]

Upon arrival of a transaction, the receiving controller attaches the tag (e.g. a time stamp plus unique node identifier, if clocks are used [Lamport 78]) and, if not having initiated a voting on a previous transaction, broadcasts a vote for this transaction to all other controllers as shown in figure 13-3(1). If we assume, that for t_A a higher priority can be deducted from the total ordering than for t_B, the three controllers proceed as follows:

- Controller B: If a vote for t_C is received prior to any vote for t_A, B broadcasts a vote for t_C. Upon arrival of t_A, B eliminates t_C and broadcasts a vote for t_A as shown in figure 13-3(2). If however the vote for t_A is received first, B broadcasts in turn a vote for t_A and discards any votes for t_C arriving later.

- Controller C: A vote for t_A is broadcast upon arrival of a vote for t_A

- Controller A: Any votes on t_C arriving at A are discarded.

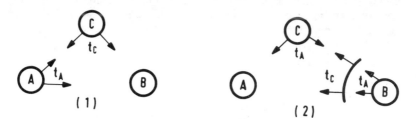

Figure 13-3: Synchronous voting as proposed in [Holler 74]

After having received votes on the same transaction (t_A in the above case) from all other
controllers, each controller (actually its associated storage processor) starts executing this
transaction.   The information needed to process the transaction locally might have been
transferred independently or piggy-backed on voting messages to the controllers.

Figure 13-4 shows a controller state transition diagram, which specifies the voting protocol for an
n-controller system.

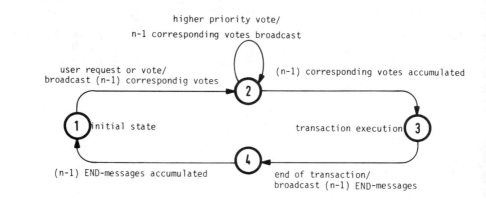

Figure 13-4: Synchronous voting: [Holler 74]; Arcs are labeled to indicate input/output

In order to allow for transaction queuing instead of rejection, a controller has to be structured as
indicated in figure 13-5. Whenever a voting procedure for a transaction is preempted on behalf
of a higher priority transaction, the status of the voting procedure is recorded in a corresponding
descriptor in a transaction queue, which allows to resume voting for a preempted request where
it had been stopped. The first element in the transaction queue corresponds to the transaction
for which voting/execution is currently in progress.

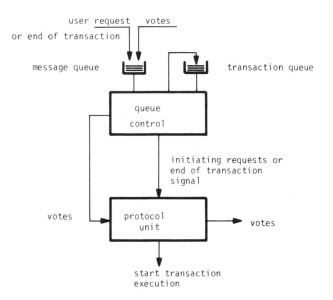

Figure 13-5: A controller for synchronous voting [Holler 74]

Synchronous voting [Ellis 77]

This procedure is in contrast to the previous one asymmetric in that it maintains a distinguished role of the initiator of a voting throughout the voting cycle. This is sketched in figure 13-6 by showing a state diagram for an initiating controller (1) and a non initiating controller (2) for a system with *n* controllers.

If a transaction is submitted to a controller for execution (user request), this controller initiates voting by broadcasting vote requests to all other controllers. If all other controllers respond with an ACK$^+$ message, the transaction is accepted for execution and the initiator broadcasts UPD-messages to initiate local transaction processing. Non initiating controllers signal end of local ntransaction processing by sending END-messages to the initiator, which after having received all END-messages returns to the initial state. Non initiating controllers always remain in the initial state, where they can acknowledge requests for vote by ACK$^+$ messages and react to UPD messages by executing the transaction locally.

Any initiating controller can, while in state 2, accept a request for vote concerning transactions, which are *compatible* with its current transaction and respond with ACK$^+$; in addition UPD messages received result in the corresponding local transaction execution regardless of the state in which a controller currently is in, since they refer to compatible requests decided upon by some other controller. Requests are compatible, if the transactions causing the requests refer to mutually non interacting readsets and writesets.

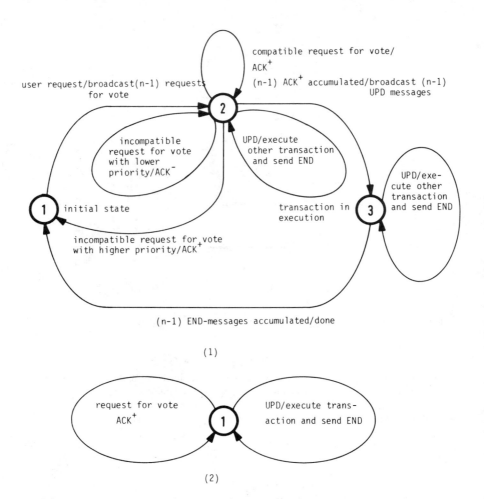

Figure 13-6: Synchronous voting procedure [Ellis 77] Arc labels are as in figure 13-4
(1) initiating controller; (2) non initiating controller

Request priorities are deducted from their total ordering which is achieved as in [Holler 74]. Figure 13-7 shows, how a conflict is solved if the scenario depicted in figure 13-2 describes a situation, where two compatible transactions initiate requests for vote:

A and C request votes for t_A and t_C concurrently (1). B acknowledges both requests immediately, because it remains in its initial state, A and C mutually acknowledge after having verified, that t_A and t_C are compatible (2). Local transaction execution is initiated (3), after having finished all local operations, end of local execution is indicated (4).

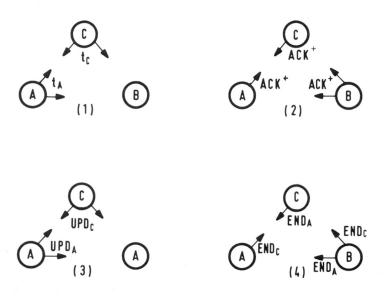

Figure 13-7: Concurrent processing of compatible transactions t_A and t_B [Ellis 77]

Asynchronous voting [Rothnie 77b, Bernstein 78]

The approach proposed for SSD-1, a System for Distributed Databases permitting redundantly distributed data, is based on a redundant update methodology, which is unique in the sense that it anticipates, that transactions can be grouped to form a set of *transaction classes* according to the readsets and writesets of the transactions. Transaction classes are predefined by the data base administrator, so that from the readset and writeset of each transaction it can be determined to which class or classes it belongs. To minimize synchronization efforts, four different synchronization protocols, $P_1,..,P_4$, are provided to assure serializability of the resulting transaction schedules and thereby internal consistency of the data base. P_1 offers least control and lowest cost and thus is most efficient, while P_4 offers the highest level of control in connection with a high degree of overhead. Protocols are selected according to the classes to which a transaction belongs by means of socalled protocol selector functions.

Mutual consistency is maintenanced (see [Thomas 78a]) by means of timestamping transactions and recording transaction time stamps in all affected data items. A change of a copy of a data item is performed only, if the time stamp of the transaction requesting the change is more recent than the time stamp of the copy. This assures, that all database copies converge to the same state once all updating activities cease (c.f. 13.1), however, temporary mutual inconsistencies may occur.

A transaction class in SDD-1, C^i_m, is defined as a set of transactions associated with a particular host m where a copy of the database is located. All transactions belonging to C^i_m are characterized by the fact, that they exclusively read data items from the read set $R(C^i_m)$ and exclusively write into the write set $W(C^i_m)$.

In SSD-1 transactions are processed in two stages according to the following model:

- During the first stage each transaction is processed locally at host m where it was initiated, using the copy of the database stored at this host. All necessary reads and writes are performed locally, while the local controller provides the local synchronization required. A list of all database changes is generated and kept. Local processing of a transaction t is considered as a primitive action L^t_n.

- As soon as stage one of a transaction has been completed, the local controller broadcasts the list of data base updates to all other controllers/storage processors. The resulting update by controller n is considered as another primitive action, denoted by U^t_n. The stream of U^t_s between each pair of controllers is assumed to be pipelined.

Primitives L^t_m and U^t_m are atomic, while the combined L and U actions of a transaction t need not be kept atomic. Thus a log in SSD-1 could be e.g., $L^1_2 U^1_1 U^1_3 L^2_1 U^2_2 L^3_1 U^3_2 U^3_3 U^2_3$

if the history of the execution of three transactions t_1, t_2, t_3 in a system with three data base copies was recorded. To obtain serializable transaction schedules, as required in order to maintain the internal consistency of the database, a construct called the L-U Graph is used to determine potential interference patterns caused by overlapping readsets and writesets among transactions in different classes. The L-U Graph contains a pair of nodes, labeled L and U for each transaction class C^i_m, the L node representing the L actions of the transactions in C^i_m while a node U represents the U actions. Arcs are drawn between L^i_m and other nodes according to the following interference types:

I1. To the U belonging to the same class (vertical arc)

I2. To U_m of another class at the same host m, if

$W(C^i_m) \cap R(C^j_m) \neq \emptyset$, $i \neq j$, or

$W(C^i_m) \cap W(C^j_m) \neq \emptyset$, $i \neq j$ (horizontal arc)

I3. To U^j_n of a class at a different host, if

$W(C^i_m) \cap W(C^j_n) \neq \emptyset$, $m \neq n$ (horizontal arc)

I4. To the U of another class at a different host, if $R(C^i_m) \cap W(C^j_n) \neq \emptyset$, $m \neq n$

Between U^i_m and other nodes:

I5. To U^j_n if $W(C^i_m) \cap R(C^j_n) \neq \emptyset$ and $m \neq n$ (diagonal arc)

Because of the strategy applied to maintain mutual consistency, which results always in that only the most recent (according to its time stamp) update is reflected in a data base copy, and because U actions are assumed to be atomic, U-U arcs which reflect intersection of write sets are of no interest.

Figure 13-8 shows as an example the L-U Graph for the transaction classes $C^1_1, C^2_1, C^1_2, C^1_3$ with

$$W(C^1_1)) \cap R(C^2_1) \neq \emptyset, W(C^1_1)) \cap R(C^1_2) \neq \emptyset,$$
$$W(C^1_2)) \cap W(C^1_3) \neq \emptyset, R(C^2_1) \cap W(C^1_2) \neq \emptyset.$$

Once the L-U graph for a given system has been constructed the protocol table for selecting one of the four protocols for each transaction class is fully specified by establishing the selection rules according to the graph topology as follows:

Classes C_1^1 C_1^2 C_2^1 C_3^1

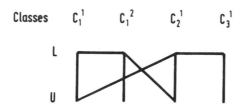

Figure 13-8: An L-U graph for four transaction classes in a three host system

S1. If L_m^i of a transaction class C_m^i is not on a cycle, or if L_m^i is on a cycle, and direct interferences with other classes are due to one of the following commutative combinations of interference types: (I2,I2), (I3,I3), (I2,I3), (I2,I5), (I3,I5), then the least restrictive protocol, P_1, is selected. P_1 simply ensures the atomicness of L_m^i by means of setting local sharable locks on the readset and local exclusive locks on the writeset of each transaction $t \in C_m^i$. No inter host communication is involved, except for broadcasting the U's to all other controllers.

S2. If L_m^i is on a cycle, and direct interference with other transaction classes is due to the combination of interference types (I4,I4) then protocol P_2 is selected for processing each transaction $t \in C_m^i$.

S3. If L_m^i is on a cycle and direct interference with other transaction classes is due to one of the following combinations of interference types: (I2,I4), (I3,I4), (I4,I5), then protocol P_3 is selected.

Protocols P_2 and P_3 are identical except for how the timestamp assigned to the vote request message, which is broadcast to all other controllers, is picked:

For each transaction $t \in C_m^i$, protocol P_2 selects the most recent timestamp from $R(C_m^i)$, while P_3 picks as a timestamp the current time TS(m), both allowing for a total ordering of transaction processing requests (c.f. 13.2).

The example given in figure 13-9 illustrates how P_2 and P_3 work. Provided of the two transactions t_A and t_C concurrently submitted, t_C holds the more recent timestamp TS(C)>TS(A), the controllers A, B, and C proceed as follows:

- if the vote request for t_C arrives at A it is queued,

- controller B if idle upon the arrival of either request sets its local clock to max(local time, TS of request) and sends an acceptance message with this new TS to the requestor; t_A and t_C irrespective of their order of arrival at B then get both accepted by B. If B is still processing a transaction t_B with a timestamp smaller than that of the incoming request, it first completes t_B and after having sent all U'_Bs accepts the new request.

- A waits until it has either received an acceptance message for t_A or a message with a larger time stamp than TS(A) from all other controllers. U messages except those with a timestamp > TS(A) and referring to the readset of t_A are executed while A is waiting.

- When A has received all necessary messages $L^{tA}{}_A$ is executed exactly as in protocol P_1.
- A resumes execution of pending U messages and acceptance requests.

This protocol assures, that by the time of t_A's local execution $L^{tA}{}_A$ t_A's readset reflects either the consistent state as of TS(A) (protocol P_2) or as of current time (protocol P_3).

Deadlocks cannot occur because preclaiming of resources is applied and conflicts are solved using the total ordering property of the timestamp mechanism.

Protocol P_4 is used to execute all transactions which are not anticipated, i.e. do not belong to any predefined class. P_4 operation is similar to that of P_2/P_3, except that the timestamp TS_F for the vote request refers to some time in the future. TS_F should be large enough, such that no controller has yet processed a transaction with a timestamp $>$ TS_F, otherwise the vote request is rejected and has to be retried, using a larger TS_F.

The formal analysis supporting the definition of the above protocols is given in [Bernstein 78,79]

The majority consensus approach [Thomas 78a].

This solution is similar to the SSD-1 approach in that mutual consistency of copies is achieved by comparing the timestamp TS(t) of each transaction t requesting to apply updates to a copy with the timestamp TS(v) associated with each data item v in the write set of t in that particular copy. An update of a data item v is applied if and only if TS(v) $<$ TS(t).

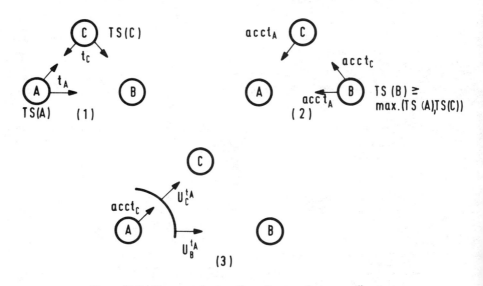

Figure 13-9: Concurrent processing of transactions according to
protocol P_2/P_3 of the SSD-1 approach

Internal consistency of a distributed multiple copy data base is maintained by means of processing each transaction according to the following protocol:

1. t obtains its readset R_t by reading the corresponding data items and their associated timestamps from a local copy of the data base. To do so the local controller has to set sharable locks on all data items in the local data base copy which belong to R_t.

2. New values for the data items in the writeset W_t are computed from the values of the data items in R_t. It is required, that $W_t \subseteq R_t$ for each t.

3. After having computed the new values of W_t, the application process submits a corresponding update request to one of the controllers. The update request specifies the new values of W_t, R_t and the timestamps associated with the data items in R_t.

4. The set of controllers votes to achieve a global acceptance or rejection of the update request.

5. If a majority consensus is achieved in favour of the acceptance of the update request, each controller/storage processor applies the update to its associated database copy as indicated above.

6. The application process is notified of how the request was resolved. If rejected, resubmission after having repeated steps 1 and 2 is possible.

The essential part of the above transaction processing protocol is the voting procedure. Voting is performed on the basis of a communication pattern known as daisy chaining (c.f. figure 13-10): A controller receiving the request votes and forwards the request together with its vote to another controller which has not yet voted, etc. until a majority consensus is reached.

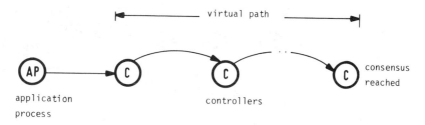

Figure 13-10: Daisy chained voting procedure

Voting rules: Upon receiving an update request the timestamps associated with the readset data items in the request are compared with the current values of the timestamps of these data items in the local data base copy.

- If each read set data item is still current and if the request is not in conflict with a pending higher priority request (e.g. with an older time stamp) the controller votes OK.

- The vote is REJECT, if any read set data item is obsolete

- The vote is PASS, if the time stamps are current but the request is in conflict with a higher priority request.

- otherwise, voting is deferred and resumed later

After having voted, each controller follows the request resolution rules:

- If the vote was OK. and a majority consensus is reached, accept the request and broadcast an accept message to all other controllers.

- If the vote was REJECT reject the request and notify all other controllers and the application process

- If the vote was PASS and a majority consensus is no longer possible, reject the request and notify all other controllers and the application process.

- Otherwise, forward the request to another controller that has not yet voted

If the request is accepted, each controller performs the local updates using the update application rules. Conflicting requests, that were deferred because of the accepted request, are rejected. If the request is rejected voting on deferred requests can be resumed.

13.3.2. Non voting solutions

Non voting solutions to the multiple copy update problem are based on explicit use of control privileges. One way to introduce explicit control privileges is to establish a master/slave relationships among controllers. The proposal given in [Alsberg 76] introduces an ordering of controllers according to their unique priorities as illustrated for the three controller example in figure 13-11, where $A>B>C$ is assumed.

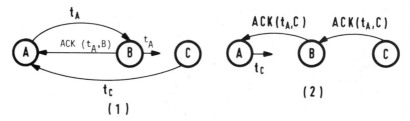

Figure 13-11: Solution based on master/slave relationship

Each transaction is sent to the highest priority controller, A in the example, which controls sequencing of conflicting transactions. Thus C has to send t_C to A, where t_A is executed.

Using daisy chaining, t_A is transferred to and processed by B and C. As soon as B and C have finished processing t_A, they acknowlege t_A. A is free to start execution of t_C after having received the aknowledgement from B (c.f. figure 13-11 (2)). Though this solution is a centralized control scheme, it introduces back up resiliency, because lower ranked controllers can take over mastership.

The *circulating token* approach as introduced in [Le Lann 77,78] allocates a unique control privilege temporarily to exactly one controller by arranging all controllers on a virtual undirectional ring (communication path). A single control token is travelling along this virtual ring from one controller to the next. This method can be used to implement either one of two different multiple copy update protocols:

1. To initiate transaction processing at all controllers/storage processors, a controller waits until it receives the control token. In the example in figure 13-12, where the virtual ring is assumed to interconnect $A \rightarrow B \rightarrow C \rightarrow A$, B holds the token (1), but, since it has no transaction, forwards it to controller C. As soon as C receives the token it broadcasts t_C to A and B and executes t_C locally (2). Remote transaction processing is acknowledged by A and B (3).

2. Instead of controlling transaction execution directly the circulating control token approach can be modified such, that the token carries a sequence number which is used to provide "tickets" to transaction requests. Every request must be ticketed. A ticket is identified by the sequence number obtained from the token. The sequence number carried by the token is incremented each time it is used to provide a new ticket. Thus tickets provide a means for establishing a total ordering of requests.

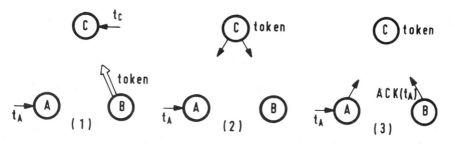

Figure 13-12: The circulating token approach [Le Lann 77]

Upon receipt of the control token, a controller draws as many tickets as there are pending requests. In order to avoid waiting for a complete token revolution, a controller is allowed to anticipate future requests and draw additional tickets [Le Lann 78]. To get rid of tickets not used during a token revolution, fake requests characterized by a no-operation code must be initialized by each controller for all unused tickets still held when the token is received again. For further extensions of this method, the reader is referred to [Le Lann 78].

Once a request is ticketed, it is broadcast to all storage processors (there is one storage processor associated with each data base copy). A positive acknowledgement is returned to the controller when the request has been stored in the waiting queue of a storage processor according to its ticket value, because of a conflict between the current locking mode (c.f. 13.3) and the intended usage mode; a negative acknowledgment is sent if the waiting queue is full.

As soon as a request moves into the first position in the waiting queue or if usage m. de and current locking mode become compatible, the coresponding storage processor sends a message to the initiating controller indicating that the data resource is allocated (A-message).

Having received A-messages from all storage processors, the initiating controller initiates local processing at all storage processors.

The above approach provides for mutual consistency through estabishing a total ordering of requests by means of ticketing; internal consistency is maintained, because of the atomicness of request execution due to the circulating token principle in connection with ticketing.

13.4. Verification of solutions

Verifying the correctness of multiple copy update solutions is a difficult and tedious, but important task. For a number of solutions only plausibility arguments are provided to prove correctness. What is needed are formal methods allowing to verify, that a given approach fulfills the following four criteria [Ellis 77b]:

1. Consistency of distributed data is maintained

2. The correct operation of the algorithm applied is not dependent on any assumptions concerning execution speeds or transmission delays being fulfilled.

3. Deadlock freedom

4. No critical blocking; i.e. all transactions requesting execution will eventually be executed

Proving the correctness of multiple copy update mechanisms amounts to verifying the correctness of the underlying protocols.

A protocol is defined as the set of rules governing the communication among a set of entities, called protocol machines, with the aim to provide certain services to some application process. In the case of multiple copy update mechanisms, the protocol machines model communicating controllers/storage processors.

A protocol description includes four basic elements:

- The specification of the protocol rules

- The specification of the protocol services

- The specification of the transmission subsystem in terms of services provided for intercommunication between protocol machines at the level of abstraction to be considered (e.g. at the interprocess communication level)

- The specification of the protocol environment, i.e. the characteristics of the protocol machines e.g. in terms of their capabilities to handle failures, reconfiguration etc.

Given the description of a protocol as defined above, protocol verification consists in proving, that the protocol rules, implemented in the specified environment and using the transmission subsystem meet the given protocol service specifications [Bremer 79].

Formal verification requires formal specification of protocol rules, protocol services, transmission subsystem and environment. For specifying protocol rules, i.e. the behaviour of protocol machines, two basic approaches have been used [Sunshine 78b]:

- The finite state machine approach. For most protocols the protocol machines behave like identical finite state machines; thus describing a protocol machine is equivalent to describing a finite state machine. Either state oriented techniques, like state transition diagrams (c.f. 13.3.1) and matrices [Bochmann 78] or high level language constructs are used [Hajek 78]. However, the state oriented approach is faced with the problem of state dimensionality when complex protocols have to be described.

- The parallel process approach. Instead of describing protocol rules by means of separate descriptions of protocol machines and transmission subsystem, this approach allows for an integrated description by means of one parallel program. An example for such an attempt consists in the use of Petri nets [Merlin 76].

As opposed to formal specification of protocol rules, almost no progress has been achieved so far in formalizing the description of protocol services. The description of transmission subsystem services raises again the problem of describing protocol services at the next lower level. Attempts have been made here to model the transmission subsystem as a stochastic process introducing the identified behaviour of the transmission subsystem as random events.

Since the analysis of the state of the art in formal description of protocols shows, that available methods are not yet advanced enough to solve the verification problem as stated above, one usually concentrates on proving general properties of protocols, like the fulfilment of the four criteria for multiple copy update protocols given earlier. Two approaches are commonly used to prove general properies:

1. State reachability analysis: general protocol properties are expressed in terms of legal system states. For the set S of states of a protocol system the relation holds:

$$S_i c \Pi_{i=1,N} S_i$$

   where S_i is the set of states of a protocol machine. To verify, that a given protocol has the desired general properies, state reachability analysis is used to show, that only such states in S are reachable, which are legal.

2. Inductive assertions: this technique has been developed for proving the partial correctness of parallel programs and may be applied to protocols described as parallel programs. So far only limited results have been produced using this technique [Brand 78].

State reachability analysis can easily be automated, if the state oriented technique for describing protocol machines is used. An obstacle, however, is the state explosion problem resulting in np-complete solutions. To cope with this, limiting assumptions are usually made, like reduction of the number of protocol machines to two, assuming a reliable communication subsystem and concentrating on only those general properties, which can be easily expressed in terms of global system states.

For the solutions presented in 13.3, as to the knowledge of the author, a formal analysis of correctness with respect to the four general properties given above is only available for the approaches given in [Ellis 77], [Holler 74] and the SSD-1 approach [Bernstein 77]. The analysis method given in [Ellis 77] is based on the formalism of L-Systems [Rozenberg 74] and was used in [Drobnik 77] to prove the correctness of the approach proposed in [Holler 74] and its derivatives.

13.5. Evaluation of solutions

The evaluation criteria which should be considered upon comparing different solutions to the multiple copy update problem can be grouped into four categories

1. Performance criteria. These are the criteria for which estimates are usually given to demonstrate the superiority of some appraoch. For an objective evaluation on the basis of

these criteria, however, it is necessary to take into account the characteristics of the specific environment in which a particular solution is to be implemented, like e.g. the kind of communication subsystem available, the types of requests which are representative for the given application etc.

Typical performance criteria are:

- Response time, mainly dependent on the amount of parallelism allowed for.
- Throughput, measured by the number of requests serviced per time unit.
- Overhead, usually expressed by the minimum/maximum number of messages to be exchanged between controllers /storage processors for resolving a given request.

2. Fault tolerance and crash recovery. This is said to be one of the more important motivations for distributed systems. By the very nature of their structure distributed systems have the principal capability to survive failures and support redundancy. Multiple copy update mechanisms must not annihilate this capability, they should provide for

- Robustness with respect to crashes of host computers, data storage components, controllers/storage processors, application processes and parts of the communication subsystem.
- Fast recovery from crashes by means of reinstallation of processes and data.

3. Correctness. This implies (c.f. 13.4) that the general properties

- Consistency
- Independence of correct execution from assumptions on relative speeds
- Freedom from deadlocks
- No critical blocking, fairness of request processing

are fulfilled. Simplicity and understandability of a solution facilitates correctness verification

4. Extensibility. Solutions should not be restricted to the fully redundant case, as far as their applicability is concerned. Furthermore, they should allow for dynamic system extension, when additional processors and data are to be added to the system.

To compare the performance of different solutions, the environment contraints must be well defined. In the following we will examine selected solutions under the following assumptions:

1. There are n copies of the database in the system, each copy being managed by a separate storage processor at a separate host. Strong consistency is required (c.f. 13.1).

2. The number of controllers is assumed to be equal to n; a controller is located at every host where a storage processor is located.

3. The average time needed by a storage processor to completely process a transaction locally is assumed to be T_r. Each transaction needs exclusive access to the database.

4. The communication subsystem is assumed to be capable of performing parallel broadcasting. The average message delay is assumed to be d.

5. The indivisible set of actions conducted by the set of controllers/storage processes exclusively on behalf of a specific transaction is called critical section. Its duration is denoted by T_c.

6. Computing times are neglected since they are assumed to be $\ll d$.

7. Communication with the requesting application process is not accounted for.

Under the above simplifying assumptions we obtain for

A. *Synchronous Voting [Holler 74]*:

The critical region includes

- broadcast request, time delay = d, n-1 messages
- accumulate votes, time delay = d, $(n$-1$) \cdot (n$-1$)$ messages
- process transaction, time delay = T_t
- desynchronization, time delay = d, $n \cdot (n$-1$)$ messages
- Average waiting time for admission to critical region, if an average of p transactions is already in the system: $W = pT_C = p(3d + T_t)$

B. *Synchronous voting [Ellis a,b]*:

The critical region includes

- broadcast request; time delay = d, n-1 messages
- accumulate acknowledgements; time delay = d, n-1 messages
- broadcast UPD messages and process transaction; time delay = $d + T_p$ n-1 messages

Additional action per request needed at initiating controller (outside critical region):

- accumulate END-messages; time delay = d, n-1 messages

  Average waiting time for admission to critical region, if an average of p transactions is already in the system: $W = pT_C = p(3d + T_t)$

  Note, that W increases, if voting on requests has to be preempted because of higher priority requests.

C. *Asynchronous voting (SDD-1)*:

The above assumptions represent the worst case environment for this approach; protocol P_4 would have to be applied for each request. Since the SDD-1 approach was designed for an environment, which allows to classify transactions according to their readsets and writesets, it will be excluded from this comparison.

D. *Majority Consensus Approach [Thomas 78a]*:

This approach is based on daisy chaining and thus with respect to performance figures highly dependent on the number of controllers involved. It will be excluded from this comparison.

E. *Centralized control privilege [Alsberg 76].*

This approach introduces a centralized component and is thus excluded from the comparison.

F. *Circulating Token with Ticketing [Le Lann 78]:*

The critical region includes

- get the ticket; if a sufficient number of tickets is anticipated: time delay $= 0, 0$ message
- If no anticipation: time delay $= 0.5(n-1)d$, 1 message
- accumulate A messages: time delay $= d$, n-1 messages
- initiate processing: time delay $= d$, n-1 messages
- process transaction: time delay $= T_t$

Additional action per request (outside critical region)

- broadcast request: time delay $= d$, n-1 messages
- accumulate acknowledgements: time delay $= 0$, n-1 messages

    Average waiting time for admission to critical region, if an average of p transactions is already in the system (exact anticipation assumed): $W = pT_C = p(2d + T_t)$

If we compare the performance figures for solutions A, B and C we obtain for the average throughput under the above assumptions:

Solution A allows to process a request every $3d + T_t$ seconds

Solution B every $3d + T_t$ seconds

Solution F (ideal anticipation) every $2d + T_t$ seconds

I.e. solution F [Le Lann 78] yields the highest throughput, provided that anticipation is exact. However, if the aniticipation of requests results in an underestimation, an additional average delay of $0.5(n-1)d$ must be added. With respect to the average response time, solution F again performs best, provided exact anticipation is possible.

As for the average number of messages exchanged per request, we can see, that there is a tie between B and F, both coming up with $4(n-1)$ messages. However, solution B will show an increase in the number of messages, if voting on requests has to be preempted because of higher priority requests.

Voting with the possibility of preemption is also one of the characteristics of solution A, but with this approach preemption only causes freezing the voting procedure status by means of storing the corresponding information in a request element in the request queue. Thus, voting for a preempted request can be resumed where it had been stopped and does not cause an increased overhead.

Parallelism and correspondingly throughput of solutions A, B and F can be significantly increased, if the above assumption 3 is relaxed and higher granularity of data resources as well as concurrent execution of requests with compatible usage and locking modes are allowed (this is true for all other solutions too). This however introduces the equivalent of global resource allocation tables to be kept at each storage processor: requests must specify all required data items and the locking mode desired. To provide for concurrent execution of requests with compatible usage and locking modes, solutions A and B are required to be able to start new voting cycles for newly arriving compatible requests regardless of the state of the voting cycle currently being executed.

Though solution A falls short of solution B and F in the performance comparison, especially w.r.t. the message overhead, it should be considered, that e.g., some ring structured local networks support broadcasts in that only a single circulating message is needed to address a set of distributed processes. In such a case as well as for $n=2$ solution A will show comparable performance.

To achieve resiliency, all solutions presented apply a timeout technique. However, a controller having detected a timeout condition can only suspect, that the process not answering has crashed. What is important is, that the set of remaining controllers obtains a consistent and identical view of the resulting new state of the system. This is supported by solution A (shown in [Drobnik 77]) in that the basic synchronous voting procedure can be applied to achieve this. Other solutions do not provide for such a means, except that for solution F a method, tailored to the circulating token mechanism, is given which allows to regenerate the control token and the virtual ring after an actual crash of a controller.

To support recovery, it must be possible to reintegrate controllers/storage processors and restore associated copies to the actual state of the database. The latter is usually achieved by maintaining a log of all changes applied to the database such, that restoring can be provided by locally performing all necessary updates once a copy is up again. If a copy was destroyed or if too many local updates would be needed to restore a copy, one of the operational consistent copies must be copied.

Once a controller/storage processor and the associated copy are up again, reintegration into the set of cooperating controllers/storage processors is necessary. Most solutions provide some specialized synchronization procedure for reintegration. Solution A allows for reintegration by having the controller to be reintegrated initialize the basic synchronization procedure [Drobnik 77], guaranteeing, that all controllers obtain an identical and consistent view of the new system state.

Correctness proofs (c.f. 13.4) are given for solutions A, B, C and (partially) for F. For the other approaches, only plausibility arguments are available.

Extensibility with respect to adding or deleting controllers/storage processors is achievable in most of the above solutions by triggering similar mechanisms as provided for handling crash/recovery. However, not all of the solutions presented are capable of handling partitioned and partially redundant distributed data bases (general case). In [Drobnik 77] it is shown, how solution A can be extended to take care of the general case. Solutions C [Bernstein 77b], D [Thomas 78a] and F [Le Lann 78] are either extensible (C) or designed (D and F) to handle partitioned distributed data bases with partial replication. It should be stressed, however, that the capability to handle the general case is usually not required for maintaining distributed system data bases.

Chapter 14. Applications and Protocols

This chapter describes a collection of protocols required for effective support of network data access. Language issues which must be considered in implementing distributed applications are also discussed.

14.1. Introduction

Computer communication networks permit users to access remote programs and data. Such access generally proves difficult because of differences in target systems and DBMSs residing on them. Conversion costs usually preclude the obvious solution of forcing all systems and application packages such as Database Management Systems (DBMSs) to conform to a common set of access and utilization conventions.

Protocols have been developed to support basic communication between both users and network accessible systems as well as between different systems. Extensive exploratory work has established the functional objectives of a collection of basic protocols (host-host, network virtual terminal, common command language for file manipulation, distributed job execution, data transfer, and network interprocess communication). Currently, a major (U.S.) Government investment is being made to develop the corresponding protocol standards.

Currently existing protocols do not provide a unified framework for accessing and retrieving remote data. Since an organization's data is increasingly recognized as one of its most valuable resources, the need for such a framework is evident. This chapter structures an initial approach for its realization.

Structuring data access protocols requires the background information on DBMSs provided in section 14.2. Section 14.3 establishes basic issues in providing a uniform user viewpoint across multiple, remote, heterogeneous DBMSs. Implementing such a viewpoint is discussed at length in section 14.4.

Given that a query or update has been processed by the target DBMSs, the resulting individual outputs must be aggregated and the collective result returned to the requesting process. This requires a protocol for preserving the meaning of data being transmitted between heterogeneous systems; the nature of the required Data Transfer Protocol is discussed in section 14.5.

Sections 14.2-14.5 scope the problem of supporting remote access to data. The merits of this approach depend on its ultimate implementability. Currently, prototype components have been implemented at the National Bureau of Standards. Accordingly, sections 14.3.5 and 14.6 contain concise overviews of an Experimental Network Data Manager (XNDM) and an Experimental Network Operating System (XNOS). XNDM provides uniform user access across remote, heterogeneous DBMSs. XNOS supports XNDM by providing a uniform mode of user and system interaction across systems.

14.1.1. Supporting program access to data

Traditional approaches to supporting program execution require co-location of the program and its data. In a networking environment, this was usually accomplished by bringing the program to the data or the data to the program. Two factors mitigate against the general applicability of this approach. The first is the difficulty of producing truly portable programs in view of the large amount of information required for characterizing the program execution environment, coupled with the tendency of vendors to produce similar, but nevertheless incompatible compilers. The second is the increasing use of Database Management Systems (DBMSs), a notably non-portable source of data.

Organizational strategic planning and exception reporting are important information processing functions whose support, in a networking environment, requires:

   i) an ability to request data from remote databases, and

   ii) a mechanism for preserving the structure of the response being transmitted between systems.

This is a problem of manifest importance; a general solution is therefore of interest.

Current teleprocessing techniques permit users to retrieve data from remote databases. A straightforward extension would support retrieval of data from multiple, remote, heterogeneous DBMSs. The implicit requirement is user knowledge of the properties of each of the accessed databases. Given the complexity of an individual DBMS, the resultant learning burden is likely to be sufficient to preclude effective routine access to multiple remote DBMSs. A different approach is required. We believe that it should mask DBMS differences from the user. Providing such a mask is a major problem since the spectrum of differences includes:

   i)   the underlying data model,

   ii) the data structures developed using this data model,

   iii) Data Manipulation Languages used for manipulating these data structures,

   iv) functionality provided by the DBMSs even if the underlying data model is the same, and

   v)   the computer systems on which the DBMSs reside.

14.1.2. Distributed applications

Currently existing protocols primarily support two party interactions in which one party is a system and the other party is a user or system. Distributed applications, in contrast, require N party interactions.

The difficulty of constructing a distributed application depends upon whether individual components existed prior to initiating application construction. If so, differing communications conventions are likely and translation technology is required. Otherwise, these differences can be eliminated through requiring individual components to conform to conventions established at application design time.

Although forced homogenization eliminates the need for translation technology we doubt its merits. This reflects the perception that future needs can rarely be anticipated in a dynamic area like computer communications. The continuing stream of new products and capabilities is a strong forcing function for heterogeneity; hence an appropriate translation technology will always be required. The following demonstrates the feasibility of using translation techniques for supporting for a large class of remote database query applications.

14.2. Database Management Systems (DBMSs)

Declining computing costs permit more effective information processing support for users and organizations through requiring less efficient utilization of these resources. The increasing interest in and sophistication of DBMSs reflects this. This section provides a brief overview stressing: need, categories, data models, and data manipulation languages.

14.2.1. The need for DBMSs

DBMSs effectively separate the logical and storage structures of data. Thus, users can access data by name and logical interrelationships rather than by location. As a result, the way in which data is physically stored can be modified without affecting program access. Moreover, the same data can be shared by several programs. (Additionally, a DBMS may provide a certain level of guarantees, e.g. access controls and security as well as useful utilities such as report writers. [Codasyl 76], particularly chapter 3, contains a useful overview of DBMSs.)

Data sharing is facilitated through using schemas. The ANSI/SPARC committee on DBMSs [ANSI/X3/SPARC 75] has identified three major schema levels: external, conceptual, and storage (internal). (Not all existing DBMSs possess exactly these three schemas.) External schemas describe the user or user program view of data. Conceptual schemas define the corporate or organization-wide view of data. Internal schemas establish access paths to the data.

These three schemas can be viewed as layers through which a request passes in actually accessing data managed by a DBMS. Consequently, processing a request requires mapping the external schema to the conceptual schema which, in turn is mapped to the internal schema.

DBMS design poses three major trade-offs:

- performance vs. understandability,
- performance vs. predictability,
- user effort vs. system effort.

DBMSs differ in their ability to support easily understood logical, i.e. user perceived, data structures. Ease of understanding usually results in reduced efficiency in accessing and storing data.

Logical data structures can be tailored to facilitate processing if the nature of the request is known. This yields better performance. It may also result in poorer performance when processing unpredictable queries involving the same data.

DBMS access can be supported at two polar extremes. The simplest, for the DBMS implementer, views the DBMS as the repository of data and requires explicit user issuance of all retrieval commands. The simplest for the user only requires specification of what data is to be retrieved and not how. Ease of use is gained at the cost of both increased processing costs and the requirement for a more sophisticated system. Declining systems costs facilitate simpler user interfaces. In any case, the processing of repetitive requests should probably be optimized.

14.2.2. DBMS differences

DBMSs can be categorized in terms of the data model which is supported and the data language provided for interacting with this data model. A data model defines the acceptable types of data structures. The three basic data models discussed below are logically based on the representation of data as record types; the network and hierarchical models also support explicit system maintenance of record type interrelationships.

Data languages can be divided into three major components: Data Definition Language (DDL), Data Manipulation Language (DML), and Data Control Language (DCL). DDLs are used to define the data structures, their components and interrelationships. DCLs permit specification of whatever access controls are provided by the DBMS. DMLs provide the means for issuing queries or updates against the database. Thus, the DDL and DCL define the organization's view of data; the DML permits user interaction with data. Discussing DML alternatives requires a fuller understanding of the alternative data models.

14.2.3. Data models

A record of type R is defined to be a linear sequence of fields that is:

$$R: f_1:T_1; \ldots; f_n:T_n$$

Two records are of the same type if the sequences of component field types T_i are identical. A record type defines the formal structure of a record. Both individual instances of a record type as well as the cardinality of the collection of instances of a record type will usually vary with time.

The three basic data models assume an underlying collection of record types. They differ in their maintenance of record type interrelationships.

14.2.3.1. The relational data model

The relational data model [Codd 70] represents data as tables. (Within this chapter, we shall carefully distinguish between the representation of data and any semantics attached to that representation.) Logically, a relation is collection of instances ("tuples") of a record type in which the sequencing of the instances and the sequencing of the fields within the record type are unimportant. Thus, two relations are equivalent (i.e. have the same "intention") if the sequence of field names and corresponding types of one relation is a permutation of the field names and types of the other, and they are identical (i.e. have the same "extension") if the sets of tuples they contain are identical.

Representing data as tables simplifies understanding the structure of the database. Logically, these tables describe entities and interrelationships among them. Interrelationships which are not represented as tables can be explicitly specified by the user via joins. Using joins provides a very flexible means for specifying interrelationships. The disadvantage is the possibility of stating semantically meaningless interrelationships, e.g. a join on the domain SNAME in the *Supplier*

SUPPLIER

SNO	SNAME	SSTAT	SCITY
1	Chen	Bad	Washington
2	Chu	Good	Boston
3	Lawrence	Good	Chicago
4	Jones	Check	Phoenix
5	Smith	Good	Boston

STOCK

SNO	PNO	QUANT
1	1	30
1	2	20
2	2	40
2	4	20
2	5	100
3	1	100
3	4	30
3	5	40
3	6	20
4	2	20
4	4	30
4	5	40

PARTS

PNO	PNAME	PCOL	PWT	PLOC
1	Screw	Black	24.0	Washington
2	Nut	Brown	30.8	Rome
3	Bolt	Blue	15.5	Boston
4	Screw	Black	30.8	Washington
5	Nut	Blue	26.4	Boston
6	Bolt	Red	10.0	Chicago

Figure 14-1: Supplier-and-parts relational schema

```
domain:    SNO         fixed bin,
           SNAME       char(15),
           SSTAT       char(8),
           SCITY       char(20),
           PNO         fixed bin,
           PNAME       char(15),
           PCOL        char(12),
           PWT         fixed bin,
           PLOC        char(20),
           QUAN         fixed bin;
relation:  Supplier    (SNO SNAME SSTAT SCITY),
           Parts       (PNO PNAME PCOL PWT PLOC),
           Stock       (SNO PNO QUANT);
```

Figure 14-2: Supplier-and-Parts relational schema definition

relation and the domain PNAME in the *Parts* relation of figure 14-1. Moreover, processing queries or updates involving user specified, semantically meaningful interrelationships may yield unsatisfactory performance if the tables are large and their expression was not anticipated.

Figure 14-1 illustrates a relation called *Supplier*, containing four columns: SNO (supplier number), SNAME (supplier name), SSTAT (supplier status) and SCITY (location of the supplier).

This relation is our representation of the real-world entity "supplier". Another relation, *Parts*, contains relevant information about the entity "parts": PNO (part number), PNAME (part name), PCOL (part color), PWT (part weight) and PLOC (where the part is stored). Information about the interrelationship between suppliers and parts is stored in the relation *Stock*: it tells us who (SNO) supplies what (PNO), and also the amount of the supply (QUANT). The corresponding schema definition (in Multics Relational Data Store (MRDS) syntax [Honeywell 78]) is given in figure 14-2. The first part of this schema definition declares the field ("domain") names and their data types, the second part defines the tables ("relations") in terms of their component fields.

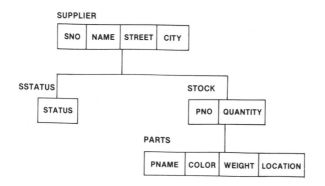

Figure 14-3: Supplier-and-Parts hierarchical schema

14.2.3.2. The hierarchical data model

The hierarchical data model [Date 77] permits data structures which are logically equivalent to a tree of record types (often termed segments within the hierarchical data model.) Thus, specified hierarchical interrelationships between one or more record types are explicitly maintained by the system. Actually, the interrelationship is really between a record instance at some level in the hierarchy and a collection of corresponding record instances at the next lower level in the hierarchy. Because of the additional interrelationship structure maintained by the hierarchical data model, processing of predictable queries is facilitated. Processing of queries involving interrelationships not explicitly defined within this data model proves correspondingly more difficult.

As an example we again consider the Supplier-and-Parts database discussed before. One possible hierarchical structure of this database is illustrated in figure 14-3. Here we have four types of records (segments): *Supplier, Sstatus, Stock* and *Parts. Supplier* is the root segment-type, it is the parent of *Sstatus* and *Stock* segment-types. The latter segment-type (*Stock*) is in turn the parent of the *Parts* segment-type. Figure 14-4 shows a sample occurrence graph for this database. It illustrates three important features of the hierarchical data model: first, each parent record occurrence can have a varying number of child occurrences connected to it, for example, the specific *Supplier* occurrence being considered (SNO=4) has one child *Sstatus* occurrence and three child *Stock* occurrences. Second, there is a single type of root segment (*Supplier*) and it can have any number of child segment-types (*Sstatus* and *Stock*). Third, each child of the root can have any number of child types, and so on, and all record occurrences must be connected to a parent unless they belong to the root segment type. For illustrative purposes, we also show (figure 14-5) the schema definition for this database, using IBM's Information Management System (IMS) database description [IBM 76] as our DDL. The first statement of this definition file assigns the name Supplier-and-Parts to the DBD ("database description"), the SEGM statements define the segment names and their lengths (in bytes) and are followed by FIELD statements giving the constituent field names, field lengths and their starting positions within the segment. The reader is referred to [IBM 76] for a complete explanation of this DDL.

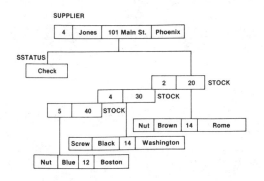

Figure 14-4: Supplier-and-Parts hierarchical occurrence graph

DBD NAME = Supplier-and-Parts
    SEGM NAME = *Supplier*, BYTES = 96
        FIELD NAME = (SNO,SEQ), BYTES = 4, START = 1
        FIELD NAME = NAME, BYTES = 15, START = 5
        FIELD NAME = STREET, BYTES = 32 ,START = 20
        FIELD NAME = CITY, BYTES = 32, START = 52
    SEGM NAME = *Sstatus*, PARENT = *Supplier*, BYTES = 8
        FIELD NAME = STATUS,BYTES = 8, START = 1
    SEGM NAME = *Stock*, PARENT = *Supplier*, BYTES = 8
        FIELD NAME = (PNO,SEQ), BYTES = 4, START = 1
        FIELD NAME = QUANTITY, BYTES = 4, START = 5
    SEGM NAME = *Parts*, PARENT = *Stock*, BYTES = 64
        FIELD NAME = PNAME, BYTES = 8, START = 1
        FIELD NAME = COLOR, BYTES = 12, START = 9
        FIELD NAME = WEIGHT, BYTES = 4, START = 21
        FIELD NAME = LOCATION, BYTES = 20, START = 25

Figure 14-5: Supplier-and-Parts hierarchical schema definition

14.2.3.3. The Codasyl data model

The Codasyl Database Task Group (Codasyl DBTG) or network data model [Codasyl 73] (we shall avoid the use of this latter term for obvious reasons, and use either Codasyl or DBTG to refer to this data model hereafter) structures data as directed graphs of record types. As with the hierarchical data model, the actual (DML level) interrelationship is between record instances rather than between types. The graph is constructed using the set concept. A set consists of two record types: owner and member. Although owner and member record types cannot be the same, a given record type can occur more than once in an access path. (A more detailed discussion of this point can be found in section 14.2.4.)

The Codasyl data model yields conceptual schemas which are relatively complex and therefore difficult to understand. However, this complexity permits efficient use of storage space. Intuitively, it also permits efficient processing of a wider range of query or update types.

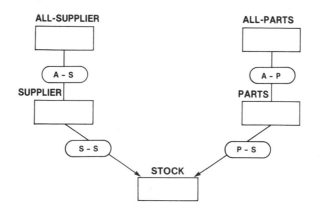

Figure 14-6: Supplier-and-Parts Codasyl schema

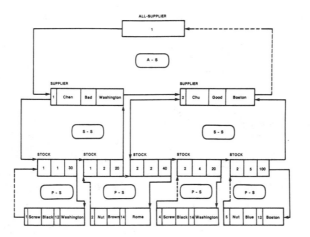

Figure 14-7: Supplier-and-Parts Codasyl occurrence graph

A possible DBTG schema for the Supplier-and-Parts database is shown in figure 14-6. The database is organized into three record types (*Supplier*, *Parts* and *Stock*). These are related through the sets S-S (owner *Supplier*, member *Stock*) and P-S (owner *Parts*, member *Stock*). The sets A-S (owner *All-Supplier*, member *Supplier*) and A-P (owner *All-Parts*, member *Parts*) serve the function of collecting all *Supplier* and *Parts* records for sequential access. (For systems supporting full DBTG capabilities, we could have eliminated the need for the record types *All-Supplier* and *All-Parts* by making A-S and A-P singular.) Figure 14-6 shows the data structure

diagram [Bachman 69] for this database. Part of the actual data model is shown in figure 14-7.
The schema itself is given in figure 14-8.

14.2.4. Data manipulation languages

Data Manipulation Languages (DMLs) provide the means for querying and updating databases.
Their comparison is facilitated through introducing the concepts of navigation and procedurality.

- Querying or updating a database is ultimately accomplished through retrieving, modifying
  or adding record instances. The prerequisite is gaining access to the appropriate records
  (or logical location within the database if a record instance is to be inserted). This process
  is referred to as *navigation*.

SCHEMA Supplier-AND-Parts.
      RECORD *All-Supplier*; LOCATION CALC USING SKEY.
          02 SKEY; TYPE FIXED 35.
      RECORD *All-Parts*; LOCATION CALC USING PKEY.
          02 PKEY; TYPE FIXED 35.
      RECORD *Supplier*; LOCATION VIA A-S.
          02 SNO; TYPE FIXED 35.
          02 SNAME; TYPE CHARACTER 15.
          02 STATUS; TYPE CHARACTER 8.
          02 CITY; TYPE CHARACTER 20.
      RECORD *Parts*; LOCATION VIA A-P.
          02 PNO; TYPE FIXED 35.
          02 PNAME; TYPE CHARACTER 15.
          02 COLOR; TYPE CHARACTER 12.
          02 WEIGHT; TYPE FIXED 35.
          02 LOCATION; TYPE CHARACTER 20.
      RECORD *Stock*; LOCATION IS SYSTEM-DEFAULT.
          02 SNO; TYPE FIXED 35.
          02 PNO; TYPE FIXED 35.
          02 QUANTITY; TYPE FIXED 35.

SET A-S; OWNER *All-Supplier*; ORDER PERMANENT NEXT.
      MEMBER *Supplier*; MANDATORY AUTOMATIC LINKED TO OWNER; KEY ASCENDING
      SKEY;

SET A-P; OWNER *All-Parts*; ORDER PERMANENT NEXT.
      MEMBER *Parts*; MANDATORY AUTOMATIC LINKED TO OWNER; KEY ASCENDING PKEY;

SET S-S; OWNER *Supplier*; ORDER PERMANENT NEXT.
      MEMBER *Stock*; MANDATORY AUTOMATIC LINKED TO OWNER; KEY ASCENDING SNO;
      SELECTION IS THRU S-S OWNER IDENTIFIED BY APPLICATION.

SET P-S; OWNER *Parts*; ORDER PERMANENT NEXT.
      MEMBER *Stock*; MANDATORY AUTOMATIC LINKED TO OWNER; KEY ASCENDING PNO;
      SELECTION IS THRU P-S OWNER IDENTIFIED BY APPLICATION.

Figure 14-8: Supplier-and-Parts Codasyl schema definition

- Once appropriate access has been gained, i.e. an access path to the required logical location within the database has been constructed, additional actions such as applying a predicate against the record instances, must be taken. *Procedurality* refers to the extent to which the user must specify how these actions are to be carried out rather than just specifying the predicate.

As an illustration of the various ways of gaining access supported by the different DBMSs, let us try, in our Supplier-and-Parts database, to locate the *Supplier* names and the names of the parts they supply. This requires accessing each *Supplier* record occurrence together with all its associated *Stock* records.

In relational calculus [Codd 71], this is done by first joining the *Supplier* and *Stock* tables on the common column sno, then selecting the appropriate columns from this combined table, as illustrated below with MRDS DML [Honeywell 78]:

```
"-range (s Supplier) (t Stock)
-select (s.SNAME t.SNO t.PNO t.QUANT)
-where (s.SNO = t.SNO)"
```

In relational algebra systems, we perform essentially the same operations, but in two separate steps (shown below in Multics Relational Data Management System (RDMS) DML [MIT 77]):

```
compose Supplier Stock -name Temp
project Temp |SNAME SNO PNO QUANT| -name Result
```

For hierarchical systems, this requires a sequential scan forward from the start of the database for all *Supplier* and all *Stock* segments as illustrated below for IBM's IMS [IBM 76]:

```
GU Supplier
NEXT GN Stock
     go to NEXT
```

The same kind of navigation is needed for DBTG systems: we traverse the *Supplier* record occurrences (by sequencing through the set A-S), followed with traversal of the occurrences of its member *Stock* records. A sample MIDS DML [Honeywell 77] sequence for this query is shown below (*dbi* is the database index and *dbc* is the status code returned by MIDS):

```
call dml_$find(dbi,"-first -path A-S",Supplier,dbc);
loop1: call dml←$get(dbi,SNAME,dbc);
if (dbc=record_not_found) then goto exit;
call dml_$find(dbi,"-first -path S-S",Stock,dbc);
     loop2:
     if (dbc=record_not_found) then do;
          call dml←$find(dbi,"-next -path A-S",Supplier,dbc);
          goto loop1;
          end;
          else call dml←$get(dbi,SNO,PNO,QUANTITY,dbc);
     call dml_$find(dbi,"-next -path S-S",Stock,dbc);
     goto loop2;
exit: . . .
```

Intuitively, the user expends the least effort when the DML does not require user specification of the access path and, moreover, only requires that the user specify the appropriate predicates rather than, in effect, write a program for their implementation. Relational calculus languages such as SQL [Chamberlin 76] (cf. 14.3.5) only require a minimum of navigation (specifying the joins to be used in interrelating tables) and are non procedural. In contrast, the Codasyl DBTG DML is highly navigational and very procedural as illustrated above.

Generally, more complex data structures require more navigation. Since multiple access paths to a given record can exist, automating this navigation process proves relatively complex. Thus, high level DMLs have been considered more extensively in the context of the relational data model.

14.3. Network virtual data managers

Currently, programs or users requiring access to a collection of remote, network accessible, heterogeneous DBMSs must formulate their queries or updates, hereafter termed requests, using the schemas and DMLs of the accessed DBMSs. Generally, the learning requirement implicit in this approach is sufficient to deter all but the most resolute user.

An alternative is to provide a common network wide virtual view of data together with the appropriate DML. Through developing the required translation technology, requests expressed via this common view can be translated to those appropriate to the system being accessed. This provides a counterpart for multiple remote DBMSs of the functionality provided by other protocols for transferring files and executing distributed jobs.

Protocols are typically specified in terms of the services provided, the lower level services which are assumed, and the message exchange protocol governing communication between peer processes on different systems [Sunshine 79]. Protocols providing a common means for querying and updating remote, heterogeneous DBMSs should be specified in the same way. However, the required translation technology must be substantially more sophisticated. Defining a uniform, network wide view of data also requires considerable care in its specification and implementation.

Two polar approaches span the spectrum of alternatives in assisting the network database accessor

   i)   requiring that the user have appropriate knowledge of each of the accessed systems, i.e. providing no assistance at all, and

  ii)   forcing a migration from the collection of presently existing DBMSs to a distributed DBMS (DDBMS).

A DDBMS may be the most desirable solution. However, the cost of a forced migration to a DDBMS is substantial since it requires database conversion – an expensive and only partially automated process. Further, if different organizational jurisdictions are involved, significant management participation may be required. The resulting implicit high cost of sharing may be sufficient to deter acceptance of DDBMS technology on purely organizational grounds. Since data structures must be tailored to support the differing requirements of two organizational units, the technical issue of achieving acceptable performance may also arise.

An intermediate alternative assists the network accessor by providing a uniform virtual view of data. This assistance is provided by a Network Virtual Data Manager (NVDM) which, logically, is intermediate between the terminal user or program requiring database access and the target DBMSs as illustrated in figure 14-9.

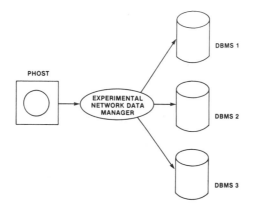

Figure 14-9: Logical view of an NVDM

The NVDM permits users to express requests in a single DML against a global schema describing a virtual network-wide view of data. Requests are decomposed into subrequests appropriate to the individual target systems, these subrequests are translated to the DML used by the target systems, processed, and the results aggregated and returned to the issuer of the request.

The advantages of having an NVDM include: reduced training costs; simpler incorporation of new DBMSs within the existing environment, extension; minimization of the need for implementing DBMSs spanning organizational boundaries; and simplifying DBMS implementation through allowing data structures to be tailored to the needs of the predominant user body. The disadvantage is the need for an appropriate translation technology. Evidently, the advantages should outweigh the disadvantages if NVDMs are to experience operational use.

Interest in NVDMs originated in the need to provide a common view of data managed by independent DBMSs. The term "independent" reflects the assumption that the entities described by two different DBMSs are logically different. For example, if two different DBMSs support warehouse inventory control systems, both may contain widgets but the widgets in one are logically distinct from the widgets in the other.

The view of data presented by an NVDM can be made formally equivalent to that presented by a DDBMS. Thus, augment each table with an additional LOCATION attribute. The resulting schema together with the NVDM DML is equivalent to that provided by a distributed DBMS with the associated DML. It follows that from the user's viewpoint, there is no difference between an NVDM and a DDBMS.

NVDMs and DDBMSs differ substantially in their implementation. The major characteristic of the difference is that the NVDM is, in effect, a second level manager of individual DBMSs. (Network operating systems [Kimbleton 78] are another interesting example of a comparable second level manager.) Thus, the NVDM must perform translation between the virtual view presented to the user and the view (global schema) supported by the individual DBMSs. Moreover, the level of functionality provided by the individual DBMSs may differ; such differences must be compensated for by the NVDM. Finally, the NVDM does not control resources; rather their control is entrusted to others (local DBMS management) and the NVDM, instead, occupies the position of a privileged user.

This section establishes major issues and alternatives in supporting a uniform, network wide view of data. The following section discusses its implementation. Together, the basic structure of a Network Virtual Data Manager (NVDM) is established. Although the user view is similar to that of a Distributed Database Management System (DDBMS), there are essential differences as discussed in 14.3.3 below. A description of an experimental implementation of an NVDM is presented in Section 14.3.5.

14.3.1. NVDM desirability and structure

We doubt the desirability of an NVDM for highly repetitive or high bandwidth applications. However, information processing applications can be divided into three categories [Anthony 65]: operational control, managerial control, and strategic planning. As one passes from operational control to strategic planning, both the bandwidth of the application and the predictability of the accessed data elements decreases. Evaluating the two factors of predictability and bandwidth, yields figure 14-10 giving our estimate of the relative utility of a Network Virtual Data Manager.

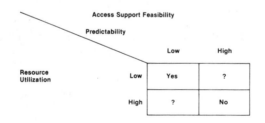

Figure 14-10: NVDM appropriateness

Thus, low bandwidth and unpredictable applications are very appropriate while high bandwidth, highly predictable applications are better served by using the DML of the target DBMS. For the two boxes containing question marks, the relative desirability of the common network viewpoint is likely to depend upon NVDM usability and efficiency. Evaluation of these performance measures requires a significant amount of operational experience.

In evaluating NVDM desirability, two major factors should be considered. The first is the high value of having the system be able to respond to queries and updates related to strategic planning via an integrated, on-line database access approach. The time savings can potentially involve orders of magnitude since the need for learning about the remote DBMS is eliminated, together with the likely requirement for active intervention by a trained programmer.

The second observation is that heterogeneity is ubiquitous. This reflects the fact that DBMS heterogeneity can be caused by:

   i)   data model differences,

   ii) differences in data semantics, e.g. data structure differences,

   iii) DBMS functionality differences,

   iv) DML differences, and

   v)   computer system differences.

Thus, an NVDM would probably still be necessary even if management required all sites to use a common DBMS package implemented on compatible systems.

Three key issues must be resolved in structuring a Network Virtual Data Manager. The first is the user's view of data, which is defined by the selected data model, the resulting virtual data structures and the DML available for manipulating these data structures. The second is the translation technology required to map operations expressed against this virtual view of data into those appropriate to the target systems. The third is the distribution of the translation process. Discussing these issues requires a clearer understanding of the sequence of NVDM processing operations which will now be described.

User → NVDM

send request expressed in a common, network wide manipulation language to the NVDM

decompose request into subrequests appropriate to individual target systems

translate subrequests from NVDM DML to DML used by target systems

NVDM → Target DBMSs

send translated requests to the target DBMSs

process subrequests by target DBMSs; if request corresponds to query, place resulting record(s) in a buffer

translate buffer contents into a common network representation used by all participating systems

(Note that this use of the term translate differs substantially from the preceding. The preceding requires translation of a Data Manipulation Language while this and the following use involve translation of data. We have avoided using separate terms to conform with existing terminology. The precise type of translation required will be clear from context.)

Target DBMSs → NVDM

transmit translated records to NVDM for aggregation; reexpress results using common network wide representation of data; and transmit to the requesting site

NVDM → User

translate buffer contents at requesting site from common network representation to the site specific representation (required to preserve the meaning of structured data being transmitted between heterogenous systems)

return result to the **requesting** process

Issuing the **send** command assumes an NVDM schema and DML together with an appropriate supporting environment. These issues are discussed at length in the remainder of this section. Translating from this global view requires a translation technology differing substantially from that usually covered under the term data translation [SDDTTG 76]; one approach to its realization is described in section 14.4.

Processing is assumed to be the province of the accessed DBMSs. **Translate**ing the result requires a means for preserving the meaning of structured data being transmitted between heterogeneous systems. This problem is structured in section 14.5; a particular implementation is also discussed.

Transmiting data between systems requires a protocol. The requirements for a Data Transfer Protocol are also discussed in section 14.5.

Translateing results from a common network representation at the requesting site is the inverse of translating partial results to a common network representation at the site where a portion of the DBMS query is processed.

Return of results to the requesting process is a function of the manner in which interprocess communication is implemented within a system and will not be explicitly addressed in this paper.

Having described the entities involved in providing a common network wide view of data together with the required processing support, we now establish a framework for understanding key issues in constructing this common network wide view.

14.3.2. Constructing the network-wide view of data

The virtual NVDM view of data consists of a Network Virtual Schema (NVS) and a Network Virtual DML (NVDML) for supporting the specification of and interaction with the NVS. It differs from that of the local DBMS in:

   i)   data structures and data models,

   ii) DMLs, and

   iii) coverage.

The first two differences are evident; the third reflects the likelihood that local DBMS management may limit the data accessible by the network user to a subset of that actually managed by the local DBMS.

Selecting a data model and designing data structures should be based on user capabilities and needs. We assume that users:

   a)   are responding to strategic planning and managerial control objectives,

   b)   have limited systems knowledge, and

   c)   are goal oriented.

Item (a) implies that users may need to access all the NVDM data. It also implies unpredictable, non-repetitive requests. Thus, conceptual simplicity must be gained by clear representations, rather than by custom tailored views (external schemas) or abstract data types [Weber 78].

Limited knowledge coupled with goal orientation implies strong user interest in problem solving and a corresponding lack of interest in learning system intricacies. If an NVDM is not simple to use, it won't be. Simplicity is dependent upon:

i)   the underlying data model which is being used,

ii) the data structures based on this data model, and

iii) the DML available for manipulating these data structures.

14.3.2.1. Selecting a data model

Two criteria for selecting a data model are:

i)   ease of use vs. efficiency, and

ii) use of existing vs. proposed data model.

Given our assumptions about the user, ease of use dominates efficiency considerations. The virtual view of data which the NVDM presents has two important implications. The first is the effective elimination of the utility of performance tuning based on the anticipated nature of the user's requests. The second is that system maintained record type interrelationships – such as those presented by networks and hierarchies – are neither feasible nor useful. Thus, the decision to use a network or hierarchy as the basic data model must be based on the decision that the corresponding information structures are simpler to understand. Given the complexity of data likely to be supported by the global schema, we doubt that such a conclusion could be supported.

Existing data models are primarily concerned with the representation of records and their interrelationships. Proposed data models include semantic considerations. Although evaluating the relative merits of proposed data models promises to be interesting, from a representational viewpoint they seem to be primarily based on: defining things (entities), establishing attributes of things, grouping things into classes, establishing attributes of classes, and defining interrelationships between classes [McLeod 79].

While representing data via records has well established limitations [Kent 79], it is nevertheless satisfactory in many, if not most instances. Since record interrelationships can be viewed as the province of data semantics, using tables as the basic data representation technique provides a reasonable basis for beginning the study of translation issues (from the viewpoint of the translator, it makes little difference whether the "user" or the "system" specifies record type interrelationships). Many data semantics issues, as we discuss later, can be studied and implemented separately.

Given that:

i)   records are the basis for data representation,

ii) the virtual view of data precludes the utility of system maintained interrelationships, and

iii) semantically meaningful interrelationships can be added as another layer (filter) as discussed in 14.3.4,

using a relational data model as the basic point of departure is reasonable.

14.3.2.2. Choosing data structures

Conceptually, the information contained within a database can be divided into two basic categories: information describing entities or things and information describing interrelationships among entities, other interrelationships or things. In the simple schema presented earlier, Parts and Suppliers are examples of entities whereas the information describing the number of parts procured from a given supplier is an example of an interrelationship.

Many database retrievals can be conceptually structured as determining attribute values of aggregates, e.g. average attribute values corresponding to a certain interrelationship among entities. For example, one might wish to determine the suppliers of red parts. This interrelationship is not explicitly contained within the schema and must therefore be derived.

Deriving complex interrelationships requires additional effort on the part of the user and provides an increased opportunity for error. Two alternatives exist:

i) incorporation of (some) interrelationships within the schema, and

ii) duplicating certain data.

The Entity-Relationship model developed by Chen [Chen 76] adopts the first approach for table based representations of data. The utility of the second approach has also been argued convincingly [Hammer 79]. For an NVDM, these approaches are essentially equivalent since the view of data is virtual.

The preceding suggests that the tables presenting the network user's (virtual) view of data should be logically structured into information describing entities and their interrelationships. Experience shows that such divisions are dependent on the viewpoint of the user [Hammer 79]. This poses a major problem in constructing database schemas. Fortunately, for an NVDM, supporting alternative views at the global schema level is feasible since all views are virtual. This virtual view also permits incorporation of additional semantics with minimal effort; the prerequisite is their definition, representation, and expression via the DML.

14.3.2.3. Selecting a DML

Given a table based view of data, two major DML alternatives exist. The first corresponds to the relational algebra and requires that the user explicitly issue commands for performing table joins, applying a predicate against the result, and selecting the necessary columns. Although this approach is flexible and, thereby, permits potentially greater efficiency in performing retrievals or updates, its procedurality is a disadvantage for the user population identified earlier. Interestingly, this procedurality is also technically disadvantageous because it is in conflict with the transaction processing approach deemed desirable by many [Gray 78].

The alternative DML type corresponds to the relational calculus and stresses specifying what data is to be accessed (rather than how) and the predicate used for selection. This is simpler for the user; it is also much more efficient for the NVDM since it permits a transaction based implementation approach. Thus, a single DML request is likely to correspond to the user's perceived request rather than just a fragment. This request can be translated and the resulting aggregate information transmitted to the target system where it is processed as an entity (cf. the discussion of "envelopes" below).

14.3.2.4. Performance considerations

NVDM performance is driven by four basic factors:

- i)   data structure effects,
- ii) the performance of the translation process,
- iii) target DBMS performance, and
- iv) distribution effects.

Data structure effects reflect the possibility that joins which seem natural for the network user may be poorly supported by the target systems. Section 14.4 contains an extensive discussion of other data structure effects.

A natural and interesting metric for measuring the performance of the translation process would compare the performance of the code resulting from translation with that produced by a trained user of a given target system. Unfortunately, such comparisons will only be meaningful after NVDMs have reached some initial stage of maturity. Current efforts such as that discussed in section 14.4 are directed toward establishing feasibility and key problem components rather than optimization.

The performance of the target system in processing a query or request is presumably fixed. However, knowledge of optimization information maintained by the target system can permit generation of equivalent queries or updates having varying performance levels.

Distribution effects reflect the degree of interaction required in processing a given request by modules located on different systems. We believe such interaction should be minimized and are in agreement with Gray's observation [Gray 78] that a transaction oriented viewpoint is appropriate. Attaining this objective when the target system uses a low level navigational and procedural DML such as the Codasyl DBTG DML requires establishing somewhat sophisticated server functions at the target DBMSs sufficient to support execution of an entire query.

14.3.3. Data integrity

Table-based data structures define the NVDM representation of data. They do not provide substantial or strong guarantees that the network user's queries or updates will be meaningful and, in the case of updates, that incorrect data will not be entered. To allay fears in the minds of local DBMS management, it is highly desirable that some guarantees be provided about limiting the accessor's view to that appropriate to the access rights which are possessed.

Integrity requires filtering DML requests. Three levels are identifiable: access controls, maintaining meaning, and simplifying specification. Access controls ensure that the access rights of the user are appropriate to the access requirements of the data specified in the request. Maintaining meaning encompasses both assuring semantic integrity of updates as well as ensuring that queries are semantically meaningful. Specification simplification seeks to simplify requests through minimizing the amount of information which must be explicitly stated by the user.

14.3.3.1. Controlling access

Access controls provide the basic mechanism defining:

    i)   who can access a given data element and,

   ii)   for each such accessor, the permitted types of access.

We distinguish between access control primitives which are provided and the guarantees that they:

    i)   work exactly as specified,

   ii)   cannot be circumvented, and

  iii)   correctly implement an articulated security policy.

Assessing these latter issues is a key component in determining the security of a system and will not be discussed in the following. Thus, our concern is with the nature of the mechanisms which can be provided to control access rather than with guarantees about the correctness of their operation.

Two major types of access controls can be identified: non-discretionary and discretionary. Non-discretionary access controls provide the means for imposing organizational constraints on data sharing. Typically, they are implemented as a collection of security levels, e.g. CONFIDENTIAL, SECRET, and TOP SECRET, together with compartments within levels, e.g. NATO, NUCLEAR. The security policy controlling their use has two major assertions:

    i)   users with the same security classification can always see the same information, and

   ii)   a user can always access information whose access requirements are dominated by his/her access authorization.

Thus, a user with a classification (TOP SECRET, NATO) could access information classified (SECRET, NATO).

Discretionary access controls provide the mechanism for supporting user controlled sharing of resources. In contrast to non-discretionary controls, there is no attempt to conform to any given security policy; instead, the objective is to provide a means for enabling users to grant access among themselves as they see appropriate. System R [Astrahan 76] provides a rather sophisticated collection of database-related discretionary access control mechanisms. An individual user can grant a wide range of access options to another user (READ, INSERT, DELETE and UPDATE tuples of a relation or, perhaps, only certain columns, and DROP entire relations). In addition, the user can also grant the GRANT right. This permits the grantee to further grant access rights which have been received. This rather fine-grained mechanism permits substantially better control over discretionary access than the password based, file oriented protection mechanisms common to many of the existing DBMSs.

The desirability of supporting both discretionary and non-discretionary access controls within a given system is evident. Their joint support requires a mediator for detecting and resolving conflicts between them. The mediator must ensure that discretionary grants are never in conflict with non-discretionary controls.

The second function of the mediator is ensuring the star property. This property states that a user with a given level of security classification can write, e.g. append, data to information at a higher classification and can read data of a lower classification. The star property is the basic consistency requirement which must be adhered to when the user is accessing data at a different security classification than his own. Through its enforcement, one can ensure that the security requirements reflected in non-discretionary access controls are not violated [Denning 76].

14.3.3.2. Maintaining meaning

Intuitively, database semantic integrity is concerned with assuring "clean" data, i.e. assuring that the data within the database is an accurate model of the organization. Traditionally, this is achieved through beginning with a semantically correct database and then assuring that subsequent updates are also semantically correct. Accomplishing the objective of semantic integrity is a complex undertaking even within the confines of an individual database. This reflects the implicit requirement that the organizational meaning of the database, i.e. its semantics, be specified.

Two major approaches to specifying database semantics exist. The more common is based on the use of assertions specifying certain interrelationships within the data managed by the DBMS. This approach has the advantage of simplicity and incremental implementability. The disadvantage is the infeasibility of determining when the collection of assertions is complete. This approach has been implemented in varying degrees by several projects [Griffiths 76], [Stonebraker 76].

The alternative approach is based on a significant extension of the concept of data type [Brodie 78]. The formal specification of these types, together with their interrelationships in a highly stylized way allows one to develop a complete specification. However, incremental specification is precluded. This approach has not yet been implemented.

The preceding approaches to semantic integrity are reasonable in the context of an individual DBMS. However, if semantic integrity is to be provided at the NVDM level, several differences exist. The most important is the fact that the NVDM does not have control over the data. Additionally, there is no way of guaranteeing that the actual databases satisfy any set of semantic integrity assertions. Moreover, semantic integrity assertions for two different databases supported by the NVDM may well be in conflict and yet be correct with respect to the system for which they have been asserted. For example, one system may require SALARY less than or equal $30,000 while another may require SALARY less than or equal $20,000. The SALARY of an individual making $25,000 would be consistent with the semantic integrity constraints of one DBMS and not with the other.

A second difference in NVDM supported semantic integrity arises from the likely limitation of network access to a subset of the data managed by an individual DBMS. As a result, there is no way of checking semantic integrity assertions spanning data accessible to the NVDM together with data which is not accessible to the NVDM.

The preceding suggests that semantic integrity in the NVDM context differs significantly from individual DBMS semantic integrity and, additionally, will be fundamentally less powerful. If this is unacceptable, an alternative is to have all semantic integrity related issues handled by the local DBMSs. Thus, semantic integrity assertions would not be checked until the translated query has arrived at the local DBMS. Unfortunately, given the present incomplete state of understanding of semantic integrity systems coupled with the fact that they do not exist as products, this approach is practically of little value.

A second approach would be to map all semantic integrity assertions from the local DBMS to the Network Data Manager while taking into account the differences in data models which may exist. Reasons cited in the first approach, coupled with the likelihood of missing data and the consequent impossibility of checking semantic integrity assertions involving such missing data render this approach unacceptable.

The third approach, which is being adopted in the context of the Experimental Network Data Manager [Kimbleton 79] described below, discards completeness as a major consideration and broadens the range of semantic integrity considerations to include both queries and updates instead of only updates. The extension to include queries reflects the desire to check that queries are basically meaningful. For example, a violation would be noted if one attempted to compare SNAME to PNAME. That is, strong domain typing is used to ensure semantically meaningful queries.

To assist in assuring the semantic integrity of updates, assertions and some data type extensions are being supported. Conceptually, these assertions can be divided into five categories: value assertions, row assertions, column assertions, intrarelation assertions, and interrelation assertions. The cost of checking the last two types of assertions is likely to be high. Accordingly, such assertions should only be made if absolutely necessary. The second principle to be followed is that whenever possible, assertion checking should minimize data retrieval requirements.

In summary, semantic integrity is likely to be an even more important concept for an NVDM than for an individual DBMS. However, significant differences exist with the result that obtaining a complete set of semantic integrity assertions at the Network Data Manager level will usually be practically impossible and may well be theoretically impossible.

14.3.3.3. Simplifying specification

The virtual view of data provided by NVDMs provides a very reasonable testbed for evaluating new, and more powerful DMLs and data models. Thus, incorporation of information describing classes, their attributes and interrelationships, and implementation of DMLs for manipulating this information is substantially simpler with an NVDM. This reflects the fact that retrieval issues can be minimized and consequently, attention can be focused on representational and manipulative issues. This facilitates studying alternative network user views of data.

14.3.4. XNDM – An Experimental Network Data Manager

To investigate the feasibility of constructing an NVDM, an Experimental Network Data Manager is currently being constructed at the National Bureau of Standards. The following presents a short overview of XNDM. A more detailed description is contained in section 14.4.6 and in [Kimbleton 79].

14.3.4.1. XNDM User Interface

The XNDM user interface consists of a Network Virtual Schema based on tables, together with a Network Virtual Data Language. The DML portion of the language consists of XNQL and XNUL. XNQL is the abbreviation for Experimental Network Query Language while XNUL abbreviates Experimental Network Update Language. This division has been established because of the significantly differing requirements implicit in supporting these two components. (The authors have also noticed that local DBMS management seems much more willing to support remote querying than remote updating!)

The XNDM Data Language is modeled after SQL [Chamberlin 76]. The primary reason for selecting SQL was its orientation toward a transaction processing style of interaction between the user and the DBMS. Additional factors supporting this decision were:

i) its relatively complete, publicly available description,

ii) its table orientation,

iii) its analysis in terms of human factors, and

iv) the likelihood that the XNDM supported local DBMSs would not use SQL since IBM systems are of limited accessibility on the Arpanet.

Figure 14-11 lists the six major classes of XNQL primitives.

Classes 1 and 2 provide the basic addressability required to support primitives of classes 3-5. Class 6, composition, supports the ability to nest queries and, thereby, facilitates a transaction processing orientation. A more detailed discussion is contained in [Wang 80].

14.3.4.2. XNDM translation

Currently, the feasibility of the required translation technology has been demonstrated. Development of an appropriate structure relating access path specification and translation is under investigation. Section 14.4 contains a detailed description of our interim understanding of this problem.

C1	Select
C2	Select . . . Where
C3	Aggregation
C4	Partition
C5	Set Operations
C6	Composition

Figure 14-11: XNQL primitive categories

14.3.4.3. XNDM distribution

XNDM implementation is distributed between the translator (resident on a PDP-11/45 as discussed below) and server modules, termed envelopes, resident on each of the target systems. The envelope serves two primary functions:

  i)   presentation of a uniform DBMS functionality within a given data model, and

  ii) support of a transaction processing oriented viewpoint.

Item (ii) is particularly important since it serves to minimize network bandwidth requirements as well as total delay.

14.3.4.4. XNDM prototype implementation

The current prototype XNDM implementation uses three Arpanet accessible computers. The host computer can be any Arpanet accessible host; currently it includes a PDP-11/45 running Unix [Ritchie 74], a Honeywell 6180 running Multics and a PDP-10 running TOPS-10. The two DBMSs are the Honeywell Multics Relational Data System (MRDS) [Honeywell 78] and Honeywell Integrated Data Store (IDS) [Honeywell 71] resident on the RADC Multics system. Translation is supported on a PDP-11/45 running the Unix operating system developed by Bell Laboratories [Ritchie 74].

14.4. Translation technology

This section considers the construction of the query management portion of NVDMs. It describes the functional nature of the task involved in the building of such systems and provides an analysis of the task. We then set forth a set of design aims for the construction of NVDMs based upon studies of the nature of the task and the operational characteristics of the application environment. A general solution approach is also outlined. A substantial fraction of the section is devoted to a detailed examination of the XNQL translator as a concrete illustration of the proposed solution methodology.

XNDM is a network virtual database management system, that is, it is a facility intended to support the use of remote DBMS capabilities in a network-wide, unified manner. Thus it provides a Network Virtual Schema (NVS), and a data manipulation language, XNQL, for the user to express data handling procedures. To the user, XNDM provides all the services that a conventional (single-host) DBMS provides. It is important to emphasize that although XNDM appears, operationally, as a state-of-the-art database manager, it is not based on, nor does it involve, the writing of a new database management system. Rather, it is built by using the existing facilities for database accessing and manipulation supplied by the individual remote DBMSs.

The above discussion emphasizes that the environment in which XNDM is run is that provided by the host database management systems (sometimes augumented in certain host DBMS deficient areas, or molded into a form more appropriate for incorporation into an NVDM). Therefore, the essential function of XNDM is the coordination of the different individual DBMS operations, not the provision and execution of these operations.

The heart of XNDM is the query language XNQL, which provides the set of commands allowing interaction with the DBMSs of other network hosts. Since we rely on the existing individual DBMSs for access and retrieval of stored data, the task of query evaluation reduces to that of translating user inputs, in the form of XNQL statements (i.e. a sequence of XNQL operations on the underlying NVS tables) into remote DBMS operations upon the data structures maintained by the individual systems.

14.4.1. Nature of the translation function

Before turning to the subject matter of this section, it is worthwhile to characterize the functions of an NVDM in (semi-)formal terms so that we shall have a more rigorous framework to base later discussions on. (Eventually we hope to express the problem in an exact mathematical form so we can apply mathematical techniques to deduce various properties for the system, e.g. correctness. Right now we shall not attempt to make the discussion precise.)

14.4.1.1. A formal definition

Following Mealy [Mealy 67], we say that a database system is a representation of some aspect of the real world, expressed in terms of a set of logical data structures (i.e. a "data model"), a set of instructions for accessing and manipulating these data structures, and a set of values constituting the inputs to and outputs from the system. We characterize a system by the relation between inputs and outputs which it determines, and also by the path by which we get from the input to the output. Our concern with the path is due to our desire to distinguish between different ways of performing the same database operation. The path information tells us both the instruction execution sequence and the state of the logical data structures which are generated along our way from the input to the output.

Consider a database system in the above sense, that is, a triple:

$$S = (E, A, V),$$

where E is a set of record types, V a set of values, A a set of "access functions" whose members are maps of the form:

$$t: E \rightarrow V.$$

(Here, as in the entire section which follows, we are confining ourselves to a much smaller context than is usually found in discussions on database systems. Specifically, we are only addressing the database retrieval, or querying aspect of the system. For general database management systems, a full set of database manipulation functions should be used in place of the access function A in the above definition for S.)

In terms of the above model, a query is defined as a composition of database access operations. Its semantics is determined by the observable sequence of data structure state transformations generated by the query during execution.

14.4.1.2. Access functions

Access functions provide the mechanisms for probing and traversing the database. Some of these allow us to locate data elements or records directly, e.g. keyed and indexed retrievals, others allow us to determine the location of data records through associations, e.g. retrieval by links.

As an example of an access function, the XNQL selection operation

"select x.QUANT from *Stock* x"

retrieves the collection of quantity values from the value set consisting of the QUANT column of the *Stock* table. The Codasyl DBTG statement

FIND FIRST *STOCK* WITHIN S-S.

has as its value set V the set of all records of type *Stock*. This is an instance of a "structural map" [Mealy 67], which is a map of the form

$t: E \rightarrow E$.

Formulated in this way, any retrieval operation can be decomposed into a record-type mapping (i.e. Mealy's "structural data map") followed by a non-record-type mapping, that is, a mapping whose result is a collection of data values rather than record-types, or, in other words, elements of the set

$W = (V - E)$.

For example, in the XNQL query

"select x.QUANT from *Stock* x, *Supplier* y
    where x.SNO $= y$.SNO and y.SNAME $=$ "Smith"",

there is an initial mapping which, given the value "Smith", yields all instances of the record(tuple)-type *Supplier*. (This can be thought of as a "direct" or "keyed" access.) It is followed by another mapping which takes tuples from the *Supplier* table, gives us a subset of the tuples from the *Stock* table (a "linked" access). A final mapping (a "projection") then yields a collection of quantity values from these *Stock* tuples.

14.4.1.3. Equivalence criterion

In terms of the above framework, the XNDM database system S, and the target host's database system S' are merely different representations of the same model of the real world. This requires that corresponding to any object in S, we can assign a unique object in S', and vice versa. In other words, there must exist a representation map, u which maps S into S':

$u: (E, A, V) \rightarrow (E', A', V')$,

and u is one-one onto [Mealy 67]. Furthermore, in order to insure that every fact derivable from one system is also derivable from the other [McGee 74], we require that for every valid query q in S, the situation shown in figure 14-12 can be made to obtain.

In the above diagram, s is the structural mapping process which allow us to derive the NVS tables from the individual remote databases:

$s: [E' \rightarrow E]$,

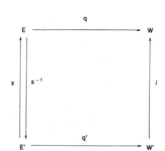

Figure 14-12: Equivalence of alternative mapping strategies

i is the identity map, and q' is the (sequence of) target commands corresponding to q. That is,

$$q' = v\,q,$$

where v is the operational translation which establishes the correspondence between the XNQL operations and the individual DBMS data manipulation commands:

$$v: [A \rightarrow A'].$$

In other words, starting with an element of the allowable class of target data structures, $e' \in E'$, one gets the same output values by applying the query q' as by applying s followed by q.

14.4.2. Translation alternatives

The previous discussion clearly shows that there are two alternative approaches to the problem of XNDM-target DBMS translation. This subsection describes these two alternatives and briefly sketches reasons for choosing one over the other.

14.4.2.1. Data structure mapping vs. DML translation

In the first approach, the desired results are obtained by transforming the target data structures into equivalent NVS representations, followed by the application of the XNQL query q on the NVS structures so generated. This way of viewing the problem emphasizes the structural aspects of the underlying databases since translation is done by reorganizing the target data into NVS schemas. The later processing of the user query q can be performed in essentially the same manner as that for any conventional relational calculus system. (There exists a large body of literature on database structural mappings, see, for example, McGee [McGee 74], Navathe and Fry [Navathe 76] and Biller [Biller 79]).

The second approach carries out the structural and query mappings (i.e. the s's and the q's) in the opposite order from that described above. Here we first establish the correspondence between q and a (sequence of) target DMLs (q'), then perform query evaluation by executing the translated query q' against the actual target data structures [Paolini 77].

14.4.2.2. Decision rationale

The first approach is unattractive for two reasons. First, it requires a large amount of data to be transferred from remote hosts to the NVDM machine to materialize the (relevant parts of) NVS tables. Since data transmission between NVDM and target sites is via communication links, this process is usually slow, sometimes unreliable or insecure, and always expensive. Secondly, we are making very ineffective use of remote DBMS services by performing a large part of the query processing inside the NVDM, instead of delegating them to the remote host.

We are thus led to the adoption of the second approach. This requires a well designed XNQL-to-target DML translator in order to be able to handle a large number of diverse target systems on a machine with relatively modest computational power and memory capacity (a PDP-11/45 with 128K core memory). This topic will not be further elaborated here as a detailed discussion of the solution approach will be taken up in a later subsection.

14.4.3. The query translation process — an informal description

The above characterizes the network query language translation problem as that of deriving the procedure v which maps the access functions A (on the class of data structures E) into a new set of access funtions A′ (on a new class of data structures E′).

A question arises here naturally: what are the basic functions such a procedure needs to perform to derive the functions A′ from A? Before going into an in-depth analysis of the various problems in devising the actual mapping procedure, let us describe intuitively how such derivation can be carried out. We shall use Codasyl DBTG as our target DBMS since it sheds more light on the subject than hierarchical or relational systems which are simpler and closer to the NVS.

14.4.3.1. Determination of query paths

A basic XNQL query retrieves specified data, the "selection list", from a database, possibly (but not necessarily) subject to some contraints — the "where clause". This must be transformed into a DBTG "query path", (a sequence of DBTG accessing primitives, i.e. FINDs) to access the target data.

Intuitively, the first step in XNQL translation is to identify the set of record-types that needs to be accessed. We begin by discovering the mapping between the set of XNQL retrieval items and constraint items and the DBTG data structures (records) of which those items are a part. Moreover, we note that in general the retrieval and the constraint items may not share common record-types. This means that we cannot access one record-type directly from the other, so we need to find some sub-structure which includes both the above sets of data items and which forms a "valid" underlying data structure for the specific XNQL retrieval request we are considering.

There are many possible definitions of what constitutes a "valid" sub-structure, none of which is completely satisfactory [Collmeyer 72]. For the sake of discussion, we shall adopt the very practical, but restrictive, approach of Lavallee et al. [Lavallee 72] and define it to be one which satisfies the criterion of a "valid covering". A covering is defined to be a connected sub-graph of the data structure diagram for the database [Bachman 69] which includes both the retrieval and the constraint record types. A covering is valid if and only if it conforms to the specifications of a confluent hierarchy (see [Collmeyer 72] for detailed discussions and examples of confluent hierarchies).

Given a valid covering, we can approach the problem of query path determination in the following way. We start with any directly accessible record-type R (i.e. member of a DBTG singular set or one with LOCATION MODE CALC) and mark it as visited. Next we visit each of the unvisited record-types adjacent to R. Then unvisited records adjacent to these records are visited and so on. The search terminates when no unvisited record-type can be reached from any of the visited ones.

This breadth-first search procedure [Horowitz 76] generates all possible paths for traversing the valid covering of the query. Usually, since more than one such path exists, we need another stage in the path formulation process – selection of the "optimal" path, to which we shall now turn our attention.

14.4.3.2. Selection of an optimal path

The objective of this stage is to find the query path that uses the least amount of resources (cpu time and secondary storage accesses). For the sake of discussion, we equate this with the number of (expected) logical record accesses. To a first approximation, this problem is separable into two parts. The first part is minimization of the number of record-types in the query path. Next, we minimize the number of record instances which must be traversed. This can be done by identifying the position of the constraining records in the path, and choosing the one where these records are as near to the entry record as possible. (An alternative and simpler way to do this is as follows. In each step of our breadth-first search we pick, whenever possible, not an arbitrary adjacent record as prescribed in section 14.4.3.1, but one which is constrained to be our next node to visit.)

Of course, the above strategy has to be improved in many ways before it can be used in a real application. First, we have assumed that the relative effectiveness of different constraining records is the same, whereas in actuality, this is usually not the case. Second, traversal of different sections of the query path usually incurs different "costs". Therefore we need a more sophisticated way of estimating resource usage than a straightforward counting of the record instances traversed [Astrahan 76], [Yao 79].

14.4.3.3. Limitations

The above approach has serious difficulties so far as actual implementation is concerned. Its basic inadequacy lies in its essential appeal to our intuitive feeling of what constitutes a "valid" sub-structure for an XNQL query. It also depends critically on our ability to show that the "meaning" (i.e. the operational effects) of the source XNQL statement is preserved by the sequence of DBTG FINDs that we produce for traversing this sub-structure.

To justify this approach, we need to view the task facing the XNQL translator in a more detailed way. We shall consider the operational results of each of the XNQL constructs and find out how to achieve the same effects with DBTG DMLs. Based upon these observations, we then devise a set of rules that describe the sequences of DBTG DMLs as a function of the NVS-DBTG schema context. Such a set of rules forms the basis of the algorithm for the translator to determine, step-by-step, the "valid" target sub-structure and the "valid" traversal path. This will be the topic of the following subsection.

14.4.4. A taxonomy of major translation issues

It is time now to look at the translation problem in more general and detailed ways. The present subsection attempts to analyze the task situation. A discussion of the XNDM solution approach will be given in section section 14.4.5.

The two basic issues involved in network virtual query translation are data schema and operation mapping. They correspond, roughly, to finding the valid covering data structure and generating the (optimal) query path, respectively, as described in the above subsection. These issues, and their inter-dependencies, will be dealt with individually in the following paragraphs.

14.4.4.1. Data schema mapping

Schema mapping provides for the connection between NVDM data structures and the various remote DBMS data structures. The most obvious such connection is that between the individual data items – the first type of mapping.

It is necessary for a network virtual data manager to be provided a means for referencing data managed by remote DBMSs. Each DBMS has some internal scheme for naming data items, but these various schema are typically different and may even be incompatible. Since it is impractical (and in many cases, impossible) to impose a common internal data item naming scheme, a network virtual name space is used, with a portion of the name space allocated to each remote DBMS. The relationship between the remote DBMS's internal name space and its portion of the virtual data item name space are used by the data mapper to transform references to NVS attributes into those for individual DBMS data elements.

The second type of schema mapping relates the NVS record types (i.e. the XNDM tuple construct) to the record types supported by the remote DBMSs. This implies that aggregation or splitting of tuples may be needed in order to map references to XNDM tables into those for the local DBMS record types. Since almost all generalized database systems contain the basic data structure corresponding to (or closely parallelling) records (e.g. records or entries in the Codasyl DBTG proposal [Codasyl 73], segments for IMS [IBM 76], logical records for IDS [Honeywell 71], relations for Ingres [Stonebraker 76] and MRDS [Honeywell 78]), the practicality of the previous two schema mapping functions is common across all individual remote DBMSs.

A third type of mapping deals with the interrelationships between the different record types. In contrast to intra-record structures, the common generalized DBMSs support widely different inter-record structures, as evidenced by the fact that almost every system has a different set of facilities for traversing the various record types within its data space.

For example, relational calculus systems [Codd 71] allow requests for subsets of the data stored in the system to be made completely in terms of first-order predicate calculus operations on the entire collection of database entry types (relations), without specifying search procedures and paths to be followed. Codasyl DBTG systems, on the other hand, provide for a very complete specification of how the search is to be conducted in terms of the exact path to be followed. It is necessary to specify the location of the next record instance from the current cursor position within the database. Relational algebra systems [Codd 71] present yet a third way of database navigation. These systems require the user to formulate a sequence of unary and/or binary algebraic operations on the underlying database relations, thereby generating the desired data subsets in a stepwise manner.

Therefore the makeup of the relevant "inter-record relationship mapper" depends heavily upon the individual local DBMS. Later in this section we shall discuss, in detail, the various issues involved in constructing such a mapper in the context of a specific system — XNDM.

14.4.4.2. Operation mapping

Operation mapping translates the XNQL table operations, namely, column and row selection, aggregation, partition, set operation and various compositions of these operations into the corresponding operations for handling target system database records and the logical interrelationships among these records.

There are four aspects to the general problem of mapping between the data manipulation operations of the various systems. The first problem we need to address is the difference in meaning (sometimes subtle, and always annoying) of primitive data manipulation operators as evidenced by the operational effects these primitives produce. A simple example of such a difference is the different degree of accuracy exhibited by the floating-point arithmetic operators for various machines [Neely 77]. Another example is the non-uniform treatment of duplicate results by the currently existing relational systems [Honeywell 78], [Chamberlin 76].

Moreover, different DMLs typically differ in the level of data aggregation allowable as a unit of manipulation [Stonebraker 75]. Some languages, notably that proposed by the Codasyl Data Base Task Group, dictate an instance-at-a-time query style. These languages contain constructs that return exactly one instance of a record each time it is called (e.g. the DBTG "find" statement). Hence, the user must execute a proper sequence of such commands in order to acquire, instance by instance, the needed information. XNQL, in contrast, is a "set-oriented" language, that is, its statements return information from the entire set of record instances satisfying the indicated condition specified in the command.

Another dimension along which query languages can vary is the degree of history sensitivity they exhibit [Backus 78]. Some DMLs include the notion of storage, so that one statement can save information and thereby affect the behavior of subsequent statements.

For example, the definition of Codasyl DBTG DML [Codasyl 73] is based upon the fundamental concept of currency, which constitutes the essential channel through which interactions between individual DMLs take place. With systems of this type, the user constructs the query a piece at a time by applying transformations on this storage space of currency indicators. This is why FIND is the most important statement for DBTG systems [Date 77]. It is logically required before each of the other statements (except STORE) so that these statements can have the right storage environment to operate in.

Languages like SQL or XNQL provide much more powerful ways for constructing complex queries. The primitives of the language operate on whole conceptual units of data (tables) and produce whole conceptual units, and we compose individual queries q and q' by first applying q and then using the result as an argument to q'. This property is very desirable since by confining the operation of individual statements to only its arguments, we do not need to worry about hidden states (contents of currency indicators and temporary storage areas, and other side effects) and the complex transitions these states undergo.

Finally, perhaps the most important characterization of a database system concerns its mechanisms for expressing associations between the different record types within the database. Some systems, among which the Codasyl DBTG [Codasyl 73] and the IBM Information Management System [IBM 76] are the best known examples, provides specific constructs (e.g. the DBTG "set" and the IMS parent-child relationship) for interrelating different record types. These data structuring constructs are used by operators (FIND NEXT and FIND OWNER for DBTG, and GET NEXT for IMS) for retrieving information contained in logically related, but different, data records.

Relational systems [Codd 70] choose, instead, to eliminate all "access path dependencies" from their data structures, and to express associations between record types explicitly in the data element values contained within the record types (relations). Prescriptions for interrelating record types are supplied dynamically in the queries issued by the user in the form of join operations on two relations over a common ("join-able") column.

The entity-relationship systems [Chen 76] take the view that record types should only be used to model real world entities. Associations among record types should model real world relationships between these entities and are part of the meta-information the system maintains about the database. The logical analysis needed to resolve the interrelationships among various record types is performed automatically by the system so the user need not express in detail how to "chain" through the different records [Shoshani 78].

14.4.5. Implementation approach

We have analyzed the various problems a network virtual data manager has to solve. We would now like to formulate a solution approach, in other words, an algorithmization of the translation process. Not all issues involved in the building of an NVDM will be considered here, nor is every facet of the proposed solution unique or optimal. Our purpose is to present one prototype, real implementation, namely, an experimental translator for our network virtual query language, XNQL. Another purpose of this subsection is to illuminate the many aspects of the problem of virtual DML translator construction based upon experiences gained from this experiment.

14.4.5.1. A translator family

Implementation of the XNQL translator is complicated by the fact that different target systems support different primitive operations and data structures; therefore we need not a single translator but a family of translators. Two approaches to their realization can be identified: construction of a collection of source-target specific translators or, alternatively, construction of a single translator for the bulk of the translation process common to all individual DBMSs, together with post-processing modules for handling the target-specific portion of the translation process.

Construction of independent translators has the advantage that design unity and run-time efficiency is more achievable with a single translator for each target DBMS. However, an entire translator is needed to support each additional target, whereas in the family approach all the translators share a core design which defines the common (target-independent) part of the translator. Each new translator in the family is obtained by building the required target-oriented functionality on top of the basic design. Therefore the bulk of the implementation effort is available across different target systems and new developments need not start from scratch.

14.4.5.2. Environmental constraints

For the XNDM application environment, easy adaptability to different target DBMSs is of primary importance. The reason is that practical use in a production environment requires that an NVDM accomodate the various evolutionary modifications to which individual DBMSs are constantly subjected [Boehm 73].

Another design constraint is that the translator only act as a mediator between the XNDM view of data and that of the remote database managers and must, therefore, interact with the target DBMSs as a user of the system. The reason for the imposition of this condition is our basic assumption that the hardware, software and human resources needed for XNDM operation are both geographically and managerially dispersed, although connected through a network. Therefore interfacing to remote facilities in any other manner would present difficulties, both operational and administrative, which would be very difficult, if not impossible, to solve.

14.4.5.3. Design goals

These operational considerations established three design attitudes toward the XNQL translator. First, it should be modular, and thereby capable of achieving a high degree of flexibility in the sense that drastic changes can be made to one module without a need to change others. Second, it should be expandable, that is, one should be able to augment the translator to handle new target DBMSs without affecting the existing modules. Third, it should confine its target dependency to as few modules as possible ("target-specificity hiding") [Parnas 72].

An important side-effect of the modular, family approach has been the insight it provides for the design of data manipulation and structuring facilities for DBMSs. It is impossible to design a simple, coherent translator family without abstracting the essential properties from various target systems and recognizing their commonalities as well as their differences.

Based upon the previous discussion, we conclude that our major task in building the query translator for an NVDM is design of a good general framework, i.e., a consistent, efficiently implementable translator allowing effective use of the target DBMS facilities.

With these system level considerations out of the way, we proceed in the next subsection with a description of the construction of a translator aimed at achieving the above goals.

14.4.6. XNQL translator specifics

So far we have been occupied with basic questions of a functional nature and the general design goals of NVDM query translation. Let us now consider a single translator in some depth, namely, that for XNQL.

The basic approach taken by the XNQL translator is to accomplish the complex semantic manipulations required for the translation by means of step-by-step transformation of an appropriately chosen internal representation of the input text. We have chosen a tree as the intermediate representation because of the requirement for flexibility in handling a wide range of target DMLs and data structures.

Each transformation takes us somewhat closer to the target query by either:

i) changing the original form of the input text to uncover the underlying "basic structure" of the query tree which characterizes the system-independent organization of the query, or

ii) reshaping the basic tree to incorporate the surface structure of the target language.

This transformational approach reduces overall translator complexity and the resulting modularization of the translator allows a simple, consistent design [DeRemer 76].

The translation process is (vertically) segmented into five phases as illustrated in figure 14-13.

Each box in the above diagram represents a major processing step. The vertical arrows represent the data dependencies between them. These boxes are further refined into sub-boxes with vertical and horizontal lines. Horizontal separations indicate the order in which the sub-boxes must be executed; vertical separations indicate the absence of such constraints.

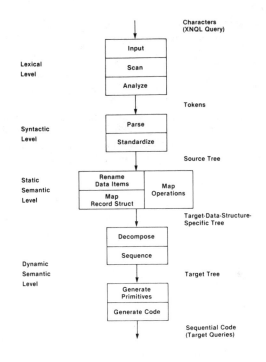

Figure 14-13: The XNQL translator as a tree transformer

For example, the "lexical level" box is divided into three components that operate serially on user inputs: one that reads the character string, one that scans the characters and one that recognizes the reserved words. An explanation of the general attributes of these five phases of the translator follows.

Lexical and syntactic analysis

The tasks of the lexical and syntactic analysis modules are conventional [Gries 71]. They produce a source(XNQL)-specific syntax tree representation of the input query. This tree contains all the information originally present in the source text as well as all the information that is inherent in the XNQL grammatical description. The source syntax tree is the first of a sequence of trees used in the translator as intermodular data structures. Each later module takes as input the tree produced by the previous module and leaves a tree that is closer to the target query by reshaping the tree, pruning source-specific information from the tree and/or incorporating target-specific information into the tree. The basic task facing the translator writer is disentangling those aspects of the source and target queries that reflect "essential" (language-independent) logical structures from those that characterize "incidental" (language-specific) representational details.

Standardization

Processing beyond the syntactic level can be made simpler if the source syntax tree is transformed into a standard form where each WHERE clause is represented as a binary tree of predicates connected by AND and OR nodes arranged in conjunctive normal form [Stonebraker 76].

Static semantic processing

Each XNQL query interacts with a data space which is the Cartesian product of several relations subject to the restriction of the "where" clause. Since frequently these restrictions are such that the Cartesian product becomes an equi-join (merging of two relations based on a common column), differences in source and target structures at the record level imply different join conditions in the queries.

The static semantic level of the translator does the processing needed to account for the first two levels of data structure differences (i.e. at and below the record level—see section 14.4.2.1), by first resolving data item name differences and then the differences in the JOINs.

The "data item renaming" module traverses the source syntax tree from the top down, replacing all leaf references to source (i.e. NVS) data items with corresponding references to target data items and depositing their attribute information at these nodes. The "record structure mapping" module then deletes all predicate nodes representing JOINs between different source relations and inserts the appropriate JOIN predicates for target records.

A third static semantic processing module, the "operator mapping" routine, converts target-system dependent operators into explicit system-specific forms to account for the kind of (primitive DML) operator differences discussed in section 14.4.4.2. For example, arithmetic and comparison operations on floating point numbers are transformed into operations in significant digit mode and interval mode, respectively.

Dynamic semantic processing

The transformations which occur at this level account for the differences in the logical structures of the source and target query languages. Since the unit of data structure for each target query may be smaller than for XNQL (e.g. each Codasyl DML statement can only involve a single record (or set) type, whereas there is no limitation to the number of different tuple types (relations) an XNQL statement can manipulate), we first decompose the query tree into sub-trees, each of which involves a single unit of data structure that a target query can handle. The "sequence" module then chains the sub-trees together in the order that the corresponding queries should be sequenced for the target DBMS and selects the execution sequence of these chains that minimizes the number of intermediate records required for processing.

Code generation

This is the final phase of the translator and output consists of the desired target DML statements that can be executed by the local DBMSs. The first module interprets each of the sub-trees along the chains produced by the "sequence" module and generates CALL statements to primitive target database operations. The second (code generation) module then expands these CALLs into sequences of actual target DML statements.

The exact form of the primitives depends upon the particular target system we are considering. Their behavior characteristics fall, in general, into the following categories: search or return the first/next instance of a specified record type, test the truth value of some predicate expression of the record type, partition all instances of a record type on the basis of some data item values, and evaluate aggregate functions for the specified record type. (These correspond roughly to the information algebra [Codasyl 62] operations of searching/returning the first/next point of a line, bundling, glumping and evaluating functions of lines.)

This extra level of indirection before the actual code generation allows us to separate out the representational details of the target DMLs and makes it possible to have a standard set of primitives for each general class of target systems, that is, Codasyl, relational calculus and relational algebra systems.

The decision to set the primitives at a fairly procedural level (namely, one record instance at a time) is due largely to our desire for flexibility and power in expressing a variety of access strategies. This allows easy incorporation of optimization modules which select the "best" access paths for the input query based upon knowledge of how the records are stored (keys, inversion, indices) [Lorie 79]. This is particularly important since the value and usefulness of XNDM in a real environment depends critically upon its performance. Experience with current relational DBMSs indicate that some form of optimization is essential in bringing performance to an acceptable level [Smith 75].

14.4.6.1. Status and interim conclusions

Work on the XNQL translator is still in progress. The current version handles the two XNQL constructs which constitute the most primitive "adequate" set for database accessing (selection of columns and selection of rows based on 1- and 2-table predicates). The target systems are:

i)   the Multics Relational Data Store (MRDS) [Honeywell 78], a relational calculus system, and

ii) the Honeywell 600/6000 Integrated Data Store (IDS) [Honeywell 71], a Codasyl-like system.

These systems were chosen because they represent, as far as NVDM implementation is concerned, the two extreme models of DBMS design. For MRDS, the translator can handle all target data structures in a very general way, but for IDS, target records with multiple owners and multiple members are excluded.

The current state of XNDM is not only unfinished but also limited in scope. Many aspects of NVDMs are left untouched. Many others have only received cursory attention, or have not been explored in sufficient detail to provide a proper understanding of the problem. For example, how should partitioned and/or replicated data be handled? How can location and replication transparency be provided? When the individual databases contain information with somewhat different (real-world) meaning, how can we resolve their differences? What can we do to improve performance, to make the system more usable, more reliable and more maintainable?

The list could be extended almost indefinitely. All of these questions are interesting and very relevant, but beyond the scope of the present paper. This paper should be viewed, then, as an interim report on an ongoing effort which needs to be advanced in many directions. We do believe it describes some of the major and so far unexplored issues in the design and implementation of network virtual data managers. Our hope is that this work will only be the beginning, and that it will stimulate other investigations into this increasingly important area [Rothnie 77], [Gray 79], [Lindsay 79].

The preceding has described an approach for supporting uniform queries across multiple, remote, heterogeneous DBMSs. A major remaining requirement is a means for transmitting the resulting (structured) data to the user in a meaning preserving way.

14.5. Data Transfer Protocols (DTPs)

This section describes a basic Data Transfer Protocol required in order to support either the transmission of data generated by a DBMS in response to a query or that generated by a process in performing an update. Key issues which must be considered are the nature of the protocol itself, translation/transformation functions which are provided to ensure the preservation of meaning, relation to other work, and supporting issues.

A data transfer protocol provides the means for moving data between possibly heterogeneous systems. Implementing one requires consideration of two major issues:

i) the nature of the protocol, and

ii) the transformations which are provided to assure preservation of meaning.

Sunshine [Sunshine 80] provides an up-to-date definition of a protocol. As discussed therein, the key features are:

- definition of the service to be provided,

- description of the entities *(site specific components)* which collectively provide these services,

- specification of the message exchange protocol used in communicating between entities, and

- identification of the lower level support functions which are assumed (equivalent to specification of the services provided by lower protocol levels)

A key component of the message exchange protocol part of a Data Transfer Protocol is the specification of intermediate data formats used in transmitting data between systems. Because of its complexity, this respresents a significant additional dimension to the commonly required message exchange protocols. This reflects the need to consider both the representation of structured data as well as the collection of messages to be exchanged.

Context for developing a DTP comes from two major sources. The first is the existing literature on File Transfer Protocols (FTPs) [Forsdick 79], [Arpan 77], [INWG 77]. Although these protocols have observed the desirability of transferring structured data, their implementations have been directed toward transmission of text (character string) or binary files. They are, therefore, inadequate for meeting the requirements which a DTP must satisfy.

A segment of the database literature has studied the problem of translating databases in detail [Navathe 76], [SDDTTG 76], [Shu 77]. The approaches which have been developed, together with the prototype implementations, have been rather powerful in their ability to handle complex data structures and their interrelationships as are commonly found in the database context. However, this power is achieved, in part, through relying on an offline approach which is appropriate when an entire database is to be moved between systems.

Given these two separate developmental threads, the issue arises as to whether a protocol can be developed which is sufficiently powerful to meet the needs for transmitting structured data between heterogeneous systems and, simultaneously, is sufficiently straightforward to permit the online operation common to database accesses. We believe the answer to the preceding question is yes! In support, the following discussion provides a detailed description of the basic nature of one Data Transfer Protocol. Although this discussion has a general, issues oriented flavor, section 14.7 describes a closely related capability implemented as part of an Experimental Network Operating System. Thus, a data point showing feasibility also exists.

14.5.1. DTP services

Defining DTP services requires considering three major issues:

- protocol invocation
- source/destination
- transformations

Within this section we shall consider only the first two of these issues. The complexity of the third is sufficient to require the relatively detailed discussion presented in the following section.

14.5.1.1. Protocol invocation

Arpanet protocols [Arpan 78] provided a basic point of departure for much subsequent protocol related work. Unfortunately, the basic model which seems to have been employed in their development assumed a rather high level of general computer communications knowledge by a terminal user.

Assuming a knowledgable user permitted the protocol implementers to substantially reduce their concern for providing a uniform environment across systems. Thus, the set of implemented commands, as well as their representation, invocation, and responses (both to note completion of normal processing as well as to signal the occurrence of an error) varied from system to system. These variations were sufficiently small to be classified as a minor annoyance by typical Arpanet users. For mission oriented users assumed to have little, if any, general interest in computers or communications per se, such annoyance can assume major proportions. Unsubstantiated comments leave the impression that the result may be a tacit decision by users to boycott the system.

Assuming a terminal user was very reasonable in the early Arpanet days and is probably still reasonable for a broad majority of users. However, developing complex distributed applications requires a process invocable protocol. This, in turn, requires some changes in the protocol design and implementation to handle the underlying asynchrony of operations. It also requires uniform responses across systems.

Handling asynchronous operations proved simple for terminal users. Effectively, one only needed to know whether type ahead was permitted. Typically, Arpanet protocols do not permit type ahead. As a result, the user must enter one parameter of the invocation sequence and wait until the appropriate response has been received to enter another. The resulting need to enter a multi-parameter command using a parameter at a time style proves difficult to program around even if a terminal emulation device such as the NBS Network Access Machine (NAM) [Rosenthal 78] is used to permit program invocation of terminal oriented protocols.

The conclusion is that Data Transfer Protocols suitable for supporting remote interaction with DBMSs must be explicitly designed to be program invocable.

14.5.1.2. Source/destination

For File Transport Protocols the source and destination were files within the file systems. This was a reasonable, if not the only choice for terminal users. Database translation, in contrast, assumed an entire database which was usually spread across a large number of files at both the source and destination. Program invocation of a DTP results in a third major source/destination type: buffers within primary memory.

We exclude databases as source/destination candidates for a DTP. Files and buffers remain. Before the rapid price declines in the cost of primary memory (one megabyte of primary memory for the IBM 4300 now costs approximately $15,000), there was an obvious distinction between files and buffers. Files were assumed to be large while buffers were small. Thus, it was reasonable to think of two separate protocols; one supporting file transfer while the other supported buffer transfer.

Distinguishing between files and buffers based on size becomes meaningless in an environment in which large systems may have primary memory sizes of 10-100 megabytes while small systems may only have 64K words of primary memory and a disk storage capacity of less than 10 megabytes. We conclude that only one protocol should be used for transferring files and buffers. The only difference occurs in specifying the explicit source or destination.   From an implementation viewpoint, this approach is very natural since implementing a protocol for transmitting structured files requires the ability to transmit structured data within a buffer.

Given the preceding, the following discussion of a Data Transfer Protocol assumes that either source or destination may be a file or buffer. The complexity of the data interrelationships which are to be supported must now be considered.

14.5.2. Data and its translation/transformation

This section addresses three major issues:

    i)   the logical complexity of data whose transmission is to be supported by a DTP,

   ii) existing approaches to translating and transforming such data, and

  iii) a specific approach based on using a Common Network Representation for data being transmitted between systems.

Data being transmitted between systems can be divided into three levels of increasing complexity of which only the first two are reasonable candidates for DTP support. These are:

- Unstructured data corresponding to transmission of some number of instances of a given data element type, e.g. text files or binary strings.

- Structured data without pointers — corresponding to transmission of a collection of structured but independent records having the same logical structure (tree representation and data element type).

- Structured data with pointers between records.

We believe that a DTP should support transfer of the first two categories of data. Although pointers are, conceptually, just another data type, significant care is required in their interpretation.   This reflects the application dependent nature of their specification and interpretation. Thus, the decision to support transfer of data in the third category may be application dependent.   A very general approach to supporting the implicit transformation requirements is contained in [Privitera 80].

Translating the first two categories of data requires considering two separate but interrelated issues. The first is the complexity of the transformations which may be performed on the data. The second is the extent to which the semantics of system data representations are "known" by the transformer and, thereby, do not have to be explicitly stated by the user.

We assume that data exists at a Sender (either file or buffer) and is to be transmitted to a Receiver (also either file or buffer). Additionally, for symmetry and conceptual simplicity, we assume that the invoker of the transfer may be colocated with the Sender, the Receiver, or may exist on a third system distinct from either Sender or Receiver. Moreover, we assume that the Receiver data may be only a logical subset of the Sender data.   That is, each Receiver data element value can be a functional image of one or more Sender data element values. This level of capability proves sufficient to handle the transformations required by XNOS. Moreover, it is sufficiently restrictive to permit the protocol to assume responsibility for data element type mappings and for mapping data structures to their linear representations (cf. the discussion of XNOS in section 14.7.

A general purpose programming language provides the most general means for performing source to destination data maps. The disadvantages of this approach are equally obvious since each different transformation requires writing a different program.

The Arpanet Data Reconfiguration Service (DRS) [Cerf 74] provided a transformation capability which was nearly as general as that provided by a general purpose programming language. Additionally, specification of the transformations was simplified by providing a compact and concise notation. However, the user was responsible for both explicitly stating the data type representations used by source and destination systems as well as for procedurally specifying the means for establishing the correspondances between the logical structure of the data, say a tree (commonly used to represent records), and the serial representation of the corresponding data elements on a storage medium.

DSCL [Schneider 75] provided a somewhat simpler means for specifying data transformations. However, the user was still required to explicitly indicate the transformations to be performed on the bit string representation of the data.

Historically, database translation has provided extensive incorporation of data type and structure semantics. However, the complexity of the requirements for supporting database translation substantially exceed those of the transformation portion of a data transfer protocol. Nevertheless, the relevant database translation literature, e.g. the University of Michigan Data Translator [Navathe 76], the Stored Data Definition Translation Task Group report [SDDTTG 76], and the Define/Convert capabilities [Shu 77] provides important insights into the levels of sophistication which can be achieved.

Instead of specifying data transformations procedurally, one would prefer to specify the source and destination record descriptions together with their interrelationship and require that the system establish the appropriate transformations. Within the context of supporting network access to data, this objective is realizable as described in 14.5.5 in the context of XNOS. Thus, the user need only specify the relevant data structures using the specification technique of the programming language being used.

14.5.3. Implementing a data translator/transformer

Data translation is required both to preserve the logical structure of data being transmitted between heterogeneous systems and to preserve the type and value of individual data elements. Structure preservation is required since different systems may store the same logical record in different ways. The structure of the data translation process is determined by:

i) the site(s) at which translation is performed, and

ii) the decision as to whether to use a Common Network Representation.

14.5.3.1. Translation implementation alternatives

Three major translation implementation alternatives exist:

i)   all translation is performed at the source, i.e. the source translates data directly to the system dependent representation used by the destination,

ii) all translation is performed at the destination, and

iii) translation is distributed between source and destination.

If either of the first two alternatives are employed, one can use direct source-destination translation.   The cost, however, if there are N heterogeneous systems, is that of building $N*(N-1)$ translators.   To reduce this cost, one may opt instead for using a Common Network Representation (CNR) and distributing the translation between sender and receiver.

Using a CNR results in translating the source data to a common representation for transmission through the network.   It is is then retranslated to the form appropriate for the destination. Apparently, this approach only requires the construction of $2N$ translators (one to and one from each of the N different system types).   If the host dependent portion of the translation process can be represented via tables, only two basic translators are required together with the appropriate code.   (This is the approach used in the discussion of XNOS described in section 14.7.)

The disadvantage of this approach, in comparison with direct sender-receiver translation, is the possibility of reduced performance.   In weighing the advantage of implementation simplicity against this possible disadvantage, two key issues are the expected bandwidth of the transmission process and the likelihood that the supported systems will change.   Since the bandwidth is likely to be limited when terrestrial communication lines are employed, the overhead of using a Common Network Representation may be negligible.   Moreover, if the characteristics or requirements of the supported systems is likely to change, the simplification resulting from the CNR approach may prove very desirable.

14.5.3.2. Translation as a distributed process

Describing the distributed translation process is facilitated by introducing some notation:

1) SSR is the Sender Storage Representation of the record and corresponds to its serial representation in the Sender_Buffer.

2) SES is the Sender Element Sequence of the record, defining the sequence in which data elements are encountered as one traverses the SSR.

3) SCNR is the Sender Common Network Representation of the record; the element sequence of the SCNR is that of the SES but the individual data elements have been translated into their common network-wide representation.

4) RES is the Receiver Element Sequence of the record.

5) RCNR is the Receiver Common Network Representation of the record.

6) RSR is the Receiver Storage Representation of the record.

Given the preceding, the translation process can be simply described as a function t: SSR $\rightarrow$ RSR.

Provided a common intermediate representation is to be used, t can be viewed as the composition of three functions, s, m and r, where s is the Sender translation function, m is the Sender-Receiver transformation function, and r is the Receiver translation function. I.e., $t = r \circ m \circ s$, where $\circ$ denotes the composition function.

Sender Translation

The Sender translation function s: SSR → SCNR. The input to the translation process consists of three components:

   i)   SSR,

   ii) a Sender Logical Record Description (SLRD) describing the SES, and

   iii) a Sender Representation Table (SRT) describing the representation of individual data element types at the Sender.

The output consists of the SCSR in sender element sequence.

Implementation of the translation process is conceptually straightforward and simply consists of:

   i)   reading the SLRD to determine the type of the next data element,

   ii) extracting the appropriate number of bits beginning from the current position of the translation pointer with offset determined by the data element type,

   iii performing the appropriate translation and concatenating the result to the existing interim SCNR,

   iv) advancing the translation pointer appropriately, and continuing the process until the SSR has been processed.

Sender-Receiver Transformation

Sender-Receiver transformation should permit:

   i)   different Sender and Receiver names for the same component,

   ii) deletion of Sender data elements (because the requestor may not have the appropriate security authorization or, alternatively, may not require a given component),

   iii) specification of a Receiver data element as a function of Sender data elements (cf. the discussion in the following section), as well as

   iv) modification of the type of a data element (for example, it may prove desirable to convert an integer data type to a real data type).

The Sender-Receiver transformation m: SCNR → RCNR. The four inputs to the transformation process are:

   i)   SCSR,

   ii) Sender Logical Record Description,

   iii) Receiver Logical Record Description, and

   iv) a Name Map Table.

The need for (i)-(iii) is evident. The Name Map Table is required to permit Sender and Receiver to use different names for the same data element and to specify the appropriate map between their data elements. Its existence adds substantial flexibility to the transformation process and, in general, supports transformation whenever the RCNR is a function of the SCNR.

The preceding discussion has not addressed the issue of where transformation is performed. Either Sender or Receiver is appropriate. Implicitly, we are assuming transformation to SCNR is performed at the source while transformation from RCNR is performed at the destination. The SCNR → RCNR map may be performed in either place. This approach should be contrasted with the approach used in a Network Operating System supported environment as described in section 14.7.

Receiver Translation

The Receiver translator r: RCN→ RSR. The inputs to this translation process are:

i)   RCNR,

ii) Receiver Logical Record Description, and

iii) Receiver Representation Table.

Logically, this translation process is the inverse of the source translation.

14.5.4. A data transfer protocol

This section describes a basic Data Transfer Protocol meeting the objectives and constraints established in the preceding. The basic service to be provided is preservation of meaning in transmitting structured data between heterogeneous systems. The entities required to provide this service are discussed at length below as is a transaction flavored message exchange protocol. Implementation of this protocol assumes a means for error free reliable transmission of data between systems. Protocols providing such functionality are sometimes termed host-host protocols; the basic requirements correspond to the services provided by levels four and five of the ISO Reference Model [ISO/TC97/SC16 N227].

We begin by describing the DTP environment and continue with a discussion of the operation of the protocol viewed as a distributed collection of processes. Thereafter, the specifics of the message exchange process are discussed.

14.5.4.1. DTP processing sequence

We assume that some process, perhaps a Network Virtual Data Manager, has generated one or more records to be transmitted to another computer system. Destination records are to be images of Sender records.

The DTP design which we will describe uses a major simplifying assumption: the elimination of options negotiation. This is achieved by requiring that all parameters be transmitted together with the record. Thus, the protocol initialization process which is usually required to ensure that Sender and Receiver are operating with compatible parameters is avoided.

DTP operation requires five separate processing phases.

- Translation of Sender Record
- Sender → Receiver Transmission
- Translation of Receiver Record
- Receiver Process Notification
- Acknowledgment to Sender

Sender and Receiver translation are logically symmetric invocations of the data transformation process discussed in 14.5.3. Sender → Receiver transmission is performed in response to an invocation of the message exchange protocol discussed below.

Process notification is required to guarantee that the appropriate process within the Receiver is notified upon completion of transmission of the record(s). If the process is in the WAIT state, this could be achieved through forcing its rescheduling for the processor. If the process is ACTIVE, a flag can be set or a message sent to an appropriate port of the process.

The acknowlegement phase is realized via transmission of a message from Receiver to Sender. Its receipt by the Sender component of the protocol is required to permit appropriate housekeeping operations, e.g. flushing of buffers before transmitting additional record(s).

14.5.4.2. DTP commands

Our discussion of a DTP assumes:

i)   protocol invocation by a process within the sender,

ii) the protocol is passed either a file name or a buffer name plus access path specifications for both Sender and Receiver which will be referred to below as SenderName and ReceiverName, and

iii) the protocol is passed a pointer to a parameter list (discussed below).

If we assume flow control is performed by a lower level protocol, only four commands are required:

Sender→Receiver
    send(Id,Sender-Location,Receiver-Location, Param-List;Return-Code)
    abort(Id)

Receiver→Sender
    received (Id)
    reject (Id)

Send is the basic command for transmitting data from Sender to Receiver. The Return-Code notifies the requesting process whether the transmission completed successfully. **Abort** is required to permit premature termination when required. **Received** indicates that transmission was successfully completed. **Reject** indicates unwillingness of the Receiver to accept (or support completion of) transmission.

The Id provides a compact mechanism for detecting duplicates and referring to a specific request. A variety of techniques exist for selecting such identifiers; one is the use of a system time stamp having sufficient resolution.

The parameter list for the DTP consists of two major components supporting record translation and transformation. The basic information requirements for their support were discussed above.

It is reasonable to ask if four commands are sufficient to support a reasonable Data Transfer Protocol. A definitive answer clearly requires user experience. However, existing knowledge indicates that the total number of required commands can be kept relatively small. Two factors support this assertion. The first is elimination of options negotiation resulting from use of a parameter list. The second is the observation that although contemporary FTPs have a large number of commands, this reflects their support of three major classes of functions:

  i)   data transfer,

  ii) file manipulation, and

  iii) remote job execution [INWG 77].

The number of commands supporting the data transfer portion of the FTP is thus substantially smaller than the number of FTP commands.

Recent work by two colleagues of the authors [Heafner 80] highlights the wide variance in commands supported by FTP protocols. In examining five different FTP specifications, a total of 170 distinct features (corresponding roughly to commands or distinguishable parts of multifunction commands) were identified. Only eight features were common to all five FTPs.

14.6. An example – the NBS experimental network operating system

The preceding has established the basic mechanisms required for exchanging structured data. Acceptance of the issues and approaches which were discussed requires assurance that they are, indeed, implementable. This section describes an Experimental Network Operating System (XNOS) implemented at the National Bureau of Standards (NBS) and providing, as a component, such a capability.

14.6.1. XNOS overview

XNOS has been described in detail in [Kimbleton 78]. Although the implementation approach described therein has been discarded to achieve compactness and efficiency, the basic collection of primitives is unchanged. The following brief discussion may be viewed as a summary.

XNOS functionality can be divided into two basic categories:

  i)   provision of a uniform user viewpoint across heterogeneous systems, and

  ii) provision of a uniform mechanism to support intersystem interaction.

Critical discussion of a network operating system requires prior establishment of the environment in which it is to be implemented. XNOS implementation assumes:

  • Prior existence of resources – precluding implementation of a new, distributed operating system and requiring, instead, use of the existing operating systems on those systems supported by the network operating system.

- Incision minimization – modifications to operating systems are strongly discouraged to encourage operational acceptance of network operating systems in a mission oriented environment.

- Offloading – to minimize local host overhead in supporting a network operating system.

- Uniform network wide resource access and control language – requiring network users to learn the XNOS command language rather than supporting direct translation between the local and remote system command languages for resource access and control.

The initial XNOS prototype implementation supported the Multics, Tenex, TOPS-10, and Unix operating systems attached to the Arpanet. Moreover, offloading was accomplished through implementing essentially all software in the programming language C on a PDP-11/45 running Unix. Figure 14-14 illustrates this implementation environment.

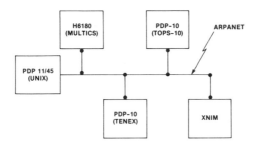

Figure 14-14: XNOS implementation environment

A user generally interacts with systems via a command language. Excluding utilities, a command language provides a basic mechanism for manipulating files and running jobs. Accordingly, XNOS provides a common command language across heterogeneous systems together with a distributed job execution capability.

The XNOS common command language for file manipulation is illustrated in figure 14-15.

The relative paucity of commands in comparison with the number usually found in an operating system command manual reflects the fact that most such commands relate to the assignment of data across devices. By definition (ours!) such commands are inappropriate for the network user interested in accessing resources and uninterested in the intricacies of systems configurations. Since the distributed job execution capability presumes no-setup jobs, only a single command is required. Multi-step jobs can be handled by stacking a series of individual commands. To facilitate user entry of such commands, a prompting facility is provided.

14.6.2. Supporting uniform system-system interactions

System-system interactions are supported within XNOS by two major functional components:

i) a relatively crude network wide interprocess communication mechanism, and

ii) a Remote Record Access mechanism for preserving the meaning of structured data being transmitted between heterogeneous systems.

Network Wide File Manipulation	
Intra-System	Inter-System
Append Compare Copy Create Delete Erase List Rename Type Undelete	Copy File A at Host A To File B at Host B

Figure 14-15: XNOS common command language

XNOS interprocess communication only provides a mechanism for two processes located in different systems to communicate. It does not provide an ability for remote process invocation and control nor does it provide synchronization capabilities. Since the existing mechanism does not represent a contribution to advancing the current state of the art, we shall not describe it further. Functionally, the primitives which it provides represent a limited subset of those provided by MSG [NSW 76]. Implementation is via Telnet links rather than raw connections, however.

A detailed discussion of XNOS Remote Record Access (XRRA) is contained in [Wood 80]. Support of meaning-preserving transmission of structured data within XNOS was constrained, to some extent, by limitations in existing Arpanet protocol implementations. Thus, the following description emphasizes the logical nature of the interaction and adds appropriate comments indicating problems requiring additional consideration.

Describing XRRA is facilitated by discussing the major sequence of processing actions which must be performed in transmitting data between a system (Sender) containing a buffer of structured data and a Receiver system. A logical overivew of XRRA is contained in figure 14-16.

XRRA assumes:

   i)   the Sender data exists within a buffer,

   ii)   a Sender Logical Record Description exists, and

   iii)   data type encodings as well as system/language dependent information describing how the graph of the record is mapped to its buffer representation exist.

Items (ii) - (iii) are assumed to be maintained by XNOS as part of XRRA on the Experimental Network Interface Machine (XNIM) indicated in figure 14-14.

Data generated by the Sender is transmitted to the XNIM, where it is converted to a Common Network Representation termed a Network Normal Form in the XNOS terminology. After

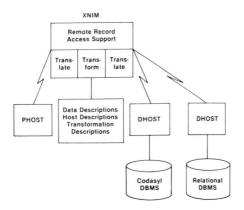

Figure 14-16: XRRA logical structure

ID	=	1.1	SNO	INT
ID	=	1.2	NAME	CHAR (15)
ID	=	1.3	STREET	CHAR (32)
ID	=	1.4	CITY	CHAR (32)
ID	=	1.5	STATUS	CHAR (8)
ID	=	1.6	PNO	LONGINT
ID	=	1.7	QUANTITY	INT
ID	=	1.8	PNAME	CHAR (8)
ID	=	1.9	COLOR	CHAR (12)
ID	=	1.10	WEIGHT	REAL
ID	=	1.11	LOCATION	CHAR (20)

Figure 14-17: Sender logical record description

conversion, a name map table is used to effect the appropriate mappings between Sender and Receiver data. Thereafter, the data is reconverted to the form appropriate to the Receiver.

Figures 14-17 to 14-19 illustrate this process. Figure 14-17 describes the record as it exists on the Sender system; figure 14-18 describes the record as it is to exist on the Receiver system; and figure 14-19 shows the name map table establishing the interrelationship between Sender and Receiver records.

ID	=	1.1	SNO	INT
ID	=	1.2	SNAME	CHAR (15)
ID	=	1.3	SSTAT	CHAR (8)
ID	=	1.4	SCITY	CHAR (20)
ID	=	1.5	PNO	INT
ID	=	1.6	PNAME	CHAR (15)
ID	=	1.7	PCOL	CHAR (12)
ID	=	1.8	PWT	REAL
ID	=	1.9	PLOC	CHAR (20)
ID	=	1.10	QUANT	INT

Figure 14-18: Receiver logical record description

SNO	=	SNO
SNAME	=	NAME
SSTAT	=	STATUS
SCITY	=	CITY
PNO	=	PNO
PNAME	=	PNAME
PCOL	=	COLOR
PWT	=	2.2*WEIGHT
PLOC	=	LOCATION
QUANT	=	QUANTITY

Figure 14-19: Name map table interrelating sender and receiver logical record descriptions

XRRA representation of boolean, binary and character data is unsurprising. Representation of reals and integers is accomplished through transformation to the equivalent ASCII character string.   This has the disadvantage of expanding the amount of space required for their representation.   It has the advantage of assuring that no information is lost in performing arithmetic operations indicated in the name map table. This reflects the possibility of using character based, arbitrary precision arithmetic packages. Note that this does not eliminate the round off errors which are inevitable in going from say, a machine with a word length of 64 bits to one with a word length of 16 bits. However, it does assure that no precision will be lost within XNOS.

The preceding has structured an integrated approach to supporting network access to data which provides both a uniform query capability across multiple, remote, heterogeneous DBMSs as well as the ability to preserve the meaning of structured data being transmitted between heterogeneous systems. The feasibility of the basic approach has been established through the ongoing implementation of prototype systems which were also discussed.

The importance of NVDMs is evident from the increasing interest in the topic [Cardenas 79], [Chu 79], [Esculier 79], [Fauser 79] and [Tsubaki 79]. We believe this interest reflects the requirement for rapid incorporation of new and more sophisticated database products within an operational environment.

NVDM design and implementation requires considering two major classes of issues: distribution management which has not been addressed in this paper and heterogeneity management which has been the focus of the paper. Distribution management deals with issues related to supporting concurrent access to multiple DBMSs and has not yet been addressed in the context of XNDM. However, the existing literature on distributed DBMSs provides substantial insight into such problems [Rothnie 77].

In general, DBMS DMLs support both queries and updates. The preceding has only considered queries since this is required to establish addressability to existing data. Considering updates requires handling modification of existing data, insertion of new record instances and deletion of existing record instances. Since the network user may only see a limited portion of the data supported by a local DBMS the problem of updating views must also be considered. Although the general solution to this problem is very difficult [Dayal 79], partial solutions sufficient for the requirements of many network users may provide an alternative.

14.7. Parameter and data representation

In this section we consider in a broader context the problems of parameter and data representation in distributed systems. Our treatment will be somewhat abstract and, unfortunately, rather superficial.

This is really a programming language design problem, although in practice it is not usually addressed in that context. The reason is that a single bit has the same representation everywhere (except at low levels of abstraction which do not concern us here). An integer or a floating point number, to say nothing of a relational data base, may be represented by very different sets of bits on different machines, but it only makes sense to talk about the representation of data when its type is known. Thus our problem is to define a common notion of data types and suitable ways of transforming from one representation of a type to another. This kind of problem is customarily addressed in the context of language design, and we shall find it convenient to do so here.

In fact, we shall confine ourselves here to the problem of a single procedure call, possibly directed to a remote site. The type of the procedure is expressed by a declaration:

P: **procedure**$(a_1: T_1, a_2: T_2, \ldots)$ **returns** $(r_1: U_1, r_2: U_2, \ldots)$.

We shall sometimes write $(a_1: T_1, a_2: T_2, \ldots) \rightarrow (r_1: U_1, r_2: U_2, \ldots)$ for short. Of course, sending a message and receiving a reply can be described in the same way, as far as the representation of the data is concerned. The control flow aspects of orderly communication with a remote site are discussed in Chapter 7 and Section 14.8; here we are interested only in data representation. The function of the declaration is to make explicit what the argument and result types must be, so that the caller and callee can agree on this point, and so that there is enough information for an automatic mechanism to have a chance of making any necessary conversions. For this reason we insist that remote procedures must have complete declarations. We assert without proof that any data representation problem can be cast in this form without doing violence to its essence.

There are three basic issues:

> *Binding*: how to *locate* the remote procedure body which is supposed to be invoked when a particular procedure is invoked, and how to ensure that the body is *compatible* with the procedure, i.e., that it has the proper type.

> *Encoding*: how to represent the arguments and results as self-contained collections of bits for transmission on the wire.

> *Conversion*: if the representation of the data at the two ends is different, how to convert from one representation to the other.

The first two issues arise in any distributed system, and for that matter in conventional systems as well, where they are dealt with, often inadequately, by the linker/loader and by the parameter passing convention(s) respectively. The third is important only in heterogenous systems.

14.7.1. Types

In order to deal coherently with these problems, we need a suitable notion of data type. Following [Morris 73] loosely, we take the view that each object or value we deal with carries a set of marks which serve to identify the abstract types of which the object is a value. For example, **integer** is such a mark in most languages; an integer value which is also an index in an array of symbol table entries might serve to represent such an entry, and as such also carry the mark *STEntry*. A mark is simply a unique identifier, which can be attached by a marking procedure whose accessibility is suitably restricted, usually to the program responsible for implementing the corresponding type. For each mark there is a predicate which tells whether its argument carries that mark; access to these predicates is not restricted.

We can now define a *type* as a predicate on values, together with a set of operations. The terms of the predicate may include the mark predicates, as well as other expressions with Boolean values. For example, the Pascal type 0..10 corresponds to the predicate **integer** $\wedge$ $0 \leq x \leq 10$. The operations of this type include $+$, $-$, $*$, $/$, $=$, $<$, $:=$ and *New*.

The reason for treating types in this way can be seen by considering the role of the type system as a primitive, but efficient program verifier. A declaration of the form

procedure $F(a: A)$ **returns** $(r: R) = S$

means that the body S has the precondition that a satisfies the predicate for A, and in turn guarantees the postcondition that r will satisfy the predicate for R. Within S, in turn, the knowledge of the formal parameter types which is provided by the declaration can be used to check that the parameters are in turn being properly passed as arguments to other procedures.

Each object or value has a representation (a collection of bits) and a set of marks; in a statically typed language it is usually not necessary to store the marks with each object, since they can be dealt with completely before execution of the program is attempted.

A simple example of all this is types for complex numbers. Several representations are possible, for instance rectangular and polar. Since these are not interchangeable either we must choose one, which can then have the mark *Complex*, or each must have its own mark, *ComplexR* and *ComplexP* respectively. The representations are the same: a record of two reals (though the fields may be named differently). The operations have the same names and type structure (but of course different implementations):

$$+, -, *, /: (Complex, Complex) \rightarrow Complex$$
$$Sin, Sqrt, \ldots : Complex \rightarrow Complex$$

14.7.2. Binding

A program may refer to procedures which are not defined within the program itself; this is an old idea which has been around since the earliest days of subroutine libraries. We can describe this situation as in the left side of figure 14-20: the program contains a set of procedure *variables*, which must eventually be *bound*, i.e., filled in with procedure *values* which are descriptors for compatible procedure bodies (on the right side of the figure) if the program is to complete successfully (at least those which are called must be filled in). The situation after binding is illustrated by the entire figure. These values can come from a variety of sources, which we classify as follows:

A *linker*, which statically examines a collection of programs, supplying procedure values by matching the name of a variable with the name of a procedure body; typically the names are taken from a single, global name space.

A *dynamic linker*, which gets control when an attempt is made to call an unbound procedure and finds a value to fill in by doing the same kind of name lookup.

The program itself, which obtains a suitable procedure value by some arbitrary computation and assigns it to the variable.

In the latter two cases it is also reasonable to consider *unbinding*, or assigning a null value to a variable. In any case, the abstract situation, as we have described it, is identical for local and remote procedures.

The need for compatibility is also identical, and it is desirable to state it precisely. Suppose we have a variable *localP*: $A_l \rightarrow R_l$ and a value *remoteP*: $A_r \rightarrow R_r$; the names of course are merely suggestive. The assignment

$$localP := remoteP$$

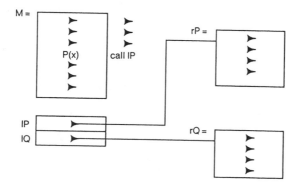

Figure 14-20: Binding a procedure identifier to a procedure body

is legal provided A_l implies A_r and R_r implies R_l. The implication of course refers to the predicates which define the types; strictly it should be

$$\forall x: (\text{Predicate}(A_l))(x) \Rightarrow (\text{Predicate}(A_r))(x)$$

This rule follows directly from the role of types in reasoning about the program. When called, *remoteP* can count on A_r but a call of *localP* need only ensure A_l, hence A_l must imply A_r. Conversely, the caller of *localP* can count on R_l but a return from *remoteP* need only ensure R_r, hence R_r must imply R_l; note that the roles of l and r are reversed for the result type. The common rule $A_l = A_r$ and $R_l = R_r$ is of course sufficient, but stronger than necessary. We reiterate that compatibility issues are identical for local and remote binding.

It is an obvious but sometimes overlooked fact that in order to talk about compatibility at all, it is necessary to have a common type system at the local and remote sites. This does *not* mean that there must be common representations. The difficulty in establishing agreement on the type system accounts for the popularity of ASCII strings as the common medium of exchange among machines, and indeed often among separately constructed programs on the same machine.

14.7.3. Encoding

In order to call a remote procedure, it is necessary to transmit the arguments to the remote machine, and later to transmit the results back to the caller. This means that the values of the arguments and results must be represented on the wire between the machines, presumably by a pile of bits which are not interpreted by the transmission mechanism. We note that the problem of obtaining such a representation is closely related to the problem of representing a value on the disk; thus a transmitted object and a permanent object stored in a file raise very similar problems. The permanent object is actually more difficult to handle in most respects, because its creator is no longer around and cannot answer questions about it when confusion arises.

To discuss a wire representation for a type T it is convenient to define another type T_w, and two procedures *Encode*: $T \rightarrow T_w$ and *Decode*: $T_w \rightarrow T$. We insist that $Decode(Encode(x)) = x$ for all values of type T. The details of T_w are private to the implementation of T, but a value of T_w will occupy a contiguous region of storage and be assignable simply by copying bits, so that it can conveniently be sent over the wire. It is important that a T_w value still carries a mark, so that *Decode* can accept it safely. As on a single machine, if the static type checking is strong enough the mark need not occupy space in the representation. In most cases, however, such confidence in the multi-machine system is not warranted, and prudence dictates that the mark should appear explicitly, so that an error in transmission, or more likely in maintaining the compatibility of the procedure binding, can be detected before any serious damage is done.

If a value contains a pointer, it may be desirable to treat the object referenced by the pointer as a *sub-object* and include it in the encoded value. This is inappropriate if the sub-object is shared, i.e., referenced by other pointers. Frequently, however, the pointer is simply a convenient way to hold a complex object together, and transmitting the object as a whole is quite reasonable. To do this, *Encode* includes the sub-object in T_w, and *Decode* creates a new sub-object in order to obtain a new pointer which it stores in the new object. [Sollins 79] gives an extended treatment of this problem.

In some cases the representation of T_w may include a *context*. This is a fancy name for a large collection of bits which we don't want to transmit. For example, a type such as **pointer to** T is really a shorthand for **pointer to** T **relative to base** b, where in the simplest case **base** means the address space of a machine. Such a pointer can be a perfectly good value on a remote machine, but it cannot be dereferenced without access to the context provided by the base. Usually this means that it must be sent back to the source machine for dereferencing, although in some cases it may be practical to transmit the entire context.

14.7.4. Conversion

When a type T has different representations T_l and T_r in the procedure caller and the procedure body, the *Encode* and *Decode* operations of the previous section are insufficient, since they are private to a particular representation. Instead, we must have some chain of conversion procedures which can turn a T_l into a T_r through a sequence of intermediate types:

$$C_1: T_l \rightarrow IT_1;\ C_2: IT_1 \rightarrow IT_2;\ \ldots\ C_n: T_{n-1} \rightarrow T_r$$

The composition of two C's is also a conversion function. Again, we insist that the C_i be lossless: if $C_i \circ C_j: T \rightarrow T$, then it must be the identity. The simplest cases are pairwise conversion:

$$C_{lr}: T_l \rightarrow T_r$$

and conversion to and from a standard representation (T_w may be an attractive candidate):

$$C_{ls}: T_l \rightarrow T_s;\ C_{sr}: T_s \rightarrow r_s;\quad C_{rs}: T_r \rightarrow T_s;\ C_{sl}: T_s \rightarrow T_l$$

with their well-known nm and $n+m$ growth functions as the number of representations increases. Given a collection of types and conversion functions, it is straightforward to find the most economical conversion, and the lossless property guarantees that a different which will yield the same results. [Wallis 80] discusses these issues further.

One attractive approach to the conversion problem is decomposition. We say that a type R is *complete* if it has operations:

$$D_1: R \rightarrow T_1;\ D_2: R \rightarrow T_2;\ \ldots\ D_n: R \rightarrow T_n \text{ and}$$
$$C: (T_1, T_2, \ldots T_n) \rightarrow R$$

where the T_i are either *basic* types such as **integer**, or simpler than R in the obvious sense. A record type, for example, can easily be made complete: the D's yield the field values, and C constructs a record value from the fields. Now, given conversion functions for the basic types, it is easy to produce conversion functions for any complete type. This problem is discussed from a different point of view in Section 14.4.

14.8. Debugging, testing and measurement

Although it is hard to argue that the problems of debugging and measurement differ qualitatively in centralized and distributed systems, in practice there do seem to be some major variations. Most of them arise from the fact that fault tolerance and partial failures are the norm for distributed systems, whereas a centralized system is typically designed to fail all at once. There is no property of distribution which makes it necessary for this to be true, but the contrast between reliable memory and unreliable communication, and between a single scheduler and autonomous processors certainly makes it natural. This entire area is poorly understoood; neither theory nor experience are developed to any significant extent. We shall therefore confine ourselves to a catalog of some important issues and a collection of anecdotes.

Global state. Autonomy, high communication latency, and low bandwidth mean that the concept of a state for the entire system, very natural in a centralized system, must be approached with caution. Short of stopping all the processors, it is not possible to find out what the system state is, and stopping all the processors is usually either impossible or at least highly undesirable. As a consequence:

A meaningful *definition* of the system state is not possible; at most we may be able to define sets of possible states.

Observation of the global state is not possible.

Observing the states of individual components is possible, but it requires resources to do this and to communicate the results. This resource consumption *interferes* with the normal operation of the system, unless additional resources are dedicated for this purpose.

On the other hand, the fact that a distributed system is often readily expandable may make it easy to provide additional resources for observation without any redesign.

Control. Debugging techniques for centralized systems often require resetting, stopping and single-stepping the system. In a distributed system it may be fundamental to the design that such operations are not possible, because the system is designed for high reliability and must not have single buttons which can stop it; this is the case on the Pluribus, for example. Even if global control of the system is not excluded on principle, it may be very difficult to implement. In a system like the Arpanet, for example, with its variety of hosts running a variety of operating systems not designed for distributed computing, there is no way to exercise control over a distributed system consisting of a collection of processes running on various hosts (although in this situation monitoring all the communication between them would be fairly easy). On the other hand, if the system is designed from scratch and uses a high-bandwidth local net for communication, it should be possible to stop the system nearly as easily as a collection of processes within a single operating system can be stopped.

Time and ordering of events. It is possible to synchronize the local clocks of elements in a distributed system with an accuracy which is limited roughly by the sum of errors which accumulate because of different clock rates in each machine, and errors arising from uncertainty about the time for communication between machines [Chapter 12, Lamport 78]. Unfortunately, the errors are often large, especially if a network becomes partitioned, and hence the concept of global time, like the concept of global state, is of limited value. Instead of a total ordering of the events which agrees with the ordering imposed by real time, we must settle for a partial order which agrees, or a total order which does not, and unless considerable care is taken, we get neither. In addition to its other uses, knowledge of the times when events occur and of their relative ordering is often critical for measurement and debugging.

Localizing failures. Typically one attempts to make the communication mechanism a global one at a low level of abstraction, so that the details of the physical facilities used to send a message are concealed. With a local broadcast net like the Ethernet, this happens at the lowest physical level; with a store-and-forward net like the Arpanet it requires a good deal of software. Above this level, however, it is not easy to localize failures in the communication system, and unless great care is taken, a clumsy process of disabling components one at a time will be required.

In the Ethernet, for example, a shorted transceiver on the cable will prevent any communication, and examining the entire cable for the short is not attractive. Fortunately, there is a device called a time-domain reflectometer (TDR), which sends a signal down the cable and measures the time at which various reflections return. Any impedance discontinuity causes a reflection, and thus a short can be localized within a foot or two. Furthermore, an active transmitter also introduces discontinuities, so that the TDR can locate a malfunctioning transmitter, and during periods of normal operation can maintain an up to date map of the physical location of stations on the cable. The latter is not a trivial matter when there are a hundred stations, and one is added or removed about once a day.

Good physical isolation is not enogh to prevent these problems. On the Arpanet there was a famous "black hole" event when the Harvard IMP's memory failed in such a way that the region storing the routing table always returned zeros. The table was represented so that all zero was a legal value indicating that every other node was directly connected to Harvard. The adaptive algorithm proceeded to broadcast this false information throughout the network, and most of the packets immediately converged on Harvard. As each one arrived, of course, it would immediately be sent out again, but this made matters worse, since the neighboring IMP which received it would just send it back again.

Test environment. As with observation, so with stimulus. Any collection of concurrent programs is difficult to test systematically, and a distributed system has the additional problems of variable communication delay and interference of the testing procedure with normal operation.

Performance bugs. An outstanding characteristic of any fault-tolerant system is that bugs which would prevent an ordinary system from working at all, and hence would be found and fixed, instead degrade the performance without affecting the functionality (hence the term, performance bugs). Since most distributed systems have a high degree of fault-tolerance, this phenomenon affects them strongly. Poorly chosen timeouts are a standard example of a performance bug, but there are many others. Situations have been observed on the Ethernet in which packets sent between a particular pair of machines were in error 80% of the time. It was not until systematic observations were made of the error characteristics of the net [Shoch 80a] that this was discovered; a 20% success rate was sufficient to provide adequate, if sluggish service. Such problems can be detected only by systematic and continued monitoring of performance at each level of abstraction. The cost of such monitoring is low if planned for initially.

14.8.1. A remote debugger

A powerful technique for debugging in a distributed system is to put the debugging software on another machine. This can be viewed as a variation on the old "world-swap" technique, in which the entire memory is written out to a reserved disk area and reloaded with the debugger; the process is reversed when it is time to run the user program again. It is simpler in that all the elements of the program state need not be sought out, preserved and restored, a process which can become quite messy when, for example, the microcode which interprets instructions is part of the "world." It is more complex in that a complete set of primitives must be provided by which the remote debugger can access the program being debugged.

Such a debugger has been implemented for the Alto (see Section 19.1). It requires about 400 bytes in the target machine to hold the *nub* which implements the primitives and the internet communication with the remote debugger, which of course is of the most primitive variety, but nonetheless is capable of interacting with a debugger anywhere in the internet (see section 19.2), not simply on the same Ethernet. The primitives required are:

read and write a single memory location;

start the program at a specified location, and stop the program;

determine whether the program is stopped;

proceed from a breakpoint.

By comparison with other ways of interfacing a debugger, this approach has only one serious drawback: since the debugger and the program have a different set of I/O devices, the user located remotely cannot observe the program's output or supply any input unless special precautions have been taken. Of course, if the terminal of the debugger is physically next to the terminal of the program's machine this is not a problem, but often it is not. Even when it is, a debugging methodology which depends on program-supplied procedures to display and modify the program's data structures is inconvenient, if not entirely impractical. This problem can be solved only by requiring the user program to do its I/O through the debugger nub.

It might be thought that the nub would be vulnerable to corruption by the program, and indeed this is true, but most other debugging interfaces have similar problems. The difficulty is often overcome by putting the interface into read-only memory, microcode, or some other inaccessible place, and this can certainly be done with the remote debugging nub also.

14.8.2. Monitoring communication

A very powerful technique for observing the behavior of a distributed system is to tap its communication. This is especially easy on a local net which uses a bus (e.g., the Ethernet) or a ring (e.g., the Cambridge ring), since all the packets pass every point, and it is easy to make provision for reading them as they go by. Although this method does require additional resources (a machine to monitor the wire), it has the charm of generating no interference at all with normal operation. Software in the monitoring machine can be written to filter the input stream (e.g., to look only at packets from a particular machine) and to arrange the data for convenient display. It must be recognized that this method is not foolproof; any errors in reception by the monitoring machine cannot be corrected by retransmission in the normal way, because the sender is not aware of the fact that there is more than one receiver. The procedures which interpret the data must take this into account by tolerating some amount of bad or missing data. This method has been applied to the Ethernet in a program called PeekPup. The most common use is simply to list the basic facts about each packet (source, destination, size, type) on the screen or in a file as it goes by; manual examination of this data yields a great deal of insight into what is going on at several different levels of abstraction. More elaborate automated analysis is of course also possible.

The same idea has been applied in the Arpanet, in the form of a trace facility which is triggered by a bit in each packet. As the traced packet passes through each IMP, an information packet is constructed and sent to a monitor machine. This method does, of course, interfere with the normal operation of the network.

14.8.3. Event logs

Perhaps the most powerful single technique for understanding the behavior of distributed systems (or for that matter, of most complex systems) is an event log. To use this technique, the program is instrumented with calls on a logging procedure at suitable points, in some way which allows the call to be bypassed at very low cost. This procedure writes a log entry which contains the time, a type code, and some data. By setting switches in the program even while it is running, the amount of information to be logged can be controlled, and perhaps the log action can be modified to collect counts or histograms instead.

This arrangement has two important properties:

> Instrumentation is always installed and can be activated at any time; hence it can be turned on at low cost, perhaps in response to an observed malfunction or dgradation in performance. Events which occur infrequently can be logged at all times, so that a record is available in case of disaster. Similarly, basic statistics of bandwidth, latency and load can be continuously accumulated.

> The perhaps complex task of analyzing the data is not done in the running system, but is deferred to a more convenient time and place. The log has enough raw data to permit many different kinds of analysis to be done.

In a distributed system, the network provides a nice place to write the log. Packets can be put on the net and addressed to a logging machine; if no such machine is present, the packets can be dropped on the floor at small cost. This scheme has had a number of applications on the Ethernet. Several hundred machines routinely run diagnostics when idle, and report the results every few minutes to a maintenance center. Another application is a general logging package called Metric [McDaniel 77], which provides procedures for putting log packets on the net, and a program for collecting the packets and doing some analysis.

14.9. Remote procedure calls

One of the major problems in constructing distributed programs is to abstract out the complications which arise from the transmission errors, concurrency and partial failures inherent in a distributed system. If these are allowed to appear in their full glory at the applications level, life becomes so complicated that there is little chance of getting anything right. A powerful tool for this purpose is the idea of a *remote procedure call*. If it is possible to call procedures on remote machines with the *same* semantics as ordinary local calls, the application can be written without concern for most of the complications This goal cannot be fully achieved without the transaction mechanism of Chapter 11, but we show in this section how to obtain the same semantics, except that the action of the remote call may occur more than once. Our treatment uses the definitions of Sections 11.3 and 11.4 for processor and communication failures and stable storage. Following [Lamport 78], we write $a \rightarrow b$ to indicate that the event a precedes the event b; this can happen because they are both in the same process, or because they are both references to the same datum, or as the transitive closure of these immediate relations. Recall that physical communication is modeled by a datum called the message; transmitting a message from one process to another involves two transitions in the medium, the *Send* and the *Receive*.

A remote procedure call consists of several events. There is the *main call*, which consists of the following events:

the call c;

the start s;
the work w;
the end e;

the return r.

The ones on the left occur in the calling machine, the ones on the right in the machine being called. The events which detail the message transmission have been absorbed into the ones listed. These events occur in the order indicated (i.e., each precedes the next). In addition, there may be *orphan* events o in the receiver, consisting of any prefix of the transitions indicated. These occur because of duplicated call messages, which can arise from failures in the communication medium, or from timeouts or crashes in the caller which are followed by a retry. The orphans all follow the call and precede the rest of the main call. Difficulties arise, however, in guaranteeing the order of the orphans relative to the rest of the main call.

14.9.1. The no-crash case

What we want is $o \rightarrow s$: all the orphans precede the start of the main call. This gives us semantics as close as we can expect to an ordinary procedure call without the machinery of transactions; the only peculiarity is that the work may be partly done several times before being completed. A straightforward sequence numbering scheme, together with explicit queuing of successive messages from the same process, will give us this property in the absence of crashes. The scheme is detailed in figure 14-21. Note that there are two separate things going on here:

- Ensure that messages are accepted in the order they are sent and duplicates rejected, to eliminate the errors of the communication medium (the sequence numbering does this);

- Ensure that for a given calling process the work is strictly serial, to give the proper semantics if the caller times out and resends the message.

It is possible to make one mechanism do both jobs, either by sequence numbering the messages separately for each process, or by serializing all the work for a processor. The reason for two mechanisms is performance:

- The sequence numbering requires some kind of stable storage, and a record of each "connection." It is expensive to maintain this information for each process, but cheap to maintain it for each processor, both because there are many fewer and because it needs to be updated only when the processor crashes.

- The serialization is logically required only for work within a single process. To apply it more broadly reduces the amount of concurrency, perhaps drastically.

This would also work in the presence of crashes if each crashed process always reattempted its call right after the crash. This could be accomplished by doing a *Save* just before each call (see 11.4.2), an idea which we reject because we are unwilling to pay two *StablePut* operations per remote call. Furthermore, this design would make it impossible to time out a call and do something else without the danger of orphans. Clearly, a realistic system must be able to do this. Other methods must therefore be adopted to deal with crashes and timeouts which do not repeat; they are considered in Section 14.9.2.

{ Remote procedures, using *Send* and *Receive* for messages, and *UniqueId* for unique identifiers.. }
type *ID* = 0..2^{64}; **const** *timeout*=...;
type *Message* = **record**
  state: (*call, return*); *source, dest*: *Processor; id, request*: *ID; action*: **procedure**; *val*: *Value* **end**;

{ The one process which receives and distributes messages }
var *m*: *Message*; **var** *s*: *Status*; **while** true **do begin** (*s, m*) : = *Receive*(); **if** *s*= *good* **then**
  if *m.state* = *call* **and** *OKtoAccept*(*m*) **then** *StartCall*(*m*)
  else if *m.state* = *return* **then** *DoReturn*(*m*) **end**;

{ Make calls }
monitor *RemoteCall* = **begin**
type *CallOut* = **record** *m*: *Message*; *received*: Condition **end**; **var** *callsOut*: **set of** ↑*CallOut* : = ( );
entry function *DoCall*(*d*: *Processor, a*: **procedure**, *args*: *Value*): *Value* = **var** *c*: ↑*CallOut*; **begin**
  New(*c*); **with** *c*↑ **do with** *m* **do begin**
    source : = *ThisMachine*(); *request* : = *UniqueID*(); *dest* : = *d*; *action* : = *a*; *val* : = *args*;
    state : = *call*; *callsOut* : = *callsOut* + *c* { add *c* to the *callsOut* set };
    repeat *id* : = *UniqueID*(); *Send*(*dest, m*); Wait(*received, timeout*) **until** *state*= *return*;
    DoCall : = *val*; Free(*c*) **end end**;
entry procedure *DoReturn*(*m*: *Message*) =
var *c*: ↑*CallOut*; **for** *c* **in** *callsOut* **do if** *c*↑.*m.id* = *m.id* **then begin**
    c↑.*m* : = *m*; *callsOut* : = *callsOut* - *c* { Remove *c* from *callsOut* }; Signal(*c*↑.*received*) **end**;
end *RemoteCall*

{ Serialize calls from each process, and assign work to worker processes }
type *CallIn* = **record** *m*: *Message*; *work*: Condition **end**
monitor *CallServer* = **begin var** *callsIn, pool*: **set of** ↑*CallIn* : = ( );
entry procedure *StartCall*(*m*: *Message*) = **var** *w, c*: ↑*CallIn*; **begin**
  w : = *ChooseOne*(*pool*) {waits if the pool is empty};
  for *c* **in** *callsIn* **do if** *c*↑.*m.request* = *m.request* **then begin** *c*↑.*m.id* : = *id*; **return**; **end**
  pool : = *pool* - *w*; *callsIn* : = *callsIn* + *w*; *w*↑.*m* : = *m*; Signal(*w*↑.*work*) **end**;
entry procedure *EndCall*(*w*: ↑*CallIn*) = **begin**
  Send(*w*↑.*m.source*, *w*↑.*m*); *callsIn* : = *callsIn* - *w*; *pool* : = *pool* + *w*; Wait(*w*↑.*work*) **end**;
end *CallServer*

{ The worker processes which execute remotely called procedures }
var *c*: ↑*CallIn*; New(*c*); *c*↑.*m.source* : = nil; *EndCall*(*c*); **with** *c*↑.*m* **do**
while true **do begin** *val* : = *action*(*val*); *state* : = *return*; *EndCall*(*c*) **end**;

{ Suppress duplicate messages. Needn't be a monitor, since it's called only from the receive loop. }
type *Connection* = **record** *from*: *Processor, lastID*: *ID* **end**; **var** *connections*: **set of** *Connection*: = ( );
function *OKtoAccept*(*m*: *Message*): Boolean = **var** *c*: ↑*Connection*; **with** *m* **do begin**
  for *c* **in** *connections* **do if** *c*↑.*from* = *source* **then begin**
    if *id* ≤ *c*↑.*lastID* **then return** false; *c*↑.*lastID* : = *id*; **return** true **end**;
  { No record of this processor. Establish connection. }
  if *action* = *UniqueID* **then return** true { Avoid an infinite loop; OK to duplicate this call. };
  { For good performance the next two lines should be done in a separate process. }
  New(*c*); *c*↑.*from* : = *source*; *c*↑.*lastID* : = *DoCall*(*source, UniqueID*, nil);
  connections : = *connections* + *c*; **return** false { Suppress the first message seen. } **end**

Figure 14-21: Algorithm for remote procedure calls

14.9.2. The crash case

The algorithm of figure 14-21 ensures $c \to o \to s \to w \to e \to r$ for any remote call. If the caller crashes (or gives up), however, and starts doing something else, it provides no guarantee that $o \to n$, where n is part of the something else. This guarantee can be provided in two ways.

Deadline with refreshing. We associate with a *root* process (one which is not working on a remote call) a deadline d, and ensure that no event in that process (including events which are part of remote calls initiated by the process) can continue past d. Now $o \to n$ can be guaranteed by waiting until after d before embarking on n. If we never set any d more than d_{max} in the future, then it is sufficient to wait for $d_{max} + e_{max}$, where e_{max} is the maximum synchronization error between clocks; we don't have to consult any recorded d to know how long to wait.

For this to work, we need

> a way to abort a process;

> some variation of clocks synchronized throughout the system.

It is sufficient to have local clocks plus an upper bound on the time a received message spent in the communication medium, but this is tantamount to having synchronized clocks [Lamport 78].

If a process has passed the deadline, it can just be aborted and the guarantee will be met. Alternatively, the deadline can be *refreshed* by consulting with the caller; this chain of consultation will run back to the root process, so that all machines involved in the current computation of the process will be refreshed. Refreshing only requires checking that there is a chain of *callsOut* entries leading back to the root, so it requires little computation. It does add some complication, but has the advantage that an expensive computation will not be abandoned because it is unlucky enough to pass its deadline.

The more serious objection to this scheme that it isn't clear how to choose the timeout interval. If it is too long, crash recovery is slowed down. If it is too short, there is too much refreshing. However, the following calculation is encouraging. Suppose that we have a system in which a disk access takes 50 ms of elapsed time and 3 ms of computing; the latter number is quite small. Also suppose that the cost of a refresh is three times the cost of a disk access (10 ms). Then to keep the cost of refreshing down to 1%, we must do 300 disk accesses per refresh; this takes 15 seconds. Delaying a crash recovery by 15 seconds does not seem too bad. Of course if communication is very slow, the real time for the refresh may be unacceptable, but even several seconds for communication time does not seem intolerable.

It is also interesting to note that the cost of timeouts is related to the reality of the possibility that pre-crash computation will continue after a crash. If all remote calls are short, they will never time out.

Extermination. An alternative approach is that after a crash, no action is taken until all outstanding activity has been explicitly stopped. Activity on the crashed machine is obviously no problem, but all remote calls must also be exterminated. Since information about which machines these are on (the *hit list*) must be kept in stable storage, it is not practical to keep it completely accurate. Instead, it must be updated periodically. When a call to a machine not on the list is made, the list must be updated before the call is started; for this reason, it is probably a good idea to use an aging scheme to delete machines from the list.

When machine A tells machine B to exterminate A's calls, B must be able to tell which of its processes are working on A's calls. Furthermore, B is responsible for any remote calls made by these workers. There are two cases:

> If B is alive, the *callsOut* list contains all its outstanding calls; it is easy to tell which ones are on behalf of A, and a list of the machines involved is returned to A and added to A's hit list. When A hits these machines, they must exterminate B's calls made on behalf of A; each call must therefore carry the whole set of machines in the call stack at the time the call is made.

> If B is recovering from a crash itself, it returns its whole hit list (or at least the unfulfilled portion remaining) to A. This will result in a certain amount of waste motion, but only when two machines recover at about the same time, and it avoids any possibility of deadlock.

Keeping the call history is unattractive, since it is an extra cost imposed even when there are no crashes. It can be avoided by making B do the exterminations for which it is responsible, rather than passing them back to A. Some care is then needed to avoid deadlock if B is recovering.

The charm of extermination is that it costs nothing unless there is a crash. The trouble with it is that if some machine on the hit list is down, or if the communication network is partitioned into two subnets which temporarily cannot communicate, it will be impossible for crash recovery to complete. This seems like an overwhelming drawback which makes it impossible to rely on extermination alone.

The other possibility is to relax the guarantee: instead of ensuring $o \rightarrow n$, we will promise only $n \rightsquigarrow o$. This means that computation may continue after a crash in real time, but there will always be some serialization in which it completes before any new activity. To implement this we use the idea of infection. Every object carries a level of infection i. Whenever a process interacts with a datum, the i of each is set to the maximum of the two. If this requires increasing the level of a process, it must be aborted or refreshed. Thus we have

$$p \rightarrow d \Rightarrow i_p \leq i_d$$
$$d \rightarrow p \Rightarrow i_d \leq i_p$$

and in general

$$p \rightarrow q \Rightarrow i_p \leq i_q$$

After a process crashes, its level is set larger than it was before the crash, and hence larger than any orphan from before the crash: $i_n > i_o$. Since $n \rightarrow o$ implies $i_n \leq i_o$, it is ruled out as desired.

Keeping a level for each datum is unattractive, especially since it has to be in stable storage. More attractive is to aggregate all the data in a single processor and keep a single level for the whole processor (and hence for every process running on that processor). The main problem with this scheme is that if there is any communication at all between two parts of a system, both will quickly rise to the same level. Since the level increases after each crash, a given processor will tend to see an increase in level every time any other processor crashes. Each such increase requires a stable storage write, as well as refreshing of some number of processes.

It may be possible to avoid this non-linearity by keeping more information in the level. Another simple scheme would keep the level as an array, one integer for each processor in the system. Now the cost of a crash is minimal, but storing and updating all the levels is non-linear. An intermediate scheme would organize the processors in some hierarchy, and keep a fixed amount of level information, in detail for processors which are changing frequently, and in large aggregates for those which are static or never communicated with. All this seems rather complicated.

The most attractive scheme is a combination of extermination with deadline or infection, since extermination is clearly preferable except when some targets cannot be reached. Extermination plus deadline allows a large d_{max} to be used; this will seldom force a long wait on crash recovery, because extermination will usually work. Extermination plus infection means that the level only needs to be increased when extermination fails; since this happens seldom, a single level will be acceptable even for a very large system.

Chapter 15. Error recovery

15.1. Introduction

The purpose of this chapter is to introduce and to define the basic concept of error recovery. In order to do so, the more general concepts of reliability are also examined. A number of highly reliable computing systems have been built in the past or are being built, e.g. JPL-STAR, Pluribus, Sift, FTSC, ESS-1A. In most cases, these systems are intended for very special applications, e.g. spacecraft flight control or telecommunications. It is likely that in the near future, reliability will become a must for a large portion of the computing market. For example, reliable systems are needed to avoid financial disasters or loss of human life. Fast progress is expected in the development of both hardware and software techniques, specially in the context of distributed systems. We have chosen to illustrate this trend by giving a description of the strategies adopted in a commercially available system (Tandem/16) and in an experimental distributed system (Delta). Recovery techniques used in the Xerox Distributed File System can be found in chapter 19.

15.2. Basic concepts and definitions

Quoting Randell [Randell 78], we will say that a fault is the mechanical or algorithmic cause of an error. An error is an item of information which, when processed by the normal algorithms of the system, will lead to a failure. A system is said to experience a failure when its behaviour is not in agreement with the system specification. Reliability is defined as the probability at which a failure does not occur. Availability differs from reliability in the sense that availability is the probability that a system will provide a requested service. For example, a computing system used in a banking application will be said available if customer operations can always be processed within 24 hours although the system may fail several times a day. The relationship between the notions of failure and system specification on the one hand and the distinction between the notions of failure and crash on the other hand have to be well understood. For example, let us imagine a system which provides external users with such primitives as "initiate operation" and "terminate operation". The system specification states that operations must be kept atomic i.e. when a fault occurs, leading to the failure of a system element, every currently executing operation must be either completed or rolled-back (undone). If the property of operation atomicity is guaranteed to be satisfied at all times then, although the system may stop functioning, it still meets its specification. Thus, it is reliable. The general approach to achieving reliable and available distributed systems is based on fault tolerance (as opposed to fault avoidance) by taking advantage of the existence of redundant hardware, software and data. In the following, we restrict ourselves to examining the issue of error recovery.

15.3. Error recovery

An error is said to have occured when part of the system state is incorrect. Therefore, the term "error recovery" is equivalent to the term "erroneous state recovery". Defining the notion of correctness for state information may be accomplished by using the notion of consistency [Eswaran 76]. The notion of atomic operation (see chapters 11 and 12) is of direct relevance to techniques which achieve fault tolerance and error recovery. The way error recovery is accommplished may depend greatly on how error detection and isolation are conducted. Clearly, if it is possible to delimit the consequences of an error, the error recovery scheme becomes simpler than when such consequences cannot be identified. The enforcement of atomic operations, in conjunction with error confinement mechanisms [Denning 76] make error recovery easier to achieve. However, one should be aware of the fact that a recovery mechanism can only cope with certain faults.

Two error recovery schemes can be considered. Backward error recovery (B-recovery) schemes utilize recovery points. A recovery point is a recording of all needed information whereby a consistent state of (part of) the system may be reinstalled. Forward error recovery (F-recovery) schemes depend on the possibility of detecting the consequences of a fault and correcting them. One may say that B-recovery implies undoing everything a system has done since the last recovery point whereas F-recovery involves doing again only those things which have been detected as being incorrect. In many systems, one may have to use both schemes, maybe at different levels of abstraction. As may be inferred from the above, error recovery (either backward or forward) is based on the utilization of some additional information, called recovery data. There exist different ways of utilizing recovery data. For example, the experimental Arpanet TCP [Cerf 74] provides for the retransmission of only the first (and maybe unique) message not being acknowledged whereas the Cyclades transport protocol [Zimmermann 75] provides for the retransmission of not only the damaged message but also all subsequent messages.

Recovery points used by B-recovery techniques serve the purpose of bringing back a process into a state which is known to be consistent. However, in systems where dependencies exist between processes, there is the problem of defining/identifying sets of individual recovery points which are globally consistent. Such sets are referred to as recovery lines [Randell 78]. Rolling back a process to a previous consistent state may result in rolling back some other processes, including the original process. This is known as the domino effect [Randell 75]. In distributed systems, the problem of identifying recovery lines may be more or less difficult to solve, depending on which types of faults and failures are considered. Furthermore, for some systems, the actual performing of a recovery line (e.g. global checkpoint) should not interfere with normal user activities. For example, global locking of a database or unnecessary roll-backs [Schlageter 80] may not be acceptable. In the following, we present two different examples of distributed transactional systems using B-recovery techniques. These two systems allow users to express transactions which should be implemented as atomic operations. Atomicity may be threatened not only because of interferences among currently executing transactions but also because of the occurence of faults and failures. Thus the need for a technique whereby it may be guaranteed that when a fault or a failure occurs, the following property holds:

(1)   either all actions of any impacted transaction will eventually be executed and intermediate states will not be seen by other transactions,

(2) or all actions, completed or not, belonging to any impacted transaction will eventually be aborted and intermediate states will not be seen by other transactions.

This latter approach has been adopted for the two systems presented below.

15.4. The Tandem/16 computing system

The Tandem/16 computing system is a multiple-computer system where every hardware component (processor, power supply, memory, I/O channel, bus) is redundant. As a result, any single failure should not result in the failure of the whole system. More information on the design goals and the hardware structure of Tandem/16 may be found in [Katzmman 78]. Services available through the operating system called Guardian are made fault-tolerant by duplicating software components. For example, access to I/O devices relies on process-pairs (a primary process and a backup process). Guardian allows for the automatic creation of a backup process each time a transaction is to be executed. At creation time, the primary begins by checkpointing the transaction execution context to its backup. When the primary fails, the backup may take over at this checkpoint. All requests (*Write*, *Read* actions) issued by a transaction are processed by the primary process. When the primary is ready to write some results to a disk file, it checkpoints all changes to its backup before writing on the file. Such a checkpoint consists in having the primary moving checkpointed portions of its data space into the backup's data space.

Between two successive checkpoints, the primary and the backup may not have identical views of the disk file being modified. In order to cope with this, a sequence number is associated with every disk file. This number is incremented at each occurence of a *Write* action on the file and is retained by the disk drive. The process in charge of doing the *Write* checks its sequence number with the copy of it stored in the disk drive memory. Only if there is a match, the *Write* is done and the sequence number is incremented. If sequence numbers do not match, a copy of the previous action's status is returned. Clearly, the writing of a new value for a data object and the writing of its associated sequence number must be indivisible.

From the description given in [Bartlett 78], one may infer that Tandem/16 is aimed primarily at surviving processor/memory failures, because each running process and its associated context are duplicated. It is more difficult to see how a Tandem/16 system may recover from a disk failure under all circumstances. It is mentioned that a logical disk volume may be recorded on two different disk drives so as to provide for a transparent duplication of data. All file *Write* actions are performed on both disk drives. However, there is the risk that the primary process and the disk drive it uses fail altogether before either the other disk drive or the backup process are made aware of the performing of a new *Write* action. In this case, the *Write* will be repeated by the backup process. Depending on the application, duplicated *Writes* may or may not be harmful.

One interesting point about Tandem/16 is the fact that computing systems embedding duplicated hardware at a macroscopic level and supporting redundant data handling techniques seem to meet the requirements of a large number of application areas in a rather cost-effective way.

15.5. Sirius-Delta

Delta is an experimental distributed data sharing system built within the framework of Project Sirius [Le Bihan 80]. One of the motivations for Delta was the investigation of techniques allowing for the implementation of reliable and atomic operations (transactions) in distributed and unreliable computing systems. We will restrict ourselves here to the description of the commit protocol which permits a correct termination of transactions in spite of processing/storage element failures and the recovery algorithm which brings any repaired processing/storage element into a correct state. The decentralized synchronization mechanism and the locking protocols used in Delta are described in chapter 12.

15.5.1. Transaction commitment

Transactions which initiate *Write, Create, Delete* actions do not update objects but only copies of objects. This is needed in order to be protected against failures interrupting the execution of transactions at random. However, for every transaction which reaches completion, it is necessary to make all modifications effective, i.e. updating of data objects must be performed. This last step must also be atomic. Special care is required if it is assumed that processing elements which host producers and consumers may fail at random.

Stated in terms of the conceptual model given in chapter 12, the problem is as follows. A transaction T which has been given ticket t and which has manipulated objects managed by a set of consumers C has reached completion. Possible intermediate rollbacks or aborts have been kept transparent to the user. Either via a software command or via a terminal control key, the user indicates his willingness to commit T. Let p be the producer in charge of controlling T when the commit command is issued (p need not be the initiator of T). The problem is that although distributed and subject to failures, a commit must be atomic. More precisely, we want to provide p and consumers in C with a commit protocol which:

(1) is reliable in case of failures;

(2) meets the requirement of mutual independence as much as possible.

In order to cope with constraint (1), a two-phase commit protocol similar to the protocol described in [Gray 78] is convenient (see chapter 11). Such a protocol is reliable in the sense that if failures occur, it is impossible for some consumers in C to commit actions belonging to T while some others decide to abort locally other actions also belonging to T. However, this protocol suffers some drawbacks:

- Because of the failure of p, either during phase 1 or during phase 2, objects may be kept locked for arbitrary large time intervals; several transactions may be rejected or made to wait because of this

- Users should be prepared to experience arbitrary large response times before they are told their transactions have been either committed or aborted.

This is against the principle of mutual independence. What this principle states is that failure of producer i should impact producer j ($j \neq i$) as little as possible. This is constraint (2). In order to meet this constraint, the original two-phase commit protocol has been modified as follows. Every "prepare-to-commit" message includes also C, the list of all consumers involved in the execution of T. This makes it possible for any consumer noticing that p is down to get in touch with other consumers belonging to C in order to decide whether to commit or to abort T. Ticket t of T is used as a common reference for such inquiries. If at least one consumer has aborted, all consumers which are up will abort (they all are running the first phase of the commit). If at least one of them has committed, all consumers which are up will commit. The only undecidable situation occurs when none of the consumers which are up has either committed or aborted and p, as well as some consumers in C are down. In this case, which is expected to occur unfrequently, consumers will have to wait until some of the failed consumers come up again (although it is possible to devise a more expensive and more reliable solution to this problem). It is not needed anymore to wait for p. Consequently, processing/storage elements which host producers may behave as memory-less elements. A subsequent benefit of this modified protocol is that the second phase ends as soon as p has received one "acknowledge commit" message from one consumer in C. This may help to reduce response time for external users.

15.5.2. Recovering from failures

For the purpose of recovering from failures (as well as for other reasons), it is necessary to maintain a journal for every partition. In fact, a journal is part of a partition. That is to say, a partition includes two subsets, one subset containing users' data objects, the other subset (the journal) containing all recovery data associated to the objects belonging to this partition Obviously, for every partition, these two subsets are implemented on different physical storage elements. Any producer may read, update, etc. a journal by submitting actions to the pertinent consumer. A journal contains four kinds of information which are the users table, images, checkpoints and a list of descriptors.

The users table: this table has one entry per user, which contains the value of the ticket corresponding to the most recent transaction committed for this user.

Images: locally, a consumer may decide at any time to copy the current state of the partition on its journal. This is called an image. An image has no system-wide significance.

Checkpoints: checkpoints are marks which have names. A checkpoint corresponds to a state which is known to be consistent system-wide (it is a recovery line).

List of descriptors: a descriptor is created by a consumer for every *Write* (*Write* includes *Create* and *Delete*) action which has reached state "prepared-to-commit".

A descriptor contains in particular the following fields:

- ticket t of the transaction which has invoked the action
- the new value of the object
- the state of the action ("prepared-to-commit", "committed", "aborted")
- a version ID if the object is replicated
- list C of all consumers involved in the commit of the transaction.

There is no reason why data objects on journals would be more reliable than other data objects. It may then be necessary to replicate journals (or parts of journals) across various partitions. For every transaction, a producer should initiate not only the actions included between the *Begin* and the *Commit* commands, but also all the actions needed to create or update descriptors on journals, as well as actions needed to update consistently replicated data objects (which may also belong to journals and data directories). Atomicity should be guaranteed. This is obtained by transforming every user *Write* action into a logical *Write* action. A logical *Write* is a compound action constructed by the executive which includes not only the user *Write* but also one *Write* action per copy in case the written object is replicated, *Write* actions necessary to update data directories (e.g. when the user *Write* is a *Create* or a *Delete*) and one *Write* action per journal which should record the descriptor corresponding to the user *Write*.

For any given transaction, at commit time, producer p which acts as the commit coordinator builds a list H containing the names of all consumers involved in the commit (C is a subset of H). When H has been built, p may initiate the commit protocol. From this point, the system behaves as described previously. This will achieve in an atomic way updating of all copies of the object, writing of a new descriptor and updating of the corresponding users table entry in all occurences of the relevant journal (and possibly an updating of directory copies).

We have already mentioned that producers may behave as memory-less elements. Consequently, the adjunction or the insertion of a producer which has failed and which has been repaired do not raise any particular problem as regards data consistency. When a consumer wants to join in the system, it begins by consulting its journal (any copy if several copies exist). Storage elements are updated by receiving first a copy of the partition which is known to be correct but late, for example the most recent image of the partition recorded on the journal. Then, the consumer goes on processing all the descriptors which are "older" than the image. Each time it encounters a *Write* action in state "prepared-to-commit", it goes on inquiring those consumers which belong to the corresponding list C in order to decide either to commit or to abort this particular action. When this is completed, the consumer sets itself to a state "up". From then, it behaves as any other consumer.

15.5.3. Unrecoverable faults and failures

It is well known that a given recovery mechanism can only cope with certain failures. With the techniques which have been presented, a correct functioning of the system is not guaranteed against all possible failures. For instance, the system does not tolerate a situation where copies of an object are not identical and the most recent descriptor has been lost. In this case, the system "looses" transactions. The probability of such situations to occur can be made as low as possible by choosing an appropriate number of copies for objects and descriptors. However, it is fundamental for the external users to be aware of the occurence of a catastrophe. To this end, each time a user enters the system, it is given the ticket or the transaction name associated to this ticket corresponding to the transaction committed most recently on his behalf. In case the name retained by the system and the name remembered by the user do not match, the user may take the appropriate decision based on the knowledge of which transaction has been committed last. In order to complete the presentation of this mechanism, it would be necessary to explain how the distributed executive performs global checkpoints, and how these checkpoints are used to install a past but consistent state when a catastrophe occurs. This requires a lengthy description beyond the scope of this section.

Chapter 16. Hardware issues[1]

16.1. Introduction

Data processing costs have in recent years declined faster than communication costs in general and data communications costs in particular. Thus, there is a tendency, in a system design, to try and decentralize computation; i.e., provide remote processing to effectively substitute computation for communication. Between 1967 and 1977 bipolar logic costs were down two orders of magnitude (measured in cents per gate)! Between 1973 and 1979 bipolar memory costs were down two orders magnitude (measured in cents per bit)! Communication costs were stable or increasing. In the future we may expect communication costs to come down. The advent of private satellites, fiber optics, and/or private carriers may cause communication costs to decrease. However, in comparison to logic and memory costs, the cost of communications has remained stable. As logic and memory costs decline even further, the push to decentralize will become even stronger. We should note that rapidly declining costs of logic and memory do not automatically mean similar performance/cost increases. There are other design and manufacturing costs that modify the decrease, with the net result that system costs decrease at a rate of 15 to 25 percent per year; i.e., the price per instruction per second decreases at a rate of 15 to 25 percent per year. Further, developments in technologies for logic systems may alter this rate.

Proponents of centralized systems claim that the concepts of distributing a system are not well developed, thus it will be difficult to actually deploy this technology. How will large data bases be distributed, updated, and synchronized? Clearly, centralized concepts are proven and well developed. Further, their development costs are reasonably well known. The cost of centralized systems is claimed to grow at a rate of $n^{1/2}$; i.e., if the cost of a system doubles, the performance goes up by a factor of four. This observation is known as Grosch's Law. It is an empirically observed law which has held up for over thirty years. This law has held up regardless of architecture.

---

1. Much of the discussions and concepts contained in the subsections 16.3, 16.4, and 16.5 are based upon real systems and experiments conducted by associates of the author. Rather than rewrite these experiments, the authors of the papers describing the experiments allowed the author to excerpt material and descriptions. For this a very substantial debt of gratitude is owed to L. D. Anderson, T. O. Wolff, L. J. Schlecta, B. R. Manning, and R. C. DeWard for permission to use their works [Anderson 79a] and [Anderson 79b]. Portions of subsection 16.3 are taken from [Thurber 77]. Lastly portions of subsection 16.7 are taken from [Thurber 80a] and [Thurber 81].

HYPERchannel and HYPERcache are trademarks of Network Systems Corporation. Z-Net is a trademark of Zilog Corporation. Shared VSS is a trademark of Masstor Corporation. CADAC is a trademark of Digital Communications Corporation. Cluster/One is a trademark of Nestar Systems Corporation. SHINPADS is a trademark of the Canadian Navy.

Distributed systems offer a number of advantages. They have the possibility of resource sharing, thus enabling a user to obtain special resources facilities without direct ownership. It is claimed that communication costs are a major cost in large systems and therefore technology economies is on the side of decentralization. The desire for interactive computation only increases the potentially high communication costs. It is claimed that microprocessors do not follow Grosch's Law and thus the cost balance would change drastically if large systems could be built from such small processors (which grow in complexity daily). Distributed systems also exhibit promise for improved system maintainability, availability and reliability. Lastly, it may be possible to update a distributed system in a piecemeal manner as technology improves.

If we believe that cost trends favor decentralization of hardware and proponents of centralized systems will lose eventually, then hardware of some form must be coming into existence for distributed systems. The purpose of this section is to describe some hardware experiments that we consider important. Many of the examples evolved out of current systems. However, the experiments have been carried out and thus exist as proof of certain capabilities or technologies.

16.2. Design issues

This chapter will consider several specific design issues as follows:

§ 16.3:   A description of a special hardware device designed to provide a kernel for an OS is described. The section begins with how the analysis was performed, how the hardware is designed and what the device accomplishes.

§ 16.4:   A description of an experiment in dedication of special functional units for a message switch is provided.

§ 16.5:   A concept for design of a computer based on the kernel of § 16.3 and the use of functional dedication concepts (§ 16.4) is provided.

§ 16.6:   Evolution of extant hardware into virtualized distributed systems is described in this section. Implementation of the described concepts could utilize hardware such as described in § 16.3.

§ 16.7:   The type of hardware available for local network and the Network Systems Corporation HYPERchannel are discussed in this section.

§ 16.8:   Lastly, some specific hardware features that could be utilized to support distributed processing are listed.

16.3. Executive control functions

This section discusses a procedure used to develop a set of executive control functions for real-time systems, the hardware implementation concept, and the developed set of primitives developed.

16.3.1. Approach

Instead of the "traditional approach" to system design shown in figure 16-1a, Freeman proposed the concept in figure 16-1b [Freeman 78] and [Anderson 79b]. The key issue is the development of decomposition elements and decomposition units. Decomposition elements can be viewed as Functional elements. Decomposition units (DU's) are the working units of the approach. They

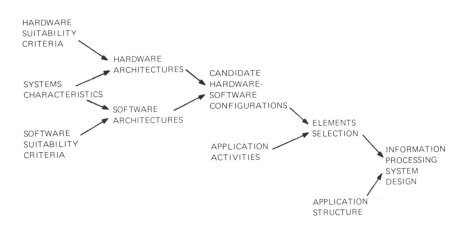

Figure 16-1a: Rejected design methodology

represent the executable entities associated with a decomposition element. Importantly, DU implementation is delayed as long as possible by the design methodology.

Using this approach a number of experiments have been performed relating to distributed systems, virtualization of distributed systems and to multiprocessing. One of these and its resulting hardware is discussed below. The system described could be used to help virtualize a distributed computer.

A system is defined as a set of concurrently executing processes cooperating via resourse utilization relationships and authorities (system structure). The elemental resources, called entities, have been grouped into four types: virtual machines, storage, communication and synchronization.

The primitives shown in figure 16-2 have been implemented on a target machine using a laboratory software test vehicle and are the basis of definition of a special purpose hardware device: SCU (System Control Unit). Two general catagories of primitives are defined: progress management and system structuring.

The system structuring primitives and their purpose (function) are defined in figure 16-3. For implementation it was assumed that all processes form a tree structure. The enable/disable primitives permit parent processes to pass the authority for resource utilization on to their descendants. If properly enabled, a named descendant may define/ release an entity, entity sharing, or entity attributes. This permits all resource usage conflicts to be identified and resolved by a common process.

The remainder of the primitives are progress management primitives. Progress management primitives enable application strategy through process cooperation while retaining the established system tree structure. The logic implementing progress management is referred to as the kernel. Two distinct subcategories exist. Primitives utilizing the macro-level instruction repertoire are called explicit primitives. Operations enabling the hardware to recognize the concept of the process but which cannot be invoked through macro-level instructions are referred to as implicit primitives.

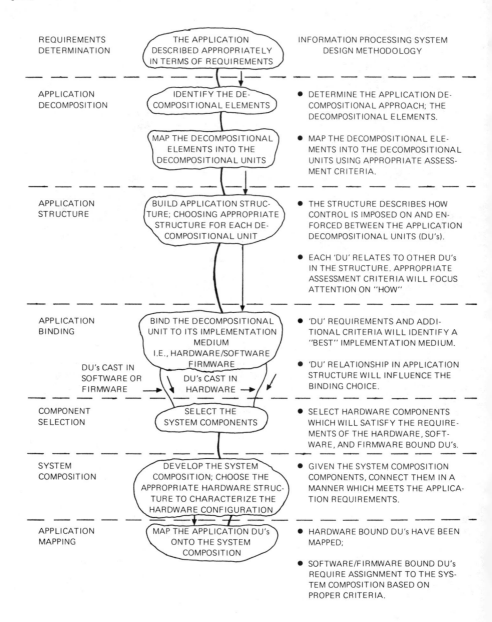

Figure 16-1b: Freeman's approach

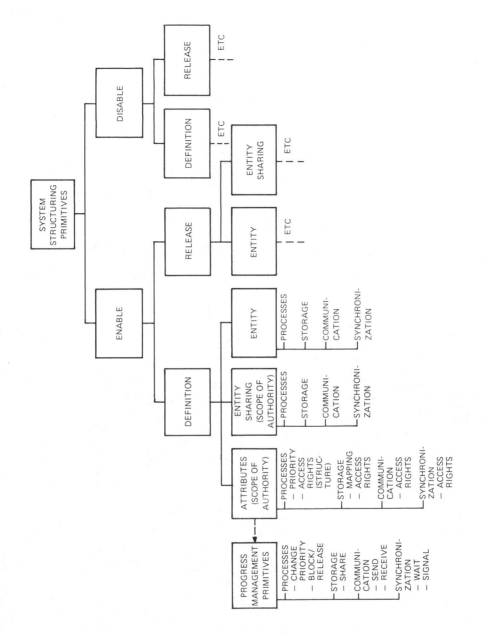

Figure 16-2: System control primitives

PRIMITIVE	FUNCTION DEFINITION
ENABLE/DISABLE ENTITY DEFINITION	ENABLES OR DISABLES STRUCTURED USE OF SYSTEM RESOURCES.
DEFINE/RELEASE ENTITY	REQUESTS OR RELINQUISHES CONTROL OF A SYSTEM RESOURCE.
ENABLE/DISABLE ENTITY SHARING	ENABLE OR DISABLES THE ESTABLISHMENT OF RESOURCE SHARING.
DEFINE/RELEASE ENTITY SHARING	REQUESTS OR RELINQUISHES RESOURCE SHARING.
ENABLE/DISABLE ATTRIBUTE CHANGE	ENABLES OR DISABLES PERMISSION FOR A PROCESS TO CHANGE CHARACTERISTICS OF RESOURCES (E.G., SEGMENT LENGTH).
DEFINE ATTRIBUTE	REQUEST CHANGE TO RESOURCE CHARACTERIS-TIC(S).

Figure 16-3: System structuring primitives

16.3.2. Hardware concept

The device implemented is called a system control unit (SCU). It provides for a kernel of an operating system. The developed hardware is designed to virtualize a distributed system (see § 16.6). The SCU is a microprogrammed device. It is implemented upon a specific piece of hardware called a MPC (Microprogrammed Controller). The special features of the primitives (See § 16.3.3 and § 16.3.4) are provided with high speed hardware assist by a tailored device called an EA (Emulation Adapter). This section describes how, in general, such hardware is built [Thurber 77].

Sperry Univac Defense Systems Division uses a Microprogramed Controller (MPC) concept to develop real-time system emulations: MPC I, MPC II, MPC III, or MPC IV. MPC provides an effective emulation capability for real-time systems due to its unique design; i.e., architecturally the MPC consists essentially of two machines working in concert. One machine is a standard piece of hardware selected from a set of standard modules. The choice of which MPC version to select is based upon consideration such as packaging, environmental, and throughput. The MPC version provides the basis for the emulation. To achieve a cost effective emulator which accounts for the machine detail design considerations, an emulation adapter (EA) is added to the MPC to provide in-hardware features (e.g., registers, memory address modes, instruction timing considerations, and unique I/O channels) which are unique to an architecture. This then enables the designer to develop an emulator which is an accurate representation of a system. Further, this design may require that detailed hardware design be done in addition to detailed microcode changes. Emulation adapters can generally be used for a class of machines (e.g., 16-bit general register machines) with minimal change, since the EA is in a sense programmable (see the emulation control word, ECW, described latter in this section).

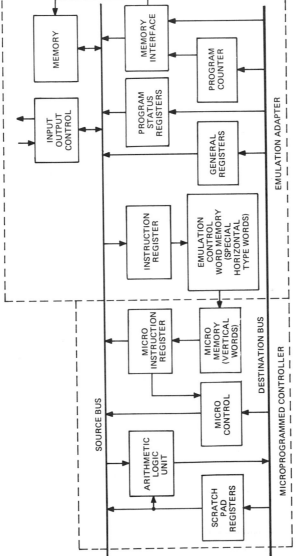

Figure 16-4a: MPC concept

Currently we have emulated over 20 different repertoires (or alternate performance levels of a given repertoire) and delivered over 1000 machines using the MPC/EA concept. From our experiences, we feel it is clear that to provide a cost effective, accurate real-time system emulation there will have to be target system specific hardware built, and the MPC/EA approach gives us a good technique to provide that hardware while keeping the MPCs unchanged as a set standard modules. Clearly, we can use a similar concept to build the SCU.

The concept of the MPC (figure 16-4a) is quite simple. It revolves around the standard building block: the Microprogrammed Controller. The MPC (figure 16-4a, figure 16-4b, table 16-1) is

15 14 13	12 11 10 9	8 7 6 5 4 3 2 1 0

	12	11	10	9	8 7 6 5 4 3 2 1 0
					EMULATION POINTER ADDRESS ONE'S COMPLEMENT
	M	I	O	U	CONTROL FUNCTION FROM EB1 OR EB2 (EMULATE BRANCH 1 OR 2)**
	0	0	0	0	RR UNARY – MODIFY ECW POINTER BITS 4–1 BY M* – NO OVERLAP***
	0	0	0	1	RR NO OVERLAP
	0	0	1	0	RR UNARY – MODIFY ECW POINTER BITS 4–1 BY M* – OVERLAP
	0	0	1	1	RR OVERLAP
	0	1	0	0	RK UNARY – MODIFY ECW POINTER BITS 4–1 BY M* – NO OVERLAP – BRANCH 1 TO INTERIM SEQUENCE
	0	1	0	1	RK NO OVERLAP – BRANCH 1 TO INTERIM SEQUENCE
	0	1	1	0	RK UNARY – MODIFY ECW POINTER BITS 4–1 BY M* – OVERLAP – BRANCH 1 TO INTERIM SEQUENCE
	0	1	1	1	RK OVERLAP – BRANCH 1 TO INTERIM SEQUENCE
	1	0	0	0	RI INHIBIT NEXT INSTRUCTION WRITE
	1	0	0	1	RI ENABLE NEXT INSTRUCTION WRITE
	1	0	1	0	UNDEFINED
	1	0	1	1	UNDEFINED
	1	1	0	0	RX INHIBIT NEXT INSTRUCTION WRITE – BRANCH 1 TO INTERIM SEQUENCE
	1	1	0	1	RX ENABLE NEXT INSTRUCTION WRITE – BRANCH 1 TO INTERIM SEQUENCE
	1	1	1	0	EX INHIBIT INDEXING – INHIBIT NEXT INSTRUCTION WRITE – BRANCH 1 TO INTERIM SEQUENCE
	1	1	1	1	RX INHIBIT INDEXING – ENABLE NEXT INSTRUCTION WRITE – BRANCH 1 TO INTERIM SEQUENCE

OPERAND MEMORY MODE

0	0	0	READ (FULL WORD)
0	0	1	WRITE (FULL WORD)
0	1	0	READ ODD WORD
0	1	1	WRITE ODD WORD
1	0	0	SPLIT CYCLE (I.E., READ, MODIFY, WRITE)
1	0	1	WRITE 0
1	1	0	READ THE BYTE SPECIFIED BY BIT 15 OF THE CONDITION REGISTER
1	1	1	WRITE THE BYTE SPECIFIED BY BIT 15 OF THE CONDITION REGISTER

*M – ONE'S COMPLEMENT OF M

**EB1 AND EB2 CONTROL ACCESS TO INTERIM ROUTINES

***RR, RK, RI, RX ARE INSTRUCTION ADDRESS FORMATS

Figure 16-4b: Emulation control word

used in the AN/UYK-20 This is a simple, vertically encoded, register-oriented machine. This provides the advantages of low cost and flexibility. Specific microinstructions can point to a second-level microinstruction, which is analogous to an instruction which acts as a nanoinstruction would act; however, it acts more like a subroutine (more precisely a procedure call). Further, this second-level instruction has as its goal the performance of the functions which are specific and unique to an architecture which is being emulated. For this reason, this portion of the machine is known as the emulation adapter. Some functions of the emulation adapter may be hardwired. Typical functions performed by the emulation adapter include format decomposition, status setting, control, and interpretation, operand fetch according to memory mode designation, etc. The emulation adapter could be

1) built from programmable logic,
2) built as an MPC with tailored firmware, etc.

INSTRUCTION FORMAT				DESCRIPTION
15–12	11–8	7–4	3–0	
F = 00	D	S	M	TRANSFER
F = 01	X			UNCONDITIONAL BRANCH
F = 02	D	S	M	ADD S2
F = 03	D	S	M	SHIFT
F = 04	D	S	M	ADD S1
F = 05	D	S	M	SUBTRACT
F = 06	D	S	M	LOGIC I
F = 07	D	S	M	LOGIC II
F = 10	D	K		ADD CONSTANT
F = 11	D	K		SUBTRACT CONSTANT
F = 12	D	K		TRANSFER CONSTANT TO D1
F = 13	D	K		TRANSFER CONSTANT TO D2
F = 14	FII	K		BRANCH
F = 15	FII	S	M	MICRO CONTROL
F = 16	FII	K		MICRO REPEAT
F = 17	D	S	M	EMULATE

DEFINITION OF FIELDS

F	FUNCTION CODE
FII	SUBFUNCTION CODE
D	DESTINATION DESIGNATOR FIELD
S	SOURCE DESIGNATOR
X	BRANCH ADDRESS DESIGNATOR
M	SUB-FUNCTION OR MODIFIER DESIGNATOR
K	CONSTANT – 8-BIT ABSOLUTE VALUE OR SUBFUNCTION CODE

Table 16-1: Microinstruction repertoire

We have chosen (to date) to build our emulation adapters from hardware due to speed considerations and the fact that generally we are attempting only a single architecture (e.g., a SCU).

A typical microinstruction repertoire is given in table 16.1. The ECW (emulation control word) format is shown in figure 16.4b (for the AN/UYK-20). The emulate microcommand causes an ECW to be read and its specified conditions to be met. Thus the sequence of events is:

<Instruction>   <User>
         is fetched and interpreted by

<Emulation Adapter>   <Emulation Tailoring>
         provided for emulation by hardware designer, uses "interim sequences" to
         decompose the instruction, fetch operands, and prepare the instruction for
         transmittal to the MPC for execution

<MPC>   <Register Oriented Machine>
         programmed by microcode (hardware) designer to act upon data placed into
         MPC scratch pad registers by the emulation adapter

<Result>   <User>
         answer from scratch pad registers is placed into appropriate positions in
         emulation adapter

The interim sequences are sequences (possibly hardwired) which provide for operand fetch, format decomposition, etc. Obviously, the most efficient design will minimize the changes required to and emulation adapter to change it from an emulator of machine A to emulation of machine B.

Further, the ECW may be viewed as either:

1) A horizontal microinstruction,

2) An extension of the vertical microinstruction, or

3) A hardwired interrupt-oriented aid to the vertical microinstruction which calls in the emulation adapter to perform emulation specific functions.

Although it is possible to make the emulation adapter and the MPC micromemory accessible to the user, to date we have not provided this capability in our machines since the ECW and micromemory are built from read-only memories.

The previous discussion assumes no overlap of microinstructions or parallelism in the MPC. In the MPC II, for example, the microinstructions are executed in a three-stage pipeline. Further, the "emulate start" command is the "last instruction" of a macro and it causes the next macro to be read and its interim sequences to be started. Thus in general the microde for a typical macroinstruction takes the form:

1) Interim Sequences (if any: parse instructions:
   specified by EB1,EB2)   obtain operands

2) Vertical Microcode   execution

3) Emulate Start (fetches next macro)   start next macro

Since the development of MPC I we have developed an enhanced version of the MPC (known as MPC II). In addition, LSI versions of the MPC II (MPC III and MPC IV) are available. Some additional MPC models are currently available but are not discussed herein. The MPC II instruction format has some monor modifications made to it to obtain the MPC III and MPC IV architectures. MPC IV and MPC II are identical (functionally) although the hardware structure is different. MPC III has more bits in the F and M (function and function modifier) fields due to the necessity to provide more function bits to control the AMD 2901 type chip. The characteristics of these MPCs are summarized in Figure 16-4c. The enhancements made to MPC I were based upon considerable analysis work which is summarized in the following paragraphs.

The emulation adapter concept is the primary feature which has yielded a decided performance edge to the MPC in contrast to other emulation approaches. The emulation adapter is an address generator which converts the MPC into an interrupt-driven system. Its primary function is to dynamically monitor the emulated machine state and produce starting addresses of microinstruction subroutines which implement the desired functions.

In the MPC, the emulation adapter is probed by means of a special microinstruction which serves as a trigger to generate the address of the next routine to be entered. This particular function is not totally unique to the MPC; however, few machines carry this function to the extent that the MPC does. One feature of the MPC which is unique is the supplementary control which is supplied by the emulation adapter. Such things as main memory cycle modes, interim-sequencing and address-generation characteristics, general register selection, macroinstruction overlapping, and condition code setting are accomplished and interpreted though the emulation adapter. In effect, the emulate instruction temporarily transfers machine control to the emulation adapter which then issues control signals to the rest of the machine in addition to supplying the branch address of the next microinstruction routine.

	MPC I	MPC II	MPC III	MPC IV
NUMBER OF BUSES	2	4	3(2)	3
NUMBER OF MICRO-INSTRUCTIONS	16	16	16	16
MICROINSTRUCTION LENGTH (BITS)	16	36	40	36
CONTROL STORE TYPE	ROM	ROM/RAM	ROM/RAM	ROM/RAM
MAXIMUM CONTROL STORE SIZE	4K X 16	4K X 72	4K X 80	4K X 72
MICRO-NESTING LEVELS	1	4	4	4
ARITHMETIC TYPES	2'S, 1'S	2'S, 1'S	2'S, 1'S	2'S, 1'S
HARDWARE RE-QUIRED	REFERENCE	SAME AS MPC I	2/3 MPC	2/3 MPC
CIRCUITS USED	GENERAL TTL	GENERAL ECL 10K	AMD 2901, AMD 2909, LSTTL PARTS	PLA'S, LS 181 ALU SLICE, AMD 2909, AMD 2914, LSTTL PARTS

Figure 16-4c: MPC attributes

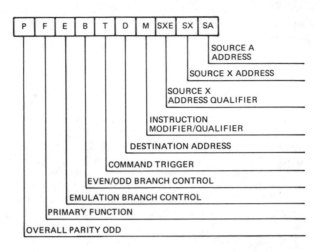

Figure 16-4d: MPC II microinstruction format

The major improvements incorporated into the MPC II reflect the extensive use of the emulate instruction, which is deleted as a special instruction, as well as the addition of facilities to relieve the following limiting characteristics of MPC I:

1) limited register addressing,

2) limited accumulator selection,

3) limited conditional branch capability, and

4) lack of parallel control capability.

The main differences between MPC II, MPC III, and MPC IV and MPC I can be seen by examining the MPC II instruction format (figure 16-4d) and the MPC I instruction format (table 16-1). Both machines have function (F) and function modifier capabilities (M). The instruction repertoires (figure 16-4d and table 16-1) differ mainly in that the emulate command (MPC I) has become a field in the MPC II (E-field). Further, the MPC II has added instruction parity (P) and an overlapped even/odd microinstruction branch capability (B). The B field allows the microcontrol store to be viewed as 4K x 32-bits or 8K x 36-bits, and this feature can be exploited in microinstruction branching during overlapped operations. A trigger field (T) was also added so that specific conditions and/or functions can be programmed for use in obtaining microinstruction parallelism; e.g., it is conceivable to initiate memory during an add microinstruction. An additional source bus (SX) and a qualifier (SXE) were added to MPC II for flexibility reasons. Additionally, a number of microsubroutine nesting levels were added to MPC I to facilitate more efficient microprograming. The resulting MPC II block diagram is shown in figure 16-4e. The system has also been equipped with a remote bus for maintenance purposes and tha ability to have a constant ROM for storage of arithmetic constants. The ECW for the MPC II is shown in figure 16-4f and the instruction repertoire in figure 16-4g. The ECW of MPC I and MPC II are similar. They both contain a microcode address; however, the MPC II contains an E/O bit to specify even/odd word addressing of the microstore. Both MPCs contain a memory operand mode control field. In MPC II the DP field is used for general register selection. The remaining fields of the MPC II provide for the format sensing (F2-F2), memory enable (M), interim sequence control (I), overlap of next instruction readup (O), and unary operation designator (U). These functions were basically encoded in the control functions of the MPC I ECW.

The above identified changes were basically determined through our experiences building emulators based upon the MPC I architecture. The three variations of the MPC II architecture are due to detailed cost/performance issues involved with parts selection to meet specific equipment requirements.

The MPC concept has been used extensively. Currently, we have emulated 12 different repertoires or alternative performance levels of a specific repertoire with the MPC I, two with the MPC II, and seven with the MPC III and three with the MPC IV. In all, we have produced over

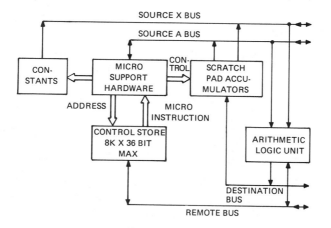

Figure 16-4e: MPC II

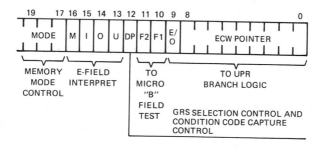

Figure 16-4f: Emulation control word

FUNCTION CODE	DESCRIPTION	MNENOMIC
00	LOAD CONSTANT	LDK
01	BRANCH	JP
02	MICRO CONTROL	MCL
03	REPEAT	RPT
04	SHIFT	SH
05	TRANSFER REMOTE	TXR
06	TRANSFER CONTROL STORE	TXC
07	UNASSIGNED	
10	ADD	ADD
11	SUBTRACT	SUB
12	LOGICAL I	
13	LOGICAL II	
14	CONDITIONAL TRANSFER SA	CTA
15	CONDITIONAL TRANSFER SX	CTX
16	CONDITIONAL SUM SA	CSA
17	CONDITIONAL SUM SX	CSX

Figure 16-4g: Microinstructions for MPC II

1000 machines which contain an emulator based upon the MPC concept. We have emulated machines as diverse as the Honeywell DDP-24 (training center 24-bit word length), the CP890 (shipboard 30-bit word length), the SKC 2070 (32-bit word length; airborne radiation hardened computer) the AN/UYK-20 (16-bit word length; shipboard computers), and the SCU.

Using an available MPC, an emulation adapter for the SCU is being developed and tested. The details of the SCU function are described in § 16.3.3 and 16.3.4. To date performance in real environments is not available.

16.3.3. Implicit primitives

16.3.3.1. Dispatch

Each active process is assigned a priority, which is used by the kernel to sequence processes eligible for dispatch on the processor. Several processes may have the same priority in which case, sequencing is In/First Out (FIFO). Dispatch involves the assignment of the processing element to the highest priority process on the dispatch list.

16.3.3.2. Event handling

Event is the term used to denote an instance of cooperation, hence the need for synchronization between two asynchronously executing processes. The act of synchronization is not visible to the macro level process directly. For example, a process which performs a **wait** operation on a semaphore will ultimately execute the next instruction regardless of whether it is temporarily suspended or continues execution. Events observed as interrupts on conventional machines will create kernel-to-process messages using the standard logical destination mechanism (see explicit primitives). Thus, events are not explicitly defined using progress management primitives. All synchronizing operations are performed on semaphores by means of the **wait** and **signal** primitives. Each instance of synchronization is represented by the assigmnent of a semaphore to each event (termed event registration) coupled with the asynchronous execution of the **wait** and **signal** operations by different processes.

16.3.4. Explicit primitives

16.3.4.1. Process management

block – Causes either the specified process (if any) or the invoking process to be removed from the dispatch list. It remains eligible for dispatch until a **release** operation is performed.

release – Causes the named process to be made eligible for dispatch, if blocked. A **release** operation will be retained (as a **signal** to an implicit private semaphore) pending execution of the next **block** operation on the named process.

priority change – Causes a change of process priority for the named process (if any) or the initiating process. Priority may only vary within the limits specified in the state vector (currently system generation parameters).

16.3.4.2. Storage management

share – Causes a specified memory page (or pages) to be shared between the invoking process and a named process. This operation permits dynamic memory sharing between processes, if established by the system structure. (Static sharing can also be established during system generation.)

16.3.4.3. Communication management

send and **receive**: All communication is performed by reference to a logical destination, as opposed to conventional real or virtual computer channels. This mechanism allows a mix of destinations, located on shared busses and point-to-point channels, to be transparent to the software. Logical device transparency is particularly important in a virtual concept, here functional allocation frequency changes due to hardware reconfiguration. Reallocation can be achieved in this environment by changing the logical destination tables in each computer. The software remains unchanged even when functions are reassigned to different computers.

Communication is in the form of process-to-process messages. The **send** and **receive** primitives are invoked regardless of the location of producer and consumer processes.

16.3.4.4. Synchronization management

Synchronization is achieved using the semaphore, a data structure composed of a counter and a queue. The semaphore operations are the P (**wait**) and V (**signal**) operations originally proposed by Dijkstra. The **wait** operation decrements the counter and, if the counter becomes negative, adds the associated process to the semaphore queue. The **signal** operation increments the counter and, if the counter remains nonpositive (includes zero), removes a process from the semaphore queue for dispatch.

In distributed processing environments, a special form of the semaphore is required to handle synchronization between processes on different computers. This semaphore, called a multi-copy global semaphore, responds to **signal** and **wait** primitives, as though it were a local semaphore (providing hardware transparency). However, this global semaphore requires special implementation techniques for queueing and updating.

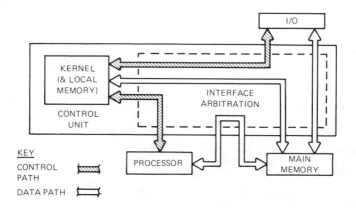

Figure 16-5: SCU block diagram

In order to gain the maximum performance for kernel primitives, a modular System Control Unit (SCU) is introduced (figure 16-5). The SCU is a hardware version of the kernel which, when added to a conventional computer, results in a process controlled computer whose structure is identical to the structure of the Virtual Machines (VM's) that will execute on it. Figure 16-6 summarizes the advantages of this approach.

HARDWARE SUPPORT

HARDWARE CAN BE OPTIMIZED

MICROPROGRAMMED FOR FLEXIBILITY

CONCURRENCY

ADD-ON MODULE

Figure 16-6: SCU advantages

This SCU consists of a microprogrammed controller for execution of the kernel primitives, high-speed local storage for the kernel data structures, and special hardware logic to boost execution speed of the kernel primitives. The kernel data structures are retained in local SCU storage and include the CPU Process Dispatch List, the set of Process State Vectors, the Logical Destination Table, the I/O Port Table and the Semaphore Data Structures. Retention of the kernel data structures in the SCU improves performance because there is no contention with main memory users and local storage, faster than main memory, can be used. Special execution logic in the SCU includes state switch hardware to facilitate rapid process switching in the CPU, virtual memory address translation logic to provide hardware enforcement of process namespace separation, and custom logic to manipulate the global semaphore data structures at high speed.

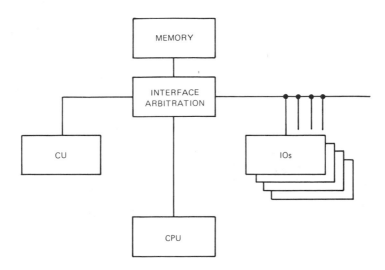

Figure 16-7: SCU relationship to a processor

As shown in figure 16-7, the SCU has control paths to the CPU and the Input/Output Controller (IOC) as well as a data path to main memory. When the CPU encounters an explicit primitive in the process instruction stream, it sends a control packet to the SCU identifying the primitive and its parameters. The CPU then enters a PAUSE state. The SCU will receive the control packet and decode the primitive operation. Depending on the primitive, one of three possible control cycles will be followed.

1. If the primitive is one which requires only a brief amount of SCU time, the primitive will be executed by the CU and the CPU will then be restarted at the next instruction of the process.

2. If the primitive is one which calls for suspension of the executing process, the SCU immediately "saves" the CPU state. selects the highest priority process from its CPU dispatch queue, initializes the CPU with the new process parameters, and restarts the CPU. The SCU then completes execution of the primitive which caused the suspension.

3. If the primitive is one which requires a longer amount of SCU time, the SCU immediately "saves" the CPU state, selects the next process, initializes and restarts the CPU, after which the suspended process is re-entered onto the dispatch queue at its current priority.

The ability to rapidly change process states on the CPU is a key feature required in this design philosophy. If the CPU process state can be changed quickly (i.e., a few microseconds), then it is reasonable to switch to a new process whenever the currently running process encounters a longer primitive. Fast state changing maximizes the amount of CPU processing time available for application processing because CPU time is never wasted performing busy waits, executive operations, or other nonproductive application processing. The SCU can quickly cause state changes because the definition of the set of processes is specified by a corresponding set of process state vectors that are stored locally in the SCU. These process state vectors are not directly accessible to any process executing on the CPU and can be accessed and/or changed only by the SCU in response to the execution of primitive operations on the CPU. The process state vectors themselves are part of the application structuring procedure and are generated offline during system generation. A process state vector contains the following information.

1) Current State – Target machine general register, program counter, status register, etc,

2) Authorities – Logical destination usage rights, semaphore usage rights, and allowable priority range,

3) Event Registrations – Hardware faults, software faults, and clock message,

4) Namespace Description – Page descriptors, and

5) Structural Relationships – Link to parent process.

The fact that the process is entirely defined by the process state vector allows a process to be dispatched on the CPU in a very efficient manner. The contents of a register located in the SCU called the Process Identifier (PID) is used to specify which process of the allowable set of processes is executing on the CPU. This PID can be thought of as an index that selects one of n process states. It specified which set of general registers, program counter, etc., are to be used by the CPU, which set of page descriptors are to be used by the Virtual Address Translator which set of authorities are to be used by the SCU in verification of access rights during primitive execution, and, which set of event registrations are to be used during the processing of events. To change the process running on the CPU, the only thing that is required is to change the contents of the PID and to perform a small amount of housekeeping in the CPU. The PID mechanism not only allows process state changes to be performed in a few microseconds, it also effectively enforces hardware separation between processes. Since the process state vector defines the entire set of machine resources and access rights available to its process and since the PID reflects only the relevant state vector, there is no way that one process can interact (i.e., interfere) with another process unless allowed to by the parameters in its process state vector. As a result, the process interfaces are hardware enforced.

ADVANTAGES

    INCREASE IN PERFORMANCE
    CONCURRENT OPERATION
    SOFTWARE SIMPLIFICATION
    STANDARDIZED INTERFACES
    USE OF LOW COST HARDWARE COMPONENTS

DISADVANTAGES

    INTERFACE OVERHEAD
    IMPLEMENTATION COMPROMISES RESULT IN HIGH LIFE CYCLE COST

Figure 16-8: Advantages of functionally dedicated processors

16.4. Functionally Distributed Architectures (FDA's)

Another interesting experiment we can consider is the addition of small inexpensive hardware to a system where the hardware is dedicated to an application function [Anderson 79a]. Figure 16-8 gives the advantages of this approach.

A simple message switch system of interest is summarized below.

The message switch was to operate in a portable environment and thus had to be light, flexible, and inexpensive. The concept was structured as in figure 16-9.

The Host Processor Adapter (HPA) provides the interface for communication lines of the network to user terminals and data processors nodes. It also provides for the arbitration for the data and control bus connecting the Line Control Units (LCU's). The LCU functions are given in figure 16-10. The LCU's are functionally identical. The LCU's and HPA utilize identical hardware layouts. The message switch was designed to enable multiple Terminal Units (TU's) or line drivers for each LCU and multiple LCU's for each network node. This permits multiple communication lines to be connected to each node and enables both network expansion and multiple message paths (reliability) to be handled more easily.

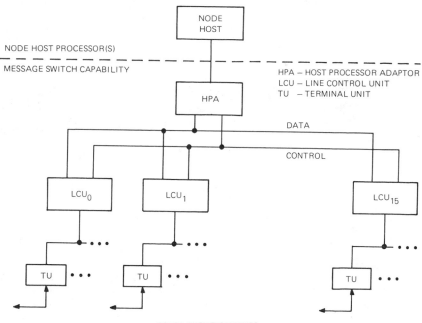

Figure 16-9: Message switch

STATUS ACCUMULATION

LINE MANAGEMENT

MESSAGE INPUT

MESSAGE OUTPUT

MESSAGE ROUTING

PROTOCOL PROCESSING

Figure 16-10: Line control unit functions

To meet the processing requirements, an interesting feature was added to the experiment, i.e., although many computers simultaneously process I/O and applications, it was necessary for this experiment to also process "control" in parallel. This was accomplished as follows. Two microprocessors were used, one dedicated to application algorithms and called the Protocol Processor (PP), the second dedicated to input/output operations and called the Character Processor (CP). A block diagram of the resulting microcomputer is shown in figure 16-11. It should be noted that memory contention is now reduced by enabling program and local data to be uniquely partitioned between microprocessors which have access to their own 4K RAM.

Figure 16-12 shows the results (summarized) of simulation runs for a fixed network configuration and communication path topology.

ORIGINAL DESIGN	OPERATION CLASSIFICATION	DUAL MICROPROCESSOR DESIGN
30%	INPUT/OUTPUT	65%
70%	CONTROL	35%
100%	TOTAL	100%
COULD NOT MEET REQUIREMENT	μP CAPACITY UTILIZED	80%

Figure 16-12: Simulation results

16.5. Control overhead

Control overhead [Anderson 79a] in a system can be very high, thus it might be conceivable to build a computer made up of processing elements which attacks this problem. Figure 16-13 illustrates such a system based upon use of microprocessors. The concept of this system is that there exists three major types of processors: communication/control, I/O, and a set of processors tailored to an application (only one of which is shown).

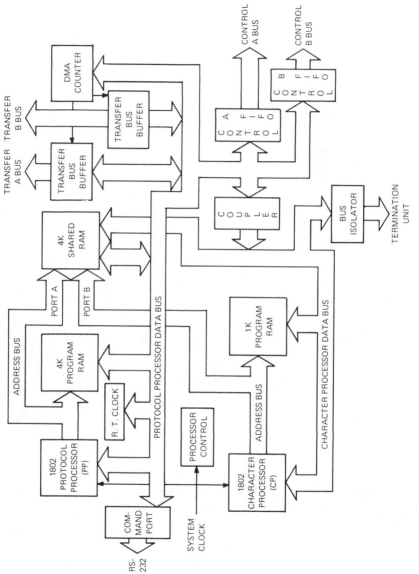

Figure 16-11: Line control microcomputer system

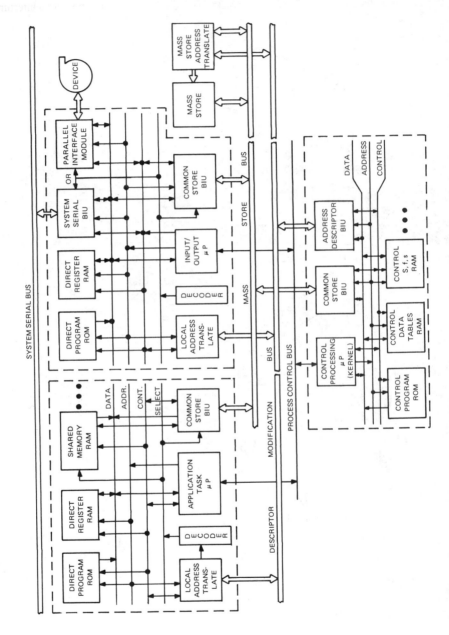

Figure 16-13: A concept to attack control overhead

The reader can see that the following capabilities are possible under this computer architecture.

1) Interrupts created either internally or externally to the computer need not cause an application task to terminate. The Kernel (Control) Processor operating on either statically or dynamically established event definition can determine and initiate the proper computer response.

2) The Kernel Processor can cause required I/O and application processes to be dispatched on their respective processing engines. The individual processor state vectors ("s") can be altered by the Kernel Processor rather than by software executing on the individual processors. Altering the state vector involves changing the descriptors which identify the process's address space, direct register set etc. The descriptor data is not available to application tasks but is held in the Kernel Processor's memory. The point in time at which dispatch occurs is triggered by the receipt of a new process name by a module's microprocessor. For example, the name change impacts the address descriptors and register set used by the function f.

3) Address translation is controlled by the Kernel Processor. Properly implemented, each task (processor) has access only to its own state space, hence data. Sharing of data can be securely controlled through the enforced use of Kernel primitives, e.g., **send/receive**.

4) Message movement is controlled by the Kernel Processor. Tight coupling (memory sharing)versus loose coupling (data movement) is transparent to the software. Tradeoff decisions (process allocation to a computer) can be altered during system generation.

5) Communication can be via messages between processors rather than shared memory.

16.6. Virtual Machines (VM) and Virtual Machine Monitors (VMM)

The concept of a virtual machine [Goldberg 79] is to provide a mechanism to isolate users and allow for the multiplexing of multiple logical machines on a single physical machine. Goldberg has been working in this area for an extended time and has proposed that virtual machines may be implemented using "distributed processors" and networks. The major considerations for this proposal are summarized in figure 16-14.

- SIMPLIFIED GROWTH AND MAINTENANCE THROUGH STANDARD INTERFACES.

- INCREASED PERFORMANCE THROUGH PARALLEL FUNCTION EXECUTION.

- SOFTWARE REUSABILITY MADE POSSIBLE BY THE REMOVAL OF MACHINE DEPENDENT INSTRUC-TIONS FROM THE APPLICATION LOGIC.

- SECURITY THROUGH ENFORCED PROCESS INTERFACE STANDARDS.

- SIMPLIFIED SOFTWARE IMPLEMENTATION NOW POSSIBLE THROUGH THE INCREMENTAL ADDITION OF HOL TAILORED APPLICATION TASK PROCESSORS.

Figure 16-14: Major factors for utilization of virtual machine concepts
in conjunction with networks

Goldberg chooses the overview model shown in figure 16-15. Further, using the three layer system model of [Thurber 78] and [Gaspar 78], application, VM network, and Communications subnetwork, descriptions of a number of systems are provided. Figure 16-16 illustrates the main features of some systems of interest.

This concept of combining virtual machine and networking technology appears quite interesting. In fact, Paradyne Corporation is said to be about to introduce a series of products designed to allow virtual machine networks to be built around IBM hardware.

BENEFITS

- EVOLVABILITY
- MODULARITY
- MACHINE INDEPENDENCE

TRADITIONAL APPROACH (EMULATION ASSISTANCE)

- PROGRAMS DEVELOPED IN SIMULATION UNDER VM
- PROTECTED PARTITIONS FOR PROGRAMS
- CAN BE RUN ON EMULATORS

VM NETWORKS

- ADVANTAGES OF VM
- ALLOWS FOR EXPANSION OF VM SYSTEM USING ADDITIONAL PROCESSORS

REQUIREMENTS

- SEPARATION OF LOGICAL AND PHYSICAL PROCESSORS
- EXTENSIVE MAPPING HARDWARE
- JOB BREAK-UP
- EMULATORS
- INCREASED LAYERING
- FUNCTIONAL MIGRATION AND HARDWARE SUPPORT

Figure 16-15: Virtual machine network concepts

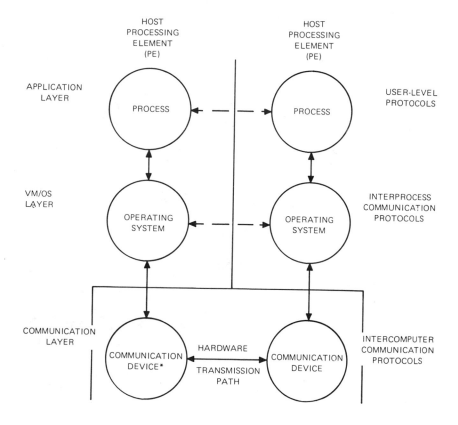

*PACKET SWITCH, CIRCUIT SWITCH (CROSSBAR SWITCH), OR BUS STRUCTURE (I/O CHANNEL)

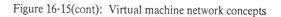

Figure 16-15(cont): Virtual machine network concepts

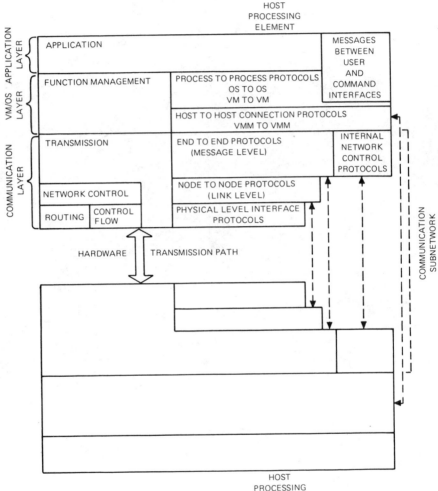

Figure 16-15(cont): Virtual machine network concepts

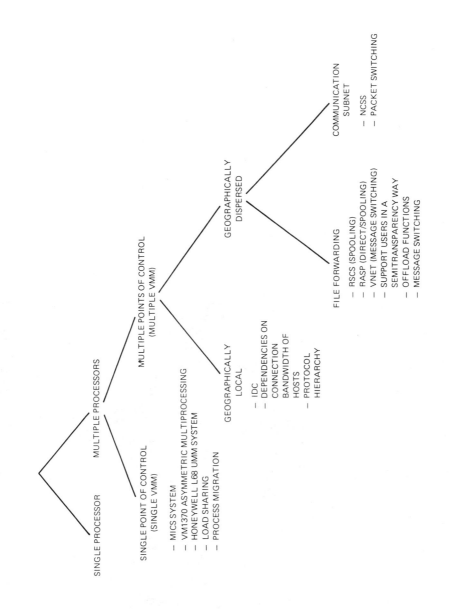

Figure 16-16: Features of virtualized distributed processors

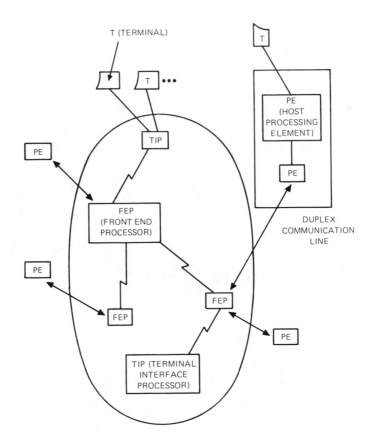

FEATURES

- IBM AND AMDAHL HOSTS
- PDP SWITCHES
- HOST TO HOST DIRECT COMMUNICATION
- TRANSPARENT COMMUNICATION (LINK/REMOTE)

Figure 16-16(cont.): Features of virtualized distributed processors

16.7. Local networks

16.7.1. Introduction

Generally, a local network is considered to be a network in which the hosts are not separated by a large geographic distance. Maybe the distance is only on the order of a few meters. Maybe it is on the order of a kilometer, but clearly, the distance is not thousands of kilometers. Because of this short distance, the applications placed on local networks may be different from the applications on a geographically separated network spread across the USA or Europe. The motives are different and the designs may be simplified. [Thurber 80] among others has identified about eighty different local network systems. Clearly, there is lot of interest in this area. The majority of these systems have an unfortunate property: they are custom built and are thus not the type of equipment that you can go out and purchase. Many have grown out of experiments. Some, particularly at universities, have grown out of necessity to connect together a large number of machines to achieve some specific computational goal.

In considering technologies local networks are the hottest current concept of "distributed processing." So let's assume for the moment that you want a local network. You have a strong desire to get one for your computer center, office of the future, etc. Where can you get one right now? What kinds can you buy? Unfortunately the answers to these questions are not particularly pleasant. For all of the emphasis in this technology area, the majority of the systems are experimental. This section will give an overview of some of the hardware you can get. Note, we said hardware. The reason is that in general you must build your own software. This should not discourage you, because at least there is hardware, and eventually there will be software.

Let's get specific. We are interested in hardware. Particularly, hardware this is in production. Where do we go? After looking around for a while, we decided that there are a variety of places to get hardware that could be a local network. This hardware exists at many system levels and thus is as hard to classify as a local network is to identify. The result of this overview is given below.

16.7.2. Application embedded hardware

Some local network hardware is not available as a specific piece of hardware; i.e., it is embedded in a system and comes as part of the system and associated application – whether you want it or not. Such system hardware may be deeply embedded in the application system, or it may be accessible so that the hardware can be configured in a local network. Or the application may be modified to exploit the known hardware characteristics.

An example of such a system is the Xerox 860 office automation system which contains an Ethernet interface embedded in the product. Many products in the area of communications or word processing have this type of characteristic.

16.7.3. Turn key systems

A number of groups provide turn key systems made of their mainframes (or minicomputers). It is to the manufacturer's advantage to provide such a product. It is also easy. If you have a networking product currently, you can develop versions of the transport mechanism designed to work in a geographically local environment. In fact, this may even simplify the design. One ring-oriented structure which provides local networking capability is the RINGNET of Prime Computer Corporation. Other system concepts such as SNA (IBM) and DECNET (DEC) could be utilized in a local network framework. Zilog's Z-Net provides local network capability for microcomputers.

16.7.4. Subsystem building blocks

With certain components, though, you may be able to build very interesting products. Such hardware may be the basis for a subsystem. Hardware available in the category of subsystems is now appearing. The most "well known" subsystem is a back end storage network known as Shared VSS (Virtual Storage System) being built by the MASSTOR Corporation. This subsystem is based upon the Network Systems Corporation HYPERchannel and HYPERcache used in conjunction with equivalent of IBM 3850 and 4341 systems to provide for a very large staged memory subsystem. The concept is quite simple. Shared VSS provides for the on-line capability to share a backend storage network with several nonhomogeneous hosts. The large data base is stored in archival storage and its movement into a host is controlled via a control processor from the archival and backing storage into a HYPERcache and eventually via the HYPERchannel into the appropriate host.

16.7.5. Components/modules

The most exciting area for local networking is the problem of interconnecting a number of nonhomogeneous computers into a network. Since the machines come from a variety of manufacturers, there is most probably no available software and the manufacturers probably try to discourage this approach for obvious reasons. But the fact remains that a majority of the produced hardware for local networking falls into this category. Competition is increasing in this area and can be expected to intensify unmercifully.

To date the most significant commercial grade hardware components or modules available to assist in the development of local networks are available from Network Systems Corporation. Almost twenty adapter types are available for the HYPERchannel, in addition to the HYPERcache. Control Data Corporation is in the process of announcing competitive hardware to Network Systems Corporation adapters and Sperry Univac has introduced military hardware to construct bus-oriented local networks. A number of manufacturers provide hardware products in this category.

16.7.6. Chips

Chips and chip sets are now becoming available that may be used to support local network construction. Western Digital is producing an X.25 chip, while Harris is developing hybrid and single chip 1553 military bus interfaces. A number of other semiconductor manufacturers are planning to introduce local network bus chips. In particular, Intel/DEC/Xerox have announced plans to jointly develop a standard local network interface chip based upon the Ethernet concept.

16.7.7. Hardware overview

We have briefly discussed a set of categories of local network hardware and some of the types of hardware that might be available in a category. What would we find if we tried to perform an exhaustive list of such hardware? It depends! Since we can not precisely define a local network, we clearly can not build an exhaustive survey. The list below provides a representative view of available off-the-shelf hardware. In each category, the hardware is listed alphabetically by manufacturer.

Application Embedded Hardware

1) ROLM's REMS (ROLM Electronic Mail System) – an electronic mail concept based around application extension of ROLM PBX (Private Branch Exchange) System.

2) Wang Mailway – an electronic mail concept based around application extensions of Wang word processors.

3) Xerox 860 – a word processing system containing an Ethernet interface.

Turn Key Systems

1) DEC DNA – if the processors were placed in close (local) proximity, DNA could be considered a local net.

2) IBM SNA and 8100 SDLC Ring – if the processors were placed in close proximity, SNA and/or the 8100 SDLC ring could be a local net.

3) Prime Computer RINGNET – a token based ring system. A similar concept, "Computer Cells", is available for multiprocessors.

4) Zilog Z-Net – a bus system which is used to connect MCZ2 computers.

Subsystem Building Blocks

1) MASSTOR Shared VSS – a backend storage network.

Components/Modules

1) AMDAX CDX – a modem-based local network concept.

2) Bolt,Beranek & Newman, Inc. (BBN) Pluribus IMP – a multiprocessor Interface Message Processor originally designed for the Arpanet.

3) Control Data's LCN – a high performance set of local network interfaces.

4) Computrol Megalink – multidrop bus based on DMA interfaces.

5) Digital Communication CAPAC – Cable Access Packet Communications System for interfacing RS 232 devices using FSK modems.

6) Digital Equipment Corp (DEC) PCL-11, DR11, etc. – a number of DEC devices PCL-11, DR11 cards, etc., could be used to build local networks.

7) Hewlett Packard (HP) DS 1000 – packet switch connections for local networks.

8) IEEE 488 Bus – built by various manufacturers; could be used to build local networks.

9) Nestar Systems Cluster/One – local network hardware for use with personnel computers.

10) Network Systems Corporation HYPERchannel and HYPERcache – the largest selection of adapters and support hardware available to build nonhomogeneous networks of large mainframes: a high-speed memory subsystem available to assist in development of backend storage networks and useful to add store-and-forward capability to HYPERchannel based systems.

11) Network Systems LNI – Local Network Interface is a PDP-11 based ring concept.

12) Sperry Univac AN/USQ-67, SHINPADS, and EPIC/DPS – AN/USQ-67 is a 640x640 circuit switch for local nets; SHINPADS is a high-speed bus structure for local nets; EPIC/DPS is a ring-based local network that may be virtualized into a centralized system concept.

13) Three Rivers Computer Packet Stream Network – contention-based coaxial system.

14) Ungermann-Bass Net/One – local net on microprocessor node hardware.

15) Wang WISE (Wang Inter System Exchange) – can be used to build local networks of Wang equipments.

Chips

1) Harris 1553 – the 1553 is a standard military serial interface. Harris is building such interfaces on modules and is developing such interfaces as single chips.

2) Western Digital X.25 – Western Digital has announced an X.25 standard chip which primarily implements HDLC.

3) Xerox/Intel/DEC – announced a joint venture to develop a standard Ethernet protocol chip.

16.7.8. Network Systems Corporation HYPERchannel

To date if you want to connect together non-homogeneous processors into a local network, the only real supplier is Network Systems Corporation.

The HYPERchannel of Network Systems Corporation is a concept for a set of building blocks to be used to build both local computer networks and backend storage networks. Originally, the goal of the company was to build backend storage networks for the "computer center of the future"; however, due to funding constraints in starting a new company, the products originally developed by the company were involved with the communication mechanism for local networks. A number of years after the original product announcements, the HYPERcache, a mechanism which can be used in conjunction with HYPERchannel to build a backend storage network, was introduced. Figure 16-17 summarizes the concept of HYPERchannel, the HYPERcache and a typical configuration of these products as a backend storage network.

The HYPERchannel itself consists of a tapped coaxial cable capable of transmitting signals over distances on the order of about 1000 meters at rates of up to 50 mhz. Connected onto this cable are devices called *adapters*. Each adapter consists of a buffered storage area along with a microprogramed processor from the device, and transmit the data to another adapter. The adapters transmit the data between each other in a special protocol (or format). This format was originally based upon a zero-insertion protocol, but was later changed to a length oriented protocol. Each adapter can connect to up to four coaxial cables in parallel. On the device side, each adapter connects to a specific type of device in a specific way. Some adapters connect to processors via I/O channels; others connect to memories via DMA (direct memory access) channels. The adapter buffers information transfers from the processor's memory and places the data into the proper format for transfer to another adapter. Additional adapter types are available which allow for connection to a channel control unit. These adapters allow for unit record equipment to be interfaced directly onto the coax via an adapter connected to their channel control unit. Such a connection may be made remotely. In such cases, the adapter connected to the processor desiring to use the unit record equipment will transfer the channel program to the adapter which will look like the channel to the channel control unit. In some cases, the operating system of the processor may be modified so that the channel program can reside on the remote adapter and be called from the processor. The HYPERchannel bus allocation scheme is based upon a prioritized carrier sense concept; i.e., any device can access the bus if no device is transmitting. If a device is locked out from transmitting for an extended period of time, a priority bias eventually asserts itself to insure access. The carrier sense concept is modified by a collision detection scheme and no acknowledgement of a transmission, a faulty NACK, or an actual collision all cause a transmission retry. Actual data transmission is done bit serial using a Manchester code.

HYPERchannel^{TM} CONCEPT

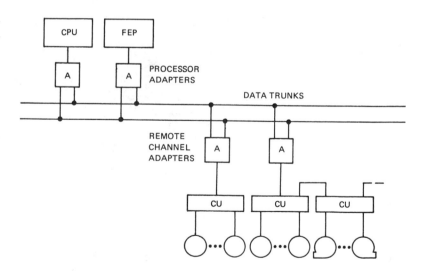

Figure 16-17: Off the shelf Network System Corporation products

HYPERcache TM CONCEPT SHOWN IN A
COMPLETE BACKEND STORAGE NETWORK

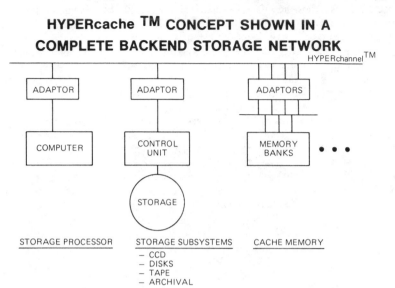

SHARED VSS TM FROM MASSTOR :
BACKEND STORAGE NETWORK

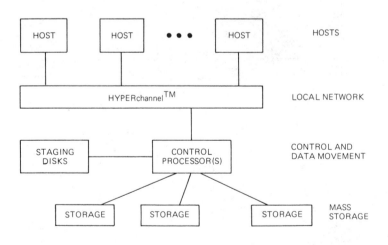

Figure 16-17 (cont.): Off the shelf Network System Corporation products

The HYPERcache is a large high speed buffer memory which connects to the HYPERchannel using a set of adapters. It is used primarily to buffer a transmission when a sender is ready but the destination is busy. It may, however, have many other uses. For one, it can be used as a centralized store and forward buffer pool. If multiple HYPERcaches are included in the network, they and be used a packet switches distributed on the HYPERchannel. Another use is to form a backend storage network where the HYPERcache is used as a buffer or staging device. A product developed around this concept is that of the Shared VSS of MASSTOR Corporation.

One complaint about the HYPERchannel has been its cost in comparison to a minicomputer. Part of this "problem" is due to the extensive cost to develop and build high speed hardware. With respect to minicomputers, e.g., the PDP-11, up to four PDP-11's can be multiplexed onto an adapter. Further it can be expected that Network Systems Corporation will begin to develop products which meet the competitive cost constraints of large user bases.

16.8. Further issues

There are a number of other systems which provide interesting hardware features to support distributed processing. These are summarized in figure 16-18.

SYSTEM	FEATURE
ETHERNET	PROCEDURE CALL MICROCODE
CM*	NONLINEAR ADDRESS TRANSFORMATION
HXOP	BIU IMPLEMENTING IN HARDWARE MICROPROGRAMMABLE FLOW CONTROL
HYPER CHANNEL	VARIETY OF INTERFACE ADAPTORS
HYPER CACHE	CENTRALIZED STORE AND FORWARD BUFFER
DPS	VIRTUALIZATION EXPERIMENTS WITH SCU
MASSTONE	A LOCAL NETWORK SUBSYSTEM

Figure 16-18: Hardware features

16.9. Conclusion

In this section a series of concepts, experiments and hardware was described.

As a caution to the reader we need to note three important distinctions:

1) What is the basic concept of the system?

2) How is the system implemented?

3) How do the hosts interface to the specific communication subnetwork?

These issues are critical to all hardware discussions which proceeded this conclusion because the system design on many of the concepts discussed were significantly compromised in implementation so. Separation of the major design features is difficult and reconstruction of solution intent may be almost impossible. Not much can be concluded about hardware. It is binary: It exists or it doesn't. There is no in between. It works properly or it doesn't. There can over a long term be no in between. The proof of distribution, decentralization, and distributed systems will be their existence and correct operation. Time will judge this issue.

Chapter 17: Hardware/software relationships in distributed computer systems

17.1. Introduction

Deciding whether a given function in a computer system should be implemented in hardware or software is one of a pair of activities which are related but conceptually distinct, and often confused with one another. The first of these activities is deciding what functionality is performed at what layers in the system. This layering, while not yet well understood, has been dealt with extensively, albeit in rather narrow contexts (such as network communications [Zimmerman 1980] and software [Goos 1975].) Less attention has been paid in the literature to the second activity, which consists of deciding on the hardware/software implementation of functionality in any particular layer. These two activities are performed in every computer system design. However, all too frequently they are carried out implicitly or by habit rather than explicitly and by systematic tradeoffs. Once the functional design of a system is complete, the layering and implementation activities should take place separately but iteratively until the desired system attributes seem to be best attained.

There are two different philosophies concerning hardware/software relationships in computer systems. The first is that systems should be designed so the hardware and software have minimum impact on one another. This view may arise when the hardware is given a priori and (perhaps consequently) hinders, as least as much as helps, the software; it may also be appropriate when the software is to reside equally well on a variety of different hardware bases [Dowson 1979]. The second philosophy is that the hardware and software should be designed together to provide maximal synergism in order that certain system attributes (such as performance, fault tolerance, or cost-effectiveness) be optimized. It is unlikely that pre-existing hardware will be ideal for the intended software-- either the software must be designed to accommodate the hardware (the usual case), or there must at least be freedom to alter the hardware, if not design it initially. With either philosophy, possible hardware/software relationships and their implications must be clearly understood. Hardware/software independence cannot be effectively achieved by simply assuming that the hardware doesn't matter.

17.2. Assigning functionality to layers

In a computer system, the layers of most frequent interest range from the user interface at the top to the ISP at the bottom, as exemplified by figure 17-1. (Note that we are refering here to the ISP *level of abstraction* [Bell and Newell 1971], as distinguished from the ISP *notation*] which can be used to describe hardware at different levels.). Layers in a computer system need not be strictly hierarchical, or even totally ordered, since the abstractions at a higher layer need not

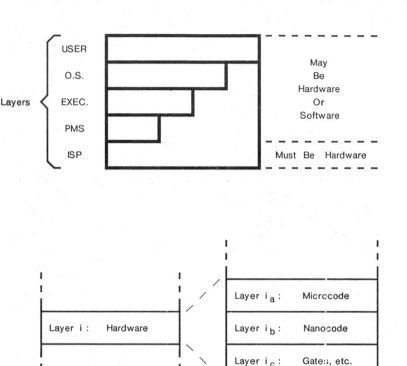

Figure 17-1: Example system layers

involve all or any of those at some particular layer below it. For example, a floating point operation could be implemented either as an O.S. utility routine available to the user layer, or as an ISP layer instruction available to all higher layers.

For the purposes of this paper, we consider software to be the instructions which are executed (or interpreted) at the ISP level and above, and hardware to be the remaining constituents of a computer system. It is important to realize that hardware *per se* is not a layer — any layer from the PMS layer up (including the executive and user layers) may be implemented in hardware, software, or a combination of the two, according to the needs of the system and its application. Consequently, it may be that certain hardware functionality at one layer utilizes lower layer software (via procedure calls, messages, etc.). Hardware appearing at any layer may be structured into sublevels, such as microcode, nanocode, and hardwired logic.

Layering is commonly carried out through the specification and design stages, but very often not reflected in the implementation (primarily for performance reasons). While layering necessarily imposes some overhead, this overhead is greatly amplified by inappropriate hardware/software relationships which fail to properly support the layering.

17.3. The implementation of functions within layers

It is generally the case that software complexity has increased far more than the complexity of the associated hardware. In some circumstances this is appropriate, but in many others it leads to what Perlis once called the "Turing tarpit", where everything is possible but nothing is easy. One reason for this inequity may be that historically, hardware was the major factor in system costs; while this is no longer generally true, design perspectives and techniques engendered by it still persist. Another major reason for the frequent imbalance in hardware/software complexity is that the hardware is intended to be relatively general purpose, while most of the software is for more specialized purposes. The requirements of generality tend to be rather vague, place few bounds on complexity, and be difficult to measure compliance with. On the other hand, special-purpose requirements vary widely, and include many combinatorial and exception cases. This notion that the hardware should be general purpose and the software special purpose arises primarily from a (usually implicit) historically based premise that certain system layers should inherently be implemented in hardware and others in software.

In a computer system, some functionality can reasonably be implemented quite analogously in either hardware or software such that its appearance and use is essentially unchanged. Some functions can be initially implemented in software, modified on the basis of experience with them, and eventually reimplemented in hardware for a variety of reasons (e.g., floating point arithmetic, the Multics protection rings). In general, the characteristics of a particular implementation may become intertwined with, and even indistinguishable from, those of the functionality being implemented. Thus, care must be taken that one implementation not reflect artifacts of another — for example, airplanes do not flap their wings, and automobiles do not have legs.

The incongruence of software-intensive and hardware-intensive implementations can be illustrated with critical regions. The classical software-intensive implementations (e.g., [Lamport 1974]) require that the hardware provide only the normal mutually exclusive single read or write access to memory. An example of a hardware-intensive implementation [Knuth 1966] utilizes indivisible queue manipulation instructions. Only with considerable effort would someone unfamiliar with both of these implementations conclude that they are alternative solutions to the same problem.

There are three major characteristics which differentiate hardware and software implementations — performance, flexibility, and cost. While these characteristics are widely recognized as the important ones in hardware/software relationships, the typical beliefs about them are over-simplified.

The most obvious factor in performance is that fewer levels of interpretation result in faster execution speed (e.g., high level language vs. microcode vs. nanocode vs. hardwired logic). However, another performance factor is that certain functionality is more easily provided by hardware than by software. For example, external access to the processor state without the participation or even the awareness of the executing process can readily be accomplished by including the necessary hardware – to perform the same functionality with software (e.g., interrupt routines which gather and output, or input and disseminate, state information) is necessarily very much slower.

Another major characteristic is flexibility, which in this context means changeability. The physical manifestation of functionality as bits in memory, rather than in more random and mechanical forms such as hardwired gates, tends to make changes easier and faster. All software is bits in memory, but so too is much of contemporary hardware – through the use of read/write and read-only random access memories (we deplore the misnomers "RAM" and "ROM"), programmable logic arrays and programmable array logic, programmable logic sequencers, etc. [Cavlan 1979]. Furthermore, some non-memory physical manifestations are more flexible than others – for example, decoded ("one-hot") state machines are considerably more changeable than the more traditional encoded variety. This approach, together with appropriate algorithmic state machine design and documentation rules (such as those of [Winkle and Prosser 1980]) have allowed programmers with no previous hardware design background to successfully make changes to a large, sophisticated machine [Jensen 1978].

The most obvious cost issue is that the recurring (i.e., replication) cost of hardware is always higher than that of software. However, specific instances require more careful analysis. For example, the hardware cost of a configuration containing j general-purpose processing elements plus k all-hardware functional elements is not clearly related to an alternative software-intensive configuration having $l \leq j+k$ processing elements.

17.4. Hardware/software relationships in distributed computer systems

While hardware/software relationships are important in most computer systems, they are even more important in a class of machines we call "distributed computers". By a distributed computer we mean a multiplicity of processors which are integrated into one computer by a conceptually singular executive, but without any activity at the executive level of abstraction or below having to depend on a unique, special entity to enforce a consistent view of the activity state on the participants [Jensen 1980]. Distributed computers appear to offer potential advantages (e.g., robustness, modularity) under certain conditions, at the cost of higher computation and communication overheads. For such systems to be cost-effective despite these overheads, unconventional hardware/software relationships which recognize executive control as a *system* rather than a software issue are important. These relationships may be manifest in both the processors and the processor interconnection mechanism.

There are two general philosophies concerning the relationship of processor and system design. The first is that the system design should be independent of the processor design. This allows the system to be compatible with existing processors and software, while at the same time permitting it to take advantage of future advances in processor technology. An additional benefit is that special-purpose (e.g., signal) processors may be accomodated without demanding that they adhere to system-dependent design constraints. On the other hand, it can be argued that the processor design should reflect the system design, because doing so can considerably improve system performance and cost-effectiveness. This is especially true for distributed computers, which are based on decentralization of control, while the current processor architectures were designed with centralized executive control in mind. Very little is known about the potential implications of decentralized executive control on processor architecture and implementation, but our research has lead us to believe that the areas most seriously impacted include: message handing; decentralized synchronization; external access to processor state; and probabilistic computations.

The commercial maturity of processor interconnection mechanisms is much less than that of processors: a smaller product base, and thus less to be compatible with; a lower sales volume, and thus less production economy of scale; and less history and thus less design inertia. These factors all reduce the barriers to be overcome when wanting to reflect the needs of distributed computers in the hardware/software relationships of processor interconnection structures. More is known in these relationships than in the processor case. To illustrate these points we will present some concrete examples which demonstrate the impacts of low level hardware design decisions on higher levels (including the software) of a computer system. They are selected from the context of bus-structured distributed systems, but corresponding cases are found in other multiple-processor configurations as well.

17.4.1. Bus bandwidth

The bandwidth of a bus in a computer system is rarely considered to have a significant effect on the higher levels of the system. However, under some circumstances bus bandwidth can affect the size and complexity of certain software structures. For example, forward error correction, or even redundant transmissions, may supplant more complex acknowledgement schemes (especially for broadcasts).

Higher bandwidth may also improve software modularity. For example, certain software partitioning approaches (e.g., Parnas' information hiding and abstract interfaces [Parnas 1977]) have been shown to improve software modularity. However, software in distributed systems is almost invariably partitioned across processor boundaries solely according to minimum communication bandwidth, and this criterion is generally not optimal for modularity.

Higher bandwidth may facilitate decentralized control, which requires considerable communication among the controllers. In a decentralized executive, much interprocess communication becomes interprocessor communication, so bus bandwidth could easily limit control functionality and performance.

17.4.2. Bus medium

It is frequently assumed that the bus medium does not have an impact on higher levels in a system. Different media, notably wire and optical fibers, have different characteristics. Therefore, the protocols used to communicate over a bus should be chosen to be either independent of the medium or optimal for a particular medium. It is not the case that a protocol which is optimized for a particular medium will perform equally well with another; furthermore, ignoring the medium when designing the protocol is likely to produce sub-optimal results for all media. One of the most distinctive characteristics of different bus media is the manifestation of errors. Wire incurs mostly poorly-characterized burst errors, due primarily to environmental electromagnetic noise radiated onto the wire, and propagated along to multiple (frequently all) devices on the bus. On the other hand, optical fiber tends to experience well-characterized, single-bit errors due to electronic (e.g., thermal) noise independently in each device receiver.

This difference impacts a number of higher level functions, including error detection, error correction, negative acknowledgment resolution, and I/O buffer managment.

The transmission error detection mechanism chosen for a fiber optics bus might be better matched to the errors which occur than that chosen for a wire bus, because of the difference in a priori knowledge about the errors. Transmission errors over fiber optics are more amenable to forward error correction than those over wire, since they are single-bit rather than bursts. However, if the bus propagation delay is short and the error rate is low (as is typical except on satellite radio buses), the bandwidth consumed by forward error correction bits may exceed that of acknowledgements and occasional retransmissions. Furthermore, the burst errors on wire suggest negative acknowledgements which call for retransmission of everything after word i, while the single-bit errors of fiber optics may permit retransmission of word i alone (provided that the bus turnaround time is low enough). The managment of I/O buffers may also be affected; replacing everything in the destination buffer from word i on (in which case the transmission length may change) may be either more or less complicated than replacing only word i; only the retransmitted part of a negatively acknowledged transmission needs to be retained in the source buffer until it is positively acknowledged, so retransmitting word i alone may release space sooner, especially if acknowledgements are deferred.

17.4.3. Broadcasts

The decision whether or not to support bus broadcasts can significantly affect higher levels of the system. We define a "broadcast" as a transmission for which the source does not know a priori that there is a single destination (i.e., their number and perhaps identities are unknown to it). This definition takes into account that unless the source knows the transmission will have only one destination, the protocol must accomodate the possibility of more than one.

A broadcast provides a lower variance of transmission arrival time over separate single-destination transmissions, and this may permit tighter real-time synchronization of the communicating entities. However, positive and negative acknowledgements which are explicit (i.e., signaled with a transmission) are difficult and expensive (and thus not frequently used) in most broadcast cases, consequently lowering the robustness of the protocol.

A software-simulated broadcast requires multiple single-destination transmissions – these must be to all possible destinations if the source is not to know which destinations are currently implemented and operational. This results not only in higher delay and variance of delay, but probably greater robustness if explicit acknowledgements are used. If broadcast is the only form of bus transmission, a software-simulated single-destination transmission requires that all destinations process the transmission to determine which one of them it is intended for. This may cause suspension of other processing in all destinations, subsequent transmissions to be missed because the destinations are busy, and consequently system performance degradation.

17.4.4. Acknowledgment deferral

Another low-level protocol decision that can impact higher levels of a distributed system is the question of whether or not to permit the deferral of acknowledgements. Acknowledgements may either immediately follow the acknowledged transmission, or be deferred to a later time. Deferral allows reduced variance of transmission arrival time (and thus perhaps tighter real-time synchronization), together with the increased robustness of acknowledgements (not normally available with broadcasts). However, deferral requires additional output buffer space to hold the transmissions which have been sent but not yet acknowledged. Furthermore, if communication is synchronous (in the sense that a sending entity stops and waits for an acknowledgement or reponse to its message) deferral results in longer suspension of the entity. This in turn may result in reduced performance, depending on the communication level involved.

17.4.5. Transmission addressing

The determination of which entity or entities should receive a transmission is based on implicit addressing through context (either local to each destination or in a global fashion), or explicit addressing. Normally, only the latter is provided (except perhaps for acknowledgments) — simulating implicit addressing requires real or simulated broadcasts (as discussed earlier) which must be processed by all destinations.

Transmissions may be explicitly addressed by their destination, source, or own ID — each has advantages, principally with respect to where information has to be changed in the event of reconfiguration for load sharing, failure, or functionality (e.g., using destination addressing, the source may change in number and identity transparently to the destination(s)). Source and transmission ID addressing are forms of broadcasts, so to simulate them using destination ID's (which is the usual facility supplied) requires simulation of broadcasts. Destination ID addressing may be either single-destination or broadcast — to simulate it given either of the others requires that all destinations process every transmission to determine which one(s) it is intended for.

Transmissions may be addressed to either physical entities (e.g., processors), or logical entities (e.g., processes or services) regardless of their physical bindings — inevitably, logical addressing is desired by the software, but only physical addressing is provided by the hardware. One way to simulate logical addressing is to maintain identical copies of binding tables in each processor. Then supporting dynamic binding (e.g., failure reconfiguration) involves a consistency problem akin to distributed data base concurrency control or dynamic routing in a packet-switching subnet. Alternatively, the software must perform a real (or simulated) broadcast of each message which every destination processor must examine to match the logical address against its own.

17.4.6. Communication support

There are varying degrees to which the hardware in a system can provide support for interprocessor communication. The hardware can provide no assistance — communication is one word at a time via programmed I/O instructions. In this case there is maximum software involvement, minimum hardware involvement, and no concurrency of communication and computation. As an alternative, the hardware can provide I/O channels, in which case the software can initialize an input or output buffer and then resume computation. However, unless the hardware provides chaining, the software may have to become involved with resetting buffer addresses, word counts, interrupt controls, etc. for each input and output communication. This type of involvement may require that the programmer have detailed knowledge of timing and other hardware details. The hardware may instead provide for Direct Memory Access (DMA), which is similar to having I/O channels, with the added advantage that a device other than the processor (in particular, a bus interface unit) can initialize buffers and initiate transfers. This has the added benefit of moving many of the details of operation from the software to the communication mechanism. It is also possible for the hardware to support both DMA and I/O buffer structures. For example, FIFO queues (in the processor's memory wherever the software desires) of pointers to incoming or outgoing messages, with suitable support for priorities, concurrent reading and writing, over/underflow protection, etc.. This type of support allows the software to set policies while relegating tactics to the hardware.

17.4.7. Bit/word/transmission synchronization

In a distributed system, transmissions normally contain "synchronization" signals for bit detection, word type recognition (e.g., control vs. data), and transmission type recognition (e.g., message vs. acknowledgement).

When synchronization, especially on a transmission basis, is static (i.e., established at discrete intervals) the potential for errors may limit transmission length (e.g., to 256 data words in HXDP). This may be inconvenient (or worse) to the software unless the hardware provides automatic packetizing, which involves additional delay (e.g., allocating the bus, adding headers, sending acknowledgements, etc.).

When the synchronization signal is selected to be something which would otherwise be an error (e.g., the modulation violation used in MIL-STD-1553 and HXDP), context must be used to determine which it is (e.g., a sync at the beginning of a transmission, but an error during a transmission). The erroneous occurrence of sync signals which are context-independent (e.g., the HDLC/SDLC "flag") can result in higher level protocol errors. Synchronization may also consume significant bus bandwidth — especially on a word basis (e.g., three bits per 16-bit word in MIL-STD-1553, a 19% overhead), but also on a transmission basis (e.g., a long preamble for a phase-locked loop).

17.5. Conclusion

The desireability of increased synergism between the hardware and software of computer systems has become a cliche, but unfortunately without being significantly reflected in practice. One of the principle aspects of our research in distributed computer systems has been to actually apply these arguments in the implementations and explore their ramifications. The examples herein were largely derived from that experience.

Acknowledgement

I am grateful to J. Duane Northcutt for his assistance preparing this paper.

Chapter 18. The National Software Works (NSW)

18.1. Introduction

The aim of the National Software Works (NSW) was to design and implement a network operating system which supports the software development process by means of providing access to a variety of tools [Geller 77]. Two classes of tools are made available to users through NSW:

- Management tools for monitoring and controlling software development project activities
- Software production aids for programmers involved in software development projects

While a variety of tools of the above kind, like editors, file systems, high level language processors, software specification and documentation systems, debuggers, simulators, emulators etc. are in use nowadays, efficient use of these aids by a majority of software developers has not yet been achieved because of various obstacles:

- not all the tools needed to efficiently improve the software development are usually available at the computersystem to be used
- interactive access to tools is not always possible, i.e. tools have to be operated in batch mode
- the operational characteristics of many tools are poor
- the user interface is not adequate or requires high skills
- different tools for the same purpose behave differently and are incompatible with respect to input and output
- tools for different tasks do not fit together
- tools accessible via resource sharing computer networks require different login procedures at different hosts and are using incompatible file systems
- access control, accounting and auditing features vary from host to host

The approach taken by NSW is to integrate tools being available in a resource sharing computer network into a *unified tool kit* under a *single monitor* with a *single file system* and make all tools uniformly accessible to programmers and project managers, respectively.

Basically there are two extremes in which a monitor, i.e. a network operating system (NOS), could provide access to distributed resources in a computer network: Either the monitor leaves all aspects of distribution visible to the user, in which case he has to assert control over the selection of resources needed to service his requests, or distribution is completely invisible and the user thus unaware of the network operations being performed on his behalf (transparency of system operation). In contrast to network operating systems like RSEXEC [Forsdick 78] NSW masks most of the details of network operation in order to ease the user's ability to combine the use of different hosts.

NSW was not designed to be a general purpose computer utility. As a consequence the set of resources which the tool kit does represent is limited, i.e. confined to incorporate only those programs which are added to the set of tools by the NSW system administration.

This very nature of the system services envisaged asks for a logically centralized administration of resources contributing to NSW operation, resulting in a NOS-concept, which does not allow for complete local autonomy of host computers w.r.t. allocation of local resources, as for instance RSEXEC does. In NSW it is the NOS which solely maintains state information concerning all of the distributed resources dedicated to the support of tool usage.

As for the implementation strategy, it was chosen to base NSW on existing local operating system functions and to include all operations not provided by available base operating systems, but required for tool administration and operation, in the software that implements the NOS. This approach allows especially in the case of different base hardware to take advantage of the large investment in proven system and application level software, though by building all software from scratch undoubtfully a better match of basic functions to the needs of NSW might have been achieved.

NSW was designed and implemented as a joint effort of Bolt, Beranek and Newman, Inc., Massachusetts Computer Associates, MIT, SRI International and UCLA, supported by the Advanced Research Project Agency of the Department of Defense and monitored by the Rome Air Development Center. Target system for the first NSW implementation was the Arpanet.

18.2. System Architecture

The design of an appropriate system architecture for NSW was confronted with two basic problems [Millstein 77]:

- a methodology was to be developed which allowed to excise existing tools from their current environment and to interface them with a NOS providing unified access to these tools

- the NOS itself and a corresponding global file system had to be constructed to integrate the tools on different hosts into a unified tool kit and to provide for global access control, accounting and auditing mechanisms.

The implementation strategy chosen caused the following design requirements:

- the modifications to existing operating systems of hosts to be integrated into NSW had to be restricted to a minimum, i.e. the NOS concept envisaged must not depend on rewriting the basic part of any operating system. Modifications of host operating systems should be restricted to adding priviledged (non-user) code

- modifications to existing tools had to be minimized, i.e. were to be small scale and contained

- solutions allowing for easy integration of existing tools must not inhibit an easy construction and installation of new tools

To cope with these requirements, NSW was conceived as a distributed system in a sense, that its components may be viewed as distributed processes cooperating to provide NSW services. These processes run on different host computers and are coordinated by the NSW monitor, which at least conceptually may be distributed as well, though the first implementation of NSW on Arpanet provides only for a monitor running on one Arpanet host.

According to the definition used in this book, a system is called a *distributed* system if and only if it applies distributed control, independent of its physical characteristics. Since the concept of NSW is based on distributed control, though its current implementational status is not, we will consider NSW as a distributed system, because it is mainly the conceptual issues we are going to discuss in the following.

The concept of NSW is not tailored to the specific requirements of a particular target system to be used as an implementation environment. As a consequence with respect to component intercommunication NSW does not rely on existing higher level communication protocols as they are already available, e.g. in Arpanet, for file transfer and communication. Instead, NSW defines its specific inter process communication protocol for inter component communication, called MSG [Thomas 76b]. MSG establishes the type of interprocess communication needed for NSW in such a way, that a variety of different computer networks may be used as target systems for implementation.

The system component providing to the user a uniform mode of access to NSW tools is the socalled Front End [Andrews 76]. One of its elementary functions is to interface various types of interactive terminals to the system via a virtual terminal protocol which causes, that all these terminals look alike to the other NSW components with respect to their communication characteristics and control functions. Triggering of local host functions by means of special control characters are intercepted before they affect the local operating system. Front End introduces a standard set of control functions to control tool operation and insulates the user of the peculiarities of different host operating systems.

All requests for NSW-specific resources (like e.g. file access) issued by tools operating on different computers must be taken care of by the NSW monitor, which is responsible for access control, accounting and auditing. As a result, no tool may request any resource from the local host operating system directly; its requests are intercepted by a NSW component called Foreman [Schantz 77] and referred to the NSW monitor via MSG. In addition, the Foreman has to provide the tool with a link to the user via MSG to the Front End. This interception of any tool's operating system calls for resource allocation/deallocation and intercommunication with other NSW components has to be accomplished by the Foreman without modification being made to local operating systems.

Another obstacle NSW is faced with is the possible heterogenity of the underlying computer network and thus the incompatibility of tool outputs and inputs. The combined use of several tools may require the output of one tool to be used as input for another tool, involving the transfer of files between different hosts. The NSW component being responsible for translation of data representations, reformatting and file movement is called the File Package [Muntz 76]

As mentioned above, the NSW components are conceptually processes which are distributed over the set of hosts constituting the target network on which NSW is implemented. Each participating host allowing for user access to NSW has a Front End, each tool bearing host has a Foreman, each host providing for NSW file storage has a File Package, and to allow for NSW component intercommunication, each host in NSW has a MSG-server process. The number of incarnations of a NSW-component at a single host, i.e. the number of processes representing executing NSW-components, may vary, e.g. a Foreman process is attached to each active tool, a Front End process to each active user. Though the functional specifications of NSW components are fixed, implementations may vary considerably for different types of host systems.

NSW component cooperation and allocation of NSW specific resources (primarily files) is controlled by the NSW monitor, the NOS of NSW, which is called the Works Manager [Millstein 77].

Works Manager is a network operating system with an associated file system designed to satisfy the following external requirements:

- support of large scale operations with respect to the number of concurrent users. As many as one thousand concurrent users are considered, resulting e.g. in a large amount of storage space to be managed for administrative purpose, like for catalogues of files, control blocks, etc.

- if large scale operation is to be supported, system failures are likely to be catastrophic and cause high costs. This asks for a fault tolerant behaviour of the Works Manager, i.e. component failures may only result in performance degradation and affect only a limited number of users.

- since NSW is designed to be implemented on existing host computers and base operating systems no special hardware to support reliability can be used.

Reliability and large scale operation ask for distributed control, i.e. distribution of the Works Manager and its associated data bases for cataloguing files, recording access rights, accounting, etc. However, since "logical unity" of the NSW monitor is required, i.e. each instance of the Works Manager realized as a seperate process has to maintain a *consistent view* of the global system state w.r.t. current resource allocation, tool operation, access rights, accounting, etc., the problem of *maintaining multiple copy data bases* comes up (c.f. Chapter 13).

To illustrate this problem in more detail let's assume that a user inserts a new file produced by one of the tools into the distributed file system controlled by the Works Manager. If the file system is partially replicated, then the Works Manager has to guarantee consistency of copies, if any, of the file to assure, that regardless of the particular file copy used a tool receives the correct input. To find the location of a copy of the file the catalogue of the file system has to be consulted. The catalogue may be regarded as part of the data base reflecting the system state. If we ask for a redundant implementation of the Works Manager and its associated data base because of reliablity and performance reasons, it is required that in our example the insertion of a new file results in a consistent update of all copies of the file system catalogue, i.e. the Works Manager processes have to apply a multiple copy update protocol for fully redundant data in order to insert the new catalogue entry. (Chapter 13)

(Note: The initial implementation of the Works Manager and NSW File System required, that both reside on a single host. The release of a prototype form of a *distributed* Works Manager and NSW File System was originally scheduled for end of 1978).

18.3. NSW components

The preceeding chapter gave an overview of the design requirements as being set by the aims of NSW and introduced the basic NSW architecture, its components and their interactions. These components will now be examined further with respect to their functions, operations and structure.

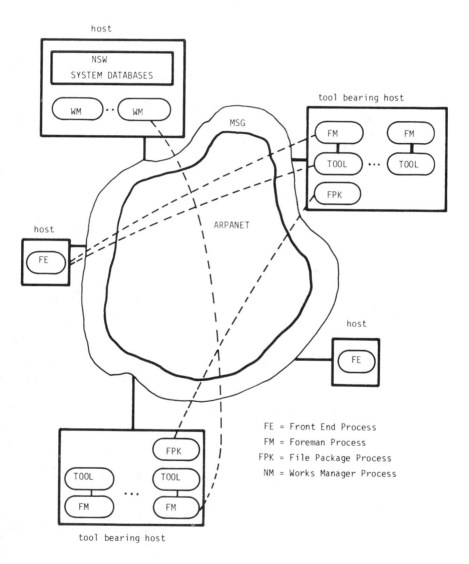

Figure 18-1: NSW components and their interaction.

18.3.1. MSG: The NSW interprocess communication facility

MSG may be regarded as the glue holding together all of the other NSW components [Thomas 76]. It is the responsibility of this component to provide for communication between the various NSW-system processes implementing Front End, Foreman, File Package and Works Manager and to allocate and activate processes of an appropriate class like File Package and Works Manager to support a specific user initiated tool operation.

Six types of communication can be identified (figure 18-1):

- Front End – Works Manager
- tool/Foreman – Works Manager
- Works Manager – File Package
- Front End – tool/Foreman
- tool/Foreman – tool/Foreman
- File Package – File Package

Other possible combinations like Front End-File Package and File Package-tool/Foreman do not represent communication paths in NSW.   (tool/Foreman indicates interception of all tool communication requests by the associated Foreman)

The above mentioned communication types show different characteristics with respect to frequency of communication, amount of information, i.e. length of messages to be transmitted, and kind of connection required.

- Front End – Works Manager

This type of communication is necessary to service user requests for resources, like e.g. run a tool, copy an existing file, delete a file, etc. and to deliver the Works Manager responses to these requests to the Front End. Requests are short (message lengths < 1000 bits) and infrequent (a few per hour). Request processing time will in general be short (order of milliseconds). Since all instances of the Works Manager (i.e. the set of distributed processes implementing the Works Manager) share a common data base, successive requests on behalf of the user need not necessarily be processed by the same Works Manager process; they can be considered as unrelated. Thus maintaining a connection (logical communication channel) for a specific pair of Front End-Works Manager processes is not necessary. Communication of this kind can be regarded as a sequence of unrelated elements, each element representing a request, followed by a brief delay (caused by processing the request) followed by a response.

- tool/Foreman – Works Manager

This type of communication follows exactly the same pattern as the previous one (i.e. its characteristics are the same). Its purpose is to transfer requests for resource allocation (on behalf of a user) from a tool to the Works Manager (example: open a file, deliver a file, create an auxiliary tool process) and to transmit the Works Manager's responses. Message length for both request and response will be < 1000 bit, request processing time is in the order of milliseconds, request inter arrival time is measurable in minutes (i.e. requests are more frequent than Front End requests).

- Works Manager – File Package

The nature of communication is similar to the above: the Works Manager forwards a request to the File Package in order to service a Front End or tool request, e.g. in case where a tool asks to open a file and provide a copy of this file at the tool's host. To transmit a copy of a file may last for up to a couple of minutes (as in the Arpanet) and thus, request processing time will be of that order of magnitude. Requests and responses result in short messages. Again the communication pattern can be characterized by a sequence of unrelated elements, each element consisting of short requests, short processing delay and short response.

- Front End-tool/Foreman

In this case Front End forwards user commands to the tool and the tool returns responses. The nature of this type of interaction turns out to be different to the above: Consecutive requests (i.e. commands) are related and must be serviced by the same tool. Service time for commands may be greater than the time passing between the response to a command and the submission of the next command. The frequency of user commands may be higher than the frequency of requests in the above types of communication. Furthermore the duration of interaction between Front End and Foreman, determined by the length of that part of a session during which a user is working with the same tool, may be very long (minutes to hours). Thus Front End-tool/Foreman communication may vary from infrequent, short request patterns to frequent, long transmissions with long durations of particular interactions.

- tool/Foreman – tool/Foreman

This is a relatively infrequent type of communication, needed for debugging tools for NSW and for multi-process tools (currently in the stage of being implemented; c.f. 18.5). Patterns of communication are expected to be analogous to Front End-tool/Foreman communication.

- File Package – File Package

The bulk of this communication will consist of files being transmitted, while a small fraction of transmission will consist of infrequent, short messages providing simple file descriptions (e.g. length and coding) to a destination File Package process. The communication pattern is thus characterized by infrequent transmissions of many bits.

Summarizing the characteristics of the above six types of communication results in three different communication patterns.

Pattern 1:

- Infrequent, short elements of interaction, the relation of successive elements being of no concern, characterizing the communication types:
                Front End – Works Manager
                tool/Foreman – Works Manager
                Works Manager – File Package

Pattern 2:

- Possibly frequent, longer elements of interaction with relationship between elements, characterizing the communication types:
                Front End – tool/Foreman
                tool/Foreman – tool/Foreman

Pattern 3:

> * Infrequent, very long elements of interaction characterizing the communication:
> File Package – File Package

These communication patterns determine an abstract model of the kind of interprocess protocol needed for NSW.

MSG supports these patterns of communication by providing two different *modes of process addressing*:

- generic addressing
- specific addressing

and three different *modes of communication*:

- messages
- logical connection
- alarms

However, MSG does not impose any restrictions on how processes use these communication modes; in particular MSG does not interpret messages, alarms or communications via connections. MSG behaves transparent w.r.t. to information transfer between processes using the MSG facilities.

Generic addressing is used to specify a functional *process class* in cases, where processes have not communicated before or where the details of past communications are irrelevant, it is restricted to the message mode of communication. A *generic address* causes MSG to select a destination process, which belongs to the specified generic class and which is willing to receive a generically addressed message. If necessary, MSG may create such a process. Generic addressing is always used to initiate pattern 1 communication.

In contrast, a *specific address* is always referring to exactly one process and may be used with all three communication patterns. Specific addressing requires that the processes which want to communicate are familiar with each other, i.e. have communicated before, either directly or through intermediary processes.

The *message mode* is the most common mode of communication among NSW processes and is used for pattern 1 and some pattern 2 communications.

The *connection mode* of communication is provided by MSG mainly to support pattern 3 and some pattern 2 communication (e.g. file transfer and terminal-like communication between Front End and tool/Foreman.

The *alarm mode* of communication is supported by MSG to allow for one process to alert another process in the case of the occurence of a specific event. The delivery of an alarm to a process is independent of any message flow to this process, i.e. messages queued for delivery do not block the delivery of an alarm. The amount of information conveyed by an alarm is restricted to a short alarm code, thus allowing for delivery of alarms even in the case of a shortage of communication and storage resources. The difference w.r.t. the concept of interrupts is mainly, that the delivery of an alarm to a process does not necessarily force a context switch.

The three modes of communication follow the same basic pattern:

- If a process wants to send a message or an alarm or to open a connection via MSG, it specifies the destination adress and a signal which MSG can use to indicate, that the respective operation has been performed

- Another process which matches the destination address performs a complementary action with respect to the type of communication initiated by the first process, i.e. indicates that it is ready to receive a message or to open a connection. It also specifies a signal which MSG can use to indicate completion of the operation

- MSG performs the communication operation and signals completion to source and destination process. In addition, MSG provides the specific address of the sending process to the receiving process

In order to make a process *addressable* within MSG, this process must be identified by a unique MSG *process* name of the form

<process name> :: = <host incarnation name> <generic designator> <specific designator>

where

<host incarnation name> :: = <host designator> <incarnation designator>

uniquely designates the host computer on which the process is running and the particular period of continuous NSW service provided by this host. The generic designator characterizes a process in terms of its functional relationship to other processes (i.e. specifies which functions a process provides). The specific designator uniquely identifies a process within a specific host. To address a process in specific address mode the process name is used, while a generic address is of the form:

<generic address> :: = <host designator> <generic designator>|<generic designator>

This generic addressing optionally allows to specify the host where the process to be selected is to reside. A generic designator e.g. may be used to specify processes providing Works Manager functions.

MSG does not automatically guarantee, that messages will be delivered to a destination process in the same order as they are sent. However, *sequencing* can be specified for each individual message as an option by the sending process. In this case a sequenced message from process A to process B will be only delivered after all previous sequenced messages from A to B have been delivered. Sequenced messages may be intermixed with non sequenced messages. To enable a receiving process in the case of an alarm to distinguish messages sent before the alarm from those sent afterwards the concept of *stream marking* is introduced: MSG guarantees that a message M carrying a stream marker, set by sending process A, will be only delivered to receiving process B after all messages preceeding M have been delivered to B and before any message sent by A after M was sent. Furthermore, MSG will notify the receiving process whenever it delivers a message carrying a stream marker. Synchronization of alarms and messages can thus be accomplished by placing a stream marker on the first message sent after the alarm.

MSG is implemented as a number of processes running concurrently on a number of different hosts and can be thought of as an extension of these hosts individual operating systems, providing a set of MSG specific system calls, i.e. a set of *communication primitives*, which can be used by other processes to establish and use interprocess communication.

The set of primitives is divided into two classes, differentiated by the meaning of the MSG reply to the primitive call: For one class the reply indicates that the primitive operation is complete, while for the other class the reply only indicates, that the call has been accepted by MSG. Only when a primitive operation of the latter class is eventually completed either successfully or not will MSG signal the initiating process using a signal specified in the primitive call. An uncompleted primitive operation is called a *pending event* and is described by

$$\langle pending\ event \rangle ::= \langle primitive \rangle \langle signal \rangle \langle disp \rangle \langle timer \rangle$$

where ⟨primitive⟩ is the operation to be performed, ⟨signal⟩ is the signal code to indicate the completed operation, ⟨disp⟩ is a pointer to a field in the process's memory where it will be indicated whether completion was successful or not, ⟨timer⟩ specifies when MSG can abort the operation.

To each process a set of pending events is associated by MSG. Primitive calls of the second class result in the addition of a pending event to the pending event set, a completed operation results in the deletion of the corresponding pending event.

Primitives creating pending events are:

(1) *SendSpecificMessage*: It causes a message, whose address has to be specified, to be transmitted to a process whose specific address is given. In addition, a signal, a return code field, a timeout interval and the type of handling (i.e. ordinary, sequenced or stream marked) have to be specified using additional parameters.

(2) *SendGenericMessage*: This primitive is like the above one, except that a generic address is specified instead of the name of a receiving process. Parameters have to be specified as in (1) except that sequencing or stream marking is not allowed. An additional parameter is introduced, which allows to indicate whether an appropriate process is to be created as a destination process if none is available, or not.

(3) *ReceiveSpecificMessage*: This is the complementary primitive to (1), issued by receiving processes. Parameters to be specified include a pointer to a local memory area for message storage and storage of the name of the sending process; all other parameters as in (1). If a pair of processes issues compatible primitive calls (1) and (3) with matching parameters, message transmission in specific addressing mode takes place.

(4) *ReceiveGenericMessage*: This is the complementary primitive to (2). Parameters are specified as in (3), except that sequencing and stream marking is not allowed.

If a pair of processes issues compatible primitive calls (2) and (4) with matching parameters, message transmission in generic addressing mode takes place.

(5) *SendAlarm*: For sending an alarm to a destination process, the destination process name, the alarmcode, a signal and a returncode field address must be specified as parameters.

(6) *EnableAlarm*: This is the complementary primitive to (5). A field to receive the alarm code has to be specified and another field where to store the sending process name. Other parameters are as in (5).

If a pair of processes issues compatible primitives (5) and (6) and if the receiving process has indicated by means of primitive Accept-Alarms (see below) to be ready for accepting alarms, then an alarm is transmitted.

(7) *OpenConn*: This primitive is used if a connection from the calling process to a specified process is to be established. In addition, the connection type (full duplex, half duplex, simplex) and an connection identifier have to be specified. A connection between two processes is established, if compatible primitives (7) are issued by both processes.

(8) *CloseConn*: This is the inverse primitive to (7)

(9) *TerminationSignal*: This primitive is used to specify a signal upon the receipt of which the process issuing this primitive is to be terminated.

The set of *primitives* that do not create pending events provides for the following calls:

(1) *StopMe*: This is used to terminate the calling process

(2) *Rescind*: The signal specified as a parameter identifies a pending event that is to be removed from the set of pending events when this call is issued

(3) *AcceptAlarms*: This is used to switch a process' state from ready to accept alarms to not ready and vice versa

(4) *Resynch*: If MSG had been rejecting sequenced or stream marked messages to the process specified after a sequencing error, this primitive is used to resume sequencing or stream marking

(5) *WhoAmI*: This primitive returns the name of the executing process in a specified area

An interhost MSG protocol is needed to support the primitives provided to processes managed by MSG. However, to deal with the kind of information to be communicated at this level of abstraction (level 2 of the System Architecture Model, c.f. Chapter 2) and how this information is communicated in a given environment, like e.g. the Arpanet, is beyond the scope of this case study.

18.3.2. Front end: the NSW user interface

Front End is the NSW component that provides terminal access via a *coherent NSW user interface* to the tools and services of the Works Manager and thus makes available a broad spectrum of services on a computer local to the user [Andrews 76]. The Front End as the user's "intelligent" work place is designed to provide commonly used tools, user interface assistance to NSW tools and services, and background intelligent agents for auxiliary tasks. The major design goals were in particular to

- provide a responsive, consistent user interface
- reduce communication costs and tool bearing host overhead
- provide terminal independent user and tool interface
- allow for low cost user interface modification and experimentation
- accomodate various classes of tools

To meet these design goals a modular design of the Front End was chosen. The major components are shown in figure 18-2. They may be separated into three classes

- Modules, comprising all programs with which the user interacts during command specification and which communicate with the tool. These include the Virtual Terminal Protocol, the Command Language Interpreter and the Process Communication Interface

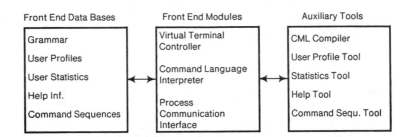

Front End Data Bases	Front End Modules	Auxiliary Tools
Grammar	Virtual Terminal Controller	CML Compiler
User Profiles		User Profile Tool
User Statistics	Command Language Interpreter	Statistics Tool
Help Inf.		Help Tool
Command Sequences	Process Communication Interface	Command Sequ. Tool

Figure 18-2: Front end components

- Databases and data structures associated with the user interface mechanism, like the grammar for driving the Command Language Interpreter, a user profile for adjusting user interaction characteristics, a help data base for supporting command specification, statistics on user interaction (for gathering data on command frequencies, error type frequencies, number of accesses to help facilities, system responsiveness, etc.), Command Meta Language (CML) source programs (specifying the user interface in a high level language called CML. When compiled, a Grammar that drives the Command Language Interpreter is obtained) and prespecified command sequences implementing high level commands.

- Auxiliary tools to allow the user or tool builder to create and evaluate the above data bases and data structures, like the CML-compiler, the user profile tool, help tool, statistics analysis programs and command sequence processor.

The Front End was designed to handle three classes of tools: nonintegrated, partially integrated and fully integrated tools.

Nonintegrated tools are simply handled by making the Front End transparent; in this case no services are provided to make the user interface more consistent. A more effective Front End can be provided if the characters that are input before a terminating character are buffered: local editing capability can be used to automatically terminate commands and their parameters with special sets of characters as required by the tool command language interpreter.

For *partially integrated tools*, the tool installer can write a user interface description in CML to take advantage of Front End services, such as help features, consistent intracommand editing characters and the user profile. The result of a successful parse of a command is a string in the command language required by the tool. Strings returning from the tool (e.g. error messages) are parsed and possibly converted or passed on to the user.

Fully integrated tools use all of the Front End services. The tool builder has to create a set of primitives for the information processing functions of the tool, a communication interface, a CML description of the user interface and a help data base. He need not be concerned with terminal control, command interpreter, providing help or user profile services. Modifications of the user interface to the tool require merely a few edits in the CML source file and recompilation of the grammar.

18.3.3. Foreman: providing the tool execution environment

The Foreman provides as the *local-to-the-tool component* of NSW a tool process (i.e. dynamic instance of a tool) with its NSW *execution environment* [Schantz 77].

Every tool process runs under the control of a Foreman; the Foreman has the responsibility for creating a tool process and subsequently removing it. In addition, the Foreman provides support for NSW resource utilization accounting.

General design aspects of the Foreman are:

- each tool must be prevented from interfering with other tools and other processes running on the same host operating system

- to achieve as much independence of the structure of any local operating system as possible, the concept of the Foreman has to be designed such, that it avoids to rely on any particular features of any system

To provide the execution environment of a tool, the Foreman has two well defined interfaces:

- an *interface between the NSW components* (e.g. Front End and Works Manager) *and the Foreman*, which is organized around the MSG message passing capability and used by the Front End and Works Manager to instruct the Foreman about handling the tool process while the Foreman uses this interface to request Front End and Works Manager services on behalf of the tool process

- an *interface between the tool process and the Foreman*, which is used to create an operating system like environment for the tool process. Through this interface the tool can invoke various functions produced by the NSW environment to augment the local operating system environment. Though this interface is well defined, it can take any of a number of different forms, depending on the implementers choice and the facilities of the host operating system. Possible types of Foreman/tool linkage include subroutine calls (as realized in the MULTICS system) and operating system calls (like SVC in IBM systems)

To illustrate the role of the Foreman in NSW, the following scenario of the beginning of a NSW session is used: Let us assume, that the user has a dedicated Front End process assigned to handle his terminal. This Front End process starts prompting the user for his login information. After the required information is accumulated, the Front End process sends these data to a Works Manager process using the generic addressing facility of MSG. The Works Manager process in turn verifies the login information and notes the full name of the Front End process which is then informed by a specifically addressed message from the Works Manager of the success or failure of the login. If the login was successful, the Front End process gathers the name of the tool the user wants to run together with all other pertinent information and sends a tool request generically to any Works Manager process. The receiving Works Manager process verifies, if the user is authorized to use the tool, and if so, retrieves the *tool descriptor* from an internal Works Manager data base. The Works Manager now sends a generic message containing the tool information and the MSG name of the Front End process to a Foreman process on the host which has been selected to run the tool process.

The Foreman process selects a workspace for the tool and establishes the tool process in this workspace. Addressing the Works Manager process specifically, the Foreman process returns the identification of the allocated workspace together with the name of the tool process which has been created; this name may be different from the Foreman process name, if the tool is not encapsulated (see below). The Works Manager process in turn sends a specifically addressed message to the user's Front End process, giving the MSG names of the tool/Foreman. Now Front End process and tool/Foreman can communicate directly using the connection mode of communication.

As the above scenario shows, the MSG facility is responsible for the allocation of Foreman processes via generic messages.   After initialization a Foreman is receptive via the ReceiveGeneric capability for Worksmanager messages commanding to initiate a new process tool. The Works Manager retrieves the host specific name for this tool from a static tool descriptor it maintains for each tool.

Prior to initiating the tool, the Foreman selects a workspace in which to run the tool. The set of workspaces at a tool bearing host is managed by the set of Foreman processes on this host. While the utilization of a workspace is completely left to the Foreman, it is the task of the Works Manager to initiate movement of files into and out of this workspace. Thus the Works Manager has to be informed by the Foreman, to which workspace a tool has been assigned.

The Works Manager keeps lists of all workspaces with currently running tools; the information stored in these lists can help a Foreman to *recover from a system crash* without losing user files left in workspaces. The tool descriptor provided by the Works Manager includes information on the nature of the tool, i.e. if the tool is a fully integrated (new) tool, a non integrated (old) tool or something in between.

A fully integrated tool will usually request NSW files directly and set up its own communication path to other components, like a Front End process; such a tool is completely aware of its operating environment. In contrast a nonintegrated tool can be *"encapsulated"* by the Foreman such, that it is unaware of its operating environment.

The tool descriptor enables the Foreman to adjust itself to provide the correct environment for the tool to be run.

Tool termination may be accomplished in two ways: either directly by the tool itself or indirectly by an explicit NSW command from the user.

Direct termination is achieved by using the primitive HALTME provided by the Foreman. A parameter indicates the type of file processing to be done by the Foreman: no file processing, saving of user specified files or automatic saving of the latest copies of modified files. Finally when all peripheral operations by the Foreman are completed and after having performed house keeping operations like closing open connections, the Foreman terminates itself using the MSG primitive StopMe.

Indirect termination is initiated by the Foreman after having received a so called FMENDTOOL message either from the Frontend or from the Worksmanager. After the tool is halted, the Foreman proceeds with the termination sequence as in the previous case.

To allow for a close *monitoring of tool execution* in terms of resource utilization and progress through its algorithm, an externally invocable Foreman function is provided for *probing the current tool execution* status. Status probing may be requested by the Works Manager or a designated Front End process. This Foreman function is invocable via an alarm (c.f. MSG) with a special alarm code being set by the requestor.

The *NSW tool execution environment* is characterized by the NSW specific facilities for *inter component communication, dynamic creation of NSW entities* (both provided by MSG) and *maintaining the NSW file system*. These facilities are in addition to similar features already available through local host operating systems which may be used in parallel if no conflict with NSW services occurs.

Tools are given access to the NSW facilities by a set of primitive operations provided by the Foreman and other NSW components. The NSW file system provides two distinct file spaces, where items can be idependently manipulated: the *sharable NSW global file space* and the *nonsharable temporary workspace* (local file space). Tools may request *copies of global files* to be placed in the *local file space* where they can be manipulated by the tool and subsequently be added to the global file catalogue upon request of the tool. Global file space operations are subject to the NSW access control mechanisms.

Global files have *unique global names* and are accessable only via the Works Manager. Files existing in the local file space can only be referenced by the tool operating in that workspace and the names of these files need not be unique in the NSW file system. To specify the relationships between NSW file names and the names of files (in terms of a local operating system) which represent local copies of NSW files a Foreman process is required to maintain a *local name dictionary*, which is usually kept as an identifiable file on the local file system.

Local files that have been created or modified during a tool session may be delivered to the global file system if they need to be permanently saved. However, this is connected with a considerable overhead caused by name conflict resolution, copying and associated synchronization and should thus be restricted to a minimum.

To keep track of subsequent modifications of copies of files in the local file space, *version numbers* are introduced. Version numbers are small integer numbers kept in a field added to the local file name. The Foreman allows a tool to specifiy version numbers when accessing files in local file space. The concept of version numbers automatically resolves local ambiguities of file names.

Associated with each file in the global NSW file space is a *semaphore-like variable*, which, when set by a tool via the Foreman on behalf of the user, warns other potential users that the file might be undergoing change. This semaphore is not a lock in a sense that it restricts the access of other users. A user can obtain an internally consistent copy of a file even if the semaphore is set, since in this case it is only a workspace copy of that file which is undergoing a change. Only in the case of a deletion request will a user be prevented from accessing a file with a semaphore set.

Tools may request that the semaphore be set when a copy is obtained from a NSW file. In this case the Works Manager presumes that the tool does not want access unless the semaphore can be set.

A tool is provided with three different sets of *file manipulation primitives*:

- primitives for *deleting, renaming and copying* files within the global name space (DELETEGLOBAL, RENAMEGLOBAL, COPYGLOBAL)
- primitives for *obtaining a local workspace copy* of a global file (GET) and depositing a local workspace file (PUT)
- primitives to *support local workspace file access* for deleting (DELETELOCAL), renaming (RENAMELOCAL), copying (COPYLOCAL), OPEN and CLOSE

Global primitives are implemented as *Works Manager procedures* which can be invoked by the Foreman, and so are the GET and PUT primitives, while the *primitives for local workspace file access* are implemented within the Foreman and supported by the local operating system.

As mentioned above one way of providing access to non integrated (old) tools via NSW is *encapsulation*. Encapsulation implies the automatic *trapping and translation* of local host operating system calls into NSW system calls.

It is the Foreman's responsibility to provide for trapping and translation. Encapsulation, allowing to use existing tools with little or no modification as NSW tools, is possible because of the similarity of the NSW system to conventional single host operating systems. In the case of a file access request encapsulation requires the Foreman to get control and translate the request into one which provides access to an NSW file. This is possible if the old tool is somehow capable of handling NSW *file name syntax*. Encapsulation cannot be discussed in terms of algorithms; it requires a detailed knowledge of the local host operating system primitive operations. Different host operating systems may require different approaches to encapsulation. Mechanisms are required, which allow the Foreman to gain control after the tool executes certain operating system primitives, but before the local operating system proceeds with the operations implementing the primitives. Especially tool initialization and termination, interactions with the file system and communication with the user will require special attention within the encapsulation component of the Foreman.

The characteristics of the communication between Front End and tool/Foreman have been described in a simplifying manner when discussing the types of communication to be provided by MSG (c.f. 18.3.1). It should be added, that the inter process communication between Front End and tool/Foreman actually requires the existence of two communication streams: one set of messages is destined for the Foreman while the other goes to the tool itself.

In the case where both tool and Foreman are integrated into one MSG process, it is the task of the Foreman to receive all incoming messages and to filter out those destined for the tool and pass them to the tool using local operating systems facilities. Alternatively if tool and Foreman are separate processes (w.r.t. MSG), it is the task of MSG to separate Foreman messages from those to the tool. In order to allow the Foreman in this case to limit the tool's use of the message passing facility, an extension to MSG is required, the description of which is beyond the scope of this case study.

18.3.4. File Package: the file handling facility for NSW

The NSW file system as a part of the tool environment is a means to make the output of one tool available as an input to another tool, regardless of the tool location and the kind of the host computer system [Muntz 76]. Thus the primary function of the File Package is the *creation of copies of* NSW *files* which are suitable as input to tools.

A secondary function of the File Package is to *import external files* into the NSW file system and vice versa and to take care of peripheral operations like reading and writing tapes, etc.

To understand the functional requirements to be met by the File Package, it is necessary to review the concepts of the NSW file system: The Worksmanager maintains a *catalogue of all files* in the NSW *global file space,* i.e. of all NSW files to which only the Worksmanager has direct access. From the logical point of view, a global NSW file is represented by an NSW name to which a list of *names of physical copies* of the file is associated. The NSW *name of a file* is syntactically uniform for the entire NSW system and is usually assigned by the user; the name of a physical file copy includes the complete network address which uniquely identifies the location of the copy within the NSW system.

Multiple physical copies of a global NSW file are logically indistinguishable, so it is of no concern to the user which copy of the file will actually be selected to fulfill his or his tool's request for access to an NSW file.

To create a new physical copy of a NSW file, which is the main function of the File Package, two instances of the File Package (File Package processes) will be involved, unless a local copy is already available at the host to which the new copy is to be assigned: a "*receiver*" File Package on the host desiring the copy and a "*donor*" File Package at the host providing the file to be copied. Of these two File Package processes involved, the "receiver" is responsible for driving the copy procedure and to create a copy with a structure, which is equivalent to the structure of the original.

The "receiver" has the right to select as the original any file from a given list of physical copies of a global NSW file. Three different situations may arise:

- A *local copy* is available at the receiver's host

- A *family copy* may be obtained, i.e. there is an original available on a foreign host supporting the local file formats (the foreign host is compatible to the local host and thus belongs to the same host "family")

- There is only an original available on a foreign host which does not support local file formats; a *translation of file formats* is required (*forced translation*)

Availability of a local copy allows for the most efficient way of copying and only one File Package process is involved in this case; the copy procedure can be implemented entirely within the local operating system.

In the case of a family copy to be obtained, the copy operation consists in encoding the source file in serial fashion and subsequently reproducing an indistinguishable file copy. This is equivalent to "saving" a file on e.g. magnetic tape, and then "restoring" it, where the "save" procedure is exactly the operation to be performed by the donor while the "restore" procedure is executed by the receiver. Within each host family a *unique "save" /"restore" encoding* has to be maintained.

In the case of incompatibility w.r.t. to file formats and data representations translation of the "donor" file has to be forced to reproduce an identical logical structure of the file copy. The approach taken in the NSW-system to provide for file translation is to introduce a standard *"intermediate language" (IL) for file encoding*: the "donor" uses IL to encode the original and the "receiver" subsequently decodes and stores the file. The specification of the intermediate language used by the File Package of NSW may be found in [Muntz 76].

Before a file copy operation can be initiated by the participating File Package processes, the "donor" may be requested by the receiver" to analyse the existing file and provide information about its physical structure. This will aid hosts requiring pre-allocation of file space and will help to insure that the created copy will be physically acceptable to the tool which requested the file (e.g. a host may see a file as sequences of logically grouped records or as a stream of bytes with no logical structure being overlaid).

Finally the File Package has to provide for a delete function to achieve the inverse of a copy operation, i.e. to delete an NSW file copy by removing the physical copy name from the hosts file catalogue.

The physical copy name of an NSW file copy has to be specified as an argument for each of the above three File Package functions. Elements of the physical copy name have to provide the name of the host, where the copy resides, the name of the directory of that host in which the local file name is recorded, the password needed to access the directory, the host dependent (local) name of the copy, information on the host dependent physical structure and information on the logical structure. As for the latter, NSW differentiates between text files, formatted text files (overprints and line-skips may be present) and binary files, consisting of sequences of n-bit bytes with all 2^n bit patterns allowed.

As indicated above the copy function of the File Package includes *file movement (file transfer)* which may be divided into three classes:

- *Importation* of files from outside the NSW system, which will be a local operation if NSW controlled file space is available locally
- *Exportation* of NSW files
- Movement of files within the NSW file space

Requests for file transfer are initiated via the Works Manager, the requestor being either a Foreman on behalf of a tool (movement within the NSW file space) or a user (importation/exportation).

The Works Manager invokes the File Package copy function using a SendGeneric message addressed to any File Package process at the same host as the requesting tool or user, specifying the following parameters:

- a list of physical copy names, giving the names of source file candidates
- the physical structure of the copy to be made

- the name of the file copy to be entered into the destination host's directory (used when exporting a file)

- a list of preferred and a list of unacceptable host families to be considered if forced translation is necessary

- the identification of a workspace at the receiving host to store an (additional) physical copy for exclusive use by tool.

NSW-controlled file space to receive the new copy need not be specified, because this file space will be selected by the receiving File Package. The "receiver" keeps track of local NSW-file spaces by means of a local "File Package Data Base".

The structure of the File Package can be thought of as consisting of three groups of modules:

- *Top level control*, comprising all modules for File Package initialization, reception of messages and alarms (via MSG) and interpretation of requests for File Package functions

- *Function controllers*, one controller being associated with each of the functions (copy, delete, analyze)

- MSG and local operating system *interface modules*

18.3.5. Works Manager: the NSW monitor

As indicated in the overall description of the NSW system architecture [Millstein 77], the Works Manager is the central (which does not necessarily mean centralized) component of NSW. It authenticates user interactions with NSW components, carries out executive commands and allocates NSW resources to users and tools (tools operating on behalf of users), the main resource of concern being the NSW file system.

The incarnation of a Worksmanager is a *server process*, which is created when a call is made by a Front End or Foreman process using the SendGeneric facility of MSG. No such server process remains continously alive; instead it only exists to service one requestor at a time and vanishes if the last request of a specific petitioner has been executed.

Worksmanager processes share a set of data structures (often called *Worksmanager Data Base*), the principle data structure being the *file catalogue*, which contains all long term data on all NSW files. Other data structures in the Works Manager's Data Base contain lists of rights, priviliges and responsibilities of users, a list of users currently logged in, a list of available and of currently running tools and other current data depicting the momentary status of NSW.

Since almost every Works Manager call results in some changes to be made to parts of the Works Manager's Data Base, access to the data base has to be interlock protected, i.e. the Works Manager processes have to be synchronized when updating the Works Manager's Data Base to provide *data base consistency*. It is the Works Manager's Data Base with its "hot" tables that gives the impression of continuity of service by the Works Manager as a logically centralized NSW component.

Works Manager functions are performed by a collection of separately callable procedures, each performing a specific function, i.e. each Works Manager call from either a Front End or Foreman results in a call on a specific procedure.

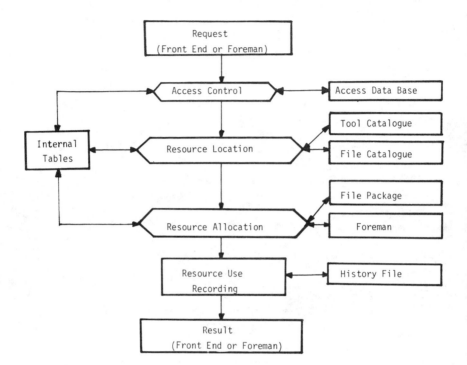

Figure 18-3: Processing of Works Manager call procedures, when a request is received from the user via the Front End, or from the Foreman acting on behalf of a tool.

A Works Manager procedure call is processed according to the flowchart given in figure 18-3.

First the *Access Data Base* is checked to determine the user's *access rights* (in both cases the request is associated with a specific user). Once the access rights are verified, the appropriate resource is located. The resource may either be an NSW file or a tool. The resource is then allocated to the user through the offices of a File Package or Foreman process. Before returning the results to the original caller, the History File is updated to reflect the resource use.

NSW provides a file system to its users which with its naming conventions, access control, protection mechanisms and primitives for manipulating, deleting and renaming files is similar to other "conventional" operating systems with the exception, that NSW *is not based on dedicated on-line storage devices* but instead uses facilities provided by host operating systems. However, the user is not required to have any knowledge of the host's individual file system used for NSW file storage. Instead he must adhere to a uniform *file system vocabulary* when referencing NSW files, regardless of what NSW component he is addressing. NSW owns on each host supporting NSW file storage (socalled Storage Hosts) one or more directories, organized to allow for maximum protection available.

As a result of the above concept, the Works Manager Data Base does not contain NSW files themselves. Every file name known to NSW has a record in the NSW file catalog, the entry giving the identifications of the hosts where file copies are stored plus the host's local identification of the file copies. The existance of multiple copies of an NSW file is normally of no concern for the user.

Some of the NSW file operations requested by the user can be done by merely making changes to the NSW file catalogue, like deleting and renaming a file or removing a semaphore used as an access lock (c.f. 18.3.3). Operations requiring access to file copies themselves are copying a file within the NSW file system as well as importing and exporting files (c.f. 18.3.4). For these operations the Works Manager calls upon the File Package.

18.4. The NSW reliability concept

Of the NSW components MSG, Foreman, Front End, File Package and Works Manager, only the Works Manager is *not intrinsically distributed*, while the others are by their nature. The Works Manager is in fact *logically singular*; making it physically singular, i.e. residing on a single host, makes NSW vulnerable to failures of that host, since access to NSW resources is only via the Works Manager. The entire NSW would be disabled because of a failure of the Works Manager. Such a single failure will not disable NSW, if the Works Manager is distributed over more than one host. To allow for distribution of *all* NSW components is the major goal of the NSW reliability concept [Shapiro 77].

The definition of reliability used for the NSW concept is centered around the *user's perception of the state of the system*:

A system is said to be reliable

- if it is available for use
- all actions reported to the user as complete are reflected in any future state of the system
- if completion of a user initiated action is not reported, then the user can probe the system and determine if it is in progress or completed. If completed, then he is informed whether completion was successful.

This definition of reliability is stronger than, e.g., the requirement that a distributed data base be consistent, since it requires that the system state be *consistent with the user's expectations*. If, for example, the user requests that a file be renamed from A to B and the Works Manager's response indicating that the renaming has been done gets lost, then the Front End will eventually report a failure to the user, though the Works Manager's Data Base may consistently reflect the change. In this case the user's expectation is not consistent with the system state. The above definition of reliability precludes such system behaviour. From the user's point of view the NSW system has two aspects. It consists of a *data base* (the Works Manager's Data Base) providing continuity of service and it consists of *processors* executing operations that modify this data base. The problem of making NSW reliable centers on keeping the Works Manager's Data Base consistent and available, and on providing reliability with respect to completion of operations, such that completion (successful or unsuccessful) is reflected in the data base and reported to the user. Since it cannot be guaranteed, that Front End hosts never fail, the latter is sufficiently supported, if the user can probe the system to determine the status of a requested operation.

Since MSG is an essential part of the environment in which NSW processes live, it plays a major role in the NSW reliability concept. MSG is assumed to be unreliable, i.e. messages transmitted by MSG may get lost, duplicated, garbled, etc. Of course, implementational effort may quantitatively reduce MSG resulting in a lessened frequency with which an error path has to be followed, but since MSG cannot be made absolutely perfect, these error paths have to be provided.

To cope with the deficiencies of MSG, the concept of *watchdog timers* is widely used in NSW. In all scenarios where a process is waiting for a message from another process a watchdog timer governs the maximum acceptable wait. To eliminate difficulties in determining the appropriate *timer intervals* (transmission time, processing time, disc access time, may vary considerably), watchdog timers are used as follows:

(1)   Upon sending a message to which it expects a reply i.e. a request, a process sets the timer interval to the sum of transmission delays and minimal processing delay to be expected.

(2)   The receiving process must send a reply within the minimum processing time anticipated by the sending process. If the reply to the message is not ready in time, a timing signal is sent instead, including status information on the curent status of the request, allowing the requestor to adjust its watchdog timer

(3)   Pattern (2) is repeated until the message reply is finally sent.

To provide for Works Manager host crash recovery, three or more sites will be selected as Works Manager hosts, each site being capable of supporting an active Works Manager and thus being able to provide the necessary secondary storage for maintaining a copy of the Works Manager Data Base. Except during crash recovery at any point in time exactly one of the Works Manager hosts will provide the *active Works Manager*, while the others are *passive*, i.e. will restrict their Works Manager related activities to keeping the data base copies consistent with the data base of the active Works Manager.

This approach will simplify the synchronization problems significantly, since all update requests originate from the active Works Manager host. If an active site crashes , all the other sites reach agreement on the latest updates received from the crashed site.   All updates already accomplished by the now dead site and reported to other components like Front Ends and Foreman are carried out at all live sites.   Finally, the users logged in at the crashed site are transferred to the elected new active Works Manager.

18.5. DAD: A debugging tool for debugging NSW

DAD stands for Do-All-Debugger; the development of this tool grew out of the need for a debugger to operate in the NSW environment [Victor 76]. DAD is an *interactive debugger* designed to provide high level languages and to allow the programmer to debug one or more cooperating processes, which may be executing on different machines with respect to each other and to the debugger. DAD could especially assist in the development and maintenance of portions of the NSW system and of NSW tools.

Another design goal was to provide a consistent interface to the user, regardless of the process being debugged using the DAD, such that commands and techniques would be the same for all machines and languages. Furthermore, the debugger concept should allow growth both with respect to commands and capabilities and to the support of new languages and machines.

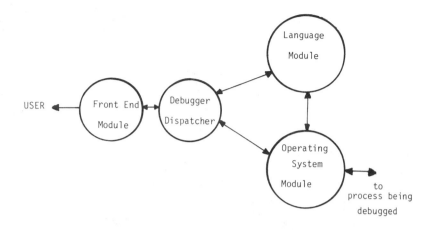

Figure 18-4: Module structure of the DAD interactive debugger

Finally, the design should allow the debugger to run in both, an NSW environment and in a stand alone operating system environment (like Tenex).

The tasks in interactive debugging fall roughly into the following categories:

- the user, i.e. the programmer, specifies a debugging action,

- the user's functional specifications are translated into calls on specific debugger routines

- the debugger routines manipulate information (i.e. read or write bits) in the address space of the program being debugged, and read/modify the program's state

- information gathered from the address space and the state information of the debugged program are interpreted and presented to the user in a way, which is ideally consistent with the programming language used.

The above tasks result in a corresponding module structure of the debugger, as depicted in figure 18-4.

These modules may or may not be executing on the same host; they interact via well defined communication protocols.   The debugger configuration may change dynamically, loading modules as appropriate to the tasks to be performed. The modules are:

- A *front end module* (FE) for all communication with the user, not to be confused with the NSW Front End, though its functions are equivalent (c.f. 18.3.2.)

- A *debugger dispatcher module* (DD) to receive the functional command specifications from the front end and to call the various routines which implement these commands. Results are transmitted back to the front end.

- *Operating system modules* (OSM), being responsible for reading and writing information from and back into the address space and state information tables of the program being debugged.

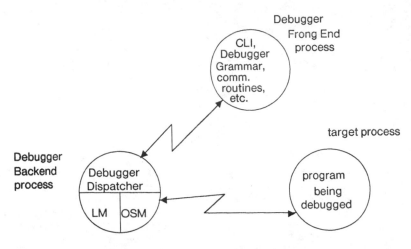

Figure 18-5: Operational structure of DAD

- *Language modules* (LM) for interpreting the information of the program being debugged in a manner compatible to the programming language in which the program was written.

The modular approach together with well defined specification for module functions and intercommunication enables DAD to be extensible:

In order to allow for the debugging of program P_{XY} being written in language X and running on machine Y, a language module X_{LM} and an operating system module Y_{OSM} are required. If instead the program is written in language N, but still running on machine Y, a combination of modules N_{LM} and Y_{OSM} is required for debugging with DAD.

In DAD the front end exists as a unique process, and the other modules, debugger dispatcher, language module and operating system module coexist in a second process, called *back end*, as shown in figure 18-5. The third process shown in this configuration is the target process (there may be several in parallel) containing the programs to be debugged.

Figure 18-6 shows a situation where an NSW implementor is interested in debugging the interaction between NSW Front End and a tool. It is assumed, that the NSW Front End is written using language L1 and is running under operating system O1 while the tool is written in language L2 and running under operating system O2. DAD will provide in this case for dynamically loading modules L1/O1 or L2/O2, depending on whether the NSW Front End or the tool is to be debugged at a particular point of time.

To interactively debug a target process, the operating system module must be able to exercise certain controls over that process, e.g., for reading from and writing into the process address space, and stopping/resuming its execution. If DAD-backend and target process run on the same machine, the operating system module exercises the required control functions by means of operating system primitives. If debugger and target process are not running on the same host, the operating system module must communicate with procedures in the target process or in a

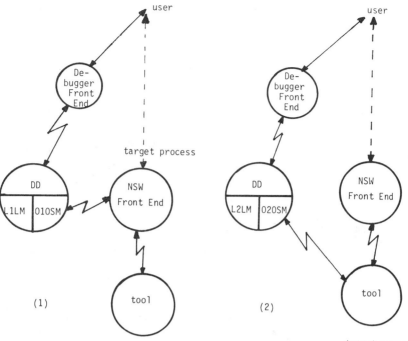

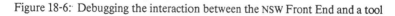

Figure 18-6: Debugging the interaction between the NSW Front End and a tool

process that has control over the target process. The procedures to be added to the target machine to implement the above functions are simple.

By providing only a small set of such function procedures on a target machine to allow for communication with an operating system module which is running on a more powerful machine, even interactive debugging of microcomputer programs is possible with previously unavailable power.

Chapter 19: Ethernet, Pup and Violet

In this chapter we describe a rather sophisticated distributed system, which maintains a collection of personal calendars and allows their owners to interact through these calendars to schedule meetings and make plans. This system makes use of a transactional file system, which in turn relies on a set of communication protocols by which it can be accessed from a variety of machines. Although these protocols support communication using a wide variety of hardware media, the one in most common use is the Ethernet network. We will describe each of these layers in turn, from the most basic to the highest.

19.1. The Alto and the Ethernet

The Alto personal computer is the main computing resource in the PARC environment we are describing [Thacker 80]. It provides sufficient computing power, local storage, and input-output capability to satisfy the needs of a single user. The standard system includes:

- An 875 line raster-scanned display.

- A keyboard and "mouse" pointing device with three buttons.

- A 2.5 Mbyte cartridge disk file.

- An interface to the Ethernet communication facility, described below.

- A microprogrammed processor that controls input-output devices and supports emulators for a number of instruction sets.

- Between 128k bytes and 512k bytes of semiconductor memory.

Such a personal computer provides substantial, predictable service to a single user. Much of the service he wants, however, cannot be provided by his machine alone, either because sharing is essential to the service or because of cost. Communication with other computers and other users is therefore needed. The communication system expands the service available to an individual, by allowing several users to share resources.

Such sharing is advantageous for two reasons. First, it allows several users to access the same data. For example, a person who composes a memorandum using text-editing facilities contained entirely in his Alto, may wish to distribute copies to several other people. He transmits the data representing the memorandum to the Altos of the recipients; each of the recipients can then read it on his Alto display. This use of communication is analogous to the use of the telephone or U.S. mail.

Communication can also be used to share resources for economic reasons. Although it is too costly to provide a hard-copy raster-scan printer for each Alto, a group of users may share a printer, transmitting to the printer the data and control information necessary to print a document. Sharing is also economical for high-capacity file storage or for special-purpose processors too expensive to replicate for each person.

At the time the Alto was designed, several computer communication networks such as the Arpa network [Kahn] had demonstrated the value of packet-switched networks for sharing resources and providing personal communication among research collaborators. A design suited for personal computers, however, has objectives rather different from those of a remote computer network such as the Arpa net:

- The transmission *speed* should be high enough that most users will not notice the presence of the network. If network bandwidth approximately matches local disk bandwidth, the user may not know or care whether a file is retrieved from a local disk or from a remote disk.

- The *size* of a network linking personal computers must not be limited. It is not unreasonable to imagine networks linking thousands of personal computers. At the same time, just two or three computers can constitute a reasonable network.

- The *reliability* of the network is extremely important when essential services such as printing depend on communication. If a user's personal computer malfunctions, he can take his disk cartridge to another one, but a network malfunction severs his access to essential services. In addition, many users are inconvenienced when the network fails, but only one when a machine fails.

- Personal computers tend to be near to each other and to the services they need, thus permitting a *local* network transmission technique for clusters of machines.

- A design for a communication system must anticipate the need for *standard communication protocols* in addition to standards for the physical transmission media. The protocols control the flow, routing, and interpretation of data in the network. Just as the design of the Alto disk controller addresses the needs of a file system, so must the design of a network address the needs of communications protocols. However, the Alto was designed at a time when experience with protocols was limited: many lessons had been learned from the Arpa protocols, but newer designs such as Pup [Boggs 80] and TCP [Cerf 74] had yet to emerge. The Alto therefore provides a general packet transport system, which has been used for a number of protocol experiments and evolutionary designs.

The Ethernet communication system [Metcalfe 76] is the principal means of communication between an Alto and other computers. An Ethernet is a broadcast, packet-switched, digital network that can connect up to 256 computers, separated by as much as a kilometer, with a 3 Mbit/sec channel. Control of the Ether is distributed among the communicating computers to eliminate the reliability problems of an active central controller, and to reduce the fixed costs which can make small centralized networks uneconomical. A standard Alto includes an Ethernet controller and transceiver. As soon as there are two Altos within a kilometer of each other, connecting the transceivers together with a coaxial cable establishes an Ethernet. Additional Altos and other computers can be connected simply by tapping into the cable as it passes by, above a false ceiling or beneath a raised floor. Connections can be made and power turned on and off without disturbing network communication. There is more discussion of the Ethernet in Chapters 4 and 16.

An Ethernet is an efficient low-level packet transport mechanism which gives its best efforts to delivering packets, but it is not error free. Even when transmitted without an error detected by the sender, a packet may not reach its destination without error; thus, packets are delivered only with high probability. A hierarchy of layered communication protocols is used to achieve reliable transmission on the Ethernet, by requiring receiving processes to acknowledge receipt of correct packets and sending processes to retransmit packets whose correct receipt is not acknowledged.

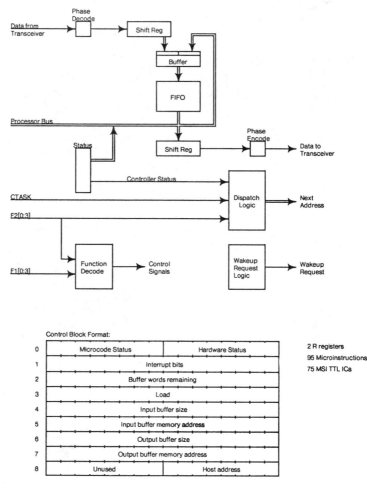

Figure 19-1: The Alto's Ethernet interface

19.1.1. Implementation

The Alto Ethernet interface (figure 19-1) contains about 75 MSI TTL ICs – it is slightly larger than the disk and display interfaces. The transceiver, on the other hand, is much smaller and less expensive than either the disk drive or the display monitor. The interface hardware consists of the following functions: phase decoder, receiver shift register, FIFO buffer and synchronizing register, transmitter shift register, phase encoder, and micromachine interface. The FIFO buffer is shared by the transmitter and receiver, so the interface is half-duplex: it can either be transmitting or receiving but not both simultaneously. This is not a severe limitation, since the Ether itself is half-duplex.

The microcode uses one medium-priority microcode task, two registers, and about 100 microinstructions. The task consumes 16% of the machine in the data transfer loops, since it runs for five cycles (one memory reference) every 5.44 ms (one Ethernet word time), doing all of its bookkeeping while waiting for the memory. To reject a packet the address filter requires 13 cycles (2.21 ms), which consumes as much as 20% of the machine in the improbable case of minimum length (2 word) back-to-back packets. The rest of the microcode is executed once per packet accepted or transmitted, and so consumes a negligible number of cycles.

Packet address filtering is done by the microcode. When the hardware has accumulated the first word of a packet, it wakes up the microcode to check the destination address byte. The microcode accepts the packet and copies it into memory if any of the following conditions is met:

- the destination address in the packet matches the *host address* field in the command block;
- the destination address is zero (in this case the packet is a *broadcast* packet, and is received by all machines);
- the host address is zero (in this case the machine is said to be *promiscuous*, and receives all packets).

Otherwise the microcode tells the hardware to ignore the rest of the current packet, and go to sleep until the beginning of the next packet.

The flexibility afforded by this filtering scheme has many applications. Any machine can substitute for another by using the other machine's address in the host address field. Promiscuity is invaluable for debugging protocols, since a machine can peek at all of the packets flowing between two others. It is also easy to study the performance of the net by monitoring all the traffic. Broadcasts are used to locate resources and to distribute globally useful information. A less desirable consequence is that the Ethernet itself provides no security; applications which need secure communication must use encryption.

Two or more Ethernet transmitters *collide* when they simultaneously decide that the Ether is free and begin transmitting. When a transmitter detects collision, it aborts transmission and waits a random time interval before trying again, so as not to collide repeatedly. As the load on the net increases, a transmitter retries less vigorously, by doubling the mean of its random interval each time it participates in a collision. This *exponential backoff* algorithm is done by the microcode and a small amount of hardware. The software zeroes the LOAD location in the Ethernet command block each time it issues an output command, and the microcode shifts a one bit into it each time a collision happens. The microcode generates a random retransmission interval by masking the LOAD location with the real time clock register, and then waiting for that interval by telling the hardware to wake it up periodically, and decrementing the interval register at each wakeup. When the register goes to zero, the microcode again tries to transmit. After 16 consecutive collisions the LOAD location overflows, and the microcode gives up and posts a failure code in the command block.

19.2. The Pup internetwork

19.2.1. Introduction

Research in network interconnection techniques has been motivated by the desire to permit communication among diverse, geographically distributed computing resources and users interconnected by a wide variety of network technologies.

It is the purpose of an internetwork architecture to provide a uniform framework for communication within a heterogeneous computing, communication, and applications environment. The work described in this paper represents one internetwork architecture, known as *Pup*, in widespread regular use within Xerox. The name referred originally to the abstract design of a standard internetwork datagram (the PARC Universal Packet), but has expanded in usage to include the whole hierarchy of internetwork protocols as well as a general style for internetwork communication.

The communications environment includes several different individual network designs. The dominant one is the Ethernet communications network, a local-area broadcast channel with a bandwidth of 3 megabits per second [Metcalfe 76]. Long-haul communication facilities include the Arpanet, the Arpa Packet Radio network, and a collection of leased lines implementing an Arpanet-style store-and-forward network. These facilities have distinct native protocols and exhibit as much as three orders of magnitude difference in bandwidth.

The applications to be supported include a wide range of activities: terminal access to the time sharing services, electronic mail, file transfer, access to specialized data bases, document transmission, software distribution, and packet voice, to name just a few. We would also like to facilitate more ambitious explorations into the area generally referred to as "distributed computing."

19.2.2. Design principles and issues

Constructing an architecture for internetwork protocols is, first and foremost, an exercise in design: identifying individual issues, exploring alternative solutions, and then knitting these pieces together to form the final result. Along the way, many compromises are made as one trades off among different criteria: functionality, efficiency, generality, ease of implementation, extensibility, and others.

In this section we enumerate some of the major design issues confronted in the development of a network architecture and describe, in general terms, the choices made in the development of Pup. (Several of these and other issues are enumerated in [Cerf 78b] and [Postel 80].) From this discussion the broad outlines of Pup will emerge; the section that follows provides more specific detail about the actual design.

19.2.2.1. The basic model: individual networks connected with gateways

As with most internetwork models, one envisions a collection of heterogeneous networks, connected with a set of *internetwork gateways* to form a loosely coupled system known generally as an *internet* [Cerf 74; Sunshine 77b; Cerf 78b]. An internet should provide the ability for any two hosts to communicate, so long as their own local networks are interconnected.

An important feature of the Pup internet model is that the hosts *are* the internet. Most hosts connect directly to a local network, rather than connecting to a network switch such as an IMP, so subtracting all the hosts would leave little more than wire. Gateways are simply hosts in the internet that are willing to forward packets among constituent networks. Thus, most of the properties of the internet are primarily artifacts of host software. The architecture must scale gracefully, and in particular must allow for the existence of a degenerate internet consisting of a single local network and no gateways.

19.2.2.2. Simplicity

One of the guiding principles in designing Pup has been the desire for simplicity. Pup is a framework for computer communications research, and simplicity is one of the best ways to minimize restrictions and maximize flexibility for experimentation. Attempting deliberately to eliminate unneeded complexity helps to keep the design open-ended. This in turn makes it easier to incorporate the existing diverse collection of networks and hosts and to accommodate new alternatives as the technology matures. Keeping the design simple helps to avoid building in technological anachronisms.

A second motivation for this principle is the desire to foster efficient implementations of the protocols in the host machines, which are typically quite small. Software overhead must be kept low in order to sustain high-bandwidth local communication, which constitutes the bulk of the traffic; yet the same software must support the full generality of internetwork communication.

19.2.2.3. Datagrams versus virtual circuits

There are two major approaches to providing an interface to packet-switched communications: accepting individual *datagrams*, or providing a higher level of service in the form of a *virtual circuit*. The two interfaces are not unrelated, since a virtual circuit interface is usually implemented within a network by the use of datagrams. In some sense, datagrams provide access to a network at a lower level, closer to its underlying capabilities. Datagrams are particularly useful in many kinds of transaction-oriented protocols. Furthermore, the task of the internet is significantly simplified if it need only transport independent, individually-addressed datagrams, without having to maintain the state required to support virtual circuits. If the internet provides a datagram interface, virtual circuit interfaces can be provided by adding appropriate mechanisms at the end points.

Therefore, the basic function provided by the Pup internet is the transport of datagrams; this simple abstraction is the foundation of Pup. The internet does not guarantee reliable delivery of datagrams (called *Pups*); it simply gives its "best efforts" to deliver each one, and allows the end processes to build protocols which provide reliable communications of the quality they themselves desire. The internet has no notion of a connection. It transports each Pup independently, and leaves construction of a connection – if that is the appropriate interprocess communication model – to the end processes. Keeping fragile end-to-end state out of the packet transport system contributes to reliability and simplicity.

19.2.2.4. Individual networks as packet transport mechanisms

Individual networks within the internet can be viewed simply as *packet transport mechanisms*. As links in the internet they give their best efforts to deliver internet packets, but they do not guarantee reliable delivery. Packets may be lost, duplicated, delivered out of order, after a great delay, and with hidden damage. A network can have any combination of bandwidth, delay, error characteristics, topology, and economics; the routing algorithm should attempt to take these characteristics into consideration.

Encapsulation is an invertible, network-dependent transformation performed on a Pup to permit it to be carried transparently through a network: an abstract Pup is presented at one end, encapsulated for transmission through the net, and decapsulated at the other end, yielding the original Pup. For some networks, encapsulation consists merely of adding headers and trailers. More elaborate transformations may be necessary to pass a Pup through other networks (for example, using low-level acknowledgments or error correction because the network has a high loss rate). Encapsulation and decapsulation take place in a *network-specific driver* in which is vested all knowledge of the encapsulation technique. The internet specification has nothing to say about encapsulation except that it be invisible.

19.2.2.5. Internetwork gateways

We distinguish two kinds of gateways: *media translators* and *protocol translators*. Media gateways are hosts with interfaces to two or more packet transport mechanisms among which they forward internet datagrams, using the appropriate encapsulation for each. These are the heart of any datagram-based internet. Protocol gateways are hosts which speak two or more functionally similar but incompatible higher-level protocols used to transport information within networks, mapping one higher-level abstraction into the other. (It's clear that a media gateway is just doing protocol translation at the link level, but the distinction is useful given the importance of internet datagrams in this architecture.)

In the Pup internet, media gateways are by definition simple, since all that is required of the translation process is that it preserve the semantics of internetwork datagrams. Protocol gateways are usually more difficult, even when the protocols are similar, since such higher-level protocols provide richer and more specialized semantics and it is not always clear how one should map the functionality of one protocol into another. Development of higher-level protocol translators between different network and internet architectures – e.g., between the Arpanet File Transfer Protocol (FTP) and the Pup-based FTP – is a thorny task, but one that must be confronted when interconnecting systems that do not share the necessary lower-level primitives.

19.2.2.6. A layered hierarchy of protocols

Layering of protocols is one of the most effective means for structuring a network design: each level uses the functions of the lower level, and adds some functionality of its own for possible use by the next level. Provided that suitable interfaces are maintained, an implementation at one level can be modified without impacting the overall structure; this helps to simplify both the design and the implementation.

Levels 4 and above

Application-defined protocols

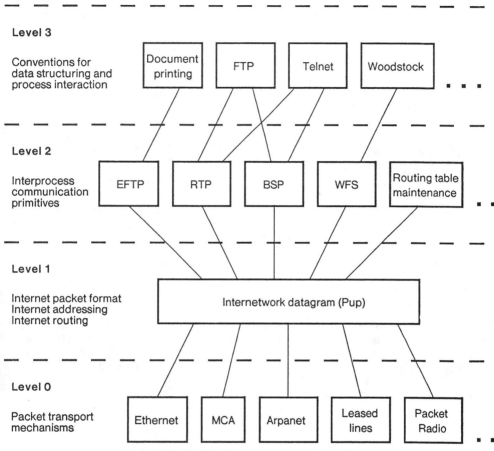

Level 3

Conventions for data structuring and process interaction

Document printing   FTP   Telnet   Woodstock

Level 2

Interprocess communication primitives

EFTP   RTP   BSP   WFS   Routing table maintenance

Level 1

Internet packet format
Internet addressing
Internet routing

Internetwork datagram (Pup)

Level 0

Packet transport mechanisms

Ethernet   MCA   Arpanet   Leased lines   Packet Radio

Figure 19-2: Pup protocol hierarchy

Pup protocols are organized in a hierarchy, as shown in figure 19-2; the details of this figure will be presented in section 19.2.3. A level represents an abstraction, to be realized in different ways in different hosts. There are four levels of interest, but there may be more than one protocol at any level except level 1, representing a different use of the underlying layers. (The numbering of layers — and, indeed, the choice of points at which to divide the layers — is arbitrary; there is no relationship between Pup's numbering and that of other designs such as the Open Systems Architecture.)

The level 0 abstraction is a packet transport mechanism. There are many realizations: an Ethernet channel, the Arpanet, the Arpa Packet Radio Network, our store-and-forward leased line network, and others. Level 0 protocols include specifications such as hardware interfaces, electrical and timing characteristics, bit encodings, line control procedures, and network-dependent packet formatting conventions. Associated with each packet transport mechanism is a convention for encapsulating Pups.

The level 1 abstraction is an internet datagram. The realization of this abstraction consists of the format of a Pup, a hierarchical addressing scheme, and an internetwork routing algorithm. There is only one box at level 1: the internet datagram protocol; it is this layer of commonality which unifies all of the different networks that might be used at level 0, and which makes available a uniform interface to all of the layers above. It is the purpose of this level to provide media independence while maintaining the common properties of the underlying packet networks.

The level 2 abstraction is an interprocess communication mechanism: a way to move bits without saying much about their form or content. Various level 2 protocols provide many combinations of reliability, throughput, delay, and complexity. These protocols can be divided into two classes according to the amount and lifetime of state information kept by the communicating end processes. Connectionless protocols support short-lived interactions; the end processes maintain little state, and usually only during the exchange of a few Pups—no more than a few seconds. Connection-based protocols support sustained interactions, generally requiring substantial state to be maintained at both ends, and for longer periods—minutes to hours.

Level 3 adds structure to the data moved at level 2, as well as conventions for how processes interact. For example, the File Transfer Protocol (FTP) consists of a set of conventions for talking about files and a format for sending them through a level 2 byte stream protocol connection. These are sometimes referred to as function-oriented protocols.

Above level 3 the dividing lines become blurred, and individual applications evolve with their own natural decomposition into additional layers. With respect to layering of protocols, Pup is similar in many ways to the Arpa Internet and TCP design [Cerf 74] and the Open Systems Architecture [Zimmermann 80]. Unlike the Open Systems Architecture (and others), Pup often has several alternative boxes which all rest on a lower level and offer different functionality and interfaces to the next higher level.

19.2.2.7. Naming, addressing, and routing

Names, addresses and routes are three important and distinct entities in an internet [Shoch, 1978]:

- the *name* of a resource is *what* one seeks,
- an *address* indicates *where* it is, and
- a *route* is *how to get there.*

A name is a symbol, such as a human-readable text string, identifying some resource (process, device, service, etc.) An address is a data structure whose format is understood by level 1 of the internet, and which is used to specify the destination of a Pup. A route is the information needed to forward a Pup to its specified address. Each of these represents a tighter binding of information: names are mapped into addresses, and addresses are mapped into routes. Error recovery should successively fall back to find an alternate route, then an alternate address, and then an alternate name. The mapping from names to addresses is necessarily application-specific, since the syntax and semantics of names depend entirely on what types of entities are being named and what use is being made of them. This is dealt with at the appropriate higher levels of protocol.

An address field, as contained in a Pup, is one of the important elements of commonality in the internet design. An end process sends and receives Pups through a *port* identified by a hierarchical address consisting of three parts: a *network number*, a *host number*, and a *socket number*. This structure reflects the attitude that the communicating parties are the end processes, not the hosts' protocol handlers; among other things, this permits alternate implementations of a higher-level protocol to coexist in a single machine. (In contrast, the Arpa Internet project [Postel 80] takes the position that the socket abstraction does not belong at the internet level; therefore, Arpa Internet addresses contain only network and host numbers. When a packet arrives, it is first demultiplexed by the *protocol type* field in the internet header; higher-level protocols such as the TCP, datagram protocol, and packet voice protocol then impose their own concept of socket if they find it useful — which, as a practical matter, they all do.)

The actual process of routing a packet through the Pup internet uses a distributed adaptive routing procedure. The source process specifies only the *destination address* and not the *path* from source to destination. The internetwork gateways route Pups to the proper network, a network then routes Pups to the proper host, and a host routes Pups to the proper socket. This routing process is associated with Level 1 in the protocol hierarchy, the level at which packet formats and internet addresses are standardized. The software implementing level 1 is sometimes referred to as a *router*. Thus, the routing table itself is kept at level 1; a very simple host (or gateway) would need only levels 0 and 1 in order to route Pups. But the routing table also requires periodic updating, as gateways exchange and distribute their current routing information; this *routing table maintenance* protocol is found logically at level 2 of the hierarchy.

Gateways provide internet routing tables to individual hosts as well as to each other. Hosts use this routing information to decide where to send outgoing packets destined other than to a directly-connected network.

19.2.2.8. Flow control and congestion control

Although the terms are often confused, *flow control* and *congestion control* attack two very different problems in packet-switched communication. Flow control is a mechanism used to regulate the behavior of a specific source and destination pair, so that the source does not send data at a rate greater than the receiver can process it. In an internet architecture, flow control remains the responsibility of the end-to-end protocols, particularly those at level 2 supporting regular stream traffic. Congestion control is a network-wide mechanism, used to control the number and distribution of packets in the network so as to prevent system overload. Internet congestion control is necessary to help protect the gateways from being burdened with excessive traffic.

The Pup datagram-based internet model does not require that the internet successfully deliver every packet that has been accepted. Therefore, an intermediate gateway which suddenly encounters a period of severe congestion is free to discard packets, although the system should be engineered to make this an uncommon event. If a gateway is forced to discard an incoming packet because of congestion, it should attempt to return some information to the source: an *error Pup* (negative acknowledgment) indicating that a packet had to be discarded in mid-route. This error Pup is simply returned to the source port, as identified in the discarded Pup; this is a good illustration of the value of including the socket number as part of the standard internet address. The source process can use this information to modify its transmission strategies—for example, to reduce its offered load (the rate at which it attempts to send Pups along the congested path) and thereby help to relieve the congestion. Long-term congestion should eventually be reflected in the routing information exchanged among gateways, discouraging subsequent traffic from attempting to pass through a badly congested area.

19.2.2.9. Reliable transport

Defining datagrams to be less than perfectly reliable is realistic since it reflects the characteristics of many existing packet transport mechanisms. Probabilistic transmission is basic to the theory of operation of network designs such as Ethernet. Even in networks nominally designed to deliver correctly sequenced, error-free packets, occasional anomalies may result from certain hardware or software failures: an Arpanet IMP may crash while holding the only copy of a packet, or an X.25 virtual circuit may be reset.

As mentioned previously, the Pup internet *always* has the option of discarding packets to relieve congestion, though this is certainly not an optimal strategy. This point is of considerable practical importance when one considers the complicated measures required to avoid deadlock conditions in the Arpanet—conditions which are a direct consequence of attempting to provide reliable delivery of every packet in a store-and-forward network [Metcalfe 73; McQuillan 77]. Packet management strategies that attempt to guarantee perfect reliability must be designed to operate correctly under *worst case* conditions, whereas strategies that have the option of discarding packets when necessary need operate correctly only under *most* conditions. The idea is to sacrifice the guarantee of reliable delivery of individual packets and to capitalize on the resulting simplicity to produce higher reliability and performance overall.

For some applications, perfectly reliable transport is unnecessary and possibly even undesirable, especially if it is obtained at the cost of increased delay. For example, in real-time speech applications, loss of an occasional packet is of little consequence, but even short delays (or worse, highly variable ones) can cause significant degradation [Sproull 78].

Reliable delivery requires maintaining state information at the source and destination. The actions of a large class of simple servers, such as giving out routing tables or converting names into addresses, are idempotent (i.e., may be repeated without incremental effects), and a client of that service can simply retransmit a request if no response arrives. These protocols reduce to a simple exchange of Pups, with an occasional retransmission by the client, but with no state retained by the server. (The server may choose to retain answers to the last few requests to improve response time, but this optimization is invisible to the protocol.)

On the other hand, many applications such as file transfer and terminal connection do depend upon fully reliable transmission. In these cases, it is perfectly reasonable to build a reliable end-to-end protocol on top of the internet datagrams. Ultimately, reliability (by some definition) is always required; the issue is where it should be provided. The Pup attitude is that it is the responsibility of the end processes to define and implement whatever form of reliable transport is appropriate to the situation.

19.2.2.10. Packet fragmentation

It is inevitable that some process will want to send an internet packet which is too large to be directlcy encapsulated for transmission through an intermediate network that has a smaller maximum packet size. This problem is usually approached with one of two forms of *packet fragmentation* [Shoch, 1979a].

With *internetwork fragmentation*, an internet-wide design specifies the operations to be performed on a packet that is too large for a network it is about to enter. The internet datagram is fragmented into a number of smaller internet datagrams, thereafter to be transported independently and reassembled at the ultimate destination. This is the approach taken, for example, in the Arpa Internet design. It requires every destination to have procedures for reassembly.

Alternatively, one may use *intranetwork fragmentation* (or *network-specific fragmentation*): when presented with an oversize packet, the network-specific driver undertakes to fragment the packet in a manner specific to that network, to be reassembled by the corresponding driver as the packet exits the network (e.g., at the next gateway). This approach confines the fragmentation and reassembly procedures to the level 0 modules of hosts directly connected to the network in which fragmentation is required.

The Pup design does not attempt to provide any form of general internetwork fragmentation. This complex issue has been simply legislated out of existence by requiring that every agent in the internet handle Pups up to a standard maximum size, using network-specific fragmentation where necessary.

19.2.3. Implementation

The preceding section has outlined some of the important properties of the Pup architecture and the internetworking issues it addresses. What follows is a more detailed description of the present design of the four major layers in the system.

19.2.3.1. Level 0: packet transport

An individual network moves network-specific packets among hosts; the addressing schemes, error characteristics, maximum packet sizes, and other attributes of networks vary greatly. An internetwork packet transport mechanism, however, moves Pups between hosts. The level 0 code which transforms a network into an internet packet transport mechanism is called a *network driver*. A machine connected to a single network, therefore, has one level 0 network driver; a gateway has one driver for each directly-connected network. Only the driver knows about the peculiarities of a network's hardware interface and low-level protocol.

The interface between levels 0 and 1 is very simple. Level 1 passes down a Pup and a network-specific host address, and the driver encapsulates the Pup and does its best to deliver it to the specified host. When a Pup arrives at a host, the driver decapsulates it and passes it up to level 1; if for any reason the Pup looks suspicious (as determined by network-specific error checking), the driver discards it.

Every packet transport mechanism must be able to accept a maximum-size Pup; if the actual network cannot directly encapsulate a packet of that size for transmission, the driver must include some form of intranetwork fragmentation. A network driver may also be asked to broadcast a packet to all other hosts on that net. On some networks this is straightforward; on others it may require use of a reverse-path forwarding algorithm [Dalal 78] or brute-force replication of the packet to each destination.

The transport mechanisms don't have to be perfectly reliable, but they should be successful most of the time—a packet loss rate of less than 1 percent is usually acceptable. A network operating for a short time in a degraded mode with a higher loss rate is harmless, so long as the probability is low that Pups will transit more than one net that is in this condition. However, if a network's inherent error characteristics are unfavorable, the driver should take steps to improve its performance, perhaps by incorporating a network-specific low-level acknowledgment and retransmission protocol.

To date, there have been five major types of networks integrated into the Pup architecture, each with a different level 0 driver.

Ethernet. Local Ethernet facilities can very easily serve as transport mechanisms for Pups: a Pup fits in an Ethernet packet with only a few additional words of encapsulation (see figure 19-3), and requires no fragmentation. These systems have good reliability, high speed, and can send broadcast packets [Metcalfe 76; Shoch 79a; Shoch 79b].

MCA. The Multiprocessor Communications Adapter (MCA), a parallel TDM bus, serves as a local network tying together a limited number of Nova computers. It has good reliability and requires no fragmentation, but does not support broadcast packets. Broadcasts are accomplished by the brute-force method—sending a copy of a broadcast packet to each of the possible hosts.

Arpanet. To cover longer distances, Pups can be routed through the Arpanet; the format for encapsulating a Pup in an Arpanet message is shown in figure 19-3. (Note that Arpanet Pup transport is based on Host-IMP protocol messages, not on Host-Host protocol streams.) Because the standard maximum Pup length is less than that of an Arpanet message, the driver itself need not fragment Pups; however, the Arpanet does perform network-specific fragmentation internally: one "message" containing a Pup may become multiple "packets" within the Arpanet. Furthermore, the Arpanet provides increased reliability through the use of its own internal acknowledgment and retransmission protocols. The Arpanet does not presently support broadcast packets; rather than sending packets to all possible Arpanet hosts, the network driver does not implement broadcasts at all.

Leased line store-and-forward network. More frequently, different local networks are interconnected over long distances through the use of a private store-and-forward network constructed using leased telephone circuits. Similar in spirit to the Arpanet, this system is used to connect internetwork gateways. Unlike the Arpanet, the system does not use separate packet switches (IMPs), but instead switches packets through the hosts themselves—that is, the connected hosts include network-specific drivers that implement a store-and-forward network. This network has its own adaptive routing procedure, independent of the internetwork routing. The system is fairly reliable and does not require low-level acknowledgments. At present, the network drivers do not fragment Pups, but they do promote small packets to the front of transmission queues at intermediate points to help improve performance for interactive traffic.

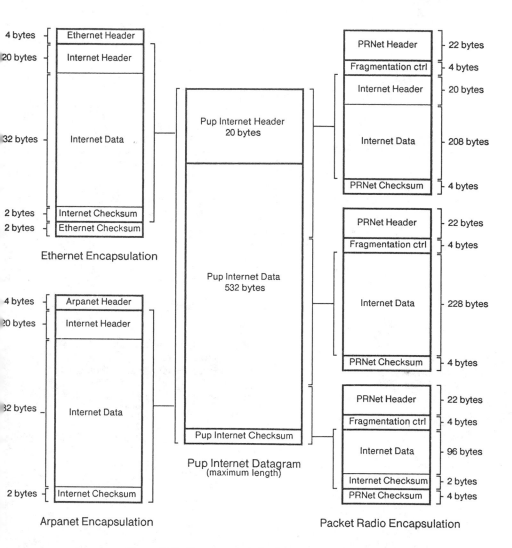

Figure 19-3: Pup encapsulation in various networks

Packet Radio network. On an experimental basis, the Arpa Packet Radio network [Kahn 78] has been used to carry traffic among local networks in the San Francisco Bay area. The Packet Radio network was integrated into the system by building a suitable level 0 network driver [Shoch 79]. The system provides good reliability; but due to the relatively small maximum packet size (232 bytes), the driver must perform fragmentation and reassembly (see figure 19-3). Though using a broadcast medium, the Packet Radio protocols do not support broadcast packets. In this case, the low-level driver includes a procedure to periodically identify Packet Radio hosts that might be running Pup software; when asked to broadcast a packet, the driver sends copies of it to all such hosts.

To date we have not used any public packet-switched networks, such as Telenet, as packet transport mechanisms. These systems usually provide only a virtual circuit interface (X.25) that requires a user to pay for functionality that may not be needed. Compared to our existing leased line network, a Telenet-based packet transport mechanism would not be cost-effective except under conditions of very light traffic volume. We would prefer to use a service that provided simple, unreliable datagrams; if there were an appropriate interface, we could dismantle our leased line store-and-forward network.

19.2.3.2. Level 1: internetwork datagrams

This is the level at which packet formats and internetwork addresses are standardized. It is the lowest level of process-to-process communication.

Pup format

The standard format for a Pup is shown in figure 19-4. The following paragraphs highlight the sorts of information required at the internet datagram level.

The *Pup length* is the number of 8-bit bytes in the Pup, including internetwork header (20 bytes), contents, and checksum (2 bytes).

The *transport control* field is used for two purposes: as a scratch area for use by gateways, and as a way for source processes to tell the internet how to handle the packet. (Other networks call this the "facilities" or "options" field.) The *hop count* subfield is incremented each time the packet is forwarded by a gateway. If this ever overflows, the packet is presumed to be travelling in a loop and is discarded. A *trace bit* is specified, for potential use in monitoring the path taken by a packet.

The *Pup type* is assigned by the source process for interpretation by the destination process and defines the format of the Pup contents. The 256 possible types are divided into two groups. Some types are *registered* and have a single meaning across all protocols; Pups generated or interpreted within the internet (e.g., by gateways) have types assigned in this space. Interpretation of the remaining *unregistered* types is strictly a matter of agreement between the source and destination processes.

The *Pup identifier* is used by most protocols to hold a sequence number. Its presence in the internetwork header is to permit a response generated within the internet (e.g., error or trace information) to identify the Pup that triggered it in a manner that does not depend on knowledge of the higher-level protocols used by the end processes.

Pups contain two addresses: a *source port* and a *destination port*. These hierarchical addresses include an 8-bit network number, an 8-bit host number, and a 32-bit socket number. Hosts are expected to know their own host addresses, to discover their network numbers by locating a gateway and asking for this information, and to assign socket numbers in some systematic way not legislated by the internet protocol.

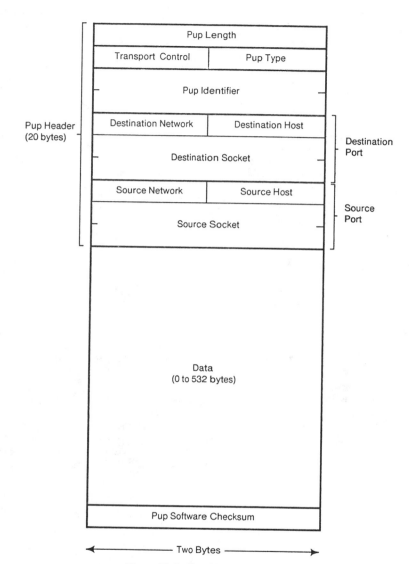

Figure 19-4: Pup internet datagram

There are some important conventions associated with the use of network addresses. A distinguished value of the network number field refers to "this network" without identifying it. Such a capability is necessary for host initialization (since most hosts have no permanent local storage and consequently no *a priori* knowledge of the connected network number), and to permit communication to take place within a degenerate internet consisting of an unidentified local network with no gateways. A distinguished value of the destination host address is used to request a broadcast. Certain values of the socket number field refer, by convention, to "well-known sockets" associated with standard, widely-used services, as is done in the Arpanet.

The *data* field contains up to 532 data bytes. The selection of a standard maximum packet length must reflect many considerations: error rates, buffer requirements, and needs of specific applications. A reasonable value might range anywhere from 100 to 4000 bytes. In practice, much of the internet traffic consists of packets containing individual "pages" of 512 bytes each, reflecting the quantization of memory in most of our computers. But just carrying the data is not enough, since the packet should accommodate higher-level protocol overhead and some identifying information as well. Allowing 20 additional bytes for such purposes, we arrive at 532 bytes as the maximum size of the data field (a somewhat unconventional value in that it is not a power of two). Thus, there may be between 0 and 532 content bytes in a Pup, so its total length will range from 22 to 554 bytes. Pups longer than 554 bytes are not prohibited and may be carried by some networks, but no internetwork gateway is required to handle larger ones.

The optional *software checksum* is used for complete end-to-end coverage — it is computed as close to the source of the data and checked as close to the ultimate destination as is possible.

This checksum protects a Pup when it isn't covered by some network-specific technique, such as when it is sitting in a gateway's memory or passing through a parallel I/O path. Most networks employ some sort of error checking on the serial parts of the channel, but parallel data paths in the interface and the I/O system often are not checked. The checksum algorithm is intended to be straightforward to implement in software; it also allows incremental updating so that intermediate agents which modify a packet (gateways updating the hop count field, for example) can quickly update the checksum rather than recomputing it. The checksum may (but need not) be checked anywhere along a Pup's route in order to monitor the internet's integrity.

Routing

Accompanying the packet format defined at level 1 are the protocols for internetwork routing. Each host, whether or not it is a gateway, executes a routing procedure on every outgoing Pup, as illustrated in figure 19-5. This procedure decides, as a function of the Pup destination port field, upon which *directly-connected network* the Pup is to be transmitted (if there is more than one choice), and it yields an *immediate destination host* which is the address on that network of either the ultimate destination or some gateway believed to be closer to the destination. Each routing step employs the same algorithm based on local routing information, and each Pup is routed independently.

Routing information is maintained in a manner very similar to the Arpanet-style adaptive procedures [McQuillan 74]. The initial metric used for selecting routes is the "hop count" — the number of intermediate networks between source and destination. The protocol for updating the routing tables involves exchanging Pups with neighboring gateways and rests logically at level 2 of the protocol hierarchy. This is an example of a connectionless protocol which doesn't require perfectly reliable transmission for correct operation. Changes in internetwork topology may cause different gateways' routing tables to become momentarily inconsistent, but the algorithm is stable in that the routing tables rapidly converge to a consistent state and remain that way until another change in topology occurs.

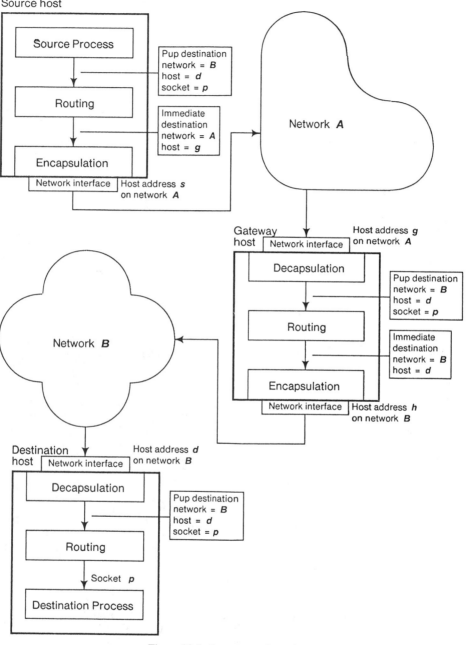

Figure 19-5: Internetwork routing

A host which is not a gateway still implements a portion of this level 2 routing update protocol: it initially obtains an internetwork routing table from a gateway on its directly-connected network, and it obtains updated information periodically. If there is more than one gateway providing connections to other networks, the host can merge their routing tables and thus be able to select the best route for packets directed to any network.

19.2.3.3. Level 2: interprocess communication

Given the raw datagram facility provided at level 1, we can begin to build data transport protocols, tailored to provide appropriate levels of reliability or functionality for real applications. These protocols generally fall into two categories: those in which a connection is established for a sustained exchange of packets, and those in which individual packets are exchanged on a connectionless basis. Connection-style protocols usually transport data very reliably, and transparently.

EFTP: the Easy File Transfer Protocol. This is a very simple protocol for sending files. Each data Pup gives rise to an immediate acknowledgment, and there is at most one Pup outstanding at a time. This protocol is an indirect descendent of the one outlined in [Metcalfe 76]. Its simplicity makes this piece of communication mechanism easy to include under conditions of very limited resources. For example, we have implemented a complete EFTP receiver in 256 words of assembly language, for use in a network-based bootstrap and down-line loading process.

Rendezvous & Termination Protocol (RTP). This is a general means to initiate, manage, and terminate connections in a reliable fashion [Sunshine 78]. In normal use, an RTP user initiates a connection by communicating with a well-known socket at some server. That server will spawn a new port to actually provide the service, and the RTP will establish contact with this port. It employs a non-reusable *connection identifier* to distinguish among multiple instantiations of the same connection and to cope with delayed packets without making assumptions about maximum packet lifetimes. RTP also synchronizes Pup identifiers for use in managing the connection.

Byte Stream Protocol (BSP). This is a relatively sophisticated protocol for supporting reliable, sequenced streams of data. It provides for multiple outstanding packets from the source, and uses a moving window flow control procedure. User processes can place *mark bytes* in the stream to identify logical boundaries and can send out-of-band *interrupt* signals. RTP and BSP combined perform a function similar to that of the TCP, with which they share a certain degree of common ancestry [Cerf 74; Postel 80].

Connectionless protocols do not attempt to maintain any long-term state; they usually don't guarantee reliability, but leave it up to the designer to construct the most suitable system. Their simplicity and ease of implementation make them extremely useful.

Echo. A very simple protocol can be used to send test Pups to an *echo server* process, which will check them and send back a reply. Such servers are usually embedded in gateways and other server hosts, to aid in network monitoring and maintenance. The server is trivial to implement on top of the level 1 facilities.

Name lookup. Another server provides the mapping from string names of resources to internetwork addresses; this is accomplished by a single exchange of packets. This service is often addressed with a broadcast Pup, since it is used as the first step in locating resources. (The name lookup service itself, of course, must be located at a well-known address. To be useful, it must be widely available; therefore it is typically replicated at least once per network.)

Routing table maintenance. The internetwork routing tables are maintained by Pups exchanged periodically among internetwork gateways and broadcast for use by other hosts.

Page-level file access. The Woodstock File Server (WFS), one of the family of file servers available on the internet, provides page-at-a-time access to a large file store [Swinehart 79]. The protocols used for this do not require establishment of a connection, but merely exchange request and response Pups that each carry both commands and file data. This arrangement supports random-access, transaction-oriented interactions of very high performance—frequently better than that obtained using local file storage, because the file server's disks are much faster than those typically connected to personal computers.

Gateway monitoring and control. There is no single network control center, but individual gateways may be queried from a monitoring program run on any user machine. With suitable authentication, the user may assume remote control of the gateway so as to perform operations such as changing parameters and loading new versions of the software.

Other connectionless protocols are used to access a *date and time server,* an *authentication server,* and a *mail check server* integrated with an on-line message system. These protocols are designed to be as cheap as possible to implement (i.e., without connection overhead) so that such servers may be replicated extensively and accessed routinely without consuming excessive resources. For example, instances of some of these servers are present in all gateway hosts so as to maximize their availability.

19.2.3.4. Level 3: application protocols

Armed with a reasonable collection of data transport protocols at level 2, one can begin to evolve specific applications at level 3. These are not discussed further here, except for the particular application treated in later sections of the chapter.

19.3. The distributed file system

19.3.1. Introduction

One of the primary functions of an operating system is providing a file storage capability (as well as allocating processor and memory resources, etc.); this section discusses an independent file facility that is *not* embedded in an operating system, but operates in a distributed environment with a number of computers of several types connected by the Pup internet; it can only be accessed over this network. A version of the system has been running for about two years.

The *distributed file system* (DFS) is so named because it is implemented on a cooperating set of *server* computers which together create the illusion of a single, logical system. The other computers in the network that use the DFS for creating, destroying, and randomly accessing files are called its *clients* (we employ the term "user" to stand only for *human* users; programs that access the DFS are always called clients).

Structuring the DFS using a set of servers is partly motivated by the economics of disk storage devices. Using rather small computers as file servers permits a wide range of file storage capacity because it is possible to expand a DFS from a single minicomputer with one disk drive to many servers, each with a number of disks. It also allows one to vary the ratio of processing power to disk capacity over a wide range to suit a variety of applications. With current disk technology, a minimal DFS (consisting of a single server with one disk drive) might hold 80 Mbytes, while a large system could consist of, say, six servers together supporting about 8000 Mbytes. This represents a range of 1:100 in storage capacity and a range of 16:1 in server computers/Mbyte of storage.

The availability of high-bandwidth local communications (the Ethernet) and distributed computers has also motivated the design of the DFS. They make it reasonable to separate the actual processing of data from the system required to store that data reliably. This separation also contributes to reliability and system robustness in the face of failures because a hardware or software problem in one computer (whether server or client) does not affect others since the only resource they share is the communications link.

Although it can store large amounts of data, the DFS is *not* itself a data-base system: it provides no built-in access mechanisms for files other than random access to sequences of bytes and pages. In fact, it does not even support user-sensible names for files. Rather, each file is "named" by a *unique identifier* (*UID*), which is essentially a large integer. However, a directory service for maintaining a map from user-sensible names into UIDs has been implemented (as a client of the DFS rather than as an integral part of it) and is discussed in section 19.3.4.

Since the DFS is intended to support applications dealing with (possibly distributed) data bases, it provides a number of important mechanisms and guarantees which they can use. The *atomic property* for file actions is by far the most important of these guarantees: A sequence of reads and writes of some set of files (probably not all residing on the same server machine) can be performed as an *indivisible, atomic* operation (see Chapter 11). Such an action sequence is called a *transaction*, and is bracketed by two special operations, *Begin Transaction*, and *End Transacion*, which are discussed more fully in section 19.3.3. All the write actions in a transaction will appear to occur simultaneously, and the information obtained by all the reads in the transaction will still be correct at the apparent time of the write. Moreover, the atomic property holds even in the presence of crashes of servers or clients; i.e., if a crash occurs, either all or none of the writes of the transaction will have been performed.

The atomic property holds even if the files involved are accessed simultaneously by more than one transaction. Read and write locks control the accesses so that the transactions do not see inconsistent views of the data When one of the transactions completes, then the other, locked-out one will be able to proceed. This has the same effect as if transactions sharing files were forced to be strictly sequential in time; thus they each see consistent data (see sections 11.1 and 11.3). These controls on sharing also create the possibility of deadlock between transactions accessing the same files. However, a lock set by one transaction can be *broken* if another transaction is trying to lock the same data and has waited too long. Thus, deadlock situations can be cleared since the atomic property allows the DFS to abort a transaction which has a broken lock.   Section 19.3.4 discusses how the lock time-out mechanism can be used by clients to maintain consistent local caches of shared data.

In the remainder of this section we discuss some of the details of transactions and accessing files using the DFS (19.3.2), how clients can use the basic mechanisms of the DFS to maintain local caches of shared data or to respond to aborted transactions (e.g., because of a server crash), and how a directory service is provided (19.3.3).

19.3.2. Access mechanics

This section describes the basic interactions between file servers and clients. Normally, application programs will not deal directly with the DFS, but will use some (more or less) standard underlying software to hide low-level details. For example, the underlying software will usually portray the DFS as a single file system even though it must be aware of the multiplicity of file servers. An application is not required to use the standard low-level software, however; it is free to treat the DFS at an abstract level that suits that application.

19.3.2.1 Client and server communications

Clients and servers converse by sending messages to one another (for the purposes of this paper we assume an underlying protocol for reliable, authenticated transmission of messages between machines on the network; see Chapter 7). To access a file a client sends a *request* message to a server; the outcome is communicated in the opposite direction by means of a *result* message. This one-to-one request-result interchange is the fundamental access mechanism. Each message includes control information, which specifies the type of message and related parameters. For example, if a client wants to read file data, it would send a message specifying the action *Read Data*, and as parameters the file's *UID*, the index of the first byte to be read, and the number of bytes to be read. In response to *Read Data*, a server would normally send a result message specifying *Here's Data* and include the bytes read from the file.

Each result message specifies the identity of the request to which it is a response, so that the client computer can match results with requests. This permits the client to initiate new requests without waiting for previous ones to be completed. However, the actual order in which the server carries out such overlapped actions is not specified, and the client needs to be able to handle results in any order. If such parallelism is unnecessary, then the client can force sequentiality by simply waiting for the response to one request before sending the next.

Instead of returning data with a result, a server may send a *reject* response (along with a reason for not fulfilling the request). For example, the requested byte range may be beyond the limits of the file, the requested access may be one this client is not entitled to make, etc. Sometimes a server sends an *unsolicited* message to a client. For example, if the server breaks a lock, it will inform the client by sending an *unsolicited* message that includes the details of the situation (see section 19.3.3.2).

19.3.2.2 Details of transactions

When a client first connects to the DFS, it sends an *Begin Transaction* request to some server (any one will do), which is then known as the *primary server* for that transaction. *Begin Transaction* serves two purposes: as with a time-sharing system, the client presents its credentials, and the server inspects them to decide whether to permit the client access to the DFS; secondly, *Begin Transaction* also begins a transaction. The server will return a result message with a unique identifier for this transaction; all further messages in the transaction will carry that identification.

Once a client has begun a transaction, it is free to request actions such as *Create File, Destroy File, Read Data,* or *Write Data.* When it is finished, the client will request a *End Transaction.* The DFS then completes the transaction, sends a response, and disconnects from that client. As a first step in carrying out a read action, the addressed server sets read locks on the data to be read. Similarly, as the first step in a write action, write locks are set on the data to be modified. As usual, a single datum may have multiple readers, or a single writer, but not both, and possession of a write lock allows one to read the data as well. Finally, when a server completes its part of a transaction, it clears all that transaction's read and write locks that the server controls.

When a client needs to access files on more than one DFS server in a single transaction, it sends an *Add Server* request to the new server with which it needs to communicate. That server will then establish a connection with the client and will report to the primary server for the transaction (which is specified as part of the *Add Server* message) so that they can coordinate later. This enables the DFS to maintain the atomic property even when multiple servers are involved in a transaction (see section 19.3.2.4). Once the *Add Server* request is accepted, the client can address file access requests to the new server directly (i.e., without generating any "hidden" communications among servers). Transactions involving any number of servers are set up in this way, and requests to them are essentially independent – there is no close coordination among servers during normal file accesses. *End Transaction* requests can be addressed only to the primary server. Along with *Add Server,* they are the only messages that cause communication among the servers involved in a transaction.

19.3.2.3 Completing transactions

This section sketches the mechanisms by which servers maintain the atomic property of transactions in the face of crashes (a more thorough explanation is given in Chapter 11). There are three main ideas: *stable storage, intentions lists,* and *multiple-server synchronization.*

We assume that a disk drive can be programmed to provide *stable storage*; i.e., that a page can be written to the disk so that if the system should crash while the write is in progress, either the write does not occur at all (leaving the previous contents of the page intact), or the write completes successfully (see 11.4). This is an atomic property for disk pages.

It should be noted that stable storage is only needed for certain system uses such as intentions lists (see below), pointer pages to clients' files, disk allocation, etc. Thus, the overhead for stable pages involves only a very small fraction of the total storage available on a disk.

An *intentions list* is a list of actions designed so that partially carrying out the list several times and then finally completing it, is the same as performing it exactly once. Intentions lists are recorded in stable storage and can be written and erased as atomic acts. (If an intentions list is larger than one page, all trailing pages are first written, then the head page. A list does not exist unless the head page exists.)

When only a single file server is involved, a transaction is completed as a three-step process. First an intentions list which completely describes the writes of the transaction is written to stable disk storage. Next the intentions are carried out. Finally, the list is erased. If a crash should occur, all existing intentions lists are (re)discovered during recovery from the crash. Each such intentions list is carried out and then erased. The effect of one or more crashes is that an intentions list may be partially carried out several times, then completely carried out once. In any case, the transaction completes correctly.

A simple implementation for intentions is obtained by representing files as pointer blocks, which contain a sequence of pointers to data pages. In this case, an intentions list can be a list of new pointer values. A transaction is then implemented by writing data only in newly allocated disk pages. When the client sends a *End Transaction* request, the addresses of these new pages are collected in an intentions list.

Multiple-server synchronization is needed to avoid a situation in which one server carries out the writes of a transaction, while another aborts the transaction due to a crash. We designate the primary server as the *coordinator* and the others involved in the transaction as *workers*. The following steps complete a transaction; they are prevented from overlapping by synchronization messages at the completion of each step:

(1) The coordinator writes a list that includes the identity of each worker and marks the list *tentative*.

(2) Each worker writes an intentions list for the transaction (covering the writes occurring at that server). The worker also includes the identity of the coordinator in the list.

(3) The coordinator changes his worker list from *tentative* to *confirmed*. This effectively completes the transaction, and the coordinator can now send a response to the client that the transaction has successfully completed.

(4) The workers carry out their intentions lists and then erase them.

(5) The coordinator erases his worker list.

During crash recovery, all coordinators' lists of workers and all workers' intentions lists are located on the crashed server's disks. When a coordinator's list is discovered, there are two cases to be considered, depending on whether the list is marked *tentative* or *confirmed*. If it is tentative, each worker of the transaction is told to delete its intentions list and then the coordinator deletes its worker list (thus aborting the transaction). If the list is marked *confirmed*, the above algorithm resumes at step (4) to complete the associated transaction. When a worker's intentions list is discovered, it is simply kept until notification is received from the coordinator to either resume at step (4) or to abort.

19.3.3. Client responsibilities

19.3.3.1. Server crashes and aborted transactions

If a client machine is to provide continuous service, it must behave correctly in the presence of aborted transactions and server crashes. The effect of an abort is that all of the write requests issued by the client since beginning the transaction are lost, and all of the read and write locks are released. The atomic property guarantees that a server crash occurring before a *End Transaction* has the same effect as an abort, while one occurring after a transaction has successfully closed has no effect.

In general, a client recovers from an aborted transaction by redoing it. This does not mean simply repeating the reads and writes of the transaction since the writes were presumably dependent on the reads, and the client may read different data the second time (all read locks have been released, so another transaction may have changed the data). Also, later read requests may have been issued on the basis of results from earlier requests. Thus, redoing a transaction includes rereading the data, repeating the intermediate calculations, and writing new results (in whatever order is appropriate for the application). Moreover, if some of the writes were based on data from human input (e.g., a teller at a bank window), then redoing it may require that the human input be resolicited. In many cases, redoing a transaction can be made more efficient, however. Assume that the client saved the results of all the read requests and the values that were written in the aborted transaction. If rereading the data yields the same input values as previously, the client can simply write the saved results from the previous calculations and need not recompute them.

A transaction may be aborted for a number of reasons (this list is not exhaustive):

(1) The server may run out of resources and deliberately abort a transaction in an attempt to recover.

(2) The transaction may have been in existence for a long time, and a write lock may have been broken by some other transaction.

(3) Some server involved in the transaction may have crashed and recovered.

(4) The server may abort a transaction because it decides that a client has crashed when it actually has not (this might happen if communications are temporarily broken and later repaired).

If a transaction is aborted for any of these reasons, it is up to the client machine to discover the situation and repair it.

A client machine will discover that a transaction has aborted in a number of ways. In the easiest case (e.g., (1) above), the server directly informs the client machine of the abortion. Alternatively, the server may reject a requested action because it has previously aborted that transaction (cases (3) and (4) can cause this).

There is one much more difficult case: A client C has sent a *End Transaction*, but before it has received a completion response, the server crashes. When the server recovers from the crash and C resends the *End Transaction*, it will receive a rejection in response because the transaction is no longer around (it either aborted or was completed as part of crash recovery). C must then figure out which case holds, *but only by inspecting data contained in the* DFS. For example, it could have written the transaction sequence number in a private file as part of the transaction. The atomic property then guarantees that the presence of the transaction number in the private file indicates that the whole transaction completed properly; its absence means that the entire transaction aborted. To avoid this overhead, the DFS servers maintain a list of the most recently completed transactions. Thus, a client can determine if a transaction completed simply by checking to see if the transaction number is on this list. However, this list is only of finite length, so a client who waits too long (on the order of days) before asking whether some transaction has completed may receive the answer "don't know" instead of "yes" or "no".

19.3.3.2 Local caches of shared data

When data is stored remotely, it is often cheaper for a client to *cache* parts of the data locally (e.g., in its main memory or on a local disk) instead of simply making requests of the DFS for every file access. By caching we mean that the client might not only hold onto data read from the DFS, but might not necessarily write data to the DFS on every logical write (e.g., to replace two overlapping writes by a single one later). However, if a client accesses shared files, caching may introduce performance problems. For example, the atomic property is enforced by setting read and write locks as a client reads and writes data. This mechanism has the undesirable effect that a client can hold data locked for long periods of time if he avoids closing a transaction.

A simple way to prevent a client from holding data locked indefinitely would be to abort a transaction whenever it has run longer than some predefined maximum. Unfortunately, clients may be unable to live within the confines of a transaction time limit. Instead of outlawing long-lived transactions, we have chosen to make three alterations to the basic locking mechanisms to make it efficient for clients to maintain local caches of shared data. Following descriptions of these changes, we give two examples of how clients may use the mechanisms to cache data.

- The first modification to the basic mechanism is to permit the *breaking* of locks which have been set for a long time. (This is weaker than aborting a transaction.) A lock is broken when two conditions are satisfied: it has been set for a long time and another transaction attempts to set a competing lock. When a lock is broken, the transaction which set the lock is notified. This notification is recorded by the server holding the locked data, and an unsolicited message is sent to the transaction client. A client may also request a list of the current set of broken read locks.

- The second modification is to permit a transaction client to clear read locks that it has set. With this change, the atomic property needs to be rephrased to read:

    at the moment a transaction completes, no data has been modified by other transactions, except possibly for any data whose read lock was subsequently cleared.

  When a client clears a read lock, he is, therefore, affirming that the data writes occurring during this transaction are not dependent on the data covered by the cleared read lock (there is an example below).

- The final modification is to prevent completing a transaction that has any broken, but uncleared locks. This dual condition on broken locks allows a client to respond to an unsolicited message that a lock has been broken by clearing the lock. A client that behaves this way (see below for an example) can thereby avoid repeating an entire transaction if non-critical read locks are broken. This modification is necessary to prevent a race condition between a client that checks for broken read locks before closing a transaction only to have some broken after checking, but before requesting a *End Transaction* request.

With these mechanisms, a client machine can maintain a local copy of data for some period of time, and become informed when the original is being changed. As shown in the following examples, this mechanism improves performance by reducing the amount of information which must be transferred between server and client, but does not provide any intrinsically new function.

Maintaining a read-only cache

Consider a specific example of an infrequently changing data base, the locations and contents of all the freight cars on a railroad. The client machine is to maintain a display terminal which shows some portion of this information, such as the location and contents of all trains destined for Paris. It is important that the displayed information correctly represents the current contents of the data base. If maximum transaction time limits were enforced, the client would have to repeatedly open a transaction, read all the data to be displayed, and close the transaction. With caching, the client initially reads all the desired information from the system. It then regularly checks for broken read locks by sending requests to the file servers involved and rereads any information whose locks have been broken (i.e., just the information that has changed).

Cache example: Updating a shared data base

Suppose that a client has a data base that changes infrequently and that the client desires to perform a transaction that first reads a substantial amount of data, then performs a long computation, and finally writes the results back to the DFS. With only a maximum time limit on transactions and no caching mechanisms, the client would proceed in three major steps:

(1) Open a transaction, read the data, and then immediately close the transaction, releasing the locks.

(2) Perform the long computation.

(3) Open a new transaction, re-read the input data and confirm that it is unchanged since read previously. If so, write the computed result back to the file system and close the transaction. If not, the client must repeat the calculation.

Caching permits the client to avoid the overhead in step (3) of re-reading the entire set of input data, to check that it has not changed. The new scenario proceeds as follows:

(1′) Open a transaction and read the input data.

(2′) Perform the long computation.

(3′) Write the results to the file system, and then check for broken read locks. If there are none (and this is probable since we assumed infrequently changing data), then the client closes the transaction.

 If there are broken read locks (it is assumed that no write locks have been broken), the client can either redo the entire transaction, or perform the following, additional steps. This increased complexity might not always be warranted, but we are assuming in this example that substantial amounts of data would have to be re-read to redo the transaction.

(4′) Clear the broken locks, re-read the data covered by those locks, and perform any reads that are dependent on that data.

(5′) Perform the long calculation, although there may be some shortcuts dependent on exactly which data was re-read.

(6′) Issue new write requests to convert the original write requests into the new answer. Then, check again for broken read locks. If there are none, just close the transaction, otherwise repeat steps (4′) through (6′).

19.3.3.3. Directories

The DFS only identifies files by their UIDs, so there is no built-in way of giving a file an alphanumeric name for users. To provide such a facility, we have implemented a *directory server*. It maintains a mapping from alphanumeric identifiers to UIDs. This mapping is represented in a normal DFS file stored in the file system. A directory server appears as an ordinary client to the

DFS. So a directory server is both a server and a client at the same time. Isolating the directory service in this way means that different implementations of directories may use different file naming schemes and still share the DFS facility. Of course, a file does not need to have an alphanumeric name – its UID can be used perfectly well by a client that needs to access it (this is typically the case for scratch files).

The directory server example brings out an interesting design issue. Consider a typical situation, such as creating a file, recording it in a directory, and storing data in it. From the point of view of the initiating client, these three actions should be atomic; either all of them or none of them should be done. The DFS atomic property guarantees this, but here the server sees two separate clients (the directory server and the initiating client) communicating from different computers. The issue is how to merge the two sets of actions together atomically.

The approach we have chosen is to permit several clients to participate in a single transaction. The directory server joins the initiating client's transaction by means of a special interchange of messages with the file server(s). To access the directory file, the directory server still addresses requests to the file server where the file resides, but the file service associates two clients with the same transaction. The initiating client needs to communicate with the directory server to coordinate opening and closing transactions, but this dialog is transparent to the file servers. Note also that the two clients may need quite different access privileges: the directory server has access to the directory file, but the initiating client does not.

19.3.4. Summary

This section has described a stand-alone file system that is accessed over a network and consists of a number of cooperating server machines. It provides a number of mechanisms to assist remote client machines to update shared files while keeping them consistent. The most important of these mechanisms, the atomic property for transactions, allows a client to encapsulate a sequence of reads and writes as an indivisible, atomic action. We also described mechanisms for enabling clients to maintain local caches of shared data and gave examples of how those facilities could be used to improve performance.

19.4. Violet: A distributed, replicated calendar system

19.4.1. Introduction

Violet was constructed as an experimental investigation into the nature of decentralized information systems. It has a number of interesting properties:

- It conceals the identity of physical resources, so that capacity and reliability could be improved without any changes to user programs.
- The user populations can in principle scale over several orders of magnitude in size without system redesign.
- It maintains a high quality bit-map display for interaction, using computing power available locally to each user.
- Each user request results in a predictable outcome, regardless of other concurrent activities.

Violet includes a general-purpose environment that makes it easy to construct decentralized user applications. The building blocks available to the architect of an application are well-defined abstractions, arranged in a hierarchy, so that simple arguments can be used to reason about the behavior of the system. The highest level of the current system is a calendar system, providing simple data base query and storage services. This system is an extremely simple data base manager, but its underlying framework is sophisticated enough to convince us that Violet's primitives are adequate to support a wide variety of applications.

The first four parts of this section provide a detailed view of Violet's architecture, and the last three parts discuss the architecture in practice. In order the seven parts are: a discussion of the implementation environment, an exposition of Violet's architecture, a description of our algorithm for replicated data, a section on sharing and locking, a discussion of Violet's performance, notes on the actual implementation, and a conclusion.

19.4.2. Environment

Every user of Violet has a personal computer, usually an Alto, connected to the Pup internet. The addressing structure of the internet is uniform, regardless of a computer's attachment point. In addition to user machines, there are file servers connected to an internetwork. Under user direction, Violet employs shared file servers to store user data. The servers provide page-level access to files: "read page" and "write page" are typical operations. The characteristics of the

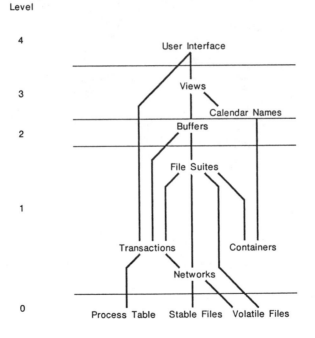

Figure 19-6: The internal structure of Violet

communications channel between client program and server determine the observed latency of the server's operations. Actual measurements reveal that the typical read latency for a 512 byte page is approximately 75 milliseconds from a file server on a directly connected network; the figure rises to 650 milliseconds for a file server connected to a remote network accessed via a 9.6 KB data circuit.

Violet uses the unique facilities of the Distributed File System [section 19.3] for data storage. Recall that operations on files are grouped into transactions, and synchronization protocols between file servers insure that either all of the actions of a transaction are performed, or none are. For example, if file A is on server X, and file B is on server Y, a transaction updating A and B will either effect changes on servers X and Y or will not change data on either of them.

19.4.3. System architecture

The system is structured in five levels. Levels correspond to components that were independently tested. Level 0 provides basic file storage facilities. Level 1 erases physical boundaries, and improves imperfect hardware to provide an idealized network virtual machine. Level 2 is a virtual memory package, and Levels 3 and 4 comprise the calendar application, with its data base manager and user interface.

To provide motivation for the abstractions, we will introduce them top down, with apologies for the occasional forward references which result. Readers may find it convenient to refer to figure 19-6, a diagram of Violet's internal structure.

LEVEL 4

User interface. Figures 19-7 and 19-8 are representative pictures of our user interface. Figure 19-7 shows a public "bulletin-board" calendar, Seminars.CSL. Figure 19-8 shows a scheduling operator applied to the union of two calendars. A pointing device is used to select menu items and calendar entries for manipulation. After a view of the calendar data base is specified, Violet paints the screen with the desired data.

All user requests are implicitly part of the current *transaction*. When a user is satisfied with his changes he can choose to commit the transaction with the commit button, shown on the screen in the figures. Violet guarantees that either all of the actions of a transaction will be performed, or none of them will. If a user is unhappy with his changes, he can choose to abort the transaction and start over again.

Violet automatically keeps the display current with changes in the data base. As long as the user's transaction is in force, it appears to the user that he is the only person using the data base. However, if another user updates data that is in the current view, the current transaction is aborted, and the screen is automatically repainted to depict the change. The detailed coordination with transaction management necessary to accomplish this is described in Section 19.4.7.

LEVEL 3

Calendar management creates and deletes calendars, and maps calendar names into file suite names (Level 1). The naming structure is fairly simple by design. Each calendar name is composed of two parts which appear as: ObjectName.GroupName. Currently we map group

```
View: Seminars.csl
```
Calendar

Violet Calendar System

January 1979

14 Sunday	15 Monday	16 Tuesday	17 Wednesday	18 Thursday	19 Friday	20 Saturday
		10:30 – 12:00 Prof. Steven Ward of MIT CSL Commons The MuNet: A Scalable Multiprocessor Architecture ---------- 14:30 – 15:30 Dr. Robert Bower, UCLA & TRW CSL Commons Very Large Scale Integrated Circuits: Evolutionary or Revolutionary for the 1980's ----------	13:15 – 15:00 Dave Gifford, CSL CSL Commons Dealer: The Architecture of Violet ----------	15:45 – 17:00 Don Scifres, GSL PARC Cafeteria Forum: Exploring the Light Fantastic ----------	15:00 – 16:00 Prof. Yutake Toyozawa GSL Conference Room #1077 Bistability and Anomalies in Resonant Scattering of Intense Light ----------	

```
 ? |   | Quit | Next Week | Previous Week | Set View | Create | Change | Delete | Commit | Abort | Copy
```

Figure 19-7: A public calendar

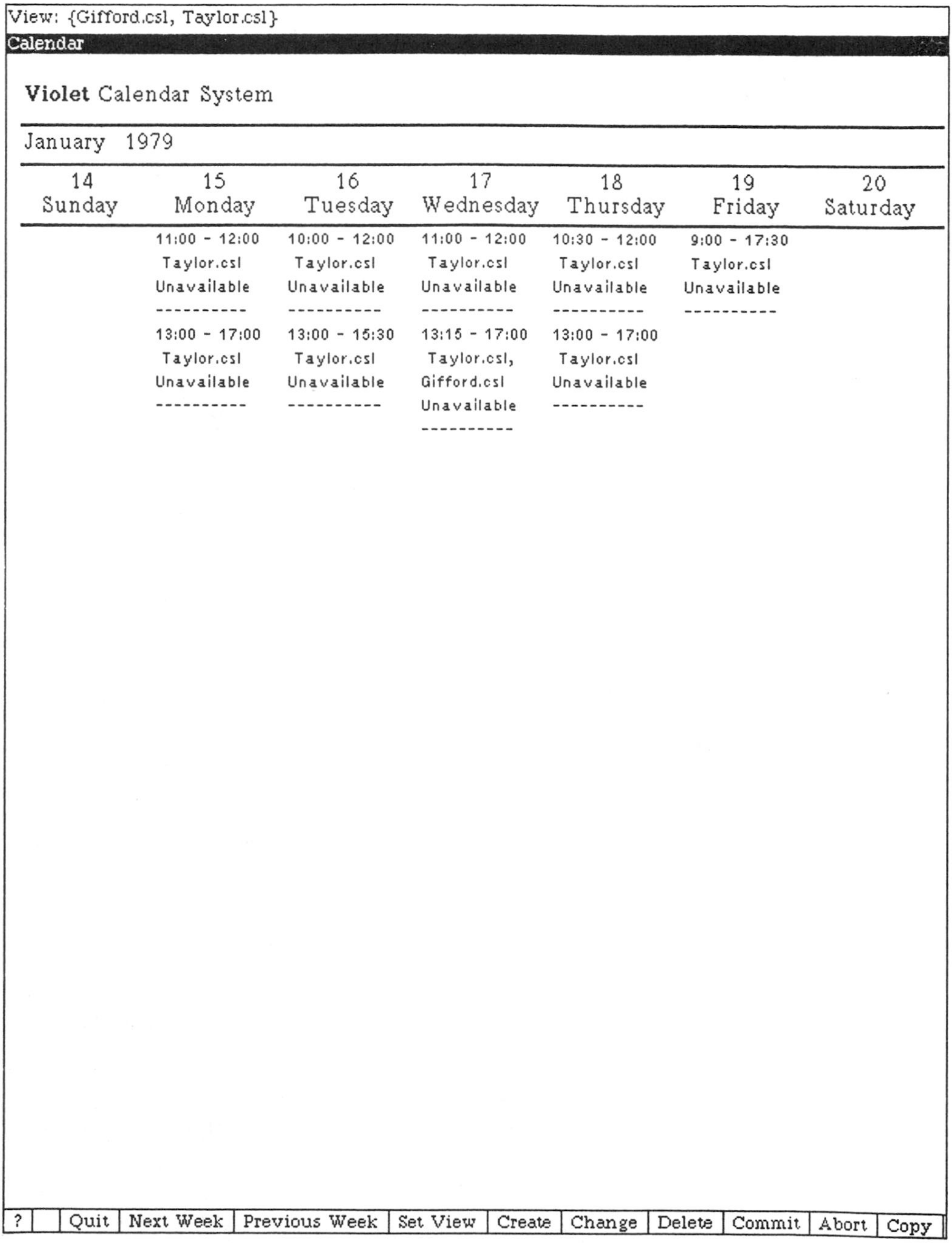

View: {Gifford.csl, Taylor.csl}

Calendar

Violet Calendar System

January 1979

14 Sunday	15 Monday	16 Tuesday	17 Wednesday	18 Thursday	19 Friday	20 Saturday
	11:00 − 12:00	10:00 − 12:00	11:00 − 12:00	10:30 − 12:00	9:00 − 17:30	
	Taylor.csl	Taylor.csl	Taylor.csl	Taylor.csl	Taylor.csl	
	Unavailable	Unavailable	Unavailable	Unavailable	Unavailable	
	----------	----------	----------	----------	----------	
	13:00 − 17:00	13:00 − 15:30	13:15 − 17:00	13:00 − 17:00		
	Taylor.csl	Taylor.csl	Taylor.csl,	Taylor.csl		
	Unavailable	Unavailable	Gifford.csl	Unavailable		
	----------	----------	Unavailable	----------		

| ? | | Quit | Next Week | Previous Week | Set View | Create | Change | Delete | Commit | Abort | Copy |

Figure 19-8: A display showing conflicts

names into containers (Level 1), and use the object name to select a file within the container. The administration of the naming environment is decentralized; by including groups we have broken the name space into pieces that can be independently managed.

Views. Tuples are related groups of information that are stored in our data base. The only tuple type we have defined corresponds to an event, and contains such fields as start time, finish time, author, event description, and so on. Sets are collections of tuples. Violet stores a set and its index in a file suite.

A view is a virtual set, synthesized from a user supplied description. The five operations on a view are create tuple, delete tuple, update tuple, get next tuple, and fetch tuple. Legal view descriptions are described by the context free grammar

> *view* :: = *base* U *view* | *base*
> *base* :: = {*view*} | (*view*) | **Calendar**

Every view operator defines fetch and update semantics, so a user can update the synthetic set provided by the view mechanism. For example, "Gifford.CSL U Taylor.CSL" describes the union of the two sets "Gifford.CSL" and "Taylor.CSL". All tuples that appear in either Gifford or Taylor appear in the union, and updates to the view are applied to both Gifford and Taylor. It would be a simple matter to define a union operator with different update semantics. The scheduling operator {*view*} synthesizes a view that groups all of the unavailable time in *view* together. Thus, "{Gifford.CSL U Taylor.CSL}" could be used to schedule a meeting between Gifford and Taylor (see figure 19-8).

LEVEL 2

Buffers provide a simulated virtual memory to Level 3, and in turn utilize file suites. The buffer manager guarantees that it always holds fresh data by registering itself with transaction management (Level 1).

LEVEL 1

Transactions. Transactions insure that a consistent set of updates are always applied to a file. Transactions guarantee serial consistency [Eswaren 76], or the illusion that there is no concurrent activity in the system. A transaction is implicitly associated with a process – although several processes in a single processor can arrange to share a transaction. Such sharing occurs in our replicated data manager when several processes cooperate to provide a single service. A process exercises direct control over its transaction, requesting that it be aborted or committed.

Supporting this abstraction requires three distinct services. First, a process-to-transaction mapping must be maintained. Second, a centralized interface for requesting transaction state changes (commit, abort) must exist. Third, a clearinghouse for messages concerning the freshness of data must be established; it must inform concerned modules that data they previously requested has become stale. To use this mechanism, modules that save state information based on reads from the data base register themselves with transaction management, and are then notified of a transaction commit or abort. This service is used by the user interface to know when the screen is out of date and should be repainted.

Network management performs two functions. First, it synthesizes full-duplex, perfect connections from a packet-switched internetwork composed of local networks and gateways which may lose or duplicate packets. Second, network management translates symbolic network server names into network addresses. Violet uses the level 2 Pup protocols.

File suites are logically arrays of bytes. The primitive operations on a file suite are create, delete, read, write, set size, and get size. File suites may be replicated for performance and reliability enhancement, as described in Section 19.4.4. Every file suite is assigned a unique name when it is created. Network management is used to communicate with the remote components of a file suite.

Containers are storage repositories for file suites, independent of specific physical storage services. A file suite's container is specified at its creation time. A file suite inherits properties from its container, including whether or not it should be replicated.

LEVEL 0

Level 0 includes the language run-time system, which supplies such necessary facilities as a segmented memory, a free-storage package, and low-level process management.

Stable files are files that can be accessed through a transactional file system. As we mentioned earlier, stable files are implemented by DFS. Because stable files are shared, it is extremely important that concurrent file operations have well-defined properties. DFS mediates access to shared files by implicitly setting locks in response to file operations.

Volatile files are files that can not be accessed through a transactional file system. Unfortunately, because of the complexity involved in providing transactions, many file systems do not implement them. An example is the one local to a user's personal computer. Section 19.4.4 describes how volatile files can be included in a file suite.

19.4.4. Replicated data

It is often desirable to replicate data for additional reliability and performance. The file suite abstraction implements a read majority, write majority algorithm [Gifford 79] for replicated data. A sketch of the algorithm is provided here, and the interested reader should consult [Gifford 79] for further details. The algorithm assumes that there is a common transactional file system across all copies of a file suite.

A file suite is composed of a number of *representatives*, each containing a copy of the suite's data. Each representative has a number of *votes*. A *majority* is a subset whose votes sum to more than half of the total number of votes assigned. Each representative also has a *version number*. A representative is said to be *current* if it contains the most recent version of the file suite.

Every file operation directed to a replicated file suite is appropriately transformed. The central invariant of our algorithm is that any majority will always contain a current representative. Conceptually, a read checks the version numbers of a majority, and actually reads from a current representative. Writes have more stringent requirements. The first step of a write is to collect a majority of current representatives. A write then applies its update to all members of this majority. In this way it assures that some majority subset is always current. In actuality, the performance of the replicated-data algorithm has been improved considerably from a naive implementation of the conceptual description provided above. Version numbers are read once per transaction. Background processes update obsolete representatives. An adaptive algorithm that measures response times of representatives attempts to forward a request to the fastest eligible representative.

An attractive property of our voting proposal is flexibility. By entrusting all of the votes to one representative a centralized scheme results; apportioning votes equally among representatives results in a completely decentralized scheme. The proposal also admits a variety of interesting configurations between the two extremes. For example, consider four representatives assigned the voting configuration ⟨2, 1, 1, 1⟩. The first representative when paired with any other representative forms a majority subset. However, the system can tolerate the failure of the first representative. As long as a majority is available, the suite will continue to function.

Using the administrative tool of vote assignment, it is possible to blend the individual strengths of representatives to achieve desired file suite properties. Heavily weighting high-reliability representatives will tend to produce a reliable suite; heavily weighting high-performance representatives will tend to produce a high-performance suite. A thorough analysis of the vote assignment problem is beyond the scope of this paper.

A representative's version number must be accurate. If a version number became incorrect, inconsistent data could potentially corrupt the entire suite. It is straightforward to use the atomic update properties of stable files to guarantee that version numbers are maintained correctly, using the following simple algorithm. When a current representative is updated by a transaction, its version number is incremented. All current representatives have the same version number, which is interpreted as the version number of the suite. When an obsolete representative is overwritten with current data, it assumes the version number of the suite.

We have also introduced the notion of a *weak representative*, one with no votes. Such a representative can be created without administrative sanction, as it will have no material effect on the system. However, it carries a version number, as does any representative, and can be included as a member of a majority subset. Thus, when placed on a high speed device, it can serve as an effective intermediate level of store. Conceptually we like to view all data that has been temporarily promoted to a different level of store as an instance of a weak representative. Such a representative can be used for access, but changes to it will not be firm until propagated backward into a majority subset. An acceptable mode of recovery for a weak representative is invalidation, because the majority invariant always guarantees that the data can be recovered from the suite. Thus, weak representatives can be stored in volatile files.

All of the replicated data machinery we have described resides in a user's local machine. Our file servers are unaware that replication of data is being performed, and are thus unencumbered. However, it is conceivable that outside assistance could improve performance. Replication servers could assume the tasks of file management, freeing user machines from their detailed knowledge of file suite replication. One could also imagine a daemon assisting file suite management in its update tasks, potentially at times of surplus communication capacity.

In sum, we see the cardinal virtue of our replication algorithm to be its simplicity. The algorithm requires no changes to file servers, and is easy to implement.

19.4.5. Sharing and locking

DFS mediates concurrent access to stable files by implicitly setting locks in response to file operations. These locks are held for the duration of a transaction and then released. Initially DFS employed traditional read and write locks that allowed for either one writer or n readers. The lock compatibility matrix for this rule is:

	No Lock	Read	Write
No Lock	Yes	Yes	Yes
Read	Yes	Yes	No
Write	Yes	No	No

If a transaction attempts to set a lock that would violate the matrix it is forced to wait.

To insure that no user monopolizes a stable file, DFS will time out a transaction if other users are waiting for a file it has locked. A transaction that times out leaves stable files unchanged because its transaction is aborted. The same mechanism insures that cyclic lock dependencies (deadlocks) will be resolved by the abortion of one of the transactions. The length of a transaction is controlled by the user, and it may consist of many interactions. As a user progresses, he acquires more locks, increasing the probability that he will conflict with another user. The net effect is to push the transaction into the lower right corner of the compatibility matrix, making the transaction less and less likely to complete.

When preparing for the first demonstration of Violet this locking strategy showed its limitations. Imagine the following scenario: there are two Violet users, each displaying the same calendar. They both have been viewing the calendar, and thus holding read locks, longer than the time-out interval in DFS. User A now updates his view, but does not commit his transaction. User A thus sets a write lock on the calendar's index, aborting User B. User B's machine, attempting to provide good service to its user, now continually asks for the index that has been denied to it. Finally, User B's machine times out User A, aborting User A's transaction. User B's machine repaints the old view of the data without User A's change. User A, having been aborted, also repaints his screen with the old information. Net progress: zero.

Two conflicting desires produce the underlying problem. First, the user interface is always trying to maintain a fresh display. Second, we want to allow a user to determine what constitutes a transaction, thus allowing him to determine how long data is unavailable. One way to solve this dilemma is to queue up all of the writes of a transaction, issuing them just before a commit. Using this strategy, User A would not acquire the write lock on the index until commit time. We use a variant of this solution, taking advantage of our transactional file system. As writes occur during a transaction, we set intention-write locks. An intention-write lock implies that the transaction will update the datum in question at commit time. The buffering of writes till commit time is a natural by-product of our transactional file system. It still appears to the issuing transaction that a write takes place immediately. When the transaction does commit, the intention-write locks are converted into commit locks, and the writes are performed. Intention-write locks are compatible with read locks. Our new compatibility matrix is:

	No Lock	Read	I-Write	Commit
No Lock	Yes	Yes	Yes	Yes
Read	Yes	Yes	Yes	No
I-Write	Yes	Yes	No	No
Commit	Yes	No	No	No

Transactions operate in the upper left three-by-three matrix. Only during commit processing will a transaction hold write locks.

We have chosen to make multiple intention-write locks incompatible. Eventually one of the transactions would commit, changing its intention-write lock into a commit lock. Thus, conflict is inevitable, and we chose not to postpone it. A direct result of our new locking mechanism is the increased availability of data. It is now always possible for users to access data, except for predictably short periods during commit processing. The increased availability of data allows for more concurrent activity.

Our locking strategy is not applicable to all environments. We have provided long transactions that may be aborted, in contrast to many existing systems that provide short transactions that will always commit. Our approach is best suited for a low contention environment with users who desire to control the length of their own transactions.

19.4.6. The performance of the architecture

File system properties

Above Level 1, Violet is similar to a typical time-sharing system. In fact, the interface to file suites is a copy of the CTSS file system interface. Thus, the *semantics* of our interface are identical to those of a centralized file system. However, our interface's *properties* are considerably different. We have identified three properties of our file system that serve to distinguish it from CTSS (or any other time-sharing like system). First, the servers that comprise Level 0 are under decentralized administrative control. Thus, the failure modes of Violet and a time-sharing system are considerably different. Second, the observed performance of file operations can range over an order of magnitude — approximately from 75 to 750 milliseconds. Third, the number of directly accessible files is for all practical purposes unlimited.

These properties provide for decentralized management of data-storage facilities, permitting a department (or other administrative unit) to assume full responsibility for its own storage needs. Of course, there is the potential for abuse. A local organization can be irresponsible in maintaining adequate server performance. For example, we often found ourselves calling colleagues to ascertain the state of a server when our system stopped responding.

The provisions for replicated data were designed in part to eliminate the undesirable properties of our decentralized hardware base. We do not have sufficient experience yet to judge how serious the problems are, or how much replication helps.

Level distribution

Retaining our basic architecture, it would be possible to reconfigure the tasks for which processors are responsible. For example, the internetwork communication path could be moved from Levels 1-0 to Levels 4-3. This alternative corresponds to "sending actions" as opposed to our current approach of "sending data", and would entail operating calendar servers. We found that the number of messages and the quantity of information that passed between Levels 1 to 0 and Levels 4 to 3 were comparable. This was a result of Violet's ability to keep pertinent calendar indexes in its virtual memory.

When assigning layers to processors the most significant effect is normally assumed to be to the cost of communication. Because our local network operates at three million bits per second, we did not find the cost of communication to be significant. The ability of the programs that compose the layers of Violet to fit in a user's local machine turned out to have the most significant effect on performance. Layers 1-4 required more main memory than many of our intended clients had available in their local machines.

19.4.7. Implementation notes

The entire Violet system was implemented in Mesa, a programming language that provides integrated processes, monitors, and condition variables. The process and synchronization facilities of Mesa are used heavily by Violet. For example, the replicated data manager is a monitor that has an instantiation for every open replicated file. Each instance employs one static process, two kinds of dynamic processes, and three condition variables.

Our abstractions are implemented as Mesa modules. We took full advantage of Mesa's class structure to evolve our implementation by specifying interfaces, filling in underlying implementations as necessary. Such step-wise development afforded us the opportunity to test our assumptions about the importance of various system components by initially implementing minimal facilities, and later returning to expand them. For example, our first implementation lacked integrated transaction management, and was difficult to comprehend. The first module to use the file system created a transaction, and was responsible for passing it to other participating modules. Exceptional conditions often resulted in the invalidation of a transaction, producing chaos. Formalizing the transaction abstraction by providing a centralized interface solved these problems.

Each abstraction is responsible for behaving correctly when it is presented with concurrent requests. There are no global locks in Violet. Rather, Violet's modules use monitors to serialize access to shared data.

The user interface is implemented by two processes. One process is dedicated to maintaining the display. It collects a display-full of information using get next tuple and fetch tuple, and paints the display. It then waits on the condition variable *ViewChanged*. The second process watches the keyboard, and when a menu item is selected, collects characters, performs the user's request, and notifies *ViewChanged*. The first process then repaints the display with the updated view. Both of these processes run in the same monitor, and procedures that enter the monitor are used to synchronize user actions with display updating. Conceptually, each button on the user's display is an entry into this monitor. This mechanism insures that user requests are not processed while the display is updating.

These processes are also used to keep the display current with changes other users make in the data base. When the user's transaction is aborted, indicating there is fresh information, a new transaction is started, and *ViewChanged* is notified. The first process then repaints the screen with fresh information. Because the transaction abort is detected at interrupt level (a network packet arrives) it is not possible for the user interface to update the display when it first learns that it is obsolete. This consideration motivated dedicating a process to display maintenance.

Testing was the hardest part of the implementation task. An annoying part of our debugging system was that we could not discern what data structures and processes were associated with specific parts of Violet. This information was not necessary for proper operation of the Mesa run-time support, and thus was not available. Furthermore, the lack of hardware protection in our personal computers has traditionally made certain kinds of problems difficult to locate. Thus, we tried to debug our system at design time, but we found that some implementation flaws were not uncovered until we ran the algorithms.

Interactive debugging tools were written to exercise the levels of Violet. Transaction and file management were operational after an afternoon's work with the Level 2 debugger. Our spontaneous transaction abort logic was tested by using several machines operating in this simplified environment. In addition to providing a debugging tool, the Level 3 debugger was our original teletype-style user interface.

19.4.8. Conclusion

Violet's structure reflects our understanding of the fundamental facilities that are required to support a decentralized user application. We very carefully factored necessary facilities into independent abstractions. The implementations of abstractions interact (e.g. transactions and file suites), but a client is always presented with independent interfaces for independent concepts. Our careful factoring reduced the complexity of Violet. For example, the code that manipulates transactions is grouped into small, pure pieces, instead of being scattered throughout the system.

Our experience with Violet has resulted in a number of observations:

- First, the primitives from which a decentralized system is to be constructed must be sound. A firm foundation offers conceptual power, as we demonstrated by synthesizing replicated files from a well-defined transactional file system.

- Second, the notion of a transaction is fundamental to a successful concurrent system. In addition to DFS servers, we utilized non-transactional servers. Weak representatives can be stored on these servers, but for general use we found them to be largely unacceptable, because their locking protocols did not provide for sufficient concurrency. In addition, our users often restart their machines when impatient, which tended to cause irreparable damage to their calendars because of uncompleted writes.

- Third, sophisticated display facilities place large performance demands on a data base system. A typical Violet screen is composed of approximately twenty tuples, and our users expect to see them appear instantaneously.

- Fourth, unifying a decentralized hardware base with a file system has a great deal of conceptual simplicity. The Level 1 framework we built would allow for the construction of a wide variety of application systems.

- Fifth, it is reasonable to expect that at any point some fraction of the resources of a decentralized system will be unavailable. We have introduced a new abstraction, the file suite, that masks partial system failures.

As we said at the beginning, we had four goals when we built Violet: configuration independence, extensibility, a flexible user interface, and consistency. We have demonstrated a system that uses simple abstractions to achieve these goals. We are confident that more ambitious systems, if attempted with a similar architecture, would also prove to be successful.

Chapter 20. Conclusion

20.1. Introduction

When I was "lucky" enough to be "selected" to provide the final remarks to the course, there was one consolation: I would be able to hear the complete series of lectures before the conclusion was to be written. As the lectures progressed two things became clear. First, there is no way to summarize the details of the course. Second, there is no conclusion to the saga that is this course; i.e., distributed systems are just begining to be practical, and there are not a large number of extant examples. After discussion during the course with other lecturers and participants, it was decided to provide a course summary which provides an overview of various categories of important issues which when grouped together form the chapter to be entitled "Concluding Remarks".

The intent of concluding remarks is to summarize and conclude this specific set of lectures without attempting to write a conclusion to the subject of distributed systems. It will be clear, however that strong conclusions will be drawn in this chapter.

The remainder of this chapter is organized into eight sections:

§ 20.2   What we have defined – This section will review the major items we defined the beginning of the course.

§ 20.3   What we think we know – The answer to many system design issues is "It depends!". During the course, we came to believe that there are some specific answers to system problems that we had solutions for. These are summarized in this section.

§ 20.4   What we conjecture- During the course it became obvious that some very strong opinions were being developed, but these opinions were not universally accepted. These strong opinions are formulated herein as conjectures.

§ 20.5   What we think we don't know – Both during the course and during the preparation meeting we discovered that the issues we were unable to answer were probably of much more relevance and difficulty than what we knew. This section will review these important issues.

§ 20.6   What we advise – During the course, we formed some strong opinions on how we would design a system. Such information is summarized in this section.

§ 20.7   What you should know – This section describes a number of important items that we feel you should be aware of.

§ 20.8   What we don't agree upon – A special section is devoted to disagreement. The lecturers are eight highly varied and complex personalities, each with strong opinions on system design. There existed during the times we were together some very vocal disagreements. The most important are summarized.

§ 20.8 Acknowledgements – Lastly, there are some individuals who were very integral to this course, but may only appear behind the scenes. This section acknowledges the people who helped make this course a success that it was.

20.2. What we have defined

The course began with a single definition: distributed system. That definition provided the most important points that would be evolved over the next two weeks. The most important idea to have gained is that a distributed system is more than distributing hardware. It consists of multiple concurrent processes, processor/memory pairs which do not share memory but communicate with other processes via messages, the concept of system wide control, etc. Clearly, lots of groups can decentralize hardware, but example extant distributed systems are rare indeed. The other important definition occurred when the subject of operating systems was broached. A theoretical space of operating systems was defined which stated with a centralized operating system and went to a hypothetically implementable decentralized global operating system. The space defined conceptual postulates, but a lack of extant operating systems which could be looked at to ascertain usefulness of characteristic features.

20.3. What we think we know

It is clear that distributed processing is more than simply distribution of appropriate hardware. The range of distribution was previously defined. It may appear that the range is network oriented, but in fact it includes distributed computers as well as networks.

We examined current system models and standards and found them to be inadequate. Grossly inadequate and oversimplified is more to the point. It appears, however, that the fact of existence of international standards is somewhat of a miracle in and of itself. Yet we felt compelled to throw out all standards and propose the reference model introduced in this course. This decision resulted from a number of simple observations including the fact that given current standards we were unable to determine what a link is in various systems we considered distributed. If someone can define a link level, then it should be well defined; i.e., you should be able to figure out what a link is.

A reference model was proposed which emphasized the issues we felt important. Contrary to other models which contain one axis, (a set of protocol levels), our model has two important characteristics. First, it has a simplified level structure. Second, it emphasizes the fact that there are other dimensions to a distributed system. There are a set of global system design and optimization issues which in general know one even bothers to address. Since, we don't know how to solve (in some cases formulate) these issues we pointed them out for intellectual honesty, but the solution is left to the student. Second, at each level of abstraction in the model there are a set of common design issues. For example, error control can be implemented at any level. As the lectures progressed, we tried to address these design issues.

We believe that eventually distributed systems will evolve into a system concept which appears as a set of locally distributed networks hierarchially linked with public data networks and satellites. It is for this reason that many of the reference models break down when viewed from our context; i.e., they do not support such system concepts.

One of the levels that will have to be developed in a distributed system is the IPC level. It appears that a large number of people know how to implement this transport oriented level. This is one of the reasons for the proliferation of so called distributed systems which really consist of simply decentralized hardware. There are many well understood ways to implement the IPC level. The medium concepts and trade off and design strategies exist to allow us to build arbitrarily complex systems.

One big problem in implementing a hierarchial system of local networks is how to construct the levels, naming, routing, etc. We suggest that you seriously study the encapsulation strategies employed in Ethernet before building a hierarchical system.

The XNOS system described and the decentralized global operating system define the endpoints of the distributed operating system spectrum; however, there does not presently exist an implementation concept or example for decentralized global operating system. Some system (concepts) close to this theoretical end point may be unimplementable and we know of no currently implemented decentralized global operating system. One important issue is the development of atomic transactions. A system model was presented which allowed the development of a concept for atomic transactions and the description of how one might go about developing a remote procedure call mechanism bassed upon the given model. An implementation for the procedure call mechanism could be developed if desired.

Throughout the course evolution is emphasized. Systems evolve! Very few revolutionary concepts go to fruition. Disquieting as it may be, the extension of this conclusion notes that at some level of abstraction, a distributed system may appear to the user just like like a centralized system. They may be indistinguishable. Does the user care? The consensus was that the user did not really care and in fact that it was probably not presently feasible or desirable to see other than a centralized system interface. Additionally, we felt that the increasing complexity of applications would insure that distributed systems would eventually become widespread via evolution of current system concepts.

At points in the course we worried about system reliability. It became apparent that the overall attitude was that it would not be out of line, in certain contexts, to allow the system to crash or to lose a few (small number) of datagrams. If the difference in design effort to increase reliability one percent was one hundred percent, for example, and current reliability was say ninety seven percent, we felt that the effort might be wasted. Interestingly, it is seldom if ever that a system designer will ever say that they know that there are times when you should lose data or crash a system. A clear statement of this principle was provided during this course. Be willing to crash! Be willing to lose datagrams! We know how to build end-to-end protocols. Depend on the end-to-end protocol to keep messages correct. Let the occasional datagram get lost to simplify algorithms. Recognize the usefulness of end-to-end protocols in crash detection recovery. Let atomic transaction concepts insure a reasonable system design and don't worry excessively about the occasional crash.

Two very complex problems are synchronization and multiple copy update. They are many strategies that can be used to solve either of these problems. Carefully define your synchronization requirement and select a solution that does not overkill the problem. Further, when considering solutions to the multiple copy update problem, rely heavily on application knowledge to simplify the solution.

Data base management systems (DBMS's) are integral to network design. Practical examples of solutions exist to these problems. Uniform views and models exist and the translations between these views have been implemented. Complex DBMS's have been made available on networks and we suggest that this work be studied before you attempt an implementation.

20.4. What we conjecture

A number of conjectures were put forth during the course:

1) There are advantages to a decentralized operating system and these advantages outweigh the disadvantages to such an extent that research should pursue decentralized operating system theory.

2) Datagram versus virtual circuit arguments are not the main issue, but whether systems should be transaction or batch oriented is the more important argument which gets simplified to datagram versus virtual circuit.

3) In a distributed system, synchronization is obtained by the ability of the synchronization mechanism to maintain a relative event order rather than an absolute event order.

4) Intuitively, we expect more of a distributed system. We expect more reliability, for example, but there is no inherent reason that a centralized system could not be as reliable as a distributed system.

5) A reasonable system model must address more than a layered structure and in fact must have three dimensions: layers, design issues common to layers, and global optimization issues.

6) System should be designed to be loaded lightly. Do not overload the system communication facilities. For example, Ethernet runs typically with a communication load in the few percent level.

7) Lastly, we conjectured that there are applications (for example certain real-time systems) under which a high degree of decentralized system wide operating system control has distinct advantages and may actually be required.

20.5. What we think we don't know

As the course was organized and began, we soon concluded that there was more that we didn't understand or know about than we felt we knew. Further, we knew details, but we didn't understand large system issues: for example, naming. Should a name space be flat or hierarchial? Does it matter? What is the impact on routing? How do name spaces change, etc.? Some of the work reported on purports strongly for hierarchial name spaces in which names, addresses, and routes all derive hierarchially and naturally from each other. Is this reasonable? A summary of some of the open issues in question form is given below. Much of this is subject to interpretation but it represents a fair consensus of the lecturer's opinions as of early 1980.

How much decentralization is required in a distributed system? What is the effect of decentralizing resources? What is the design trade off space and design parameter choices? Under what conditions are distributed systems better than centralized systems? How can one optimize design decisions? How does one relate the individual parameters of our reference model for trade of purposes? Can taxonomy spaces be developed which relate individual design parameter spaces to distributed systems? Are such spaces meaningful. Given that we do not have a large number of identified systems that we classify as distributed, how we can obtain performance experience with real systems? Can we extrapolate design parameters from systems which satisfy somme but not all of our definition? How can we verify the operation and performance of a distributed system? Some features such as fault tolerance not only provide a capability (fault tolerance and thus fault masking) but also make verification difficult (faults may be masked)? Do we know enough to establish realistic measurement and verification and verification schemes? Do we really know what a distributed system should do?

There are some very challenging design problems associated with distributed systems. Some of the problems, such as the remote procedure call, can be implemented using certain model assumptions. Will we need different hardware approaches than generally found in a centralized system to implement such features? or, must we be satisfied with lower speed problem solutions comforted in the knowledge that we have obtained other benifits such as resource sharing?

As we discussed our system model, we discovered that the closer we got to the hardware, the more we knew; i.e., the closer we got to applications the less we knew. In fact, what we could say about applications was very little. What applications are suitable for distributed systems? Are there applications which require distributed systems? Can the application tell whether a system is a distributed? At what level does a system look distributed?

We also discovered after a quick look at applications, that we did not know much about the operating system level. What should an operating system look like? Should we replicate an operating system and call that a distributed operating system? Is the space of decentralization introduced useful? How can one design a decentralized global operating system? Are the decentralized analogs of the design issues and alternatives that one could parameterize for a centralized operating system? What about protection, is it different (easier or harder in a distributed system? Do we really understand flow control, congestion, etc.?

It should be clear to the reader that we know far less than the literature and most proponents of distributed systems would lead us to believe.

20.6. What we advise

Do not give up, fair reader. Press on and you will be rewarded for your persistence. For all our previous indecisiveness, we will make some strong statements in this section. We will provide you with some advice, experience, and conjectured truisms which will solve your problems.

In a design be careful making symplifying assumptions based upon interconnection technology, topology, or lower levels. Use of X.25 and other standards may be dangerous to your system because their design parameters may not match yours and anyway standards are not standards. Some standards are more equal than others.

Fairness in a system is application and hardware dependent and may not be the most important parameter.

Do not overload the system.

Hardware matters but absolute hardware cost may not be important. Seriously observe the concepts of life cycle costing.

Distributed systems may be easily constructed because a transport mechanism may be simply erected on top of current hardware then there remains the minor issue of operating systems and applications.

XNOS represents a way in which operating systems and data base management systems can be developed based upon compatibility and other pragmatic constraints.

Don't go to heroics to make lower levels have an ultra reliable design: fault tolerance can be spread throughout the design and you should seriously trade off the cost of losing an occasional (infrequent) datagram. The choices for synchronization techniques are many and the system requirements need to be carefully defined to provide an intelligent selection criteria for selection of a technique for a specific system.

Encryption may occur at any system level or combination of system levels depending upon your design criteria.

There are enough theoretical solutions/choices for us to select a reasonable solution to the multiple copy update problem.

Terminal (device) emulation is too inefficient to be considered practical.

If you want to convince your management of the usefulness of distributed processing, then do not build the system on top of extant hardware or software. The performance will not be available and the result will be very discouraging. Manufacturers should take note of this lament.

Some of the lecturers have strong opinions or biases. The reader should note that if you argue religion you may not converge on a solution. Portions of this course are strongly influenced by religion and the reader should carefully check and consider all positions to avoid an unwanted or unnecessary conversion and its required attendant excise. Portions of this course are purely the author's unbiased opinions.

20.7. What you should know

If you were to come away from this course with only three facts/opinions, what should they be. After careful consideration we suggest the following:

1) It is truly difficult to define precisely terms and concepts. As careful as we tried to be we may have been inconsistent in usage. Further, we had trouble with ideas as simple as link. Because of these difficulties, we tried very hard to make two items precise and understandable. These are our definition of a distributed system and our reference model. These should receive careful consideration.

2) Distributed systems are not simply networks.

3) Distributed systems include distributed computers.

20.8. What we don't agree upon

After spending many hours together there are a number of points which we never could agree upon. Given thousands of years more to argue, we would still not agree. These items are presented for your consideration and individual decision:

1) Whether decentralized control is important.

2) What is the NOS/GOS spectrum and wherein should your design reside.

3) What is the best design technique for a NOS/GOS.

4) To what extent is global synchronization important.

5) What is the best technique for global synchronization given a specific design goal.

6) The extent to which hardware is important.

7) The degree of fairness that a system should have.

20.9. Acknowledgements

A number of people made major contributions to the success of this course. A summary of the contributions is given below. The lectures wish to acknowledge and thank the following individuals and groups:

Professor Dr. H. Siegert and Professor Dr. M. Paul for their organization and guidance during the course. A special debt of gratitude is due to these gentlemen for the cordial treatment of the lecturers and their families during the course activities.

Ms. Weber, Dr. Halfar, Ms. Heilmann and the staff at the University for their able assistance.

The Technical Unviersity of Munich and the European Community for their sponsorship.

The participants and discussants who made the course the success that it was.

Xerox Corporation for allowing Dr. Lampson use of the facilities to produce the course notes and final book copy.

Sara Dake, Dr. Lampson's secretary, who did a large part of the work required to assemble this book.

Lastly, Dr. Butler Lampson. Dr. Lampson is listed as book editor, but that simple title does not reflect his contribution. During the time span of this course Dr. Lampson took eight widely varying sets of notes and chapters in all kinds of crazy formats, time frames, etc., and generated in a timely fashion two important documents: the course notes (for the first course) and the book (for the final presentation of the course). Without his persistence and patience, this book would not exist. Personally and for all the other lecturers, we thank Dr. Lampson for his volunteer effort.

References

Abbreviations

Berkeley Workshop	*Berkeley Workshop on Distributed Data Management and Computer Networks.*
CCC	*Computer Comunications Conf.*
CLCN	*Conf. Local Computer Networks.*
DCS	*Data Comunication Symp.*
ICCC	*Int. Conf. Computer Communication*, Toronto.
ICDPS	*Int. Conf. Distributed Processing Systems*, IEEE, Huntsville, Alabama.
ICERASAD	*Int. Conf. Entity-Relationship Approach to Systems Analysis and Design*, Los Angeles, Calif..
ICVLDB	*Int. Conf. Very Large Data Bases.*
ISOS	*Int. Symp. Operating Systems*, IRIA, Rocquencourt, France.
SCNP	*Symp. Computer Network Protocols*, Universite de Liege, Liege, Belgium.
SCNPTA	*Symp. Computer Network Protocols: Trends and Applications*, National Bureau of Standards.

[Abraham 80]   Abraham, S.M., Dalal, Y.K., Techniques for Decentralized Management of Distributed Systems, *COMPCON 80*, (Spring 1980), 430-437.

[Akkoyunlu 74]   Akkoyunlu E., Bernstein, A., Schantz, R., Interprocess Communication Facilities for Network Operating Systems, *Computer* 7, 6 (1974).

[Alsberg 76]   Alsberg, P.A., Day, J.D., A Principle for Resilient Sharing of Distributed Resources, *Proc. 2nd Int. Conf. Software Eng.*, San Francisco, CA., (Oct. 1976).

[ANSI 79]   Further Refinements to the Proposed Datagram Interface [for X.25], *Computer Communication Review* 9, 1 (Jan. 1979), 25-31.

[ANSI/X3/SPARC 75]   Study Group on Data Base Management Systems: Interim Report, *FDT (Bull. ACM SIGMOD)* 7, 2 (1975).

[Anderson 75]   Anderson, G.A., Jensen, E.D., Computer Interconnection: Taxonomy, Characteristics, and Examples, *Computing Surveys*, (Dec. 1975).

[Anderson 79a]   Anderson, L.D., DeWard, R.C., Functionally Distributed Microcomputer Architecture, *Proc. IEEE Microprocessor Workshop*, Johns Hopkins Applied Physics Lab, (Mar. 1979).

[Anderson 79b]   Anderson, L.D., et. al., Partitioning For Virtual Machine Efficiency, *COMPCON 79*, (Fall 1979).

[Andrews 76]   Andrews, D., Irby, C., Poggio, A., Watson, R., User Interface System for a Computer Network Marketplace, Augmentation Research Center, SRI International, Menlo Park, California, (Nov. 1976).

[Anthony 65]   Anthony, R., Planning and Control Systems: A Framework for Analysis, Division of Research, Graduate School of Business Administration, Harvard University, (1965).

[Arpanet 78]   *Arpanet Protocol Handbook*, NIC 7104, Network Information Center, SRI International, Menlo Park, California, (1978).

[Astrahan 76]   Astrahan, M.M., et. al., System R: Relational Approaches to Database Management, *ACM Trans. Database Sys.* 1, (1976), 97-137.

[BBN 80]   Bolt Beranek, & Newman, System Dev. Corp., Formal Description Techniques For Network Protocols, National Bureau of Standards Report, ICST/HLNP 80-3 (June 1980).

[Bach 79]   Bach, M.J., Goguen, N.H., Kaplan, M.M., The Adapt Data Translation System and Applications, *Proc. 4th Berkeley Workshop*, (Aug. 1979), 51-71.

[Bachman 69]   Bachman, C.W., Data Structure Diagrams, *Data Base* 1, 2, (1969).

[Backus 78]   Backus, J., Can Programming Be Liberated from the von Neumann Style? A Functional Style and Its Algebra of Programs, *Comm. ACM* 21, (1978), 613-641.

[Badal 78]   Badal, D.Z., Popek, G.J., A Proposal for Distributed Concurrency Control for Partially
                  Redundant Distributed Data Base Systems, *Proc. 3rd Berkeley Workshop*, (Aug. 1978), 273-285.

[Ball 76]   Ball, J.E., *et. al.*, RIG, Rochester's Intelligent Gateway: System Overview, *IEEE Trans. Software
                  Eng.* 2, 9 (Dec. 1979), 312-328.

[Bartlett 69]   Bartlett, K.A., Scantlebury, R.A., Wilkinson, P.T., A Note On Reliable Full-duplex
                  Transmission Over Half-duplex Links, *Comm. ACM* 2, 5 (May 1969), 260-265.

[Bartlett 78]   Bartlett, J.F., A "Non Stop" Operating System, *11th Hawaii Conference on System Science* 3,
                  (Jan. 1978), 103-117.

[Baskett 77]   Baskett, F., Howard, J.H., Montague, J.T., Task Communication in DEMOS, *Operating Systems
                  Review* 11, 5, (Nov. 1977), 23-32.

[Bell 71]   Bell, G., Newell, A., *Computer Structures*, McGraw-Hill, (1971).

[Belsnes 76]   Belsnes, D., Single-Message Communication, *IEEE Trans. Communication* COM-242, (1976),
                  190-194.

[Bernstein 78a]   Bernstein, P.A., *et. al.*, The Concurrency Control Mechanism of SDD-1: A System for
                  Distributed Databases, *IEEE Trans. Software Eng.* SE-44, 3, (May 1978).

[Bernstein 78b]   Bernstein, P.A., Shipman, D.W., A Formal Model of Concurrency Control Mechanisms for
                  Database Systems, *Proc. 3rd Berkeley Workshop*, (Aug. 1978).

[Bernstein 77]   Bernstein, P.A., *et. al.*, The SDD-1 Redundant Update Algorithm (the general case), Computer
                  Corporation America, Cambridge, MA, Tech. Rep CCA-77-09, (Dec. 1977).

[Biller 79]   Biller, H., On the Equivalence of Data Base Schemas – A Semantic Approach to Data
                  Translation, *Information Sys.* 4, (1979), 35-47.

[Bochmann 78]   Bochmann, G.V., Finite State Description of Communication Protocols, *Computer Networks* 2,
                  4/5, (Sept./Oct. 1978).

[Bochmann 79]   Bochmann, G.V., Vogt, F.H., Message Link Protocol, *Computer Communication Review* 9, 2,
                  (Apr. 1979), 7-39.

[Boebert 78a]   Boebert, W.E., *et. al.*, Design Issues in A Distributed Executive, *Proc. IEEE Compsac*, (1978).

[Boebert 78b]   Boebert, W.E., Franta, *et. al.*, Kernel Primitives of the HXDP Executive, *Proc. IEEE Compsac*,
                  (1978).

[Boebert]   Boebert, W.E., *et. al.*, Communications in the HXDP Executive, *IEEE Trans. Software Eng.*, (to
                  appear).

[Boehm 73]   Boehm, B.K., High Cost of Software, In *Proc. Symp. on High Cost of Software*, Naval
                  Postgraduate School, Monterey, Calif., (1973).

[Boggs 80]   Boggs, D.R., *et. al.*, Pup: An Internetwork Architecture, To appear in *IEEE Trans.
                  Communication*, (1980).

[Boorstyn 77]   Boorstyn, R.R., Frank, H., Large-Scale Network Topological Optimization, *IEEE Trans.
                  Communication* COM-25, (January 1977), 29.

[Brand 78]   Brand, D., Joyner, W.H., Verification of Protocols Using Symbolic Execution, *Computer
                  Networks* 2, 4/5, (Sept./Oct. 1978), 351.

[Brandt 72]   Brandt, G.J., Chretian, G.J., Methods to Control and Operate a Message Switching Network,
                  Proc. Symp. Networks and Teletraffic, Brooklyn Polytechnic, (Apr. 1972).

[Bremer 79]   Bremer, I., Drobnik O., Specification and Validation of a Protocol for Decentralized Directory
                  Management, IBM Research Report No. RC 7880, (Sept. 1979).

[Brinch Hansen 78] Brinch Hansen, P., Distributed Processes: A Concurrent Programming Concept, *Comm. ACM*
                  12, 11 (Nov. 1978), 934-941.

[Brodie 78]   Brodie, M., Specification and Verification of Data Base Semantic Integrity, Technical Report
                  CSRG-91, Univ. of Toronto, Comp. Sci. Dept., Toronto, Canada, (Apr. 1978).

[Bunch 80]   Bunch, S.R., Day, J.D., Control Structure Overhead in TCP, *Proc. SCNPTA*, IEEE Cat. No.
                  80CH1529-7C, (May 1980), 121-127.

[Burruss 80]   Burruss, J., Features of the Transport and Session Protocols, NBS Report ICST/HLNP-80-1, (Mar.
                  1980).

[Cardenas 79]   Cardenas, A.F., Pirahesh, M.H., The E-R Model in a Heterogeneous Data Base Management
                  System, *Proc. ICERASAD*, Los Angeles, CA, (1979), 648-654.

[Cavlan 79]   Cavlan, N., Durham, S.J., Field-Programmable Arrays: Powerful Alternatives to Random
                  Logic, *Electronics*, (July 5, 1979).

[CCITT 77a]   CCITT Recommendation X.25, Interface Between Data Terminal Equipment (DTE) and Data
                  Circuit Terminal Equipment (DCE) for Terminals Operating in the Packet Mode on Public
                  Packet Networks, Geneva, (1977).

[CCITT 77b]   CCITT Provisional Recommendations X.3: Packet Assembly/Disassembly Facility (PAD) in a
                Public Data Network;
                X.28: DCE/DTE Interface for a Start-stop Mode Data Terminal Equipment Accessing the Packet
                Assembly/Disassembly Facility (PAD) in a Public Data Network Situated in the Same Country,
                Geneva, (1977).

[CCITT 78a]   Recommendation X.75, Terminal and Transit Call Control Procedures and Data Transfer
                System on International Circuits Between Packet Switched Data Networks, Geneva, (1978).

[CCITT 78b]   Recommendation X.121, International Numbering Plan for Public Data Networks, Geneva,
                (1978).

[CCITT 79]   Revised Recommendation X.25, Preface and Level 3, CCITT COM VII, 384-E, Geneva, (Aug.
                1979).

[CCITT 80]   CCITT Rapporteur Report, X.25, Characteristics of Concern to Transport Services Working
                Paper, ANSI Document Number X 3S37-80-32R, (Apr. 1980).

[Cerf 72]   Cerf, V.G., et. al., An Experimental Service for Adaptable Data Reconfiguration, IEEE Trans.
                Communications COM-20, (1972), 557-564.

[Cerf 74]   Cerf, V., Kahn, R., A Protocol for Packet Network Intercommunication, IEEE Trans.
                Communications COM-20, 5 (1974), 637-648.

[Cerf 78a]   Cerf, V., et. al., Proposal for an Internetwork End-to-End Transport Protocol, INWG 96.1, also
                in Proc. SCNP, (Feb. 1978).

[Cerf 78b]   Cerf, V., Kirstein, P.T., Issues in Packet-Network Interconnection, Proc. IEEE 66, 11, (Nov.
                1978), 1386-1408.

[Chamberlin 76] Chamberlin, D.D., et. al., SEQUEL2: A Unified Approach to Data Definition, Manipulation,
                and Control, IBM J. Res. & Develop. 20, (1976), 560-575.

[Chaum 78]   Chaum, P.L., Fabry, R.S., Implementing Capability-Based-Protection Using Encryption,
                University of California, Berkeley, Electronics Research Laboratory, Memorandum UCB/ERL
                M78, (July 1978).

[Chen 74]   Chen, R.C., Bus Communication Systems, PhD Dissertation, Carnegie-Mellon University,
                (1974).

[Chen 76]   Chen P.P.-S., The Entity-Relationship Model – Toward a Unified View of Data, ACM Trans.
                Database Sys. 1, (1976), 9-36.

[Cheriton 79]   Cheriton, D.R., et. al., A Portable Real-Time Operating System, Comm. ACM, (February 1977),
                105-115.

[Chlamtac 80]   Chlamtac, I., et. al., Performance Issues in Back-end Storage Networks, Computer 13, 2, (Feb.
                1980), 18-31.

[Chu 74]   Chu, W.W., Ohlmacher, G., Avoiding Deadlock in Distributed Data Bases, Proc. ACM Nat.
                Conf. (Nov. 1974), 156-160.

[Chu 79]   Chu, W.W., To, V.T., A Hierarchical Conceptual Model for Data Translation in a
                Heterogeneous Database System, Proc. ICERASAD, Los Angeles, CA, (1979), 647.

[Clark 78]   Clark, D.D., Pogran, K.T., Reed, D.P., An Introduction to Local Area Networks, Proc. IEEE 66,
                11 (Nov. 1978), 1497-1516.

[Clark 80]   Clark, D.D., Svobodova, L., Design of Distributed Systems Supporting Local Anatonomy,
                COMPCON 80, (Spring 1980), 438-444.

[Codasyl 62]   Codasyl Development Committee, An Information Algebra, Comm. ACM 5, (1962), 190-204.
[Codasyl 73]   Codasyl Data Description Language Committee, DDL Journal of Development, (1973).
[Codasyl 76]   Codasyl Systems Committee, Selection and Acquisition of Data Base Management Systems,
                (1976).

[Codd 70]   Codd, E.F., A Relational Model of Data for Large Shared Data Banks, Comm. ACM 13, (1970),
                377-387.

[Codd 71]   Codd, E.F., Relational Completeness of Data Base Languages, Data Base Systems, R. Rustin,
                ed., Prentice-Hall, (1971), 65-98.

[Cohen 77]   Cohen, J.M., Moses, H.E., New Test of the Synchronization Procedure in Non-inertial Systems,
                Physical Review Letters 39, (Dec. 1977), 1641-1643.

[Cohen 79]   Cohen, D., Postel, J.B., On Protocol Multiplexing, Proc. 6th CCC, (Nov. 1979), 75-81.
[Collmeyer 72] Collmeyer, A.J., Implications of Data Independence on the Architecture of Database
                Management Systems, ACM SIGFIDET Workshop on Data Description, Access and Control,
                Denver, Colorado, (1972), 307-321.

[Cornafion 79] Cornafion Group, A Critical Study of Different Flow Control Methods in Computer Networks,
                Computer Communication Review 9, 3, (July 1979), 23-32.

[Crocker 72]   Crocker, S.D., et. al., Function Oriented Protocols for the ARPA Computer Network, Proc. AFIPS Conf. 40, (May 1972), 271-279.

[Crowther 73]   Crowther, W.R., McQuillan, J.M., Walden, D.C., Reliability Issues in the ARPA Network, Proc. 3rd DCS, (1973).

[Date 77]   Date, C.J., An Introduction to Database Systems, 2nd Ed., Addison-Wesley, (1977).

[Davidson 77]   Davidson, J., et. al., The Arpanet Telnet Protocol: Its Purpose, Principles, Implementation and Impact on Host Operating System Design, Proc. 5th DCS, (Sept. 1977), 4-10 – 4-18.

[DaviesDP 79]   Davies, D.R.H., et. al., A Transport Service; Post Office Packet Switching Study Group Report, BIG/CP 7, (Apr. 1979). Available from The Data Communication Protocols Unit, c/o The Computer Laboratory, Corn Exchange St. Cambridge, CB2 3QG, England.

[DaviesDW 72]   Davies, D.W., The Control of Congestion in Packet-Switching Networks, IEEE Trans. Communications COM-22, (June 1972), 546.

[DaviesDW 79]   Davies, D.W., et. al., Computer Networks and Their Protocols, Wiley, N.Y., (1979).

[Day 79a]   Day, J.D., Resource Sharing Protocols, Computer (Sept. 1979), 47-55.

[Day 79b]   Day, J.D., Grossman, G.R. Howe, R.H., WWMCCS Host to Front End Protocols: Specifications Version 1.0, Digital Technology Inc., Doc. 780 12 C-INFE 14, (Nov. 1979).

[Dayal 78]   Dayal, U., Bernstein, P.A., On the Updatability of Relational Views, Proc. 4th ICVLDB, West Berlin, (1978), 368-378.

[DenningDE 76]   Denning, D.E., A Lattice Model of Secure Information Flow, Comm. ACM 19, (1976), 236-243.

[DenningPJ 76]   Denning, P.J., Fault-tolerant Operating Systems, Computing Surveys 8, 4, (Dec. 1976), 361-386.

[Dennis 66]   Dennis, J.B., Van Horn, E.C., Programming Semantics for Multiprogrammed Computations, Comm. ACM 9, 3, (Mar. 1966), 143-155.

[Deppe 76]   Deppe, M.E. and Fry, J.P., Distributed Data Bases – A Summary of Research, Computer Networks 1, (1976), 130-138.

[DeRemer 76]   DeRemer, F.L., Transformational Grammars, Compiler Construction: An Advanced Course, L.F. Bauer and J. Eickel, eds., Springer-Verlag, (1976), 121-145.

[Di Ciccio 79]   Di Ciccio, V., et. al., Alternatives for Interconnection of Public Packet Switching Data Networks, Proc. 6th DCS, (Nov. 1979), 120-125.

[Diffie 76]   Diffie, W., Hellman, M.E., New Directions in Cryptography, IEEE Trans. Information Theory IT-22, 6, (Nov. 1976), 644.

[Diffie 77]   Diffie, W., Hellman, M.E., Exhaustive Cryptanalysis of the NBS Data Encryption Standard, Computer, (June 1977), 74.

[Dijkstra 74]   Dijkstra, E.W., Self-stabilizing Systems in Spite of Distributed Control, Comm. ACM 17, 11, (Nov. 1974), 643-644.

[Donnelley 76]   Donnelley, J.E., A Distributed Capability Computing System, Proc. 3rd ICCC, (Aug. 1976), 432-440.

[Donnelley 78]   Donnelley, J.E., Yeh, J.W., Interaction Between Protocol Levels in a Prioritized CSMA Broadcast Network, Proc. 3rd Berkeley Workshop, (Aug. 1978), 123-143. Also in Computer Networks 3, (February 1979), 9-23.

[Donnelley 79]   Donnelley, J.E., Components of a Network Operating System, Proc. 4th CLCN, (Oct. 1979), IEEE 79CH 14464C, 1-12, Also in Computer Networks 3, 6, (Dec. 1979), 389-400.

[Donnelley 80]   Donnelley, J.E., Fletcher, J.G., Resource Access Control in a Network Operating System, To appear in Proc. ACM Pacific 80, (Nov. 1980).

[Dowson 79]   Dowson, M., Collins, B., McBride, B., Software Strategy for Multiprocessors, Microprocessors and Microsystems, (July/Aug. 1979).

[Drobnik 77]   Drobnik, O., Verfahren zur Sicherung der Operationalen Integrität in verteilten Datenbasen bei dezentraler Kontrollstruktur, Ph.D. Thesis, Universität Karlsruhe, (1977).

[desJardins 78]   desJardins, R., White, G., ANSI Reference Model for Distributed Systems, COMPCON 78, (Sept. 1978), 144-149.

[ECMA 79]   ECMA, HDLC: Elements Of Procedure, Document TC9-ECMA-49, (May 1979), 27.

[EMCA 80]   Standard EMCA (European Computer Manufacturers Association) Transport Protocol, Final Draft, EMCA/TC 24180167, (July 1980).

[Ellis 77a]   Ellis, C.A., A Robust Algorithm for Updating Duplicate Databases, Proc. 2nd Berkeley Workshop, (1977).

[Ellis 77b]   Ellis, C.A., Consistency and Correctness of Duplicate Database Systems, Operating Systems Review 11, 5, (Nov. 1977).

[Enslow 78]   Enslow, P.H., What is a "Distributed" Data Processing System? Computer 11, 1, (Jan. 1978), 13-21.

[Esculier 79]   Esculier, C., Glorieux, A.M., The Sirius-Delta Distributed DBMS, *Proc. ICERASAD*, (1979), 616-624.

[Eswaran 76]   Eswaran, K.P., *et. al.*, The Notions of Consistency and Predicate Locks in a Database System, *Comm. ACM* 19, 11, (Nov. 1976), 624-633.

[Everest 74]   Everest, G.C., Concurrent Update Control and Data Base Integrity, *Data Base Management*, Klimbie, J.W., Koffeman, K.L. eds., North Holland, (1974), 241-270.

[Fabry 74]   Fabry, R.S., Capability-based Addressing, *Comm. ACM* 17, 7, (July 1974).

[Fanent 77]   Fanent, R.A., The National Software Works: Operational Issues in a Distributed Processing System, *Proc. ACM Nat. Conf.*, Seattle, (Oct. 1977), 53-58.

[Farber 73]   Farber, D.J., *et. al.*, The Distributed Computing System, *COMPCON 73*, (1973), 31-34.

[Fauser 79]   Fauser, U., Neuhold, E.J., Transaction Processing in the Distributed DBMS-POREL, *Proc. 4th Berkeley Workshop*, (1979), 353-375.

[Feinler 76]   Feinler, E., Postel, J., File Transfer Protocol for Arpanet, *Arpanet Protocol Handbook*, (1976 Edition), 117-235. National Technical Information Service, Acc. No. AD-AO297964.

[Feldman 78]   Feldman, J.A., Low, J.R., Rovner, P.D., Programming Distributed Systems, *Proc. ACM Nat. Conf.*, (Dec. 1978), 310-316.

[Fletcher 75]   Fletcher, J.G., *et. al.*, Computer Storage Structure and Utilization at a Large Scientific Laboratory, *Proc. IEEE* 63, 8, (Aug. 1975), 1104-1113.

[Fletcher 78]   Fletcher, J.G., Watson, R.W., Mechanisms for a Reliable TimerBased Protocol, *Computer Networks* 2, (1978), 271-290.

[Fletcher 79a]   Fletcher, J.G., Serial Link Protocol Design: A Critique of the X.25 Standard, Level-2, Lawrence Livermore Laboratory, Report UCRL 83604.

[Fletcher 79b]   Fletcher, J.G., An Arithmetic Checksum for Serial Transmissions, Lawrence Livermore Laboratory, Report UCRL-82569, (May 1979).

[Fletcher 80]   Fletcher, J.G., Watson, R.W., Service Support for Network Operating System Services, *COMPCON 80*, (Spring 1980), 415-424.

[Folts 78]   Folts, H.C., Karp, H.R., eds., *Data Communication Standards*, McGraw-Hill, (1978).

[Forsdick 75]   Forsdick, H.C., A Comparison of Two Schemes That Control Multiple Updating of Data Bases, MIT Research Report, (1975).

[Forsdick 78]   Forsdick, H.C., Schantz, R.E., Thomas, R.H., Operating Systems for Computer Networks, *Computer* 11, 1, (Jan. 1978), 48-57.

[Forsdick 79]   Forsdick, H., McKenzie, A., FTP Functional Specification, Bolt Beranek and Newman Inc., Cambridge, Mass., Report No. 4051, (Aug. 1979).

[Frank, 70]   Frank, H., Frisch, I.T., Chou, W., Topological Consideration in the Design of the ARPA Network, *Proc. AFIPS Conf.* 36, (May 1970), 581.

[Franta 79]   Franta, W.R., Rahimi, K., A Posted Update Approach to Concurrency Control in Distributed Data Base Systems, *Proc. 1st ICDPS*, (Oct. 1979).

[Fratta 73]   Fratta, L., Gerla, M., Kleinrock, L., The Flow Deviation Method: An Approach To Network Design, *Networks* 3 (1973), 97.

[Freeman 78]   Freeman, H.A., System Design Methodology – A First Step, *COMPCON 78*, (Spring 1978).

[Garcia-Molina 78] Garcia-Molina, H., Performance Comparison of Two Update Algorithms for Distributed Databases, *Proc. 3rd Berkeley Workshop*, (Aug. 1978), 108-119.

[Garlick 77]   Garlick, L., Rom, R., Postel, J., Reliable Host-to-Host Protocols: Problems and Techniques, *Proc. 5th DCS*, (Sept. 1977).

[Gaspar 78]   Gaspar, A., Lamm, P., A Simulated Data Communication Network, *Computer Communication Review* 8, 4, (Oct. 1978).

[Gelenbe 78]   Gelenbe, E., Sevcik, K., Analysis of Update Synchronization for Multiple Copy Data-Bases, *Proc. 3rd Berkeley Workshop*, (Aug. 1978), 69-90.

[Geller 77]   Geller, D.P., The National Software Works: Access to Distributed Files and Tools, *Proc. ACM Nat. Conf.*, Seattle, (Oct. 1977), 39-43.

[Geller 78]   Geller, D.P., Sattley, K., NSW User's Reference Manual, System Version 3.1., Massachusetts Computer Associates Inc., Wakefield, Mass., Report No. CADD-7811-1411, (Nov. 1978).

[Gerla 77]   Gerla, M., Kleinrock, L., On The Topological Design of Distributed Computer Networks, *Electrical Communication* 49, (1974), 48.

[Gien 78]   Gien, M., A File Transfer Protocol, *SCNP* (Feb. 1978), (D5-1)-(D5-7).

[Gien 79]   Gien M., Zimmermann, H., Design Principles for Network Interconnection, *Proc. 6th DCS*, (Nov. 1979), 109-119.

[Gifford 79]   Gifford, D.K., Violet: An Experimental Decentralized System, *Operating Systems Review* 13, 5, (Dec. 1979).

[Gimpelson 74]   Gimpelson, L.A., Network Management: Design and Control of Communication Networks, *Electrical Communication* 49, (1974), 4.

[Goldberg 79]   Goldberg, R.P., *et. al.*, Virtual Machines and Distributed Processing, *Proc. Workshop for Informatik, E.U.*, München, (15-16 March 1979), Springer-Verlag, (1979), 199-227.

[Goos 75]   Goos, G., Hierarchies, *Software Engineering: An Advanced Course*, Springer-Verlag, (1975).

[Grange 79]   Grange, J.L., Gien, M., eds., *Flow Control in Computer Networks*, North Holland, (1979).

[Grapa 77]   Grapa, E., Belford, G.G., Techniques for Update Synchronization in Distributed Data Bases, Center for Advanced Computation, University of Illinois, (1977).

[Gray 75]   Gray, J.N., Lorie, R.A., Putzolu, G.R., Granularity of Locks in a Shared Data Base, *Proc. ICVLDB*, (1975).

[Gray 78]   Gray, J.N., Notes on Database Operating Systems, *Operating Systems: An Advanced Course*, Goos, G., Hartmanis J., eds., Springer-Verlag, (1978), 393-481.

[Gray 79]   Gray, J.N., A Discussion of Distributed Systems, IBM Res. Rep., IBM Res. Lab., San Jose, Calif., (1979).

[Gries 71]   Gries, D., *Compiler Construction for Digital Computers*, Wiley, New York, (1971).

[Griffiths 76]   Griffiths, P.P., Wade, B.W., An Authorization Mechanism for a Relational Database, *ACM Trans. Database Sys.* 1, (1976), 242-255.

[Grossman 79]   Grossman, G.R., Hinchley, A., Sunshine, C.A., Issues in International Public Data Networking, *Computer Networks* 3, (1979), 259-266.

[Gupta 77]   Gupta, M. M., Saridis, G. N., Gaines, Brian R., *Fuzzy Automata and Decision Processes*, (1977).

[Hajek 78]   Hajek, J., Automatically Verified Protocols, *Proc. ICCC 78*, Kyoto, Japan, (Sept. 1978).

[Hammer 79]   Hammer, M., McLeod, D., On Database Management System Architecture, University of Southern California Computer Science Dept., TR 4, Los Angeles, California, (April 1979).

[Havender 68]   Havender, I.W., Avoiding Deadlock in Multi-Tasking Systems, *IBM Syst. J.* 2, 7, (1968).

[Haverty 78]   Haverty, J.F., Rettbert, R.D., Inter-Process Communication for a Server in Unix, *COMPCON 78*, (Sept. 1978), 312-315.

[Heafner 80]   Heafner, J.F., Nielsen, F.H., A Linear Programming Model for Optimal Computer Network Protocol Design (submitted for publication).

[Herman 78]   Herman, D., Verius, J.P., Universite de Rennes, An Algorithm for Maintaining the Consistency of Multiple Copies, *Proc. 1st ICDPS*, (Oct. 1978).

[Hertweck 78]   Hertweck, F., Raubold, E., Vogt, F., X.25 Based Process/Process Communication, *Proc. SCNP*, (Feb. 1978), C3.1-C3.22.

[Hess 79]   Hess, M.L., Brethes, M.S, A Comparison of Four X.25 Public Network Interfaces, *ICC 79 Conf. Record* 3, (June 1979), 38.6.1-38.6.8.

[Hoare 74]   Hoare, C.A.R., Monitors: An Operating System Structuring Concept, *Comm. ACM* 17, 10, (Oct. 1974), 549-557.

[Hoare 78]   Hoare, C.A.R., Communicating Sequential Processes, *Comm. ACM* 21, 8, (Aug. 1978), 666-677.

[Hohn 80]   Hohn, W.C., The Control Data Loosely Coupled Networks Lower Level Protocols, *Proc. AFIPS Conf.* 49, (1980).

[Holler 74a]   Holler, E., Multiple Copy Files in Computer Networks, Kernforschungszentrum Karlsruhe, Report KfK 1734, (February 1974).

[Holler 74b]   Holler, E., Koordination kritischer Zugriffe auf verteilte Datenbanken in Rechnernetzen bei zentraler Ueberwachung, Ph.D. Thesis, Universität Karlsruhe, (1974).

[Holler 77]   Holler, E., Drobnik, O., Integrität, Ausfall und Wiederanlauf redundanter Prozessdatenbasen in verteilten PDV-Systemen, 2. Fachtagung "Prozessrechner 1977", Augsburg, März (1977), (in German).

[Holt 78]   Holt, A.W., Myers, J.M., An Approach to the Analysis of Clock Networks, Boston University Report, (July 1978).

[Honeywell 71]   Honeywell Information Systems, *Integrated Data Store*, Order No. BR69, Rev. 1, (Dec. 1971).

[Honeywell 77]   Honeywell Information Systems, *Multics Integrated Data Store Reference Manual*, Draft, (Oct. 1977).

[Honeywell 78]   Honeywell Information Systems, *Multics Relational Data Store (MRDS) Reference Manual*, Order No. AW53, Rev.2, (Oct. 1978).

[Horowitz 76]   Horowitz, E., Sahni, S., *Fundamentals of Data Structures*, Computer Science Press, Woodland Hills, Calif., (1976), 293-295.

[IBM 76]   IBM Corp. *IMS/VS Version 1. General Information Manual*, IBM Program No.5740-XX2, (Apr. 1976).

[Ichbiah 79]   Ichbiah, J.D., *et. al.*, Rationale for the Design of the of the ADA Programming Language, *SIGPLAN Notices* 14, 6, (June 1979), Part B.

[IFIP 79]   IFIP Working Group 6.1., Implications of Recommendation X.75 and Proposed Improvements for Public Data Network Interconnection, *Computer Communication Review* 9, 3, (July 1979), 33-39.

[INWG 77]   A Network Independent File Transfer Protocol, Prepared by the High Level Protocol Group, IFIP, International Network Working Group, HLP/CP 1, (December 1977).

[ISO 76]   ISO, High Level Data Link Control: Frame Structure, Document IS 3309, (1979).

[ISO 77]   ISO, High Level Data Link Control: Frame Structure, Document IS 4335, (1977).

[ISO 79]   Reference Model of Open Systems Interconnection, ISO/TC 97/ SC16 N 227, (Aug. 1979).

[Israel 79]   Israel, J.E., Mitchell, J.G., Sturgis, H.E., Separating Data from Function in a Distributed File System, *Proc. 2nd ISOS*, (Oct. 1978).

[Jacobs 78]   Jacobs, I.M., Binder, R., Hoversten, E.V., General Purpose Packet Satellite Networks, *Proc. IEEE* 66, 11, (Nov. 1978), 1448-1467.

[Jensen 78]   Jensen, D.E., The Honeywell Experimental Distributed Processor An Overview, *Computer* 11, 1, (Jan. 1978), 28-39.

[Johnson 75]   Johnson, P.R., Thomas, R.H., The Maintenance of Duplicate Databases, Network Working Group, RFC 677, NIC 31507, (Jan. 1975).

[Jones 77]   Jones, A.K., Software Management of Cm* – A Distributed Multiprocessor, *Proc. AFIPS Conf.* 46, (1977).

[Jones 78a]   Jones, A.K., Protection Mechanisms and the Enforcement of Security Policies, *Operating Systems: An Advanced Course*, Springer Verlag, (1978), 228-251.

[Jones 78b]   Jones, A.K., The Object Model: A Conceptual Tool for Structuring Software, *Operating Systems: An Advanced Course*, Springer Verlag, (1978).

[Kahn 72]   Kahn, R.E., Crowther, W.R., Flow Control in a Resource Sharing Network, *IEEE Trans. Communication* COM-20, (June 1972), 539.

[Kahn 78]   Kahn, R.E., *et. al.*, Advances in Packet Radio Technology, *Proc. IEEE* 66, 11 (Nov. 1978), 1468-1496.

[Kaneko 79]   Kaneko, A., *et. al.*, Logical Clock Synchronization Method for Duplicated Data Base Control, *Proc. 1st ICDPS*, (Oct. 1979).

[Katzman 78]   Katzman, J.A., A Fault-Tolerant Computing System, *11th Hawaii Conf. System Sciences* 3, (Jan. 1978), 85-102.

[Kent 77]   Kent, S., Encryption-based Protection for Interactive User/Computer Communication, *Proc. 5th DCS*, (Sept. 1977), 5-7/5-13.

[Kent 79]   Kent, W., Limitations of Record-Based Information Models, *ACM Trans. Database Systems* 4, (1979), 107-131.

[Kerr 76]   Kerr, I.H., *et. al*, A Simulation Study of Routine and Flow Control Problems in a Hierarchially Connected Network, *Proc. ICCC*, Toronto, (Aug. 1976), 495.

[Kimbleton 76] Kimbleton, S.R., Mandel, R.L., A Perspective on Network Operating Systems, *Proc. AFIPS Conf.* 45, (1976), 551-559.

[Kimbleton 78] Kimbleton, S.R., Wood, H.M., Fitzgerald, M.L., Network Operating Systems – An Implementation Approach, *Proc. AFIPS Conf.* 47, (1978), 773-782.

[Kimbleton 79] Kimbleton, S.R., Wang, P.S.-C., Fong, E., XNDM: An Experimental Network Data Manager, *Proc. 4th Berkeley Workshop*, (Aug. 1979), 3-17.

[Knuth 76]   Knuth, D.E., Additional Comments on a Problem in Concurrent Programming Control, *Comm. ACM*, (May 1976).

[Lagally 78]   Lagally, K., Synchronization in a Layered System, *Operating Systems: An Advanced Course*, Springer-Verlag (1978), 252-278.

[Lamport 74]   Lamport, L., A New Solution of Dijkstra's Concurrent Programming Problem, *Comm. ACM* 17, 8, (Aug. 1974).

[Lamport 78]   Lamport, L., Time, Clocks and Ordering of Events in a Distributed System, *Comm. ACM* 21, 7, (July 1978), 558-565.

[Lampson 73]   Lampson, B.W., A Note on the Confinement Problem, *Comm. ACM* 16, 5, (Oct. 1973), 513-515.

[Lampson 80]   Lampson, B.W., Sturgis, H.E., Crash Recovery in a Distributed Data Storage System, To appear in *Comm. ACM* (1980).

500 REFERENCES

[Lantz 79]   Lantz, K.A., Rashid, R.F., Virtual Terminal Management in a Multiple Process Environment, *Operating Systems Review* 13, 5, (Dec. 1979), 86-97.

[Lantz 80]   Lantz, K.A., RIG, An Architecture for Distributed Systems, University of Rochester, Dept. of Computer Science Report, (May 1980). (To appear in *Proc. ACM Pacific 80*, Nov. 1980).

[Lauer 79]   Lauer, H.C., Needham, R.M., On the Duality of Operating System Structures, *Operating System Review* 13, 2 (Apr. 1979), 3-19.

[Lavallee 72]   Lavallee, P., Ohayon, S., Sauvain R., Non-Procedural Access to DMS Databases, *Proc. 19th Intl. XDS User's Meeting*, (Dec. 1972).

[Le Biham 80]   Le Biham, J., et. al., Sirius: A French Nationwide Project on Distributed Databases, *ICVLDB*, (Oct. 1980).

[Le Lann 77]   Le Lann, G., Distributed Systems - Towards a Formal Approach, *Proc. IFIP Congress*, Toronto, North Holland Publishing Company, (Aug. 1977), 155-160.

[Le Lann 78a]   Le Lann G., Le Goff H., Verification and Evaluation of Communication Protocols, *Computer Networks* 2, 4 (Feb. 1978), 50-69.

[Le Lann 78b]   Le Lann, G., Algorithms for Distributed Data Sharing Systems which use Tickets, *Proc. 3rd Berkeley Workshop*, (Aug. 1978), 259-272.

[Le Lann 79]   Le Lann, G., An Analysis of Different Approaches to Distributed Computing, *Proc. 1st ICDPS*, (Oct. 1979), 222-232.

[Lee 77]   Lee, C., Shastri, R., Distributed Control Schemes for Multiple-Copied File Access in a Network Environment, *Proc. COMPSAC*, (1977), 722-728.

[Lesser 79]   Lesser, V. R., Erman, Lee D., An Experiment in Distributed Interpretation, *Proc. 1st ICDPS*, (Oct. 1979).

[Levy 78]   Levy, J.V., Buses, The Skeleton of Computer Structures, *Computer Engineering: A DEC View of Hardware Systems Design*, C.G. Bell, et. al., (eds.), Digital Press, Maynard, Mass, (1978), 269-299.

[Lin 79]   Lin, W.K., Concurrency Control in a Multiple Copy Distributed System, *Proc. 4th Berkeley Workshop*, (1979).

[Lindsay 79]   Lindsay, B. G., et. al., Notes on Distributed Databases, IBM Research Report RJ2571, IBM Research Laboratories, San Jose, California, (July 1979).

[Liskov 79]   Liskov, B., Primitives for Distributed Computing, *Operating Systems Review* 13, 5, (Dec. 1979), 33-42.

[Livesey 79]   Livesey, J., Inter-process Communication and Naming in the Mininet System, *Compcon 79*, (Spring 1979), 222-229.

[Lorie 79]   Lorie, R. A., Nilsson, J. F., An Access Path Specification Language for a Relational Data Base System, *IBM J. Res. & Develop.* 23 (1979), 286-298.

[Lu 79]   Lu, S.C., Lee, L.N., A Simple and Effective Public Key Cryptosystem, *COMSAT Tech. Rev.* 9, 1 (Spring 1979), 15.

[Luczak 78]   E.C. Luczak, Global Bus Computer Communication Techniques, *Proc. Networking Symp.*, (1978), 58-71.

[Mahmoud 76]   Mahmoud, S., Riordon, J.S., Protocol Considerations for Software Controlled Access Methods in Distributed Data Bases, *Proc. Int. Symp. Computer Performance, Modelling, Measurement and Evaluation*, ACM SIGMETRICS and IFIP WG., (Mar. 1976), 241-264.

[Mao 80]   Mao, T.W., Yeh, R.T., Communication Port: A Language Concept for Concurrent Programming, IEEE *Trans. Software Eng.* SE-6, 2 (Mar. 1980), 194-204.

[Manning 78]   Manning, E.G., On Datagram Service in Public Packet-Switched Networks, *Computer Networks* 2, (1978), 79-83.

[Maruyama 78]   Maruyama, K., Designing Reliable Packet-Switched Communication Networks, *Proc. ICCC*, Kyoto, (Sept. 1978).

[Mathison 78]   Mathison, S.L., Commercial, Legal, and International Aspects of Packet Communications, *Proc. IEEE* 66, 11 (Nov. 1978), 1527-1538.

[McDaniel 77]   McDaniel, G.A., Metric: A Kernel Instrumentation System for Distributed Environments, *Operating Systems Review* 11, 5 (Nov. 1977), 93-99.

[McGee 74]   McGee, W. C., A Contribution to the Theory of Data Equivalence, *Data Base Management*, J. W. Klimbie, K. L. Koffeman, Eds., North-Holland, Amsterdam, (1974), 123.

[McLeod 79]   McLeod, D., King, R., Applying A Semantic Database Model, University of Southern California Computer Science Department, TR 5, Los Angeles, California, (Aug. 1979).

[McQuillan 74] McQuillan, J. M., Adaptive Routing Algorithms for Distributed Computer Networks, Bolt Beranek and Newman Report 2831, (May 1974).

[McQuillan 77] McQuillan, J.M., Walden, D.C., The Arpanet Design Decisions, *Computer Networks* 1, 5 (Sept. 1977).

[McQuillan 78a] McQuillan, J.M., Cerf, V.G., Tutorial: A Practical View of Computer Communications Protocols, *IEEE* Catalog No. EHO 137-0, (1978).

[McQuillan 78b] McQuillan, J.M., Enhanced Message Addressing Capabilities for Computer Networks, *Proc. IEEE* 66, 11, (Nov. 1978) 1517-1526.

[Mealy 67] Mealy, G. H., Another Look at Data, *Proc.* AFIPS *Conf.* 36, (1967), 525-534.

[Menasce 78] Menasce, D.A., et. al., A Locking Protocol for Resource Coordination in Distributed Databases, *ACM Sigmod*, (June 1978).

[Merkle 78] Merkle, R. C., Hellman, M.E., Hiding Information and Signatures in Trap-Door Knapsacks, IEEE *Trans. Information Theory* IT-24, (Sept. 1978), 525.

[Merlin 76] Merlin, P., A Methodology for the Design and Implementation of Communication Protocols, *IEEE Trans. Communication* COM-24,5 (June 1976).

[Metcalfe 76] Metcalfe, R. Boggs, D.R., Ethernet: Distributed Packet Switching for Local Computer Networks, *Comm.* ACM 19, 7 (July 1976), 395-404.

[Morris 73] Morris, J.H., Protection in Programming Languages, *Comm.* ACM 16, 1 (Jan. 1973), 15-21.

[MIT 77] MIT, Information Processing Services, *The Relational Data Management System Reference Guide*, 1st Ed., (June 1977).

[Millstein 77] Millstein, R.E., The National Software Works: A Distributed Processing System, *Proc. ACM Nat. Conf.*, (1977), 44-52.

[Minoura 78] Minoura, T., Maximally Concurent Transaction Processing, *Proc. 3rd Berkeley Workshop*, (Aug. 1978), 206-214.

[Minoura 79] Minoura, T., A New Concurrency Control Algorithm for Distributed Database Systems, *Proc. 4th Berkeley Workshop*, (1979).

[Mullery 75] Mullery, A.P., The Distributed Control of Multiple Copies of Data, IBM Research Report, RC 5782, (August 1975).

[Muntz 76] Muntz, C.A., Cashman, P.M., File Package: The File Handling Facility for the National Software Works, Massachusetts Computer Associates Inc., Wakefield, Mass., Report No. CADD-7602-2011, (February 1976).

[Navathe 76] Navathe, S. B., Fry, J. P., Restructuring for Large Databases: Three Levels of Abstraction. *ACM Trans. Database Systems* 1, (1976), 138-158.

[Needham 78] Needham, R.M., Schroeder, M.D., Using Encryption for Authentication in Large Networks of Computers, *Comm. ACM* 21, 12 (Dec. 1978), 993-998.

[Needham 79] Needham, R.M., Adding Capabilities Access to Conventional File Service, *Operating Systems Review* 13, 1 (Jan. 1979), 3-4.

[Neely 77] Neely, P. M., Implementation Independent Arithmetic: Speculation for Discussion, *Software-Practice and Experience* 7, (1977), 461-468.

[Nessett 79a] Nessett, D., A Protocol for Buffer Space Negotiation, *Proc. 4th Berkeley Workshop*, (Oct. 1979).

[Nessett 79b] Nessett, D., A Survey of Congestion Control Issues in Store and Forward Networks, Lawrence Livermore Laboratory, Livermore, CA., Report UCRL-83551, (Nov. 1979).

[Nessett 80] Nessett, D., Watson, R.W., The Secure Management of Capabilities in a Distributed Operating System, Lawrence Livermore Laboratory, (June 1980).

[NSW 76] National Software Works Semi-Annual Technical Report, CADD-7603-0411, Mass. Comp. Assoc., Wakefield, Mass., (1976).

[NSW 76] NSW Protocol Committee, MSG: The Interprocess Communication Facility for the National Software Works, BBN Report No. 3483; also available as Massachusetts Computer Associates Document No. CADD-7612-2411 (Dec. 1976).

[Opderbeck 78] Opderbeck, H., Common Carrier Provided Network Interfaces, *Operating Systems: An Advanced Course*, Springer-Verlag, (1978), 482-507.

[Paolini 77] Paolini, P., Pelagatti G., Formal Definition of Mappings in a Database, *Proc. ACM-SIGMOD Int. Conf. Mngt. Data*, New York, (Aug. 1977), 40-46.

[Papadimitriou 77] Papadimitriou, C.A., Bernstein, P.A., Rothnie, J.B., Some Computational Problems Related to Database Concurrency Control, *Proc. Conf Theoretical Computer Science*, University of Waterloo, Waterloo, Ontario, Canada, (August 1977).

[Parnas 72] Parnas, D. L., On the Criteria To Be Used in Decomposing Systems into Modules, *Comm. ACM* 15, (1972), 1053-1058.

[Parnas 77] Parnas, D. L., Use of Abstract Interfaces in the Development of Software for Embedded Computer Systems, Naval Research Laboratory Report 8047, (1977).

[Parnas 79]	Parnas, D.L., Designing Software for Ease of Extension and Contraction, *IEEE Trans. Software Eng.* SE-5, 2, (Mar. 1979), 128-137.
[Pearson 80]	Pearson, G., Burruss, J., Service Specification of Transport and Session Protocols, National Bureau of Standards Report ICST/HLNP-80-2, (Mar. 1980).
[Peebles 75]	Peebles, R.W., Manning, E.G., A Computer Architecture for Large Distribued Data Bases, *Proc. ICVLDB,* (Sept. 1975), 405-427.
[Peebles 77]	Peebles, R., Concurrent Access Control in a Distributed Transaction Processing System, prepared for the Brown University Workshop on Distributed Processing, (Aug. 1977).
[Peebles 80]	Peebles, R., Dopirak, T., Adapt: A Guest System, *COMPCON 80,* (Spring 1980), 445-454.
[Pliner 77]	Pliner, M., McGowan, L., Spalding, K., A Distributed Data Management System for Real-Time Applications, *Proc. 2nd Berkeley Workshop,* (May 1977), 68-86.
[Poh 79]	Poh, S., Stoneburner, P., Wood, D., A Performance Study of a Network Frontend, *Proc. 6th DCS,* (Nov. 1979), 126-136.
[Pohlig 78]	Pohlig, S.C., Hellman, M.E., An Improved Algorithm for Computing Logarithms Over GF(p) and Its Cryptographic Significance, *IEEE Trans. Information Theory* IT-24, (Jan. 1978), 106.
[Popek 78]	Popek, G.J., Kline, C.S., Design Issues for Secure Computer Networks, *Operating Systems: An Advanced Course,* Springer-Verlag, (1978), 517-546.
[Popek 79]	Popek, G.J., Kline, C.S., Encryption and Secure Computer Networks, *Computing Surveys* 11, 4 (Dec. 1979), 331-356.
[Postel 79]	Postel, J., An Internetwork Message Structure, *Proc. 6th DCS, IEEE* 79CH 1405-0 CSC B/C (Nov. 1979), 1-7.
[Postel 80a]	Postel, J.B., DoD Standard Internet Protocol, RFC 760, IEN 128, USC Information Sciences Institute, (Jan. 1980).
[Postel 80b]	Postel, J.B. DoD Standard Transmission Control Protocol, RFC 761, IEN 129, USC Information Sciences Institute, (Jan. 1980).
[Pouzin 76a]	Pouzin, L., Virtual Circuits vs. Datagrams Technical and Political Problems, *Proc. AFIPS Conf.* 45, (June 1976), 483-494.
[Pouzin 76b]	Pouzin, L., Flow Control in Data Networks Methods and Tools, *Proc. 3rd ICCC,* (Aug. 1976), 467-474.
[Pouzin 78]	Pouzin, L., Zimmerman, H., A Tutorial on Protocols, *Proc. IEEE* 66, 11 (Nov. 1978), 1346-1370.
[Privitera 80]	Privitera, J., Data Transformations: Specification and Correctness, NBS SP 500- (in preparation), National Bureau of Standards, Washington, D.C., (1980).
[Rabin 78]	Rabin, M., Digitalised Signatures, *Foundations of Secure Computing,* Academic Press, New York, (1978).
[Rahimi 79]	Rahimi, S.K., Franta, W.R., A Posted Update Approach to Concurrency Control in Distributed Data Base Systems, *Proc. 1st ICDPS* (Oct. 1979).
[Ramirez 79]	Ramirez, R.J., Santoro, N., Distributed Control of Updates in Multiple-Copy Databases: A Time Optimal Algorithm, *Proc. 4th Berkeley Workshop,* (1979).
[Randell 75]	Randell, B., System Structure for Software Fault Tolerance, *IEEE Trans. Software Eng.* SE-1, 2 (June 1975), 220-232.
[Randell 78]	Randell, B., *et. al.,* Reliability Issues in Computing System Design, *Computing Surveys* 10, 2 (June 1978), 123-165.
[Rashid 80]	Rashid, R.F., An Interprocess Communication Facility for Unix, Department of Computer Science, Carnegie-Mellon University, (Mar. 1980).
[Reed 77a]	Reed, D.P., A Protocol for Addressing Services in the Local Net, MIT Laboratory for Computer Science, LNN 5 (February 15, 1977).
[Reed 77b]	Reed, D.P., Kanodia, R.K., Synchronization with Eventcounts and Sequences, *Operating Systems Review* 11, 5, (Nov. 1977).
[Rinde 76]	Rinde, J., Tymnet: An Alternative to Packet Switching Technology, *Proc. 3rd ICCC,* (August 1976).
[Rinde 77]	Rinde, J., Virtual Circuits in Tymnet II, Tymshare Inc., (Oct. 1977).
[Ritchie 74]	Ritchie, D. M., Thompson, K., The Unix Time-Sharing System, *Comm. ACM* 17, (1974), 365-375.
[Rivest 78]	Rivest, R.L., Shamir, A., Adelman, L., A Method Of Obtaining Digital Signatures and Public Key Cryptosystems, *Comm. ACM* 21, 2 (Feb. 1978), 120.
[Roberts 76]	Roberts, L. G., International Interconnection of Public Packet Networks, *Proc. 3rd ICCC,* (Aug. 1976), 239-245.

[Roberts 78] Roberts, L.G., The Evolution of Packet Switching, *Proc. IEEE* 66, 11 (Nov. 1978), 1307-1313.

[Rosen 79] Rosen, E.C., The Updating Protocol of the Arpanet's New Routing Algorithm: A Case Study in Maintaining Identical Copies of a Changing Distributed Data Base, *Proc. 4th Berkeley Workshop*, (1979).

[Rosenberg 74] Rosenberg, Y., Theory of L-Systems: From The Point of View of Formal Language Theory, *Lecture Notes in Computer Science* 15, Springer Verlag, (1974).

[Rosenkrantz 78] Rosenkrantz, D.J., Stearns, R.E., Lewis, P.M., System Level Concurrency Control for Distributed Data Bases, *ACM Trans. Database Sysems* 3, 2 (June 1978).

[Rosenthal 78] Rosenthal, R., Lucas, B. D., The Design and Implementation of the National Bureau of Standards' Network Access Machine, NBS SP 500-35, National Bureau of Standards, Washington, D.C., (1978).

[Rothnie 77a] Rothnie, J.B., and Goodman, N., A Study of Updating in a Redundant Distributed Database Environment, Technical Report No. CCA-77-01, Computer Corporation of America, 575 Technology Square, Cambridge, Massachusetts 02139, (Feb. 15, 1977).

[Rothnie 77b] Rothnie, J.B., Goodman, N., Bernstein, P.A., The Redundant Update Methodology of SDD-1: A System for Distributed Databases (The Fully Redundant Case), CCA Report 77-02, (June 1977).

[Rothnie 77c] Rothnie, J. B., Goodman N., A Survey of Research and Development in Distributed Database Management, *Proc. 3rd ICVLDB*, Tokyo, Japan, (1977), 48-62.

[Rybczynski 76] Rybczynski, A., et. al., A New Communication Protocol for Accessing Data Networks, The International Packet Mode Interface. *Proc. AFIPS Conf.* 45, (1976), 477-482.

[Sahin 78] Sahin, K.E., Connectivity Patterns In Large Computer Networks: Impact Response Routing With Selcuk Procedure, *Proc. Networking Symp.*, (1978), 53-57.

[Saltzer 78a] Saltzer, J.H., Naming and Binding of Objects, *Operating Systems: An Advanced Course*, Springer-Verlag, (1978), 99-208.

[Saltzer 78b] Saltzer, J.H., Research Problems of Decentralized Systems with Largely Autonomous Nodes, *Operating Systems Review* 12, 1 (Jan. 1978), 43-52. Also in *Operating Systems: An Advanced Course* Springer-Verlag, (1978), 583-591.

[Schantz 77] Schantz, R.E., Millstein, R.E., The Foreman: Providing the Program Execution Environment for the National Software Works, Bolt, Beranek and Newman Inc., Report No. 3442, First Revision, (Jan. 1977).

[Schlageter 78a] Schlageter, G., Locking Protocols in Distributed Databases, *Int. Conf. Management of Data*, Milano, Italy, (June 1978).

[Schlageter 78b] Schlageter, G., Synchronisation durch Locking in verteilten Datenbanken. Informatik Fachberichte 14: Datenbanken in Rechnernetzen mit Kleinrechnern. GI Fachtagung, Karlsruhe, (1978), Springer Verlag.

[Schlageter 80] Schlageter, G., Dadam, P., Reconstruction of Consistent Global States in Distributed Databases, *Int. Symp. Distributed Databases*, (Mar. 1980), North-Holland, 191-200.

[Schneider 75] Schneider, G. M., DSCL-A Data Specification and Conversion Language for Networks, *Proc. ACM SIGMOD*, (May 1975), 139-148.

[Schwartz 77] Schwartz, M., *Computer-Communication Network Design and Analysis*, Prentice Hall, (1977).

[Schwartz 80] Schwartz, M., and Stern, T.E., Routing Techniques Used in Computer Communication Networks, *IEEE Trans. Communications*, (Apr. 1980).

[SDDTTG 76] Stored-Data Description and Data Translation: A Model and Language, Report of the Stored-Data Definition and Translation Task Group of the Codasyl Systems Committee, (1976).

[Seguin 79] Seguin, J., et. al., A Majority Consensus Algorithm for the Consistency of Duplicated and Distributed Information, *Proc. 1st ICDPS*, (Oct. 1979).

[Sekino 75] Sekino, L.S., Multiple Concurrent Updates, *Proc. ICVLDB*, (1975), 505-507.

[Shamir 78] Shamir, A., A Fast Signature System, MIT Laboratory For Computer Science, Report No. MIT/LCS/TM-107, (July 1978).

[Shannon 49] Shannon, C. E., Communication Theory of Secrecy Systems, *Bell Sys. Tech. J.* 28, (1949), 657.

[Shapiro 77] Shapiro, R.M., Millstein, R.E., NSW Reliability Plan, Mass. Computer Assoc. CA-7701-1411, (June 1977).

[Shapiro 78] Shapiro, R.M., Millstein, R.E., Failure Recovery in a Distributed Data Base System, *COMPCON 78*, (Spring 1978), 66-70.

[Shoch 78] Shoch, J.F., Inter-Network Naming, Addressing, and Routing. *COMPCON 78*, (Spring 1978), 72-79.

[Shoch 79]	Shoch, J.F., Tactics and Strategy for Packet Fragmentation in Internetwork Protocols, *Computer Networks*, (1979).
[Shoch 80a]	Shoch, J.F., Hupp, J.A., Performance of an Ethernet Local Network, A Preliminary Report, *COMPCON 80*, (Spring 80), 315-322.
[Shoch 80b]	Shoch, J.F., Cohen, D., Taft, E.A., Mutual Encapsulation of Internetwork Protocols, *Proc. SCNPTA*, IEEE Cat. No. 80CH1529-7C, (May 1980).
[Shoshani 78]	Shoshani, A., CABLE: A Language Based on the Entity-Relationship Model, University of California Lawrence Berkeley Lab., Report UCID-8005, Berkeley, California, (Jan. 1978).
[Shu 77]	Shu, N. C., Housel, B. C., Taylor, R. W., Ghosh, S. P. and Lum, V. Y., EXPRESS: A Data Extraction, Processing and Restructuring System, *ACM Trans. Database Systems* 2, (1977), 134-174.
[Sieworek 74]	D.P. Sieworek, Modularity and Multi-Microprocessor Structures, *7th Ann. Workshop on Microprogramming*, (Oct. 1974).
[Simmons 77]	Simmons, G.J., Norris, M.J., Preliminary Comments on the MIT Public Key Cryptosystem, *Cryptologia* 1, 4 (1977), 406.
[Simmons 79]	Simmons, G.J., Symmetric and Asymmetric Encryption, *Computing Surveys* 11, 4 (Dec. 1979), 305-330.
[Sloan 79]	Sloan, L.J., Limiting the Lifetime of Packets in Computer Networks, *Proc. 4th CLCN*, (Oct. 1979), IEEE, 79CH1446-4C, 111-118. (Also in *Computer Networks* 3, 6 (Dec. 1979), 435-446.)
[Smid 79]	Smid, M.E., A Key Notarization System for Computer Networks, U.S. NBS Report SP 500-54, (Oct. 1979).
[Smith 75]	Smith, J. M., Chang, P. Y.-T., Optimizing the Performance of a Relational Algebra Database Interface, *Comm. ACM* 18, (1975), 568-579.
[Sollins 79]	Sollins, K.R., Copying Complex Structures in a Distributed System, MIT LCS TR-219, Laboratory for Computer Science, MIT, Cambridge, Mass., (May 1979).
[Sproull 78]	Sproull, R.F., Cohen, D., High Level Protocols, *Proc. IEEE* 66, (Nov. 1978), 1371-1385.
[Stearns 76]	Stearns, R.E., Lewis, P.M, Rosenkrantz, D.J., Concurrency Controls for Database Systems, *Proc. 17th Ann. Symp. Foundations Computer Science*, (1976), 19-32.
[Stonebraker 75]	Stonebraker, M., Held G., Networks, Hierarchies, and Relations in Data Base Management, Mem. No. ERL-M504, Electronic Research Lab., College of Engineering, University of California, Berkeley, California, (March 1975).
[Stonebraker 76]	Stonebraker, M., Wong, E., Kreps, P., Held, G., The Design and Implementation of Ingres, *ACM Trans. Database Systems* 1, (1976), 189-222.
[Stonebraker 77]	Stonebraker, M., Neuhold, E., A Distributed Database Version of Ingres, *Proc. 2nd Berkeley Workshop*, (May 1977).
[Stonebraker 78]	Stonebraker, M., Concurrency Control and Consistency of Multiple Copies of Data in Distributed Ingres, *Proc. 3rd Berkeley Workshop*, (Aug. 1978), 235-258.
[Stucki 78]	Stucki, M.J., *et. al.*, Coordinating Concurrent Access in a Distributed Database Architecture, *4th Workshop on Computer Architecture for Non-Numeric Processing*, (Aug. 1978).
[Sunshine 75]	Sunshine C. A., Interprocess Communication Protocols for Computer Networks, DSL Techinical Report 105, Stanford University, (Dec. 1975), 268 pages.
[Sunshine 76]	Factors in Interprocess Communication Protocol Efficiency for Computer Networks, *Proc. AFIPS Conf.* 45, (1976), 571-576.
[Sunshine 77a]	Sunshine, C.A., Source Routing and Computer Networks. *Computer Communications Review* 7, (Jan. 1977).
[Sunshine 77b]	Sunshine, C.A., Interconnection of Computer Networks. *Computer Networks* 1, 3 (1977).
[Sunshine 78a]	Sunshine, C.A., Dalal, Y.K., Connection Management in Transport Protocols, *Computer Networks* 2, 6 (1978), 454-473.
[Sunshine 78b]	Sunshine, C.A., Survey of Protocol Definition and Verification Techniques, *Computer Networks*, 2, 4/5, (Sept./Oct. 1978).
[Sunshine 79]	Sunshine, C., Formal Techniques for Protocol Specification and Verification, *Computer*, (Sept. 1979), 20-27.
[Swan 77]	Swan, Richard J., A Modular Multi-Microprocessor, *Proc. AFIPS Conf.* 46, (1977).
[Swinehart 79]	Swinehart, D., McDaniel, G., Boggs, D., WFS: A Simple Shared File System for a Distributed Environment, *Operating Systems Review* 13, 5, (Dec. 1979), 9-17.
[Thomas 73]	Thomas, R. H., A Resource Sharing Executive for the Arpanet, *Proc. AFIPS Conf.* 42 (1973), SJCC 155-163.

[Thomas 76a]   Thomas, R.H., A Solution to the Update Problem for Multiple Copy Databases which uses Distributed Control, BBN Report 3340, (July 1976), Bolt, Beranek and Newman Inc., 50 Moulton St., Cambridge, Massachusetts 02138.

[Thomas 76b]   Thomas, R.H., Schaffner, S.C., MSG: The Interprocess Communication Facility for the National Software Works, Bolt, Beranek and Newman Inc., Report No. 3483, (revised Dec. 1976).

[Thomas 78a]   Thomas, R.H., A Solution to the Concurrency Control Problem for Multiple Copy Databases, *COMPCON 78*, (Spring 78).

[Thomas 78b]   Thomas, T.H., Schantz, R.E., Forsdick, H.C., Network Operating Systems, Rome Air Development Center Technical Report TR-78-117, (Mar. 1978), also Bolt Beranek and Newman Report 3796.

[Thornton 79]   Thornton, J.E., Overview of the HYPERChannel, *COMPCON 79*, (Spring 1979), 262-265.

[Thornton 80]   Thornton, J.E., Back-end Network Approaches, *Computer* 13, 2 (Feb. 1980), 10-17.

[Thurber 72]   Thurber, K.J., et. al., A Systematic Approach to the Design of Digital Bussing Structures, *Proc. AFIPS Conf.* 41, (Fall 1972).

[Thurber 77]   Thurber, K.J., Kregness, G.R., Emulation Considerations for Tactical Real-Time Computer Systems, *COMPCON 77*, (Fall 1977), 372-377.

[Thurber 78a]   Thurber, K.J., Computer Communication Techniques, *Computer Architecture News* 7, 3 (Oct. 1978).

[Thurber 78b]   Thurber, K.J., G.M. Masson, *Distributed-Processor Communication Architecture*, Lexington Books (D.C. Heath), Lexington, Massachusetts, (1978).

[Thurber 80a]   Thurber, K.J., A Survey of Local Network Hardware, *COMPCON 80*, (Fall 1980).

[Thurber 80b]   Thurber, K.J., Freeman, H.A., Tutorial: Local Computer Networks, IEEE Computer Society, Long Beach, California, (Sept. 1980).

[Thurber 81]   Thurber, K.J., Architecture and Strategies for Local Networks: Examples and Important Systems, *Advances in Computers* 20, Yovitts, M.C., ed., (1981).

[Traiger 78]   Traiger, I.L., et. al., Transactions and Consistency in Distributed Database Systems, IBM Research Report RJ2555, IBM Research Laboratory, San Jose, California, (June 1978).

[Tsubaki 79]   Tsubaki, M., Hotaka, R., Distributed Multi-Database Environment with a Supervisory Data Dictionary Database. *Proc. ICERASAD*, (1979), 625-646.

[Tsuruoka 78]   Tsuruoka, K., Hattori, M., Correctness of Distributed Logical Clock Synchronization Method, *19th Ann. Conf. Records of IPS*, Japan 4J-1, (Aug. 1978), 945-946 (in Japanese).

[USAF 73]   USAF, MIL-STD-1553: Military Standard Aircraft Interval Time Division Multiplex Bus, (1973).

[Victor 76]   Victor, K.B., The Design and Implementation of DAD: A Multiprocess, Multimachine, Multilanguage Interactive Debugger, Augmentation Research Center, Stanford Research Institute, Menlo Park, California, Draft, (Aug. 1976).

[Walden 72]   Walden, D., A System for Interprocess Communication in a Resource Sharing Network, *Comm. ACM* 15, 4 (Apr. 1972), 221-330.

[Walden 79]   Walden, D.C., McKenzie, A., The Evolution of Host-to-Host Protocol Technology, *Computer*, (Sept. 1979), 29-35.

[Wallis 80]   Wallis, P.J.L., External Representations of Objects of User-Defined Type, *Trans. Prog. Lang. Sys.* 2, 2, (Apr. 1980), 137-152.

[Wang 80]   Wang, P. S. C., The Design of a Database Access Protocol, (in preparation).

[Ward 80]   Ward, S.A., Trix: A Network-oriented Operating System, *COMPCON 80*, (Spring 1980), 344-349.

[Watson 70]   Watson, R. W., *Timesharing System Design Concepts*, McGraw-Hill, (1970).

[Watson 78]   Watson, R. W., The LLL Octopus Network: Some Lessons and Future Directions, *Proc. 3rd USA-Japan Computer Conf.*, San Francisco, (Oct. 1978), 12-21.

[Watson 79a]   Watson, R. W., Delta-t Protocol Preliminary Specification, Lawrence Livermore Laboratory, Livermore, CA, Rep. UCRL 52881, (Apr. 1980).

[Watson 79b]   Watson, R.W., Fletcher, J.G., An Architecture for Support of Network Operating System Services, *Proc. 4th Berkeley Workshop*, (Aug. 1979), 18-50. (Also to appear in *Computer Networks*, 1980.)

[Watson 80a]   Network Architecture Design Issues: With Application to Backend Storage Networks, *Computer*, 13, 2 (Feb. 1980), 32-49.

[Watson 80b]   Watson, R.W., Timer-based Mechanisms in Reliable Transport Protocol Connection Mangement: A Comparison of the TCP and Delta-t Protocol Approaches, *Proc. SCNPTA*, IEEE Cat. No. 80CH1529-7C, (May 1980).

[Watson 80c]   Watson, R. W., Comments on the EMCA Transport Protocol, Contributors to ISO, SC-16, (Aug. 1980).

[WatsonW 79]   Watson, W.B., Simulation Study of the Traffic Dependent Performance of a Prioritized, CSMA Broadcast Network, *Proc. 4th CLCN*, (1979) 67-74. Also in *Computer Networks* 3, 6 (Dec. 1979), 427-434.

[Weber 78]   Weber, H. A., Software Engineering View of Data Base Systems, *Proc. 4th ICVLDB*, West Berlin, (1978), 36-51.

[Wecker 79]   Wecker, S., Computer Network Architectures, *Computer* (Sept. 1979), 58-72.

[White 76]   White, J.E., A High-Level Framework for Network-Based Resource Sharing, *Proc. AFIPS Conf.* 45, (1976), 561-570.

[Winkel 80]   Winkel, D., Prosser, F., *The Art of Digital Design*, Prentice-Hall, (1980).

[Wittie 79]   Wittie, L.D., A Distributed Operating System for a Reconfigurable Computer Network, *Proc. 1st ICDPS*, (Oct. 1979), 669-678.

[Wood 80]   Wood, H. M., Kimbleton, S. R., Remote Record Access: Requirements, Implementation and Analysis, NBS SP 500- (in preparation), National Bureau of Standards, Washington, D.C. (1980).

[Wulf 72]   Wulf, William A., Bell, C., Gordon, C.mmp – A Multi-Processor, *Proc. AFIPS Conf.* 41, (1972).

[Yao 79]   Yao, S. B., Optimization of Query Evaluation Algorithms, *ACM Trans. Database Systems* 4, (1979), 133-155.

[Zimmermann 75]   Zimmermann, H., The Cyclades End-to-End Protocol, *4th DCS*, (Oct. 1975).

[Zimmermann 80]   Zimmermann, H., The ISO Model of Architecture for Open Systems Interconnection, *IEEE Trans. Communication*, (April 1980).

Index

CONPAR 81

Conference on Analysing Problem Classes
and Programming for Parallel Computing
Nürnberg, June 10–12, 1981

Proceedings

Editor: **W. Händler**

1981. XI, 508 pages. (Lecture Notes in Computer Science,
Volume 111). ISBN 3-540-10827-0

From the Contents: Programming and structure changes in
parallel computers. – Tree machines and divide-and-con-
quer algorithms. – Queue machines: an organization for
parallel computation. – Operating systems support for the
finite element machine.– Automatic program restructuring
for high-speed computation.– Language support for designing multilevel computer systems. – Parallel structures for
vector processing. – Language design approaches for parallel
processors.– Reconciling data flow machines and conventional languages. – On language constructs for concurrent programs. – Generation of dataflow graphical object code for
the Lapse programming language.– Cellular algorithms and
their verification.– The development of fast cellular pattern
transformation algorithms using virtual boundaries. – Cellular algorithms for binary matrix operations. – Analysis of
concurrent algorithms – SAUGE: How to use the parallelism of sequential programs. – A transformational approach
for developing parallel programs.– A methodology for programming with concurrency. – On synchronization and its
specification. – Nonnumerical aspects of computations on
parallel hardware. – Compiling in parallel. – Finding the
maximum, merging and sorting in a parallel computation
model. – Parallel computations in information retrieval.–
Recurrence semigroups and their relation to data storage in
fast recurrence solvers on parallel machines. – Parallel algorithms for the convex hull problem in two dimensions. – On
basic concepts in parallel numerical mathematics.– Iterative
methods for the solution of elliptic difference equations on
multiprocessors. – Hierarchical discrete systems and realisa-
tion of parallel algorithms. – Solving two modified discrete
poisson equations in 7 logn steps on n^2 processors. – A
parallel algorithm for solving band systems and matrix
inversion. – Parallel evaluation of correlation time-of-flight
experiments. – Parallelization of a minimization problem for
multiprocessor systems. – Design and development of concurrent programs. – Binary trees and parallel scheduling
algorithms.– New variants of the quadrant interlocking factorisation (Q.I.F.) method.

Springer-Verlag
Berlin
Heidelberg
New York

Microcomputer System Design

An Advanced Course

Trinity College Dublin, June 1981
Editors: **M. J. Flynn, N. R. Harris, D. P. McCarthy**

1982. VII, 397 pages. (Lecture Notes in Computer Science, Volume 126). ISBN 3-540-11172-7

In order to use microcomputers effectively, system designers require a broad knowledge of computer hardware, interfacing, software, and design tools.
Covering both theory and practice the microcomputer system design course described in this volume integrates the hardware and software sides of microcomputers. It includes the revised notes of a course which spanned development from silicon technology to software. It brought together current techniques in LSI/VLSI design, computer structures and languages, showing their application to, and implications for, microcomputer system design.

S. Osaki, T. Nishio

Reliability Evaluation of Some Fault-Tolerant Computer Architectures

1980. 46 figures, 2 tables. VI, 129 pages. (Lecture Notes in Computer Science, Volume 97). ISBN 3-540-10274-4

The computer's increasingly important role in the world today has made system breakdowns costly and dangerous, often to the point of serious societal disorder. To aid in the design and operation of systems with a higher degree of reliability, the authors of this work investigate stochastic models of fault-tolerant computer architectures using a unique modification of regeneration point techniques in Markov renewal processes. They also provide numerical examples of performance-related reliability measures to allow comparisions of fault-tolerant computer architectures from the viewpoint of reliability and performance. The interesting results gained from such comparisions are discussed with relation to their applicability to the design of system configurations.
An appendix is included, outlining the Markov renewal processes used throughout the book to analyze stochastic models of fault-tolerant computer architecture.

Springer-Verlag
Berlin
Heidelberg
New York